The Motor Vehicle

The Motor Vehicle

Tenth Edition

K. NEWTON
MC BSc ACGI AMInstCE MIMechE
Late Assistant Professor, Mechanical and Electrical
Engineering Department,
The Royal Military College of Science

W. STEEDS
OBE BSc ACGI FIMechE
Late Professor of Mechanical Engineering,
The Royal Military College of Science

T. K. GARRETT
CEng FIMechE MRAes
Sometime Editor of *Automobile Engineer*

BUTTERWORTHS
London Boston Durban Singapore Sydney Toronto Wellington

First published by Iliffe & Sons Ltd 1929
Eighth edition by Iliffe Books 1966
Ninth edition 1972
   Reprinted 1973
   Reprinted by Newnes-Butterworths 1975
   Reprinted 1978
Tenth edition by Butterworth Scientific 1983
   Reprinted 1985, 1986

British Library Cataloguing in Publication Data

Newton, K.
  The motor vehicle.—10th ed.
  1. Motor vehicles
  I. Title II. Steeds, W. III. Garrett, T. K.
  629.2   TL145

  ISBN 0-408-01157-2

Photoset by Butterworths Litho Preparation Department
Printed in England by Mackays of Chatham Ltd., Kent

Preface to the Tenth Edition

In the preface to the 9th Edition, Professor Steeds welcomed me as joint author, a task that I had taken up at the earlier invitation of the by then deceased Professor Newton. Now, owing to the death of Professor Steeds shortly before the current revision fell due, I have been left with the considerable task of revising the whole of the work. That it is such a major undertaking is due to three factors: first, the sheer size of the work, owing to enormously painstaking efforts that have been directed consistently over 50 years by the late Professors Newton and Steeds into covering in depth in this book the whole of the field; secondly, the great accumulation of knowledge and experience that they have recorded within it with each successive revision; and, thirdly, the rapidity with which major technological advances have been made over a broad front since the 9th Edition was prepared.

These advances have necessitated the rewriting of virtually whole chapters, for example those on petrol and diesel fuel injection, the carriage unit, steering mechanism, and suspension principles and systems. Moreover, considerable additions and changes have been made to the chapters on engine details, such as bearings, pistons, cylinder heads, and carburettors, and to those on transmissions, both manual and automatic, and clutches, axles, wheel hubs and brakes. A section has been added, too, on the relative merits of various types of transmission – belt and chain – used for driving main and auxiliary equipment on road vehicles. As regards trends for the future, the new section on stratified-charge engines, in Chapter 17, will be of especial interest.

The principles laid down by Professors Newton and Steeds have been followed. That is, in the revised sections, not only are details of the latest advances presented, but also the history of the stages of evolution leading up to them have, where practicable, been outlined. In some instances it has been spelled out – for example, in the sections on pistons and rings – while, in others, the student can discover them by reading through a chapter – for instance, that the high camshaft of the Humber *Super Snipe* was an intermediate stage between the move from low to overhead camshafts, to reduce the inertia and elasticity of the valve actuation train.

Above all, the book has been written in simple language so that, despite the complexity of some of the topics, the student will have no difficulty in understanding them. Indeed, it is intended as a volume that the student can buy at the very beginning of his preliminary training, knowing that it will serve him faithfully as a constant source of information that he cannot obtain from any other single book, until he has passed his examinations at the end of his final, and most advanced, courses. That it has in the past succeeded in this aim has been confirmed by the number of designers and others in senior executive positions who have commented to me that, even after their many years experience in the industry, they still keep this book and use it constantly as a source of reference on automotive design technology.

T.K.G.

Contents

Contents

Units and Abbreviations

Calorific value	kilojoules per kilogram	kJ/kg
	megajoules per litre	MJ/l
Specific fuel consumption	kilograms per kilowatt hour	kg/kWh
Length	millimetres, metres, kilometres	mm, m, km
Mass	kilograms, grams	kg, g
Time	seconds, minutes, hours	s, min, h
Speed	centimetres per second, metres per second	cm/s, m/s
	kilometres per hour, miles per hour	km/h, mph
Acceleration	metres-per-second per second	m/s^2
Force	newtons, kilonewtons	N, kN
Moment	newton-metres	Nm
Work	joules	J
Power	horsepower, watts, kilowatts	hp, W, kW
Pressure	newtons per square metre	N/m^2
	kilonewtons per square metre	kN/m^2
Angles	radians	rad
Angular speed	radians per second	rad/s
	radians-per-second per second	rad/s^2
	revolutions per minute	rev/min
	revolutions per second	rev/s

SI units and the old British units:

Length	1 m = 3.281 ft	1 ft = 0.3048 m
	1 km = 0.621 mile	1 mile = 1.609 km
Speed	1 m/s = 3.281 ft/s	1 ft/s = 0.305 m/s
	1 km/h = 0.621 mph	1 mph = 1.61 km/h
Acceleration	$1\ m/s^2 = 3.281\ ft/s^2$	$1\ ft/s^2 = 0.305\ m/s^2$
Mass	1 kg = 2.205 lb	1 lb = 0.454 kg
Force	1 N = 0.225 lbf	1 lbf = 4.448 N
	(1 MN = meganewton = 1 million newtons)	
Torque	1 Nm = 0.738 lbf ft	1 lbf ft = 1.356 Nm
Pressure	$1\ N/m^2 = 0.000145\ lbf/in^2$	$1\ lbf/in^2 = 6.895\ kN/m^2$
	$1\ bar = 14.5038\ lbf/in^2$	$1\ lbf/in^2 = 0.068947\ bar$
Energy, work	1 J = 0.738 ft lbf	1 ft lbf = 1.3558 J
	1 J = 0.239 calorie	1 calorie = 4.186 J
	1 kJ = 0.9478 Btu	1 Btu = 1.05506 kJ
		(1 therm = 100 000 Btu)
	1 kJ = 0.526 CHU	1 CHU = 1.9 kJ
Power	1 kW = 1.34 hp	1 hp = 0.7457 kW
Specific fuel consumption	1 kg/kWh = 1.645 lb/bhp h	1 lb/bhp h = 0.6088 kg/kWh
	1 litre/kWh = 1.316 pt/bhp h	1 pt/bhp h = 0.76 litre/kWh
Calorific value	1 kJ/kg = 0.4303 Btu/lb	1 Btu/lb = 2.324 kJ/kg
	1 kJ/kg = 0.239 CHU/lb	1 CHU/lb = 4.1868 kJ/kg

Part 1

Fundamentals

Chapter 1

Engineering drawings

A knowledge of the principles of mechanical drawing, sufficient to enable simple engineering drawings to be understood, is of great use to all who have to deal with things mechanical. It is not practicable, perhaps not possible, to describe by means of a written description alone a piece of mechanism as intricate as the motor car. Drawings enable this to be done and, since they are used extensively in all engineering literature, it is thought advisable to begin this book with an outline of the principles of mechanical drawing and, by giving a number of examples, accompanied by photographs and descriptions of the objects they represent, to assist the reader to understand those that appear later in the book.

There are several ways of depicting objects by means of drawings. One is by *perspective views* such as are seen in Figs. 1.15 to 1.17. These views are similar to photographic views and show the object as it appears to an observer, as far as this is possible on flat paper. They can be made very lifelike by suitable shading, but are comparatively difficult to draw, and their field of usefulness, in engineering, is somewhat limited. The best method of depicting engineering objects is by means of a number of *orthogonal projections* or *engineering views*. We will therefore proceed to consider how such views are obtained.

1.1 Engineering view of an object

An engineering view of an object along any 'line of sight', that is, from any particular point of view, is obtained as follows: The plane paper on which the view is to be drawn is placed behind the object perpendicular to the line of sight. All the points in the outline of the object are then 'projected' on to the paper by drawing lines from them perpendicular to the paper. If the points where these perpendiculars strike the paper are marked, the resulting figure is the orthogonal projection of the object along the line of sight chosen. The process is not confined to the outline of an object but is extended to any features on its face which it is desirable to show. The lines drawn from the points in the object perpendicular to the paper are known as *projection lines* and obviously are parallel lines. Now, since the rays of light that reach the eye from an object placed at a great distance are very nearly parallel, an engineering view of an object can be obtained by placing the object at a great distance. With small objects it will be found sufficient to place them about six feet away and to close one eye.

1.2 Examples of orthogonal projection

The method of obtaining the orthogonal projection of a cube along a line of sight perpendicular to one of its faces is shown in Fig. 1.1, which is a perspective view of the operation. The view obtained on the paper is in reality a square, but the perspective shown in the Figure distorts it into a rhombus. It should be noticed that the sides of the cube, which are parallel to the line of sight, appear in the projection simply as lines.

Fig. 1.2 shows the projection of a cylinder along a line of sight parallel to its axis. The view obtained is a circle, but here again the perspective distorts it – into an ellipse. When the line of sight is perpendicular to the axis of the cylinder the view obtained is a rectangle as shown in Fig. 1.3 where, owing to the perspective, it appears as a parallelogram. The

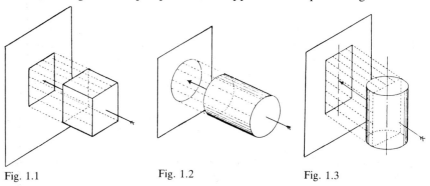

Fig. 1.1   Fig. 1.2   Fig. 1.3

diameter of the circle representing the end view of the cylinder is equal to the breadth of the rectangle representing the side view of the cylinder. The length of the rectangle is equal to the length of the cylinder. The rectangle of Fig. 1.3 gives no indication that it is a view on the curved surface of a cylinder. This may be done by shading the view. Shading, however, is not much used in engineering drawings.

A little consideration will show that the orthogonal projection of a sphere along any line of sight is a circle. The projection of a cone along a line of sight perpendicular to its axis is a triangle. Consider now the projections of a circular disc. When the line of sight is perpendicular to the disc the view is obviously a circle. When it is parallel to the surface of the disc the view is simply a straight line. In any intermediate position, when the line of sight is inclined to the disc, the view is an ellipse. If any difficulty is experienced in realising this the reader should cut out a disc of cardboard and test it for himself. Having done this he should have no difficulty in realising that the projection of a cylinder along a line of sight inclined to its axis is as shown in Fig. 1.4; the circular ends of the cylinder being seen as ellipses. Next consider a cylinder having one end cut at an angle to the axis. The actual shape of the slanting end is an ellipse. When such a cylinder is looked at along a line of sight as shown in Fig. 1.5, the elliptical end will appear less elliptical and may actually appear circular. Again if difficulty is experienced in realising this it should be tested experimentally by cutting out an ellipse in cardboard. It will be found that from one particular point of view the ellipse will appear circular. When the line of sight is parallel to the slanting end the view will be as in Fig. 1.6.

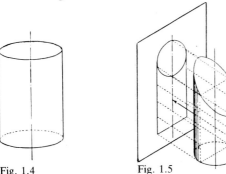

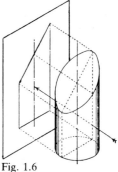

Fig. 1.4   Fig. 1.5   Fig. 1.6

A single perspective view often conveys a good idea of the general shape of an object, but a *single* engineering view fails in this respect. A rectangle, for example, might be a view of a cylinder, or of a square or triangular prism, or of a rectangular piece of tin-plate. It is therefore necessary in most cases to give more than one enginering view of an object. With simple objects two views may be sufficient, with most three are necessary, but in the case of complicated objects a number of views is required. Each one of these will be an engineering view obtained by projection as previously described.

The lines of sight along which the three views necessary with most objects are taken, are three mutually perpendicular lines. This may be illustrated by considering a simple house. A view of a house from the front, another from one end, and a third looking down on it from above, will give sufficient indication of the general shape of the house. These views are called the *front view* or *front elevation*, the *end* or *side view*, and the *plan* respectively and, provided that they were labelled so that the lines of sight along which they were taken could be recognised, they might be placed anywhere on the drawing paper. The relative positions of the views on the paper can, however, be used to indicate the lines of sight along which the views have been taken. The relative position of the views on the paper thus becomes a matter of importance, and there are three systems or conventions determining those positions. These systems will now be explained.

1.3   Relationship of the views on the paper

To explain how the various views come to occupy certain definite positions on the paper we will consider the object shown in the photograph Fig. 1.7. This object is a cubical block having two diagonally opposite corners bevelled off and having a cylindrical projection on one end and a square projection on the opposite end.

There is no difficulty in placing one view of this object on the paper; we have merely to place the paper behind the object perpendicular to the line of sight and to project the view as shown in Fig. 1.8. It will be observed that one face of the object has been placed parallel to the paper in obtaining this view, or in other words the line of sight chosen is perpendicular to one of the faces of the object. We now want to get a view of the object along a line of sight at right angles to the previous one. Such a line of sight is shown at AB, and in order to get the view along this line of sight on to the paper the latter must be placed behind the object perpendicular to the line of sight. To do this imagine the paper bent round at right angles as indicated in Fig. 1.9. The view can then be projected as seen. The third line of sight, perpendicular to the other two, is shown at CD, and in order to get this view on to the paper the latter must be bent round underneath the object (Fig. 1.10) until it is perpendicular to the line of sight. The view can then be projected as shown.

Now, when the paper is bent in this manner, the three portions on which the views have been projected occupy the same position as the two walls and the floor of the corner of a square room. This should be clear from Fig. 1.10, where X is the front wall, Y the side wall and Z the floor. When the paper is folded back into the flat again it should be clear that the three

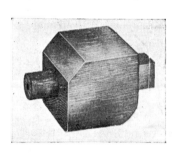

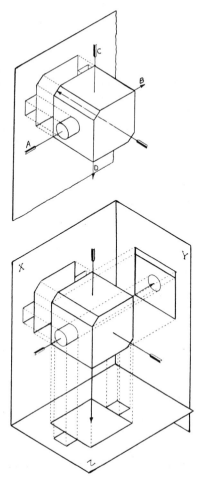

Fig. 1.7 (*above*)
Fig. 1.8 (*right*)
Fig. 1.9 (*below*)
Fig. 1.10 (*below right*)

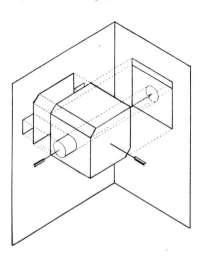

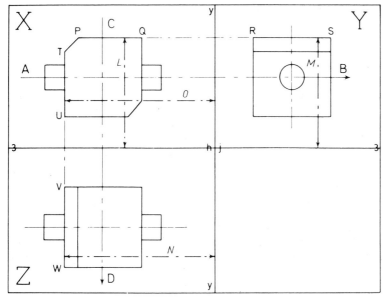

Fig. 1.11

views will occupy the positions shown in Fig. 1.11, where X is the front view, Y the side or end view and Z the plan. The line *yy* is the fold by which the paper was positioned for the projection of the end view. This line, however, can also be considered as the view, on the wall X, of the wall Y as seen when looking along the first line of sight in obtaining the front view. Similarly the line *zh* represents the fold by which the plan view was obtained. This line also can be considered as the view, on the wall X, of the floor Z. Again the line *jz* represents the view, on the wall Y, of the floor Z and it should be clear that *zh* and *jz* form a continuous straight line so that *zz* can be taken as representing the floor line while *yy* represents the side wall Y.

Consider now the top surface of the object. This is represented in the front view by the line PQ and in the end view by the line RS. The distance between this surface and the floor is the distance *L* in the front view and the distance *M* in the end view.

Since the surface can be at only one distance from the floor the distances *L* and *M* must be equal, and therefore if PQ is prolonged as shown, it will coincide with RS. Similarly the end surface of the object is shown in the front view by the line TU and in the plan by the line VW. The distance of this surface from the side wall Y is given in the front view by the distance *O* and in the plan by the distance *N* and again, since the surface can be at one distance only from the side wall, those distances must be equal, and if TU is prolonged as shown it will coincide with VW. The lines PQ and RS are in projection and, in fact, the whole of the two views of which the lines PQ and RS are part are in projection. Similarly the lines TU and VW and the whole of the views to which they belong are also in projection. If the line of sight AB, along which the end view was obtained, is drawn in the front view as shown, then it should be clear that the projection lines connecting corresponding points in the front and end views are all parallel to that line of sight. Similarly the projection lines connecting the front view with the plan are parallel to the line of sight CD seen in the front view and along which the plan view was obtained.

When the front view, the end view and the plan are obtained in the manner described above, the relationship of the views is said to be according to the English convention or system. In that system, therefore, the view that appears *underneath* the front view is a view obtained by looking down on the *top* of the object, and the view that appears on the *right*-hand of the front view is a view obtained by looking on the *left*-hand end of the object. If a view appeared on the left hand of the front view, then that view would be a view obtained by looking on the right-hand of the object. These two end views would be identical as far as the outline of the object was concerned, but they would differ in the details seen. Thus, for the object considered above, one end view would show the cylindrical projection and the other end view would show the square projection.

The second method of relating the views is generally known as the *American method*, and is derived thus. The front view is obtained by placing the paper in *front* of the object, perpendicular to the line of sight. Then, imagining the paper to be transparent, the view is drawn on the side of the paper remote from the object. The view on the left-hand end of the object is next obtained by bending the paper round in *front* of that end until it is perpendicular to the line of sight. The view is again drawn on the side of the paper remote from the object and again the paper has to be imagined to be transparent. Similarly with the plan, the paper is bent round over the top of the object and the view drawn on the side of the paper remote from the object.

The process is shown in perspective in Fig. 1.12. In this system the object is always behind the paper and one looks 'through' the view on the paper to the object behind. This is the opposite to the procedure in the first system where the paper was always behind the object and one looked through the object on to the view.

When the paper is bent back into the flat the three views occupy the positions shown in Fig. 1.13. The view on the *left*-hand end of the object

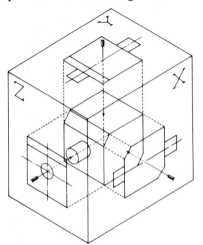

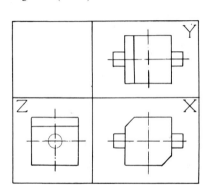

Fig. 1.12 (*left*)
Fig. 1.13 (*below*)

here appears on the *left* of the front elevation, and the plan or view from *above* appears *above* the front elevation. Each pair of views, that is, the front elevation and end view, and the front elevation and plan, is in projection just as in the first system.

The third method of relating the views is a mixture of the two previous systems. Thus the English system is followed with regard to the plan, which therefore appears underneath the front elevation, but the American system is followed with regard to the end views.

Present day practice leans towards the use of the third system, which is sometimes known as the *mixed system*, but after a little practice no difficulty should be experienced in following drawings made on any one of the systems. In this book views are generally placed according to the mixed system.

1.4 Sectional views

We have, so far, considered views on the outside of objects, but very often the internal shape has to be shown. This may be done in two ways: by means of dotted lines or by means of 'sectional' views. Dotted lines are also used to show the shape of a part of an object when it is hidden by another part. Dotted lines are difficult to follow, however, and except with comparatively simple things their use leads to confusion.

A sectional view is obtained by cutting an object into two pieces and looking on the cut surface of either piece. It is sometimes necessary to cut an object in this way in order to find out its internal shape, but usually the process is an imaginary one carried out only in the mind of the draughts-man.

In the consideration of the components of a motor car the internal parts are, generally speaking, the more interesting ones, and the sectional view is of great use. A large number of examples will therefore be considered in order that the reader may become familiar with sectional views—

(1) Fig. 1.14 shows a gudgeon pin (see Section 6.12), a simple hollow cylindrical pin that acts as a pivot; (*a*) is a perspective sketch of a sectioned pin, and the corresponding engineering sectional view is seen at (*b*); (*c*) is an ordinary side view in which the inside shape is shown in dotted lines.

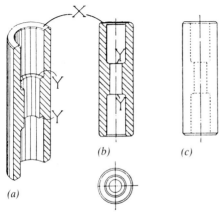

(*b*)   (*c*)

(*a*)

Fig. 1.14

The pin is thickened at the middle to stiffen it. Observe that the straight line X in (*b*) represents the surface X seen in (*a*). Similarly, the lines Y Y in (*b*) represent the ledges Y Y in (*a*) where the thickened middle part of the pin ends. The metal actually cut through is indicated by cross-hatching it.

(2) Fig. 1.15 shows a simple piston; (*a*) is a perspective view of the piston in section; (*b*) the corresponding engineering sectional view; (*c*) an outside end view, and (*d*) a plan. Observe the lines L, M and N in (*b*) which represent the ledges L, M and N in (*a*) where the thickness of the wall, or *skirt*, of the piston changes.

(3) Fig. 1.16 shows a flywheel in section, (*a*) in perspective and (*b*) as an engineering view. The flywheel is formed into a hollow cone at P to form part of a clutch. Observe the lines A, B, C, D and E in (*b*) which represent the corresponding surfaces similarly lettered in (*a*). The end view of this flywheel is simply a number of concentric circles, since the whole object is

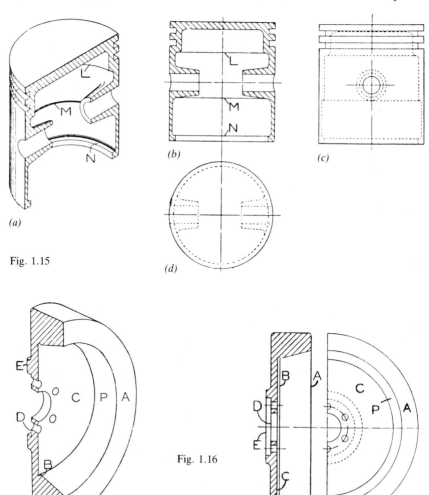

(a)

Fig. 1.15

(b)

(c)

(d)

Fig. 1.16

(a)

(b)

circular. When this is so an end view is not usually given but is left to the imagination.

(4) Fig. 1.17 shows another piston. The ceiling, or *crown*, of the piston appears in the perspective view (*a*) to be very thick, but actually it is not, the apparent thickness being due to the fact that a rib, or *web*, of metal runs across the middle of the piston to stiffen the crown, and this thin web has been cut lengthwise through the middle in making the section. In the engineering view (*b*) the true thickness of the crown is emphasised by leaving the web AAAA blank. This is a recognised convention adopted by draughtsmen. There is a second web, B in (*d*) (running at right angles to the web A), which is cut across by the section. In (*b*) this web is cross-hatched where it is sectioned, however, as no false impression is thereby given. The lines CC in (*b*) represent the sides of this web where they curve down into the skirt of the piston.

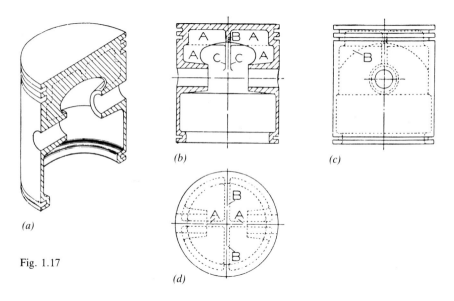

(a) (b) (c) (d)

Fig. 1.17

(5) Fig. 1.18 shows the inlet valve cage of a 150 hp Ricardo tank engine, which had an overhead inlet valve and a side exhaust valve. The lower part of the cage is cylindrical and fits in a hole in the cylinder casting, a gas-tight joint being obtained by means of the conical seating A. The cage is held in place by studs and nuts which pass through three lugs integral with it; these lugs are seen at B and two can be seen in the photograph of the complete cage. There is a second conical seating C for the valve to seat upon. The stem of the valve is guided in the long guide D, and the coil springs that close the valve are housed in the recess E. The cage is connected by the flange F with the induction pipe and the fuel-air mixture is drawn in, when the valve is depressed off its seat, through the arrowed passage shown in Fig. 1.18. It will be seen that a certain amount of obstruction to the flow of the gases is caused by the valve guide which projects into the gas passage. At the back of the cage is an arm H provided with a fulcrum pin upon which a rocker lever pivots.

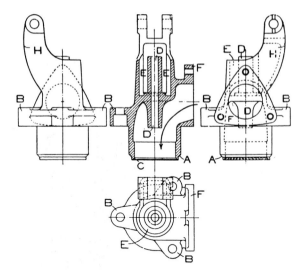

Fig. 1.18

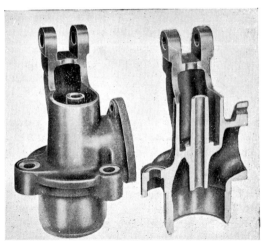

(6) Fig. 1.19 shows a plunger type oil pump used in the Ricardo engine. Its action is similar to that of the oscillating cylinder engines used on toys. The plunger is free to slide up and down in the cylinder which is formed in the member sectioned in black, and that motion is imparted to it by a crank pin which works in the hole in the end of the plunger. The cylinder is free to oscillate inside the casing, being cylindrical and a free fit therein. Suitable suction and delivery ports are provided in the casing as shown.

In the position shown in the drawing both ports are closed, but if the crank pin is turned in the direction of the arrow the cylinder will be oscillated clockwise, and the right-hand port will be put into communication with the cylinder. Since the plunger is moving up the cylinder, oil will be drawn in through the port. As the plunger approaches the top of its stroke the cylinder is oscillated back to the central position and the suction

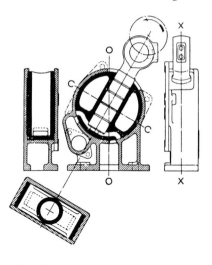

Fig. 1.19

port is closed. Continued motion of the crank pin causes the cylinder to oscillate further, thus opening the delivery port, and since the plunger is now moving downwards, oil is forced out of the cylinder. As the plunger approaches the bottom end of its stroke the cylinder is oscillated back to the central position and the delivery port is closed. The cycle is then repeated, if the crank pin continues to revolve. The grooves in the plunger serve to prevent the escape of oil. Note that the plunger is shown in outside view because nothing more would be shown if it were sectioned. This is frequently the case, and such things as shafts, bolts, spindles, wheel spokes, etc. are, as a rule, shown in outside view and not in section, although they would actually be cut through if a section were made.

In the photograph two of the studs, by means of which the pump is secured to the crank case of the engine, can be seen. A stud is a cylindrical piece of steel with a screw thread at each end. One end is screwed into one of two pieces that have to be secured together, the stud projects through a hole in a flange of the other piece which is then held in place by a nut which is screwed on the other end of the stud. Studs are meant to become a fixture in the part into which they are screwed; if the two pieces are required to be separated the nut is removed from the outer end of the stud and one piece is lifted off. Studs are used in preference to screws when bolts and nuts cannot be used and when the parts may have to be separated frequently. If a screw were used the constant screwing up and unscrewing would soon wear out the thread in the hole, and this cannot be easily rectified. When a stud is used it is the thread on its end that will be worn, and this is easily remedied by fitting a new stud. Thus it is important that studs should remain fixed in the part into which they are screwed, when their nuts are unscrewed; if they do not steps should be taken to secure them. This is especially important when studs are screwed into soft metals such as aluminium.

1.5 Draughtsmen's conventions

Conventional methods of depicting certain things such as screw threads, gear teeth, etc., are often employed by draughtsmen and these, unless mentioned, may be puzzling when met for the first time.

Four methods of showing a V screw thread on the end of a rod are shown in Fig. 1.20. Of these only the second and fourth indicate the 'hand' of the thread, a right-handed thread being shown. These methods are also used for screwed holes, the lines being dotted unless the part is in section. In the latter case the method shown in Fig. 1.21 may be used.

Diagonal lines as shown at A in Fig. 1.22 are frequently used to indicate flats formed on cylindrical pieces. In the figure they are used to show two of the four flat faces of the squared end of a shaft, such as might be used when a handle had to be fixed to the shaft rotationally. A common method of securing a wheel is by a *key*, which is a piece of metal as indicated at B. This is sunk for about half its depth in a recess C formed in the shaft, and then projects into a groove or keyway formed inside the boss of the pulley. An alternative form of key is shown at D; this is a Woodruff key. Keys are sometimes indicated by diagonal lines as shown. Another method of securing two pieces together rotationally is by means of a splined shaft. This is in effect a shaft on which a number of keys are formed integrally, but the keys are then called *splines*. The appearance of a splined shaft is shown in Fig. 1.23. They are sometimes indicated by diagonal lines also. (The curves at the ends of the recesses, as at A, are due to the use of a circular cutter in the manufacture.)

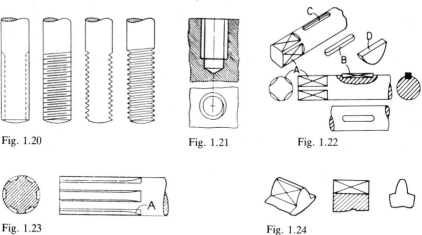

Fig. 1.20   Fig. 1.21   Fig. 1.22

Fig. 1.23   Fig. 1.24

Diagonal lines are also used to indicate the teeth of gear wheels, as shown in Fig. 1.24, and the teeth of 'positive clutches' (see Section 21.1). The teeth of gear wheels are frequently not drawn fully but are indicated by dotted circles, as shown in Fig. 22.1, page 475.

Chapter 2

Bearings and gearing

When a shaft has to revolve it must be supported in bearings that will allow of the desired rotation. The simplest bearing is just a cylindrical hole formed in a piece of material and in which the shaft is a free fit. The hole is usually lined with a brass or bronze lining, or *bush*, which not only reduces the friction in the bearing but also enables an easy replacement to be made when wear occurs. Bushes are usually a tight fit in the hole in which they fit. To reduce the friction to the lowest amount, ball-and-roller bearings, in which 'rolling' friction replaces the 'sliding' friction that occurs in 'plain' bearings, are used.

Considering the shaft shown in Fig. 2.1, it will be seen that two bearings are provided. This is almost universally done because otherwise the single bearing would have to be of an inordinate length. It will also be observed that the bearings shown are capable of withstanding only loads that are perpendicular to the axis of the shaft. Such loads are called *radial* loads, and the bearings that carry them are called *radial* or *journal bearings*. That part of a shaft that actually lies within a bearing is called a *journal*. To prevent the shaft from moving in the axial direction shoulders or collars may be formed on it or secured to it, as shown in Fig. 2.2, which shows the loose collar secured by a grub screw P. If both collars are made integral with the shaft then obviously in order that the shaft may be put into position the bearings must be split or made in halves, the top half, or *cap*, being put on and bolted in place after the shaft has been put in. The collars

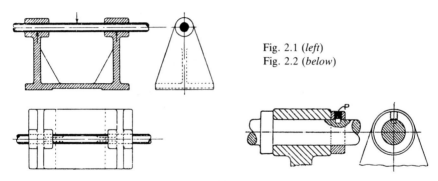

Fig. 2.1 (*left*)
Fig. 2.2 (*below*)

or shoulders withstand any end thrusts, and bearings that do this are termed *thrust bearings*.

Figs. 2.3 to 2.8 show various forms of ball-and-roller bearings. Fig. 2.3 shows a single-row journal or radial ball bearing. The inner race B is a ring of steel case-hardened (provided with a hardened surface layer but having a soft centre or core) with a groove or track formed on its outer circumference for a number of hardened steel balls to run upon. The outer race A is another ring which has a track on its inner circumference. The balls fit between the two tracks, thus enabling the outer race to turn relatively to the inner one, the balls meanwhile rolling round the tracks. The balls are kept from rubbing against each other by some form of cage. Such a bearing, as its name *radial* implies, is meant to withstand chiefly radial loads; they will usually, however, withstand a considerable amount of axial thrust and are often used as combined journal and thrust bearings. Both the inner and the outer races are then secured in the end direction between nuts and shoulders or by other means. When the bearing is used simply to take radial loads one of the races is left free axially. Some journal-thrust ball bearings can take thrust loads only in one direction; care has therefore to be taken when assembling these to ensure that they are properly placed to take the thrust load.

Fig. 2.4 shows an SKF self-aligning ball bearing. The outer race is ground on the inside to form part of a sphere whose centre is on the axis of the shaft. Hence the axis of the inner race and shaft may be displaced out

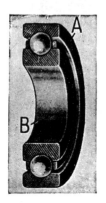
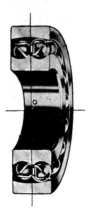
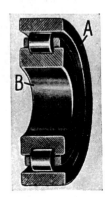

Fig. 2.3 Fig. 2.4 Fig. 2.5

of parallel with that of the outer race without affecting the action of the bearing. Two rows of balls are used. Such bearings are desirable where the deflection of a shaft or frame cannot be limited to a negligible amount. They are often used in back axles.

An example of a parallel-roller journal bearing appears in Fig. 2.5. The tracks on the races A and B are now cylinders and cylindrical rollers take the place of the balls. Roller bearings can withstand heavier radial loads than equivalent-sized ball bearings, but obviously the one shown cannot withstand any end thrust. By providing lips or shoulders on both inner and outer races a parallel-roller bearing can be made to withstand small end thrusts and this is sometimes done. If, however, the tracks and rollers are made conical, giving a taper-roller bearing, then large end thrusts can be taken in one direction. A taper-roller bearing is shown in Fig. 2.6. It may be pointed out that the angles of the cones forming the races and the rollers have to be such that when the bearing is assembled all the cones have a common apex lying on the axis of the shaft.

Roller bearings in which the length of the rollers is equal to several times their diameter are called *needle-roller bearings*. Often these have no cage, the rollers completely filling the space between the inner and outer races. An example is seen at H in Fig. 24.2.

Fig. 2.7 shows a *single thrust bearing*. The tracks are now formed on the inner faces of two discs, A and B, so that an end thrust can be carried. In Fig. 2.8 a *double thrust race* or *bearing* is seen, in which two sets of balls are provided so that thrusts in either direction can be taken; the races A and C abut against shoulders or nuts on the revolving shaft while the central race B is fixed in the stationary housing. The balls may be carried in a cage, but whereas this is almost universal with journal bearings, thrust bearings are often not provided with cages. Thrust bearings are not capable of taking radial loads; these, therefore, have to be taken by journal bearings.

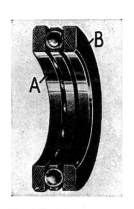

Fig. 2.6   Fig. 2.7   Fig. 2.8

From the point of view of the user the most important point concerning ball-and-roller bearings is the necessity for absolute cleanliness. Dirt, dust, particles of metal and water will quickly destroy them. In machining, the holes in which outer races fit should be truly cylindrical and the outer race should usually be a fairly free fit. The inner race, which is normally the revolving one, should, on the other hand, be a tight fit on its shaft.

Greases containing animal fats must not be used in ball bearings as the acids usually contained in these lubricants destroy the races and balls. Most oil companies put up greases which are suitable for ball bearings and their recommendations should be accepted.

In general, unless bearings are overloaded as a result of bad design or gross overloading of the vehicle, or are exposed to water or dust, they will give no trouble and may easily outlast the rest of the vehicle.

2.1   Types of toothed gearing

Toothed gearing, which is used to transmit motion of rotation from one
shaft to another, assumes various forms according to the relative positions
of the shafts. When the shafts are parallel the gears are called *spur gears*,
and are cylinders with teeth cut on the outside or the inside according to
whether they are external or internal gears. Examples of such gearing are
shown in Figs. 2.9 and 2.10 respectively. In these cases the teeth are seen to
be cut parallel to the axes of the gears. Such teeth are called *straight* to
distinguish them from those shown in Fig. 2.11 which, being parts of
helices, are called *helical teeth*. Owing to the inclination of helical teeth

Fig. 2.9   Fig. 2.10

there is an axial or end thrust on each gear tending to separate them
axially. These end thrusts have to be resisted by suitable thrust bearings.
The end thrust is avoided in *double helical gearing* (Fig. 2.12) where the
thrust from one half of a tooth is counteracted by that from the other half.
In all the forms of spur gearing the forces between the teeth in contact tend
to separate the gears radially. These forces have to be taken by the journal
bearings of the shafts.

   When their axes intersect, shafts are connected by *bevel gearing*. Bevel
gears are cones with teeth cut upon them. The teeth may be straight, giving
straight-toothed bevel gears, as shown in Fig. 2.13, or spiral, giving *spiral
bevel gears* (Fig. 2.14). With straight-toothed bevel gears, since the forces
between the teeth in contact tend to separate the gears both radially and
axially, thrust bearings must be fitted behind each gear. When spiral teeth
are used the axial forces on the gears may tend to separate them or to make
them mesh more deeply; it depends upon the angle of the spiral, whether it
is right-handed or left-handed, and upon the direction of rotation. With
spiral bevel gears, therefore, it is usual to fit double thrust bearings.

   When the shafts are neither parallel nor intersect they may be connected
by either *skew, worm* or *hypoid gearing*. A pair of skew gears is illustrated
in Fig. 2.15. These are usually cylindrical, being then identical with helical

Fig. 2.11 (*above*)
Fig. 2.12 (*right*)

Fig. 2.13 (*left*)
Fig. 2.14 (*below*)

toothed spur gears, but one of them is sometimes hollowed out like a 'worm wheel' so that it embraces the other, as this gives a better contact between the teeth and results in an increased efficiency.

The ordinary type of worm gearing is shown in Fig. 2.16. The worm (at the top) may be considered as part of a screw having a number of threads. If the wheel is considered to represent a nut it will be seen that if the worm is prevented from moving in the axial direction and then it is rotated, the worm-wheel also will have to revolve. This type is known as *parallel worm gearing*, the worm being a parallel screw. There is another type in which the worm is shaped to embrace the wheel, instead of being parallel. It is known in its general application as the *Hindley*, *hour-glass* or *globoidal* type, but in its application to motor cars as the *Lanchester worm*, since Dr. Lanchester developed if for that application. In both types of worm gearing there are both radial and axial forces acting on the worm and the wheel tending to separate them. The directions of these forces change when the direction of the motion is reversed and, besides journal bearings, double

Fig. 2.15 (*left*)
Fig. 2.16 (*below*)

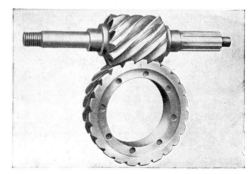

Fig. 2.17

thrust bearings have to be fitted to both worm and wheel. The efficiency of worm gearing depends to a very great extent on the quality of the materials used, the accuracy and degree of finish and on the lubrication. When these factors are right the efficiency is very high (commonly about 95 to 99%).

The efficiency of good spur gearing is also very high, bevel gears are slightly less efficient and skew gears least efficient of all.

An example of hypoid gearing is shown in Fig. 2.17, from which it will be seen that the chief difference between it and spiral bevel gearing is that the axis of the pinion is placed lower than that of the crown wheel so that the axes of the gears do not intersect. If desirable the pinion axis may be placed above the crown wheel axis. There are two chief advantages claimed for the hypoid gear over the spiral bevel, greater quietness and greater strength; it is possible to make the pinion larger than that of spiral bevel gears having the same gear ratio and same size of crown wheel. If this increased strength is unnecessary then the hypoid gears can be made smaller than the corresponding spiral bevel gears. There is a sliding action in the direction of the length of the teeth of hypoid gears that is absent in bevel gearing and this makes lubrication of the teeth a more difficult matter so that special lubricants frequently have to be used with hypoid gearing.

2.2 Gear ratio of toothed gearing

When two shafts are connected by toothed gearing of any of the types described, the ratio between the speeds of those shafts will always be constant. This constant ratio is called the *gear ratio*. In all the types of gearing considered when one wheel drives another the gear ratio between them will be the *inverse* ratio of the numbers of teeth in the wheels. Thus if a wheel A drives a wheel B then—

$$\frac{\text{Speed of A}}{\text{Speed of B}} \equiv \frac{\text{Number of teeth in B}}{\text{Number of teeth in A}}$$

and the bigger wheel goes slower than the smaller one. This will be clear when it is realised that in any given time as many teeth of the wheel A as of the wheel B, pass the point (P) where the teeth mesh together. Now suppose the speeds of the wheels are S_a and S_b rev/min and numbers of teeth N_a and N_b. Then the number of teeth of A that pass the point P in one minute is $N_a \times S_a$ while for B the number is $N_b \times S_b$ and these are equal, thus—

$$N_a \times S_a = N_b \times S_b \quad \text{or} \quad S_a/S_b = N_b/N_a$$

The rule applies to worm gearing, the number of teeth in the worm being equal to the number of threads or starts it has. The number of starts is easily seen by looking at the worm from the end.

Chapter 3

Some fundamental principles of mechanics

The subject of mechanics deals with the action of forces on bodies and with the motion that results from such action. A knowledge of the fundamental principles of mechanics is therefore necessary if the working of the various components of an internal combustion engine and vehicle is to be properly understood, and if the reasons for the adoption of certain constructions are to be appreciated.

3.1 Mass, force and motion

In mechanics, a *body* means a certain amount of 'stuff' or 'matter', and it is the quantity of matter in a body with which we are principally concerned. This quantity is called the *mass* of the body, and it may conveniently be measured by means of weights and scales, the measurement being in reality a comparison with that of a standard body arbitrarily chosen.

Bodies are either at rest or in motion, both states being considered relatively to some body of reference, usually the earth. The motion of a body may be very complicated, but it can always be separated into two component motions of a simple character – *motion of translation* and *motion of rotation*. In the first every point of the body moves in a straight line. In the second all the points in the body move in concentric circles, that is, the body revolves about a fixed axis. It will be convenient to consider these motions separately.

3.2 Motion of translation

Motion of translation is either uniform or variable. If it is uniform then the body will traverse equal distances in equal intervals of time, and the measure of the speed of the body is the distance covered divided by the time taken. If the motion is variable the speed changes from instant to instant, and dividing the distance covered by the time taken will only give the average speed during the interval. In mechanics speeds are usually measured in metres per second, and a speed of 20 metres per second is usually written 20 m/s. For high speeds, kilometres per hour (km/h) is more convenient.

When the speed of a body is changing, the rate at which it changes is called the *acceleration* of the body. Accelerations may be either uniform or variable. If uniform they may be measured by measuring the increase or decrease in the speed in a given time interval. If the speed of a body increases by 1 m/s in one second, then the acceleration is one metre-per-second per second for which the SI abbreviation is 1 m/s². Variable accelerations need not be considered here.

Forces, in mechanics, are any actions that tend to move a body from a state of rest or to alter the motion of a moving body. Altering the motion of a body means either increasing or decreasing its speed or changing the direction in which it moves. Forces are recognised as acting in definite directions or along definite 'lines of action' and at definite 'points of application'.

In the SI system, the unit of force is called the newton (note the small initial n) and it is the force that will give a body whose mass is unity an acceleration of 1 m/s². As the unit of mass in the SI system is the kilogram, a newton is the force that will give a mass of one kilogram an acceleration of one metre-per-second per second and this unit is denoted by the symbol N. For large forces a unit of 1000 N may be used and this is denoted by the symbol kN.

3.3 Newton's Laws of Motion

The superstructure of mechanics has been raised upon three axioms first enunciated by Sir Isaac Newton and known as his *Laws of Motion*. They are—

(1) Every body continues in its state of rest, or of uniform motion in a straight line, except in so far as it is compelled, by external impressed forces, to alter that state.

(2) The acceleration produced by a force acting on a body is directly proportional to the magnitude of the force, inversely proportional to the mass of the body and takes place in the direction of the line of action of the force.

(3) To every action there is an equal and opposite reaction.

Certain corollaries follow from the first of these statements.

If a body at rest is caused to move, a force must have acted upon it; if a body in uniform motion in a straight line is caused to go faster or slower or to deviate from the straight line, a force must have acted upon it.

A body can move in a curved path only so long as a force acts upon it to deflect it from the straight path.

If a body is at rest or is moving uniformly in a straight line, then either there are no forces acting upon it or the forces that are acting upon it are *in equilibrium*, that is, they neutralise each other so as to have no net effect or *resultant*.

From the second axiom it will be seen that if the force acting on a given body is doubled, then the acceleration also will be doubled, while if a given acceleration is to be produced in each of two bodies, and the mass of the first is twice that of the second, then the force that must be applied to the first must be twice that which must be applied to the second.

The third statement will be made clear by an example. If a body rests upon the ground it acts downwards on the ground with a force equal to its weight, but the ground also acts upwards on the body with an equal force. Again, if a lorry hauling a trailer pulls on the tow-rope with a force P, it is evident that the rope tends to pull the lorry backwards with an equal force P.

3.4   Inertia forces

Consider a body acted upon by a force P as shown in Fig. 3.1. The force will accelerate the body in the direction PQ, and is spent in overcoming the disinclination of the body to change its state of motion, or briefly, in overcoming the inertia of the body. The inertia of a body that is accelerated (or decelerated) by a force P, may be expressed as a force P_1 equal to P and acting at the 'mass centre' of the body in a direction opposite to the force P, but it must be observed that the force P_1 is an internal force and not an external one.

The mass centre of a body is a point in the body such that if the line of action of any force acting on the body passes through the point, the force has no tendency to rotate the body. Or, it is that point at which the whole of the matter in the body may be considered to be concentrated. The more familiar phrase *centre of gravity* (CG) should be used only in the case of gravitational forces.

It follows from the first definition that if a force acts on a body and the line of action of the force does not pass through the mass centre of the body then the force will have a tendency to rotate the body. This may be seen as follows. In Fig. 3.2 the force P acting on the body produces a linear acceleration in the direction PQ. The internal inertia force expressing the

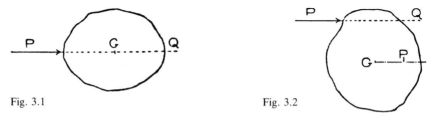

Fig. 3.1   Fig. 3.2

disinclination of the body to be accelerated is an equal and opposite force P_1 acting at the mass centre G. Then clearly the two forces P and P_1 have a tendency to turn the body in a clockwise direction. It must be remembered that the force P_1 is an internal one. If it were an external force the body would not be accelerated at all in the direction PQ, since the two forces would produce equal accelerations in opposite directions which would cancel out. The tendency to rotate, however, would remain.

3.5   Couples

Thus the only effect of two equal external forces that act upon a body in opposite directions is to rotate the body. Such a pair of forces is called a *twisting moment, torque* or *couple*. When motion of rotation alone is being considered we are concerned with couples rather than with forces.

The tendency of two forces, constituting a couple, to rotate the body upon which they act is proportional to the magnitude of the forces and to the perpendicular distance between their (parallel) lines of action. If the magnitude of the forces is *P* and the perpendicular distance between their lines of action is *l*, then the magnitude of the couple is $P \times l$. Since forces are measured in newtons and distances in metres, a couple will be measured in units of newtons × metres; this unit is called a newton-metre and is denoted by Nm.

It is now necessary to turn to motion of rotation.

3.6 Rotational motion

The rotational motion of a body may be either uniform or variable. If it is uniform it may be measured by ascertaining the number of revolutions made in a given time. The speed would then be obtained as so many revolutions per minute or per second (rev/min or rev/s) and this is the common method of measuring rotational speeds; however in the SI system, angles are measured in radians and so the unit of angular speed is one radian per second, or 1 rad/s. Revolutions per minute will undoubtedly continue to be used however.

If the rotational speed is variable, then the measurement of the number of revolutions made in a given time will give only the average speed during the interval. When the rotational speed of a body is increasing or decreasing, the rate of increase or decrease – that is, the rotational or angular acceleration – may be measured, if it is uniform, by measuring the increase or decrease in the angular speed during a given time interval. The angular acceleration will then be obtained as so many rev/min per minute; in SI units angular accelerations will be measured in radians-per-second per second, or rad/s^2.

We may now consider Newton's three laws as they apply to rotational motion—

(1) Every body continues in its state of rest or of uniform rotation about an axis fixed in direction, except in so far as it is compelled by external impressed couples, or by a force whose line of action does not pass through the mass centre of the body, to alter that state.

(2) The angular acceleration produced by a couple acting on a body is directly proportional to the magnitude of the couple, inversely proportional to 'the moment of inertia of the body about the axis about which the acceleration occurs', and takes place in the plane of the couple.

(3) To every couple there is an equal and opposite reactionary couple.

In considering the first of these it should be noted that the rotational motion of a body is not affected by any motion of translation the body may have and *vice versa*. Thus corresponding to uniform motion in a straight line when translatory motion is being considered we have, for rotational motion, uniform rotation about an axis that always remains parallel to its original position, i.e., that is fixed in direction.

Certain corollaries follow from the first statement—

(a) If a body at rest is caused to rotate, a couple must have acted upon it.

(b) If a body that is rotating uniformly about a fixed axis is caused to go faster or slower a couple must have acted upon it.

(c) If a body is rotating about a certain axis and the direction of that axis is changed, a couple must have acted upon it.

(d) If a body is at rest or is rotating uniformly about an axis fixed in direction, then either there is no couple acting on it or the couples that act upon it neutralise each other and have no net effect or resultant. The body is then in rotational equilibrium.

3.7   Moment of inertia of a body

If the statement in (b) above is compared with the second statement in Section 3.3, it will be found that in place of the mass of the body there is now the 'moment of inertia of the body about the axis about which the angular acceleration occurs'. This quantity however, unlike the mass of a body, depends upon the shape of the body and on the position of the axis of rotation. This may perhaps be made clearer as follows.

Suppose a definite weight of steel is taken and is formed first into a long shaft of small diameter, and secondly into a flywheel as shown in Fig. 1.16. Then it should not be difficult to realise that while it will be comparatively easy to grasp the shaft and to twist it to and fro about its axis (an operation involving continual angular acceleration and deceleration of the shaft) it will be impossible to twist the flywheel to and fro at anything like the same rate. This is because the moment of inertia of the flywheel is very large compared with that of the shaft, although the weights (and masses) of the two are equal; this, in turn, is because the matter composing the shaft is disposed in such a way that it is all quite close to the axis of the shaft, whereas in the flywheel most of the matter is situated at a considerable distance from the axis. The effect, as regards rotational inertia, of each particle of matter in the bodies is dependent on the distance of that particle from the axis of rotation. (Actually the effect *varies* as the square of the distance, so that if the distance of one particle is twice that of another the effect of the first is four times that of the second.) It is possible to find an equivalent radius at which all the particles composing the body may be considered to act. This equivalent radius is called the *radius of gyration* of the body about the axis concerned, and the moment of inertia of the body is equal to the mass of the body multiplied by the *square* of the radius of gyration relative to that axis.

The torque reaction of a back axle is an example of the third axiom, and this is considered in Section 26.4.

3.8 Resolution of forces

A force can be represented by a line drawn in the proper direction and of length proportional (on any convenient scale) to the magnitude of the force, but the representation is not complete until an arrowhead has been inserted to indicate the direction in which the force acts. Thus the line PQ in Fig. 3.3, being 20 mm long, represents a force of 100 N to a scale of 1 mm to 5 N. If now a parallelogram PAQB is drawn upon PQ as diagonal it can be shown that if the lines PA and PB represent forces (to the same scale as for PQ) then the forces PA and PB acting together are equivalent to the force PQ and might replace that force without affecting the action in any way. The forces PA, PB are called the *components* of PQ, and the process of finding them is called the *resolution of forces*. Usually it is required to resolve a force in two directions which are at right angles; the parallelogram then becomes a rectangle.

3.9 Constrained bodies

So far we have considered the action of forces upon bodies that are free and unconstrained; we pass on to the consideration of bodies that are constrained so that they can move only in definite paths determined by the constraining influence. An example of a constrained body is an axle carried in bearings; the body can have only rotational motion. Another example is a piston in a cylinder; which can have only motion in a straight line.

It will be found that the motions of the parts of mechanisms are all constrained motions. However, the motion of a constrained body can be considered exactly as if the body were unconstrained, provided that the forces introduced by the constraints are considered. These forces, however, can generally be found by considering the equilibrium of the body in the direction in which motion is prevented by the constraint. An example will make this clear.

Fig. 3.4 shows a body A constrained by guides BB so that it can move only along the straight line XY, while a force P acts upon it as shown. Then, since no motion is possible in the direction perpendicular to XY there can be no resultant force acting on the body in that direction. The force P, however, has a component Q in that direction: the constraint must therefore supply a force equal and opposite to Q. This is supplied by the reaction Q_1 acting on the body – the pressure between the body and the guide.

Since we know that there is equilibrium in the direction perpendicular to XY, when we are considering the motion of the body we need not consider the forces, or components of forces, that act in that direction, but can confine our attention to the forces, and the components of forces, that act parallel to XY.

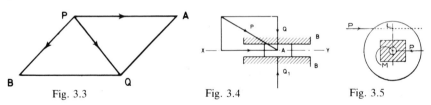

Fig. 3.3   Fig. 3.4   Fig. 3.5

As another example, consider a body pivoted on a fixed axis. The constraint is such that the body cannot have any motion of translation. There cannot, therefore, be any resultant force acting on the body. If a force P acts on the body as shown in Fig. 3.5, then the constraint (in this case the bearings in which the axle turns) will supply an equal force, acting parallel and in the opposite direction to P so that the only resultant action on the body is a couple, which can only produce rotational motion. (The force supplied by the bearings is an external force quite different from the internal inertia force shown in Fig. 3.2.) The magnitude of the couple is, of course, $P \times$ (distance LM). The force supplied by the bearings is often so much taken for granted that instead of speaking of the couple PP it is usual to speak of the product $P \times$ (LM) as the 'moment of the force P about the axis M'.

3.10   Centrifugal force

A common form of constraint is that which compels a body in motion to move in a circle. Since the direction of the motion is then continually changing (being always tangential to the circle), it follows that a force must be continually acting to produce the change. This force is supplied by the constraint; for example, if a cord attaches a body to a centre the force is the pull the cord applies to the body; it acts always towards the centre and is a centripetal force; its reaction is the pull applied by the body to the cord and it acts away from the centre, being the *centrifugal force* (CF). Its magnitude is directly proportional to the mass of the body and the square of the linear speed, and inversely proportional to the radius of the circle.

$$CF = \text{mass} \times (\text{linear speed})^2/\text{radius}$$
$$= \text{mass} \times (\text{angular speed})^2 \times \text{radius}$$

In SI units the mass will be in kilograms, the angular speed in radians per second and the radius in metres; the CF will then be in newtons.

3.11   Friction

If a body is placed upon a flat horizontal table it will be found that in order to move the body over the surface of the table at a *uniform* speed a force must be applied to it. Since the speed is uniform the body is in equilibrium, and there is no resultant force acting on it. It follows, therefore, that acting somewhere on the body there must be a force equal and opposite to the applied force, and the only place where such a force can exist is between the surfaces in contact. This force between the surfaces in contact is called the *force of friction*. If the applied force is increased then the difference between it and the frictional force will go to accelerate the body. If the applied force is decreased, then the difference between it and the frictional force will go to decelerate the body and ultimately to bring it to rest.

The magnitude of the frictional force depends upon several factors. The first is the materials of which the surfaces are composed. The friction between two blocks of wood is greater than between two blocks of steel, other factors being the same. The second factor is the condition of the surfaces, whether rough, smooth or polished, clean or dirty, dry or oily.

The third factor is the force acting between the surfaces in contact, but it is only the force perpendicular to the surfaces that affects the friction. This perpendicular force between the surfaces is called the *normal force*, the normal to a curve or surface being a line at right angles to the curve or surface.

The frictional force may be expressed in terms of the normal force, and a quantity that depends upon the kind and condition of the surfaces and which is known as the *coefficient of friction*. Thus if—

$$F = \text{force of friction}$$
$$P = \text{normal force}$$
$$\mu = \text{coefficient of friction,}$$
$$\text{then } F = \mu \times P.$$

In the consideration of any actual contact between two bodies, the kind of surface and the condition of the surfaces will not usually alter, so that the coefficient of friction in any particular case is usually a constant.

The above relation does not include any factor depending on the area of the contact or on the velocity of sliding. This is because those factors do not greatly affect the frictional force. If the force acting between two surfaces is kept constant, then altering the area of the contact will alter the *pressure* between the surfaces and the amount of wear in a given time, but it will not alter the frictional force. When the velocity of sliding is increased the frictional force will generally be decreased, but unless the increase in the velocity is large, the effect on the frictional force will be negligible. The value of the coefficient of friction varies from as low as 0.01 up to as much as 0.8 and more. Some values in particular cases are given in connection with clutches. (See Section 19.7).

It must be borne in mind that it is the *normal force* between the surfaces that determines the magnitude of the frictional force. If, therefore, a force acts upon a body at an angle to the contact surfaces it is the component of that force perpendicular to the surfaces that has to be considered.

When the above relation between the normal and the frictional force holds, the friction is called *solid friction* to distinguish it from the friction that occurs in liquids, which is known as *fluid friction*. If two bodies are separated by a complete film of oil or other fluid the frictional force between them depends on the laws of fluid friction. These are quite different from those of solid friction and are dealt with in Chapter 15.

Although, as already mentioned, an increase in the velocity of sliding has very little effect on the frictional force, yet if that velocity becomes zero, so that the bodies are at rest relatively, an appreciable change occurs in the frictional force between them, the change being an increase. This fact is allowed for by using a slightly higher coefficient when the bodies are at rest than when they are sliding. The coefficient that applies to the state of rest is generally called the *static* coefficient, and that applying to the state of motion the *kinetic* coefficient.

3.12 Work and energy

To lift a weight from the ground on to a table requires the expenditure of energy. The weight of a body is a force which has to be overcome when the body is lifted and the product of the force and the distance is a measure of the work done. In the SI system, unit work is done when a unit force (1 newton) is overcome through a unit distance (1 metre); this unit is called a *joule* and is denoted by the symbol J. When a force moves one body over the surface of another against the force of friction, work is done. If a force of P newtons acts upon a body and the point of application of the force moves a distance of L metres *in the direction of the force* then the force does P × L joules of work.

No work is done by a force unless its point of application moves in the direction of the force. Thus, if there is no friction, no work is done in moving a body over a horizontal surface, since the motion is perpendicular to the only force acting, that is, the weight of the body. If a force acts on a body along a line of action making an angle with the direction in which the body moves, then it is only the component of the force in the direction of the motion which does work. When a force acts to assist the motion of a body the force is said to do work on the body. When a force opposes the motion of a body the phrase 'work is done against the force' is used.

The energy expended in lifting a weight is not lost, but is stored as *potential* energy, and may be obtained again. By means of suitable apparatus the weight in falling to its original level could be made to drive a dynamo and generate electric current or to raise the temperature of a quantity of water. When a force does work on a body by accelerating the body, the work done is stored as energy of motion or *kinetic energy*, which may be obtained again by bringing the body to rest. Energy may thus exist under many different forms. We have, for example, potential energy, kinetic energy, heat energy, electrical energy, the energy of light and sound, chemical energy and strain energy (the energy stored in a compressed spring is stored by virtue of the strain or deformation of the material of the spring). Energy existing in one form can generally be changed into energy in another form, but there are limitations to these processes about which more will be said when we come to consider heat engines.

3.13   Power

Although the same amount of work is done when a weight is lifted through a height, whether the process occupies one second, one minute, or one year, the *rate* at which the work is done varies with the time taken. When we say that one engine is more powerful than another we mean that it can do a greater quantity of work in a given time, that is, that it can work at a greater rate. The 'power' of an engine thus expresses the 'rate at which it can work'. In the British system of units, the unit of work was the ft lb and the unit of time the second, so the unit rate of working would logically be a rate of 1 ft lb per second. This unit, however, was too small to be used conveniently by engineers, who therefore used a unit called the *horsepower* (hp). One horsepower is a rate of working of 550 ft lb per second or 33 000 ft lb per minute. It was introduced by James Watt and was meant to represent the rate at which a good horse could work continuously. The SI unit of power is the watt, W, which is one joule per second, 1 J/s, or 1 Nm/s. One horsepower is 745.7 W. The metric horsepower 1 PS = 75 kgf m/s ≈ 736 W. From this, it can be seen that SI units are not necessarily the same as other metric units.

3.14 Principle of the conservation of energy

This principle states that although energy may be changed from one form to another, yet it cannot be destroyed or lost; it may pass out of control and be unusable yet it still exists. For our purposes the principle can be stated in the following way—

$$
\begin{Bmatrix} \text{Rate at which} \\ \text{work is done on} \\ \text{a machine at one} \\ \text{end} \end{Bmatrix} = \begin{Bmatrix} \text{Rate at which} \\ \text{work is performed} \\ \text{by the machine at} \\ \text{the other end} \end{Bmatrix} + \begin{Bmatrix} \text{Rate at which} \\ \text{energy is stored} \\ \text{within the machine} \end{Bmatrix} + \begin{Bmatrix} \text{Rate at which} \\ \text{energy is used in} \\ \text{overcoming fric-} \\ \text{tion within the} \\ \text{machine} \end{Bmatrix}
$$

Part 2

The Engine

Chapter 4

General principles of heat engines

The petrol or oil engine, which is the source of power with which we are immediately concerned, is a form of internal combustion 'heat engine', the function of which is to convert potential heat energy contained in the fuel into mechanical work.

It is outside the scope of the present volume to go deeply into the physical laws governing this conversion, for a full study of which a work such as A. C. Walshaw's *Thermodynamics for Engineers* (Longmans-Green), should be consulted. It will not be out of place, however, to give a brief outline of the general principles.

4.1 Heat and work

A quantity of heat is conveniently measured by applying it to raise the temperature of a known quantity of pure water.

The unit of heat is defined as that quantity of heat required to raise the temperature of unit weight of water through one degree, this quantity depending, of course, on the particular unit of weight and the temperature scale employed.

The Continental European and scientific temperature scale has been the Centigrade scale, now called *Celsius* because of possible confusion with the French meaning of the word *centigrade* – one ten thousandth of a right angle. The interval between the temperatures of melting ice and boiling water (at normal pressure) is divided into one hundred, though the unsatisfactory Fahrenheit scale, which divides the foregoing interval into 180 divisions, has been the commercial standard in Britain and the USA.

It is thus necessary to define by name three different units of heat as follows –

The British Thermal Unit (Btu): The heat required to raise the temperature of 1 lb of water through 1°F. (1 Btu = 1.05506 kJ).

The Pound Calorie or Centigrade Heat Unit (CHU): The heat required to raise the temperature of 1 lb of water through 1°C. (1 CHU = 1.9 kJ).

The Kilogram Calorie: The heat required to raise the temperature of 1 kg of water through 1°C. (1 calorie = 4.186 J).

The first and second of these units are clearly in the ratio of the Fahrenheit degree to the Centigrade degree, or 5:9, while the second and third are in the ratio of the pound to the kilogram or 1:2.204. Thus the three units in the order given are in the ratio 5, 9, 19.84, or 1, 1.8, 3.97. Now, as mentioned in Section 3.12, we use the *joule*, which approximately equals 0.24 calories.

The *therm*, formerly used by Gas Boards, is 100 000 British thermal units (Btu).

To recapitulate briefly some definitions already given –

4.2 Work

If work is done by rotating a shaft, the quantity of work is the product of the torque or turning moment applied to the shaft in newton metres, multiplied by the angle turned through measured in radians. One revolution equals 2π radians.

4.3 Joule's equivalent

Dr. Joule was the first to show, in the middle of the last century, that heat and work were mutually convertible one to the other, being, in fact, different forms of energy, and that when a definite quantity of work is expended wholly in producing heat by friction or similar means, a definite quantity of heat is produced. His experiments, confirmed and corrected by others, showed that 778 foot-pounds produce one Btu, or 1400 foot-pounds produce one CHU.

This figure is called *the mechanical equivalent of heat*, though it would perhaps be better to speak of the *thermal equivalent of work*. For though the same equivalent or rate of exchange holds for conversion in either direction, while it is comparatively simple to convert to heat by friction the whole of a quantity of work supplied, it is not possible, in a heat engine, to convert to mechanical work more than a comparatively small percentage of the total *heat* supplied. There are definite physical laws which limit this percentage – or *thermal efficiency* as it is called – to about 50% or less in the best heat engines that it is practicable to construct.

4.4 Thermal efficiency

The thermal efficiency is governed chiefly by the range of temperature through which the working fluid, be it gas or steam, passes on its way through the engine.

This range of temperature is greater in internal combustion engines than in steam engines, hence the former are inherently capable of higher thermal efficiencies, that is to say, they are capable of converting into work a higher percentage of the total heat of the fuel with which they are supplied than the latter. Even so, the physical limitations are such that the thermal efficiency of a good petrol engine is only about 25%. The remaining 75% of the heat supplied, which is *not* converted into work, is lost in the exhaust gases and cooling water, and in radiation.

4.5 Calorific value

When unit weight of any fuel is completely burnt with oxygen (pure or diluted with nitrogen as in the air), a certain definite quantity of heat is liberated, depending on the chemical composition, that is, on the quantities of the fundamental fuels, carbon and hydrogen, which one pound of the fuel contains.

To determine how much potential heat energy is being supplied to an engine in a given time, it is necessary to know the weight of fuel supplied and its calorific value, which is the total quantity of heat liberated, when unit weight of the fuel is completely burnt.

The calorific values of carbon and hydrogen have been experimentally determined with considerable accuracy, and are usually given as—

Carbon   33 000 kJ/kg, or 14 200 Btu/lb
Hydrogen   144 300 kJ/kg, or 62 100 Btu/lb

The calorific value of any fuel, consisting, as all important fuels do, of a known proportion of carbon, hydrogen and incombustible impurities or diluents, may be estimated approximately on the assumption that it consists simply of a mixture of carbon, hydrogen and incombustible matter, but the state of chemical combination in the actual fuel leads to error by this method, and the only accurate and satisfactory means of determination is experimentally by the use of a suitable calorimeter.

Average petrol consists approximately of 85% carbon and 15% hydrogen by weight, the lighter fractions containing a higher percentage of hydrogen than the heavier. Refined petrol contains no measurable impurities or diluents. Its gross calorific value is about 46 000 kJ/kg, or 19 800 Btu/lb.

Liquid fuels are usually measured by volume, and therefore it is necessary to know the density before the potential heat supplied in any given case can be determined, for example:

A sample of petrol has a calorific value of 46 000 kJ/kg; its specific gravity is 0.72. How much potential heat energy is contained in 8 litres?

($1\,cm^3$ of water weighs $1\,g$).
Weight of 8 litres $= 8 \times 0.72 = 5.76\,kg$.
Thus, the potential heat in 8 litres $= 5.76 \times 46\,000 = 264\,900\,kJ$.

4.6 Power

Power is the *rate* at which work is done, 1 hp being defined (by James Watt) as a rate of working of 33 000 ftlb per minute, or 550 per second. (1 hp = 745.7 W).

Problem: What is the thermal efficiency in the following case?

An engine develops 22.4 kW and consumes 10.25 litres of fuel per hour, the calorific value being 46 000 kJ/kg and the specific gravity 0.72.

Potential heat supplied per hour $= 10.25 \times 0.72 \times 46\,000 = 339\,300\,kJ$.

Since $1\,W = 1\,J/s$, work done per hour $= 22.4 \times 60 \times 60 = 79\,950\,kJ$.

Therefore the thermal efficiency is $\dfrac{79\,950}{339\,300} = 23.6\%$

4.7 General method of conversion of heat to work

All heat engines convert heat into work by the expansion or increase in volume of a working fluid into which heat has been introduced by combustion of a fuel either external to the engine, as in a steam engine, or internally by the burning of a combustible mixture in the engine itself, a process giving rise to the phrase *internal combustion* (*ic*) *engine*.

Thus, in all so-called *static pressure engines*, as distinct from turbines, it is necessary to provide a working vessel, the volume of which is capable of variation, work being done on a moving portion of the wall by the static pressure of the working fluid as its volume increases. In general both the pressure and temperature fall with the increase of volume.

4.8 Practical form of working vessel

In practice it has been found that for mechanical and manufacturing reasons the most satisfactory form of working chamber is a straight cylinder closed at one end and provided with a closely fitting movable plug or 'piston' on which the work is done by the pressure of the steam or gases. This arrangement is common to steam, gas, oil and petrol engines.

4.9 Rotary and reciprocating engines

The motion of the piston in the cylinder of the above arrangement is, of course, in a straight line, whereas in the majority of applications the final motion required is a rotative one.

Very many attempts have been made to devise a form of chamber and piston to give rotary motion directly, but practically all have been mechanical failures, the chief weaknesses being excessive friction and difficulty in maintaining pressure tightness. A design that achieved a limited degree of success was the NSU Wankel engine, described in Section 8.7. The universally established 'direct acting engine mechanism' with connecting rod and crank is, however, unlikely to be generally replaced in the near future. Thus in most applications the reciprocating motion of the piston must be converted to rotation of the crank by a suitable mechanism. The most important of these mechanisms are—

(1) The crank and connecting rod.
(2) The crank and cross-slide as used in the donkey pump and small steam launch engines.
(3) The 'swash plate' or 'slant' mechanism.
(4) The 'wobble plate' or Z crank.

The second of these is not used in the applications with which we are concerned, owing to its undue weight and friction loss, and the third is, in general, confined to pumps and compressors for the conversion of rotary into reciprocating motion.

The Michell crankless engine, though not produced commercially, used the swash-plate in conjunction with the Michell thrust bearing which has eliminated the chief objection to the swash-plate, namely, excessive friction and low mechanical efficiency.

The first-mentioned mechanism is practically universal in internal combustion engines owing to its simplicity and high mechanical efficiency. We thus arrive at the fundamental parts common to all reciprocating engines having a crank and connecting rod, though the new rocking piston variant, Section 17.18, is of considerable interest.

4.10 Cylinder, piston, connecting rod and crankshaft

These fundamental parts of the conventional engine are shown in simple diagrammatic form in Fig. 4.1.

In this figure the crank is of the single web or 'overhung' type, as used in many steam engines, and certain motor cycle engines, but the double-web type, with a bearing on each side of the crank, is practically universal for internal combustion engines. This is illustrated in Fig. 4.2, which shows a cross-section through the cylinder, piston and connecting rod of the engine. A flywheel is mounted on the end of the crankshaft. The form and construction of the parts are considered later, only sufficient description being given here to enable their functions to be understood.

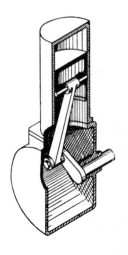
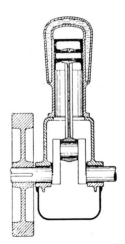

Fig. 4.1 (*left*)
Fig. 4.2 (*right*)

Cylinder. The ideal form consists of a plain cylindrical barrel in which the piston slides, the movement of the piston or 'stroke' being, in some cases, somewhat longer than the bore, but tending to equality or even less since the abandonment of the Royal Automobile Club (RAC) rating for taxation purposes. (See Section 4.16). This is known as the *stroke:bore ratio*.

The upper end consists of a combustion or 'clearance' space in which the ignition and combustion of the charge take place. In practice it is necessary to depart from the ideal hemispherical shape in order to accommodate the valves, sparking plug, etc., and to control the process of combustion.

Piston. The usual form of piston for internal combustion engines is an inverted bucket-shape, machined to a close (but free sliding) fit in the cylinder barrel. Gas tightness is secured by means of flexible 'piston rings' fitting closely in grooves turned in the upper part of the piston.

The pressure of the gases is transmitted to the upper end of the connecting rod through the 'gudgeon pin' on which the 'small end' of the connecting rod is free to swing.

Connecting rod. The connecting rod transmits the piston load to the crank, causing the latter to turn, thus converting the reciprocating motion of the piston into a rotary motion of the crankshaft. The lower end, or 'big end', of the connecting rod turns on the crank pin.

Crankshaft. In the great majority of internal combustion engines this is of the double-web type, the crank pin, webs and shaft being usually formed from a solid forging. The shaft turns in two or more main bearings (depending on the number and arrangement of the cylinders) mounted in the main frame or 'crankcase' of the engine.

Flywheel. At one end the crankshaft carries a heavy flywheel, the function of which is to absorb the variations in impulse transmitted to the shaft by the gas and inertia loads and to drive the pistons over the dead points and idle strokes. In motor vehicles the flywheel usually forms one member of the clutch through which the power is transmitted to the road wheels.

The foregoing are the fundamental and essential parts by which the power developed by the combustion is caused to give rotation to the crankshaft, the mechanism described being that of the *single-acting engine*, because a useful impulse is transmitted to the crankshaft while the piston moves in one direction only.

Most steam engines and a few large gas engines work on the *double-acting* principle, in which the pressure of the steam or gaseous combustion acts alternately on each side of the piston. The cylinder is then double-ended and the piston takes the form of a symmetrical disc. The force acting on the piston is transmitted through a 'piston rod' to an external 'cross-head' which carries the gudgeon pin. The piston rod passes through one end of the cylinder in a 'stuffing-box' which prevents the escape of steam or gas.

4.11   Method of working

It is now necessary to describe the sequence of operations by which the combustible charge is introduced, ignited and burned and finally discharged after it has completed its work.

There are two important 'cycles' or operations in practical use, namely, the 'four-stroke', or 'Otto' cycle as it is sometimes called (after the name of the German engineer who first applied it in practice), and the 'two-stroke', or 'Clerk' cycle, which owed its early development largely to Sir Dugald Clerk.

The cycles take their names from the number of single piston strokes which are necessary to complete a single sequence of operations, which is repeated continuously so long as the engine works.

The first named is by far the most widely adopted except for small motor cycle and motor boat engines, and for large diesels, for though it leads to greater mechanical complication in the engine, it shows higher thermal efficiency, and therefore greater economy in fuel. This cycle will therefore be described first, the two-stroke cycle being left until Chapter 10.

4.12   The four-stroke cycle

Fig. 4.3 shows in a diagrammatic manner a four-stroke engine cylinder provided with two valves of the 'mushroom' or 'poppet' type. The cylinder is shown horizontal for convenience.

The inlet valve (IV) communicates through a throttle valve with the carburettor or vaporiser, from which a combustible mixture of fuel and air is drawn. The exhaust valve (EV) communicates with the silencer through which the burnt gases are discharged to the atmosphere. These valves are opened and closed at suitable intervals by mechanisms, which will be described later.

The four strokes of the complete cycle are shown at (*a*), (*b*), (*c*) and (*d*).

Below the diagrams of the cylinder are shown the corresponding portions of what is known as the *indicator diagram*, that is to say, a diagram which shows the variation of pressure of the gases in the cylinder throughout the cycle. In practice such diagrams can be automatically recorded when the engine is running by a piece of apparatus known as an *indicator*, of which there are many types.

The four strokes of the cycle are as follows—

(*a*) *Induction stroke – exhaust valve closed: inlet valve open*
The momentum imparted to the flywheel during previous cycles or rotation by hand or by starter motor, causes the connecting rod to draw the piston outwards, setting up a partial vacuum which sucks in a new charge of combustible mixture from the carburettor. The pressure will be below atmospheric pressure by an amount which depends upon the speed of the engine and the throttle opening.

(*b*) *Compression stroke – both valves closed*
The piston returns, still driven by the momentum of the flywheel, and compresses the charge into the combustion head of the cylinder. The pressure rises to an amount which depends on the 'compression ratio', that is, the ratio of the full volume of the cylinder when the piston is at the outer end of its stroke to the volume of the clearance space when the piston is at the inner (or upper) end. In ordinary petrol engines this ratio is usually between 6 and 9 and the pressure at the end of compression is about 620.5 to 827.4 kN/m² , with full throttle opening.

$$\text{Compression ratio} = \frac{V_s + V_c}{V_c} \qquad V_s = \frac{\pi}{4} D^2 \times L$$

(*c*) *Combustion or working stroke – both valves closed*
Just before the end of the compression stroke, ignition of the charge is effected by means of an electric spark, and a rapid rise of temperature and pressure occurs inside the cylinder. Combustion is completed while the piston is practically at rest, and is followed by the expansion of the hot gases as the piston moves outwards. The pressure of the gases drives the piston forward and turns the crankshaft thus propelling the car against the external resistances and restoring to the flywheel the momentum lost during the idle strokes. The pressure falls as the volume increases.

(*d*) *Exhaust stroke – inlet valve closed: exhaust valve open*
The piston returns, again driven by the momentum of the flywheel, and discharges the spent gases through the exhaust valve. The pressure will be

slightly above atmospheric pressure by an amount depending on the resistance to flow offered by the exhaust valve and silencer.

It will thus be seen that there is only one working stroke for every four piston strokes, or every two revolutions of the crankshaft, the remaining three strokes being referred to as *idle strokes*, though they form an indispensable part of the cycle. This has led engineers to search for a cycle which would reduce the proportion of idle strokes, the various forms of the two-stroke engine being the result. The correspondingly larger number of useful strokes per unit of time increases the power output relative to size of engine, but increases thermal loading.

4.13   Power, speed and rating

The work done on a moving piston, from our foregoing definition, is the product of the force in newtons (or pounds) acting on the piston head, and the distance in metres (or feet) through which the piston moves.

If the force on the piston is variable, which is the case in all internal combustion engines, then the total movement or stroke may be divided into a number of parts, each portion of the movement being then multiplied by the value of the force during that movement, and the total work obtained by summation. What amounts to the same thing is to determine the mean force on the piston throughout the stroke and then multiply it by the length of the stroke.

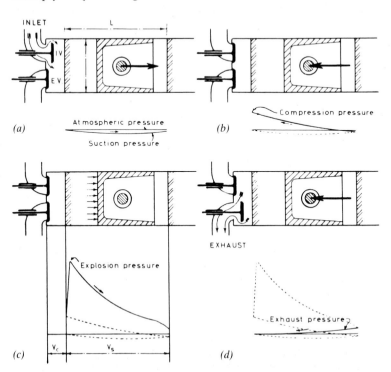

Fig. 4.3 The four-stroke cycle

The mean force on the piston is the mean intensity of pressure, or mean effective pressure (mep) (now measured in kilonewtons per square metre, kN/m^2), multiplied by the piston area – the cross-sectional area of the cylinder, in square metres. This mean effective pressure is determined from the indicator diagram, if available, in the following manner.

Referring to Fig. 4.3, the four small pressure diagrams show the variation of gas pressure during the four strokes, the pressure on the induction and exhaust strokes being exaggerated for clarity. Approximate average figures for the *mean* pressures throughout each stroke are as follows—

(1) Induction $14 kN/m^2$ below atmosphere.
(2) Compression $207 kN/m^2$ above atmosphere.
(3) Combustion $1040 kN/m^2$ above atmosphere.
(4) Exhaust $14 kN/m^2$ above atmosphere.

Now it must be remembered that the pressures are driving the engine, and are *positive*, only on the combustion stroke, being against the engine or negative on the three remaining strokes.

Thus the resultant mean *effective* pressure is

$$1040 - (207 + 14 + 14) = 805 kN/m^2$$

In practice the suction and exhaust pressures with full throttle are so small compared with those on the remaining strokes that they hardly show on a full-throttle indicator diagram, which reduces to the form shown in Fig. 4.4.

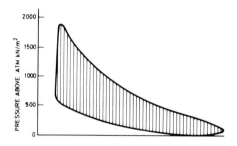

Fig. 4.4

It will now be realised that the mean effective pressure can be obtained from the mean height of the shaded area (Fig. 4.4). If the area of the figure, obtained in any convenient manner, is divided by its length, the result will be its mean height in, say, millimetres (or inches). This height is then multiplied by the scale of the spring used in the indicator, thus giving the mean effective pressure in kilonewtons per square metre, or pounds per square inch.

The *negative work* involved in the suction and exhaust strokes, which is usually too small to estimate from the indicator diagram, is regarded as part of the mechanical losses of the engine, and is known as the *pumping work*.

4.14   Factors governing the mean effective pressure

The mean effective pressure depends primarily on the number of potential heat units which can be introduced into the cylinder in each charge. When the volatile liquid fuels are mixed with air in the chemically correct proportions, the potential heat units per cubic metre of mixture are almost exactly the same in all cases, being about $962\,kcal/m^3 = 4.050\,MJ/m^3$ at standard temperature and pressure.

The 'volumetric efficiency' represents the degree of completeness with which the cylinder is re-charged with fresh combustible mixture and varies with different engines and also with the speed.

The 'combustion efficiency' represents the degree of completeness with which the potential heat units in the charge are produced as actual heat in the cylinder. Its value depends on a variety of factors, among the more important of which are the quality of the combustible mixture, nature of fuel, quality of ignition, degree of turbulence, and temperature of cylinder walls.

Lastly, the 'thermal efficiency' governs the percentage of the actual heat units present in the cylinder which are converted into mechanical work.

In engine tests the phrase 'thermal efficiency' is taken comprehensively to include combustion efficiency as well as conversion efficiency, as in practice it is impossible to separate them.

They are further combined with the mechanical efficiency where this cannot be separately measured, as 'brake thermal efficiency'.

It can be shown theoretically that the conversion efficiency is increased with an increase in compression ratio, and this is borne out in practice, but a limit is reached owing to the liability of the high compression to lead to detonation of the charge, or *pinking* as it is popularly called. This tendency to detonation varies with different fuels, as does also the limiting compression ratio which, with low grade fuel, generally lies between 6 and 7½. With better fuels a higher compression ratio (8 to 9½) is possible, owing to the greater freedom from risk of detonation. (See Chapter 14).

It thus follows that for the same volumetric efficiency, compression ratio and thermal efficiency the mean effective pressure will be practically the same for all liquid fuels. This is borne out in practice.

The thermal efficiency of an internal combustion engine of a given type does not depend very much on the *size* of the cylinders. With small cylinders, the loss of heat through the jacket may be proportionately greater, but the compression ratio may be higher.

The highest mean effective pressure obtained without supercharging, and using petrol as fuel, is about $1103.6\,kN/m^2$, but this is exceptional and very little below the theoretical maximum. A more normal figure to take in good conditions with full throttle is about $896\,kN/m^2$.

4.15   Work per minute, power and horsepower

Let p = mean effective pressure, N/m^2.
   D = diameter of cylinders, m.
   L = length of stroke, m.
   N = revolutions per minute.

f = number of effective strokes, or combustions, per revolution per cylinder, that is, half for a four-stroke engine.

n = number of cylinders.

Then

Force acting on one piston = $p\dfrac{\pi D^2}{4}$ newtons

Work done per effective stroke = $p\dfrac{\pi D^2 L}{4}$ newton-metres = joules

Work done per revolution = $p\dfrac{\pi D^2}{4}Lf$ joules

Work done per minute = $p\dfrac{\pi D^2}{4}LfN$ joules

Since the SI unit of power is the *watt* (W), or one joule per second, the power per cylinder in SI units is—

$$\frac{p\pi D^2 LfN}{4 \times 60}\ \text{W}$$

and for the whole engine—

$$= \frac{p\pi D^2 LfnN}{4 \times 60}\ \text{W}$$

Incidentally, since 1 hp is defined as the equivalent of 550 ft lbf of work per second, Section 4.6, it can be shown that the formula for horsepower is precisely the same as that for the power output in watts, except that p, D and L are in units of lbf/in^2, in and ft, and the bottom line of the fraction is multiplied by 550.

4.16 Piston speed and the RAC rating

The total distance travelled per minute by the piston is $2LN$. Therefore, by multiplying by two the top and bottom of the fraction in the last equation in Section 4.15, and substituting S – the mean piston speed – for $2LN$, we can express the power as a function of S and p: all the other terms are constant for any given engine. Since the maximum piston speed and the bmep (see Section 4.20) tend to be limited by the factors mentioned in Section 4.19, it is not difficult, on the basis of the dimensions of an engine, to predict approximately what its maximum power output will be.

It was on these lines that the RAC horsepower rating, used for taxation purposes until just after the Second World War, was developed. When this rating was first introduced, a piston speed of 508 cm/s and a bmep of 620 kN/m^2 and a mechanical efficiency of 75% were regarded as normal. Since 1 hp is defined as 33 000 lbf work per minute, by substituting these figures, and therefore English for SI metric dimensions in the formula for work done per minute, Section 4.15, and then dividing by 33 000, we get the output in horsepower. Multiplied by the efficiency factor of 0.75, this reduces to the simple equation—

$$\text{bhp} = \frac{D^2 n}{2.5}$$

For many years, therefore, the rate of taxation on a car depended on the square of the bore. However, because it restricted design, this method of rating for taxation was ultimately dropped and replaced by a flat rate. In the meantime, considerable advances had been made: mean effective pressures of 965 to $1100 \, \text{kN/m}^2$ are regularly obtained; improved design and efficient lubrication have brought the mechanical efficiency up to 85% or more; and lastly, but most important of all, the reduction in the weight of reciprocating parts, and the proper proportioning of valves and induction passages, and the use of materials of high quality, have made possible piston speeds of over $1200 \, \text{cm/s}$.

4.17 Indicated and brake power

The power obtained in Section 4.15 from the indicator diagram (that is, using the mep) is known as the *indicated power output* or *indicated horsepower* (ipo or ihp), and is the power developed inside the engine cylinder by the combustion of the charge.

The useful power developed at the engine shaft or clutch is less than this by the amount of power expended in overcoming the frictional resistance of the engine itself. This useful power is known as the *brake power output* or *brake horsepower* (bpo or bhp) because it can be absorbed and measured on the test bench by means of a friction or fan brake. (For further information on engine testing the reader is referred to *The Testing of Internal Combustion Engines* by Young and Pryer, EUP.)

4.18 Mechanical efficiency

The ratio of the brake horsepower to the indicated horsepower is known as the *mechanical efficiency*.
Thus—

$$\text{Mechanical efficiency} = \frac{\text{bpo}}{\text{ipo}} \quad \text{or} \quad \frac{\text{bhp}}{\text{ihp}} = \eta$$

in SI units or BS units respectively.

and bpo or bhp = mechanical efficiency $\times$ ipo (or $\times$/ihp)

$$= \frac{\eta p D^2 S}{305.56} \quad \text{or} \quad \frac{\eta p D^2 S}{168\,067}$$

$$= \frac{\eta p D S n}{305.56} \quad \text{or} \quad \frac{\eta^2 S n}{168\,067}$$

4.19 Limiting factors

Let us see to what extent these factors may be varied to give increased power.

It has been shown that the value of p depends chiefly on the compression ratio and the volumetric efficiency, and has a definite limit which cannot be exceeded without supercharging.

The diameter of the cylinder D can be increased at will, but, as is shown in Section 4.23, as D increases so does the weight per horsepower, which is a serious disadvantage in engines for traction purposes. There remain the piston speed and mechanical efficiency. The most important limitations to piston speed arise from the stresses and bearing loads due to the inertia of the reciprocating parts, and from losses due to increased velocity of the gases through the valve ports resulting in low volumetric efficiency.

A compression of large numbers of engines of different types, but in similar categories, shows that piston speeds are sensibly constant within those categories. For example, in engines for applications where absolute reliability over very long periods is of prime importance, weight being only a secondary consideration, piston speeds are usually between about 400 and 600 cm/s, and for automobile engines, where low weight is much more important, piston speeds between about 1000 and 1400 cm/s are the general rule. In short, where the stroke is long, the revolutions per minute are low, and *vice versa*.

4.20   Characteristic speed power curves

If the mean effective pressure (mep) and the mechanical efficiency of an engine remained constant as the speed increased, then both the indicated and brake horsepower would increase in direct proportion to the speed, and the characteristic curves of the engine would be of the simple form shown in Fig. 4.5, in which the line marked 'bmep' is the product of indicated mean effective pressure (imep) and mechanical efficiency, and is known as *brake mean effective pressure* (bmep), or shortly as *brake mean pressure*. Theoretically there would be no limit to the horsepower obtain-

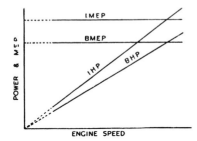

Fig. 4.5

able from the engine, as any required figure could be obtained by a proportional increase in speed. It is, of course, hardly necessary to point out that in practice a limit is imposed by the high stresses and bearing loads set up by the inertia of the reciprocating parts, which would ultimately lead to fracture or bearing seizure.

Apart from this question of mechanical failure, however, there are reasons which cause the characteristic curves to vary from the simple straight lines of Fig. 4.5, and which result in a point of maximum brake horsepower being reached at a certain speed which depends on the individual characteristics of the engine.

Characteristic curves of an early four-cylinder engine of 76.2 mm bore and 120.65 mm stroke are given in Fig. 4.6. The straight radial lines tangential to the actual power curves correspond to the power lines in Fig. 4.5, but the indicated and brake mean pressures do not, as was previously assumed, remain constant as the speed increases.

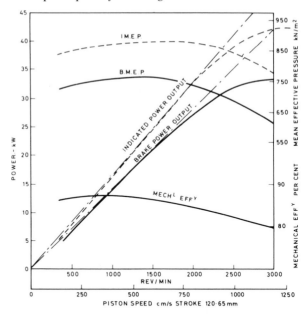

Fig. 4.6 Power curves of typical early side-valve engine, 3-in bore and 4¾-in stroke (76.2 and 120.65 mm)

On examining these curves it will be seen first of all that the mep is not constant. It should be noted that full throttle conditions are assumed – that is, the state of affairs for maximum power at any given speed.

At low speeds the imep is less than its maximum value owing partly to carburation effects, and partly to the valve timing being designed for a moderately high speed; it reaches its maximum value at about 1800 rev/min, and thereafter decreases more and more rapidly as the speed rises. This falling off at high speeds is due almost entirely to the lower volumetric efficiency, or less complete filling of the cylinder consequent on the greater drop of pressure absorbed in forcing the gases at high speeds through the induction passages and valve ports.

When the mep falls at the same rate as the speed rises, the horsepower remains constant, and when the mep falls still more rapidly the horsepower will actually decrease as the speed rises. This falling off is even more marked when the bmep is considered, for the mechanical efficiency decreases with increase of speed, owing to the greater friction losses. The net result is that the bhp curve departs from the ideal straight line more rapidly than does the ihp curve. The bmep peaks at about 1400 rev/min, the indicated power at 3200 and the brake power at 3000 rev/min, where 33.5 kW is developed.

4.21 Torque curve

If a suitable scale is applied, the bmep curve becomes a 'torque' curve for the engine, that is, it represents the value, at different speeds, of the mean torque developed at the clutch under full throttle conditions – for there is a direct connection between the bmep and the torque, which depends only on the number and dimensions of the cylinders, that is, on the total swept volume of the engine. This relationship is arrived at as follows:

If there are n cylinders, the total work done in the cylinders per revolution is—

Work per revolution $= p \times \frac{\pi}{4} D^2 \times L \times n \times \frac{1}{2}$ joules

(see Section 4.15), if L is here the stroke in metres. Therefore the work at the clutch is—

Brake work $= \eta \times p \times \frac{\pi}{4} D^2 \times L \times n \times \frac{1}{2}$ joules.

But the work at the clutch is also equal to the mean torque multiplied by the angular distance moved through in radians, or $T \times 2\pi$ newton-metres per revolution if T is measured in SI units.
Therefore—

$$T \times 2\pi = \eta \times p \times \frac{\pi}{4} D^2 \times L \times n \times \frac{1}{2}$$

$$\text{or,} \quad T = \eta\, p \times \frac{(\frac{\pi}{4} D^2 \times L \times n)}{4\pi}$$

Now $\frac{\pi}{4} D^2 \times L \times n$ is the total stroke volume or cubic capacity of the engine, which may be denoted by V. Therefore we have—

$$T = \eta\, p \times \frac{V}{4\pi}$$

where $\eta\, p$ is the bmep and $\frac{V}{4\pi}$ is a numerical constant for the engine, so that the bmep curve is also the torque curve if a suitable scale is applied.

In the case of the engine of Fig. 4.6, the bore and stroke are 76.2 mm and 120.65 mm respectively, and V is 2.185 litres.

$$\text{Thus,} \quad T = \eta p \times \frac{2.185}{4\pi}$$

and the maximum brake torque is—

$$T = 762 \times 0.1753 = 133.6\,\text{Nm.}$$

It is more usual to calculate the bmep (which gives a readier means of comparison between different engines) from the measured value of the torque obtained from a bench test.

Indicated mean pressure and mechanical efficiency are difficult to measure, and are ascertained when necessary by laboratory researches.

Mean torque, on the other hand, can be measured accurately and easily by means of the various commercial dynamometers available. The necessary equipment and procedure are in general use for routine commercial tests. It is then a simple matter to calculate from the measured torque the corresponding brake mean pressure or bmep—

$$\eta p \text{ or bmep} = T \times 4\pi/V$$

The usual form in which these power or performance curves are supplied by the makers is illustrated in Figs. 4.7 and 4.8, which show torque, power, and brake specific fuel consumption curves for two Ford engines, the former for a petrol unit and the latter a diesel engine. In both instances, the tests were carried out in accordance with the DIN Standard 70020, which is obtainable in English from Beuth-Vertrieb GmbH, Berlin 30. The petrol unit is an overhead camshaft twin carburettor four-cylinder in-line engine with a bore and stroke of 90.8 by 86.95 mm, giving a displacement of 1.993 litres. Its compression ratio is 9.2 to 1. The diesel unit is a six-cylinder in-line engine with pushrod-actuated valve gear and having a bore and stroke of 104.8 mm by 115 mm respectively, giving a displacement of 5948 cm^3. It has a compression ratio of 16.5 : 1.

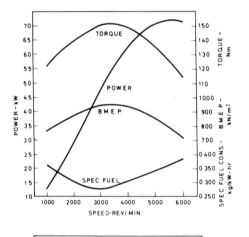

Fig. 4.7 Typical performance curves for an overhead camshaft, spark-ignition engine. High speeds are obtainable with the ohc layout

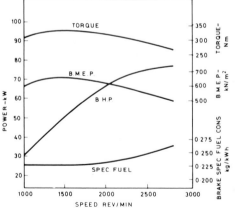

Fig. 4.8 Performance curves of a diesel engine. The fact that torque increases as speed falls off from the maximum obviates the need for excessive gear-changing

For both, the specific fuel consumption is given in terms of weight. This is more satisfactory than quoting in terms of volume, since the calorific values of fuels per unit of volume differ more widely than those per unit of weight. It can be seen that the specific fuel consumption of the diesel engine is approximately 80% that of the petrol engine, primarily due to its higher compression ratio. Costs of operation, though, depend not only on specific fuel consumption but also on rates of taxation of fuel. The curves show that the lowest specific fuel consumption of the diesel engine is attained as the fuel:air ratio approaches the ideal and at a speed at which volumetric efficiency is at the optimum. In the case of the petrol engine, however, the fuel:air ratio does not vary much, and the lowest specific fuel consumption is obtained at approximately the speed at which maximum torque is developed – optimum volumetric efficiency.

The fuel injection rate in the diesel engine is regulated so that the torque curve rises gently as the speed decreases. A point is reached at which the efficiency of combustion declines, with rich mixtures indicated by sooty exhaust. This torque characteristic is adopted in order to reduce the need for gear changing in heavy vehicles as they mount steepening inclines or are baulked by traffic. The heavy mechanical components, including the valve gear as well as connecting rod and piston assemblies of the diesel engine, and the slower combustion process, dictate slower speeds of rotation as compared with the petrol engine.

The bearing of the shape of these curves on the choice of gear ratios is dealt with in Chapter 20, but an important difference between the petrol engine and the steam locomotive and the electric traction motor must here be pointed out.

An internal combustion engine cannot develop a maximum torque greatly in excess of that corresponding to maximum power, and at low speeds the torque fails altogether or becomes too irregular, but steam and electric prime movers are capable of giving at low speeds, or for short periods, a torque many times greater than the normal, thus enabling them to deal with gradients and high acceleration without the necessity for a gearbox to multiply the torque. This comparison is again referred to in Section 20.9.

4.22 Commercial rating

The performance curves discussed so far represent gross test-bed perform-ance without the loss involved in driving auxiliaries such as water-pump, fan and dynamo. For commercial contract work corrected figures are supplied by manufacturers as, for example, the 'continuous' ratings given for stationary industrial engines.

Gross test-bed figures, as used in the USA, are sometimes referred to as the *SAE performance*, while Continental European makers usually quote performance as installed in the vehicle and this figure maybe 10 to 15% less. See also Fig. 7.7.

4.23 Number and diameter of cylinders

Referring again to the RAC formula (see Section 4.16), it will be seen that the power of an engine varies as the square of the cylinder diameter and directly as the number of cylinders.

If it is assumed that all dimensions increase in proportion to the cylinder diameter, which is approximately true, then we may say that, for a given piston speed and mean effective pressure, the power is proportional to the square of the linear dimensions. The weight will, however, vary as the cube of the linear dimensions (that is, proportionally to the volume of metal), and thus the weight increases more rapidly than the power. This is an important objection to increase of cylinder size for automobile engines.

If, on the other hand, the *number* of cylinders is increased, both the power and weight (appropriately) go up in the same proportion, and there is no increase of weight per unit power. This is one reason for multi-cylinder engines where limitation of weight is important, though other considerations of equal importance are the subdivision of the energy of the combustion, giving more even turning effort, with consequent saving in weight of the flywheel, and the improved balancing of the inertia effects which is obtainable.

The relationship of these variables is shown in tabular form in Fig. 4.9, in which geometrically similar engine units are assumed, all operating with the same indicator diagram. Geometrical similarity implies that the same materials are used and that all dimensions vary in exactly the same proportion with increase or decrease of cylinder size. All areas will vary as

VARIABLE	A	B	C	ENGINE
PISTON SPEED	I	I	I	
STROKE	I	2	I	
REV/MIN	I	$\frac{1}{2}$	I	
BORE	I	2	I	
TOTAL PISTON AREA	I	4	4	
POWER	I	4	4	
MEAN TORQUE	I	8	4	
VOLUMETRIC CAPACITY	I	8	4	
WEIGHT	I	8	4	
POWER / WEIGHT	I	$\frac{1}{2}$	I	
MAX. INERTIA STRESS	I	I	I	
MEAN GAS VELOCITY	I	I	I	

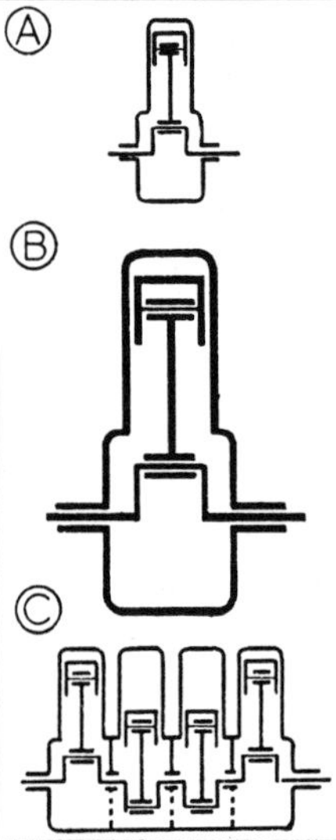

RELATIVE VALUE OF VARIABLES IN SIMILAR ENGINES [FOR SAME INDICATOR DIAGRAM]

Fig. 4.9

the square of the linear dimensions, and all volumes, and therefore weights, as the cube of the linear dimensions. These conditions do not hold exactly in practice, as such dimensions as crankcase, cylinder wall and water jacket thicknesses do not go up in direct proportions to the cylinder bore, while a multi-cylinder engine requires a smaller flywheel than a single-cylinder engine of the same power. The simplified fundamental relationships shown are, however, of basic importance.

It can be shown on the above assumptions that in engines of different sizes the maximum stresses and intensity of bearing loads due to inertia forces will be the same if the piston speeds are the same, and therefore if the same factor of safety against the risk of mechanical failure is to be adopted in similar engines of different size, all sizes of engine must run at the same piston speed, torque, power and weight, and gas velocities through the valves.

4.24 Power per litre

This basis of comparison is sometimes used in connection with the inherent improvement in performance of engines, but such improvement arises from increase in compression ratio giving higher brake mean pressures, the use of materials of improved quality, or by tolerating lower factors of safety or endurance. The comparison ceases to be a comparison of similar engines, for with similar engines the power per litre (or other convenient volume unit) may be increased merely by making the cylinder smaller in dimensions, and if the same total power is required, by increasing the number of the cylinders. Thus in Fig. 4.9 all the three engines shown develop the same power per unit of piston area at the same piston speed and for the same indicator diagram, but the power per litre of the small-cylinder engines is double that of the large cylinder, not because they are intrinsically more efficient engines but because the smaller volume is swept through more frequently.

Thus, high power per litre may not be an indication of inherently superior performance, whereas high power per unit of piston area is, since it involves high mean pressures or high piston speed or both, which are definite virtues provided that the gain is not at the expense of safety or endurance.

4.25 Considerations of balance and uniformity of torque

In the next Chapter consideration is given to the best disposition of cylinders to give dynamic balance and uniformity of torque, which are factors of vital importance in ensuring smooth running.

Chapter 5

Engine balance

Any moving mass when left to itself will continue to move in a straight line with uniform speed. If a heavy mass is attached to a cord and swung round in a circle a pull, known as *centrifugal force*, will be felt in the cord. This force represents the tendency of the mass to move in a straight line. Owing to the presence of the cord the mass is compelled to move round in a circle, its tendency to move in a straight line being overcome by the pull of the cord, as explained in Section 3.10.

Thus any mass revolving in a circle sets up an outward pull acting in the radial line through the centre of rotation and the centre of the mass. For example, the crankpin of a car engine revolves in a circle round the centre of the main bearings, and sets up a force on those bearings acting always in the direction of the crankpin. If this force is not *balanced* a vibration of the whole engine will be set up, in time with the rotation of the crankpin. This vibration will be more or less apparent according to the rigidity with which the engine is bolted to the frame.

The mathematical expression for centripetal acceleration (see Section 3.10) is $\omega^2 r$, where ω is the angular speed of the mass about the centre of rotation at a radius r. If ω is expressed in radians per second (there are 2π radians in one revolution) and r is measured in metres, then the acceleration is given in metres/sec^2.

The corresponding force in newtons, inwards on the mass, outwards as a reaction on the bearing, is given by—

$$F = M\omega^2 r$$

but if $2\pi N/60$ is substituted for ω, we have—

$$F = M \times \frac{4\pi^2 N^2}{60^2} \times r$$

which can be reduced to—

$$F = \frac{MrN^2}{91.1}$$

where r is expressed in metres and N in rev/min.

For example, suppose the crankpin and big end of an engine of 0.127 m stroke weigh together 1.8144 kg and the engine is turning at 3000 rev/min, then, if there were no provision for balance, the reaction on the main bearings would be—

$$F = \frac{MrN^2}{91.1}$$

$$= \frac{1.8144 \times 0.0635 \times 3000^2}{91.1}$$

$$= 11\ 400 \text{ newtons}$$

due to revolving masses only.

It is, however, possible to balance the disturbing force by means of a balance 'weight' or mass, placed diametrically opposite the crankpin. (It is more correct to speak of 'mass' in connection with running or dynamic balance, since the forces are not due to 'weight' which is the attractive force of gravity.) In engines it is not possible actually to place this balance mass in the same plane as the crankpin, and it must therefore be divided into halves placed symmetrically on each side. If the balance mass is placed at the same distance as the crankpin from the crankshaft axis then it must be of the same amount; if the distance is twice as great the mass must be halved. Thus, in Fig. 5.1, $B \times r_1$, must equal $M \times r$.

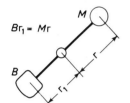

$Br_1 = Mr$

Fig. 5.1

Actually this force, with that due to the crank webs, would be balanced either against an opposed crank and big end, or by balance extensions to the crank webs. That part of it due to the big end of the connecting rod would represent part of the total inertia load on the big-end bearing.

5.1 Practical balancing

There is no mathematical difficulty in balancing revolving masses, and with simple disc forms or short crankshafts a static test is often sufficient. The part to be balanced is mounted on a true spindle (or its own journals) and placed on straight and carefully levelled knife edges or slips.

It will then roll until the heaviest side comes to the bottom. By attaching small counterweights until it remains indifferently in any position the error may be ascertained, and correction made by adding balance masses or removing excess metal as may be most convenient.

If the part has considerable axial length, there may be unbalanced couples which a static test will not reveal – it is not possible to ensure that Br_1 of Fig. 5.1 is in the same plane as Mr, though by a static test they may have been made equal. Such couples can be revealed and corrected only by means of a dynamic test during which the shaft or rotor is run up to speed and the couple or moment is shown by rocking or 'pitching'. Many ingenious dynamic balancing machines have been produced and are in use to measure and locate the plane of the imbalance in order that it may be corrected.

The degree of accuracy with which the correction is made is a question of the time and cost that may be expended.

The dynamic balance of complete rotational assemblies is usually carried out with great care, and may be dependent on the selected positioning of nuts and bolts. In reassembling or refilling a fluid flywheel, for instance, care should be taken to replace plugs in the same holes from which they were removed. An article on crankshaft balancing appeared in *Automobile Engineer*, Vol. 56, No. 20.

5.2   Balance of reciprocating parts

The movement of the piston backwards and forwards in the cylinder is known as a *reciprocating movement* as opposed to the *rotative movement* of the crankshaft, flywheel, etc. The reciprocating parts of a motor engine are the piston, gudgeon pin and as much of the connecting rod as may be considered to move in a straight line with the piston (usually about one-third of the connecting rod is regarded as reciprocating, the remainder, including the big end, being considered as a revolving mass).

Now the reciprocating parts, which we will refer to simply as the *piston*, have not a uniform motion. The piston travels in one direction during the first half of a revolution and in the opposite direction during the second half. Its speed of movement in the cylinder increases during the first half of *each* stroke (that is, twice every revolution) and decreases during the second half of each stroke, the speed being greatest and *most uniform* about the middle of each stroke. To change the speed of a body requires a force whose magnitude depends on the mass of the body and the rate at which the speed is changed, that is, the acceleration. This may be realised by holding an object in the hand and moving it rapidly backwards and forwards in front of the body. (See Chapter 3.)

The speed of the piston is *changing* most rapidly (that is, the acceleration is greatest) at the ends of the stroke, and it follows that the force required to change the motion is greatest there also. At the middle of the stroke the speed is not changing at all, so no force is required.

The necessary force is supplied by a tension or compression in the connecting rod. If the connecting rod were to break when the piston was approaching the top of the cylinder, the engine running at a high speed, the piston would tend to fly through the top of the cylinder just as, if the cord broke, the mass referred to earlier would fly off at a tangent. Now the reaction of this force, which is required to slow the piston at the top of its stroke and to start it on its downward stroke, is transmitted through the connecting rod, big-end bearing, crankshaft and main bearings to the engine frame, and sets up a vibration. This is dealt with more fully in Sections 5.11 and 5.12.

At the two ends of the stroke the piston produces the same effect, that is, the same force, on the crankpin as if it were simply a revolving mass concentrated at the crankpin and, consequently, it may be balanced at these points by a revolving balance mass placed opposite the crankpin as in Fig. 5.2. Supposing that such a balance mass B_2 is placed on the extended crankshaft webs, of sufficient mass to balance completely the reciprocating parts. The forces set up by the movement of the piston act in a vertical direction only, that is, in the line of the stroke. They will have their greatest value at the ends of the stroke, in opposite directions, and become nothing in the middle of the stroke. Referring to Fig. 5.3, as the crankshaft revolves the centrifugal force *F* or the balance mass, acting always radially outwards from the shaft centre, has a decreasing effect or 'component' in the direction of the line of stroke, but an increasing one in a horizontal direction at right angles to the line of stroke. The decrease in the vertical component corresponds exactly to the decrease in the force set up by the piston. At the centre of the stroke the piston exerts no inertia force since its speed is momentarily steady, and the balance mass exerts no force in a vertical direction, since its crank is horizontal. The addition of this rotating balance mass then balances the engine completely in the vertical direction. Consider, however, the horizontal effect produced. The balance mass introduces a horizontal component force F_h (Fig. 5.3), which varies from zero when the piston is at either end of the stroke to a maximum when the piston is in the middle of the stroke when, as the crank is horizontal $F_h = F$.

This horizontal effect is exactly equal to the original vertical effect due to the piston which it was sought to balance, and thus the only result of attempting to balance the reciprocating parts completely, by means of a revolving mass, is to transfer the disturbance from the vertical to the horizontal direction without altering its amount. In some cases this may be an advantage, but the engine is in no sense properly balanced.

In a single-cylinder engine a compromise is arrived at by adding a balance mass equivalent to a portion (usually half) of the reciprocating parts. This leaves the remainder unbalanced in a vertical direction, but the horizontal effect is only that due to the smaller balance mass. If half the piston is balanced the result is a vertical and a horizontal effect, each equal in amount to half the original unbalanced effect. If a greater balance mass is used the vertical imbalance is less, but the horizontal is greater.

It is quite impossible to balance an ordinary single-cylinder engine completely by the addition of balance masses to the revolving crankshaft.

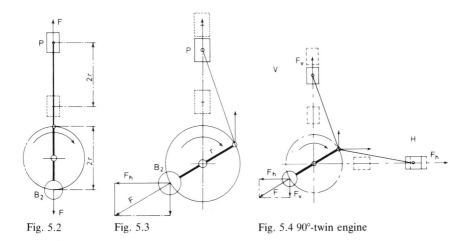

Fig. 5.2   Fig. 5.3   Fig. 5.4 90°-twin engine

Consider a 90° twin engine, that is, one which is provided with two equal cylinders having their centre lines at right angles to each other in the same plane and both connecting rods driving on to a common crankpin. Suppose that the engine is placed with the centre line of cylinder V vertical as in Fig. 5.4. The centre line of cylinder H will then be horizontal.

We will assume that the revolving parts (that is, the crankpin, etc.) are already completely balanced by the addition of a suitable balance mass opposite the crankpin, incorporated in the extended crank webs.

A further balance mass is now required for the reciprocating parts. This is placed opposite to the crankpin and is of sufficient mass to balance the *whole* of the reciprocating parts of *one* cylinder. As already explained, this will secure complete balance in the vertical direction and further, as the mass turns into the horizontal position, it will supply the increasing horizontal balancing force F_h required by the cylinder H. In other words, when one set of reciprocating parts requires the full balance mass the other requires nothing, and in intermediate positions the resultant effect of the two sets of reciprocating parts is always exactly counteracted by this single balance mass.

An engine of this type can therefore be balanced completely for what are known as the *primary forces*. The effect of a short connecting rod is to introduce the additional complications of what are known as *secondary forces*, which are dealt with in the latter portion of this Chapter for the benefit of those readers with a mathematical turn of mind who may wish to study the matter further.

5.3   Other V twin engines

V twin engines in which the angle between the cylinders is not 90° but some smaller angle occupy a position intermediate between the 90° twin and the single-cylinder engine, primary balance being approached more nearly as the angle between the cylinders approaches 90°.

5.4   Horizontally-opposed twin

In engines of the flat-twin-cylinder type, the reciprocating parts are not balanced by means of revolving masses, but one set of reciprocating parts is made to balance the other set by making them operate on two diametrical-ly-opposed crankpins. The pistons at any instant are moving in opposite directions and the inertia forces oppose and balance each other.

Owing to it being impracticable to arrange the cylinder centre lines in the same vertical plane, there is a small unbalanced twist or couple. This is indicated in Fig. 5.5, which is a plan view of the engine. The inertia forces *F F*, being equal, have no resultant force, but since they do not act along the same line they constitute a couple. The magnitude of this couple, which tends to oscillate the engine in a horizontal plane, increases as the distance *d* increases.

5.5   Side-by-side twin with cranks at 180°

Fig. 5.6 shows a side-by-side twin engine with cranks at 180°. The motion of the pistons is still opposed, but in addition to the fact that the couple is increased owing to the greater distance *d* between the cylinder centre lines, this arrangement is not so good as the opposed twin because the secondary forces due to the shortness of the connecting rod do not balance. This will be understood after a study of the effect of the secondary forces which are dealt with in Section 5.12. The inertia force F, due to the piston which is on its inner dead point, is greater than the inertia force F^1, due to the other piston which is at its outer dead point. With the usual ratio of connecting rod length to crank length F is about 60% greater than F^1, the difference being twice the secondary force due to one piston. Balance is, in fact, obtained only for primary forces and not for secondary forces or for primary couples.

5.6 Four-cylinder in-line engine

Suppose, however, a second side-by-side twin, which is a 'reflection' of the first, is arranged alongside in the same plane and driving the same crankshaft as in Fig. 5.7. The couples due to the two pairs are now clearly acting in opposite directions, and their effects will be opposed so that there will be no resultant couple on the engine as a whole. The engine is then

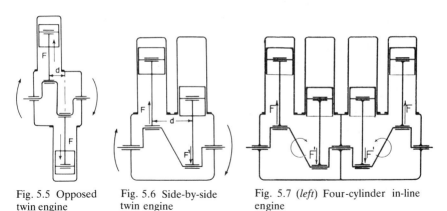

Fig. 5.5 Opposed twin engine

Fig. 5.6 Side-by-side twin engine

Fig. 5.7 (*left*) Four-cylinder in-line engine

balanced for everything except secondary forces, which in a four-cylinder engine can be dealt with only by some device such as the Lanchester harmonic balancer, illustrated in Fig. 5.11.

It should be clearly realised that it is only the engine as a whole that is balanced, and that the opposition of the two couples is effective only by virtue of stresses set up in either the crankshaft or crankcase or both.

5.7 General method of balancing

This method of balancing by opposing forces and couples represents the general method of balancing multi-cylinder engines, the cylinders and cranks being so disposed that as far as possible or expedient the various forces and couples, both primary and secondary, may be made to neutralise each other throughout the engine as a whole. The best dynamic balance is not, however, always consistent with the best distribution of the power impulses and a compromise must therefore sometimes be made, as will be seen later. Another consideration is that of bearing loads due to the dynamic forces, and here again it may be desirable – as in high-speed racing cars – to tolerate some degree of dynamic imbalance in order to reduce the load factor on a particular bearing.

5.8 Couples due to revolving masses

Referring again to Fig. 5.7, it will be appreciated that the *revolving* masses at each crank in give rise to couples in just the same way as the reciprocating masses, except that here it is an 'all-round' effect instead of acting only in the vertical plane. The revolving couple is unbalanced in Fig. 5.6, while in Fig. 5.7 the two opposite couples are opposed exactly as indicated by the arrows for the reciprocating effects, and the shaft and crankcase assembly must be so stiff as to avoid whip under the combination of the two independent disturbances.

5.9 Balanced throws

The stresses and whip due to the revolving masses may be reduced by adding counterweights to the individual throws, as shown in the crankshaft illustrated in Fig. 6.13, thus eliminating the couples.

In the modern highly-rated engines, serious crankshaft whip has been eliminated only by the addition of these balance masses. They may be incorporated in the forging or be separately attached. Clearly their employment makes the crankshaft construction more expensive and in straight six- and eight-cylinder engines they may give rise to another trouble, namely *torsional vibration* of the crankshaft.

5.10 Torsional vibration

Under the combustion impulses the shaft alternately winds and unwinds to a small extent, and as with all types of strain and vibration there is a certain natural frequency of this action. The longer and more slender the shaft and the larger the crank masses incorporated in it, the lower will this natural frequency be, and it may be so low as to equal the frequency of the combustion impulses at some particular engine speed. Resonance will then occur between the forced impulses and the natural frequency of the shaft vibration giving rise to dangerous torsional strain.

Such vibrations may be damped out by the use of a vibration damper as shown in Fig. 7.4.

5.11 Secondary forces and couples

It was indicated in Section 5.2 that the motion of the piston could be regarded as the vertical component of the motion of the crankpin, and this is known as *simple harmonic motion*. If the connecting rod were infinitely long and thus always parallel to the cylinder axis, or if the crank and cross-slide mechanism referred to in Section 4.9 were used, the piston, moving in its straight line of stroke, would have this simple harmonic motion.

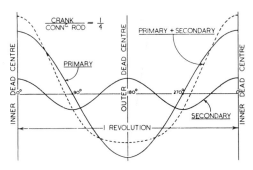

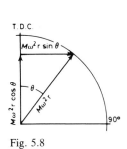

Fig. 5.8   Fig. 5.9

At any position of the piston, measured by the crank angle θ from its top dead centre as shown in Fig. 5.8, the accelerating force required for the piston would be $M\omega^2 r \cos\theta$, while the horizontal force $M\omega^2 r \sin\theta$, which would represent the horizontal component of the centrifugal force of a *revolving* mass, obviously has no existence in the context of reciprocating mass, since the piston has no displacement, velocity or acceleration at right angles to the axis of the cylinder. This 'primary' disturbing force is drawn in Fig. 5.9 as a full line having its maximum value when $\theta = 0°$ and $180°$. Its direction must be considered in relation to the forces on the bearings of the connecting rod, which provides the necessary accelerating force and transmits the reactions to the crankpin and main bearings.

5.12   Effect of short connecting rod

In an actual engine, owing to the shortness of the connecting rod, the motion of the piston is *not* simple harmonic, and its acceleration and the corresponding accelerating force require for their calculation other terms in the expression, of which only the 'second harmonic' is of importance in the present connection.

The total accelerating force is then—

$$F = f_1 + f_2$$
$$= M\omega^2 r \cos\theta + M\omega^2 r.\frac{r}{l}\cos 2\theta$$
$$= M\omega^2 r \left(\cos\theta + \frac{r}{l}\cos 2\theta\right), \text{ where } l \text{ is the length of the connecting rod}$$

between centres.

The ratio r/l is usually about ¼, and this value has been assumed in Fig. 5.9, the lower full line representing the secondary disturbing force which, it will be seen, has twice the frequency of the primary.

At the inner dead centre the secondary is in the same direction as the primary, while at the outer dead centre they act in opposite directions.

To use a familiar term, the 'dwell' of the piston is longer at the outer dead centre than it is at the inner (or top of the stroke), owing to the fact that the swing of the connecting rod neutralises to some extent the swing of the crank.

To obtain the total disturbing force on the bearings the primary and secondary forces must be added, as shown by the broken line, but it is convenient and in many ways more enlightening to consider them separately, so that the conditions of balance in respect of primary and secondary forces, and primary and secondary couples may be assessed.

Thus, if the four-cylinder engine of Fig. 5.7 is considered, it will be seen that when pistons 1 and 4 are at their inner dead points, 2 and 3 are at the outer position, the corresponding values of θ being 0 and 180. The primary forces and couples are balanced as indicated in Fig. 5.7, while if the direction of the secondaries is examined with the help of Fig. 5.9, it will be found that all four act together, outwards at both dead centres and inwards at mid stroke. They thus give rise to a total unbalanced force equal in magnitude – with a 4:1 connecting rod ratio – to a single primary force, and vibrating with twice the frequency.

In Fig. 5.10 are shown in diagrammatic form the conditions of balance for various arrangements of a four-cylinder engine with flat crankshaft. The reader should have no difficulty in checking the conditions of balance with the help of the curves in Fig. 5.9, if care is taken to avoid confusion as to the directions in which the primary and secondary disturbing forces act. The longer arrows represent the primary forces and the shorter the secondary.

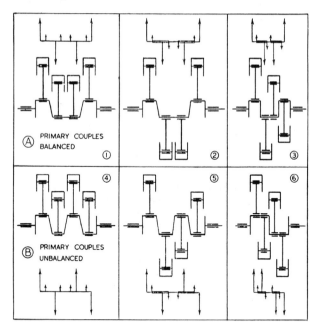

Fig. 5.10 Balancing diagrams for four cylinders

They are drawn side-by-side for clarity, but actually both act along the axis of the cylinder. The double coupling lines indicate the 'arms' of the secondary couples, while the primary couples will be clear.

The following points should be noted—

The balance of primary forces and couples depends on the crankshaft arrangement. Primary forces are balanced in all the six cases, while primary couples are balanced with the 'mirror-image' crankshafts A but not with the zigzag shafts B. With the arrangements B the tendency to bend or whip the shaft due to inertia forces is less, and if a third bearing is provided, the inertia loading on this bearing is less than with the arrangements A.

The balance of secondary forces and couples depends on cylinder disposition. No. 2 in Fig. 5.10 is the only arrangement with complete dynamic balance for primary and secondary forces and couples.

5.13   Firing intervals

It will be seen that No. 2 is also the only layout in which all four pistons are at their inner dead centres simultaneously. This makes it impossible to distribute the firing impulses at intervals of half a revolution, as is proper, because at least two pistons would be at the end of their compression strokes together, and this would result in the cylinders firing in pairs at intervals of one revolution. The smoothness of torque would then be no better than that of the 180° twin of Fig. 5.5. For this reason, arrangement No. 2 is not used in practice in spite of its perfect balance.

Arrangement No. 3 takes its place. Past examples were the Jowett *Javelin* and Lancia *Flavia*. It will be found that all the arrangements except No. 2 permit of half-revolution firing intervals, and the reader may find it instructive to write down the alternative firing orders for which the camshafts might be designed.

5.14   Compactness of engine

Arrangements Nos. 1 and 4 provide the most compact engine transversely to the crankshaft, while No. 6 forms the shortest engine with the simplest shaft, but has large unbalanced couples. No. 3 is a compact and favourable arrangement with perfect balance except for secondary couples, which are not a serious objection.

With suitable form of crank webs, arrangement Nos. 2 and 5 can be made more compact in the axial direction than can Nos. 1 and 4.

Nos. 4 and 5 would be the most expensive crankshafts to manufacture, and would normally be provided with three bearings, while Nos. 3 and 6 are particularly favourable to the two-bearing construction.

The most widely adopted form of the four-cylinder engine is No. 1 of Fig. 5.10 by virtue of its general compactness, symmetrical manifolding, possibilities of economic manufacture and convenience of installation in the chassis, combined with accessibility. The secondary forces remain unbalanced, however, and it is natural that engineers should have turned their attention to the problem of balancing these.

5.15   Harmonic balancer

A most ingenious device for accomplishing this object is the Lanchester harmonic balancer, which was used in early days in Lanchester, Vauxhall and Willys four-cylinder engines, and has been employed in numerous instances to cure vibration troubles in stationary and marine engines.

If suitable bob-weights are mounted on two shafts geared together to turn at the same speed in opposite directions, it is possible to produce the effect of a reciprocating mass having simple harmonic motion.

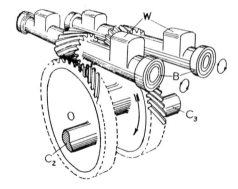

Fig. 5.11 (*left*) Lanchester harmonic balancer

Fig. 5.12 (*below*)

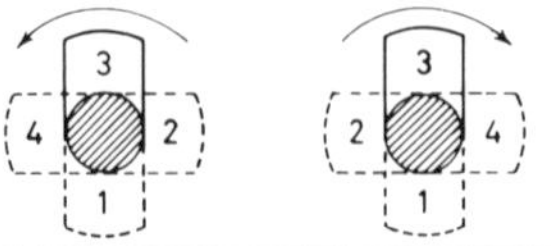

Crank angle from T D C	CYL^s 1&4	180	225	270	315	0
	CYL^s 2& 3	0	45	90	135	180
Position of Bob-weights		1	2	3	4	1

If the device is arranged to run at twice crankshaft speed, and is suitably proportioned, it may be made to balance the sum of the secondaries due to the four pistons.

One form of the device is shown in Fig. 5.11. C_2 and C_3 are the two inner crankpins of an ordinary four-throw shaft with three bearings.

The crank webs on each side of the centre bearing are circular in form and provided with helical gear rings which drive at double crankshaft speed the two cross-shafts carried in bearings B.

Each of these shafts carries for symmetry two bob-weights W, each of which is proportioned to develop a centrifugal force equal to the secondary inertia force of one piston, so that the four bob-weights together neutralise the combined secondary forces due to the four pistons. Since the cross-shafts revolve in opposite directions, it will be seen on referring to Fig. 5.12 that in the horizontal direction the two pairs of bob-weights neutralise each other, while they combine in the direction of the piston movement to give a reciprocating effect in opposite phase to the secondary piston disturbance. Thus complete dynamic balance of the engine is obtained.

5.16   Meadows' harmonic balancer

An interesting practical layout of the harmonic balancer is that fitted by the Henry Meadows company to certain of their four-cylinder compression-ignition (ci) engines.

This is designed as a unit assembly interposed between the bottom of the crank case and the lower sump, which may be fitted in applications where improved balance and freedom from transmitted vibration may be important considerations.

Two parallel longitudinal shafts are driven from the crankshaft by duplex roller chain and helical gearing, in opposite directions and at twice crankshaft speed.

There are four plain bushed bearings of the camshaft type to each shaft.

The necessary imbalance of the shafts is obtained partly by grinding one side of each shaft between the bumped-up bearing journals, and partly by the addition of small bob-weights to which correction can readily be made by grinding as necessary. The bob-weights just clear the bearing bores during assembly.

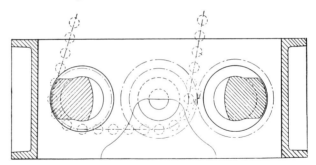

Fig. 5.13

Fig. 5.13 shows the arrangement in a diagrammatic manner. The shafts are shown in the position at which the imbalances act outwards in opposition, producing no resultant horizontal force since none is required.

In the vertical direction the forces are added as in the Lanchester device described in Section 5.15.

The balance of six- and eight-cylinder engines is dealt with in Chapter 7.

5.17 Flexible mountings

An engine which is perfectly balanced for forces and couples in the sense described above will have no tendency to move, or to transmit vibration to the frame or foundation to which it is attached, as a result of the sources of disturbance so far enumerated.

Small imperfections of actual balance may be troublesome in extreme circumstances, but the presence of the unbalanced secondary inertia forces in four-cylinder engines not provided with harmonic balancers may involve considerable vibration troubles.

This type of simple, inexpensive engine construction is particularly popular for medium-size cars, at the expense of the admittedly superior mechanical properties of the six, which at one time appeared likely to oust the four from favour.

Resonant vibration of body panels, or 'boom,' arising from the unbalanced secondaries, intensified by frameless or unitary chassis construction, has forced designers to direct their attention to methods of engine mounting to ensure that improved comfort in riding and silencing shall not be offset by fatiguing vibration effects.

5.18 Torsional disturbances

Further disturbing effects, not capable of internal balance by the methods described above, are due to driving and inertia *torque* reactions. As regards high frequency torque reactions from the rear wheels – Newton's third law – these tend to be smoothed out if there is a torque converter in the drive-line.

Useful torque cannot be transmitted from the engine as a result of the internal gas pressures without a corresponding torsional reaction on the engine mass, arising through a piston and bearing side-thrust.

This has a mean value determining the power at any instant, and a series of harmonics representing the fluctuations of torque on the crankshaft that are due to the variable gas pressures and their effective action.

These harmonics are a source of torsional vibration of the engine on its mounting, the frequencies ranging from the '½ order' or cycle frequency of the individual cylinders, to the higher orders. If the indicator diagrams of the several cylinders were precisely similar, there would be no ½ order or half engine speed frequency, apart from camshaft effects.

'Inertia torque reaction' arising quite independently from gas pressures, may be visualised as the reaction of torque applied to the crankshaft by the flywheel to effect the piston accelerations. The connecting rod obliquities and piston side-thrusts develop the inertia torque and its reaction, which can be most noticeable under overrun conditions. Frequencies are the 1st, 2nd, 4th, 6th, etc., but only the 1st and 2nd are important.

Angular fluctuations about the longitudinal axis of the crankshaft can be balanced by contra-rotating flywheels or other contra-rotating components. This is not generlly done, although Dr. F. Lanchester incorporated this feature in some of his engines, *circa* 1895, and an experimental installation on a Volvo 144S car was described in the August 1970 issue of *Automobile Engineer*.

5.19   Modes of vibration, natural frequency, forcing frequency and resonance

Any mass of finite dimensions, free to move in space, possesses six degrees of freedom: three of translation along, and three of rotation about, three mutually perpendicular axes. These axes may be arbitrarily chosen, in relation to the crankshaft axis, which has no significance while the engine is at rest, or may be the three 'principal axes of inertia' of the engine mass, both sets passing through the mass centre of the unit.

The former may have no fundamental relation to the rotational inertias of the unit, but are convenient for calculations connected with static and transient loads due to dead weight, road shocks, cornering, braking and, if the crankshaft axis is chosen, driving thrust and torque reaction due to mean torque and impulsive clutch engagement from which clutch judder may arise.

Any 'mode of motion' may be resolved into a number or all of these translations and rotations, the modes of motion becoming 'modes of vibration' when regular periodic forces and torques are applied.

Engine mountings must be designed to completely constrain the power unit against these static and vibrationary loads and disturbances, with the maximum degree of insulation of the body structure from noise and transmitted vibrations of uncomfortable frequency.

The number of modes of vibration, each with its natural frequency, of the various parts and accessories of an automobile is practically infinite, and many of these modes have frequencies liable to resonant vibration with 'forcing' vibrations emanating from the engine.

Natural frequency is determined by the mass or inertia and the stiffness (as of a spring) of the constraint. The stiffer the constraint in relaton to the mass or its rotational inertia, the higher will be the frequency. Any component of the mounting may be called on to constrain two or more modes of motion, hence the value and simplicity of bonded rubber mountings.

Should the forcing frequency at some particular engine speed be equal to the natural frequency of the whole or part of the frame or body on which the engine is mounted, resonance will occur, and the amplitude of vibration, without damping, may theoretically become infinite.

Fig. 5.14 shows the theoretical proportion of the applied force or amplitude of movement which is transmitted from the 'exciter' to the support for different ratios of forcing frequency to natural frequency F/f, the *frequency* of the transmitted vibration being the same as the forcing frequency.

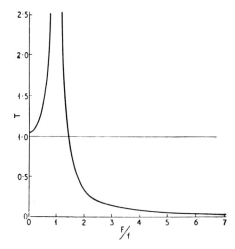

Fig. 5.14 Transmitted vibration

It will be seen that when F/f is unity, the transmitted vibration amplitude T theoretically becomes infinite. In practice inherent damping always limits the amplitude, but it is in some instances necessary to incorporate positive steps to prevent excessive movement under certain conditions.

When F/f is increased to three by reducing f, only one-eighth of the forcing amplitude or force is transmitted.

Thus for insulation of vibration a low natural frequency, i.e., a soft mounting, is required, but a compromise may be necessary with the greater stiffness likely to be needed to take the various static and transient loads enumerated above. Road shock loads, for instance, may greatly exceed the dead weight.

5.20 Principal axes of inertia

If a long, fairly regular object, such as a potato or a lump of firm plasticine, is pierced with a knitting needle in the general direction of its greatest length, an axis of rotation may be obtained about which the moment of inertia is small compared with those about axes generally at right angles to it (see Section 3.7).

There is a particular axis, passing through the mass centre, about which, owing to the general proximity of all the mass particles, the moment of inertia is a minimum for the solid. This is one of the principal axes. The two others, also passing through the mass centre, complete a trio of mutually perpendicular principal axes. Of the second and third axes, one will be the axis of maximum inertia and the other will have an intermediate value. These three principal axes, which may be described in reference to a power unit as the axes of natural roll, pitch and yaw, are the axes about which torsional oscillation can be initiated without introducing lateral or translational forces, and are the axes about which the mass, if supported in a homogeneous elastic medium (such as soft rubber or jelly) and with gravitational forces balanced, would take up component rotations when disturbed by any system of applied torques.

5.21   Importance in the design of engine mountings

These principal axes are important in the design of engine mountings, particularly the fore-and-aft 'roll' axis, which ordinarily lies at an angle of 15 to 30° with the crankshaft axis, sloping downwards from front to rear as indicated in Fig. 5.15. Ideally, the mountings should be so disposed as to confine rotation to this axis, so that torsional vibrations may be constrained without introducing lateral forces. If rotation about any other axis is imposed by the mountings, such lateral forces will arise, and may require additional constraints.

It will be noticed that, assuming lateral symmetry, the principal axis intersects the crankshaft axis near the centre of the flywheel housing, so that mountings placed on the sides of the housing could deal with torsional vibrations about the principal axis as well as with direct 'bump' loads. The front mounting would be placed high, as near to the principal axis as possible, and would take the balance of the bump loads as determined by the position of the mass centre. In the Chrysler mounting shown in Fig. 5.16, all reactions are distributed between the front and rear mountings, snubbers only being provided at the flywheel housing.

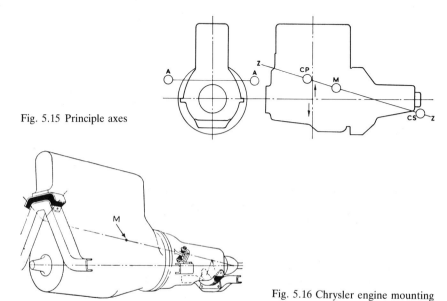

Fig. 5.15 Principle axes

Fig. 5.16 Chrysler engine mounting

Fig 5.15 also indicates the *centre of percussion*, CP. The position of the CP is determined by the distribution of the mass relative to the rear suspension or pivot point, which in effect is the *centre of suspension*, CS. Usually it will lie near the central transverse plane of the engine, which is the plane in which the resultant of the unbalanced secondaries in a four-cylinder engine acts. If CP can be located exactly in this plane by suitable choice of CS and mass distribution, and if the front mounting can also be so placed, there will be neither pitching *moment* due to the secondary disturbing force nor reaction at the CS. The principle is similar to that applicable to a door stop, which should be positioned at the centre of percussion so that, if the door is suddenly blown open against it, the hinges are not overloaded.

In practice, it is rarely possible to arrange for exact coincidence as described above, but the central plane is a structurally desirable, though not always convenient, location for the front mountings. These are indicated at AA in Fig. 5.15, widely spaced to deal with torsional vibrations about the axis ZZ.

This percussion system appears to be an ideal means of dealing with pitching disturbances; road shocks and cornering loads would be shared by the attachments at CS and AA in a ratio determined by the position of the mass centre M.

A V arrangement of links with rubber-bonded bushes, with the link centre lines meeting on the principal axis and so utilising the principle of the instantaneous centre may be used, or else a type of front V-mounting of 'compression-shear' units.

The arrangement used for the mounting of the three-cylinder Perkins diesel engine in a light van chassis is shown in Fig. 5.17.

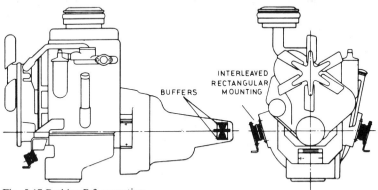

Fig. 5.17 Perkins P-3 mounting

Both vertical and horizontal primary out-of-balance couples are present in this engine, and to obtain insulation against these as well as the 1½ order torque harmonic it was necessary to use a suspension giving a high degree of rotational flexibility about all axes. This was achieved by using a V arrangement of sandwich mountings very close to the centre of gravity (or mass centre) with the front rubber sandwich mounted so that its compression axis passes approximately through the centre of gravity. The degree of insulation obtained is excellent. Engine movement under shock torque reaction, and when passing through resonance on starting and stopping, is quite large, but has not proved troublesome. A pair of circular sandwich units pitched to give greater torque control may be used at the front instead of the rectangular form.

A great variety of rubber-to-steel bonded units to provide the many different constraints required, has been produced by Dunlop Polymer and a few of these are shown in Fig. 5.18. The illustration includes early unbonded cushions, bonded double shear and compression-shear mountings, a bonded eccentric bush, rubber-steel compression spring, and others.

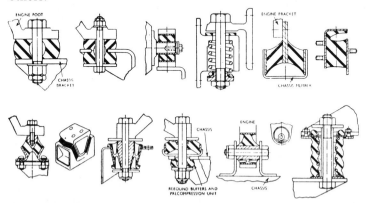

Fig. 5.18 Metalastik elastic engine mountings by Dunlop Polymer

It is possible to design units capable of resisting various combinations of compression, shear and torsional loads, with appropriate variation in the elastic properties of the rubber obtained by a suitable mix.

Though no mathematical treatment has been attempted here, the reader will have realised that for quantitative analysis of inertias, modes of motion and vibration frequencies, advanced and difficult mathematics are required, combined with experimental measurement.

Recourse must be had to trial and error in the development of actual mountings, which can only approximate to ideal arrangements.

Authoritative articles on the subject have been published in the *Proceedings* of the engineering societies and in *Automobile Engineer*, and the interested reader is referred to the comprehensive treatment given in an important paper by M. Horovitz read before the Automobile Division of the Institution of Mechanical Engineers in November, 1957. The present authors are much indebted to the author of this paper, to Metalastik Ltd. (now Dunlop Ltd., Polymer Engineering Division) for technical information, and to the Council of the Institution for permission to abstract material from their *Proceedings*.

This paper, *The Suspension of Internal-combustion Engines in Vehicles*, includes a full mathematical appendix and a useful bibliography.

Volume 43 of *Automobile Engineer* contains an article giving details of methods for determination on inertias and other authoritative matter, and *Engine Installation* by H. C. Harrison in Volume 46 of the same journal is of great interest.

Chapter 6

Constructional details of the engine

Chapter 4 described the conventional arrangement of cylinder, reciprocating piston, and connecting rod mechanism of the ordinary internal combustion engine. This construction is, with the exception of occasional isolated attempts to develop the swash plate or similar mechanisms, so generally adopted that it may be regarded as definitely established as the most satisfactory arrangement for all static pressure, as distinct from turbine engines. Many factors have contributed to this stabilising of design, including mechanical success and reliability, suitability for economic production and standardisation, and widespread familiarity and experience in maintenance requirements.

The requirements for continuous and economic production are stabilised and well-understood design features, and thus new ideas and inventions, however mechanically sound and desirable they may be, must conform with these powerful commercial considerations before widespread use becomes possible. Popular prejudice – in some countries more than others – is also a factor militating against revolutionary features. Many advanced designs have proved to be before their time from the point of view of the availability of suitable materials and manufacturing processes and after lapsing for a period have been revived as a result of advances in production technique.

The present Chapter is confined to descriptions of the conventional and well-tried fundamental parts and the various assemblies of these which are used in current multi-cylinder four-stroke engines with notes on their comparative merits.

Since the poppet valve still remains a feature almost as general as the crank and connecting rod, its construction and operation are covered in Section 6.27.

Sleeve and rotary valves and other special engine constructions, which represent the perennial search for engineering improvement and advance rather than current practice, are dealt with in Chapter 8, while Chapter 7 is devoted to types of engine having six or more cylinders.

6.1   General engine parts

What may be classified as 'general' engine parts will first be described, followed by the poppet valve and its various possible positions and methods of operation. General cylinder construction, which depends on the location of the valves, will follow and, finally, descriptions of typical four-cylinder engines will be given.

6.2   The piston

The piston performs the following functions—

(1) Forms a movable gas-tight plug to confine the charge in the cylinder
(2) Transmits to the connecting rod the forces generated by combustion of the charge
(3) Forms a guide and a bearing for the small end of the connecting rod, and takes the lateral thrust due to the obliquity of that rod.

For the designer, the major problem is catering for the variation in operating temperatures – from starting from cold at sub-zero to maximum output in tropical climates, as well as the smaller, yet still large, variations encountered in any one locality. Additionally, the weight of the piston must be kept to a minimum to reduce vibration and the inertia loading on bearings, and to avoid friction and other losses entailed in accelerating the pistons in both directions. Consequently, although cast-iron pistons have been employed, to minimise the effects of differential expansion between the piston and cylinder, these are now found only in a few two-stroke engines. This is because of their superior resistance to the higher temperatures generated in that cycle, especially adjacent to the exhaust ports.

6.3   Thermal considerations

Almost all modern engines have aluminium alloy pistons. Because the aluminium alloy is of lower strength than cast iron, thicker sections have to be used so not all the advantage of the light weight of this material is realised. Moreover, because of its higher coefficient of thermal expansion, larger running clearances have to be allowed. On the other hand, the thermal conductivity of aluminium is about three times that of iron. This, together with the greater thicknesses of the sections used, enables aluminium pistons to run at temperatures about 200° C lower than cast-iron ones. Consequently, there is little or no tendency for deposition of carbon – due to thermal breakdown of lubricant – beneath the piston crown or in ring grooves. So important is this that sections thicker than necessary for carrying the mechanical loads are in many instances used to obtain a good rate of cooling by heat transfer.

The thermal flow in a piston is from the crown, out to the ring belt, whence the heat is transferred through the rings to the cylinder walls and thence to the coolant. A small proportion is transferred down to the skirt and then across the bearing surfaces – between the skirt and cylinder walls – but this is not of such great significance, partly because of the relative remoteness of the skirt from the source of heat and partly its fairly light contact with the cylinder walls. Some heat is also taken away with the lubricant but, again, this is not a very significant proportion unless the underside of the crown is positively cooled by a jet of oil or some other system. Highly-rated engines – for example, some turbocharged diesel units – as well as engines with large diameter pistons and those operating on the two-stroke principle, may have oil-cooled pistons.

6.4   Design details

Some typical pistons for heavy-duty engines are illustrated in Figs. 6.1 and 6.2. From Fig. 6.1, it can be seen that thick sections are used and there are no abrupt changes in section which could form barriers to heat flow. The aim has been not only to keep local temperatures below the level at which the mechanical properties of the material begin to fall off significantly but also to maintain fairly uniform thermal gradients to avoid thermal fatigue cracking, especially adjacent to exhaust valves.

In Fig. 6.2 is illustrated a multi-piece oil-cooled piston, which may have either a forged steel or a Nimonic crown. Oil in this instance is taken up an

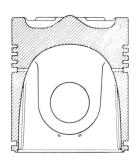
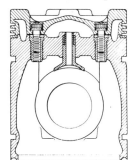

Fig. 6.1 (*left*)
Fig. 6.2 (*right*)

axial hole in the connecting rod and, through a spring-loaded slipper pick-up, into the space between the crown and skirt portions. It drains back through holes not shown in the illustration. With this design, the two parts are secured together by set-bolts inserted from above, so the crowns can be removed for attention in service without disturbing the remainder of the reciprocating assembly.

For light duty engines it used to be common practice to employ pistons the skirts of which were split by machining a slot up one side. The object was to enable the cold clearance between skirt and cylinder bore to be reduced without risk of seizure when hot. Later, as ratings increased, T-shape slots, as illustrated in Fig. 6.3, were used, the head of the T excercising an influence over thermal flow as well as on the resilience of the

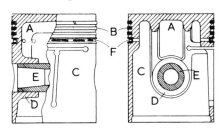

Fig. 6.3 Early light alloy piston

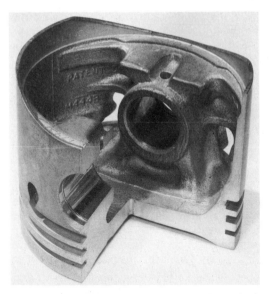

Fig. 6.4 In the Hepolite W-slot piston, there is one slot in each face. It extends along the base of the oil control ring groove and, as shown in this illustration, its ends are swept round the gudgeon pin bosses

skirt under radial compressive forces. Nowadays, engines are generally too highly rated for T-slotted skirts. The modern equivalent is the piston with slots machined through the base of its bottom ring grooves. In some instances, the ends of these extend a short distance downwards, as in Fig. 6.4 which shows the Hepolite W-slot piston.

More highly-rated engines on the other hand have no slots, being of what is termed the *solid skirt type*. In many instances, these have steel inserts, as shown in Fig. 6.5, to help to limit the expansion, by tying the skirt in locally. Virtually all pistons are cam-ground to non-circular shapes. They are also profiled top to bottom to compensate for the differing degrees of thermal expansion due to both the thermal gradients and the variations in local thicknesses of metal needed to meet the requirements for transmitting the gas and inertia loading down from the crown to the gudgeon pin bosses. In general, the diameter on the axis of the gudgeon pin is smaller than that on the thrust axis. This is because the region around the pin is so rigid that it could not deflect enough to accommodate tightening hot clearances. Cutting a slot in the bottom ring groove on each side, on the thrust axis, channels heat into the minor axis and gives the skirt on the thrust axis the additional flexibility required for running with tighter clearances.

Large clearances, causing piston slap when the engine is cold, are relatively harmless. Hot slap, on the other hand, can shorten fatigue life, impair the sealing of the rings and, assuming it is persistent, cause sufficient noise to induce driver-fatigue. In engines with wet liners, it can also cause cavitation erosion due to resonant vibration of the liners. A remedy sometimes adopted is to offset the gudgeon pin slightly. However, this tends to be more effective the lower the engine speed and, because of inertia effects, can even be detrimental at high speeds.

If the clearances are too small, thermal expansion may cause excessive contact pressures at the rubbing surfaces between piston and cylinder bore. The result can be scuffing or seizure. These effects are usually local, hence the need for the complex profiling mentioned two paragraphs previously. For a solid skirt piston, the thermal expansion pattern is generally as follows. The crown tends to expand as a solid disc, carrying with it the rigidly attached gudgeon pin bosses. Consequently, the upper part of the skirt, being not only cooler but also less rigid, tends to be drawn in to an oval shape by the outward movement of the bosses. On the other hand, the bottom of the skirt, especially of a rigidly constructed piston for a diesel engine, may deflect in the opposite sense from the upper part. The reason for this contra deflection is not positively understood, but it is probably due to pivot action about the mid portion.

Steel inserts, of course, as in Fig. 6.5, considerably modify the thermal expansion pattern, so the designer has to pay attention to the rigidity with which the skirt is attached to the crown. Slots machined in the base of the oil ring groove, by forming a barrier to thermal flow, significantly reduce thermal expansion of the skirt. They also of course affect the flexibility of the connection between the skirt and crown and hence the degree and mode of deflection.

The most commonly-used material for pistons is an aluminium alloy containing 10 to 12% silicon, which has a coefficient of thermal expansion of $19.5 \times 10^6/°C$, as compared with 23×10^6 for aluminium and 11×10^6 for cast iron. A hypereutectic alloy containing about 19% silicon, 1.2% nickel and 0.5 to 0.6% of each of cobalt and chromium is also available for applications in which an even lower coefficient of expansion – 17.5×10^6 – is required. It is sometimes used where cooling may not always be good, for example in portable engines for power tools.

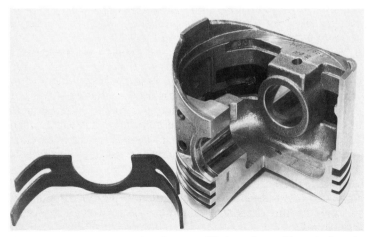

Fig. 6.5 Hepworth and Grandage Pyrostrut III piston. Its steel insert is shaped so as to exert the greatest degree of control over thermal expansion near the crown of the piston

6.5   Slipper and articulated pistons

For applications in which running temperatures are relatively constant and therefore large cold clearances are acceptable, slipper type pistons can be used. These have no skirt, the function of which is performed by two thrust pads separated from the crown and supported directly by the gudgeon pin bosses, Fig. 6.6(*a*). With this arrangement, the shape of the piston in plan view can be virtually a true circle, which improves the oil film distribution and bearing characteristics. Such a piston is sometimes termed the *crosshead type* because of the duty performed by the thrust pads. Slipper type pistons are also made in which the thrust pads are not separated from the crowns, other than perhaps by slotting in the lower ring groove.

The articulated piston is one in which the thrust pad portion, but generally in the form of a skirt, is carried independently on the gudgeon pin, Fig. 6.6(*b*). For very highly rated engines, the crown can be of iron or a ferrous alloy, while the skirt is aluminium. Because the skirt can be of

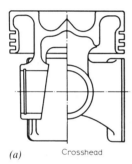

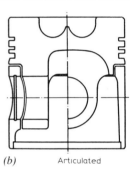

Fig. 6.6

(a)   Crosshead

(b)   Articulated

virtually uniform stiffness and its running temperature is little higher than that of the lubricating oil, the clearance can be small and its bearing properties good. Moreover, by virtue of the articulation of the skirt, pivoting freely about the gudgeon pin, the lateral thrust loading tends to be well distributed over a large bearing area, while the crown remains stable and supported by its rings. Both the pistons in Fig. 6.6 are for diesel engines.

6.6   Combustion chamber in piston

Because of the need for a working clearance between the crown of the piston at TDC and the lower face of the cylinder-head casting, a conventional combustion chamber tends to take the form of a flat disc, and consequently to have a high surface-to-volume ratio. This, as explained at the end of Chapter 11, is liable to lead to unacceptably high proportions of unburnt hydrocarbons in the exhaust. Moreover, if the compression ratio is high, the very close tolerances necessary to ensure that it is equal in all cylinders can be difficult to maintain. This has led to the development of bowl-in-piston combustion chambers, similar to those previously found only in diesel engines.

With this arrangement, not only is a compact chamber obtained in which relatively close control of turbulence is possible, but also the maintenance of close tolerances between the flat area around the bowl and the equally flat lower face of the cylinder head is not too difficult, since both surfaces are easy to machine all over. A good example is the Austin-Morris O-Series engine, described in Section 6.52. The valve layout, for actuation by an overhead camshaft, can be extremely simple, and the gas flow is not impeded by the proximity of the boundary of the combustion chamber, except at TDC. With the sparking plug close to the centre, a uniform spread of combustion is obtained. Obviously the rate of heat transfer to the piston is greater than with more conventional designs, so the positioning of the rings relative to both the crown and each other is critical and the optimum must be determined by development testing.

The modern tendency is to form the combustion chamber partly in the piston crown and partly in the head. Typical examples are the Jaguar V-12 and Rover 2.3/2.6 engines described in Sections 7.15 and 7.10 respectively. The advantages relative to the total combustion chamber in piston are: heat flow problems eased and a minimum of unburnt hydrocarbons in the exhaust.

6.7   Piston rings

Piston rings tax the skills mainly of the metallurgists and production engineers. The main functions of piston rings are—

(1) To form a pressure seal, preventing blow-by of the gases, including combustion products at high temperatures.
(2) The transfer of heat from the piston to the cylinder walls.
(3) Control of the flow of oil in adequate quantity to the skirt and to the rings themselves, while preventing excessive amounts from entering the combustion chamber.

Fine-grain alloy cast iron has proved superior to any other material for this purpose. Its merits arise from its excellent heat- and wear-resistance inherent in its graphic structure. Two typical material specifications are given in Table 1. The medium-duty material is recommended for second compression rings, while the heavy-duty material is for top rings.

A ring of the HG10 material will not lose more than 20% of its original free gap when heated at 350°C for 6½ hours enclosed in a sleeve the bore

Table 1—CHEMICAL COMPOSITION, PER CENT

	Hepolite HG10 (medium duty)	Hepolite HG22C (heavy duty)
Total carbon	3.40 – 3.90	2.70 – 3.30
Combined carbon		0.50 – 1.10
Silicon	2.10 – 2.90	2.00 – 3.00
Sulphur	0.00 – 0.10	0.00 – 0.10
Phosphorus	0.40 – 0.80	0.00 – 0.50
Manganese	0.40 – 0.90	0.50 – 0.90
Chromium	0.00 – 0.40	0.50 – 0.85
Molybdenum	0.00 – 0.40	0.00 – 0.40
Vanadium		0.00 – 0.40

size of which is equal to that of the cylinder bore, and then air-cooled. One of the HG22C material, on the other hand, will lose no more than 10% in the same circumstances. Their tensile strengths (BS 4K6) are respectively minima of 278×10^6 N/m^2 and 587×10^6 N/m^2.

Piston rings are mostly cast in the open condition and then cam-turned to a profile such that, when they are closed to fit into the cylinder, their peripheries are a true circle. Final machining is done with the ring in the closed condition. An earlier method of manufacture, now discontinued, was to start with a circular ring and then open it out by peening its inner periphery.

Gaps have been cut to various shapes, some of which are shown in Fig. 6.7. Now, however, the simple square cut has superseded all others. This type does not wear a vertical ridge in the cylinder, since rings tend to rotate.

6.8   Ring sections

Cross-sectional depth is determined by the radial stiffness required, though it is necessary also to ensure that the bearing areas between the ring and the sides of its groove are adequate. Thickness, although it also has an influence on radial stiffness, is primarily determined by the bearing pressures required between the outer face of the ring and the cylinder wall.

Simple rectangular-section rings, though often with modified face profiles, are mostly used. However, some others have been introduced with varying degrees of success. One is the L section, Fig. 6.8(*a*). This, when radially compressed into its groove, twists into a dished configuration owing to the absence of material in its upper inner corner to resist the compression induced by the bending. As a result, the lower corners come more forcibly into contact with the cylinder wall and lower side of the groove. Thus both the sealing and oil control characteristics of the ring are improved, though the heat transfer may not be quite so good. At the same time, because of the relative freedom with which gas pressure can act on the top of the ring, flutter and blow-by tend to be inhibited.

The wedge section ring and groove, Fig. 6.8(*b*), was developed to obviate ring sticking in compression ignition engines. It was said to be especially suitable for two-stroke engines. When it bottoms in its groove, there must be a side clearance of at least 0.0254 mm.

In Fig. 6.8(*c*), the Cords ring is illustrated. This comprises four dished and gapped alloy steel washers assembled in a manner such that the upper and lower ones are flexibly in contact with the sides of the groove. It is claimed to be especially suitable for use in worn bores.

6.9   Oil control rings

In the early days of the internal combustion engine, only one compression ring was used. Subsequently, two were found to seal better, and later even three were used. As speeds increased, greater quantities of lubricant had to be supplied and the problem of controlling it had to be faced. In the first instance, this was done simply by using a lower ring having a narrow face-width, to increase its contact pressure. Then stepped, or bevelled or taper-faced rings were employed and, ultimately, grooved and slotted rings, similar to that in Fig. 6.8(*d*), were adopted.

The typical oil control ring of this type, shown in the illustration, has two narrow lands bearing at a relatively high, but controlled, pressure on the cylinder walls to scrape off the oil that is surplus to requirements for lubrication. The holes, or slots, in the base of its channel section allow the oil removed to flow into the base of the groove, in which there are more holes to allow it to drain back down the cylinder to the crankcase and sump. Often the lower outer corner of the groove is chamfered and holes are drilled from the chamfer to the interior of the skirt, again for drainage. To improve the wear resistance of the narrow faces of the rings, these faces are generally chromium-plated.

Fig. 6.7 (*above*) Piston rings

Fig. 6.8 (*right*)

Because of the high speeds and bore:stroke ratios of modern engines, a copious supply of oil is flung up the cylinder bores, so the radial pressure exerted by oil control rings has had to be intensified. Consequently, a ring comprising a helical coil spring, in compression, is often interposed between the oil control ring and the base of its groove, Fig. 6.9. Humped, or crimped, strips of spring steel exerting a radial pressure on these rings are rarely used now because they are inadequate for such high speeds and loads.

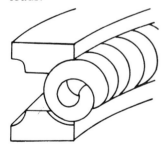

Fig. 6.9

The narrow faces, or lands, of the grooved and slotted rings are difficult to chromium-plate, so three-piece oil control rings, such as that in Fig. 6.10, are now widely employed. These comprise, in effect, the two lands of the grooved and slotted ring with a spacer between them. Initially, these were of cast iron, but now steel strip is used because it is easier to produce and to plate, and is lighter. In the Hepolite SE ring illustrated, there are two rails and the expander and spacer between them are integrated to form a single component. Such a ring has the additional advantages that it is stronger and less prone to breakage than a cast-iron ring. Moreover, it can conform more easily to worn bores.

Fig. 6.10

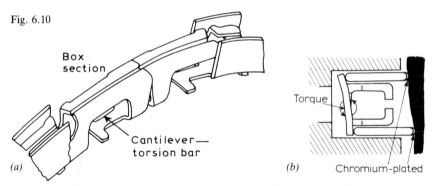

From the illustration it can be seen that the two rails are spaced apart by a rigid box section pressing and are forced radially outwards by a series of tiny cantilever springs formed in the base of the box section. The rails seat on lateral spurs, one each side of the end of each of the cantilever springs, which, if one rail lifts or sinks further than the other, act as rectangular section torsion bars to accommodate this differential deflection. Since each cantilever spring is independent of the others, failure of any one would have only a marginal effect on the performance of the ring.

6.10 Ring belt design

Most modern petrol, and even some diesel, engine pistons have only two compression and one oil control ring, all above the gudgeon pin. Previously, for very many years, the most common arrangement was three compression rings above the gudgeon pin and one oil control ring below. With the removal of one compression ring, space became available above the pin for the oil control ring. Locating it there also had the advantage that, at the high speeds and ratings of modern engines, the consequently increased supply of oil for lubrication of the skirt, especially for solid-skirt pistons, was desirable. Moreover, the ring grooves are now all in the part of the piston where metal sections are in any case thick and therefore less likely to be unacceptably weakened by their presence.

The top compression ring is generally chromium-plated for wear and corrosion resistance, as described in Section 6.11. An alternative is a sprayed molybdenum coating on the periphery of the ring to improve its scuff resistance. The outer faces of either type are generally either angled slightly – taper-faced – or lapped, to a barrel profile, to facilitate bedding in.

Spacing of rings is important, in that the lands must be thick enough to avoid their breaking up under the dynamic loading applied by the rings. The height of the land above the top ring is generally greater than the widths of the others because of the high temperatures at which it may operate which, under extreme conditions, can significantly reduce the strength in this region. For very heavy duty engines, a steel band may be bonded into the piston to carry the rings. Bonding is preferable to casting it in integrally because of the high tensile loads that would be produced at the steel-aluminium interface on cooling from the casting temperature. With bonding, the ring band can, if necessary, be shrunk on.

6.11   Cylinder bore wear and corrosion

The life of an engine between re-bores of the cylinders is determined by both abrasion and corrosion wear, the chief factors in the former being the nature of the prevailing atmospheric conditions and the efficiency of the air and oil filtration, while the latter is due to corrosive products of combustion formed during the warming-up period, and is most apparent in engines whose duty involves frequent starting from cold. Piston, piston rings and cylinder bore have to be considered together, and intensive metallurgical and engineering research is continuously devoted to the associated problems of blow-by, wear and corrosion of cylinder bores, and excessive oil consumption through pumping action due to lateral movement of the rings in their grooves.

The most widely used method of finishing cylinder bores is plateau honing. A typical machining sequence is as follows: turn to size with a diamond-tipped tool, to obtain an exceptionally clean-cut finish; coarse silicon carbide hone, plunging the tool in and out of the bore to establish two opposite-handed sets of spiral markings and thus a criss-cross pattern of extremely fine scratches; a final fine honing operation to leave only the deepest of the scratch marks, with smooth plateaux between them. The residual scratches, or minute grooves, serve to retain the lubricant, while the plateaux form the bearing surfaces to take the loading. As a result, total glazing of the bore – which would tend to prevent oil from adhering to the surface – is obviated and therefore scuffing prevented.

Chromium plating of rings or bores, and provision of 'dry' or 'wet' liners of special irons centrifugally cast, are methods of attack which are used singly or in combination, with varying degrees of success and commercial justification.

Chromium plating of bores has produced remarkable results in reducing both abrasion and corrosion wear, so reducing bore wear that life between re-bores has been extended to four or five or even more times normal experience. It is, however, costly, and running-in is a lengthy process, though assisted by the matt or slightly porous finishes used.

Application of hard chromium plating to rings rather than bore is effective in protecting both ring and bore. With the considerable difference in the hardnesses of the moving parts, abrasive particles tend to be so deeply absorbed by the softer material that they do not wear the harder.

There seems little doubt that the exceptional hardness of chromium provides protection against the lapping effect of a soft piston on the theory indicated above, while a hard plated ring has much the same effect in the reverse direction on a moderately soft liner – it is too hard either to pick up abrasive particles and act as a lap, or to be lapped by a 'loaded' bore, but has on the contrary a burnishing action on the bore.

Experience and user opinion appear to confirm the value of pre-finished chromium-plated liners in cases of heavy-duty engines in dusty atmospheres, the increased initial cost being more than balanced by reduced maintenance expenditure.

Centrifugally-cast, pre-finished liners of alloy cast iron, or made of steel tube, are very resistant to corrosion wear for applications involving frequent starting from cold, and give specially long life where abrasive conditions are adverse. These dry liners are finished to very close tolerances, and can be supplied if required to give a slip fit to aid easy renewal. They are sometimes copper-plated on their external surfaces to aid both assembly and heat flow to the water jackets.

With the pre-finished type of liner the bores in the block must be finished to a very high degree of accuracy in order to avoid distortion of the liners on assembly, the thickness of these being of the order of 2.5 mm, and not providing for re-bore.

Wet liners are made much thicker, as their necessary stiffness, reinforced by joint flanges, must be self-contained. They are usually more easily renewable than the dry type, and for two-stroke engines the necessary scavenge air ports may be readily cast in. The two types are illustrated in Figs. 6.28, 6.30 and 10.10, and may be seen in various other illustrations of complete engine assemblies.

6.12   Gudgeon pin

The gudgeon pin is of case-hardened steel; usually it is hollow and the conventional way of supporting it in two internal bosses on the piston walls is shown in Fig. 6.3. Many different ways of securing the gudgeon pin against end movement have been tried and abandoned, the device now most generally used being the spring circlip. Sometimes tightness of fit is relied upon, and phosphor bronze or aluminium pads may be placed at the ends; these will not damage the cylinder should endways movement occur. An alternative arrangement is to secure the pin in the small end of the connecting rod and allow it to turn in long piston bosses without bushes, while a 'floating' pin has also been used which is free to turn in both rod and piston, end pads being fitted. When the connecting rod is free on the gudgeon pin, a phosphor bronze bush has to be provided; this bush is a tight fit in the eye of the rod. The small end bush develops very little wear and requires renewal only at long intervals.

In view of the very heavy alternating loading of the gudgeon pins of compression-ignition engines, special care is taken to avoid risk of fatigue cracks originating at the surface of the bore, by broaching or honing or rapid-traverse grinding with the object of eliminating circumferential tool marks. The external bearing surface is finished to a very high degree of accuracy to ensure correct fit in the piston and connecting rod.

6.13   Connecting rods

Most connecting rods are medium carbon steel stampings. For special applications, however, they may be forgings, and aluminium alloys or even titanium may be used. Very highly stressed rods – for example in racing car engines – are sometimes machined all over to improve fatigue strength and to reduce weight to a minimum. Fairly recent developments are the application of malleable and SG irons and even steel castings.

As mentioned previously, the big end is usually split and has a separate cap, so that it can be assembled, together with its bearing, on to the crankpin. The cap is secured to the rod by either two or four bolts and nuts.

In the small-end eye, there is usually a force-fit phosphor-bronze or lead-bronze bush, either solid or metal-backed. The gudgeon pin generally either floats axially between circlips in the piston or is located by an interference fit in the piston bosses. Alternatively, the bearing bush and circlips are dispensed with and the pin is either a press fit in the small end or the eye is split and the pin secured by a pinch bolt.

6.14   Bearing bushes

Except in certain applications, such as some motor-cycle engines, big-end and main journal bearings are in halves – otherwise a fabricated crankshaft would have to be used so that they could be assembled on to it. One-piece cylindrical bushes are, however, used for camshaft, rocker and spiral gear bearings. In some instances these bushes are simply strips of bearing material, produced by wrapping them round a mandrel without actually joining their abutting ends.

6.15   Bearing materials

Undoubtedly whitemetal has the best bearing properties. However, its fatigue strength is limited, so other alloys have to be used for many modern highly-rated engines. Properties of bearing metals are set out in Table 2.

Babbitt invented whitemetal in 1839. It contained 83% tin, 11% antimony and 6% copper. The hard copper-antimony particles suspended in a matrix of soft copper-tin alloy give good wear resistance plus the ability to embed solid abrasive particles that would otherwise wear the shaft. Additionally, whitemetal will conform readily to inaccuracies of the shaft profile and to accommodate deflections of the shaft. Because of its low melting point, high spots in the bearing interface cause this material to soften and flow slightly to relieve excessive local pressures, instead of seizing.

Because of the increasing price of tin, there has been a tendency to use lead babbitts – which have properties similar to those of tin babbitts.

Originally, whitemetal bearings were cast in their housings. Later, they were made in the form of thick shells, sometimes in a thick bronze backing, and could therefore be more easily replaced. In either case, it was necessary first to bore them in the engine and then to scrape them manually, using prussian blue marking, to obtain a good fit.

6.16   Thin-wall bearings

In the mid nineteen-thirties the thin-wall, or shell-type, bearing was introduced for cars in the UK. This had been developed originally in the USA for aero-engines and then cars. The whitemetal was applied as a very thin lining on a steel backing about 1.5 mm thick. This had two main advantages: first, the steel backing gave good support to the whitemetal, and therefore the fatigue strength of the bearing was good; and secondly, the bearings could be made with such precision that, provided that their housings were equally precisely machined, they could be assembled without the need for skilled manual fitting. Moreover, they were equally easy to replace in service.

Table 2—POPULAR GLACIER BEARING MATERIALS

Lining material (steel-backed)	Nominal composition					Sapphire fatigue rating**	Fatigue strength	Seizure resistance	Corrosion resistance	Embeddability and conformability	Hardness HV5	Typical usage
	Al	Cu	Pb	Sb	Sn							
Tin babbitt	–	3.5	–	7.5	89	4500	2	10	10	9	27	Gas turbine, industrial gearbox, electric generators, petrol engines etc.
Lead babbitt	–	–	84	10	6	4500	2	9	10	10	16	Large industrial machinery, petrol engines (lower cost than tin)
Tin-aluminium	60	–	–	–	40	8500	4	9	10	9	27	Low- and medium-speed diesel, cross-head, reciprocating compressor
Tin-aluminium	79	1	–	–	20	1400	7	7	10	8	35	Medium- and high-speed diesel units, petrol engines
Tin-aluminium	93	1 (+1% nickel)	–	–	6	16000	8	5*	10	6	45	Medium- and high-speed diesel
Copper-lead	–	70	30	–	–	17000	8	5*	5	7	40	Medium-speed diesel, petrol engines
Lead-bronze	–	73.5	25	–	1.5	18000	9	4*	5	5	50	Medium-speed diesel and turbo-blowers***, petrol and high-speed diesel engines
Lead-bronze	–	73.5	22	–	4.5	18000	9	3*	5	4	55	Medium- and high-speed diesel
Lead-bronze	–	80	10	–	10	18000	10	2	5	2	100	Small-end and rocker bushes for petrol and medium- and high-speed diesel engines
Aluminium-silicon	88.5	1	–	–	(+10.5% silicon)	18000	9	8*	10	4	56	Highly-rated high-speed diesel engines

*These ratings apply to the base material.
Commonly, these alloys are supplied with a layer 0.0254 mm thick of electro-deposited lead–10% tin to improve seizure resistance to a rating of 10 initially.
**Sapphire rating is the dynamic load in lbf/in² which can be withstood by an oil-lubricated bearing with minimal misalignment in a 2-in diameter sapphire test rig for more than 3×10^6 load cycles; test temperature 110 to 130°C, depending upon load.
***Turbo-blowers have cast lead-bronze lining, Glacier GL26 (Pb 26% Sn 2%) with properties similar to lead-bronze.

6.17 Stronger materials

In the meantime, engine speeds, and with them gas and inertia loadings, had been increasing. Additionally, diesel engines were becoming popular for commercial vehicles. Consequently, there was a demand for stronger bearing materials. Solid bronze shells had been used, and this entailed hardening the shafts to prevent rapid wear. For heavy-duty applications, the new thin-wall bearings, with copper-lead and lead-bronze bearing materials on steel backings, were used. Of these materials, the latter is the stronger, but its conformability is worst. In both, the lead is held within the matrix, so that it is immediately available to smear on the bearing surface. The difference between the two is that in one case the matrix is pure copper and in the other it is the stronger copper-tin alloy. With the harder bearing materials, the crankshafts must be hardened, usually within the range 350 to 900 Vickers.

6.18 Corrosion of bearings

Unless engine oils are changed at fairly frequent intervals, copper-lead and lead-bronze bearings are liable to corrode. The lead phase is attacked by organic acids and peroxides that develop as a result of degradation of the oil at high temperatures. Weakening of the bearing structure and fatigue failure of the copper matrix ensue.

To protect these bearings from corrosion, a lead-tin overlay is almost invariably applied to their surfaces, by electro-plating to a nominal thickness of 0.025 mm. Such a plating also improves both seizure-resistance and bedding-in and, provided the environment is favourable, it can last the life of the engine. However, abrasive dirt can score the overlay and allow the corrosive elements to penetrate to the lining material. The lead-based overlay does not corrode because it is protected by a tin content, which is generally of the order of 10% – the minimum acceptable is 4%.

6.19 The aluminium bearing alloys

Although aluminium-tin bearings were introduced in the mid nineteen-thirties, no more than 6% tin could be used, otherwise fatigue strength was unacceptably reduced. Because of the hardness of this alloy, the shafts had to be hardened; this problem, however, was overcome by the end of the Second World War by overlay plating with alloys of lead with tin, copper or indium. The main incentive for using aluminium is its low cost relative to that of copper. Additionally, its melting point is low enough for easy casting and application in the manufacture of bearings.

By 1950, the Glacier Metal Company Ltd., appreciating the fact that overlay plated copper-lead, lead-bronze and 6% tin-aluminium linings were expensive, intensified their efforts to develop a better material. The outcome was the introduction in 1951 of a reticular tin-aluminium alloy, containing 20% tin. This development, a joint project between Glacier and the Tin Research Institute, was a major advance.

The problem of reduction of fatigue strength was overcome by preventing the tin from remaining as grain boundary films – it's natural tendency –

in the aluminium. Instead the tin forms continuous films along the edges of the grains of aluminium but not across their faces, thus forming a network structure – hence the term *reticular tin*. Essentially, this development was made possible by the perfection by Glacier of a cold roll-bonding process, instead of casting, for attaching the material to a steel backing.

Increasing the tin content up to as much as 40% improves resistance to scuffing and seizure. However, additions beyond 20% reduce the mechanical strength of the alloy.

More recently, with the increasing use of turbocharging for diesel engines, an even stronger aluminium alloy bearing material has been developed by Glacier. It is an 11% silicon-aluminium alloy, similar to that used for pistons, but with the hard silicon particles much more finely dispersed in the aluminium matrix. This fine dispersal makes the alloy very ductile, improves its fatigue strength and bearing properties, and renders it suitable for lining on to a steel backing. The material is normally overlay-plated to improve running-in and surface properties. Protection against corrosion is unnecessary, since neither aluminium nor silicon are affected. A 1% addition of copper in solution in the aluminium matrix helps to strengthen it.

6.20   Typical connecting rods

A typical connecting rod of the bronze bush type formerly used for a car and truck engine is shown in Fig. 6.11. The castellated nuts are locked by split pins; or, alternatively, plain nuts may be secured by tab washers turned up against the flats. In some designs, with a view to saving weight and reducing the number of loose parts, studs screwed into the body of the rod are used in place of bolts. A is the forged steel body of the rod and C the cap, originally part of the same stamping. B is the bronze small-end bush and D the split big-end bush lined with whitemetal.

A big end of the floating-bush type is illustrated in Fig. 6.16. This type is sometimes employed with a built-up crankshaft and is mounted on the crank pin during assembly of the crank. The steel bush A is held firmly between the cap and body of the connecting rod in the usual way, and the bronze bush B rotates or 'floats' relatively to both the steel bush or rod and the crank pin, there being thus two lubricated surfaces under relative motion resulting in distribution of wear and, under certain conditions, in decreased frictional resistance.

A sturdy piston and connecting rod assembly for a high-speed compression-ignition engine is illustrated in Fig. 6.12(a). This design is used in the Meadows 10.35-litre direct-injection engine, the rated power of which is 130 bhp at maximum governed speed of 1900 rev/min. The engine has been in extensive use in a variety of marine and mobile industrial applications, and the design may be regarded as well tried.

The piston runs in a dry alloy-iron centrifugally-cast liner, and is provided with three pressure rings, plus two scraper rings, one above and one below the gudgeon pin.

The exploded details of the connecting rod, which is of patented design, show the construction clearly. The joint face of the cap is inclined to the axis of the rod at 35°, in order that the overall width of the dismantled big

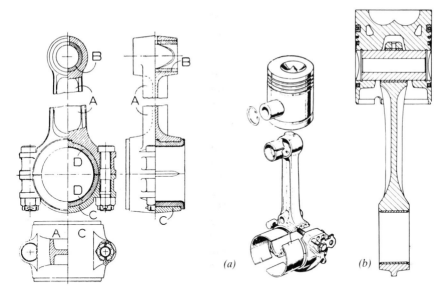

Fig. 6.11   Fig. 6.12

end may be small enough for withdrawal through the bore of the cylinder; and also, in marine and similar applications, that the big-end cap and bolts may be readily accessible through inspection covers on the side of the crankcase.

The cap is secured by four big-end bolts, the two upper ones being screwed into cylindrical nuts housed in the transverse hole through the rod, this hole also serving the purpose of a locating hole on the machining jigs. The cap is accurately registered by the fitted centre portion of the bolt shanks, which also serve to take, in shear, a large portion of the load transmitted from the cap to the rod during the inertia tension loading of the rod on the exhaust and induction strokes. The robust ribbing of the cap, the twin tab washers, and the axial drilling of the rod for gudgeon pin lubrication may be noticed. Two additional holes parallel to the bolt holes are for jig location and additional registering dowels, as may be found desirable.

For diesel engines, in which the gas loading is generally more severe than the inertia loading, chamfered small-end bosses are often employed, as in the Perkins T 6.3543, Fig. 6.12(b). This makes the bearing areas in the critical opposite halves of the bush in the rod and the bosses in the piston as large as practicable for a given cylinder bore dimension.

6.21   The crankshaft

This is usually a steel forging and, except in rare cases, is in one piece. However, cast crankshafts are gaining ground.

The number of bearings varies from two in a few small engines up to one between every pair of cranks. Thus in a four-cylinder engine there may be two, three or five bearings. The first gives a very compact arrangement and facilitates the use of ball or roller bearings, but a very stiff crankshaft is required, involving large diameter pins and greater frictional losses at the big ends. A larger number of bearings enables the dimensions of the crankshaft to be cut down without danger of whip, but the cost is increased, and great care must be taken to ensure correct alignment of all the bearings. The usual number with four cylinders was three but the five bearing layout is now becoming the general rule. This is because of the high compression ratios, bmep's and rotational speeds – and therefore inertia loadings – of modern engines.

Fig. 6.13 Forged crankshaft with balanced webs

The form of the bearing is very similar to the big end, the upper half of the bush being carried in a transverse web in the upper half of the crank case, while the cap carrying the lower half of the bush, which has to take the full force due to combustion, is secured to this web by bolts or studs. Examples of solid forged crankshafts for four-cylinder engines are shown in Figs. 6.13 and 6.14.

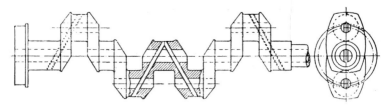

Fig. 6.14 Five-bearing shaft for ci engine

Fig. 6.13 illustrates a precision-finished, forged crankshaft as supplied by Laystall Engineering to various engine makers. The extended crank webs supply the opposing couple required in each half of the shaft to balance the revolving couple due to the pair of crank pins and big ends. The bearing loads are thereby reduced as compared with the expedient of relying on mirror symmetry of the whole shaft to balance these couples.

Fig. 6.14 illustrates a stiffly-designed shaft for a four-cylinder ci engine. Balance masses are omitted from the throws in this case, as reduction of weight is important, and the crankcase structure is made sufficiently stiff to resist the revolving couples which require to be mutually opposed.

6.22 Cast crankshafts and camshafts

The development of moulded crankshafts and camshafts, notably by such specialist automobile firms as the Ford Motor Company and the Midland Motor Cylinder Company, and by the Ealing Park Foundry for a wide range of industrial engines, has represented a great advance in metallurgical control and foundry technique.

The result is an application of special cast irons to components for which ordinary cast irons are quite unsuitable.

For highly-stressed shafts in power units of high performance or minimum weight, high tensile alloy steels will still have preference, but for ordinary production power units the casting process has outstanding advantages in producing complicated forms requiring the minimum of machining, apart from certain merits inherent in the material itself.

The chief of these are the resistance to fatigue and the excellent wearing properties of cast iron, and its capacity to withstand a given flexure with lower induced stress owing to the lower value of its elastic modulus.

Thus any misalignment of bearings due to crankcase distortion will cause a lower stress in a cast shaft than in a forged steel one of the same dimensions.

Internal damping properties under torsional oscillation are superior to those of a steel shaft, and appropriate heat treatment results in values of the ultimate strength comparable with medium alloy steels.

The material used by Ford may be described in a general way as 'copper-chromium-iron' with high carbon and some silicon, hence the descriptive name 'high carbon, high copper, chromium silicon cast steel' used by some writers. The correctness of the designation 'steel' is open to question, depending as it does on the amount and condition of the carbon present. The total proportion of alloys present amounts to about 5.5%, the remainder being iron.

An authoritative paper on nodular cast iron, with special reference to its suitability for crankshafts, was presented to the Institution of Mechanical Engineers in April 1954 by S. B. Bailey. (See *Proc I. Mech. E.*, Vol. 168.)

An illustration of the moulded crankshaft for a Ford V-eight engine is given in Fig. 6.15, from which it will be realised that the casting process

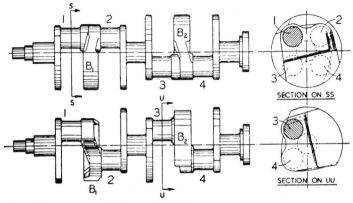

Fig. 6.15 Cast crankshaft for Ford V-eight

aids the economic production of a shaft of very complicated form. The purpose of the balance weights B_1 and B_2 is explained in Section 7.13, where the general arrangement of V-eight engines is described. Machining is normally confined to the journals and crankpins and the drilling of the oil ways, the balance being corrected by the drilling of lightening holes and rough grinding of the webs as required.

The use of 'chills' for local hardening of cam faces is referred to in Section 6.25.

6.23   Built-up crankshafts

Two examples of the built-up type of crankshaft are shown in Figs. 6.16 and 6.17. In Fig. 6.16 is shown one throw of a crankshaft in which the crank webs are permanently shrunk on to the journals; the case-hardened crank-pins being secured in the split webs by the clamping bolts shown. The big-end bush is described in Section 6.20.

The other example, Fig. 6.17, is the crankshaft of a special racing engine. The webs of the shaft are formed of circular discs A and B, the A discs having as an integral portion the journals C while the crankpins D are integral with the B discs. The B discs are a tight fit on the journals C and

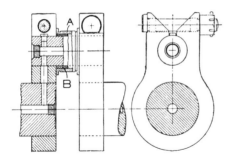
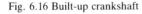

Fig. 6.16 Built-up crankshaft

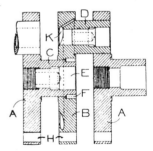

Fig. 6.17 Built-up crankshaft

are secured thereon by means of plugs E. The large ends of the latter are slightly tapered and are forced into the correspondingly tapered holes of the journals, thereby expanding the latter firmly inside the B discs. Dowel pins F fitting in holes drilled half in the journals and half in the B discs give added security against relative motion of those parts. Similar tapered plugs are used to secure the crankpins in the A discs but no dowel pins are used. When taking the shaft to pieces, plugs are screwed into the holes in the journals, thus forcing out the plugs E. To ensure correct alignment of the journals an accurately-ground rod is passed through holes H formed in the discs, during assembly of the shaft.

6.24   Surface-hardening of shafts

The term *case-hardening*, though also applicable to the nitriding and chill casting processes, is normally used for the time-honoured process of carburising the surface layer of a suitable low carbon steel to obtain a high carbon case. The carburising or carbon supplying agent may be solid, liquid, or gaseous. Subsequent quenching and heat treatment is applied with the object of producing a high degree of hardness in the case while maintaining strength and toughness in the core. Case-hardening steels are low carbon steels containing alloys which assist both the carburising process and the requirements of the core.

The depth of case is dependent on time, temperature, and composition of the steel. The time required ranges from a minimum of about a quarter of an hour in the cyanide bath to several hours in box hardening with solid carburising agents. In complicated forms such as crankshafts, though selective hardening of pins and journals is possible, the high temperatures involved and the subsequent quenching are liable to lead to quite unmanageable distortion, since the temperature of the whole component must be raised above the critical change point.

Nitriding is a similar process in that the chemical composition of the surface layer is altered, but by the production of very hard nitrides of iron and certain alloying metals, of which aluminium and chromium are effective in producing extreme hardness in the case, while molybdenum increases the toughness and depth of penetration.

The nitriding agent is ammonia gas, which decomposes into hydrogen and nitrogen at the furnace temperature of about 500°C.

The process occupies from one to two days, and is thus a slow one compared with the rapid production methods described below. No quench is required.

The great advantage compared with carburising is the exceptional degree of hardness obtainable and the relatively low temperature necessary, this being below the change point of the parent steel. This has the double merit of reducing or preventing distortion, and permitting the normal annealing and heat treatment processes of alloy steels to be carried out beforehand, without risk of subsequent interference.

Another surface hardening process is termed *New Tufftriding*. The best results are obtained with low alloy steels containing aluminium and, perhaps, chromium, tungsten, molybdenum, vanadium or titanium. Treatment of a crankshaft generally takes about two hours, during which it is immersed in a bath of molten sodium cyanate at a temperature of 570°C.

Both nitrogen and carbon are released from the salt. Nitrogen, being more soluble than carbon in iron, diffuses deeply into the surface, forming needles of ductile iron nitride. Simultaneously, hard iron carbide particles are formed at or near the surface and act as nuclei for the precipitation of some of the diffused nitrogen, forming a tough compound zone. While this hard surface zone increases resistance to wear, galling, seizure and corrosion, the tough iron nitride needles diffused below the surface present a multitude of barriers to crack propagation and therefore increase fatigue resistance.

6.25 Chill casting

The process known as *chill casting* is a long-established one and is now being applied to the selective hardening of the cam surfaces of moulded camshafts.

By the insertion into the mould of suitably-shaped iron 'chills', rapid cooling of the necessary surfaces can be effected. This results in the formation of a high proportion of combined carbon, that is of very hard carbide of iron as distinct from the free graphitic form. The hard cam surfaces can then be ground in the usual way.

Fig. 6.18 illustrates such a camshaft made by the Midland Motor Cylinder Company in their Monikrom iron. The proprietary name indicates the three important alloying elements – molybdenum, nickel and chromium.

Fig. 6.18

A very valuable feature of this method of production is the incorporation of integral gear-wheel blanks, the finished gears showing, after prolonged tests, wear-resisting qualities fully comparable with the usual alternative materials.

6.26   High-frequency induction hardening: flame hardening

Heating by the induction effects of high-frequency alternating current, of parts possessing electrical conductivity, is now used in a great variety of applications.

In the surface hardening of steel automobile parts frequencies of 2000 to 10 000 Hz are generally used for normal heavy work, and very much higher values of a 'radio' order for specially light parts requiring small penetration.

The heating is followed immediately by a quench, and the process represents the physical hardening of a suitable medium or high carbon steel in contrast to the casing processes described in Section 6.24. The general mass of the material below the surface layers remains at normal temperature and is unaffected by the operation, owing to the extreme rapidity with which the heating and quenching are accomplished.

The process requires the installation of equipment constructed to deal with large numbers of particular components, the Tocco equipment, handled in this country by the Electric Furnace Company, having reached a very high degree of specialised, high-production development.

The authors are indebted to the above company for information.

The process consists in the application to the individual crank pin or journal, or whatever part is to be hardened, of a copper muff or inductor block – split as necessary – which forms part of a high-frequency, high-current electric circuit.

There is a clearance space between the muff and the shaft into which high-pressure jets of quenching water may be introduced. Frequencies of the order of 2000 to 10 000 Hz, and currents up to 10 000 amperes are used, and the surface of the part is heated to the hardening temperature in a period of only a few seconds by the induced eddy currents, the quenching water being then introduced over a period of seven to ten seconds, the time cycle depending on the depth of penetration required.

The equipment has been developed to handle every type of automobile component made of alloy steel requiring surface hardening, and the elaborate automatic controls enable the required depth and hardness of the modified surface layer to be precisely controlled.

For rapid, precise and large-scale local hardening of suitable steels the process would seem to have no equal where the cost of equipment is justified by the large quantity of work to be dealt with.

The well-known firm of Birlec has been developing this class of apparatus in this country.

The Shorter process and equipment represent a successful attempt to introduce precision control into the use of the oxy-acetylene torch for local flame heating followed by rapid quenching.

The equipment varies in elaboration according to the nature and quantity of output, but various types of push-button apparatus have been introduced for the purpose of providing the necessary relative motion of work and torch, with the timed follow-up of the quenching sprays.

For some classes of work, particularly of the largest size where output is limited, the Shorter equipment is probably somewhat more flexible than the highly elaborate but very convenient and accurate Tocco apparatus. The Shorter process is now handled by the British Oxygen Company.

6.27 Engine valves and detail

General engine parts having now been described, the poppet valve will be dealt with before cylinder construction is considered.

The cone-seated poppet valve is still, in spite of its defects and its reputation as a source of weakness in the internal combustion engine, in practically universal use, and when in proper condition there is no better form of pressure seal to the cylinder. Once described as a 'mechanical monstrosity and a metallurgical miracle', the poppet valve is increasingly being required to perform miracles and is succeeding as a result of metallurgical progress and improved heat treatment techniques.

Failure may arise from a variety of causes singly or in combination. Higher-lift cams and stronger springs, higher maximum engine speeds associated with spring surge, impose higher mechanical stresses on head and stem.

High temperature effects include general oxidation, serious distortion and the corrosive effects due to lead compounds from the highly-leaded anti-knock fuels. Local cracking and flaking of carbonised deposits leads to 'guttering' and rapid local failure of valve seat and lip. Corrosion fatigue effects combined with operating stresses produce ultimate failure of the head.

Generally, the material selected is that which most economically meets the critical requirements – for exhaust valves, these are generally strength, creep resistance and corrosion resistance at high temperatures. An Austenitic steel is a common choice, but since this has a high coefficient of thermal expansion, the stem may have to be tapered in order that it shall become parallel despite the thermal gradient along its axis under operating conditions. An alternative now increasingly adopted is to friction-weld the head, especially if it is of a very expensive material, to a stem of a material having suitable bearing qualities and coefficient of expansion. Inlet valves, running much cooler, are generally of a cheaper material such as En51 or 52. A comprehensive article on steels for exhaust valves was published in the March 1962 issue of *Automobile Engineer*.

6.28   Protection of valves by special coating processes

Economic conditions of cost and supply that may arise in both peace- and war-time conditions have prompted much research and development in the direction of applying special coatings to valve steels of the less expensive and more readily obtained varieties.

The principal alloying elements are nickel, manganese, cobalt, chromium and silicon, but certain combinations of these, while giving excellent results, are expensive and may involve supply difficulties. Molybdenum, tungsten and titanium are less frequently used.

6.29   Brightray and Nimonic alloys

The nickel base alloys, Nimonic 75 and 80, and BAC Brightray, all containing 20% chromium with 70 to 80% nickel as base, showed excellent resistance to the corrosive deposit effects of high lead content fuels during the Second World War, but cost and limitation of supply prohibited their general use.

Successful developments have taken place in the application by flame welding techniques of a Brightray coating to certain of the less expensive iron base alloys, such as Silchrome I and Silchrome XB.

It is reported that the deposition requires no flux, is not difficult, and if applied to the seat, lip and edge of crown gives high resistance to corrosion and cutting by high speed gases. Machinability is good.

6.30   Production surfacing by Aldip process

This is a large-scale, highly-mechanised process developed by General Motors.

The current method appears to involve the preliminary finish machining of the valve seats and the rough grinding of the stems followed by the application of the metal coating as a paste, by spraying, or by the placing of a ring or washer on the valve seat. Carried in an elaborate jig the batch of valves is then immersed for a few seconds in a molten flux bath at 760°C. Then the jig is passed to an air blast fixture where surplus aluminium is blown off. The final result is a smooth, permanently adhering coating which does not require a further finishing process.

Photomicrographs of the coating show that an aluminium overlay covers a layer of iron-aluminium alloy, which appears to provide the resistant properties required to improve valve life. Production techniques and sequences of considerable elaboration have called for extensive experiment before large-scale economic development was achieved, but current experience shows improvement in life of coated relative to uncoated valves averaging 100%.

6.31 Poppet valve

Fig. 6.19 shows a typical general arrangement of a poppet valve in position in the cylinder casting – side-valve layout.

The valve head A rests on a conical seating formed in the cylinder casting, the angle of the cone being usually 45°, though occasionally a flatter angle, of about 30°, is used. Flat-seated valves, though they have been tried in many instances, have not proved as satisfactory as the cone-seated type.

The stem passes through a guide G supported in the cylinder casting, the guide being cast iron, or even case-hardened steel, and a push fit in the casting. In some cases the renewable guide is dispensed with, the stem passing through a plain hole in a suitable boss in the casting. This construction is inferior, however, since wear at the inlet valve guide causes leakage of air into the induction system and rectification is then troublesome.

The valve is closed and pressed on to its seating by a spring, usually helical, which abuts against a washer and bears on a washer resting on a split collar C, or on a cotter pin which passes through the lower end of the valve stem. Thus the gas pressure on the head of the valve assists the spring in pressing the valve firmly on its seating when closed, gas tightness being readily secured by careful grinding of the valve to its seating.

The valve is opened by positive mechanical means which will be described later, the lift being usually about one-fifth of the diameter of the seating.

The description of sleeve valves and typical rotary valves is deferred until Chapter 8, as these types pass through periodical phases of popularity and inventive productivity without succeeding in establishing themselves in general use and production.

6.32 Special valve seat inserts

The use of valve seat inserts is of course essential in the aluminium alloy heads. These inserts are generally of special sintered heat-resistant cast irons, or 'Stellited' steel. Stellite is a class of extremely hard alloys containing – according to the particular application – varying proportions of cobalt, chromium, tungsten and carbon, but without iron. It is applied by a flame-welding process as a facing to the contact portion of the steel valve seat ring. It may also be applied to the conical face of the valve.

The Centri-lock insert is an under-cut stepped ring of special centrifugally-cast iron. The machining tolerances are very closely controlled so that the interference on each diameter will hold the seat securely when it is pressed in. Figs. 6.20 and 6.21 illustrate these inserts.

6.33 Layout of valves and form of combustion chamber

The requirements to be met in the design of the cylinder head and location of valves are numerous and conflicting, and the search for the successful compromise has led to the designing, patenting and production of a very great number of different forms and arrangements, often with puzzling anomalies and inconsistencies in performance between different examples possessing apparently the same virtues.

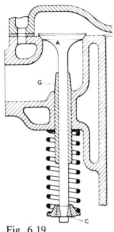

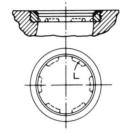

Fig. 6.19   Fig. 6.20 Stellited seat   Fig. 6.21 Centri-lock seat

The basic requirements to be met are indicated in Table 3. They are stated very simply, but the five main requirements given under each lettered heading, with the necessary means of provision, cover the more important factors to be reconciled.

Fig. 6.22 illustrates four conventional arrangements which are in wide general use, and Fig. 6.23 and later illustrations give examples or variations of these.

Fig. 6.22(*a*) is the once popular side-valve construction with all valves in line, the detachable head being of the turbulence type providing for compression or squish turbulence produced as the piston closely approaches the flat portion of the cylinder head. Valve diameter and adequate valve port cooling are in conflict, as with all valves in single-line arrangements, unless the longitudinal pitch of the cylinders is increased; and volumetric efficiency is further limited by the changes in direction of the gas flow and restricted entry to the bore. Requirements A (3) and (4), in Table 3, are reasonably well met, though flame travel is long. Requirement B (2) is *not* met, and the high surface:volume ratio of the head, if combined with undue turbulence and over-cooled jackets, militates against economy. Requirements C and D are well met on the whole. Incidentally, in recent years the real significance of squish turbulence has been questioned: after all, why should the gases not move progressively from between the approaching parallel flat faces, rather than wait there to be squirted, or squished, out at top dead centre. On the other hand, as the piston descends again, a reverse squish action certainly does occur.

Fig. 6.22 (*b*) should give good volumetric efficiency as a large diameter inlet valve may be used, and the valve port gives direct access to the bore.

High compression ratio can be readily provided.

Other characteristics are similar to (*a*), though the construction is likely to be more expensive owing to the mixed direct and push-rod valve gear.

In both cases combustion is initiated in a hot region and the end-gas is well cooled on a shallow flame front.

Diagram (*c*) illustrates the very widely used overhead valve (ohv) arrangement with vertical valves in single line, permitting the use of simple

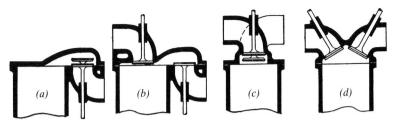

Fig. 6.22

push-rod and rocker gear. The wider cylinder pitch at the main bearings sometimes permits of an increased length of combustion chamber, known as the 'bath-tub' type, to accommodate larger valves. The width is usually less than the bore in modern designs to provide increased compression ratio and some compression turbulence.

At (*d*) is shown the classic approximation to the ideal hemispherical head which is used in many high performance designs. Large diameter inlet valves with free entry can readily be provided and with careful port design and possibly some degree of masking of the lower side of the inlet valve, there should be fair general turbulence though compression or squish turbulence is absent. Flame travel is short, and high compression ratio can be readily provided by a domed piston crown, but this adds to surface area.

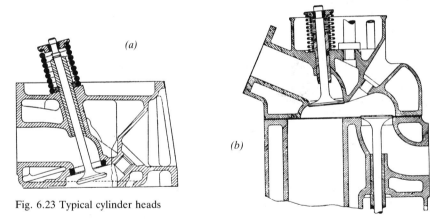

Fig. 6.23 Typical cylinder heads

If four valves of smaller diameter are used the combustion chamber takes the 'penthouse' form, and it is somewhat easier to accommodate the sparking plug on the cylinder centre line.

Valve gear is somewhat complicated and expensive, twin camshafts with push rods and rockers being the most commonly employed arrangement. The two diagrams of Fig. 6.23 may be taken to represent in each case one or more well-known makes.

6.34   Cylinder head – some overall design considerations

The choice between cast iron or aluminium for the cylinder head is not simple. Aluminium has the advantages of light weight, high thermal conductivity, and ease of production to close tolerances by gravity or

Table 3—PERFORMANCE AND CONSTRUCTION

Objective	Requirements	Means of provision
A Power output Smooth running	(1) High compression ratio. (2) High volumetric efficiency. (3) Rapid and efficient combustion. (4) Freedom from pinking (see Section 14.10).	Small volume of combustion chamber. Early closing of inlet valve. Large inlet valve, suitable valve timing, limited pre-heating. Short flame travel, adequate turbulence, good plug scour. Short flame travel, well cooled 'end-gas', suitable plug position.
B Fuel economy (low specific fuel consumption or high thermal efficiency)	(1) High compression ratio. (2) Low surface:volume ratio. (3) Efficient use of weak fuel:air mixtures. (4) Adequate pre-heating.	Small volume of combustion chamber, etc. Hemispherical form of combustion chamber. Short flame travel, adequate turbulence, good plug scour. Hot jackets and induction manifold.
C Economical manufacture	(1) Economy in machining. (2) Simple castings. (3) Simplified details. (4) Ease of assembly.	Elimination of unnecessary joints and attachments. May conflict with above. Simplified design. Standardisation. Sub-, and main assemblies.
D Ease of maintenance	(1) Accessibility. (2) Easy renewal of parts. (3) Ease of decarbonising and valve grinding (4) Limited weight of components.	Detachable head. Separate cylinder block. Renewable valve and tappet guides and cylinder liners. Unit assembly of head and valves. Sub-, and main assemblies.
E Low emissions	(1) A limited compression ratio, for NO_x. (2) Efficient use of weak air:fuel ratios, for low CO. (3) High ratio of volume: superficial area, for low HC. (4) Smooth combustion chamber, free from crevices, for low HC.	A complex series of measures needed, as described in Sections 11.58–11.65

low-pressure diecasting. On the other hand, aluminium is more expensive than iron, tooling for large quantity production is costly, porosity in the finished casting can present difficulties, aluminium is more easily damaged in service and rather more prone to gasket blow-by failure, corrosion may present problems – especially where there are copper components in the cooling system – and heat-resistant valve seat inserts are essential.

Cast iron is inherently stiffer, and therefore contains noise better, and is cheaper. On the other hand, the labour costs in making the moulds and cores are higher, and more labour may be required for removing the sand cores, and for fettling.

An outstandingly good cylinder-head design is that of the *Dolomite Sprint*, Fig. 6.24. Since it exemplifies the best solution to many of the problems, it will be described here. It is of aluminium and has four cylinders, four valves per cylinder, and a single overhead camshaft. The exhaust valves are inclined 16° to one side of the axis of the cylinder and the inlets 19° to the other side. Their seats are in a penthouse-type combustion chamber.

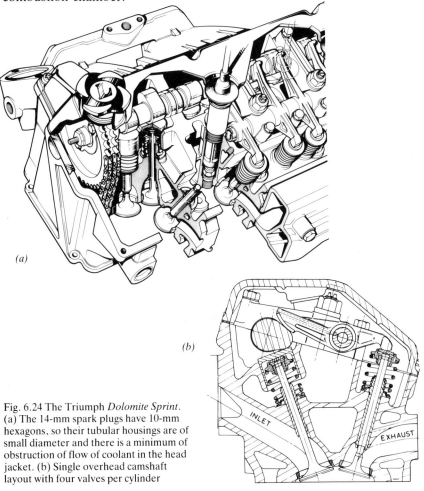

(a)

(b)

Fig. 6.24 The Triumph *Dolomite Sprint*.
(a) The 14-mm spark plugs have 10-mm hexagons, so their tubular housings are of small diameter and there is a minimum of obstruction of flow of coolant in the head jacket. (b) Single overhead camshaft layout with four valves per cylinder

Since the engine, when installed, is tilted 45° towards the exhaust side, the inlet valve ports then slope steeply downwards. This facilitates cold starting, in the following manner. As the crankshaft is turned, any fuel remaining unevaporated in the manifold runs down into the cylinder, where it is evaporated by the heat generated during the subsequent compression stroke. Mixing is further assisted, at TDC, by the squish effect between the flat area surrounding the slightly dished portion of the crown of the piston and the flat lower face of the casting, each side of the pairs of valves. Because of the steepness of the slope of the inlet ports, this fuel runs down positively into each cylinder in turn so that, once the first cylinder fires, the others will pick up immediately. The penalties for a slope that is either inadequate or too steep are respectively mixtures that are either too weak or too rich to fire in sequence.

A single camshaft, with eight cams, serves all the valves. Each cam actuates first an inlet and then an exhaust valve. However, whereas the inlet valve is actuated directly, through the medium of an inverted bucket tappet, the exhaust valve is opened by a rocker, one end of which follows the cam and the other bears on a pallet, or thick shim, seated in a recess in the top face of the valve spring retainer. A similar pallet is interposed between the exhaust valve spring retainer and its tappet.

To reduce the velocity of sliding between the rocker and cam, the pad on the end of the rocker is curved. This, however, tends to increase the velocities of both opening and closing of the valve and therefore has to be taken into account in the design of the cam profile.

The sparking plug is very close to the centre of the top of the combustion chamber, for efficient combustion. As a result, it has not been possible to make the diameter of the two inlet valves much larger than that of the exhausts but, to compensate for this, their lifts are greater – 8.712 mm as compared with 7.798 mm.

To span the distance between the camshaft and the exhaust valves, the rockers have to be long. Consequently forged En8 steel, instead of the usual cast iron, rockers are used. Because of the relatively poor bearing characteristics of steel, however, oil from a radial hole in the rocker bearing is fed down a groove on top of the rocker arm to the cam follower pad. To obviate any possibility of oil dripping down and getting into the exhaust valve guide, where it could form carbon deposits, a heat-resistant flexible seal is fitted over the upper end of the guide.

As can be seen from Fig. 6.24, the upper half-bearing for the camshaft and the semi-circular clamp for the rocker shaft are machined in a single long diecast aluminium bearing cap secured on the plane of the inclined joint face of the valve gear cover by a bolt at each end. With this arrangement, the valve actuation gear can be fitted to the cylinder head, forming a self-contained sub-assembly, with valve clearances set, all ready for mounting on the engine.

The cylinder head holding down studs on the inlet side of the head are inclined 74° relative to the cylinder gasket joint face, and this brings their upper ends out through the diecast cap, adjacent to the rocker shaft and at right angles to the inclined seating face. Consequently, when the head is tightened down, the stud pulls the clamp tightly down on to the rocker shaft so that there is absolutely no possibility of fretting fatigue between the cap and shaft. Set bolts, perpendicular to the cylinder head gasket joint face, hold down the exhaust side of the head. With this overall arrangement, the head can be removed in service without disturbing the valve gear.

The inlet valves are of Silchrome, while the exhausts are either Nimonic 80A with Stellite tips on the ends of their stems, to prevent undue wear, or of En18 with Nimonic 80A heads welded to them. All stems are chromium-plated to reduce the rate of abrasive wear in the guides.

Sparking plugs of the conical seating type are fitted, because they are screwed into bosses at the lower ends of tubular housings cored vertically in the head casting, where plug washers would be difficult both to place and to retrieve. The gap between the upper end of each of these cored housings and the valve gear cover is spanned by an aluminium tube with elastomeric seals moulded around both its ends. The lower seal is a tighter fit in the head casting than is the upper one in the valve gear cover, so that the tube will not pull away from the head when the cover is removed. Although 14-mm plugs are fitted, their hexagons are of 10-mm plug size, so that the tubular housings can be of small diameter. This, in turn, restricts as little as possible the water passages around the plug bosses.

The good thermal conductivity of the aluminium head, together with generous cooling passages around the valve seats account for the absence of valve sinkage when unleaded fuel is used. Lead in fuel is thought to act as a lubricant between the valve and its seat, so with unleaded fuel and elevated temperatures the rate of wear of less well cooled seats can be high with the result that the valve sinks into them.

A four-valve head layout was chosen because this engine was required to have high performance. So far, no positive proof of why the four-valve layout is so efficient has been put forward. However, the central positioning of the plug probably contributes, and the scavenging on a broad front – through a pair of exhaust valves – may also help.

6.35 Cylinder block and crankcase arrangement

Until about 1925, cylinder heads and blocks were generally integral, and in highly rated aero-engines, notably the Rolls-Royce Merlin, the arrangement was still in use throughout and after the Second World War. However, with road vehicles, the need for frequent servicing and economy of manufacture led to the adoption of the separate cylinder head casting. But, with the introduction of turbocharging and the consequent development of high gas-pressures and temperatures, the designers of the Leyland 500 diesel engine, Fig. 6.25, reverted to the combined head and block casting, bolted to a separate crankcase.

The elimination of the cylinder head gasket disposes not only of the barrier to the conduction of heat, but also of the thick sections of the adjacent faces of the two separate castings, which can cause thermal distortion of the structure. In particular, with this layout, the cylinder bores and valve seats should be relatively free from distortion. The absence of cylinder head retaining studs should also help in this respect, as well as give the designer greater freedom in arranging the valve and porting layout and cooling passages. Large covers bolted on each side of the block facilitate the cleaning of sand from the cooling passages after the casting operation. However, despite all these potential advantages, the design proved extremely difficult to develop to the point of complete satisfaction in practice.

Other cylinder block and crankcase arrangements appear in Figs. 6.26 to 6.30. The black sectioning represents cast iron and the cross-hatching aluminium alloy. While the figures are simplified and to a great extent diagrammatic only, each is represented by one or more examples in past or present practice.

That shown in Fig. 6.26 is the conventional arrangement used in large engines of the highest quality, where it is not essential to economise in machining and fitting. Here a monobloc cylinder casting, with overhead valves in a detachable head, is bolted to a two-part aluminium alloy crankcase split on or below the crankshaft centre line. The maximum degree of accessibility is provided for valves, pistons and bearings.

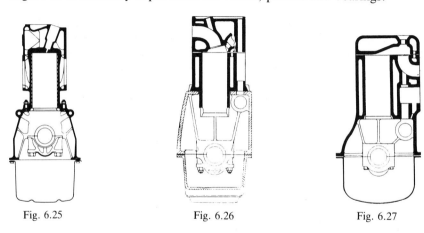

Fig. 6.25   Fig. 6.26   Fig. 6.27

Fig. 6.27 shows the side-valve arrangement of what has been the most widely used construction but which is now generally superseded by the overhead valve arrangement shown in Figs. 6.28 and 6.29 with various camshaft arrangements. Modern designs simplify the cylinder block casting and improve accessibility of valves and rockers. A single monobloc casting in iron or in aluminium alloy – in which case wet cylinder liners are used – extends from the head joint face to usually well below the crankshaft centre line, forming a rigid beam structure of great depth and stiffness. Well ribbed webs tie the crankcase walls together and carry the main and camshaft bearings. The bottom is closed by a light sump which is often ribbed for cooling purposes and may carry the main oil filters. For examination and overhaul, pistons and connecting rods must be withdrawn upwards through the bores unless removed bodily with the crankshaft.

The corresponding overhead-valve construction is illustrated in Fig. 6.28, which shows a low camshaft for push rod and rocker operation of the valves. A dry liner is indicated in this case. The valves all lie in the same longitudinal plane.

End assembly of the crankshaft is provided for in the construction of Fig. 6.29. When arranged for three bearings, the centre bearing is mounted in a

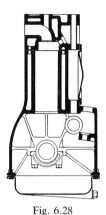
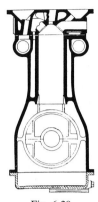
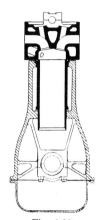

Fig. 6.28   Fig. 6.29   Fig. 6.30

circular housing of diameter exceeding the diameter of the crank webs. The old Lea-Francis design was of this construction, which provides a rigid and accurately aligned support for the crankshaft. It had high twin camshafts to operate the inclined overhead valves, which were pitched transversely.

Figs 6.30 and 10.10 show two examples of wet liner construction, one for a medium-powered petrol engine and the other for a blower-charged, poppet-exhaust two-stroke ci engine. The air gallery and scavenge ports of the latter will be noticed. Water joints are made with synthetic rubber rings (as indicated) and gas pressure joints usually by separate gasket rings to each bore. A light alloy main casting is indicated in these two cases.

6.36   The aluminium crankcase

Aluminium alloy has always been a potentially attractive material for crankcases. This is because of its light weight, good thermal conductivity, prospect for good cooling and, if aluminium pistons could be used in aluminium bores, the absence of differential expansion would enable tighter clearances to be adopted in the bores. However, until recently, this light metal has failed to gain wide acceptance because it has been necessary to fit cast-iron liners, primarily owing to the unsatisfactory bearing properties of aluminium pistons in bores of the same material. This has increased the cost of production with a material that, in any case, is expensive. Moreover, there have been other problems, including the risk of electrolytic corrosion and of the head welding to the block, as well as a high noise level and, when diecasting is used because of its suitability for large quantity production, a large rejection rate owing to porosity.

Some European manufacturers, however, with access to relatively cheap supplies of aluminium, and others throughout the world who produce expensive cars, as well as Rootes – later Chrysler, now Talbot – have used sand-cast crankcases and cylinder blocks. The Rootes car, the Hillman *Imp*, was a special case, since weight reduction was of prime importance as the engine and transmission were to be installed at the rear. An open top deck layout was chosen because, originally, diecasting was envisaged.

Fig. 6.31 The diecast aluminium block of the Chevrolet Vega has 6.35-mm thick cylinder walls, and most of the other walls are 4.826 mm thick

Fig. 6.32 The open-deck design, with siamesed cylinders, was adopted for the diecast aluminium crankcase of the Vega so that the dies could be easily withdrawn

There are four iron liners, which are preheated to 204°C before they are inserted in the mould, for the aluminium to be cast around them. To key the liners in the aluminium, their outer peripheries have spiral grooves 0.331 mm deep machined around them at 3.18 mm pitch. When cast in, they are arranged in two siamesed pairs – otherwise the block would be unduly long – so water can flow transversely between only the central two cylinders and across the ends of the block.

Renault, too, have used cylinder blocks with wet cast-iron liners for many years. One of their later developments has been the 1.47-litre R16 model, in which a high pressure aluminium diecast cylinder block and crankcase is employed. Although most of the walls are only 4 mm thick, the casting is well ribbed and flanged for stiffness. The liners are closely spaced in the open-top casting, and there are five main bearings – the *Imp*, being a much smaller unit, 875 cm^3, has only three bearings. An interesting feature of the Renault engine is the employment of an aluminium head too.

In 1971, General Motors announced the Chevrolet Vega 2300 engine with a diecast all-aluminium crankcase and cylinder block, Figs. 6.31 and 6.32, reported in *Automobile Engineer*, August 1970. Developments that have made this possible include the Accurad method of diecasting, described in the November 1969 issue of *Automobile Engineer*. This entails control of the cooling of the metal so that areas remote from the point of injection solidify first, and a two-stage injection process, the second stage of which effectively compensates for shrinkage of the metal. Secondly, a new alloy, termed A390, has been introduced by Reynolds Metals, and this combines good fluidity in the molten condition with fine dispersion of silicon after heat treatment, which gives good bearing properties and ease of machining – large particles wear the tools and tear from the surface of the alloy. It contains 16 to 18% silicon, 4 to 5% copper and 0.45 to 0.65% magnesium.

Diecasting is employed because of its suitability for large quantity production and its accuracy: the latter minimises subsequent machining and enables thin walls to be incorporated – as little as 4.826 mm, but 6.35 mm for the bores – thus economising in material. The finished block for this 2.3-litre engine weighs only 36 lb, as compared with 87 lb for the cast-iron block of the comparable Chevrolet L-4 engine. However, because it is diecast and provision must therefore be made for withdrawal of metal cores, the open top deck form, with siamesed cylinders, has to be used.

Diecast aluminium heads have not yet been used by any manufacturer in quantity production, because of the problem of withdrawal of the cores. Experiments, though, have been made with two-piece castings joined by means of adhesives or by electron beam welding. A cast-iron head, however, makes up for any lack of stiffness of an aluminium block with an open top deck and helps to contain the noise of combustion and from the overhead camshaft and valve gear. On the Vega, it is secured by ten long bolts screwed into bosses at the bases of the cylinders, so that the bores are rigidly held in compression.

The cylinder bore treatment in the Vega, to form a wear-resistant and oil-retaining surface, and to prevent scuffing, comprises exposure of the hard silicon particles by an electro-chemical etching process. In addition, the skirts of the pistons are coated with iron by a four-layer electrodeposition process, to render the bearing surfaces compatible with those of the bores. The coats, in order of application, are: zinc, copper, iron and tin. Zinc bonds well to aluminium, the copper prevents removal of the zinc by the iron plating process and the tin prevents subsequent corrosion of the iron and helps in running in. The iron coating is 0.019 mm thick.

6.37   Camshaft drive

Whatever the type of valve used it is necessary in the four-stroke engine to drive it from a camshaft which runs at half the speed of the crankshaft, as each valve is required to function only once in two revolutions of the crankshaft. The necessary gearing for this purpose is placed, with few exceptions, at the front of the engine, that is, at the end remote from the flywheel and clutch. The camshaft or camshafts may be driven by gears, chains or toothed belts, while a few overhead camshafts have had a 'coupling rod' drive. Fig. 6.33 shows diagrammatically some typical arrangements of two-to-one drive for both low and high camshafts.

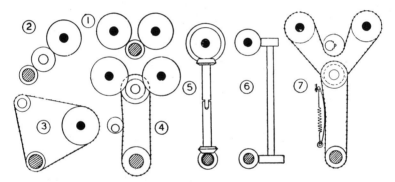

Fig. 6.33

No. 1 shows the simplest possible arrangement of direct gearing for either one or two camshafts. The wheel on the camshaft has twice as many teeth as the crankshaft wheel, and therefore revolves at half the speed of the latter. Where, as is often the case, the distance between the two shafts is considerable, this arrangement requires undesirably large gear wheels, and this has led to the adoption of the arrangement shown at 2. Here an intermediate idler wheel is interposed between the crankshaft wheel and the camshaft wheel. This idler wheel may be of any convenient size, as the number of teeth in it does not affect the gear ratio. The camshaft now revolves in the same direction as the crankshaft, whereas in the former arrangement it did not.

A chain drive is shown at 3. The single chain drives the auxiliaries in addition to the camshaft, the drive thus being a triangular one, but if the chain is passed round only the crankshaft and camshaft sprockets, the shorter run thus obtained is less prone to whip.

At 4 is illustrated a combined chain and gear drive for twin high camshafts. The chain sprocket ratio is 1:1, and the 2:1 ratio is provided by the gearing.

An automatic chain tensioner of the Coventry eccentric type is indicated. The axis of rotation of the jockey chain wheel can swing eccentrically round the spindle on which it is mounted to take up slack in the chain, the desired pressure on the back of the chain being adjustable and automatically maintained by the clock-type spring, the inner end of which is secured to the mounting spindle and the outer end to the drum which carries the jockey-wheel bearing.

A later development is the Renold hydraulically-actuated tensioner, Fig. 6.34(a). When assembled, the cylinder casting is secured by two bolts to the front wall of the crankcase, and inserted into it is a plunger, carrying the neoprene-faced slipper together with the spring-loaded piston which forces the slipper lightly into contact with the chain. When the engine is

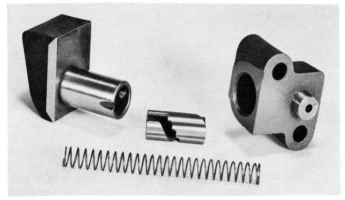

Fig. 6.34(a) The ratchet device on the plunger of the Renold hydraulic chain-tensioner prevents the chain from going too slack when the oil pressure is low

started, oil from the pressure-lubrication system, ducted into the cylinder of the adjuster, forces the slipper firmly against the chain. The piston has a spiral ratchet-toothed slot in its skirt, in which registers a peg projecting radially inwards in the bore of the plunger: its function is to limit the backlash, that is, movement of the slipper away from the chain.

Various means of driving overhead camshafts are illustrated at 5, 6 and 7 in Fig. 6.33. Diagrams 5 and 6 show vertical shafts driven by bevel and skew gears respectively. In either case the 2:1 ratio may be obtained in one or two steps as may be most convenient. In the latter case particularly, ratios 3:2 and 4:3 are advantageous.

It will be noticed that in the case of the bevel gears a tongue and slot arrangement is provided so that expansion of the cylinder block will not affect the meshing of the gears. This provision is not strictly necessary with skew gears, though the slight axial movement of the vertical gear that may place will result in a slight variation of timing between the hot and cold conditions.

No. 7 is the layout on the Jaguar in-line engine, which has stood the test of time. The 2:1 ratio is divided between the two stages, the tooth ratio of the four chain-wheels being 21:28 × 20:30. This tends to distribute the wear and maintains uniformity of pitch. Another advantage is that small sprockets can be used.

For the lower chain, a nylon-faced damping slipper bears on the driving strand, to prevent thrash due to torsional oscillations. On the earlier models, a spring plate tensioner bore on the slack strand, but this was subsequently superseded by the Renold hydraulic tensioner. For manual adjustment of the tension in the upper chain, the jockey sprocket is mounted on an eccentric spindle, as described in detail in *Automobile Engineer*, May 1956.

Renold also produce a commendably simple double-acting tensioner, comprising a central cast housing with twin parallel bores in which are horizontally opposed plungers, each with a shoe on its outer end. Two coil springs in compression push the plungers lightly outwards until the shoes contact the inner faces of both the taut and idle runs of the chain. At the same time, oil splashing into a pocket on top of the housing is drawn continually, by the motions of the plungers due to fluctuations in the drive, through a non-return valve to fill their bores. Movement of one plunger inwards in its bore instantly seats the non-return valve, causing the other to move in the opposite direction so that the light contact with both runs is continuously maintained.

Another type of tensioner is that used in the Jaguar V-12 engine, Section 7.17, supplied by the Morse Chain Division of Borg-Warner Ltd. Of the four runs of chain between the sprockets – on the crankshaft, two camshafts and the jackshaft – three are controlled by damper pads and the fourth by the tensioner. Because these four runs form a strand 1.674 m long, an extremely accurate and effective tensioning is essential.

The Morse tensioner, Fig. 6.34(b), supports the run of chain over most of its length – its shoe is approximately 28 cm long – so the force per unit area on the shoe is small, and undue noise and wear are therefore avoided.

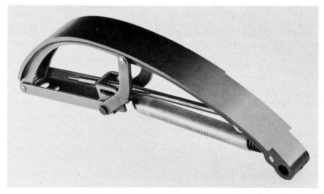

Fig. 6.34(b) The Morse chain-tensioner is a simple spring-loaded mechanical device

Moreover, the shoe is a nylon moulding and therefore does not require a separate facing. Nylon, of course, has a low coefficient of friction and, in this application, fillers are added to improve both the stiffness and wear characteristics. It is also resistant to oil, fuels and temperatures of 150°C and even higher. Furthermore, its flexibility increases with temperature, so, when the engine is warm, the tensioner readily conforms to changes in shape of the chain run throughout its life. Finally, so that the chain cannot go slack and, possibly, ride over the sprocket, a one-way device is incorporated in the tie that holds the shoe in the bowed condition. A tendency for the chain to go slack can arise, of course, in the event of a backfire, or some other form of uneven running, or when the engine is turned backwards by hand, for timing.

From Fig. 6.34(b), the form that the one-way device takes can be seen. The tie comprises a steel channel section, which is attached to one end of the bowed shoe, and a plain tie-rod and tensioning spring parallel to it, which is attached to the other end, these parts being all connected, near the centre, by a small U-section bracket pivot-mounted in the channel. A pair of arms extend, one from each end of the pivot pin, and are attached mid-way between the ends of the bowed shoe, to afford additional support. The tie-rod is a clearance fit in the hole in the base of the U, and the line of action of the spring is such that it tends to cause the bracket to swing about the pivot pin. This locks the tie-rod by friction in its clearance hole so long as there is a load tending to straighten the bowed shoe, but leaves it free to slide further into the hole if that load is released altogether, so that the shoe can bow further to take up the slack in the chain. Both the bracket and the tie-rod are, of course, of case-hardened steel. The friction lock can be released in service, by the use of a key which engages in a slot in the bracket, to rotate it about its pivot until the rod is free in its hole. Around the spring is a nylon sleeve, to damp out vibrations and thus contribute to quietness and reliability.

Fig. 6.35 The outer surface of the internally-toothed belt drive for the camshaft can be used to drive the water pump and fan. Such a belt is wider than a chain

Another recent development is the PowerGrip toothed belt, which is now widely used as a camshaft drive. Its advantages include relative silence and complete absence of stretch and slip, but it does add to the length of the engine. The drive, Fig. 6.35, is manufactured by the North British Rubber Company under licence from the United States Rubber Company.

Its continuous flexible belt comprises a stranded cable or braided core, of high tensile steel or glass fibre – with a coating of synthetic rubber such as neoprene closely bonded to the core – and carrying shallow rubber teeth integral with its inner face. The construction is described in British patent No. 618 172. The drive is transmitted through transversely grooved pulleys of cast iron or steel, and the whole assembly is usually either screened or totally enclosed, both for safety and to keep it clean.

Whichever form of core is used, it is wound around the base of the vulcanising mould, on a thin lining of wear resistant material which forms the skin of the teeth and inner face of the belt. To avoid distortion of the belt, the cables alternately may be twisted clockwise and anti-clockwise. Clearance is left between adjacent convolutions to allow of penetration of the vulcanising compound. By this construction the core, on the pitch line of the belt, can coincide closely with the pitch lines of the mating pulleys, the teeth of which have no addendum. Thus change of pitch on engagement is avoided.

6.38   Camshaft brakes and compensating cams

As each cam follower passes from the front to the back of the cam at the point of maximum lift, the effect of the valve spring changes from a resisting effort to a driving effort, and the direction of the torque in the camshaft (as far as that cam is concerned) is abruptly reversed. If the camshaft is long, this sudden reversal of torque results in considerable torsional whip, while if the torque on the camshaft as a whole (taking all the cams into consideration) reverses, then, if there is any backlash in the camshaft drive, noise will result from the blow as the backlash is suddenly taken up. This is avoided in some high-class engines by fitting a lightly loaded friction brake, as shown in Fig. 6.36, which exerts a continuous small resisting torque sufficient to prevent this torsional 'flick' or whip. The small amount of friction necessary is often provided by the lubricated

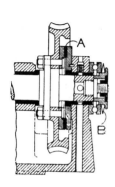

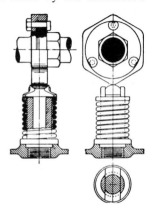

Fig. 6.36 (*left*)
Fig. 6.37 (*right*)

contact of a metal or fabric disc A against the rim face of the camshaft wheel, contact being maintained by a light compression spring or washer B.

Another means of avoiding the trouble is the use of a compensating cam operating a special spring-loaded tappet. The lobes of the cam are so designed in number, shape and spacing as to compensate the fluctuations of impulse of the main cams and thus ensure an approximately even torque on the camshaft. A design suitable for twin overhead camshafts for a six-cylinder engine, with spring-loaded 'lag-tappet', is shown in Fig. 6.37, and a similar application to a four-cylinder engine has been used.

6.39 Camshaft bearings

Camshaft bearings do not call for any special comment. In the majority of engines they consist of plain bushed or unbushed holes in suitable bosses in the crankcase casting, the diameter being great enough to enable the shaft to be inserted. In many instances, the bearings are successively larger in diameter, from one end to the other, to facilitate insertion and withdrawal of the shaft.

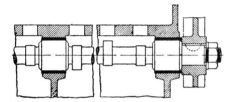

Fig. 6.38 Camshaft bearings

Such plain bearings stand up well to the impulsive loads that arise in the operation of the cams, they are inexpensive to manufacture, and are silent in operation. In the higher class of engine, where it is desired to reduce the frictional torque to a minimum by reducing the diameter of the bearings, and also to provide adjustment for wear, the bearing bushes, usually white metal lined, are split, and provided with separate caps in a similar manner to the main bearings of crankshafts. The former arrangement is shown in Fig. 6.38, and the latter in Fig. 6.47.

6.40 Adjustment of valve timing

Clearly, with a one-piece shaft, relative variation of the inlet and exhaust valve timing or of individual cylinders is impossible, but all events can be advanced or retarded together. Where two camshafts are used, however, the exhaust and inlet valve timings, of course, can be varied independently.

Generally, the camshaft wheel is keyed or, perhaps, splined to the shaft in a position such that, when certain marked teeth are meshed, the timing is most suitable for the particular engine. The smallest amount by which the timing may then be advanced or retarded is one tooth pitch, corresponding to, say, 10 to 15° of crank angle. Occasionally, finer adjustment is provided as shown in Fig. 6.39, where the cam wheel rim is formed separately from its boss, and a series of 'vernier' holes is drilled through the flanges of the two members so that they can be bolted up in relative

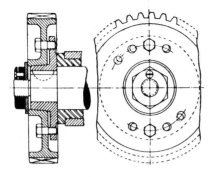

Fig. 6.39 Vernier timing adjustment   Fig. 6.40 Valve timing

angular positions which vary by a small fraction of a tooth pitch. While this adjustment is useful, especially during development work, it is not usually essential since, once established, the optimum timing is reproduced in each engine during manufacture.

A timing diagram forms the subject of Fig. 6.40. The five events shown are—

(1) Inlet valve opens.
(2) Inlet valve closes.
(3) Spark passes.
(4) Exhaust valve opens.
(5) Exhaust valve closes.

These events do not take place exactly at the dead centres, but rather earlier or later as the case may be. Thus, in order to get the exhaust gases clear of the cylinder as early as possible the angle *d* is, on the average, about 50°, and as much as 70° in some racing engines. Very little of the useful pressure is lost since the piston is near the end of its stroke, while the total time available for the escape of the exhaust gases is very much increased.

The angle *e* is from 0 to 10 or 12°, *a* from 10° early to 15° late, while *b* is from 20 to 40° late, in order to take advantage of the 'ramming' or inertia effect of the rapidly moving gases in the induction pipe.

The spark occurs about 20 to 40° early when fully advanced, and approximately at TDC when fully retarded.

When the angle *e* is greater than the angle *a* there is said to be 'overlap', that is, the exhaust valve closes after the inlet valve has opened. The purpose of this is to take advantage of the momentum of the high velocity exhaust gases in producing a scavenging vacuum after the piston has reached TDC.

6.41   Operation of the valves

The valves are operated from the camshaft in a variety of ways according to their disposition, but only in a few cases of overhead camshafts do the cam faces act directly on the valve stems. In the great majority of cases some form of cam follower or tappet is interposed beween the cam and valve stem. In many cases, including some arrangements with overhead valve layouts and a few with side valves, a rocker is introduced, the leverage of which usually increases the lift of the valve in relation to the cam eccentricity. This enables the overall diameter of the camshaft to be kept small, and reduces the frictional and inertia forces.

Four typical methods of operation are shown in outline in Figs. 6.41 and 6.42, namely, side valves, Fig. 6.41(*a*), overhead valves operated by push rods from a camshaft in the crankcase as in Fig. 6.41(*b*), while Fig. 6.42 shows three examples of the overhead camshaft. Direct operation of the cam on the valve stem (*a*) introduces heavy side-loading, which is largely obviated in (*b*). The arrangement at (*c*), Fiat 130, is used, with various methods of tappet adjustment, on many overhead camshaft engines, to relieve the valve of all side loading.

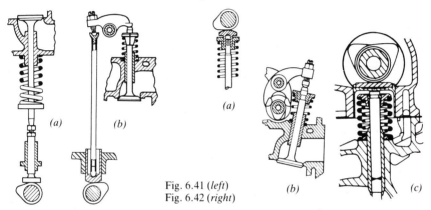

Fig. 6.41 (*left*)
Fig. 6.42 (*right*)

With side valves the interposition of a tappet only is required between the cam and the valve stem. The tappet slides vertically in its guide, which is sometimes of bronze or cast iron and renewable, while the foot follows the cam profile.

In modern simplified designs, as will be seen in the illustrations showing push-rod gear, the tappet is of simple bucket form, as shown in Figs. 6.41 and 6.43, moving in a plain reamed hole in the iron crankcase.

6.42   Forms of cam follower

There are three forms of tappet foot or cam follower in general use, namely—

(1) Solid curved foot (obsolescent).
(2) Mushroom or flat follower.
(3) Bucket type.

These are illustrated in Fig. 6.43. A is the tappet guide, B the adjustable tappet head by means of which a suitable small clearance is maintained between the tappet and valve to allow the latter to seat properly. C shows a curved foot follower operating a push rod enclosed in an oil-tight case. E shows a flat follower with its centre line offset from the centre of the cam. This offset causes the tappet to rotate and so reduces the amount of sliding between the cam and tappet foot with consequent reduction of wear. At F is shown the 'bucket' type of follower. This is very widely used in current designs, the material being cast iron. A bucket type follower, inverted over the valve stem and spring, is used in many overhead camshaft layouts.

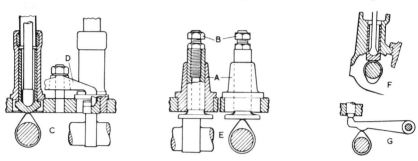

Fig. 6.43 Forms of cam follower

The rocker type of follower G is sometimes introduced between the cam and tappet to reduce the side thrust on the latter and in some cases to increase the lift in relationship to the cam throw. This, again, is used in some overhead camshaft arrangements.

D is a clamping bridge employed to hold a pair of tappet guides in position. The roller type of follower, popular at one time because of reduced friction, was liable to become eccentric through wear, with consequent variation in tappet clearance. Another example using needle roller bearings to correct this trouble may be seen in Fig. 10.10.

Theoretically the clearance should be kept at the minimum possible value that will allow the valve to seat under all conditions. With side valves, the minimum clearance usually occurs when the engine is hot, as the downward expansion of the valve stem is greater than the upward expansion of the cylinder block. With overhead valves and push rods the clearance is usually a minimum with the engine cold, as the rods tend to keep relatively cool, while the upward expansion of the cylinder block has the effect of increasing the clearance, owing to the rise of the rocker pivot. With overhead camshafts the clearance will usually be a minimum when the engine is hot. Minimum clearances are usually about 0.1 to 0.2 mm.

6.43　Overhead valves

The push rod and rocker method of operation is illustrated in Fig. 6.44(*a*). The upper end of the push rod which is usually of tubular section for lightness is provided with a cup C in which fits the ball end of the rod B, which is screwed and lock-nutted to the rocker for purposes of adjustment. The construction in which the rounded end of the push rod bears in an inverted cup formed in the rocker is somewhat less favourable for lubrication. The rockers may be mounted on ball or needle-roller bearings, as here indicated at A, or they may be threaded on a tubular bearing bar running the whole length of the head and carried in suitable brackets. Light coil springs are usually threaded on in addition, in order to reduce noise by taking up end shake.

Except in the more simplified engines, means of adjusting the tappet clearance are provided, as shown in Figs. 6.44(*a*) and (*b*), and 6.45. Fig. 6.44(*b*) is an illustration of the inverted tappet of the Vauxhall arrangement, a method of adjustment that is particularly easy to effect in service on engines of the overhead camshaft layout: alternatives are the interposition of hard shims or washers between the inverted bucket type tappet and either the cam as in Fig. 6.42(*c*), or the valve stem as in Fig. 7.9. With the Vauxhall system, access is gained through a hole in the side of the tappet to a grub-screw. This screw is inclined 5° 30′ relative to the flat top of the

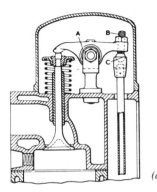

Fig. 6.44(a) (*left*) Push rod and rocker
Fig. 6.44(b) (*below*) Vauxhall screw type adjuster

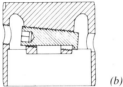

(a)   *(b)*

valve stem, and a flat is machined at a corresponding angle, but in the opposite sense, on its periphery in such a way that it is parallel to, and seats on, the end of the valve stem. Rotation of the screw through 360° gives adjustment of 0.0762 mm.

The interesting valve spring arrangement of the old Standard *Vanguard* engine is shown in Fig. 6.46. The inner valve spring is relieved of the duty of accelerating the rocker, push rod and tappet during closure of the valve, this action being performed by the auxiliary outer spring, the spring washers being so arranged that the clearance is always concentrated at the top of the valve stem. A slot S is provided for insertion of the feeler guage during adjustment of the clearance.

The arrangement makes for reduction of noise as the clearance is taken up between only one pair of surfaces. The simple and effective provision for assembly by means of the key-hole drilling of the main spring washer may be noted.

Fig. 6.47 shows a well-thought-out and executed design, incorporating a single overhead camshaft with inclined valves and rockers. The camshaft is mounted above the rockers, which are of the third order of lever, thereby increasing the valve lift in relation to the cam throw. A further advantage of a long rocker is obtained, namely, that the 'draw' or sliding of the rocker toe on the end of the stem is less for a given valve lift, thus minimising wear. The rockers A are machined from the solid to give maximum strength with lightness, and they incorporate an oil trough in which the cam roller runs, thus ensuring excellent lubrication. The rockers are mounted on bearing spindles B carried in independent forked brackets C. The portion of the pin B on which the rocker bears has a considerable eccentricity in relation to the end portions which are clamped in the brackets, so that by rotation of the spindles in the brackets the clearance between the roller and concentric portion of the cam, which represents tappet clearance, can be adjusted. Attention may be drawn to the arrangement of light steel sleeve and soft packing around the valve stem, which prevents excess oil reaching the stem and also avoids air leakage into the induction port, a source of trouble when adjusting the carburettor for idling.

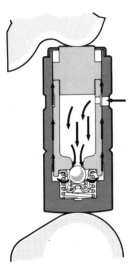

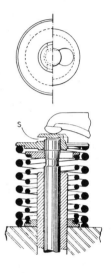

Fig. 6.45 (*left*) Hydraulic tappet for the Ford *Escort*

Fig. 6.46 (*right*) *Vanguard* valve springs

6.44 Hydraulic self-adjusting tappets

Self-adjusting – in America, termed *zero-lash* – tappets have two main advantages: they compensate automatically for variations of tappet clearance as a result of both wear and differential thermal expansion of the metal components of the crankcase, cylinder head and valve actuation mechanism, and they reduce noise due to tappet clatter. The principal design aim – in addition to the obvious ones such as keeping the inertia and rates of wear on both the barrel and ends as low as possible – is the avoidance of aeration of the oil owing to the severe shaking to which it is subjected inside the tappet. In general, the remedy is to allow leakage from the top of either the tappet or its oil supply system, so that any air or vapour present vents out. At the same time a well supported camshaft, to keep vibration as low as possible, and cam design to reduce to the minimum the instantaneous acceleration levels of the tappets help.

The Ford hydraulic tappet, Fig. 6.45, is designed for effective operation up to 7000 rev/min crankshaft speed. It comprises a hollow cylindrical body, closed at its lower end and having a thimble-shape plunger inserted in its upper end. The top of the plunger is closed by a hardened cap, on which bears the end of the rocker, while the lower end of the body housing the plunger functions as the cam follower.

Interposed between the base of the plunger and the lower end of the body is a fairly stiff coil spring, which presses the plunger up against the rocker during the dwell periods following each closure of the valve. Between the upper end of this spring and the base of the plunger is clamped the flange around the open end of a top hat shape pressing that houses a non-return ball valve. The ball is seated on a port in the end of the plunger by a light coil spring interposed between it and the base of the pressing and, during actuation of the tappet, by the hydraulic pressure below it.

When the tappet is lifted by the cam, the actuation load is transmitted from the cam follower through the oil, trapped by the ball valve, between the lower end of the body and the base of the plunger, and on through the plunger itself to the rocker. The oil comes from the main pressure lubrication system. It passes from the hollow five-bearing camshaft, through a duct in the cylinder head, to an annular groove round the body of the tappet, on through a radial hole to an annular groove round the plunger, and finally through another radial hole into its centre. A second annular groove, lower down around the periphery of the body, Fig 6.45, serves as an oil reservoir and spreader for assisting in the lubrication of the lower end of the tappet, which of course is subjected to the greatest side thrust, especially under start-up conditions when the faces of the cam and follower are relatively dry.

When the poppet valve closes, and the load is therefore released from the tappet, the spring in the base of the tappet pushes the plunger up to take up any clearance, and oil flows from the central cavity in the plunger past the non-return valve into the chamber in the base, to replace that which has leaked out during the opening of the poppet valve and to compensate for any changes in clearance that would otherwise be taking place gradually owing to thermal expansion or contraction of the metal parts. A controlled degree of leakage, between both the body and plunger and the body and the tappet housing bore, lubricates the ends of the tappet.

6.45   Alternative rocker arrangements

Fig. 6.48 shows an American construction of extreme simplicity suitable for large-scale economic manufacture. The rocker is a simple steel pressing of light weight and great strength, taking its bearing on a spherical spacer retained by the self-locking nuts on individual mounting studs. The push rods are of light tubular construction working in close fitting guides formed by simple drillings in the upper deck of the head casting. The push rods are thus able to provide the necessary constraint to maintain transverse alignment of the rockers.

Tappet adjustment is effected by the retainer nuts. In layouts using bucket type cam followers, it may be provided by the employment of self-adjusting tappets of the type such as that in Fig. 6.45. Alternatively selective assembly by push rod length may be used.

Lubrication may be through the support studs from a longitudinal gallery, from the hydraulic tappets through the push rods, or by oil mist and splash.

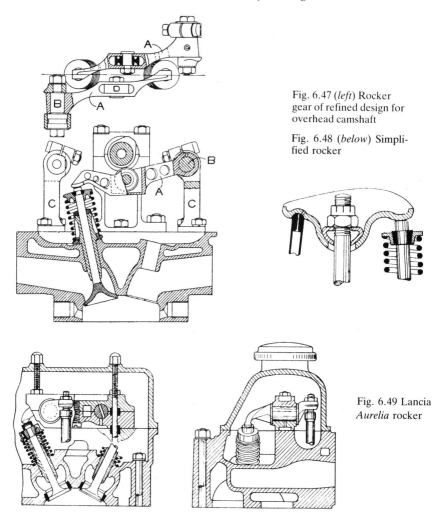

Fig. 6.47 (*left*) Rocker
gear of refined design for
overhead camshaft

Fig. 6.48 (*below*) Simplified rocker

Fig. 6.49 Lancia
Aurelia rocker

Fig. 6.49 shows the typically original rocker arrangement used on the
Lancia *Aurelia*, which facilitates the combination of hemispherical heads
having longitudinally inclined valve stems, with a single camshaft in a
V-type engine. The rocker axes are transverse, and individual bearing
blocks are mounted longitudinally for each cylinder, for the pair of
rockers.

The tendency to 'off-set tilt' is thus greater than in conventional
arrangements, but is catered for by the bearing surface and close fit of the
large diameter rocker collars.

6.46   Auxiliary drives

The following auxiliaries are common to both petrol and diesel engines,
and provision for their drive must be made: oil pump, water pump,
dynamo and fan. For certain countries, a compressor may also be needed

for air injection into the exhaust manifold, to control emissions. On petrol engines, the fan, impeller type water pump, compressor and dynamo or alternator do not call for an exact speed ratio, so some of these may have a common belt drive. Valve gear, ignition distributor and diesel injection pump require an exact ratio of 2:1 or 1:1 according to the cycle used. Such auxiliaries as exhauster and rotary blower are usually, though not necessarily, driven through longitudinal shafts by gearing or chain, while superchargers may be operated by either of these positive means or independently by engine exhaust.

In petrol engines, it is convenient to mount distributor and oil pump on a vertical or inclined shaft driven by 1:1 skew gearing from the camshaft, as shown in Fig. 6.53.

Magnetos are now rare, but were commonly driven with the water pump from a transverse shaft at a speed depending on the number of sparks provided per revolution by the magneto and required per revolution by the engine.

6.47   Typical all-round chain drive

A typical all-round drive employing duplex roller chain is illustrated in Fig. 6.50, which shows the auxiliary drive of an early AEC compression-ignition engine. This type of drive is popular, and has the great advantages of adaptability to any convenient position of the auxiliaries and light

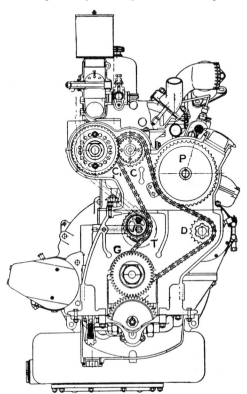

Fig. 6.50 AEC chain drive. A typical 'all-round' chain drive for a high-speed diesel engine

weight, but for the larger diesel engines gearing is preferred, despite the need for close tolerances on centre-to-centre spacing.

The crankshaft carries a spur gear G for the 1:1 drive for the oil pump, while behind it is the twin sprocket for the chain. The 2:1 ratio for the injection pump drive is obtained by the large sprocket P while the 2:1 camshaft ratio is obtained by means of the spur gears C and C_1, of which the gear C is a twin gear having springs so disposed between the two parts as to impart relative rotational movement for the purpose of taking up backlash. The slight increase in pressure on the driving side of the teeth is not detrimental, and quiet running is obtained.

The gear C_1 is coupled to the camshaft by a 'vernier' coupling of the type described and illustrated in Section 6.40 and Fig. 6.39. The sprocket D drives the dynamo at 7/6 engine speed. The automatic tensioner T is of the eccentric type described in Section 6.37.

6.48   All-gear and mixed drives

An all-gear drive of high quality is shown in Fig. 6.51 which illustrates the rear end drive typical of Meadows diesel engines. All the gears have helical teeth. A generously proportioned detachable pinion, in the form of a thimble, is clamped between the flywheel and the flange on the crankshaft. To centre the flywheel, its spigot registers in the open end of the thimble. Thus, the assembly is rigid and positive, while wear of the pinion does not involve replacement of the shaft.

The 2:1 reduction is obtained by a compound train of ratios 4:3 and 3:2, while the gears for the camshaft and injection pump are C and P respectively. D is the dynamo gear running at 1½ times crankshaft speed, or higher if required. If a blower or exhauster is provided, it is driven from the pump gear.

The camshaft and pump gears are flange-mounted, with slotted bolt holes for timing adjustment.

Fig. 6.52 illustrates a somewhat unusual combination of chain and gear drive used on the Thornycroft KRN6 diesel engine. A three-row roller

Fig. 6.51 Typical Meadows timing gears
at rear of engine

Fig. 6.52 Thornycroft timing gears

chain drives an intermediate wheel and the dynamo drive sprocket, and is tensioned by a Renold spring-loaded eccentric unit. The compound intermediate wheel is formed by bolting to the back of the driven sprocket a helical gear which, on one side, meshes with the camshaft wheel and, on the other, with the gear driving the injection pump and auxiliary compressor. Provision is made in the construction for either right- or left-hand assemblies.

6.49   Complete assembly

Some descriptions of complete engine assemblies follow in order that the relationship of the various components and the general arrangement of the engine may be clearly understood.

6.50   Vauxhall 'square' engines

The abandonment by the Treasury of the RAC horsepower formula for taxation purposes (see Section 4.16) freed design as regards stroke:bore ratio. Power developed per unit of piston area then became of relatively little significance as a fundamental criterion of performance. In the UK the first quantity-produced car engines in which full advantage was taken of the new-found freedom were the Vauxhall *Wyvern* and *Velox* units – September 1952 issue of *Automobile Engineer*.

These engines were described as *square* – a term indicating that the bore and stroke are equal. Actually, the dimensions in this case were 79-mm bore and 76-mm stroke – slightly over-square. The *Wyvern* was a 1.5-litre four-cylinder engine and the *Velox* a 2.75-litre six-cylinder unit. A compression ratio of 6.4:1 was adopted for both.

Fig. 6.53(*a*) shows the cross-section of the six-cylinder unit, but in general is the same for both, while (*b*) is the longitudinal section of the other. Many components were common to both. Because of the short stroke, there was considerable overlap between the journals and crank-pins, giving a stiff shaft, all main journals being 53.975 mm diameter. With such a large bore, the big ends were split normal to the axes of the rods, instead of diagonally, but could nevertheless be withdrawn upwards through the cylinder.

This is a typical example of the traditional overhead valve layout, operated by push rods and chilled cast-iron tappets. The flat piston crown directs a squish, or turbulence, towards the plug, giving good scour while at the same time ensuring adequate cooling of the end-gas in the quench area – large quench areas, incidentally, are avoided in modern engines because of the problem of exhaust gas emissions, discussed in Section 11.58 *et seq.*

A pipe of quadrilateral section, with slots in it, is inserted longitudinally in the cylinder head to direct coolant over the hot areas of the combustion chamber – the exhaust valve seats and sparking plug bosses. The thermostatic control of the hot-spot manifold is shown to a larger scale in Fig. 6.54.

A later version of this engine incorporated several changes, including cylinder head holding-down studs extending the full depth of the casting on both sides – increasing the cross-section, and so the stiffness, of the casting.

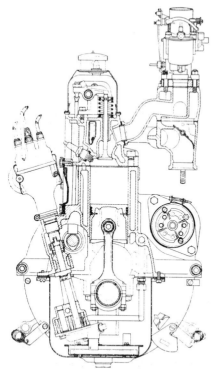

Fig. 6.53 Vauxhall 'square' engines

(a)

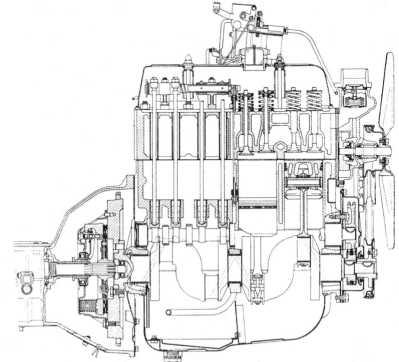

(b)

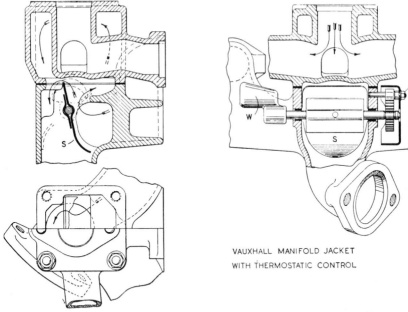

VAUXHALL MANIFOLD JACKET
WITH THERMOSTATIC CONTROL

Fig. 6.54

Also, the air intake manifold branches slope down from the head, so that any liquid fuel drawn from the carburettor under cold conditions tends to collect on the exhaust heated hot-spot, where it is evaporated instead of being carried straight into the cylinder. This arrangement also enables the height of the bonnet to be reduced.

In general, with a square or over-square type of design, the rotational speed for a given piston speed can of course be higher, or *vice versa*. Although, by adopting a low rotational speed, it is possible to reduce inertia stresses and friction losses, the modern trend is towards high speeds, to obtain corresponding gains in power per litre.

Whereas, in 1935, stroke:bore ratios were commonly in the range of 1.36:1 to 1.75:1, they are now mainly less than 1:1, an extreme example being the 997 cm³ Ford *Anglia* engine, at 0.61:1. Exceptions are some of the transversely installed engines, where short length, and therefore a smaller bore, is the prime requirement.

Not only can the short stroke engine, for the same stresses, run about 14 to 15% faster than the long stroke unit, but also the breathing can be improved, because of the larger area available for valve ports. However, there are certain disadvantages: at these higher speeds, the volume of the air drawn in per unit of time is greater and therefore a carburettor with a larger choke has to be used which, in turn, means that the velocity of air flow through the choke at low speeds of operation is correspondingly slower. This makes it more difficult to obtain satisfactory torque at low speeds, and some problems may be experienced in starting. In any case, the longer the stroke, and therefore crank throw, the greater is the mean torque applied to the crankshaft per unit of pressure on the pistons.

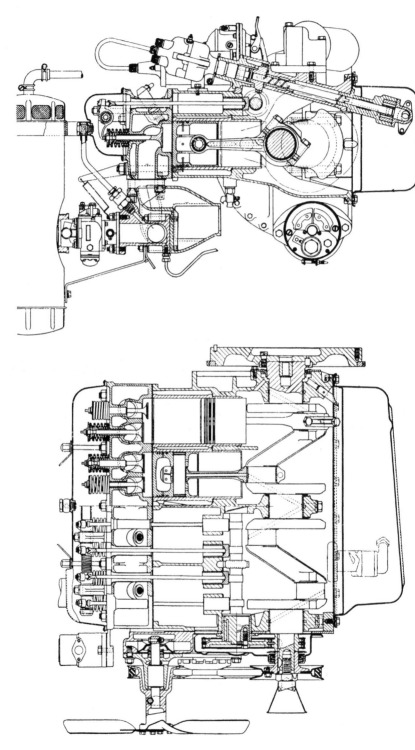

Fig. 6.55 Standard *Vanguard* engine

Piston weights increase approximately as the cube of the bore and this, together with the increased angularity of the connecting rods at mid stroke, increases the magnitude of the secondary out-of-balance forces – dependent on the inverse ratio of the length of the connecting rod to the stroke.

6.51   Standard *Vanguard* four-cylinder engine

An interesting medium-powered four-cylinder engine of conventional 'production' layout was the Standard *Vanguard* 2088 cm^3 power unit, Fig. 6.55. A great merit of this wet-liner construction is the simplification of the foundry work on the cylinder block, with accompanying speed and accuracy of production. The increased machining required is largely confined to the liners which, in turn, enable closely specified material of the most suitable type to be used. Replacement of liners is a simple operation. A disadvantage, however, is the loss of stiffness owing to the absence of a top deck on the block.

The engine has a bore and stroke of 85 mm × 92 mm and a compression ratio of 6.8:1. Its performance curves are given in Fig. 6.56 and the valve timing diagram in Fig. 6.57. The torque and bmep curves fall somewhat steeply after the very good peak figure at 2300 rev/min. Sealed crankcase breathing arrangements, with draw-off pipe (provided with a restriction orifice) to the inlet manifold, can be seen. These provide a through air-flow from the air cleaner, by means of an external pipe.

The general construction of deep cast-iron cylinder block with light pressed steel sump and detachable cylinder head will be noticed, while the stiff crankshaft and generous journal and crankpin diameters ensure ample freedom from troublesome vibration. A diagonally split big end facilitates withdrawal through the bore. The interesting valve spring arrangement is shown in enlarged detail in Fig. 6.46 and described in Section 6.44. A Solex downdraught carburettor feeds an aluminium alloy inlet manifold. Further interesting particulars will be found in *Automobile Engineer,* Vol. 48, No. 9.

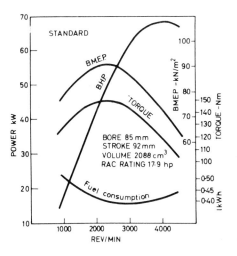

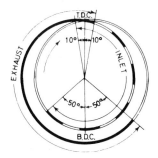

Fig. 6.56 (*left*) *Vanguard* performance curves

Fig. 6.57 (*below*) *Vanguard* timing

6.52   Austin-Morris O-series engine

The 1700 and 1994 cm^2 O-series engine (Fig. 6.58), at the time of its introduction, was an outstanding example of good modern design. Its bore is 84.45 mm, and the strokes are 75.87 and 89 mm respectively for the smaller and larger capacity versions. With a 9:1 compression ratio – an option of 8:1 is available for countries having low grade petrol – the

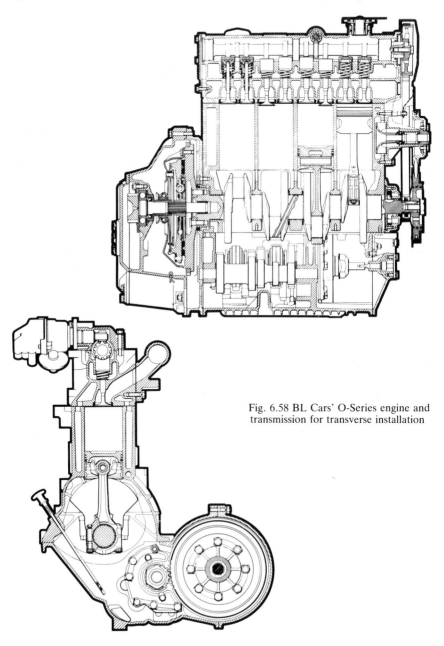

Fig. 6.58 BL Cars' O-Series engine and transmission for transverse installation

1.7-litre version develops 87 bhp at 5200 rev/min and the 2-litre unit 93 bhp at 4900 rev/min. Their maximum torques are 131.5 Nm at 3800 rev/min and 152.67 Nm at 3400 rev/min. (See Fig. 6.59).

With vertical in-line valves, an inexpensive single overhead cast-iron camshaft installation has been possible, the cams acting directly on inverted bucket-type cast-iron tappets. The latter relieve the valves of all side and offset loading due to the motion of the cams. Three bearings carry the shaft, and their lower and upper halves are machined in the aluminium head and valve gear cover castings respectively. Because of the low inertia and high rigidity of this valve gear, the valve crash speed is 7000 rev/min. Since the camshaft is driven by a toothed belt, the overall length of the engine is a little greater than would otherwise have been possible, had a chain been used, with the siamesed cylinders. This joining of all cylinders is sometimes frowned upon because, inevitably, it leads to uneven temperature distribution and variations in stiffness around them. However, Leyland Cars have adopted this feature in a number of engines over many years and say that they have experienced no difficulties attributable to it.

The cylinder head is an LM8 WP aluminium alloy gravity die casting. It has a totally-flat machined lower face, broken only by the valve ports, with their seat inserts, and the apertures for the sparking plugs, oil ducts and coolant transfer passages. This layout, again, is possible only by virtue of the use of vertical valves and the incorporation of combustion chambers in the form of shallow depressions in the crowns of the pistons. Its four inlet and four exhaust ports are arranged alternately along one side, to keep the temperature distribution as uniform as possible. The sparking plugs are along the opposite side, so access to them is easy.

Noise tests have shown this engine to be 6 dB quieter than the old B-Series which it replaces. This is attributed to the use of a cast aluminium valve gear cover – instead of pressed steel – the absence of push rods and rockers, the use of a toothed belt drive for the camshaft, the formation of the combustion chambers in the pistons, the resultant minimum variations of compression ratio from cylinder to cylinder, the stiffness of the cast-iron

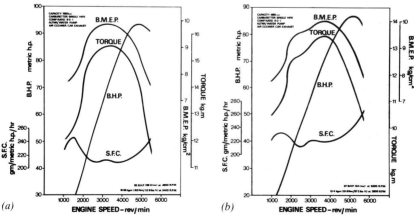

Fig. 6.59 Performance curves for BL Cars' Austin-Morris O-Series engine (a) 2-litre, (b) 1.7-litre versions

cylinder block, and the use of aluminium alloy pistons having steel inserts to control their thermal expansion.

Because of the absence of a tappet chest and camshaft bearings in the crankcase, this component is of commendably simple and symmetrical design. This, together with a deep skirt, vertical external ribbing of the water jacket between the cylinders, the siamesing of the cylinders, and the profiling of the water jacket to wrap around each of them, has made the crankcase and cylinder block casting uncommonly stiff, again contributing to noise reduction.

The five-bearing crankshaft is of nodular cast iron. An increase in fatigue life of about 60% is claimed by virtue of fillet rolling the junctions between the ends of the pins and journals and the sides of the webs. Because the shaft is cast, it has been possible to make the counter-weights integral with it. They provide total primary balance on the 1.7-litre and 80% balance on the 2-litre unit.

Timing is checked electronically, by means of a light-emitting diode (l.e.d.) on one side, beamed towards a photoelectric cell on the other of a disc with a radial slot in its periphery. This disc is bolted to the crankshaft, but the l.e.d. and photoelectric cell are separate pieces of servicing equipment. The advantage of this system, using as a datum the impulses generated when the light shines through the slot on to the photoelectric cell, is that the ignition can be checked at all engine speeds. Such a facility is necessary where, to satisfy exhaust emission requirements, the spark advance does not bear a simple relationship to speed. The valve timing is: inlet opens 19° before top dead centre (BTDC), closes 41° after bottom dead centre (ABDC); exhaust opens 61° before bottom dead centre (BBDC), closes 15° after top dead centre (ATDC).

6.53   ADO 15 power unit

The great success of the BMC – now BL Cars – *Mini* range heralded the adoption by many other manufacturers of the transverse engine installation, coupled with front-wheel-drive. This layout is extremely compact, especially as regards overall length of the car, so that exacting requirements of adequate space for both comfortable seating and luggage are successfully met.

The 848 cm³ four-cylinder engine may be regarded as a derivative of the Series A 948 cm³ unit (see *Automobile Engineer*, Vol. 50, No. 7); the following notes on the special features of the smaller engine are abstracted from a comprehensive description of the complete vehicle in *Automobile Engineer*, Vol. 51, Nos. 4 and 5.

The series A block and head are employed without alteration, a new crankshaft giving the reduced stroke of 68 mm. Thus with a bore of approximately 63 mm, the stroke-bore ratio is 1.08:1 which is nearly square.

To accommodate the larger bore in the limited length of block, siamesing of the cylinders in pairs and off-setting of the connecting rod big ends by 3 mm is resorted to, with no detriment to the running. The big ends of the connecting rods are diagonally split, and the gudgeon pins are clamped in the small-end eye, a construction which, it is considered,

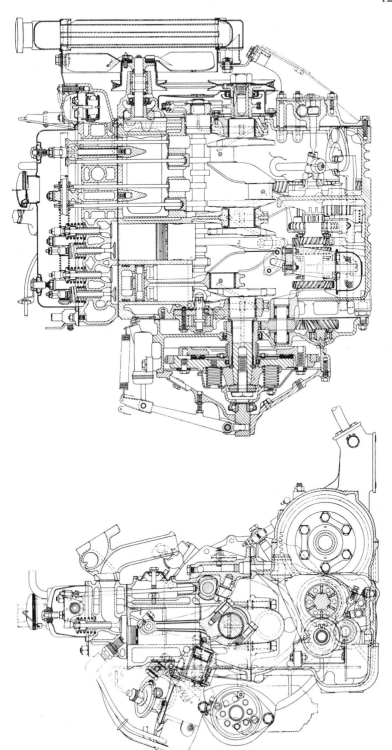

Fig. 6.60 BMC ADO15 power unit

contributes to silence as there is only one clearance to develop possible knock.

The sturdy forged crankshaft carries integral balance weights, and the short stroke results in considerable crankpin/journal overlap. All these features make a valuable contribution to smooth running and may be seen in Fig. 6.60.

The compression ratio is 8.3:1, achieved by using taller pistons to compensate for the shorter stroke.

The joint between cylinder block and sump is on the crankshaft centre line, as this affords free access to the big ends and provides a deep and rigid housing for the transmission.

The camshaft is of normal design, driven by a single roller chain of 10-mm pitch. To take the driving load and provide for wear, the front end bearing is a steel-backed whitemetal-lined shell, while the other two are of the plain type running in bores machined directly in the block. The Hobourn-Eaton oil pump is driven co-axially by a slot and peg in a counter-bore.

The bucket type cam followers and cup-ended push rods are now common practice, but the rockers are of novel construction, being formed from a pair of light steel pressings by projection and spot welding. This results in a considerable saving in weight as compared with the usual stamping, and may be compared with the pressed form shown in Fig. 6.48. The rocker bearings are Clevite 8 wrapped copper-lead bushes.

Curves of engine performance, measured at the flywheel, are reproduced in Fig. 6.61.

Those shown by full lines are for the engine to BL's standard specification. The gross performance, shown by dotted lines, is measured under conditions similar to standard, except that the air filter is removed and manual controls are employed for the carburettor and ignition.

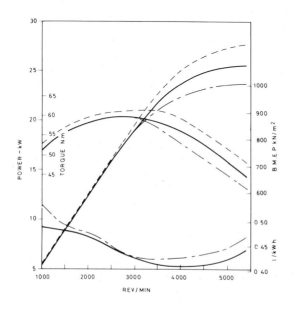

Fig. 6.61 BMC ADO 15 performance curves

Chain-dotted lines are used to indicate the performance as installed; the engine specification then differs from that for the standard curves in that the cooling fan is fitted, and the car's exhaust system replaces that of the test-bed installation. The results are obtained with an SU semi-down-draught carburettor.

It is of interest that the gross power output of 27.55 kW at 5500 rev/min is slightly greater than that of the Austin A40, which has a Zenith carburettor and produces 26.85 kW at 4800 rev/min, and less than that of the Morris *Minor 1000*, which is 29.8 kW at 5000 rev/min. The higher specific output of the ADO 15 unit, 32.6 kW/litre as against 28.4 for the A40 and 31.5 for the *Minor,* is mainly attributable to the proportionately larger valves, which have made possible an upward extension of the speed range. While the respective maximum piston speeds of the two 948 cm^3 engines are 1220 cm/s and 1270 cm/s, that of the ADO 15 unit is 1250 cm/s. The ADO 15 has a maximum gross bmep of 910 kN/m^2, about average for an engine of this type.

6.54 Engine position

In recent years, the traditional front engine and rear-wheel-drive layout has been abandoned by many manufacturers, at least for their small cars, where space is at a premium. The rear engine and rear-wheel-drive layout has advantages of compactness, and therefore more space for occupants, and good traction in slippery conditions and uphill – this is because a high proportion of the weight is on the driven wheels – but there is a marked tendency to oversteer, and the luggage space is severely restricted owing to both the need for a low bonnet for satisfactory forward range of vision and the limited space between the front wheel arches, which have to accommodate the steered wheels in the full lock position.

Front-wheel-drive, on the other hand, does not have these disadvantages, though the steering lock may be slightly restricted: moreover, in the fully laden condition, the weight distribution tends to equalise between the front and rear, instead of becoming even more asymmetric. With both layouts, of course, the absence of a propeller shaft is helpful for the body designer, but the additional constant velocity joints in the drive to each wheel, and the more complex suspension arrangements, add to the cost.

6.55 Under-floor engines

The under-floor layout is of course widely employed for public service vehicles. Horizontally-opposed, and even V, layouts have been used for this type of installation, but more commonly a vertical engine is adapted by making special arrangements for all parts and accessories affected by the changed gravitational conditions. Principal among these, of course are the sump and lubrication system.

Most of the well-known oil-engine builders have developed designs on these lines, and the arrangement would seem to have the merit that maintenance operations of any particular type can be confined to one or other side of the vehicle, with the additional facilities provided by access doors. An example is given in Fig. 6.62, which shows in cross-section the

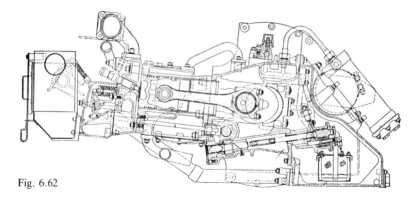

Fig. 6.62

8-litre six-cylinder direct-injection diesel built and operated by the Birmingham & Midland Motor Omnibus Company Ltd.

On the other hand, there is the Bedford YQR chassis, which has a vertically installed engine, under the floor midway between the front and rear axles. The advantages are: quietness, good weight distribution, the floor is flat and clear for placing the entrances wherever desired, and an engine common to a wide range of vehicles can be used. Access for servicing is gained through a hatch in the floor. This layout is suitable only for buses, coaches and, perhaps, pantechnicons and vehicles such as mobile shops.

6.56   Panhard Dyna 55 engine

Many years ago the Panhard company developed a 12-cylinder horizontally-opposed air-cooled engine for aircraft, and it was illustrated in *Automobile Engineer,* Vol. 43, No. 8. Because of its flat layout, it would have been eminently suitable for under-floor installation, possibly in an eight-cylinder form, for commercial vehicles. Although the advent of the gas turbine ruled it out for aircraft, the basic concept survived, but in twin-cylinder form, for a front-wheel-drive car, a racing version of which was successful in its class in the 1953 le Mans race.

A cross-section of the car engine is shown in Fig. 6.63. An interesting feature is the valve gear layout, derived from the 12-cylinder version. Torsion-bar springs and roller cam-followers are used. The rockers are similar to that in Fig. 6.48, but are of cast iron, instead of simple pressings, and the tappets are more positively locked. Full details are in *Automobile Engineer*, Vol. 48, No. 4.

With a bore of 85 mm and a stroke of 75 mm, the swept volume is 851 cm^3. The maximum power output is 31.3 kW at 5000 rev/min, while the maximum bmep and torque are respectively 94 kN/m^2 and 63.7 Nm, at 3500 rev/min.

A feature of the aluminium alloy cylinders is that their heads are integral. Dry liners are fitted, and the fins are of generous area for good heat-transfer.

A three-piece crankshaft is employed. One piece is the central web, while the other two each comprise a journal, web and crankpin. After the

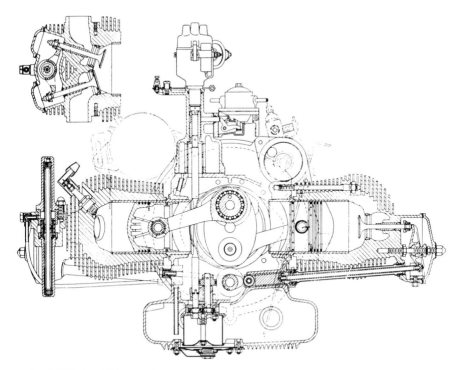

Fig. 6.63 Panhard Dyna engine

roller bearing big ends have been threaded on to the pins, the whole crankshaft assembly is completed by pressing the ends of the crankpins into the holes in the central webs. Plugs pressed into the ends of the pins prevent them from deflecting radially inwards under dynamic loading and thus allowing the joints to loosen. An axial hole in each plug is tapped to receive the end of a taper-seating bolt used to tighten a dished pressed steel plug into the other end of the hollow pin, to seal it.

To balance the rotating couple due to the offset of the cylinder axes, masses are secured by cheese-head screws, and located by dowel pins, to the outer faces of the crank webs. These masses also partly balance the reciprocating inertia of the pistons. The whole crankshaft and connecting rod assembly is inserted through a large oval aperture in the front end of the crankcase, which therefore has no horizontal or vertical joints to give trouble by leaking.

6.57 Citroën Visa engine

A more modern horizontally-opposed twn-cylinder air-cooled engine is that of the Citroën Visa and LNA models. This is a 652 cm³ unit, with a bore and stroke of 77 and 70 mm respectively. Its compression ratio is 9:1 and its maximum power and torque are 26.8 kW at 5500 rev/min and 51.5 Nm at 3500 rev/min.

An unusual feature is the use of three bearings to carry the crankshaft. As can be seen from Fig. 6.64, the third bearing is in fact a support for the rather long nose of the crankshaft, which is necessary for carrying the cooling fan. To have shortened the shaft and brought the fan closer to he engine presumably would have made it impossible to collect the air efficiently from the whole of the 360° sweep of its blades for directing it over the two cylinders. Unsupported, such a long nose would be liable to vibrate at certain crankshaft speeds, and this would have made the gear drive to the camshaft noisy.

The cylinders, which have separate heads, are of aluminium alloy. Their bores are spray-coated with Nicasil – a ceramet obviously containing nickel and silicon – which was originally developed for the Citroën version of the Wankel engine. There are of course no cylinder liners.

The ignition system is entirely electronic. It comprises two proximity detectors, a vacuum sensor, a computer and a coil. As can be seen from

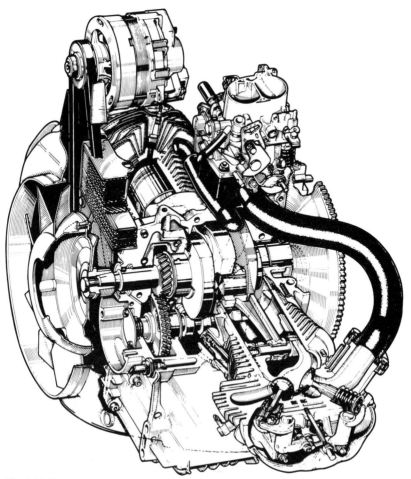

Fig. 6.64 Citroën Visa engine

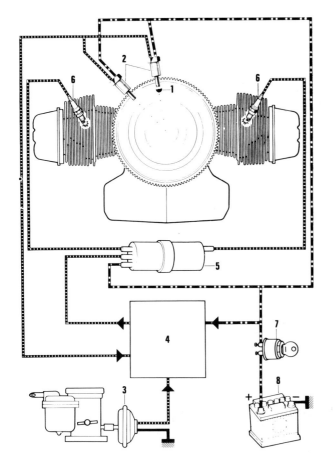

Fig. 6.65 Citroën Visa electronic ignition system

1 Peg on flywheel
2 Proximity sensors
3 Vacuum sensor
4 Micro-processor
5 Ignition coil
6 Spark plug
7 Ignition switch
8 Battery

Fig. 6.65, the proximity detectors sense the passing of a metallic pin attached to the flywheel, to obtain an accurate indication of both the rotational speed of the engine over the critical period within which the spark must occur, and the datum point relative to which the spark must be timed. The vacuum sensor, connected to the carburettor choke, gives an indication of induction air flow and therefore engine load. All three sensors pass signals to the computer, which calculates the spark timing required. The computer also regulates the primary current to the coil, to ensure that the secondary voltage is appropriate under all conditions of operation.

With this system, there are no adjustments to be made. Nor are there any moving parts subject to wear. Consequently, the shape of the advance curve remains constant throughout the life of the engine. Moreover, this curve can be exactly matched to the continually changing requirements of the engine. The outcome is low fuel consumption, minimum exhaust gas pollution, and good low-speed torque and acceleration .

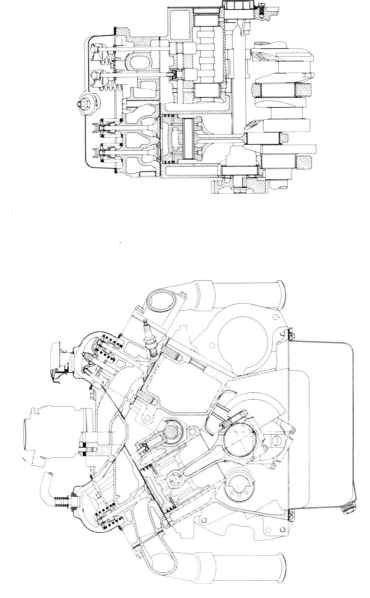

Fig. 6.66 Features of the Ford *Corsair* V-four engine include the balancer shaft, a shallow bowl-in-piston combustion chamber, and push-rod actuation of the valves

6.58 Ford V-four engines

With the adoption of the over-square cylinder proportions, together with the need for longer main bearings to cope with higher ratings, there has been a tendency for in-line engines to become long. This, and a demand for low bonnet profiles – to improve forward range of vision and hence safety – has led to the adoption of the V-four layout by some manufacturers. Besides compactness, there are also advantages of ridigity of the cylinder block, crankcase and of the short crankshaft. Moreover, because of the wide spacing of the cylinders, there is plenty of room for coolant passages around them and for ample separation of the hot regions around the exhaust valves.

A good example is the Ford range, Fig. 6.66, comprising the 1662 cm^3 and 1995 cm^3 Corsair engines, with common bore dimensions of 93.66 mm and strokes of 60.3 and 72.4 mm respectively. To enable connecting rods common to the whole range to be fitted – centre-to-centre length 143.3 mm – the gudgeon pin of the engine with the longer stroke is 60.3 mm closer to the crown and the piston has a shorter skirt than that of the other. Bowl-in-piston combustion chambers have been adopted, and the lower face of the cylinder head is entirely flat, except for shallow machined recesses around the valve heads. The combustion chambers are completely machined and therefore of accurately controlled form, finish and volume. Local recesses are machined in the cylinder crowns, to clear the valves at and near top dead centre.

The spheroidal graphite cast-iron crankshaft is carried in three 63.5 mm diameter aluminium-tin or copper-lead bearings. Crankpins 60.2 mm diameter are employed.

Between the cylinder banks, the angle of the V is 60°. With a firing order of 1R 3L 4L 2R, this gives equally-spaced firing intervals and the primary forces are in balance, but a secondary couple remains. This couple is balanced by weights on a separate shaft, parallel to and driven at the same speed as the crankshaft, but in the opposite direction, Fig. 6.66. A 60° angle, of course, is ideal with the V-six engines, the blocks of which are made on the same production line. The balance of this engine is dealt with in Section 7.11.

In standard form, both engines have the Autolite 36 IV down-draught carburettor. There is, however, a GT version of the larger engine, which is equipped with a Weber 32/36 DF AV progressive choke twin down-draught carburettor, the two chokes feeding into a common riser bore.

Chapter 7

Six-, eight- and twelve-cylinder engines

The desire for a more uniform turning moment and better dymanic balance has led to the production of six-, eight- and even twelve-cylinder engines where questions of first cost are not of primary importance. The effective driving effort of an ordinary four-stroke single-cylinder engine extends, when friction is taken into account, over only about 150° of crank movement, and, as in a four-cylinder engine the power strokes are at intervals of 180°, or half a revolution, it follows that there are appreciable periods when the shaft is receiving no useful torque whatever, and the stored energy of the flywheel is called on to supply the deficiency. At low speeds the flywheel does not contain sufficient energy to tide over the idle periods without undue variation of speed and hence jerky running and high transmission stresses are set up.

Remembering that the number of power strokes per revolution is equal to half that of the cylinders, it will be seen that in a six, the intervals between power strokes, if the cylinders and cranks are so disposed as to render them equal, have a duration of 120° of crank angle, while in an eight the interval is 90°. There is thus an appreciable overlap in the former and a very considerable one in the latter. The result is great improvement in the smoothness of running and a lighter flywheel may be employed.

7.1 Six cylinders

Fig. 7.1 illustrates the normal arrangement of cranks in a six-throw crankshaft, the full number of bearings, namely seven, being here shown. The cranks are 120° apart in pairs, the halves being arranged to give 'looking-glass' symmetry, in order to give opposition of the inertia couples as explained in Chapter 5. The circle diagram shows the two alternative crank arrangements consistent with the above symmetry.

In what may be called a left-hand shaft, No. 1 crank is on the left when looking from the front of the engine, with 3 and 4 vertical. Cranks 1 and 6 may clearly be interchanged with 2 and 5 giving a shaft of the opposite hand. Both these arrangements are met with in practice.

7.2   Dynamic balance

Just as three equal and symmetrically distributed revolving masses in one plane will be in dynamic balance, since their combined centre of gravity is clearly at the centre of rotation, so six equal and symmetrically distributed revolving masses which do not all lie in one plane will be in dynamic balance provided that the couples due to the distances between the planes of revolution cancel out. This cancelling out is attained with the arrangement illustrated, provided that the corresponding throw spacings are the same and the throws uniform. Dynamic balancing of crankshafts is carried out by the majority of makers to correct for slight errors in weights and sizes of the various throws.

In like manner the primary reciprocating effects balance, since these represent the vertical components of corresponding revolving effects. This will perhaps be realised better if *standing* balance is considered, where the only forces are vertical ones due to gravity. A six-cylinder engine, even if quite frictionless, will remain at rest in any position of the crank provided the moving parts of all cylinders are uniform in weight. Further, the secondary effects cancel out, as may be ascertained from Fig. 5.9, by a careful combination of the forces in correct phase. The six-cylinder engine is, in fact, capable of complete balance for both primary and secondary forces and couples, thus eliminating vibration from this cause.

7.3   Firing order

To obtain good *distribution* of the fuel to all cylinders it is desirable and usual to arrange the inductions alternately in the front and rear halves of the engine. An examination of the circular diagram of Fig. 7.1 will make clear that the possible firing orders, to satisfy this condition, are 1 5 3 6 2 4 and 1 4 2 6 3 5 for the two arrangements of cranks. These are the most

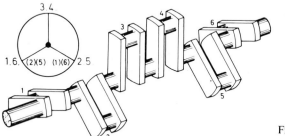

Fig. 7.1

usual in practice, but others are sometimes met. Thus, from the point of view of torsional oscillation, it may be desirable in some cases to have two cylinders in one half of the engine firing in succession in order to prevent the 'unwinding' of the shaft between power impulses. This problem is referred to later.

7.4   Eight cylinders

Here the proper interval between power strokes is 90°. A 'straight eight' may clearly be formed by placing two fours end to end with their flat crankshafts at right angles, as in the upper diagram of Fig. 7.2. Each set of four cylinders is then in balance for primary forces and couples as explained in Chapter 5, but there remains the secondary effect. This secondary effect acts downwards when the cranks are horizontal and upwards when they are vertical; thus, while the downward secondary effect of one half of the engine opposes the upward effect of the other half there remains, with the 'double four' arrangement, an unbalanced couple, tending to pitch the engine in the longitudinal plane.

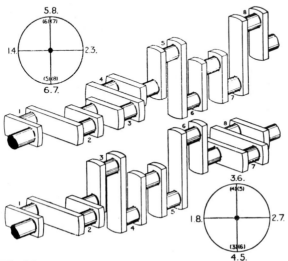

Fig. 7.2

This may be eliminated by adopting the 'split four' arrangement shown in the lower diagram of Fig. 7.2. Here the downward secondary effect of two pistons at each end of the engine 1, 2 and 7, 8 opposes the upward effect of 3, 4, 5 and 6 without introducing a couple. This arrangement is in complete balance for primary and secondary forces and couples.

7.5 Firing order

There are clearly many possible orders of firing with eight cylinders arranged as shown in Fig. 7.2, but the more usual are 1 7 3 8 4 6 2 5, 1 5 2 6 4 8 3 7 and 1 6 2 5 8 3 7 4. Other crank arrangements are met with in special cases, particularly for racing purposes, where considerations of bearing loads may be of greater importance than exact dynamic balance. With adjacent cranks in phase, as in the case of 4 and 5 in the lower diagram (Fig. 7.2), the centrifugal and inertia forces of the moving parts of both cylinders act always together, producing very heavy loads on the intermediate bearing. If adjacent cranks are placed 180° apart as far as uniformity of turning moment permits, the mutual balance of opposing cranks is more direct, and bearing loads and crank case stresses are much reduced. Such arrangements result, however, in there being unbalanced couples.

7.6 Balanced webs and torsional oscillation

Another method of reducing bearing loads and crankcase stresses is to balance the individual throws for rotational effects by adding extended webs and balance weights, it being impossible, except in the 90° V engine, to deal with reciprocating effects in this way. But, as previously mentioned, while this expedient may cure shaft and crankcase *whip*, it is very liable to increase the risk of torsional oscillation of the shaft, because heavy masses revolving with a slender shaft make the natural torsional or twisting vibration a relatively slow one – slow enough in some cases to give rise to dangerous and uncomfortable resonance with the torque variations. An aircraft shaft of relatively slender proportions, with such attached balanced weights, is shown in Fig. 7.3.

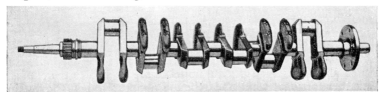

Fig. 7.3 Crankshaft with balanced throws

To reduce torsional vibration, a vibration damper may be mounted at the front end of the crankshaft. A damper of the Lanchester type is illustrated in Fig. 7.4(*a*). It consists essentially of a flywheel member A, of 20 to 30 mm diameter, according to the size of engine, driven through a friction disc clutch, the inner plate member B of which is keyed to the front end of the crankshaft. The friction is adjusted by the springs acting on the presser plate C so as to be insufficient to transmit to the heavy rim A the high torsional acceleration during the winding up and unwinding of the crankshaft as the torsional impulses are applied to the cranks. Thus the torsional wind and rebound are absorbed in friction in much the same way as in the case of a spring damper, and serious resonant vibrations are suppressed, reducing noise, premature wear and failure of chain drives, tensioners and even, possibly, the crankshaft.

Fig. 7.4(*b*) shows a simple bonded rubber insert type of damper. A more recent development in the UK is the introduction of dampers in which the rubber is held in place by compression between the inertia ring and the hub, instead of by bonding. Dampers of this type have long lives, and timing marks and V-belt grooves can be incorporated on the inertia rings. Rubber dampers are, in general, limited to engines of about 13 litres swept volume or less.

An alternative damper is the viscous type which, though more expensive than the rubber type, is extremely reliable. It has been described in *Practical Solution of Torsional Vibration Problems* Volume 4, by Ker Wilson (Chapman & Hall). Basically the unit comprises an annular flywheel, sealed in a metal casing. Fig. 7.4(*c*). The space between the two is filled with a silicone fluid of high viscosity. Since the casing rotates and oscillates with the crankshaft, while the flywheel tends to maintain a steady-state motion, there is a considerable viscous drag in the fluid between the two: thus, energy of vibration is dissipated as heat.

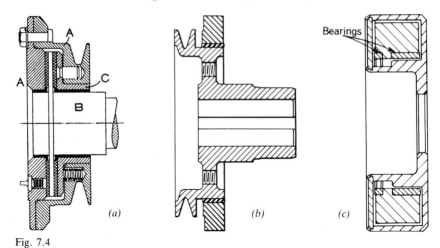

Fig. 7.4

7.7   Difficulties met in design

Sixes and straight eights are liable to three important troubles in running
and performance. These may be summarised as bad gas distribution, high
fuel consumption and torsional oscillation. The second is partly a consequence of the first and partly due to the rather lower thermal efficiency
obtainable in cylinders of small size, owing to the relatively greater losses
to the jackets and other causes. Bad distribution is one of the most elusive
difficulties with which designers have to contend. Although a correct and
homogeneous mixture may leave the carburettor, it is highly improbable
that it will reach all the cylinders in exactly equal quantity or of similar
composition. Thus it may be necessary to employ an unduly rich carburettor setting, with correspondingly high consumption, in order to
prevent starvation of certain of the cylinders. This trouble is present even
in four-cylinder engines, and is accentuated in sixes and eights, where the
induction manifolds present far greater difficulties. It is almost impossible
for a designer to form a reliable forecast of the probable behaviour of any
given arrangement of single or twin carburettor, and induction pipe
arrangement, taken in conjunction with a particular firing order.

The third difficulty of torsional oscillation has already been referred to.
These difficulties and the extra cost of manufacture of the six have enabled
the reliable and economical, though less smooth-running, four-cylinder
engine to maintain its popularity in the smaller powers, and for medium-
sized commercial vehicles.

7.8   Humber *Super Snipe* engine

The layout of this engine (Figs. 7.5 and 7.6) – like that of the Armstrong
Siddeley *Sapphire*, *Automobile Engineer*, December 1953 – represents an
intermediate stage in the trend of development from low to overhead
camshaft. An interesting, but expensive, alternative is that of the Lea
Francis 2.5-litre engine, Fig. 6.33 and *Automobile Engineer*, June 1952.

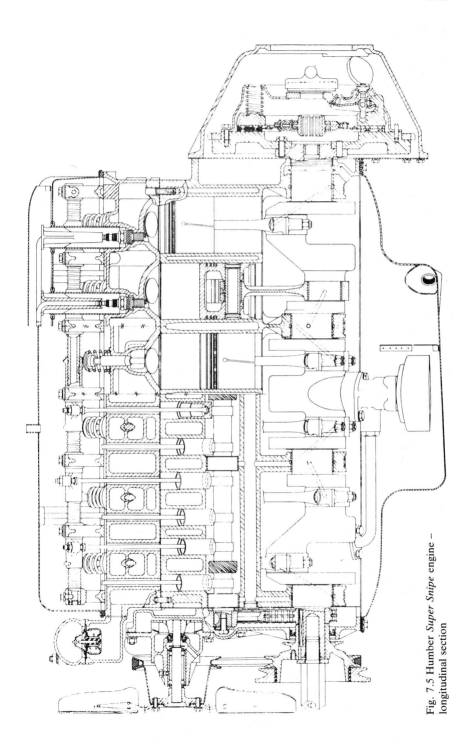

Fig. 7.5 Humber *Super Snipe* engine – longitudinal section

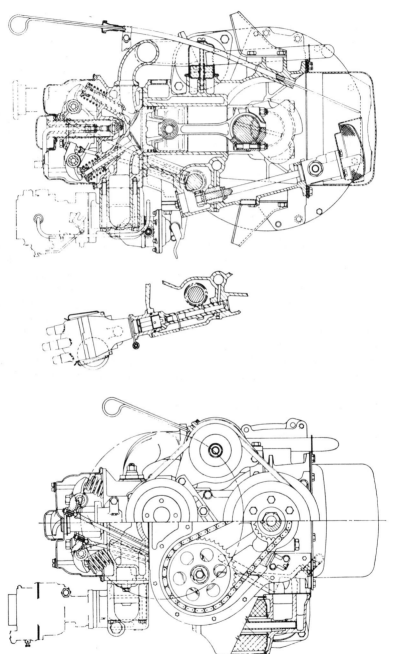

Fig. 7.6 Humber *Super Snipe* engine – transverse sections

For the *Super Snipe* 2965 cm³ unit, the over-square bore/stroke arrangement was chosen to give a lower piston speed of 13.2 m/s at maximum power. It also permits a crankshaft with overlapping pins and journals, thus ensuring a very rigid crank free from torsional weakness. Both these points contribute to the smooth running of the engine. The combustion chamber is of the hemispherical type, shallowed down to give a flat topped piston for the chosen compression ratio of 8:1. With the shallow type of head, smooth combustion is assured as the flame front build-up is quenched by the piston top before roughness is initiated.

Large valves (3.556 mm inlet throat diameter, 3.048 mm exhaust throat diameter) are possible, and with the uninterrupted gas flow characteristic of this hemispherical type of head, good filling is achieved. The low expansion aluminium alloy piston has two compression rings and a scraper, the top ring being chromium plated, the second ring stepped.

Both rings are 1.98 mm thick and 4.06 mm wide, giving the fairly high wall pressure necessary with over-square engines. The 23.8-mm diameter gudgeon pin is fully floating and located with circlips.

A high camshaft position is a fundamental requirement of this type of engine. Short pushrods are necessary for high speed of operation to obtain high power output. Moreover, they have to be inclined to actuate rockers on two shafts – the alternative to overhead camshafts for actuating inclined valves in hemispherical heads. The camshaft layout adopted has the advantages of a relatively short drive and ease of tappet adjustment. Details of the valve timing – for good torque at low speeds and high power output at high speeds – are: inlet opens 20° BTDC, closes 46° ATDC; exhaust opens 52° BBDC, closes 14° ATDC.

A water-heated aluminium alloy inlet manifold is used to feed two separate galleries formed in the cast-iron cylinder head. Each gallery feeds three cylinders.

The performance figures shown in Fig. 7.7 are obtained with a single Zenith 42 WIA down-draught carburettor.

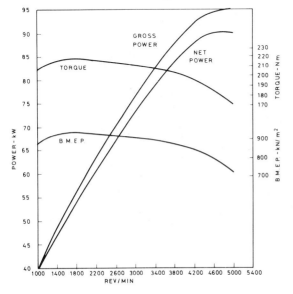

Fig. 7.7 Humber *Super Snipe* performance curves

Gross power output is 96.7 kW at 4800 rev/min giving 32 kW per litre and maximum torque of 219 Nm developed at 1800 rev/min.

The general arrangement drawings of Figs. 7.5 and 7.6, and the performance curves, Fig. 7.7, give a very clear picture of the power unit, which may be amplified by the following notes.

The cylinder block is cast iron and the engine mounting point is rearward of the front face and therefore nearer to the centre of gravity of the unit. This, coupled with the deep section of the block, provides a rigid and vibration free unit when installed.

To reduce noise and wear, the camshaft and bucket type tappets run in an oil bath. Particular attention has been paid to the valve gear to avoid unnecessary deflections. Short solid push rods operate cast-iron rockers on induction-hardened shafts.

The four-bearing forged crankshaft has integral balance weights and bearings of 63.5 mm diameter, the crank pins being 50.8 mm diameter, giving a valuable crankpin/journal overlap of 15.875 mm. A Metalastik torsional damper is fitted at the front end.

The Hobourn-Eaton oil pump (see Section 15.13) has a delivery of 2½ gallons per 1000 revolutions. A separate positive feed is taken to both the oil pump drive gear and the distributor drive gear. This drains back to the camshaft gallery together with the rocker surplus. Standpipes and cast-in weirs maintain the level in the gallery and the overflow returns to the sump.

7.9   Jaguar 2.4-litre engine

In deciding on post-war policy, Jaguar Cars Ltd. faced the problem of reconciling the conflicting claims of a variety of factors.

The great reputation built up by pre-war models for outstanding performance and elegant design at moderate selling price, suggested a continuance of the production of both six- and four-cylinder models to power the two sizes of vehicle. The six-cylinder XK engine of 3.5-litre capacity had been an outstanding success.

In deciding whether the smaller engine should be a six or a four many factors had to be weighed. Rationalisation of manufacture, export markets, particularly the USA, and considerations of balance and vibration problems likely to arise with the unitary body construction that it was intended to use, led to the final choice of the six. Cost and weight were at some slight disadvantage relatively to the four, but smoothness of torque and freedom from troublesome vibrations were regarded as over-riding considerations, particularly as it was possible to achieve a considerable degree of rationalisation in manufacture and provision of spares by altering one principal dimension only, namely the stroke. The consequential modification to connecting rods, crankshaft, cylinder block and pistons have been satisfactorily achieved, and interchangeability of cylinder heads, valve gear and smaller components, such as bearing shells, will ensure economies in manufacture and maintenance.

The main features may be seen in elevation in Fig. 7.8 and in the cross-sectional views of Fig. 7.9. With the stroke reduced to 76.5 mm but

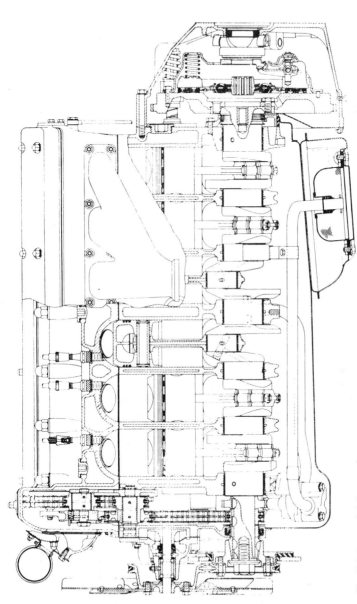

Fig. 7.8 Jaguar 2.4-litre engine

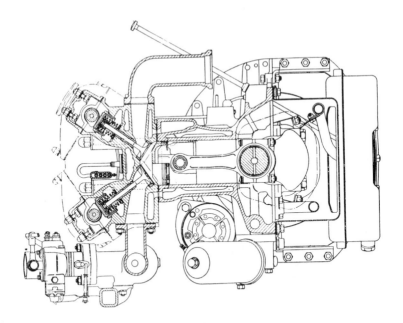

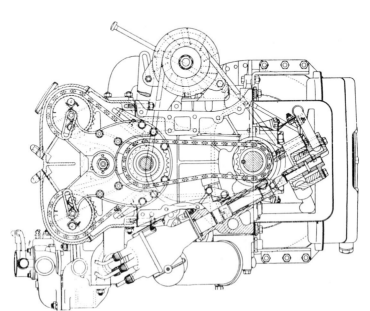

Fig. 7.9 Jaguar cross-sections

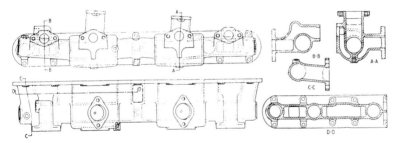

Fig. 7.10 Jaguar induction manifold

with the same bore of 83 mm as the 3.5-litre engine, the cylinders are under square, the stroke:bore ratio being 0.92.

The cylinder block is a relatively simple chromium iron casting extending to the crankshaft centre line, and closed by a deep pressed-steel sump. No liners are used, and the freedom from wear which has been Jaguar experience will no doubt be greatly helped by the chromium-plated rings used in the top grooves (see Section 6.11).

Features of the camshaft drive are referred to in Section 6.37, and the direct skew-gear drive to the distributor shaft is of interest. The small number of teeth – only ten – and the large helix angle on the crankshaft gear will be noted, though not apparent in the conventional view of this gear in the longitudunal section, but the driving conditions at the teeth will be quite favourable for the two-to-one reduction. The driving gear is of case-hardened steel and the driven gear on the distributor-pump shaft of phosphor bronze.

The torsional vibration damper is a Metalastik rubber-to-metal bonded, inertia-ring type.

Fig. 7.10 shows the design of the aluminium alloy induction manifold which is fed by two Solex B 32-PBI-5 down-draught carburettors.

With 24 mm chokes the performance curves shown in Fig. 7.11 are obtained. These represent a conservative tuning which could be consider-

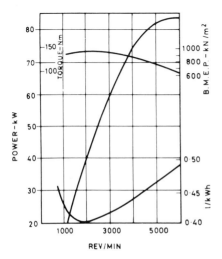

Fig. 7.11 Jaguar performance curves

ably improved if desired. Fuel supply is by SU high pressure electric pump, and the air cleaner is a long cylindrical type of AC manufacture.

The lubrication system incorporates a Hobourn-Eaton pump of a type described in Section 15.13 and a full-flow Tecalemit externally mounted filter. The somewhat unusual drilling of the crankpins, which has the effect of forming a useful sludge trap, may be noted.

A most informative and fully illustrated article will be found in *Automobile Engineer*, Vol. 46, No. 5.

7.10   Rover 2.3/2.6-litre E-Series engines

In this design, the aim has been to reduce the number of components to a mimimum consistent with the achievement of a high level of performance and reliability. The alternative swept volumes have been obtained by the use of crankshafts having different throws. Consequently, the bore is 81 mm for both, while the strokes are 76 mm for the 2350 cm^3 version and 84 mm for the 2597 cm^3 unit. Their compression ratios are common at 9.25:1, the pistons having dimensions different from their crowns-to-gudgeon-pin axes. These engines are illustrated in Fig. 7.12. and their performance curves reproduced in Fig. 7.13.

The power outputs are 91.7 kW and 107 kW at 5000 rev/min, while the torques are respectively 182 Nm at 4000 rev/min and 203 Nm at 3750 rev/min. In both instances twin SU HS6 carburettors are employed.

Commendable features of the design are the head and the block. The layout of the low pressure diecast aluminium head is in many respects similar to that of the Triumph *Dolomite Sprint* but since high, rather than sporting performance was required, only two valves per cylinder are used. Each pair is actuated by a common cam, which bears directly on an inverted bucket type tappet over the inlet valve and on a rocker for actuation of the exhaust valve.

The rockers in this engine are of cast iron, so their bearing properties are such that no special provision has to be made for the lubrication of their ends, splash and mist being adequate. Valve clearances are adjusted – as on the *Sprint* and O-Series engines – by pallets, or thick shims, seating in recesses machined on top of the spring retainers.

The included angle of the the valves is 40°, which gives a compact penthouse combustion chamber with good crossflow characteristics – the incoming wave of fresh mixture helps to sweep the burnt gases before it, out through the exhaust. Shallow dished piston crowns form the bottom portions of the combustion chambers. With such a large included angle between the valves, there is also plenty of space between the ports for the provision of adequate water cooling. Both the inlet and exhaust valves have identical springs except in that, to cope with the inertia of the additional mass of the rockers, a smaller supplementary spring is fitted inside the main one on each exhaust valve. The valve-head diameters are: inlet 42 mm, and exhaust 35.6 mm.

For simplicity of assembly and servicing, the camshaft bearings and tappet slideways are machined in a single high-pressure aluminium diecasting. Because of the precision with which this type of casting can be produced, oilways can be accurately cored in it and machining is reduced to

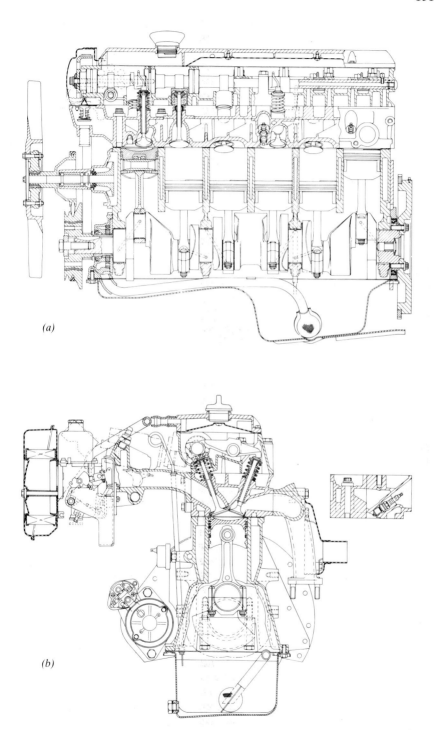

(a)

(b)

Fig. 7.12 The Rover 2600 six-cylinder engine shown in (a) longitudinal and (b) cross sections

a minimum. Unlike that in the *Sprint*, this casting extends the full width of the head, so the structural stiffness of the assembly is greater. It is bolted down on to a liquid sealant to prevent oil leaks. Having no flexible gasket in this joint face obviates the risk of tappet clearances closing due to settlement in service.

A steel-cored composite gasket is interposed between the head and cylinder block. The fourteen 12-mm set bolts that secure the head are tightened by the SPS Technologies system. With this system a machine with an electronic control and air motors tightens the bolts, sensing both the angle through which each is turned and the torque applied, stopping the tightening the instant the bolt begins to yield. A full explanation can be found in *Automotive Engineer*, Vol. 3, No. 3, 1978. Because the bolts are tightened so accurately, no retightening is required in service.

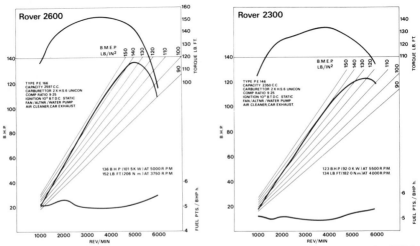

Fig. 7.13 Performance graphs for the Rover 2600 and 2300 six-cylinder engines. Net (DIN) installed condition

A toothed belt drives the cast-iron camshaft, which runs in seven 51-mm diameter bearings line-bored directly in the diecast carrier. Since the contact breaker and distributor, mounted horizontally, is driven by a spiral gear machined on this shaft, it is high up and therefore extremely accessible.

The cast-iron exhaust manifold is secured by two bolts per port to the head. No gasket is used, so a common source of failure has been eliminated.

A cast-iron crankcase and cylinder block has been employed to give the engine a good degree of rigidity and durability. Since the contact breaker and distributor unit and camshaft are on the head, the Hobourn-Eaton multi-lobe eccentric rotor oil pump is on the front end of the crankshaft, and the water pump centrally positioned above it, the crankcase layout is symmetrical. This obviates thermal distortion problems, facilitates both casting and machining and contributes to rigidity and noise reduction. Uncommonly large vertical ribs on the outer faces of the water jackets, and extension of the skirt well below the level of the crankshaft further stiffen the unit. A plate extending rearwards from the 6-litre sump is bolted up to the clutch bellhousing to prevent sag of the engine and transmission unit.

An En16T forged steel crankshaft, with four main journals is employed. Had seven journals been incorporated, it would have been possible to use a lighter shaft but, now that low fuel consumption is an important consideration, the additional friction and oil drag would have been unacceptable. The 50.5-mm diameter pins and 70.38-mm journals are induction hardened. They run in copper-lead bearings the surfaces of which are lead-indium flashed to assist running in.

A damper comprising a rubber spring element and a tuned annular mass is fitted to the front end of the crankshaft. Grooves are machined in the periphery of the annulus to take the V-belt drive for the fan and water pump, and to the alternator, which therefore form part of the damping system. To limit the power absorbed by the fan, it has a viscous coupling.

7.11   Ford V-six range

The transverse section of this engine is virtually identical to that of the V-four range, Fig. 6.66, except in that there is no counterbalance shaft and the inlet manifold is, of course, different. Obviously, too, the considerations that led to the adoption of this layout are similar to those set out in

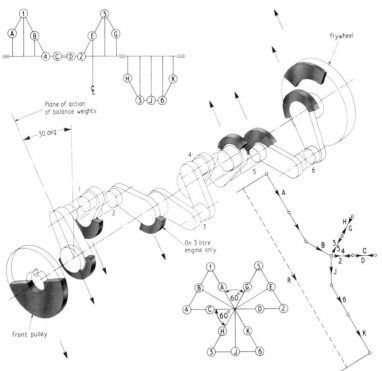

Fig. 7.14 Disposition of the balance weights on the crankshaft of the Ford V-six engine, with a diagrammatic layout of the arrangement of the crankpins (numbered 1 to 6) and the crankshafts (lettered A to K). Top left is a diagram of the rotational couples; bottom right is a vector diagram of the couples

Section 6.58, the need for compactness as regards overall length being even greater.

As in the V-four range, there are two sizes of V-six. They are the 2.5- and 3-litre units, and their bore and stroke dimensions are respectively the same as those of the 1662 and 1995 cm³ V-four engines – 93.66 mm bore by 60.3 and 72.4 mm stroke. For the 3-litre unit, the mean piston speed at 4750 rev/min, maximum power, is 1145 cm/s.

How complete primary balance is obtained is illustrated in Fig. 7.14. Diagram (*a*) shows the disposition of the counter-weights, (*b*) the arrangement of the six crankpins, (*c*) the rotating couples, and (*d*) is a vector diagram. The cylinders are numbered 1 to 3 from the front in the right-hand bank, and 4 to 6 in the left-hand bank, so the firing order is 1 4 2 5 3 6. Since this engine has a six-throw crankshaft, the cylinders in the right hand bank are offset forward relative to those in the other.

The 2.5-litre engine has an Autolite 38 IV down-draught carburettor, with an automatic choke unit sensitive to coolant temperature. On the other hand, the 3-litre engine has a Weber 40 DF AI twin venturi down-draught carburettor: each venturi serves a three-branch section of the induction manifold. At the top of the riser bores is an air balance slot. A W-shape diffuser in the riser bores helps to promote uniform distribution of the charge. Again, an automatic choke unit sensitive to coolant temperature is employed. The use of down-draught carburettors offsets to some extent the advantage of low overall height of the engine – most in-line engines now have side-draught carburettors – but very thin pan-cake-shape air filters and silencer units have been developed for this type of layout. A detailed description of this engine was published in the May 1966 issue of *Automobile Engineer*.

7.12   The V-eight

An objection brought against the straight eight engine, in addition to the liability to torsional oscillation of the crankshaft, is its great length, and an alternative arrangement of eight cylinders is the V-eight, employing two banks of four cylinders each, at right angles. This arrangement, long known and used in various applications, has established an overwhelming preponderance over alternative types in the USA for automobile purposes.

Following earlier pioneer designs, large-scale development was initiated by Cadillac in 1914, and aircraft and tank development produced air-cooled types. The flat or single plane crankshaft was used in these early constructions, but in 1926 Cadillac, and in 1932 Ford, introduced the 90° arrangement, the improved balance of which is described below. Side valves gave place to overhead valves from 1949 onwards.

The early Ford 30 hp and 22 hp engines are well known in this country, but their power output proved rather higher than the general demand required, with the result that the popular Ford models, as indeed of all makes, in Britain subsequently had the in-line engines. The situation in the USA has been different. The insatiable demand for increased power, and the earlier availability of 100 octane fuels, has resulted in the production by all the big groups of overhead-valve V-eight engines of rated maximum outputs from 160 to 300 hp, with compression ratios from 8:1 upwards, that of the Packard 300 hp being 10:1.

The cylinder dimensions are under square, with few exceptions, averaging about 95.25 mm bore and 82.55 mm stroke, giving a piston displacement of about 4.75 litres.

7.13 Balance and firing intervals of V-eight

With the single plane crankshaft, the 90° firing intervals are obtained by the disposition of the cylinders in two banks at right angles, whereas with the two-plane shaft, four of the intervals are due to cylinder disposition and four to crank arrangement.

The flat crankshaft is a simpler and, therefore, with comparable production methods, a less expensive form to make, but the dynamic balance of the engine is inferior to that obtained with the right angle disposition of cranks. The former arrangement is, for balancing purposes, treated as two ordinary four-cylinder engines sharing the same crankshaft, each set of four pistons being self-balanced for primary forces and couples, while the secondaries remain unbalanced in each bank. This gives a combined resultant secondary force for the whole engine which is zero in the 'vertical' direction, but has, in the 'horizontal' direction a value 40% greater than that corresponding to one set of four pistons since the horizontal components combine in the ratio $\sqrt{2}:1$, while the vertical components neutralise each other.

When the right-angle disposition of adjacent cranks is adopted, the engine is treated for balancing purposes as four 90° V twins, and the primary forces are counteracted by means of revolving masses in the manner described in Section 5.2. The combined primary reciprocating effect of the two pistons, operating on the same crankpin and with their lines of stroke at right angles, is equivalent to the mass of one piston revolving at the crankpin, and the balancing problem is reduced to that of a revolving system.

In the V-eight crankshaft illustrated in Fig. 6.15 the thinner webs adjacent to the journals may be regarded as circular disc webs each corrected to neutralise half of the actual revolving mass at each crankpin, that is, half the pin and one of the big ends.

The heavy masses B_1 and B_2 each incorporate in effect two of these corrected disc webs, together with further masses to balance both the adjacent *equivalent* revolving masses representing the effect of the two pistons on each pin.

If component couples in the plane of the paper for the lower view are considered, it will be realised that the arm of the couple due to cranks 1 and 4, which form a clockwise component couple, is greater than the arm of the component couple due to cranks 2 and 3, acting in the contrary sense. This is corrected by giving the masses B_1 and B_2, which act in intermediate planes, a bias to assist their opposition to cranks 1 and 4. This bias accounts for the unsymmetrical form of the masses.

Since the balance of the pistons involves masses incorporated in the crankshaft, it will be realised that not only should the piston masses be held to close tolerances among themselves, as in the four-cylinder engine, but also that their relation to the crankshaft must be carefully checked.

7.14   Secondary balance with two-plane shaft

The secondary balance with the right-angle shaft is superior to that of the flat shaft.

It will be found that adjacent pairs of pistons in each bank, moving in the same longitudinal plane, operate on cranks at right angles. Thus when one piston is at the position corresponding to $\theta = 0$ (see Fig. 5.9) its neighbour in the same bank has $\theta = 90°$, and the corresponding secondary forces will be opposed.

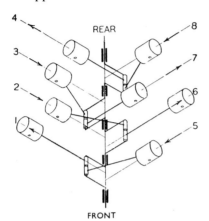

Fig. 7.15 Diagram of V-eight

Fig. 7.15 shows the disposition of the cylinders and cranks, the shaft being indicated with five main bearing journals in order to make clear the relative disposition of the throws. The arrows represent the secondary disturbing forces in the configuration shown, and it will be seen that these are self-balanced in each bank, for both forces and couples.

7.15   Construction of V-eight

A cross-section of the early Ford side-valve engine is given in Fig. 7.16, which shows the salient special features. The two banks of cylinders and the crankcase are formed in a single monobloc casting, the sump which forms the lower half of the crankcase being a light steel pressing.

Detachable heads with side valves operated from a single camshaft are conventional features, while the somewhat inaccessible position of the tappets and valve springs is mitigated by the special construction adopted. The tappets are non-adjustable, and the valve stems have a wide splayed foot which minimises wear at this point. The valve stem guide is split along its centre line for assembly around the valve stem, and the whole assembly may be withdrawn upwards through the cylinder block after removal of a retainer of flat horseshoe form. Precision gauging during assembly is claimed to render adjustment between periodical regrindings unnecessary, and so enables a simpler construction to be adopted.

A twin down-draught carburettor is fitted to a unit induction manifold and cover, renderng the whole assembly compact and of clean exterior form. Numbering the off-side cylinders 1, 2, 3, 4 and the near-side 5, 6, 7, 8, as in Fig. 7.15, the near-side choke feeds numbers 1, 6, 7 and 4 while the

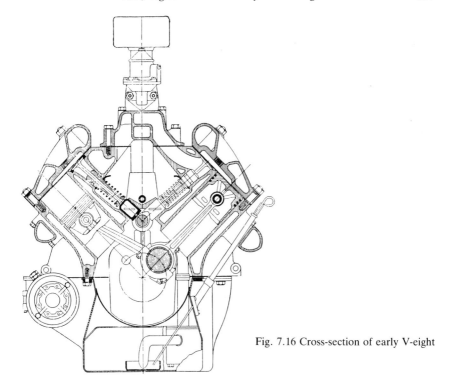

Fig. 7.16 Cross-section of early V-eight

off-side choke feeds 5, 2, 3 and 8. The firing order is 1 5 4 8 6 3 7 2, resulting in a regular interval of half a revolution between cylinders fed from the same choke. The induction tracts are symmetrically arranged, but are not equal in length for all cylinders.

Mounted at the rear of the induction manifold may be observed the crankcase breather and oil-filler, up which passes the push rod for operating the AC fuel pump.

7.16 A British V-eight engine

A most interesting V-eight unit, because it is designed for production in large numbers and in conjunction with an in-line four-cylinder engine, is that used in the Triumph *Stag, Automobile Engineer,* July 1970. An in-line version, comprising in effect one bank of the V-eight unit, but incorporated in a different crankcase, is that of the 1708 cm^3 Saab 99, *Automobile Engineer*, September 1968. This engine was subsequently used in the Triumph *Dolomite* range. The bore and stroke dimensions of the Saab version were originally 83.5 × 78 mm, but the bore was subsequently increased to 87 mm, giving a swept volume of 1850 cm^3.

For the 2997 cm^3 V-eight unit (Fig. 7.17), the bore is 86 mm and the stroke 64.5 mm. This gives a mean piston speed of 11.83 m/s at 5500 rev/min, at which the maximum power, 108 kW, is developed. The valve overlap and lift of the V-eight are larger than those of the in-line engine, helping to give a much higher maximum torque – 235 Nm at a speed of

3500, instead of 137.3 Nm at 3000 rev/min – but steeper flanks to the torque curve.

With a V-angle of 90° – the four cylinder version is canted over at 45° – and a two-plane crankshaft, complete balance can be achieved. The first and fourth crankpins are displaced 90° from the second and third. Cylinders 1, 3, 5 and 7 are in the right-hand bank and numbers 2, 4, 6 and 8 in the left-hand one, so the firing order is 1 2 7 8 4 5 6 3. In the right-hand bank, the cylinders are set 19.8 mm forward of those in the left. At the

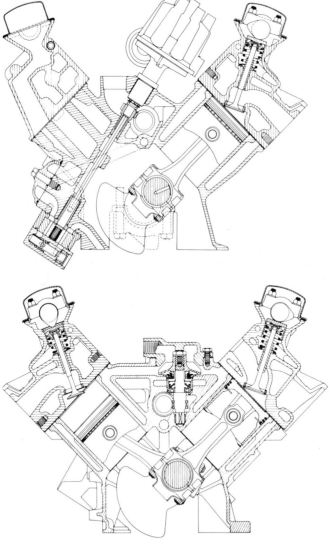

Fig. 7.17 The Triumph *Stag* V-eight engine has an inclined drive for the oil pump and ignition distributor, while the water pump, also driven from a spiral gear on the camshaft, is vertically incorporated between the banks of cylinders, thus economising on overall length and simplifying the drive arrangement

front end of the crankshaft, a Holset viscous coupling limits the torque transmitted to the fan to 6.56 Nm and its mean speed to 2400 rev/min, thus reducing waste of power when the engine is operating at high speed.

There are several other features of special interest. First, the auxiliary drive layout is common to both the V-eight and the four-cylinder units: a jackshaft rotating at two-thirds crankshaft speed and carried in the base of the V – an arrangement possible because of the use of the overhead camshaft layout – is driven by the timing chain for the camshaft of the left-hand bank. machined on the jackshaft are two spiral gears, one to drive the spindle for the water pump installed vertically in the V, and the other for the spindle driving the ignition distributor – inclined towards the left in the V – and the oil pump, which is on the left, near the base of the crankcase, Fig. 7.17. With this layout, the water pump does not add to the length of the engine, as it would if mounted horizontally in front. Apart from this, the drive to each single overhead camshaft is a simple run of chain from the crankshaft to camshaft pulleys with, in each case, a Renold hydraulic tensioner and a nitrile rubber-faced arcuate guide bearing against the slack run and a nitrile rubber-faced flat damping strip on the taut driving run.

So that the valve gear can be completely assembled on the head before it is mounted on the block, but without impairing accessibility for tightening the cylinder head on the block, five bolts and five studs are used to secure the two: the bolts are perpendicular to the joint face, but the studs are inclined at an angle of 16½° relative to the axes of the cylinders and, to sustain the component of the tightening force parallel to the joint face, they are a close fit in reamed holes in the head.

The in-line valves are inclined at an angle of 26° inwards, and wedge-shape combustion chambers are employed. Each exhaust valve comprises a 21-4 N steel head welded to an En18 stem. These seat on the Brico 307

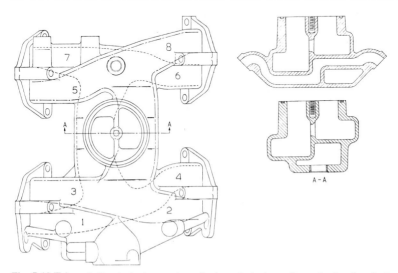

Fig. 7.18 Triumph *Stag* induction system. Section A-A shows the water heating ducts and the upper section shows an alternative exhaust gas heating passage to meet US emission control requirements

sintered iron inserts in the aluminium head – the use of sintered powder components saves a lot of machining. To clear the heads of the valves, and to form part of the combustion chambers, the crowns of the pistons are slightly dished.

Two Stromberg 175-CDS carburettors are mounted on top of the manifold. Each discharges into an H-shape tract, one serving number 2, 3, 5 and 8 cylinders and the other numbers 1, 4, 6 and 7, so that the induction impulses occur alternately in each, Fig. 7.18. A balance duct is cored in the wall between the two risers.

All the coolant leaving the cylinder heads passes through passages cored beneath the inlet tracts, leaving through the thermostat housing, which is integral with the manifold, Fig. 7.18, section AA. To satisfy emission regulations in the USA, an alternative exhaust heated manifold can be supplied. It has an 82.55-mm wide transverse passage, which communicates with the exhaust ports of numbers 3 and 5, and 4 and 6 cylinders, the gas leaving again through a port at the front. The alternative arrangement is shown in the scrap view above section AA, Fig. 7.18. In addition, a thermostatically-controlled warm air intake system is incorporated. This type of device is described in Section 11.62.

7.17   Jaguar 5.3-litre V-twelve

Obviously, success with any design depends on meeting the requirements of a distinctly identifiable sector of the market. A high proportion of Jaguar cars is sold in the USA and for this reason the 60° V-twelve layout was decided upon. First, it offers something different from the common run of V-eights in that country. Secondly, with a swept volume of $5343\,\text{cm}^3$, its potential is ample both to provide enough power for use with automatic transmissions and to offset limitations imposed by current or foreseeable future measures for avoiding atmospheric pollution by exhaust gas constituents. Thirdly, it is inherently in balance and, with six equally placed firing impulses per revolution, it is not only free from torsional resonances but also smooth running.

In this Chapter, it will be possible to outline only a few interesting features of the design, Figs. 7.19 and 7.20, but a full description was published in the April 1971 issue of *Automobile Engineer*. To save weight, aluminium castings are used for the cylinder block and heads, the sump, oil cooler, timing cover, coolant pump casing, tappet carriers, camshaft cover, induction manifolds, coolant outlet pipes, thermostat housings and the top cover of the crankcase. Although the crankcase was designed so that it could be diecast, sand casting is currently employed. With an open top deck and wet liners, simple cores can be used and the sealing of the liners, by compressing them between the head and the block, is relatively easy; on the lower seating flanges, Hylomar sealing compound is used to prevent any possibility of leakage of water into the crankcase. The length of the liners between these flanges and the upper ends is only about 44.4 mm, so problems due to differential expansion of the iron liners and aluminium block are reduced to a minimum, while the hottest portions of the liners are in direct contact with the water.

Cast-iron main bearing caps are used, and they are each held down by four studs. This ensures adequate rigidity, for avoidance of crankshaft rumble. It also reduces to a minimum variations in clearance due to thermal expansion.

A shallow combustion chamber depression in the crown of the piston, beneath the completely flat face of the cylinder head, was found to give a clean exhaust gas – originally, a deep chamber with clearances machined beneath the valves was tried. To reduce emissions it was also found necessary to lower the compression ratio to 9:1 from the 10.6:1 originally conceived. The stroke:bore ratio is 0.779 to 1 (70 mm to 90 mm) and the maximum torque is 412 Nm at 3600 rev/min – even between 1100 and 5800 rev/min the torque does not fall below 325 Nm. The gross bmep of 1110 kN/m^2 is quoted, and the maximum bhp is 272, or 202.5 kW at 5850 rev/min.

A single overhead camshaft is used for each bank. This is more compact, simpler, lighter and less costly than the twin overhead camshaft layout.

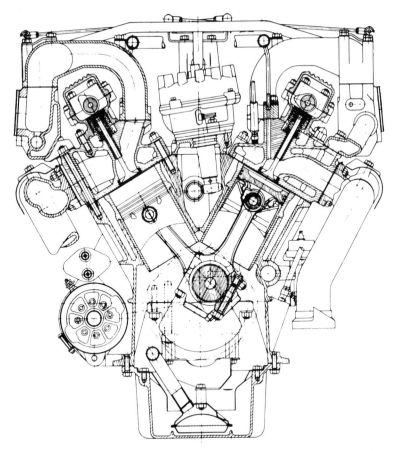

Fig. 7.19 Transverse section of the Jaguar V-twelve engine showing how the problem of differential expansion between the aluminium crankcase and the iron liners is minimised by incorporating the flange high up around the periphery of the liner

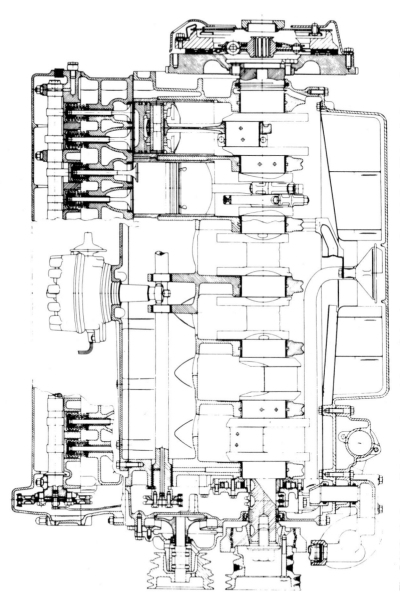

Fig. 7.20 On the Jaguar V-twelve engine, cast-iron main bearing caps are used, each being held down by four studs screwed into the aluminium crankcase

Moreover, the timing drive is simpler: a single two-row roller chain passes round the drive sprocket on the crankshaft, the two camshaft sprockets and, in the base of the V, the jackshaft sprocket for driving the Lucas Opus contact breaker and distributor unit. A Morse tensioner bears against the slack run of the chain and a damper strip against each of the other runs between the sprockets. This tensioner is described in Section 6.37.

For the lubrication system, a crescent type oil pump is interposed between the front main journal and the front wall of the crankcase, its pinion being splined on a sleeve which, in turn, is keyed on to the crankshaft. The advantages of this type of pump are its short length and that the fact that axial clearance within the housing – in this installation, 0.127–0.203 mm – is much less critical than that of the more common gear type pump.

At 6000 rev/min, this pump delivers 72.7 litres/min. Normally, half of this output goes through a filter to the engine, while the other half passes through the relief valve, which lifts at 483 kN/m^2, to the oil cooler integral with the filter housing at the front end of the sump. The return flow from the base of the radiator to the water pump inlet passes through this cooler, lowering the temperature of the oil by about 22°C and increasing that of the water by only just over 1°C.

7.18 Jaguar with May Fireball combustion chamber

Early in 1976, the May Fireball combustion chamber was announced. Then, however, except for a few papers presented before learned societies in various parts of the world, little more was heard of it until mid 1981, when Jaguar introduced their V-twelve HE engine, the letters 'HE' standing for 'high efficiency'. This engine is exactly the same as that described in the previous section except in that it has the May Fireball combustion chamber, together with some recalibration of the petrol injection and modifications to the ignition system. Thus, Jaguar is the first manufacturer to develop the May system to the point of actual series production.

Basically, the May system is designed to burn very weak mixtures and thus, by ensuring that there is plenty of excess air, converting all the fuel to CO_2 and H_2O. This not only ensures that thermal efficiency is high, it also reduces exhaust emissions. It does this in three ways: first, as just mentioned, the formation of CO is prevented; secondly, piston crown temperatures are low – in fact down by about 100°C – partly because of the excess air, so the top land clearance can be kept small and this helps further to reduce hydrocarbon emissions which tend to be generated by quenching of the flame in clearances such as this; thirdly, because of the relatively low peak combustion temperatures, the generation of oxides of nitrogen is minimal.

To burn these weak mixtures, a high compression ratio is necessary and this, by increasing the thermodynamic cycle efficiency, also contributes considerably towards reduced fuel consumption. However, the high compression ratio alone is not enough: the other requirements are a controlled degree of turbulence of the charge, to distribute the flame, and a high-energy spark to start the combustion off vigorously.

With the May Fireball combustion chamber there are two zones in the cylinder-head casting. One is a circular dished recess in which is the inlet valve, and the other, extending further up into the cylinder head, accommodates both the exhaust valve and the sparking plug. Because the compression ratio is required to be high, the combustion chamber has to be fully machined, otherwise both the tolerances and clearance spaces would be too large. Below is the flat crown of the piston – instead of the previously slightly-dished crown of the earlier version of this engine.

As the piston comes up to TDC in the final stages of compression, it forces the mixture out of the inlet valve recess through a channel guiding it tangentially into the deeper recess beneath the exhaust valve, Fig. 7.21. This generates a rapid swirling motion in that recess which, once the flame has been initiated by the spark, helps to spread it throughout the mixture.

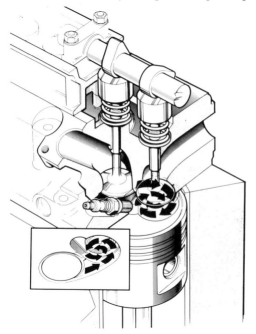

Fig. 7.21 Jaguar V-twelve HE combustion chamber. Inset: underside view of the swirl pattern

The spark plug, however, is screwed into a small pocket adjacent to the passage through which the mixture flows from the inlet to the exhaust valve regions. In this pocket, it is not only sheltered from the blast of swirling gas but also is in a position such that the fresh mixture that has just come in through the inlet valve is directed on to it. Consequently, it is supplied with an ignitable mixture; also, the nucleus of flame around the points will have time to develop and expand without being blown out, or quenched, before it can generate enough heat to be self-sustaining.

Most of the detail development work has been aimed at getting the guide channel between the inlet and exhaust valve pockets just right for inducing the optimum swirl. Incorporation of a ramp in this channel was found to give the best results.

At steady speeds at part throttle, with the compression ratio of 12.5:1, air:fuel ratios of 23:1 were burned consistently well, but richer mixtures were found to be necessary for transient conditions experienced on the road. Obviously, the Lucas digital electronic fuel-injection system had to be recalibrated to suit the lean burn requirements, but otherwise it is the same as used by Jaguar in the earlier version of the engine.

To ignite such weak mixtures, a high-energy spark is required. The reliable, constant energy ignition module introduced for the XK 4.2 engine was utilised, but given a more powerful amplifier to raise its output from 5 to 8 amp. Within the distributor, a magnetic pick-up has been incorporated. Then a twin coil system – both coils being Lucas 35 C6 units – was developed, the secondary coil being used solely as a large inductor and mounted ahead of the radiator to keep it cool. The outcome of all this work is a system that will provide accurately-timed ignition for 12 cylinders at 7000 rev/min – no mean achievement. On 97-octane fuel, the engine produces 223 kW (299 bhp) at 5500 rev/min. Its maximum torque is 44.05 kg at 3000 rev/min.

Chapter 8

Sleeve-valve and special engines

Interest in the reciprocating sleeve valve has persisted throughout the history of the automobile engine, and though not now so widely used as in the early days of the Burt-McCullum and Knight patents, the single sleeve still has many strong adherents, while later metallurgical advances made possible such exacting and successful applications of the single sleeve as the Bristol Perseus and Napier Sabre aircraft engines.

The double sleeve has become obsolete owing to its greater cost of manufacture and greater viscous drag as compared with the single sleeve and though the qualities of the Daimler-Knight, Minerva, and Panhard engines are proverbial, it does not appear likely that the double-sleeve arrangement will experience revival.

The sleeve valve, as the name implies, is a tube or sleeve interposed between the cylinder wall and the piston ; the inner surface of the sleeve actually forms the inner cylinder barrel in which the piston slides. The sleeve is in continuous motion and admits and exhausts the gases by virtue of the periodic coincidence of ports cut in the sleeve with ports formed through the main cylinder casting and communicating with the induction and exhaust systems.

8.1 Burt single-sleeve valve

The Burt-McCullum single-sleeve valve is given both rotational and axial movement, because with a single sleeve having only axial reciprocation, it is impossible to obtain the necessary port opening for about one-quarter of the cycle and closure for the remaining three-quarters, if both inlet and exhaust are to be operated by the same sleeve. It will be found that a second opening occurs when the ports should be shut. The sleeve may be given its combined axial and rotational motion in a variety of ways, one of which is illustrated in Fig. 8.1. This shows an arrangement of ball-and-socket joint operated by short transverse shafts in a design due to Ricardo, and the same mechanism was used in the Napier Sabre engine. The ball B is mounted on a small crank pin integral with the cross-shaft A which is driven at half-engine speed through skew gears from the longitudinal shaft

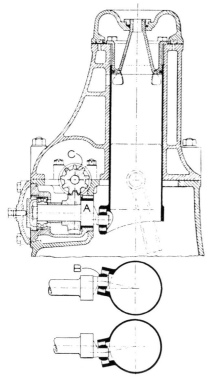

Exhaust Ports   Inlet Ports

(a)

(b)

Sleeve   Ports

(c)   S

(d)

(a) Exhaust just closing and inlet about
to open
(b) Maximum port opening to induction
(c) Top of the compression stroke, S
being the maximum 'seal' or overlap
of the ports and cylinder head
(d) Maximum opening to port

Fig. 8.1 Ricardo actuation mechanism for   Fig. 8.2 Single-sleeve porting
Burt McCullum sleeve valve

C. Clearly the sleeve receives a vertical movement corresponding to the
full vertical throw of the ball B while the extent of the rotational movement
produced by the horizontal throw of the ball depends upon the distance
between the centre of that ball and the axis of the sleeve.

8.2   Arrangement of ports

The form and arrangement of the ports are arrived at as the result of
considerable theoretical and experimental investigation in order that the
maximum port openings may be obtained with the minimum sleeve travel.
This is important, as the inertia forces due to the motion of the sleeve, and
the work done against friction, are both directly proportional to the
amount of travel. Fig. 8.2 shows an arrangement of ports wherein three
sleeve ports move relatively to two inlet and two exhaust ports, the middle
sleeve port registering in turn with an inlet and an exhaust port. The
motion of the sleeve ports relatively to the fixed cylinder ports is the
elliptical path shown. In the figure, the sleeve ports are shown in full lines
in their positions relative to the cylinder ports (shown in broken lines) at
various periods of the cycle. In practice it is usual to provide five sleeve
ports and three inlet and exhaust ports.

8.3   Advantages and disadvantages of sleeve valves

The great advantages of the sleeve valve are silence of operation and freedom from the necessity for the periodical attention which poppet valves require, if the engine is to be kept in tune. Hence sleeve valves have been used in cars of the luxury class where silence is of primary importance. The average sleeve-valve engine has not shown quite such a good performance as its poppet valve rival in maintenance of torque at high speeds, owing chiefly to the somewhat restricted port openings obtainable with reasonable sleeve travel. Hence sleeve-valve engines have not figured prominently in racing, although some very good performances have been made from time to time. Sleeve-valve engines share with rotary valve types reduced tendency to detonation owing to the simple symmetrical form of the combustion chamber with its freedom from hot spots, and shortness of flame travel. The construction also lends itself well to high compression ratios without interference between piston and valves. The disadvantages of gumming and high oil consumption experienced with early sleeve-valve designs have been successfully overcome, but there is some element of risk of serious mechanical trouble in the event of piston seizure, which dangerously overloads the sleeve driving gear.

8.4   Rotary valve

Many types of rotary valve have been invented, either to act as distribution valves only, or to perform the double function of distribution and sealing.

Their great mechanical merit is that their motion is rotative and uniform, and the stresses and vibration of the reciprocating poppet or sleeve valve are eliminated. They are suitable for the highest speeds, and the limitation in this direction is determined by the inertia stresses in the main piston, connecting rod and bearings. A high degree of mechanical silence is obtained.

The performance shown by the two proprietary makes described in the following paragraphs has proved conclusively that from thermodynamic and combustion points of view they have outstanding qualities as compared with the conventional poppet valve construction. In both the Cross and Aspin engines in the single-cylinder motor-cycle form, exceptionally high compression ratios with freedom from detonation with fuels of quite low octane value have been obtained. The corresponding bmep reaches figures of the order 1100 to $1240 \, kN/m^2$. The quite exceptional outputs per litre arising from the combination of extreme rotational speeds with these pressures should be considered in the light of the remarks in Section 4.24.

The remarkable freedom from detonation under a combination of high compression ratio and low octane fuel – a combination usually disastrous in a normal engine – is no doubt largely due to the general coolness of the combustion chamber, its smooth form and freedom from hot spots. Further, the high compression ratio probably results in complete evaporation of the fuel before ignition, and it is believed that this inhibits the formation of the peroxides referred to in Section 14.10. This may be consistent with observation that tetra-ethyl lead, which is also regarded as an inhibitor of such formation, appears to have little effect in these cool engines.

To offset these remarkable characteristics there are, unfortunately, considerable mechanical difficulties in pressure sealing and providing adequate lubrication of the valves without excessive waste to the cylinder and the exhaust ports. Considerable progress was made towards final success in these directions, and advances in metallurgy, and extended trials of different combinations of materials, may well result in the general supersession of the poppet valve – if lead-free fuel becomes mandatory – by the rotary form.

8.5   Cross rotary-valve engine

The valve of the Cross engine normally runs at half engine speed, but by duplicating the inlet and exhaust ports through the valve it may be readily designed to operate at one-quarter engine speed.

The valve housing is split about the centre-line of the valve, the halves being held in resilient contact with the valve. The bottom half of the valve housing is usually an integral part of the cylinder, which is not bolted to the crankcase, but allowed to press upwards against the valve, such pressure being proportional to the gas pressure in the cylinder.

In cylinder sizes above 200 cm³ a controlled valve loading scheme is adopted so that the pressure on the valve by the housing is only just sufficient for adequate sealing.

The lubrication of the valve is brought about by pumping oil on to one side of the valve and removing it with a scraper blade on the other side, an essential part of the mechanism being a non-return valve which prevents oil from being sucked into the induction side of the valve.

In cases where it is not possible to have a completely floating cylinder, the lower part of the valve housing is spigotted into the top part of the cylinder, suitable sealing rings being provided.

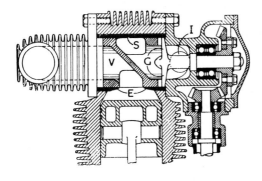

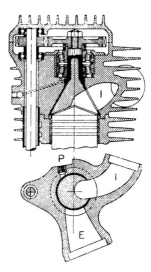

Fig. 8.3 (*above*) Cross rotary valve

Fig. 8.4 (*right*) Aspin engine

Cross engines usually use an aluminium cylinder without liner. The piston rings, being made from very hard steel, act not only as the means of pressure sealing, but as bearers to prevent the piston touching the bore. The cylinder bore wear with this construction is negligible.

Fig. 8.3 is a sectional view of an early type of valve for a 500cm^3 motor-cycle engine, having vertical shaft and bevel drive for the valve. V is the cylindrical valve operated by the dogs G on the half-speed shaft. The induction port is indicated at I, and S is the tunnel liner in which the valve rotates. In this design sealing is obtained by the resilient port edges E of the liner, which is so machined as to maintain an elastic pressure on the rotating valve.

This sealing pressure is transmitted through the valve body to the upper casting and back to the crankcase through two long holding-down bolts.

Various materials have been tried for the valve and liner, a combination of nitri-cast-iron valve running in a liner of bronze or nitralloy steel having given good results.

The makers report that this engine has developed a bmep of 1344kN/m^2 at 4000 rev/min with a fuel consumption of 0.228 kg/kWh.

For further details of these interesting engines the reader should refer to a paper by R. C. Cross in Vol. XXX of the *Proceedings of the Institution of Automobile Engineers*.

8.6   Aspin engine

Like the Cross engine, the Aspin engine has shown the most striking performance in the single-cylinder, air-cooled motor-cycle form, an engine of 67 mm bore and 70.5 mm stroke with a compression ratio of 14:1 having developed 23.5 kW at the remarkable speed of 11 000 rev/min. When developing 15.64 kW at 6000 rev/min the fuel consumption was recorded as 0.1946 kg/kWh.

The general construction of this single-cylinder engine should be clear from Fig. 8.4. The valve consists of a nitrided alloy-steel shell partly filled with light alloy, within which a cell is formed to constitute the combustion chamber. As the valve rotates the cell is presented in turn to the inlet port I, the sparking plug P and the exhaust port E. During compression, ignition and combustion the cell is on the cool side of the cylinder, and after ignition the plug is shielded from the hot gases. These conditions play a great part in the thermodynamic properties of the engine. In this early engine a double-thrust Timken roller bearing was provided to take the bulk of the upward thrust due to the gas load, only a carefully regulated amount being carried direct on the conical surface.

A four-cylinder Aspin engine, of 4.6 litres, was developed for heavy duty, and in Fig. 8.5 are shown sectional views of its head construction. Water cooling was incorporated for the rotor, which was of fabricated steel construction, faced with lead-bronze alloy, and running in a cast-iron cylinder head.

For full descriptions and analysis of performance of these engines, the reader should refer to articles by Louis Mantell and J. C. Costello in Volumes 34 and 35 of *Automobile Engineer*.

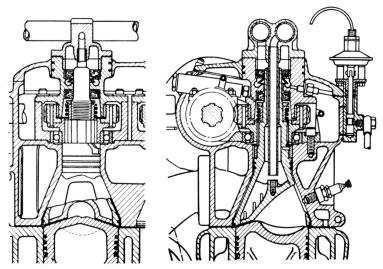

Fig. 8.5 Four-cylinder Aspin engine

8.7   NSU Wankel rotary engine

The information that follows is an abstracted summary of the comprehensive technical articles by R. F. Ansdale, AMIMechE, in *Automobile Engineer*, Volume 50, No. 5 and Dr-Ing. Walter Froede in Volume 53, No. 8. An article by Felix Wankel on the performance criteria of this type of engine is in Volume 54, No. 10 of the same publication.

This enterprise in the long search for a successful design of rotary pressure engine introduces no new principle or thermodynamic cycle. The four events of the four-stroke cycle take place in one rotation of the driving member.

The general profile of the straight working chamber is of epitrochoid form, a group of curves of the cycloid family, the geometry of which is fully discussed in the articles under notice.

The general construction of a single-rotor type, known as the KKM version, with three-lobed rotor, is shown in Fig. 8.6.

The rotor provides three equal working spaces, and clearly an exhaust release will occur each time an apex seal overruns the leading edge of the exhaust port E, that is, three times per revolution of the rotor, and this exhaust will continue until the following seal reaches the trailing edge of the port.

Induction will have commenced in the same space about 60° of rotor movement earlier.

There are thus three complete four-stroke cycles per revolution of the rotor in different working spaces, but all fired by the same sparking plug as maximum compression is reached.

The stationary shell pinion is fixed in the casing, and the annulus mounted at the centre of the rotor, and carried on needle rollers on the periphery of the shaft eccentric or crank, engages and rolls around the fixed pinion. With 24 and 36 teeth on the pinion and annulus respectively, the main shaft will make three turns for one turn of the rotor, this giving a complete cycle for each revolution of the main shaft. The driving impulses transmitted to the shaft thus correspond to those of a normal two-cylinder four-stroke engine.

There is a rotating primary imbalance due to the eccentric path of the rotor, but this is readily dealt with by means of two symmetrically mounted flywheels, suitably drilled to provide the countervailing imbalance. Suitable balancing provision for the cooling water and oil is incorporated.

The most interesting and informed articles on which these notes are based give an extensive description of the construction an related experience with the various sealing devices, and also performance curves and figures of the pioneer KKM unit in comparison with a normal piston engine.

Fig. 8.6 shows longitudinal and cross-sections of a typical unit, and Fig. 8.7 gives views of three different forms of rotor. Recesses in the curved faces are provided to obviate strangling of the charge during passage from one zone to the next.

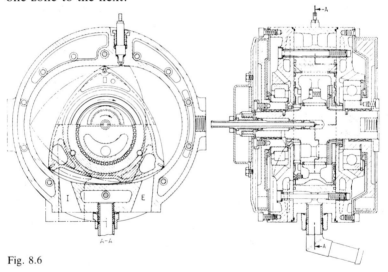

Fig. 8.6

The form of these faces, subject to the necessary compression ratio being provided, is not limited to any particular profile.

Cooling has not presented many problems, because the complex movements of the rotor, and the resultant changing accelerations, tend naturally to circulate the oil and so to cool the interior. The circulation thus set up contributes greatly to the cooling.

Most of the development problems have been associated with reducing the rates of wear of the apex seals and bore, and improving the efficiency of combustion.

As regards wear the problems have been solved. Tojo Kogyo has developed seals made of glass-hard carbon, which run in hard chromium-plated aluminium bores. NSU have used a proprietary metallic seal called IKA, and they have also used a cermet, called Ferrotic, which is mainly

Fig. 8.7

iron and titanium carbide sintered. Both these seals have been used in aluminium silicon bores that have been coated with nickel in which are uniformly embedded closely-spaced, fine particles of silicon carbide.

The potential for the solution of the combustion problems is more open to doubt, having regard to the existing and pending legislation on both exhaust emissions and fuel economy. With such an attenuated form of combustion chamber, efficient combustion is difficult to achieve, though there should be no undue tendency towards the formation of oxides of nitrogen. While all the European manufacturers have abandoned production of Wankel engines, Tojo Kogyo have introduced new twin-rotor engines for their *Mazda* cars, and NSU are continuing research and development on their project.

The torque of this type of engine falls off at low speeds. However, in this respect it does not differ so much from some high-performance sports car engines of conventional design.

A diesel version of the Wankel engine was developed by Rolls-Royce Ltd. It has been described in a paper by F. Feller, *Proc. I. Mech. E.* 1970–71, Vol. 185, 13/71. Basically, it comprises two units, a small one incorporated integrally in the casing above a larger one. The larger one acts as a compressor, supercharging the other, which is the power unit. With this arrangement, compression and expansion ratios as high as 18:1 can be obtained, and the surface:volume ratio in the combustion chamber is about the same as that of an equivalent reciprocating piston engine.

In this unit, the restriction, or throat, formed between the two portions of the combustion chamber as the rotor sweeps past top dead centre, is used to generate the turbulence required for burning weak mixtures in the pocket, or depression, in the periphery of the rotor. To obtain this effect, the pocket is shaped like a cricket bat, foreshortened with its lower end bifurcated like the section of the base of the Saurer combustion chamber, Fig. 9.7. As the channel represented by the handle of the bat passes the restriction, the compressed gas is forced along it, directing a jet at the base, which divides the flow into two turbulent eddies rotating in opposite senses. These eddies, of course, swirl one each side of the chamber represented by the foreshortened blade of the bat.

Another special feature of the Rolls-Royce version is its tip seals. These are shaped so that gas pressure forces the trailing seal into contact with the wall of the chamber. Specific fuel consumptions of the order of 0.232 to 0.2433 kg/kWh are expected. Although the useful speed range of this engine is narrow, this may be overcome by the use of automatic transmission.

A survey of various types of rotary combustion engine, including brief comments on development work by Renault on two-stroke and four-stroke versions, is given in a serial article by R. F. Ansdale, AMIMechE, in *Automobile Engineer*, Volume 53, No. 11 and Volume 54, Nos. 1 and 2. The thermodynamics have been dealt with by D. Hodgetts, BSc, AMIMechE, in Volume 55, No. 1 of the same journal.

Chapter 9

The compression-ignition engine

One of the most remarkable engineering developments has been the rapid advances made in the application of the compression-ignition principle to engines for transport purposes, particularly on road and rail. The earliest work on this type of engine was done by two Yorkshiremen, W. D. Priestman and H. Ackroyd Stuart.

These engines are now generally described as 'diesel' engines in honour of Dr. Rudolph Diesel, the German engineer who was responsible for most of the pioneer invention and development work with large stationary units, and 'heavy oil engines' from the higher specific gravity and less volatile – and therefore less flammable – nature of the fuels which they are capable of using. The phrase *compression-ignition* (ci) is tending to be preferred by authorities in this field, because the essential characteristic of the type, as compared with the volatile fuel spark ignition engine, is thereby clearly indicated.

This essential feature is the ignition of the fuel, when injected at or near the inner dead centre, by the high temperature of the air charge after compression through a volume ratio of not less than 12 or 13:1, and rising in some cases to as much as 20:1 or more.

9.1 Temperature produced by compression

The resulting temperature depends on the temperature at the beginning of compression and the amount of heat loss during compression.

With an effective compression ratio of 14 from the point of closing of the inlet valve, an initial temperature of 60°C, and assuming no heat loss – true *adiabatic* compression – the resulting temperature at inner or top dead centre would be 675°C. These conditions would be approximately attained at full load and full speed, and a temperature of 675°C would be more than sufficient to ignite the fuels used, which have self-ignition temperatures in air at atmospheric pressure ranging from 350°C to 450°C, these temperatures of self-ignition being lower at the high pressure prevailing during injection.

Under light load and at starting, the conditions are less favourable. At starting from cold the prevailing temperature in the engine at the commencement of compression will be that of the atmosphere, say 15°C, and the heat loss during the relatively slow compression in a cold cylinder may prevent the temperature rising much above 400°C. This might prove insufficient to ignite certain fuels, and in some engine designs arrangements are made to provide a higher compression ratio when starting than for normal running, in order to ensure that ignition will be obtained.

The temperature reached does not depend on the initial *pressure* of the charge, except to a slight degree indirectly, owing to the proportionately greater heat loss with a less dense charge. Thus, throttling the induction does not lower the compression temperature attained provided the initial temperature and volumetric compression ratio are the same. It is important to bear this in mind when studying the action of the pneumatic governor described later.

If the induction is unrestricted except by the normal throttling effect of the inlet valve, the pressure at commencement of compression will be from 89.6 to 103.4 kN/m² absolute, depending on the speed and breathing characteristics of the engine. The pressure at the end of compression will depend on this initial pressure, the effective compression ratio and the amount of heat loss, its value ranging in different designs and according to the conditions from 3100 to 3800 kN/m² or more.

Piston ring leakage will naturally reduce both the pressure and temperature at the end of compression. Thus far the cycle of operations differs from that in the petrol engine in that air only is compressed and a much higher compression ratio is used.

Shortly before top dead centre the liquid fuel is injected and ignites and burns in the heated air in the compression space. The combustion is not, as in the spark ignition engine, the burning of a more or less homogeneous mixture of air and vaporised fuel, but rather a process in the early stages, of surface combustion of the liquid droplets which develops at a later stage, and to a varying degree in different designs, into a more or less rapid explosion. The variation of pressure during this process depends on the method of injection, whether it be by means of a high pressure air blast or simply by the agency of a mechanical pump, and on the form of the combustion chamber and conditions of turbulence.

9.2   Air blast injection

This method constituted the true diesel method as originally used in large stationary and marine engines, and involved the following features. The compression pressure was about 3450 kN/m², and the fuel was measured and delivered by a mechanical pump to the annular space behind a small conical injection valve placed in the centre of the cylinder head and arranged to open outwards. To this space was applied an air pressure of 5516 to 6895 kN/m² from air storage bottles charged by a compressor which was usually incorporated in the engine itself.

At the correct moment the injection valve was lifted off its seat and the high-pressure blast air drove the fuel in at a very great velocity, when it mingled with the combustion air in the cylinder and was ignited by the high temperature of this air caused by the high compression. It must be realised that the volume of liquid fuel delivered each cycle is an extremely small one, but the accompanying bulk of blast air, which was from 2 to 3% of the total air, lengthened the injection period with the result that the pressure did not rise during combustion, but was merely maintained at approximately the compression pressure as the piston moved outwards until combustion was completed.

The compression indicator diagram is shown at *a* in Fig. 9.1, the black dot indicating the approximate point of commencement of injection. The maximum pressure is about 3447, and the mean pressure about 690 kN/m^2, if the fuel injected corresponds to about three-quarters of the air present, representing about 30 to 40% excess air over that chemically necessary. The diagram marked *c* is obtained on part load with reduced fuel supply.

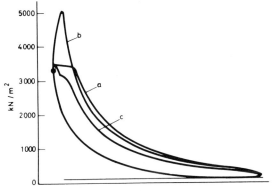

Fig. 9.1 Indicator diagrams of compression-ignition engine

The maximum pressure is the same, but the rate of combustion does not keep pace with the piston movement, and the pressure falls somewhat irregularly until combustion is complete.

These conditions represent approximately, combustion at constant pressure, and led to the adoption of that assumed condition of combustion in the hypothetical 'diesel cycle' in thermodynamic discussion.

9.3 Mechanical injection

The high-pressure compressor required for the blast air was a costly and somewhat troublesome auxiliary, and absorbed considerable power, thus making the overall mechanical efficiency of the engine somewhat low. Further, storage bottles for the blast air were necessary, and the apparatus was far too cumbersome for motor vehicle use. Even with large land and marine diesel installations, mechanical injection by means of a jerk pump has almost wholly replaced the air blast method, which must be regarded as obsolete.

With mechanical injection the air blast is entirely dispensed with, and the oil is forced in from a pump through a sprayer or pulveriser, comprising one or more fine holes in a suitable nozzle. Very difficult conditions have to be met. The volume of liquid to be injected is very small and must be injected at a very high velocity in order that it may be thoroughly atomised and yet be capable of penetrating through the whole volume of air present.

The jet must also be so disposed and directed that a stream of liquid is not likely to impinge on the cylinder wall or piston, where rapid carbonisation could occur – an exception is the system adopted for the MAN engines, in which the fuel jet is deliberately impinged on the hot wall of the bowl-in-piston combustion chamber to facilitate evaporation. Section 17.16 and Fig. 17.17.

The injection of a small volume at high velocity implies a very short *period* of injection, and this results in the action approximating closely to an explosion with a more rapid rise in pressure and a much higher maximum pressure as shown at *b* in Fig. 9.1, which represents a typical full load diagram with mechanical injection. This higher maximum pressure makes the ratio of mean pressure to maximum pressure even less favourable than in diagram *a*, which already compares unfavourably in this respect with the petrol engine.

9.4   Power-weight ratio

The above ratio of mean to maximum pressure is the determining factor in the value of the power:weight ratio, since the power depends on the mean pressure while the sturdiness and therefore weight of the parts will depend on the maximum pressure to be provided for. Thus, the compression-ignition engine is inherently heavier than its rival the petrol engine, owing to the very factor which results in its superior economy, namely, the higher compression and expansion ratio. As the petrol engine seeks to improve its fuel consumption by employing special fuels which permit of a higher compression ratio being used, so this difference tends to disappear, and safety and cost of the fuel and general engine performance will become the determining factors. Metallurgical improvements and advances in manufacturing techniques are available equally to both types.

9.5   Injection and combustion processes

Extensive research has been and is being carried out to determine the best methods of injection and form of combustion chamber to give smooth and complete combustion of the injected fuel and suppression of the characteristic 'diesel knock' which gives rough and noisy running or the high speed mechanical injection engine.

The problem is to inject into the cylinder an extremely small volume of liquid fuel in such a manner and into such an environment that every minute particle of oil shall be brought into immediate contact with its full complement of heated air, in order that combustion shall be rapid and complete without being so sudden as to give rise to rough running.

There are two general alternatives – either to cause the fuel to penetrate by its own velocity to all parts of the combustion chamber and find the air required, or to give the air itself such a degree of swirl or turbulence that it will seek out the fuel as it enters. The former represents the process of direct or open chamber injection in which any movement the air may possess is fortuitous or due to masking of the inlet valve, while the second covers the many designs of swirl or pre-combustion chamber arranged to give either ordered swirl or general turbulence to the air during injection of the fuel.

The merits and de-merits of the two general systems will be discussed when the details of the arrangements are described.

9.6 Three phases of combustion

Ricardo has recognised and described three phases of combustion. These are illustrated in Fig. 9.2 which shows a form of indicator diagram differing from the form in Figs. 4.4 and 9.1, in showing the pressures plotted on a continuous crank angle base instead of on a stroke base. With the

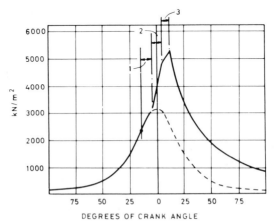

Fig. 9.2 Fundamental phases of combustion in mechanical-injection ci engine

crankshaft turning steadily at some measured speed, the crank angle base becomes also a *time* base and, as time is an important factor in combustion processes, very useful information can be obtained from such diagrams, though they cannot be used for the calculation of power output unless they are first reduced to a stroke base by a suitable graphical process. These crank angle diagrams can be obtained by means of indicators of the 'Farnborough' and 'cathode-ray' types.

9.7 Delay period

Referring to Fig. 9.2, the commencement of injection is indicated by the dot on the compression line about 15° before dead centre. The period 1 is the 'delay' period during which ignition is being initiated, but without any measureable departure of the pressure from the air compression curve which is continued as a broken line in the diagram as it would be recorded if there were no injection and combustion.

9.8 Second phase

This delay period occupies about 10° of crank angle and is followed by a second period of slightly less duration during which there is a sharp rise of pressure from 3102 to over 4826 kN/m². This period represents a phase of rapid flame-development and combustion of the whole of the fuel present in the cylinder and approximates to the 'constant volume' combustion of the vaporised fuel in the spark ignition engine. The steepness of this rise – here about 200kN/m^2 per degree of crank movement – is a determining factor in causing diesel knock, or rough running. In general, though the form of the combustion chamber has an important influence, the longer the delay period the steeper will be the second phase and the rougher the running, as a greater proportion of fuel is present. The nature of the fuel, the temperature and pressure of compression, and initial rate of fuel injection are all factors in deciding the length of the delay period apart from the form of the combustion chamber.

With the majority of engines the running is rougher at light loads and idling, as the lower compression temperature and smaller quantities of fuel injected increase the delay period, but this is not universal. Ricardo has shown that this period tends to be constant in time, thus occupying a greater crank angle at higher speeds and calling for injection advance, while the second phase covers more nearly a constant crank angle, as in a given engine it is dependent on turbulent displacement, the speed of which will increase with engine speed.

9.9   Final phase of combustion

The third phase involves combustion of the fuel as it issues from the sprayer holes, and represents the only phase over which direct control can be exercised by control of the rate of injection. With air blast injection this period could be largely determined by the blast pressure, and the characteristic flat top to the diagram could be obtained; but with mechanical injection most of the fuel is already in the cylinder before this stage is reached, and control is less certain.

It should be appreciated that the diagram in Fig. 9.2 is hypothetical, and that the three phases are not in general so sharply distinguishable one from the other.

9.10   Types of combustion chamber

Typical forms of combustion chamber are shown in Figs. 9.3 to 9.8. These illustrations are diagrammatic and are a selection from the many forms that have been invented and introduced with varying degrees of success. In the UK, the swirl or ante-chamber has very generally given place to direct or open chamber injection, and combustion chambers are now formed largely as a hemispherical or toroidal recess in the piston crown, except for the smallest compression ignition engines required to operate at high speeds. In the latter, the minute quantities of fuel injected have to burn completely in very short periods of time.

9.11   Direct injection

Fig. 9.3 illustrates the direct injection or open chamber type, in which the fuel is sprayed through two or three fine holes at a high velocity, and requiring injection pressures of $27\,580 \text{kN/m}^2$ or more. The resulting 'hard' jet enables the fuel to penetrate the dense air and find the necessary oxygen for combustion, aided in most cases by some residual swirl or turbulence set up during the induction stroke by the masking of the inlet valve, as is indicated in Fig. 9.7. The merits of this type are that a moderate compression ratio of 13 or 14:1 may be used, no auxiliary starting devices such as heater plugs or cartridges are necessary, and the smaller sizes of engine can be started by hand-cranking from cold, provision being made for releasing the compression until the engine is rotating at sufficient speed.

The form of the combustion chamber with a moderate ratio of surface to volume is favourable to the reduction of heat loss, and engines of this type show good fuel economy and high mean pressure. Maximum pressures tend to be high, however, and there is a somewhat greater tendency to

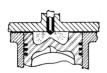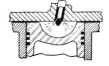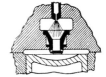

Fig. 9.3 Direct injection   Fig. 9.4 Benz

rough running. The indicator diagram approaches in form to 'constant volume' rather than to 'constant pressure' combustion. The injectors with their minute spraying holes – about 0.2032 mm – and high pressures, require highly skilled technique in production and most careful provision for filterng the fuel.

Direct injection engines have not generally been considered capable of quite such high speed or so tolerant of poor fuel as the pre-combustion or ante-chamber types, but their easy starting and high thermal efficiency have produced many converts as the more difficult injection technique has been mastered.

9.12   Pre-combustion chamber

Fig. 9.4 shows the pre-combustion chamber type developed largely by the Benz firm and used in several Continental European designs. The action gives an approximation to the characteristics of air blast injection and limits the maximum pressure. The pre-chamber represents about 40% of the total clearance space, and the fuel is injected into this air and partly burned, the spread of ignition being helped by the turbulence arising from the passage of the air through the communicating pepper-castor holes during compression.

The products of this partial combustion and the remaining fuel are then forced by the excess pressure in the pre-chamber back through the communicating holes at high velocity as the piston commences to descend. The high turbulence thus created aids the final flame-spread and combustion in the main cylinder, while the piston is protected from the high initial pressure which would arise from too rapid combustion of the whole fuel charge. This system has the disadvantage that there is considerable cooling loss during passage of the air through the communicating holes, and due to the high surface:volume ratio of the combustion chamber.

The cooling effect is mitigated by partially isolating the inner lining of the chamber from the main body of metal as shown in the figure, but even so a higher compression pressure is necessary to obtain satisfactory starting with (in the majority of designs) the further help of heater plugs. Though engines employing this arrangement are in general free from rough running and high maximum pressures, and give a clean exhaust, they have not shown either such good economy or high output as more modern types.

9.13   Controlled air swirl

His investigations and experience with these and other types, and a realisation of their defects, led Ricardo to develop the principle of ordered turbulence or swirl of the air. His initial work was carried out on a single sleeve valve engine, as this gave the greatest possible freedom in choice of form of the combustion chamber.

He quickly discovered that by arranging for the air to enter the inlet ports in a partly tangential direction, a rotational swirl or vortex about the cylinder axis could be formed, which persisted throughout the compression stroke and that, owing to the conservation of angular momentum in a free vortex, the rotational speed of the vortex became increased as the air entered the smaller diameter of the combustion chamber. If injection then took place in a direction at right angles to this ordered swirl, as shown in Fig. 9.5, a very complete and rapid distribution of fuel throughout the whole mass of air was obtained, it being possible to use a relatively soft and finely atomised jet with low injection pressure. This construction has been successfully applied to a range of medium speed stationary engines by Brotherhood, and a fuel consumption as low as 0.2188 kg/kWh has been obtained.

9.14   Comet swirl chamber

A fairly genuine prejudice against the sleeve valve led to the development by Ricardo, in conjunction with AEC and other firms, of the Comet chamber, which is illustrated in Fig. 9.6.

Different designs vary in detail, and the twin turbulence recesses in the piston crown are a later development.

The usual shape of chamber is spherical with a single tangential entry passage. With this design heater plugs are unnecessary. An important feature of the Ricardo patents is the semi-isolated hot plug forming the lower part of the chamber, the purpose being the mitigation of the heat loss

Fig. 9.5 Vortex

Fig. 9.6 Comet

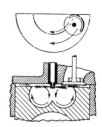

Fig. 9.7 Saurer

to the jackets, which loss gives rise to higher specific fuel consumption, as in the pre-chamber arrangement.

Comparative tests of AEC transport engines with open and Comet chambers showed lower fuel consumption and better low-speed torque with the former but better high-speed torque with the latter.

Another application to the Ricardo Comet chamber, enabling easy starting to be obtained without a heater plug, is the Pintaux injector nozzle developed jointly by CAV and Ricardo. This is illustrated and described in Section 19.19.

9.15 Saurer dual-turbulence system

This system combines the effect of what has been aptly termed the *squish* of the air trapped between the piston crown and cylinder head, with rotational swirl produced by masking the inlet valve, as indicated in Fig. 9.7. In the actual construction there are two inlet and two exhaust valves, and the two directions of swirl are superimposed in the doughnut-shape recess in the piston head. The injector has four radially directed holes and only a moderate injection pressure is called for owing to the relatively large diameter of these. With a compression ratio of 15, no heater plug is required to obtain easy starting, and the delay period, owing to the good turbulence, is short. Similar systems are now widely used by most manufacturers.

9.16 Perkins direct injection engines

The earlier Aeroflow design of Perkins P type engines is now replaced by the direct injection system. This simpler and more economical type is shown in Fig. 9.8. The general design follows familiar lines, a deep unit crankcase and cylinder block with dry cylinder liners being used. An interesting feature is the arrangement of the drive for the CAV distributor type injection pump, which incorporates a flange-mounting at the top of a nearly vertical shaft in the manner familiar with the ignition distributor of the petrol engine: in fact, it takes little more room than the latter.

High speeds are obtainable with modern design and materials. A small engine in the Perkins range, the 4/99, is capable of a maximum speed of 4000 rev/min. The Volkswagen light diesel engine runs up to 5000 rev/min at full load.

9.17 Injection equipment

The nature of the problem in providing fuel injection equipment for compression-ignition engines can be illustrated by quoting some of the parameters that have to be met with the small cylinder sizes now prevalent.

Engines with indirect injection into swirl-type combustion chambers are now as small as 0.35 litres/cylinder. The full load fuel delivery requirement is of the order of $20 \, mm^3$ per stroke and that for idling about 15% of this, or about 3 to $4 \, mm^3$ per stroke. For a four-cycle engine of this size running up to 5000 rev/min, these minute quantities have to be injected with precision and regularity at a frequency of up to 2500 per minute.

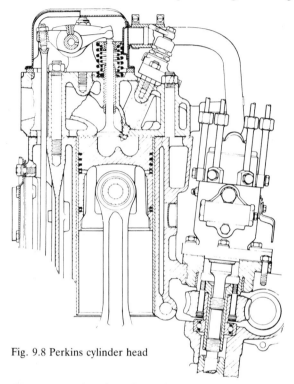

Fig. 9.8 Perkins cylinder head

Moreover, the duration of each injection, even at full load, must not exceed some 30 to 35° of crankshaft, implying a time period at maximum speed and load of only one thousandth of a second.

Direct injection engines, although currently not quite so small, present even more difficult problems owing to the need for shorter injection periods and higher injection pressures. A direct injection engine of 0.5 litres/cylinder running up to 3000 rev/min would need a maximum injection pressure at full load speed of at least 500 bar to force the fuel through injection orifices of no more than 0.20 mm diameter – assuming that four holes are required to give adequate distribution. Moreover these holes need to be drilled to an extremely close tolerance to ensure equality of flow between individual nozzles.

Therefore, highly specialised manufacturing techniques not met with in any other industry are required, with the result that the majority of injection equipment is supplied by a handful of manufacturers scattered over the world, most coming from two major manufacturers – Lucas CAV and Robert Bosch – and their licensees. The only significant exceptions are two US engine makers – General Motors and Cummins – who produce their own equipment peculiar to their engines.

Broadly speaking, the fuel injection system used for both direct and indirect injection diesel engines comprises individual injectors – one for each cylinder – a high-pressure injection pump of rotary or in-line configuration and having an integral governor, and a filtration system to remove contaminants from the fuel. In the following Sections we look in greater detail at these components.

9.18 Pintle type nozzle

This type of nozzle (Fig. 9.9) is used with pre-chamber and swirl types of combustion system, because these do not need the high energy jet characteristic of the hole-type nozzle. The orifice through which the fuel is discharged into the combustion chamber is an annulus formed by an extension of the valve needle – the pintle – projecting into the single axial hole. The pintle has a biconical profile, shown clearly in the enlarged section, Fig. 9.10. This profile can be varied to produce the angular dispersion characteristics required of the emergent spray, to suit the particular combustion chamber.

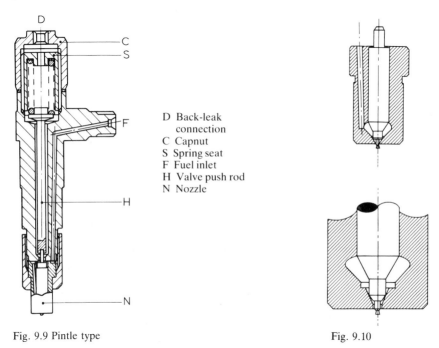

D Back-leak
   connection
C Capnut
S Spring seat
F Fuel inlet
H Valve push rod
N Nozzle

Fig. 9.9 Pintle type   Fig. 9.10

When the valve is closed, a parallel portion of the pintle, just beneath the conical seat, protrudes into the hole, and there is a small clearance between it and the hole. During the first part of the valve opening motion – known as the *overlap* – while this parallel portion is lifting out of the hole, it restricts the area of the orifice. This limits the quantity of fuel injected during the combustion delay period, reducing the initial rate of combustion and therefore noise – especially beneficial under idling conditions. All pintle nozzles have some overlap, but those for the more modern engines have an extended overlap, and are termed *delay type* pintle nozzles.

A particular advantage of the pintle nozzle for small high-speed engines is the the orifice area increases with the valve lift so, in effect, the nozzle is self-adjusting over the wide range of flow rates required as load and speed change. This of course cannot be achieved with the fixed-area hole type nozzle.

9.19 Pintaux nozzle

The Pintaux nozzle was developed jointly by CAV Ltd. and Ricardo & Co. Engineers (1927) Ltd., and is applicable only to the Ricardo Comet type cylinder head. This nozzle was designed primarily to enable cold starting to be obtained without the use of heater plugs.

With the normal type of pintle nozzle the spray is coaxial with the injector, and the direction of injection found most advantageous for all-round engine performance is that indicated in the diagrams of Fig. 9.11, which is downstream on the opposite side of the swirl chamber from the throat entry.

Investigation has shown, however, that under starting conditions the hottest zone of the chamber is outside this spray path and nearer the centre of the chamber on the opposite side. By directing the spray into this zone considerably improved starting can be obtained without the use of heater plugs.

This direction does not, however, give the best all-round engine performance, and the construction of the nozzle has been so contrived that at the low speeds of starting, when the injector needle is only partly lifted, the main orifice is largely blanked by a cylindrical portion of the needle

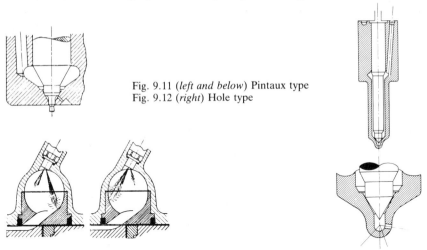

Fig. 9.11 (*left and below*) Pintaux type
Fig. 9.12 (*right*) Hole type

point, and the bulk of the delivery is discharged through the oblique hole shown in the enlarged view of the nozzle. At normal running speeds the cylindrical portion is lifted clear, and about 90% of the delivery issues in the normal manner, but preceded by a small pilot charge which promotes quieter running.

9.20 Hole type nozzles

The hole type of nozzle, Fig. 9.12, is invariably used with direct injection combustion chambers, in which the fuel has to be distributed radially through a number of holes. Generally, too, the spray energy level is higher and the droplet density lower than in indirect injection engines: this is to compensate for the lower degree of swirl.

Most widely used with such combustion chambers is the multi-hole type. This has between two and six holes more or less symmetrically arranged on a wide angle cone, as shown in the inset to Fig. 9.13. These holes are drilled normally to the spherical surface of the tip, breaking through the inner surface, which too is of spherical form and is concentric with the outer one so that the lengths of the holes are equal. To avoid leakage of the fuel into the combustion chamber between injections, the volume enclosed between the valve seat and the tip has to be as small as practicable. This volume is known as the *sac*.

In the 'closed' type of nozzle which, for vehicle engines, has now entirely superseded the 'open' type, the valve is a conically-ended needle, the cylindrical upper portion of which is close fitting in the nozzle body, to guide it concentrically with the valve seat. Alternatively, as with the Gardner design shown in Fig. 9.14, it is guided in a separate nozzle holder. In each instance the valve is closed by a spring mounted in the nozzle holder, Figs. 9.10, 9.13, 9.14 and 9.15.

A valuable feature of this design is the differential lifting force obtained because the diameter of the guide is larger than the effective diameter of the seat. The valve will begin to lift only when the fuel pressure, acting on the area comprising the difference between that of the guide and the seat, overcomes the force of the spring. As soon as the lift begins, the pressure acts instantly upon the whole of the guide area, so the valve rises rapidly to its limit stop and the flow to the nozzle orifice is unrestricted. A less

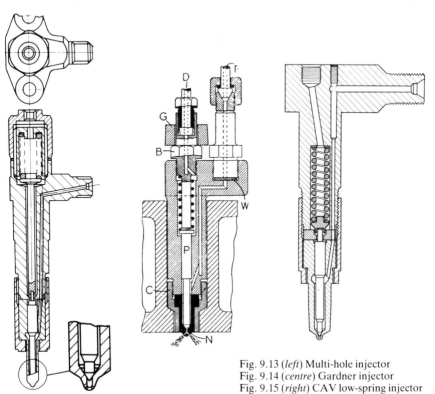

Fig. 9.13 (*left*) Multi-hole injector
Fig. 9.14 (*centre*) Gardner injector
Fig. 9.15 (*right*) CAV low-spring injector

favourable effect of this differential feature is that the valve will not return to its seat until the pressure has fallen to a value such that the spring force can overcome the pressure acting upon the whole guide area. This means that the closing pressure will always be lower than that at which the valve is opened. The closing pressure in fact often becomes the controlling parameter, since too low a setting may allow combustion gases to enter the nozzle at the end of injection and this can lead to carbon fouling of the interior. This effect can be minimised by reducing the mass of the moving parts, as has been done with the low spring injector, Fig. 9.15.

With the now obsolete 'open' type nozzle, there was no valve to control injection, which began as soon as the fuel pressure at the open end of the hole exceeded the gas pressure in the combustion chamber and ceased when it fell again below that of the gas pressure. One or more non-return valves prevented gas pressure from forcing the fuel to flow in the reverse direction.

9.21　Injector asemblies

Some typical injector assemblies are illustrated in Figs. 9.9, 9.13, 9.14 and 9.15. In each, provision is made for collecting and returning to the supply pipe any leakage of fuel between the differential valve and its guide.

This leakage is reduced to a minimum by the extreme precision and lapped finish of the stem and guide assembly, tolerances of the order of 0.0025 mm being common. Valves and bodies must be kept in pairs, never being interchanged.

In Fig. 9.9, the nozzle N is of the pintle type. H is the spindle transmitting the spring load to the differential valve and, on removal of the protecting screw-cap C, the spring load can be adjusted by the screw S which is locked simply by tightening the cap C against the body.

In the Gardner injector (Fig. 9.14) the spring acts directly on the differential valve or plunger P. The upper end of the spring seats on the breech plug B, on top of which bears the holding down yoke G. N is the nozzle and C the nozzle cap, while W is a very fine gauze filter washer provided as a final precaution against choking of the tiny spray holes.

In both, the fuel enters at F, and leakage past the valve is led away at D, to be returned to the main fuel intake.

Turbocharging, which commonly implies cylinder pressures higher than with natural aspiration, can result in gas entering the nozzle, unless opening, and hence closing, pressure is set undesirably high. This problem can be largely overcome using the 'low spring' injector, Fig. 9.15, the moving parts of which have a smaller mass. The effect is a more rapid closure of the valve, as can be seen in the comparative needle lift diagram, Fig. 9.16.

9.22　CAV Microjector

The CAV Microjector first went into large-scale production in 1981. It was developed because of the rapidly increasing demand for small diesel engines, especially for cars, and because the existing types of injector were too bulky for this type of installation and were unsuitable for metering and

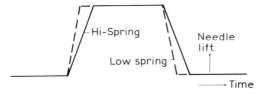

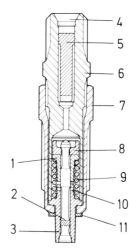

Fig. 9.16 Needle lift diagram

1 Lift stop	7 Capnut
2 Nozzle valve	8 Collar
3 Nozzle body	9 Spring
4 Inlet	10 Feed ports
5 Edge filter	11 Sealing washer
6 Nozzle holder	

Fig. 9.17 General arrangement of the CAV
Microjector

spraying satisfactorily the small quantities of fuel required per stroke. Such engines, ranging from about 1.6 to 3 litres swept volume, can have cylinders as small as 0.4-litre capacity, and they are virtually all of the pre-chamber type.

With both the pintle and Pintaux type injectors, a major disadvantage is the need for a back-leak pipe to allow fuel to be displaced back as the pintle lifts inwards, in a direction opposite to that of the flow of injected fuel. In the Microjector, this requirement is obviated by the use of a poppet valve opening in the direction of flow. Also, the whole injector has been made smaller, since gas pressure in the cylinder assists the spring in holding the poppet valve on its seat.

As explained in Section 9.19, the Pintaux type injector was developed to facilitate cold starting with the Ricardo Comet combustion chamber. Consequently, an experimental predecessor to the Microjector had the auxiliary hole for injection into the hottest part of the combustion chamber during cranking. However, with the development of greatly improved glow-plugs for cold starting assistance, the auxiliary hole became unnecessary and, with a single hole closed by a poppet valve, all risk of entry of foreign matter into the injector was obviated and production was simplified.

The construction of the Microjector can be seen from Fig. 9.17. Fuel from the injection pump flows through the edge-filter into the nozzle holder, and on into the spring chamber. When the pressure rises sufficiently to overcome the spring and gas forces on the poppet valve, this valve is lifted, and the fuel flows through the spring and the diametral holes, or feed-ports, in the nozzle body, past the helical grooves in the lower guide, and on past the valve seat. If the pressure is high enough, the valve will continue opening until the lift stop has descended on to the upper end of the nozzle body; otherwise it will float in an intermediate position. When injection ceases, the valve closes under the influence of both the spring and the gas pressure, the latter of course being the combustion pressure and therefore much higher than the compression pressure against which it was initially opened.

With this design, the reciprocating masses are small and gas blow-by into the nozzle is not a problem. Also, the jet pattern is such that the droplet size is smaller and the fuel more finely and widely distributed within the chamber than with the Pintaux type. Consequently the vaporising time, and therefore ignition delay, are shorter, so both the mechanical and combustion noises are less too.

Some features not immediately apparent in Fig. 9.17 are as follows. The collar by means of which the spring assembly is retained, is fitted by passing the top of the valve stem through a hole not shown in the illustration, drilled eccentrically in the collar, and then sliding it radially to centre it on to its smaller-diameter seating, which can be seen in the illustration. The poppet valve is guided in the nozzle body by both the central land between its two waisted portions and the lower land in which spiral grooves are machined to allow the fuel to pass through. Had these grooves been parallel to the axis of the valve, they would have tended to have worn grooves in the nozzle body. The lower end of the valve is a close fit in the body, to prevent combustion products from getting near or entering the conical seat a few millimetres above. Between the seat and the lower end of the valve, the profile is such as to maintain the required spray characteristics as the valve lift is progressively increased. Finally, the thread around the lower portion of the capnut is similar to that of a 14-mm sparking plug so the unit is very compact and easy to install on the cylinder head.

9.23 Injection control

For the high-speed automobile engine, the 'jerk' type of constant stroke plunger pump is widely employed. The term *jerk* indicates the sudden impulse given to the fuel at the instant of injection, followed at the appropriate moment by a sudden collapse of pressure, causing injection to cease in an abrupt manner to prevent dribble.

The volume of the high-pressure system and the inherent compressibility of the fuel, however, leads to a complicated sequence of events in which the pressure developed by the injection pump is propagated along the high-pressure pipe. This pressure wave has a travel time that is significant in terms of the whole injection period. Moreover, the pressure waves are reflected backwards and forwards along the system from its closed, or partially closed, ends both during and after the injection. Therefore it is not possible to predict the behaviour of an injection system by simple calculations. In fact, complicated mathematical solutions, rendered feasible by the use of digital or analogue computers, are now used to supplement and assist in the protracted experimentation necessary to develop an injection system for each particular application.

9.24 The in-line injection pump

Since the merger of the CAV and Simms, the range of classic in-line pumps manufactured in the UK has been rationalised into three basic types, covering the requirements of the smallest to the largest engines for vehicles. These are the Minimec, the Majormec and the Maximec, Fig. 9.18, in increasing order of size and output capability. The maximum

Fig. 9.18

horsepowers per engine cylinder obtainable with these pumps are respectively 40, 60 and 100. Throughout this rationalised range the basic constructional features are similar, so it will be necessary to describe only one – the Minimec pump.

9.25   Construction of the Minimec pump

The six-cylinder version, with an integral governor, is shown in Fig. 9.19. It is also available in three-, four- and eight-cylinder forms. For some applications, however, the pump and governor are in separable housings.

Although the main housing is a light alloy casting in which the camshaft, tappet assemblies and control gears are contained, the pumping element assembly is carried in a one-piece steel pumping head. This design feature provides good sealing capability and stiffness, as compared with the traditional all-aluminium arrangement. Moreover it obviates relaxation problems due to differential thermal expansion.

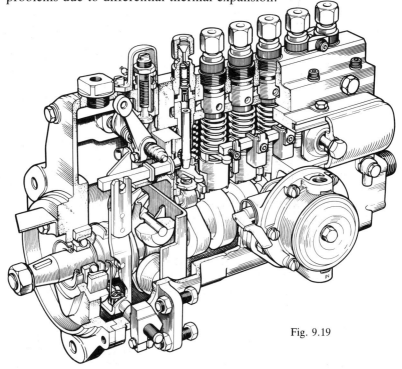

Fig. 9.19

The alloy steel camshaft has a large base diameter, for longitudinal stiffness. It is carried in ball or roller races mounted in the cast-iron end-covers. In the example illustrated, the cover at the governor end is in the form of a flange for direct mounting on the engine timing case, so that the drive gear can be fitted directly to the camshaft. Alternatively, the pump may be mounted on its base, in which case the drive will be transmitted through a jackshaft and couplings. Pumps with separable governors do not have through shafts, and therefore may be driven or flange-mounted only at the end remote from the governor.

To reduce the length of the pump to a minimum, the cams are as close together as possible, and they actuate roller tappets reciprocating in bores machined in the main housing. These tappets are prevented from turning by flats on their peripheries, against which register steel keep-plates, one between each pair. Their upper ends carry shims for adjustment of angular phasing between the delivery lines, to make good any differences arising out of manufacturing tolerances.

In the upper steel body, each pumping element assembly comprises the plunger and barrel, the latter being held down against a shoulder by the screwed-in delivery valve holder. The feed gallery is drilled longitudinally to interconnect the outer ends of the radial inlet ports in the barrels, and the fuel passes into the gallery from the free end. In the body, the plunger and tappet return-springs are retained during assembly by spring plates, which then rest upon the upper faces of the tappet shims.

For controlling fuel delivery, arms pressed on to the lower ends of the plungers register in vertical slots, or forks, in which they slide during the plunger stroke, Fig. 9.20. These forks are mounted on the square section control rod, which slides axially in bearings at each end of the housing. When the control rod is moved by the governor output lever, it rotates each plunger to control the delivery volume, as described in detail in Section 9.26. On assembly, each fork can be adjusted relative to the others, to equalise the delivery from all of them, and they are finally clamped to the control rod with set-screws. Access for this adjustment is gained through the front cover.

The delivery valve holder contains the valve and its spring, the function of which is described in Section 9.28, and at its upper end is the conical seat and screw connection for the high-pressure pipe line. A clamp between each pair of delivery valve holders prevents them from rotating during attachment of their pipes.

In Fig. 9.19, the assembly is shown with a feed pump driven by an eccentric on its camshaft. Alternatively, the feed pump may be driven from the engine camshaft. In either case, its outlet is connected through a filter, described in Section 9.32, to the pump inlet.

The camshaft and tappets are lubricated by engine oil. All the larger pumps, and increasing numbers of smaller pumps, are connected to the engine lubricating oil supply. The remaining small pumps have an initial fill

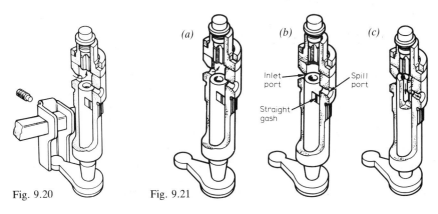

Fig. 9.20   Fig. 9.21

(a)   *(b)*   *(c)*

Inlet port

Spill port

Straight gash

of engine oil, which needs to be changed periodically owing to gradual dilution with fuel oil. Measures taken to reduce this leakage, past the elements, are described in Section 9.27.

9.26   Operation of the pumping elements

Towards the upper end of the plunger, a straight gash, inclined relative to the axis of the plunger, Fig. 9.21, communicates through radial and axial drillings with its upper end. In the barrel are two radial ports, one termed the *inlet port* and the other the *spill port*. They are not necessarily diametrically opposite one another, and are positioned so that the top face of the plunger, as it moves upwards, covers the uppermost port (or both if they are diametrically opposite) at a point when it approaches its maximum velocity, as determined by the cam profile. Consequently, the fuel that has entered the pumping space during the downward stroke is then cut off from the feed system so, during the remainder of the stroke, it is pressurised and forced through the delivery valve to the high pressure pipe. Displacement continues until the previously-mentioned straight gash begins to uncover the spill port whereupon, because of the interconnecting holes between the gash and top end, pressure will start to collapse and displacement of fuel therefore cease. Fuel displaced during the remainder of the stroke is returned to the fuel system.

The instant when the port, or ports, are just closed by the top face of the plunger is known as the *cut-off point* – in terms of plunger lift or cam angle – and the instant of just uncovering of the port by the plunger gash is known as the *spill point*. Obviously, the volume displacement of fuel, between cut-off and spill, can be varied from zero to a maximum, by rotating the plunger relative to the barrel, since this changes the spill point by moving it up or down the inclined edge of the gash. The rotation is effected, independently of the reciprocation, by the mechanism described in Section 9.25. With the arrangement described, the cut-off point of course is constant, regardless of fuel delivery. When the control rod, actuated by the governor, rotates the element, the delivery is increased or decreased by retarding or advancing the spill point in terms of lift or cam angle.

What has just been described is the normal arrangement. However, it is also possible to obtain constant termination of displacement of fuel by inclining the top edge of the plunger and having a circumferential spill groove. Intermediate effects can be obtained by inclining both edges. A slot can be milled in the upper face, in a position beyond that for the normal maximum displacement so that, by retarding the spill point, the injection can be retarded for cold starting. With such an arrangement, provision must also be made for supplying excess fuel, as described in Section 9.40.

9.27   Control of element leakage

At this point it is appropriate to describe the method of restricting leakage past the pumping elements. A circumferential groove is machined below the gash, in the plunger, Fig. 9.22. This groove connects with a spiral groove extending up towards but not breaking through the top face of the plunger. Fuel leaking downwards from the upper part of the plunger during pumping reaches this groove, which is so placed that, during the high-pressure injection part of the stroke, it is in communication with the feed system through the inlet port. The leakage is therefore prevented from progressing to the lower part of the barrel where it would pass into the cambox and dilute the lubricating oil.

9.28   Delivery valve

The delivery valve, shown in Fig. 9.23, serves an important purpose. It is a spring-loaded mitred-seating non-return valve, guided in its body by a close-fitting grooved shank. Its function is to prevent the pressure waves reflected back from the injector, during or after injection, from interfering with the subsequent injection cycle. The large fluctations in pressure due to these waves would cause the pipe line to be partially emptied between injections, or would prevent complete filling of the pumping space in the element in readiness for the next injection.

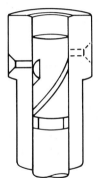

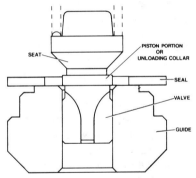

Fig. 9.22 CAV pumping element, spiral groove design

Fig. 9.23 Delivery valve and guide, with valve open

If, however, a simple valve were to be used it would, after closure, reflect the same pressure waves forward to the injector, probably causing secondary injections. Therefore, a plain cylindrical portion known as the *unloading collar* is machined on the valve, immediately below the seat. This, on closure of the valve, withdraws a predetermined volume of fuel from the line, thus moderating the forward reflections sufficiently to avoid secondary injection. The magnitude of this unloading volume has to be carefully chosen to match the parameters of the system.

Unloading also significantly affects the quantity of fuel that is delivered over a speed range with the pump control rod in a fixed position. So, to modify the shape of the torque-speed curve of the engine, a flat or other restricting passage is sometimes machined across the unloading collar.

9.29   Advance devices

An optional feature is a *centrifugal advance device*. This may be required for engines with a wide speed range, to improve performance by optimising injection advance. An example, mounted on the drive end of the Minimec pump, is illustrated in Fig. 9.19. It angularly displaces the camshaft relative to the drive shaft, or gear, as a function of speed. This displacement is determined by the centrifugal force produced by masses acting through cams or wedges to vary the relative angle between driving and driven members.

9.30   Majormec pump

As stated before, this pump is basically of the same construction as the Minimec. The pump and governor housings, however, are always separable to accommodate a variety of governors, and the pump must be driven from the end remote from the governor. Six- and eight-cylinder models are currently available.

9.31   Maximec pump

This is an up-rated and strengthened, long-life version developed from the Majormec unit. It was introduced to meet the requirements for engines of the largest cylinder sizes and highest ratings. To extend the maximum pressure capability and to reduce radiated noise, the cambox has been made extremely rigid. The length and diameter of the tappets have been increased, and the camshaft is carried in large taper roller bearings. This pump is available in four-, six-, eight- and twelve-cylinder forms. The six-cylinder unit is shown in Fig. 9.24.

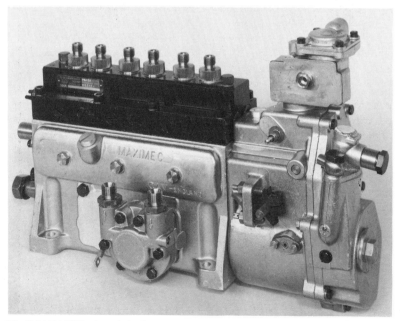

Fig. 9.24 CAV Maximec injection pump

9.32 CAV paper element filter

Filter elements of cloth, felt and other materials have been used, but an extremely efficient unit is the paper element filter produced by CAV. Its element comprises a double spiral of creped paper, V-convoluted and wound on to a core. This is contained in a cartridge, or metal canister.

The special filter paper is treated with resin, and is of high strength when wet. It has been shown that by reducing abrasive wear, the use of such a filter can increase the life of a fuel injection pump element by a factor of five. The spiral convoluted construction gives a large filtering area, and the life – limited by choking – is comparable to that of the older cloth or felt types.

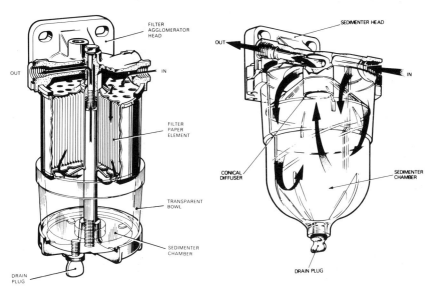

Fig. 9.25   Fig. 9.26

This CAV filter is designed also to trap water droplets, which agglomerate on the clean side of the element. It does so by virtue of the fact that the flow is downwards, so that the water falls into the base which, if required, can be fitted with a transparent bowl, or sleeve, of large volume, as shown in Fig. 9.25.

An additional water separator, for interposing upstream in the feed system, is also available for applications where severe water contamination is likely. This is shown in Fig. 9.26.

9.33   Control of engine speed

Generally some form of governor is used to control both the maximum and idling speeds of compression-ignition engines. This is necessary to limit the inertia stresses that arise from the acceleration of the massive moving parts and to maintain idling stability – since the system is inherently unstable at a fixed pump control setting.

With the petrol engine, a single 'authority' – the carburettor – is of course responsible for delivering a correct mixture, while the air flow, in effect, controls the petrol flow. In the compression-ignition engine, on the other hand, the air drawn in is normally dependent on the breathing characteristics of the cylinders, and varies with speed and operating temperature in a manner characteristic of the engine – the actual quantity of air drawn in per induction stroke decreases with increase of speed, as in a petrol engine.

The fuel delivered per injection is determined, quite independently, by the characteristics of the pump. Therefore, for a fixed control position, it will not fall sufficiently, as speed increases, to match the reduction in quantity of air drawn in per stroke. Consequently the 'matching' of the characteristics of engine and pump is difficult where it is necessary to provide for running at varying speeds at any fixed accelerator position or where, without limiting maximum torque at any speed, excessive fuel must not be injected – with its attendant waste, smoke and smell – at any combination of speed and accelerator position.

9.34   Mechanical or centrifugal governor

If the governor is designed merely to limit maximum speed, movement of its sleeve cannot take place until the centrifugal force developed by the revolving masses is sufficient to overcome the load of the control spring. Therefore it cuts down the fuel supply only at the pre-determined maximum speed.

Below this maximum, the accelerator pedal directly actuates the pump control rod. Lost motion arrangements allow the governor to over-ride the foot control at maximum speed. Another spring comes into action when the accelerator pedal is raised and the governor idling stop is reached. This type is known as an *idling-maximum* or *two-speed governor*.

Alternatively, direct connection between the accelerator pedal and pump control rod is dispensed with, so that all movements of the rod are performed by the governor under the control of a governor spring, the compression in which is determined by the position of the accelerator pedal. With such a system, the speed of the engine and vehicle is fixed by the position of the pedal, and the governor actuation spindle then moves the control rod to the position required to maintain, under the prevailing road conditions, the speed corresponding to the compression of the governor spring. This constitutes an *all-speed governor*.

In the Gardner execution of this type of governor, shown in Fig. 9.27, the mechanism is linked with an injection advance control which gives to one of a pair of helical driving gears a slight axial movement. This correspondingly changes the phase between the pump shaft and the driving shaft. The result is injection advance dependent on pedal position – which is not necessarily the same as on engine speed.

In Fig. 9.27, the arrows indicate the movements that would increase speed and injection advance. C is the chain sprocket on the engine camshaft, G_1 the wide camshaft gear and G_2 the sliding gear on the pump-shaft. S is a stopping lever acting directly on the pump control rod and M is a speed screw operated by hand, or remote control, to maintain

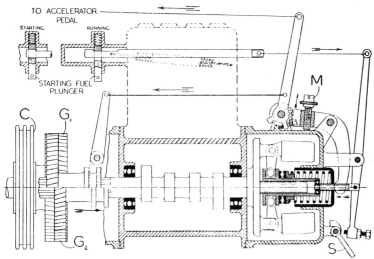

Fig. 9.27 Diagram of Gardner control

any steady speed desired. The last-mentioned feature is convenient for stationary or marine applications, or for testing.

9.35   Vacuum governor

Although formerly popular on the smaller engines, the vacuum governor has now become virtually obsolete. It fell out of fashion owing to inconsistency and ease of unauthorised adjustment. Moreover, it was associated with a risk of uncontrolled runaway should the engine inadvertently be caused to run backwards, for instance when stalled on a hill. Now, such engines have simplified forms of mechanical governor or, with distributor-type pumps, in-built hydraulic or mechanical governors.

9.36   Hydraulic governor

An hydraulic governor for in-line pumps was, until recently, manufactured by CAV but it has now been replaced by cheaper mechanical governors in association with the rationalised pumps described in Sections 9.24 to 31. Its unique feature was an ability to give very low idling speeds which, owing to the large amplitudes of rocking motion at low resonant speeds following the universal adoption of flexible mountings for road transport engines, became impracticable without it.

9.37   CAV governors for in-line pumps

The range of CAV governors covers the requirements for all the types of pump already described, and some are suitable for use with more than one of them. Each is basically an all-speed type, but those for road vehicles have the special characteristics required for this duty.

Fitted only to the Minimec pump and shown with it in the cut-away view, Fig. 9.19, is the GE. This is the simplest of the range. The centrifugal weight unit consists essentially of two dumb-bell like masses, driven by a U-shape member attached to the camshaft, carrying slippers sliding on inclined faces of a member that moves axially on an extension of the camshaft.

More recently, CAV has introduced an alternative governor, known as the C type. Its lever and spring-loading system, common with that of the GE unit, can be seen in Fig. 9.28, but the components peculiar to the C unit are shown more clearly in Fig. 9.29.

A cage having six pockets drives the weight unit. It is either riveted directly to the camshaft flange or, as in Fig. 9.28, has a cush drive to isolate it from torsional oscillations of the camshaft. Two, three, four or six weights can be fitted, pivoting on the outer inside corner of the pocket. A finger on each weight engages the sliding sleeve, which transmits the centrifugal force through a thrust race to the spring loading mechanism.

A compound leaf spring is employed. It is loaded against the thrust sleeve by a roller assembly which, moved up and down by a forked lever, runs between the spring and a fixed ramp attached to the governor cover. The forked lever is actuated by a linkage system connecting it to the driver's pedal.

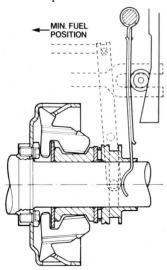

← MIN. FUEL
POSITION

Fig. 9.28 CAV C type governor

Movement of the roller not only regulates the reaction to the centrifugal force, and hence the position of the thrust sleeve at a given speed, but also varies the rate of the spring by shortening its effective length as the load is increased. By appropriate selection of ramp angle and position, the governor characteristics can be made to suit individual requirements at idling, intermediate and maximum speeds, without the need for auxiliary damping devices.

The movement of the thrust sleeve is transmitted to the pump control rod through the pivoted lever shown dotted in Fig. 9.28. Thus, this governor is of the all-speed variety, the driver setting the equilibrium speed

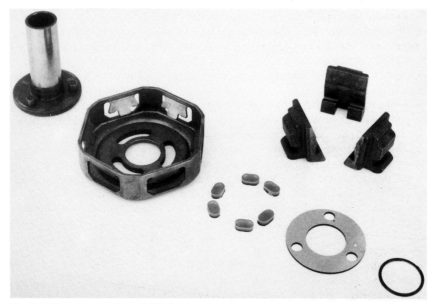

Fig. 9.29 Components of the CAV C type governor

by directly selecting the load on the spring. The variable-rate feature compensates for the normally unfavourable square law characteristic of a centrifugal governor, otherwise the governing would become progressively sharper as speed is increased, which is undesirable for road vehicles.

A former variant of the GE, known as the GX unit, had a conventional swinging weight unit to give additional governor force for some duties. The GM unit is a somewhat larger governor with two or four swinging weights, for the Majormec and Maximec pumps. It can have the leaf-spring loading system, as used with the GE and C, or an alternative tension spring, both having the variable spring-rate feature.

More recently, the GCS governor has been introduced for the more exacting duties of the Majormec and Maximec pumps. It is shown, with a boost control above, mounted on the Maximec pump in Fig. 9.24. The weight unit is that of the C type already described, however the thrust sleeve is not directly connected to the pump control rod but actuates it through an hydraulic servo, using engine oil as the pressure medium. In this way, high control rod forces are obtained without the need for large centrifugal forces. As a result, the compact and high quantity production C unit can be utilised.

9.38 Boost control

The incidence of turbocharging of vehicle engines has led to the need for a boost control. Such devices are available as an option for most of the previously-described governors.

Turbocharger characteristics are such that the maximum fuel the engine can take at low speeds is less than that at higher speeds. It is difficult to match this requirement with the natural delivery against speed characteris-

tic of the injection system, except with very moderate degree of turbocharging. Moreover, the slight lag in the response of the turbocharger,
when accelerating the engine rapidly from idling, causes an unacceptable
puff of smoke owing to excessive fuel delivery.

Both these difficulties may be overcome by replacing the fixed maximum
fuel stop in the normal governor by a moving stop whose position is a
function of boost pressure. This can be arranged to match the maximum
delivery of the pump to the ability of the engine to consume fuel without
smoke, both at steady speeds and when accelerating.

Such a device is attached to the top of the CAV GCS governor on the
Maximec pump illustrated in Fig. 9.24, and sections are shown in Fig. 9.30.
It is known as the BC 50. Manifold pressure, applied to the upper surface
of a rolling diaphragm attached to a guided spindle, acts against a spring.

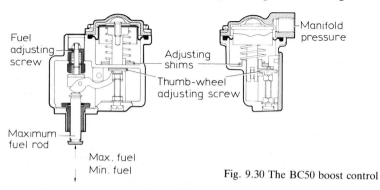

Fig. 9.30 The BC50 boost control

Movements establishing equilibrium are transmitted by a rocking lever to
another spindle, which replaces the normal fixed fuel stop. The limits of
the movement and the ultimate maximum position can be adjusted. Also
shown in the section is an optional spring-loaded stop for the maximum
fuel rod, which varies the maximum fuel as a function of governor force
and therefore of speed, thus providing a facility for shaping the delivery
curve over the upper part of the speed range – after the boost control has
reached its maximum position.

9.39   Torque control

Shaping the curve of maximum fuel against speed, so that the torque curve
falls as speed increases, can also be effected with any of the governors by
replacing their usual fixed maximum fuel stop by a spring-loaded stop
similar to that of the boost control. This is a common requirement for
tractor engines.

9.40   Excess fuel

An excess fuel feature is commonly provided to improve the cold starting
of the engine. Legislation requires that, to prevent excessive smoke
emission, this facility cannot be used by the driver whilst the vehicle is
moving.

The additional movement of the control rod for obtaining extra fuel is effected by a latch mechanism in the governor, which allows the normal maximum fuel stop to be over-ridden. However, it can be brought into operation only if the driver leaves his seat to operate it. This device, usually on the pump, is designed to latch out automatically as soon as speed rises after starting. Additionally, the design is usually such that the driver cannot set the device permanently into the excess fuel position. To meet all these requirements, several ingenious mechanisms, too detailed to describe in a few words, have been produced.

To satisfy requirements for excess fuel conditions, it is possible to retard the beginning of fuel injection, by modification to the pumping elements. This is done by milling a slot in the appropriate position in their upper faces.

9.41 CAV DPA pump

With the development of the smaller diesel engines, manufacturers soon realised that the cost of a multi-line fuel injection pump of the classic type was becoming a prohibitive proportion of the total engine cost, and that progress depended on the development of smaller, simpler and less costly equipment. Many other advantages are offered by the distributor type of pump, on which much development work has been done since its introduction. A schematic diagram of the complete system is shown in Fig. 9.31.

The DPA pump, manufactured by CAV and its licensees for some years, has more recently been developed further to increase its capability and to meet the special demands for compression-ignition engines for light vehicles and cars. It has a single pumping element, which serves all cylinders. Distribution to the individual injectors is effected by a rotor

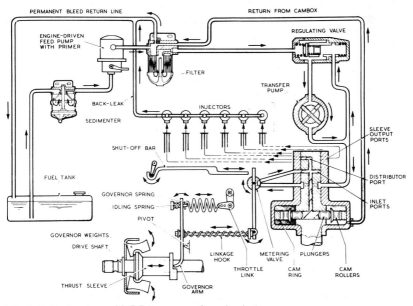

Fig. 9.31 Fuel system with DPA pump and mechanical governor

having a single inlet, and delivering in turn to the appropriate number of outlets. This ensures both uniformity of delivery to all injectors and in-built and exact uniformity of interval between successive injections. There are no adjustments to be made or maintained.

The pumping element consists of two plain opposed cylindrical plungers in a diametrical hole in the rotor head, an extension of which forms the distributor. An axial hole drilled in this extension connects the pumping chamber with a radial hole which registers in turn with radial delivery ports, one for each cylinder of the engine, in a steel sleeve in the 'hydraulic head', which is in an aluminium housing containing also the governor and control mechanism.

Fuel is delivered by a transfer pump through the pressure regulating and metering valves and an inlet port to force the pumping plungers apart with a metered volume of fuel. They are returned, to effect the injection, by lobes in an external cam ring, which is stationary except for a small angular movement within the pump housing to give automatic advance to the injection timing when required. The arrangement of the ducting for the incoming fuel is the inverse of that for delivery: that is, there is one radial hole in the hydraulic head and there are as many radial holes in the distributor rotor as there are engine cylinders, each passing the fuel into the axial hole, as shown in Fig. 9.32.

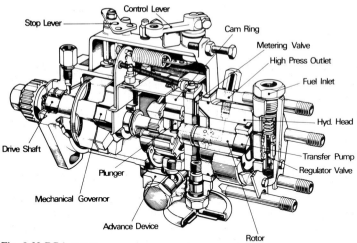

Fig. 9.32 DPA pump

Hardened rollers carried in sliding shoes are interposed between the pumping plungers and cam ring. Cam-shape lugs on the sides of the shoes register in corresponding slots in two rotatable side plates, to provide the adjustable 'maximum fuel stop' by limiting the outward movement of the pumping plungers, as shown in Figs. 9.33 and 9.34.

No ball or roller bearings, or return springs are required for the location or control of the moving parts, which are lubricated by the fuel oil delivered under controlled pressure by the transfer pump.

By virtue of these features of construction, significant reductions in cost and gains in performance have been obtained. The small mass of the

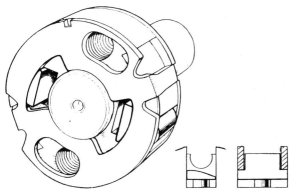

Fig. 9.33 The adjusting unit assembled for fitting

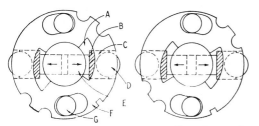

A   Cam-shaped slot
B   Lug on roller shoe
C   Roller shoe
D   Roller
E   Plunger
F   Adjusting plate
G   Locking screw hole
   in shoe carrier

Fig. 9.34 The method used to adjust the maximum travel of the plungers

pumping elements and absence of return springs for the pumping plungers enable higher speeds to be attained. Currently, the limit is about 12 000 deliveries per minute, the controlling factor being the ability to recharge the pump between successive injections. The only adjustment to be made by the engine builder is that of the maximum delivery stop, but even this is normally preset during testing of the pump by its manufacturer.

9.42   Governing metering and timing adjustment of the DPA pump

Variation of delivery with load is effected by the metering valve under the control of an 'all-speed' governor of either the mechanical or hydraulic type, the former having important merits of precision and flexibility of control, while the latter, Fig. 9.35, is more compact, simpler and less costly. A variant of the mechanical governor is available, which governs at idling and maximum speeds only.

The standard all-speed governors operate on the principles referred to in Sections 9.36 and 9.37. The accelerator pedal movement does not control directly the quantity injected, but only the *position* at which spring-load balances centrifugal force or hydraulic pressure. The required speed of the engine is then maintained automatically, no matter what the load, gradient or gear ratio of the transmission.

A mechanical governor is most commonly used. It is shown diagrammatically in Fig. 9.31 and, annotated appropriately, in Fig. 9.32. The hydraulic version differs only in that the mechanical governor and its attachment to a rotating metering valve is replaced by a reciprocating metering valve – spring-loaded by the control lever – which responds to a speed-sensitive pressure generated by the transfer pump.

With both types of governor, metering is effected by opening communication through a variable orifice between the transfer pump – under regulated pressure – and the injection plungers for an interval of time determined by the period of registration of each rotor inlet port, in turn, with the single port in the hydraulic head. This period of course varies with rotor speed, but the governor – mechanical or hydraulic – automatically adjusts the variable orifice so that, within that period, the required volume of fuel is delivered.

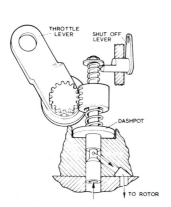

Fig. 9.35 Hydraulic governor

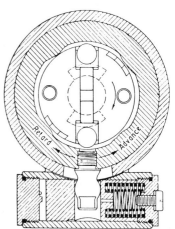

Fig. 9.36 The injection timing is controlled automatically by moving the cam ring

With either mechanical or hydraulic governoring, the pump is basically stable in the fixed metering valve condition – equivalent to fixed rack with the in-line pump. This is because, during the fixed angle of registration of the filling ports, the volume of fuel metered is inversely proportional to speed: for example, as speed is reduced by an increase in load, the time period for filling or metering is increased, and more fuel is metered. By virtue of this characeristic, good governing is obtained with relatively light forces.

The speed-dependent automatic injection timing advance device consists of a piston, subjected to transfer pressure, moving in a housing mounted under the pump body. Its motion, transmitted through a ball-ended screw, rotates the cam ring. Equilibrium is maintained by coaxial springs opposing the force of transfer pressure on the piston, Fig. 9.36. This timing device can be fitted to both the hydraulically- and mechanically-governed versions.

Fig. 9.37(*a*) and (*b*) show diagrammatically the operation of the regulating valve during priming, both when the transfer pump is at rest and during normal running. For priming, the separately-mounted fuel-feed pump is operated by hand and the free plunger piston is in equilibrium between the low pressure feed and the light priming spring. When the transfer pump

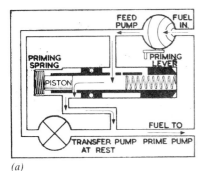
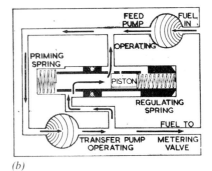

(a)   *(b)*

Fig. 9.37 Regulating valve

becomes operative, the stiffer regulating spring is in equilibrium between it and the high-pressure feed.

The spring characteristics and orifice arrangement determine the final torque/speed and advance/speed characteristics of the engine, and can be varied to suit the application. For diagrammatic convenience the valve is shown in the horizontal position. The actual setting in current models may be seen in Fig. 9.32.

9.43   Additional DPA features

A more recent development is the four-plunger pump, in which the two plungers of the standard pump are augmented by a further two for obtaining a higher rate and more rapid termination of injection. This requirement has arisen, in particular, to enable engines to meet stringent smoke, noise and emission legislation without sacrifice of power output.

The pump offers greater flexibility in choice of the injection-pressure pattern, by increasing the displacement rate without increasing mechanical stresses. For example, it has been found that engine timing can be retarded up to 6° without increase in smoke and with advantages in respect of both noise and emission levels. Alternatively, where stringent legislation does not apply, this pump can be used to give an increase in performance by providing higher injection pressure and increased fuel delivery within established reliability limits.

It is available for either four- or six-cylinder engines. The major difference by comparison with the standard pump is in the rotor head assembly. From Fig. 9.38 it can be seen that an additional pair of plungers is provided, and the spacing is 90° for four-cylinder engines, or 60° and 120° for six cylinders. This of course is to suit the spacing of the cam lobes. The four-plunger pump is suitable for engine applications up to about 20 kW/cylinder.

The standard device previously described advances injection as a function of speed, as indicated by the transfer pressure. It is commonly arranged to give a sharp retard when the engine, and therefore the pump, is rotated at cranking speeds. This is to optimise timing for cold starting – an alternative to excess fuel.

This same device can be arranged to advance injection with reduction of load, instead of speed, when necessary to counter the natural characteristic of the pump. This is done by utilising a pressure signal dependent on metering valve position.

To meet the requirements laid down by legislation, particularly regarding gaseous emissions, an injector-advance device sensitive to both speed and load has become necessary. A more recent development, therefore, has been the introduction of advance devices sensitive to both speed and load signals independently. In some instances these devices are designed to have non-linear characteristics.

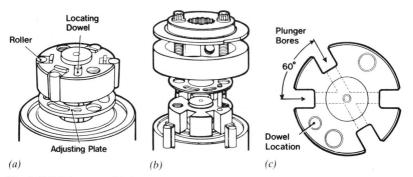

Fig. 9.38 DPA pump with four-plunger head and rotor. (a) Roller and shoe assemblies, (b) head and rotor assembly, (c) end view of rotor

With the DPA pump, provision can be made for delivering excess fuel. Although the optimisation of timing for cold starting is usually sufficient for direct injection engines and all but the smallest indirect injection units, generally the latter have either combustion chamber heater plugs or external devices for heating induction air during cold starting. With the introduction of very small indirect injection engines for cars and light vehicles came a need for both optimum timing and excess fuel, since the high surface:volume ratio of the small cylinders leads to particular difficulty in cold starting. Features are therefore incorporated for excess fuel to be both supplied and cut off automatically.

9.44   Representative designs of ci engine

An outstandingly successful example of the direct injection type is the Gardner LW engine, built in three-, four-, five- and six-cylinder forms, all of 107.95 mm bore and 152.4 mm stroke to develop about 13.67 kW per cylinder at maximum governed speed of 1700 rev/min with a best bmep of about 703.27 kN/m^2.

The meticulous care and skill devoted to the manufacture of the engines and injectors have resulted in an engine of proved reliability which has been adopted as the power unit by a large number of commercial vehicle manufacturers. To meet the challenge of the demand for a still lighter and higher speed engine, the makers, Norris Henty & Gardners Ltd., later produced the 4 LK engine of 95.25 mm bore and 133.35 mm stroke, which develops 39.5 kW on a rising curve at 2000 rev/min governed speed.

At the bare engine weight (without electrical equipment) of 261 kg, the specific weight is 6.61 kg/kW. This engine is in successful use in the lighter types of commercial vehicles, replacing the 3 LW unit which develops about the same power but at a lower speed. The fuel pump used on all Gardner engines was originally of a type modified to incorporate special priming levers. The arrangements for altering the compression at starting are as follows.

A compression control lever is provided for each pair of cylinders as shown at L in Fig. 9.39. This operates a gear quadrant meshing with a gear pinion mounted on the end of a control shaft C lying under the push rod end of the valve rockers.

The shaft C carries radial cams for lifting each inlet valve rocker through the adjusting studs S and a face cam F, which in one position of the lever L moves the rocker of No. 1 inlet valve to the left against the coil spring R, thus bringing the offset portion O of the rocker end over the valve stem. This offset end is stepped so as to increase the tappet clearance to about 1.5 mm. There is a further slight increase due to the tilting of the push rod as its cupped upper end moves over with the rocker.

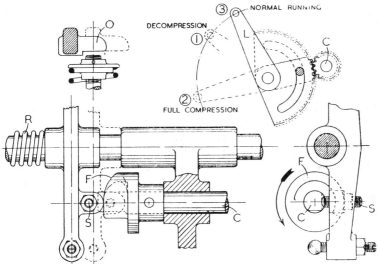

Fig. 9.39 Gardner compression control

The effect of this increase of tappet clearance is to make the closing of the inlet valve earlier, and thus give an effective compression ratio corresponding to the full swept volume of the cylinder.

The accompanying later opening and reduced lift of the valve do not, at the low speed of cranking, have any appreciable strangling effect on the induction.

The radial cams are provided for all cylinders, and consist simply of clearance flats on the control shaft C, rotation of which causes the adjusting studs S to ride on to the cylindrical portion and so raise the rockers. The corresponding positions of the control levers are shown in the diagram in Fig. 9.39.

The first position (1) gives complete decompression by holding the inlet valves off their seats during initial cranking. Position (3) is the normal running position with the starting control cut out.

The face cam is ordinarily provided for No. 1 cylinder only, and is brought into action in position (2) of the lever to give higher compression in that cylinder in order to obtain the first impulse. The control levers may be operated by a common grouped control or independently, as may be most suitable for the particular installation. It may be found convenient to keep a pair of cylinders decompressed until the starting cylinders have got well away.

Fig. 9.40 shows an exterior view of the near side of the 5 LW engine. A feature which should be noted is the deep and rigid crankcase structure extending well below the crankshaft centre line. The sump is an electron

Fig. 9.40 Gardner 5LW engine

casting. The cylinder block is in two separate portions of three and two cylinders, and the special CAV injection pump is assembled from corresponding units. On the injection pump are five priming levers, one for each cylinder, to actuate the plungers in the pump. The delivery pipes to the injectors are of approximately equal length.

9.45 Perkins P3 diesel engine

The application of the compression ignition engine to lighter vehicles was originally delayed by the fact that injection and combustion difficulties increase greatly with diminution in size of cylinder. This has stimulated interest in the use of a reduced number of cylinders for the lower powers.

The Perkins P3 engine has been developed as a substitute or conversion unit for certain tractors and light commercial vehicles where the flat torque characteristics and operational economy of the diesel engine are decisive

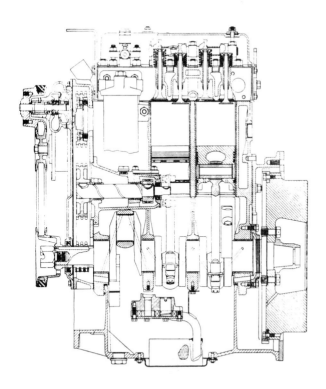

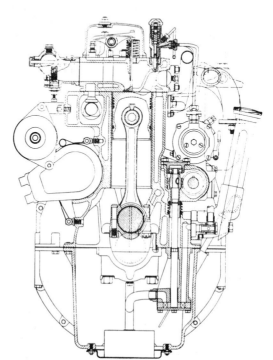

Fig. 9.41 Perkins P3 engine

factors in the choice of the power unit. Suitably limited power is obtained without the difficulties that are experienced with small cylinder and injection equipment, and a simplified servicing system and rationalised manufacture are made possible by the use of standardised general engine parts in the P3, P4 and P6 engines.

The P3 is half the P6 engine, the special parts required being confined to those depending on the length of the engine, such as crankshaft, cylinder block and sump.

The overall dimensions have proved very convenient for installation in the space occupied by the alternative petrol engine, and the high reputation of the engine has led to a considerable demand for the P3 as a conversion unit both in the UK and abroad.

Longitudinal and cross-sectional views of the engine are shown in Fig. 9.41, from which the sturdy and yet compact design will be noted. Dry cylinder liners are fitted into a nickel or chromium cast iron block which extends from the head face to the crankshaft centre-line in the conventional manner.

The bore and stroke are 89.9 mm and 127 mm respectively and the connecting rods are 228.6 mm long between centres.

The sturdy four-bearing crankshaft is of forged steel, the four main journals being Tocco hardened.

With three cranks at 120° pitch there are no primary or secondary unbalanced reciprocating forces, and the rotating couple is balanced by the two attached balance weights on the end crank webs. Primary and secondary reciprocating couples remain to be absorbed by the engine mounting, and this disadvantage and the massive flywheel required to absorb the variations in turning moment are the penalties to be paid for the convenience of the three-cylinder lay-out.

9.46 Thornycroft 11.33-litre diesel

This engine was intended for the heaviest commercial applications, particularly in undeveloped areas.

Designed robustly with the view of its installation in the naturally aspired form (KRN6) or turbo-blower supercharged (KRN6/S), the design follows well established principles in the construction of British direct-injection engines.

The general construction follows that shown in Fig. 6.26 adapted to diesel requirements with dry cylinder liners and crankcase extended well below the crankshaft centre line. This construction, while involving more, but readily accessible, machining processes, is also well adapted to variations of assembly, handing and mounting for special requirements; the separate components are lighter and more easily handled.

The crankshaft is without integral balance weights in order to save weight, but at the moderate speeds involved, mirror symmetry, combined with the generous proportions of the shaft and crankcase ensures vibration-free running. A torsional vibration damper of the Holset steel-rubber bonded type is bolted to the first crank web as will be seen from Fig. 9.42. The crankshaft is nitride hardened on journals and pins.

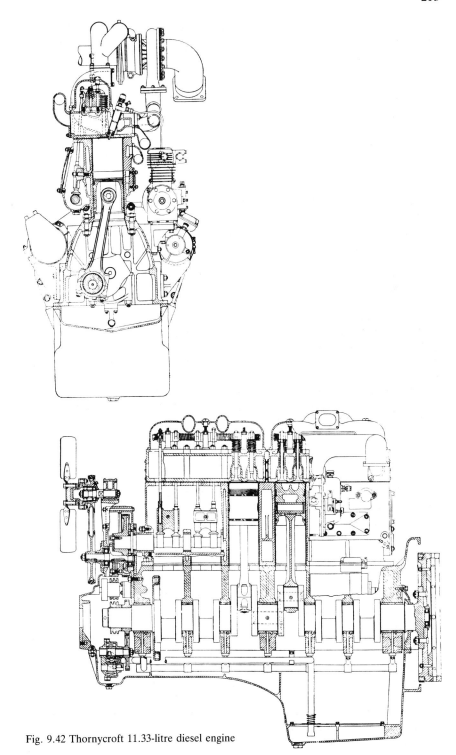

Fig. 9.42 Thornycroft 11.33-litre diesel engine

Steel-backed, prefinished, copper lead lined bearings are used through-out, with the exception of the small end of the connecting rod, where a phosphor bronze bush is fitted. A floating gudgeon pin is end-located by Seeger circlips. The camshaft bearings are of aluminium alloy.

The Wellworthy pistons are of tin-plated Lo-Ex aluminium alloy, and are of the solid skirt type, with an offset toroidal cavity in the crown. The valve gear follows conventional design, the valve stems working in phosphor bronze guides in the cast-iron cylinder head.

The timing gear, which is of mixed chain and gear design, is described in Section 6.48. The case is separate from the main crankcase casting, to facilitate the provision of right- or left-hand assemblies – referred to above.

Performance curves and further particulars are given in Chapter 13 on Supercharging, and the reader will find a comprehensive description in *Automobile Engineer*, Vol. 47, No. 2.

9.47   Comparative merits of spark ignition and ci engines

In spite of the inherent disadvantages of greater weight and bulk per horsepower and rougher running, the ci engine has fully consolidated its position. Greater economy, greater security from risk of fire, and with modern bearing materials and methods of manufacture a degree of general reliability which is not less than that of the petrol engine, are definitely attained.

The injection equipment, provided proper care is taken with filtration of the fuel, is proving itself more reliable than the electrical equipment of the spark-ignition engine. Overheating troubles are less for, owing to the higher thermal efficiency, the heat losses, both to the jackets and to the exhaust, are smaller than with the petrol engine. Flexibility, silence and smooth running still leave something to be desired, but as knowledge of the injection and combustion processes increases, so will the smoothness of performance improve.

Because of the greater gas-loadings, diesel engine components are heavier, and therefore the engines themselves bigger, than comparable petrol engines. Moreover, in a diesel engine cylinder, since there is only an extremely brief interval after the start of injection for the fuel to mix with the air, only about 75% of the total throughput of air can be burnt. Otherwise, because of local concentration of rich mixture, black smoke will be emitted from the exhaust. Consequently, for a diesel engine to produce the same power as a petrol unit, either it must have a larger swept volume or, if it is required to be of the same size, a larger charge must be forced into its cylinders. This is usually done by turbocharging.

The injection pump is more difficult both to accommodate and to drive than the ignition contact breaker-distributor unit. Another factor that makes the diesel engine larger is that, in commercial vehicle operation, it has to operate with even greater reliability for long distances, and therefore must be sturdier. The problem of compactness has been solved by some manufacturers by adopting the V-six or V-eight layout. Since the arguments for the use of the V layout have been outlined already, in connection with the petrol engines, Section 6.58, there is no need to repeat them here. For commercial vehicles, the main difference is that the compact form is required in order to leave the maximum possible space free for the load-carrying platform. There are also some types of installation, for example, transverse rear engine, where a power unit of short length reduces the angularity required in the drive line to the rear axle. Among the engines of this type are the AEC 800 unit, described in *Automobile Engineer*, October 1968, the Cummins V-six and V-eight engines, and the Perkins V-8.510 unit, described in *Automobile Engineer*, January 1967.

First cost of both engines and injection equipment remains high, owing to the meticulous care required in manufacture, but for the commercial user whose vehicles cover a high annual mileage, particularly on long runs, saving in fuel costs results in a rapid recovery of initial expenditure.

In special cases it may be possible to approach, by raising the compression ratio of the petrol engine, the efficiency of the ci engine, but this is possible only by the use of very expensive and special fuels, as the requirements of the vapour compression (spark-ignition) engine become increasingly exacting with increase of compression ratio, though rotary valve engines appear to be exceptions to this generalisation.

For equal thermal efficiency the spark-ignition engine does not require quite such a high compression ratio as the ci engine, and maximum pressures would be about the same. Thus weight per unit of cylinder volume would tend to be the same.

The question of fuels for compression-ignition engines is dealt with in Chapter 14.

Chapter 10

The two-stroke engine

The limitations of power output given by the four-stroke cycle for a cylinder of given size running at a given speed have led designers to seek an alternative cycle which should eliminate the idle exhaust and charging strokes which occupy one complete revolution of the crankshaft. These two strokes and the corresponding crankshaft revolution may be regarded as interpolated between the active firing stroke and the idle, though necessary, compression stroke of the following cycle.

If the exhaust of the old charge and the introduction of the new could be accomplished while the piston is passing the outer or bottom dead centre without sacrificing any great portion of the combustion or compression strokes, then a useful working stroke would be obtained for every revolution of the crankshaft instead of every alternate revolution, and the engine would develop twice the power of the four-stroke cycle engine provided the speed, mean effective pressure, and mechanical efficiency remained the same. In most cases very much less than this doubled power is obtained, for it is quite impossible with the ordinary two-stroke engine to obtain such high mean effective pressures as with the four-stroke cycle for reasons which will be explained presently. Nor is the mechanical efficiency of the two-stroke engine so high when the pumping losses are included with the mechanical friction losses. The net result is that most two-stroke engines give only from 10 to 40% more power than four-stroke types of the same piston displacement running at the same speed, while fuel economy is in most cases greatly inferior to that of the four-stroke engine.

However, greater mechanical simplicity and consequent cheapness of manufacture, more uniform turning moment arising from the smaller interval of time between the combustion impulses, leading to a reduction in the necessary weight of the flywheel, and greater mechanical silence, have made the two-stroke engine popular in cases where moderate power is required and where high fuel economy is not essential. Its widest fields of application at present, apart from certain large stationary and marine types, are to the small motor cycle and to the small motor boat, in which latter application it is usually made in the twin-cylinder water-cooled form.

To return to the means of obtaining a complete cycle of operations in two strokes or one revolution of the crankshaft it will be found that as the crankshaft turns from 45° before the outer or bottom dead centre to 45° after it, that is to say, through one-quarter of a revolution, the piston 'dwells' within less than one-eighth of its stroke from the bottom dead point. This quarter revolution, or in some cases considerably more, is devoted in two-stroke engines to the exhaust of the old charge, usually through a port or ports cut through the cylinder wall and communicating with the exhaust pipe or silencer, when the port or ports are uncovered by the top of the piston towards the bottom end of its stroke.

The exhaust gases escape for the most part by virtue of the excess of their own pressure over that in the silencer or atmosphere, but the final clearing or 'scavenging' of the cylinder, since it cannot be done by the return of the piston, as in the four-stroke engine, must be accomplished by the introduction under a slight pressure of scavenge air. This scavenge air may or may not carry with it the necessary fuel for the succeeding combustion, the variations between the many designs of two-strokes in use consisting in the means employed for the introduction of the scavenge air and fuel. In all cases, however, the whole or major part of the scavenge air is introduced while the exhaust ports are open, and if this air carries with it the fuel vapour, as is the case with volatile liquid or gaseous fuels, there is a serious risk of loss of some portion of the fuel charge through the exhaust ports. In cases of bad design the proportion becomes excessive and is one of the main reasons for the high fuel consumption of the two-stroke engine.

The introduction of the scavenge air with or without fuel requires some form of scavenge pump which may consist of a separate pump cylinder with its piston operated from the crankshaft and usually of somewhat greater capacity than the working cylinder, or the main crankcase may be made air-tight and the displacement of the under side of the main piston be used to form a pump of the same displacement capacity. A third system is to use a rotary blower of the displacer type or a high-speed centrifugal fan, just as in supercharging a four-stroke engine.

In recent years, the paramount requirement for fuel economy and the passing of laws restricting the proportions of unburnt hydrocarbons in the exhaust, Section 11.58, have precluded the installation of two-stroke petrol engines in road vehicles. Another factor has been the inherent tendency of these engines, in some forms, to fire irregularly under idling and light load conditions, as pointed out in Section 10.4. Consequently, most of the examples described in this Chapter are primarily only of historical interest, so far as automotive application is concerned.

However, now that four-stroke diesel engines are increasingly common-ly turbocharged to improve overall economy, objections to the blown two-stroke diesel on grounds of its complexity are to some extent nullified. Moreover, some manufacturers believe that to meet future legislation requirements even petrol engines will need injection equipment instead of carburettors. So, in view of the potential for drastically reducing hydrocarbon emissions by injection after the inlet ports are closed, and the demands for higher power from smaller, lighter engines, together with low specific fuel consumption, a revival of practical interest in the two-stroke unit could occur.

10.1   Three-port two-stroke engine

Fig. 10.1 shows in simple diagram-form the Day three-port engine. The exhaust port is shown at E, this being uncovered by the piston after completion of about 80% of its stroke. The transfer port T, through which the charge is pumped from the crankcase, opens slightly later than the exhaust port, as shown in 1, to reduce the risk of hot exhaust gas passing into the crankcase and igniting the new charge. It follows that the transfer port is closed by the rising piston slightly before the exhaust port, so that the final pressure in the cylinder, and therefore the total quantity of charge (consisting of a mixture of burnt gases, air and fuel vapour) is determined not by the pump delivery pressure but only by the extent to which the

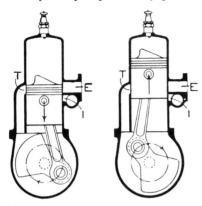

Fig. 10.1 Three-port two-stroke engine

throttling and pulse effects of the exhaust pipe, silencer, etc., raise the cylinder pressure above that of the atmosphere. The piston head is specially shaped to deflect the entering gases to the top of the cylinder. This is known as *cross-flow scavenge*.

The piston rises and compresses the charge, after which it is ignited and expands in the usual way. The indicator diagram takes the form shown at (*a*) in Fig. 10.2, which differs from that of the four-stroke cycle only in the rather more sudden drop of pressure as the exhaust ports are uncovered and the elimination of the 'bottom loop' showing the exhaust and suction strokes. This bottom loop is replaced, of course, by the indicator diagram, shown at (*b*), obtained from the crank case or scavenge pump cylinder. There is no possibility of eliminating this pump work from either the four-stroke or the two-stroke cycle – in one case it is done in alternate revolutions in the main working cylinder, and in the other in every revolution in the scavenge pump cylinder. Indeed, the 'phased pump' type of two-stroke engine, of which a later example is the Trojan design as shown in Fig. 10.5, may be regarded as a V-twin four-stroke engine in which the positive work is concentrated in one cylinder and the negative pumping work is done in the other, instead of each cylinder doing half of both.

To return to the Day type of engine (Fig. 10.1), it is necessary now to describe how the charge is drawn into the crankcase from the carburettor.

As the piston rises, a partial vacuum is formed in the crankcase, the pressure becoming steadily lower until, near the top its stroke, the rising piston uncovers the induction port 1, which communicates with the carburettor, as shown in 2. Air rushes in to fill the vacuum and carries with it the petrol from the jet necessary to form a combustible mixture. It will be realised that the suction impulse on the jet is a violent one of short duration – the very worst from the point of view of obtaining a correct and homogeneous mixture – while the time interval during which the induction port is open is also unduly short from the point of view of the inspiration of a full charge of air. Fig. 10.2 (c) shows a typical timing diagram of the various port openings and closings expressed in degrees of crank angle.

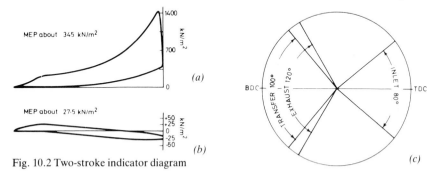

Fig. 10.2 Two-stroke indicator diagram

An alternative to the piston-controlled induction port which is used in many two-stroke heavy-oil engines is the light spring-controlled automatic air valve. This valve remains open for practically the whole of the upward or suction stroke of the piston, ensuring higher volumentric efficiency though at the cost of an additional moving part. The American Gray motor, extensively used for marine work in the water-cooled form, employs both port and automatic valve.

10.2   Reverse-flow scavenge. DKW engine

An interesting and successful example of the three-port engine using 'reverse-flow' or 'inverted' scavenge is the German DKW small car engine. This is a twin cylinder unit of 76mm bore and 76mm stroke, using crankcase displacement, but having twin transfer ports, one each side of the exhaust port, and imparting a tangential and upward flow to the entering charge.

The piston deflector is dispensed with, thus eliminating pressure and inertia tilt due to lack of symmetry – a source of two-stroke rattle – and the direction of scavenge flow becomes somewhat as indicated in Fig. 10.3. By the provision of ports through the piston skirt the transfer passages are kept short, but as an additional change of direction is involved it is doubtful if the transfer resistance is appreciably reduced as compared with the arrangement of Figs. 10.1 and 10.4.

The makers carried out comparative tests of the two methods of scavenge, and at 3000 rev/min they improved the bmep by 14% by converting to the reverse-flow system.

The Villiers Company successfully applied this principle, but in a modified form, using two pairs of transfer ports and two exhaust ports in

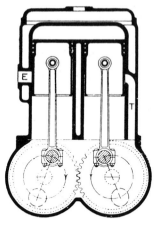

Fig. 10.3 (*left*) DKW engine
Fig. 10.4 (*right*) Lucas engine

their well-known air-cooled motor-cycle engines. From their 249 cm³
engine 8.95 kW has been obtained at 5000 rev/min, which represents a
bmep of 427.5 kN/m².

10.3 Special constructions of two-stroke engine

The loss of efficiency arising from the loss of new charge through the
exhaust ports, which occurs in these simple port constructions, has led to
the use of a double-piston form of engine in which two pistons working in
twin barrels side by side share a common combustion chamber and
sparking plug. There is, of course, only one impulse or firing stroke per
revolution, no matter what particular arrangement of connecting rods and
cranks is employed. The Lucas engine (Fig. 10.4) is now no longer made
but it had interesting and ingenious features.

The two pistons drive independent connecting rods operating on separate cranks, which are arranged to run together by means of gear teeth cut
in the periphery of the circular crank webs. The flywheel and clutch are
connected to one of these cranks only, so that half the power necessarily
passes through the gear teeth. The cranks clearly revolve in opposite
directions, and use is made of this fact to obtain complete primary balance.
Each crank assembly is provided with revolving balance weights corresponding to the whole of the revolving and reciprocating parts for one line.
This ensures primary balance in the vertical plane as explained in Chapter
5, while the unwanted horizontal effects of the two revolving balance
weights neutralise each other, exactly as in the Lanchester harmonic
balancer, which, however, deals with secondary unbalanced forces.

With the twin cylinder-barrel in this arrangement one piston may be
used to control the transfer port T while the other uncovers the exhaust E,
and in this way the new charge has to traverse the full length of both barrels
before there is any possibility of its escaping out of the exhaust port.

Further, it is possible, by suitably meshing the gear wheels, to arrange that the exhaust port is given a 'lead' which results in its opening *and* closing somewhat ahead of the corresponding events of the transfer port, thus tending to give a more complete cylinder charge. If this is done, however, the advantage of exact primary balance will be affected.

10.4 Separate phased pump

The reader will have realised, in considering the characteristics of simple crankcase displacement, that the swept volume available for induction is the same as that of the main cylinder, namely, the piston area multiplied by the stroke, and, moreover, that the charge is not transferred to the cylinder simultaneously with the pump displacement, but in a rush after pre-compression. This causes the indicated pumping work to be high, and though some of this energy is no doubt usefully applied to producing a warmed and homogeneous mixture as a result of the turbulence, there is risk of admixture with the old charge and loss of fuel through the exhaust port.

Both the quantity and, especially at light loads, the quality of the mixture suffer, leading to limited power output and high specific fuel consumption.

These considerations have led many designers to have recourse to the separate charging pump, which is driven usually by a separate crank placed in appropriate phase relationship with the main crank.

10.5 Trojan engine

The redesigned Trojan engine retained a twin-barrel construction success-fully used in the original model, but, instead of crankcase compression scavenge, the phased charging pump was adopted, in combination with piston-controlled tansfer and exhaust ports.

As result of this change, a normal lubrication system can be used, and the necessity for pressure sealing of the crankcase is obviated.

In early development of the new engine, a mechanically-driven, cylin-drical distribution valve was used, but this was subequently replaced by light, spring-blade automatic valves.

The general construction should be clear from the two sectional views given in Fig. 10.5, while Fig. 10.6 shows to a larger scale the details of the interesting automatic valves.

The bore of the working barrels is 65.5 mm and of the charger cylinders 96.8 mm, the stroke of all being nominally 88 mm, but owing to the off-set cylinder axes, the actual stroke is fractionally greater than twice the crank throw in each case, different off-sets being used for the three bores.

The nominal swept volume of the power cylinders is therefore 1186 cm^3, or the equivalent of two cylinders of 92.6 mm bore, while that of the pump cylinders is 1293 cm^3, thus providing a 9% displacement margin.

The effect of the cylinder off-sets, combined with the relative position of the leading edges of the ports, is to give the exhaust period, with a duration of 106°, a lead over the 104° inlet period, of about 22°, the overlap being about 83°.

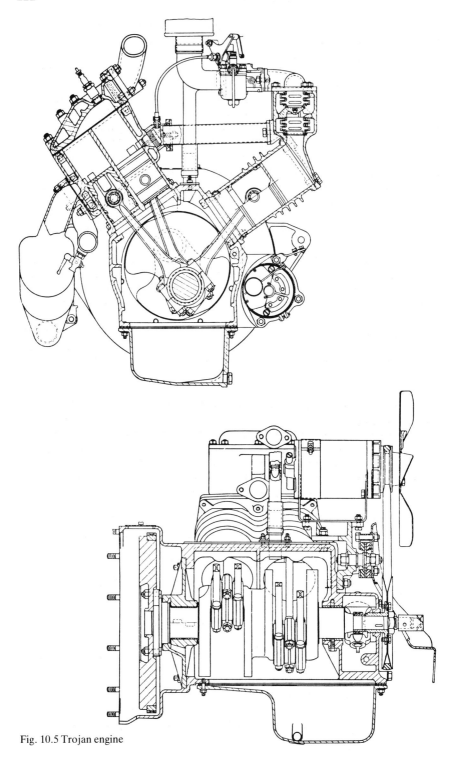

Fig. 10.5 Trojan engine

The off-set of the pump axis not only reduces the obliquity of thrust on the delivery stroke, but advances the stroke timing by about 8° relatively to the 90° at which the cylinders are set. By the use of a single transfer pipe and twinned inlet ports for the two sets, No. 1 charging cylinder delivers to No. 2 pair of working bores and *vice versa*.

All the six connecting rods are identical, and each pair of aluminium alloy main pistons with their small ends are made identical in weight with the corresponding cast-iron piston of the charging cylinder. Dynamic balance is thus secured on the principle described in the latter part of Section 5.2, the necessary balance masses being incorporated in the cast crankshaft of Mehanite iron. There is a slight discrepancy due to the off-set bores, and the secondaries remain unbalanced, but neither of these gives rise to serious vibration.

One cage of the automatic valve assembly is shown partly exploded in Fig. 10.6. The upper inlet cage is identical with the lower delivery cage, the 'air-flow' being radially outwards in both cases.

Two tiers each of three spring blades V form the valves, which bear on faces machined to an eccentric radius on the outside of the aluminium alloy body B. The pressed steel retainers R exercise a minimum constraint for the location of the spring blades, which have less free curvature than have the retainers, with the result that when blown open by the air-flow the blades are strained against the retainers, and spring back sharply to the closed position on reversal of the flow. The rolled ends of the blades minimise friction under the relative motion. The total area of the six ports is about 6.45 cm².

The flame trap, consisting of four thicknesses of gauze, may be noticed at the junction of the transfer pipe and transfer port, with a petrol priming pipe to aid starting.

A representative set of performance curves is shown in Fig. 10.7, a most valuable feature being the excellent maintenance of torque at low speeds. This results in very good top gear performance, reflected in satisfactory mpg consumption figures, though the specific fuel consumption on the bench is higher than normal four-stroke figures.

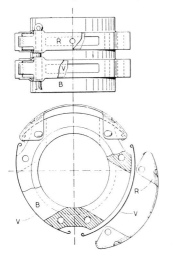

Fig. 10.6 (*left*) Trojan automatic valves and cage

Fig. 10.7 (*below*) Trojan performance curves

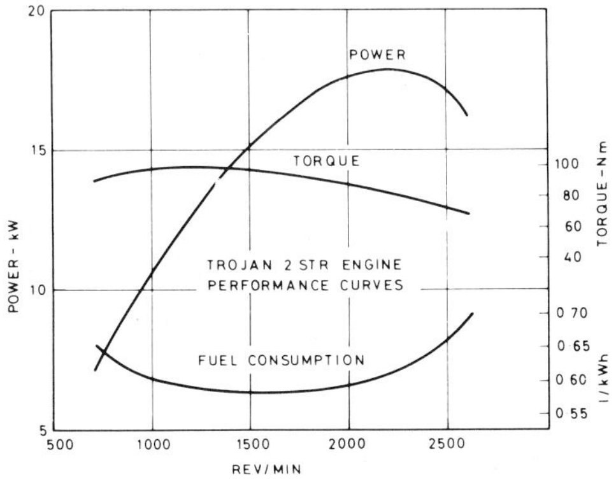

10.6 Kadenacy system

The scavenging systems of large two-stroke diesel engines, essentially of the stationary constant speed type, have been the subject of intensive theoretical investigation and practical experiment.

An authoritative work by P. H. Schweitzer, *Scavenging of Two-stroke Cycle Diesel Engines,* and published by The Macmillan Company of New York, deals exhaustively with the mathematical and practical aspects of design involved in the efficient utilisation of exhaust gas energy in scavenging and charging engines with and without blowers.

The phrase 'Kadenacy effect' has been extensively and somewhat loosely used to describe pulse phenomena that have been utilised with varying degrees of success in different designs, often showing little similarity with the patent specifications.

In Schweitzer's work the Kadenacy system is described as basically the development of a high degree of vacuum in the cylinder by the sudden and very rapid release of the charge through sharp-edged exhaust ports of large area, this depression being sufficient to aspire the new charge without the necessity of a positive blower or pump.

Kadenacy British Patents Nos. 308,593 and 308,594, which relate to small engines of the automobile type, cover a variety of claims relating to cylinder porting, a somewhat elaborately ported piston working in a cylinder provided with inlet and exhaust belts each ported round the full circumference of the cylinder as shown in Fig. 10.8 (*a*) and several claims of a different nature involving the use of light automatic non-return valves in both inlet and exhaust ports, a mechanically-operated sleeve valve as shown in Fig. 10.8 (*b*) and a mechanically-operated inlet valve.

An opposed-piston design is also covered.

The early type of deflector piston, liable to distortion and to cause two-stroke rattle, is replaced by flat-topped pistons in all cases.

The possibility of dispensing with a scavenge blower is suggested in the valve operated designs, but not with the simple ported constructions, except under favourable conditions of steady speed and load.

Poppet exhaust-valve engines such as the General Motors and Foden designs can hardly be said to use the above fundamental Kadenacy principle, the Kadenacy effect in these instances being rather a sustained extractor effect due to the moving column in the exhaust, as in the four-stroke engine with valve timing overlap.

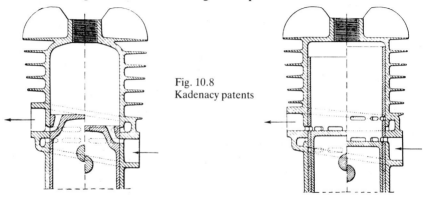

Fig. 10.8
Kadenacy patents

10.7 Loop scavenge, Schnuerle system

The term *loop scavenge* is associated with Schnuerle and other patents, and is usually indicated diagrammatically as shown in Fig. 10.3 applied to the DKW engine, in which case the less common designation *reverse flow* is used.

Schnuerle patents cover also a variety of exhaust pipe systems in which the extractor and non-return effects of a volute form initiating vortex flow are described.

These ideas were developed and exploited in the small two-stroke engines used in Continental Europe for the popular family car of small cost.

10.8 Exhaust pulse charging

Though not fully applicable to the variable speeds and loads of automobile engines, this important development by Crossley Bros. and H. D. Carter, described in *Proc. Inst. Mech. E.*, Vol. 154, should be mentioned.

In multi-cylinder stationary diesel engines, by providing a 'tuned' exhaust system, the high-pressure pulse from the initial exhaust of each cylinder is utilised to 'pack up' the fresh charge in an adjacent cylinder which has reached the last portion of the exhaust port opening period.

Thus the first portion of a new, relatively low-pressure charge may be caught as it is entering the exhaust pipe, where the mean pressure again may be low, and be forced back into the cylinder to raise the density of the charge finally trapped. In a single-cylinder engine it may be possible to produce a suitable wave pulse by reflection from an appropriate face of the exhaust manifold.

10.9 Uniflow scavenging. Opposed-piston engines

Uniflow scavenging occurs in any design in which the inlet and exhaust ports or valves are situated at opposite ends of the cylinder bore, as in the poppet exhaust and sleeve-valve constructions, but more particularly, and with simpler cylinder construction, in the opposed-piston engine.

10.10 Compression-ignition two-stroke engine

Since in the compression-ignition engine no fuel enters the cylinder until all ports and valves are closed, and cannot therefore be lost through the exhaust ports, one of the greatest objections to the two-stroke cycle is eliminated, and it is with this type of engine that the cycle tends to make greatest progress.

There is another important merit of the high-compression ci engine in its application to the two-stroke form. The high expansion ratio results in lower exhaust temperature and reduced waste heat, and thus the inherent cooling difficulties of the cycle arising from doubled heat flow are less than with the petrol engine.

This factor, combined with the unidirectional scavenge with cool air over piston head and valves, appears to have justified the development work that has been devoted over the years to the port scavenge, poppet valve exhaust two-stroke engine, which attained a considerable degree of success.

At first sight the type appears to perpetuate one of the chief weaknesses of the four-stroke engine, the highly stressed and heated exhaust valve, in addition to the mechanical complication of camshaft and valve operating gear. Experience seems to show that, owing to the favourable conditions described above, the valves give remarkably little trouble.

10.11   Rotary blower and poppet exhaust valves

An interesting example of this construction is the three-cylinder General Motors engine shown in Fig. 10.9. In the six-cylinder form this engine was used during the Second World War in a variety of military applications, including the Sherman tank.

The engine illustrated has a bore and stroke of 107.95 and 127 mm, and a compression ratio of 16:1. The continuous rated output is 47.7 kW at 1600 rev/min with a fuel consumption of 0.2735 kg/kWh while the maximum output is given as 59.6 kW at 1800 rev/min.

The corresponding values of the bmep are 482.6 and 572.3 kN/m² respectively. These ratings would be applicable to marine propulsion or similar duties.

The high camshaft and the three-lobed Roots blower are driven by gearing at the flywheel end of the engine, damping and cushioning devices being incorporated. The camshaft is duplicated by a balancing shaft, both carrying bob-weights which produce a reciprocating effect in a similar manner to that of the Lanchester harmonic balancer, but in this case arranged to produce a couple to balance the primary reciprocating couple due to the three pistons. In the figure the bob-weights are shown in false phase for convenience.

The direct injection system is employed, a combined pump and sprayer unit of special construction being mounted between the two exhaust valves and operated by a rocker from the camshaft.

Very complete information on this engine is given in the work by Schweitzer, referred to in Section 10.6.

10.12   Foden six-cylinder two-stroke ci engine

An interesting example of the same general system is the Foden engine.

A full description of the FD.6 Mk. I engine, with an account of its behaviour on the road will be found in *Automobile Engineer*, Vol. 39, No. 4 and in *Bus and Coach*, Vol. 20, No. 238. Later reports have been published from time to time in the technical press, but the reports mentioned give detailed descriptions of the engine.

The injection pump and control unit consists of a high-speed model of a CAV pump, combined with a hydraulic H-type governor, which gives remarkably sensitive and accurate control.

The later engines were straightforward and logical developments of the earlier versions. The bore was increased from 85 to 92 mm, thin shell aluminium-tin bearings replaced the original thick shell whitemetal bear-

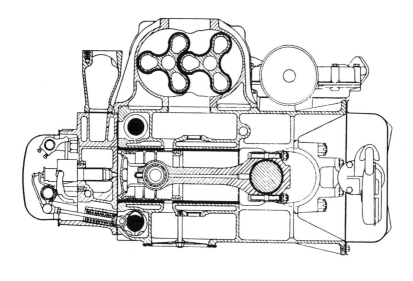

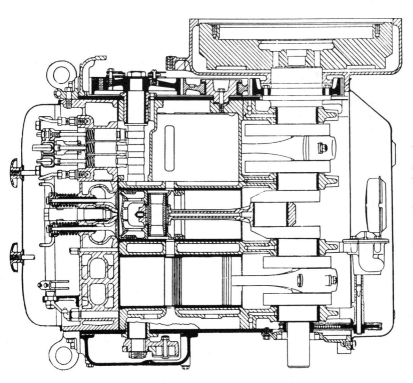

Fig. 10.9 General Motors blower-charged ci engine

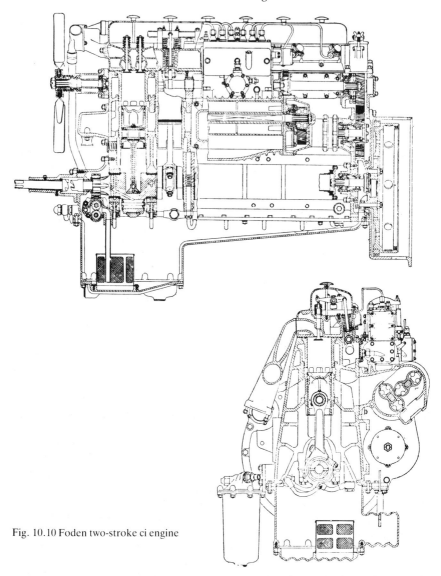

Fig. 10.10 Foden two-stroke ci engine

ings and the cylinder head and liner design was altered so that each cylinder had a separate head. Also, the Mark VII six-cylinder engine was exhaust turbocharged and intercooled.

As a measure of the advance in design of this particular engine, a comparison of the later performance figures with those obtained from the Mark I engine is interesting. Although the physical dimensions of the engine remained practically unchanged, the power increased by 79%, the torque by 82%, the specific weight decreased by 40% and the specific fuel consumption improved by 10.7%.

An output of 35kW per litre at 2200 rev/min, a specific weight of 3.837 kg/kW, an overall length of less than 1.2192 m and weight, without electrical equipment, of 635 kg, compare most favourably with most advanced designs of four-stroke diesel engines.

The maximum value of bmep is 1069 kN/m² at 1300 rev/min and the best specific fuel consumption is 0.218 kg/kWh.

At maximum rev/min the piston speed is about 6% less than in corresponding four-stroke types, and this, combined with the unidirectional loading of the connecting rod, makes the rod and bearing load-factors more favourable. Since every upward stroke is a compression stroke, and the gas load exceeds the inertia load up to about 3500 rev/min, there is no reversal of stress in the connecting rod, or big-end cap loading. The fluctuations of torque throughout each revolution are consequently much less, and a lighter flywheel can be used, with direct gain in liveliness and ease in gear changing.

The general construction of the FD.6 Mk. I engine may be studied from the longitudinal and cross sections of Fig. 10.10.

Centrifugally-cast wet liners are used in an aluminium alloy monobloc casting, with two cast-iron heads, each covering three bores.

The various pressure and water joints are made with copper gasket rings and synthetic rubber sealing rings respectively, the joint faces of the liners standing proud of the block to ensure the proper degree of nip on the various washers.

The air delivery gallery supplies air to each bore through a series of ports formed to impart tangential swirl in a clockwise direction, seen from above, the injector delivering fuel from a single-hole nozzle downstream into the air. The toroidal recess in the piston crown has the effect of increasing the rotational swirl when the piston reaches the top of the stroke, on the principle of the conservation of angular momentum in a space of reduced diameter, as utilised by Ricardo in the cylindrical head of sleeve-valve engines.

Tin-plated cast-iron pistons are fitted, and the great length of these above the gudgeon pin will be noted. This makes them admirably fitted to perform the crosshead function of the piston without risk of tilt, and provides generous bearing area with an excellent wearing material. It also helps to minimise small end bearing temperatures.

The arrangement of piston rings is of interest as illustrating two-stroke requirements.

The top ring is a composite 'flame' ring designed to give gas sealing for the full depth of the top land and incorporating the ring groove for the first normal pressure ring, which is provided with a snug to prevent relative rotation. The flame ring serves to prevent the top edges of the scavenge ports being exposed to the cylinder gases earlier than the nominal instant when they are overrun by the top of the piston and the gas pressure is sufficiently reduced. Two further pressure rings – they are all of taper section – are provided above the gudgeon pin, and below are the air-chest seal ring to prevent blow-by of scavenge air to the crank chamber as the piston rises, and a normal oil scraper ring. All the rings have integral cast snugs or dowel pegs to prevent circumferential movement and ensure that the joints ride along one or other of the port bars.

The continuous compression loading of the connecting rod is reflected in the arrangement of the gudgeon pin and piston bosses, the latter being stepped in order to give the maximum bearing area on the underside combined with the fullest possible support of the pin against bending. Provision is made for pressure lubrication of the pin through central drilling of the rod, to ensure continuous maintenance of an oil film under the somewhat more difficult conditions when no reversal of load occurs. An oil-jet for piston cooling is incorporated, and in view of this provision, the thickness of the piston crown is limited in order to reduce the heat flow to the piston rings and lands.

The diagonally split big ends may be noticed. This is now general practice in ci engines, and reflects the continuous increase in crank pin and main journal diameter in the search for improved crankshaft stiffness and reduced intensity of bearing loads. The diagonal split enables the lateral width of the big end to be made small enough for upward withdrawal through the bore.

10.13   Blower and scavenging

The blower is of the Roots type with two-lobe rotors and runs at twice engine speed, average boost pressure is about 34.474 kN/m², sufficient with the Kadenacy extraction effect to give thorough scavenge and exhaust valve cooling, followed by a degree of supercharge which enables four-stroke values of the bmep to be maintained.

The twin exhaust valves, of moderate diameter, are driven by push rod and rocker gear of the normal type, but roller cam followers, running on needle-roller bearers, are employed.

Fig. 10.11 shows the interesting timing of the valves and cylinder ports, the early opening of the exhaust valves aiding the thorough scavenge without unduly delaying the commencement of compression. The effective

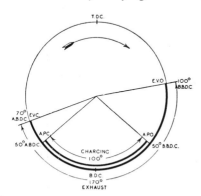

Fig. 10.11 Foden ci engine valve and port timing

expansion ratio is appreciably less than in the average four-stroke compression-ignition engine, but some of the remaining energy is usefully employed in the wave extraction due to the carefully designed exhaust ducts, which extend independently for about 15.46 mm from the ports.

The camshaft and auxiliary driving gear is at the rear of the engine and, having helical gears, is of similar construction to that described in Section 6.48, though with a 1:1 ratio for the camshaft and injection pump shaft. To conform with the best practice, ball-and-roller races are housed in spigotted bronze castings fitted on studs, instead of being carried directly in the aluminium alloy casting. The whole timing gear is robust and well designed.

Careful arrangements are made for vigorous circulation of the cooling water, with jets directed to the potential hot spots around exhaust valves and injectors. The direct cooling of the valve guides will be noticed.

An indication of the remarkable coolness of the exhaust is the successful use of an aluminium alloy exhaust manifold.

10.14 Crankshaft balance and firing order

The crank throws are phased 120° apart in two sets of three, the two sets being out of phase by 60° to give 60° firing intervals, six in each revolution.

This sets the opposing primary and secondary couples slightly out of phase, as the shaft is not in exact mirror symmetry. However, the resulting slight tendency to pitch and yaw is of negligible effect, though of some technical interest. The engine is quite free from critical vibration within the normal speed range.

The firing order is 1 5 3 4 2 6, repeated each revolution. Performance curves for the FD.6 Mk I, Mk. VI and Mk. VII engines are given in Fig. 10.12. They show exceptionally good maintenance of torque at high speed, and the improvement in bmep and power of the late Marks is an outstanding achievement.

As stated earlier, all marks of engines after the Mark I were fitted with individual heads. Mark III and all later engines have thin shell bearings and a larger diameter crankshaft. At this point the fuel injection pump was also

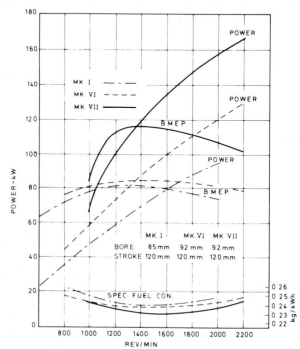

Fig. 10.12 Foden ci engine performance curves

modified for engine oil lubrication in place of the fuel oil lubrication which had been used hitherto. The lubricating oil pump and water circulating pump speeds were also increased at this stage. Mark VI and VII engines had the cylinder bore increased to 92 mm, these two engines being similar in all mechanical details except that the Mark VII was fitted with a CAV turbocharger and intercooler.

An external view of the FD.6 Mk. VII engine is given in Fig. 10.13.

Fig. 10.13 External view of Foden two-stroke ci engine

The intercooler and the connecting trunk between the supercharger and the Roots blower have been removed so as not to mask the engine details.

The authors are much indebted to the makers of the engine for information and for drawings from which the illustrations were prepared.

10.15   Opposed-piston engine

The Lucas and Trojan engines, with parallel cylinder barrels, may be described as *uniflow opposed-piston engines* since the scavenge air flows continuously from the inlet ports uncovered by one piston to the exhaust ports uncovered by the other, the two pistons moving towards each other for compression and away from each other for expansion.

More usually, however, the description is confined to the construction incorporating a single straight cylinder barrel in which the two pistons move in opposite phase towards and away from each other.

This involves either two crankshafts phased by gearing or equivalent means, or a single crankshaft to which the power of one piston is transmitted directly, and that of the other by means of a pair of side connecting rods, or alternatively by means of a symmetrical reversing rocker system for each piston.

Side return rods involve either a three-throw crankshaft, a crank and two eccentrics with smaller throws (Harland & Wolff), or the special arrangement used in the successful Fullagar marine diesel, in which, in each unit pair of cylinders, oblique tie rods connect the pairs of pistons which move in phase, suitable crossheads and slides being provided to take the side thrusts. Thus two cranks and two connecting rods serve four pistons. In the return rocker arrangement a two-throw shaft with offset rockers is sufficient for each cylinder.

These have been exemplified in (1) the Junkers Jumo aircraft engine, (2) the Oechelhauser horizontal gas unit even earlier and the more recent Peugeot-Lilloise single-line stationary type made under Junkers licence and (3) a number of recent designs and proposals of which the Commer TS.3 is the best known. The return connecting-rod method, if applied to a multi-line design, would clearly involve a crankshaft of prohibitive complexity and flexibility, with a lack of symmetry leading to balancing difficulties.

When first installed for electric generating purposes in Johannesburg, the Oechelhauser gas engines gave considerable trouble through the distortion of crankshafts and side rods arising from pre-ignition due to dirty gas.

The large gas engine, though important in its day in the utilisation of blast-furnace gas, is obsolete as a prime mover.

The third of the constructions listed above, namely the return rocker arrangement with a single crankshaft, has been the subject of many patents and designs.

Two of these, which are of special importance and interest, are illustrated in Figs. 10.14 to 10.16.

Fig. 10.14 shows the Sultzer engine produced in about 1936 which exhibited features of historic interest as representing a design by an experienced firm of repute, in which the opposed-piston rocker arrangement is combined with a phased reciprocating scavenge pump, in a manner that will be clear from the illustration.

The admission and discharge of air to the scavenge pump, the capacity of which is considerably in excess of the displaced volume of the main cylinders, is by automatic valves of the reed type.

The bore and combined stroke are 90 mm and 240 mm respectively, giving a volume of 1527 cm^3 per cylinder, the maximum rating under intermittent full load conditions being 22.4 kW per cylinder at 1500 rev/min. This corresponds to a bmep of 586 kN/m^2.

Phasing of the pistons, to give a lead to the exhaust, is accomplished by the disposition of the rocker pins and their arc of movement. With clockwise rotation of the crankshaft, it will be noticed that the right-hand rocker has passed its dead point while the left-hand one is just on it, the 180° disposition of the cranks being maintained for balancing purposes.

The Commer TS.3 compression-ignition engine was a post Second World War example of the opposed-piston and rocker construction which was in production and successful use for about 20 years.

Instead of the phased pump, a Roots blower is used for scavenging, this being more in line with later two-stroke practice. The engine has three cylinders of 82.55 mm bore and a combined stroke of 203.2 mm giving a swept volume of 3262 cm^3.

At 2400 rev/min the maximum output of 78.3 kW is obtained, corresponding to a bmep of 414 kN/m^2.

The maximum value of the bmep is $724\,kN/m^2$ attained at $1350\,rev/min$. The minimum specific fuel consumption claimed is $0.232\,g/kWh$, an excellent result.

The forged crankshaft has four main bearings and six crankpins in pairs opposed at $180°$, and for each crank pin there is a normal connecting rod, a rocker, and a short swinging piston link, and piston. Except for the couple arising from the distance between the planes of the two connecting rods of each pair, and the corresponding offset of the two arms of the rocker, the two sets of reciprocating masses are in dynamic balance (see Section 5.4), but heavy pin loading in each set of reciprocating parts is involved in all examples of this construction because of the large masses. Reversal of loading due to inertia forces is less likely to occur than in a four-stroke engine, as compression is met on each inward stroke. Thus running should be quiet at some sacrifice of the benefit to lubrication of thrust reversal. It

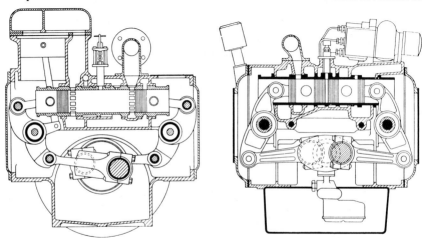

Fig. 10.14 Sultzer opposed-piston engine   Fig. 10.15 Commer TS.3 ci engine

will be noticed that the rockers in the Commer design are longer than the centre distance between cylinder and crankshaft, but owing to the reversal of the porting relative to the direction of rotation, lead of the exhaust piston is again provided. Figs. 10.15 and 10.16 show the general lay-out of this engine arranged in such a manner as to make it very suitable for under-floor installation.

Full details will be found in *Automobile Engineer*, Vol. 44, No. 8.

There is also an interesting article by R. Waring-Brown in Vol. 47 of the same journal.

10.16   Comparison of advantages

From the foregoing descriptions it will be realised that the high performance two-stroke engine cannot claim greater mechanical simplicity than its four-stroke competitor, and it is still doubtful whether it will ever achieve equally favourable specific fuel consumption.

Approaching 100% higher output for a given space and weight appears to be achieved, though progress in supercharging of the four-stroke engine

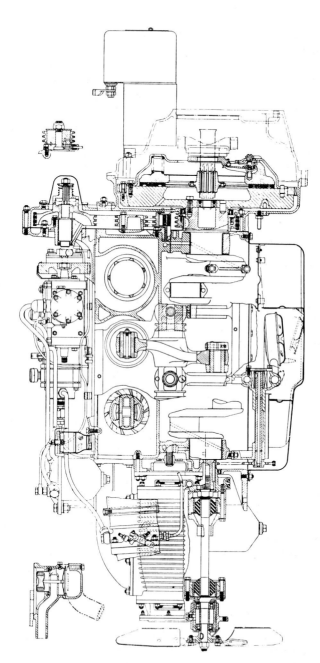

Fig. 10.16 Commer TS.3 opposed-piston ci engine

may reduce the advantage once more. Waste heat difficulties may well be the ultimate determining factor with both types.

Smoother torque and more favourable bearing load factors are inherent advantages which the two-stroke cycle will always be able to claim, and these should react favourably on maintenance and operational acceptability. Higher rotational speeds and smoother torque will react favourably on transmission design and endurance, and the advantages of a lighter flywheel in facilitating gear changing and aiding rapid acceleration have already been mentioned.

Chapter 11

Carburation and carburettors

The term *carburation* may conveniently be applied to the whole process of supplying to the engine continuously a suitable combustible mixture of vaporised fuel and air. A mixture carrying just the necessary air for complete combustion, in accordance with the chemical composition of the fuel, is not by any means the best in all circumstances, as will be seen later, but the study of the main principles involved is simplified if constant mixture strength in the chemically correct proportions is assumed to be the object sought.

The complete process of carburation in modern jet carburettors may be divided broadly into three stages as follows –

(1) Continuous measuring out in correct proportions of liquid fuel and air for combustion.
(2) *Atomisation* or breaking up into very fine spray of the liquid stream and its intimate and uniform mixture with the air current.
(3) Provision of the necessary *latent heat of vaporisation* to the liquid fuel so that the mixture may form a homogeneous vapour preparatory to ignition.

The perfect carburettor would fulfil all these requirements under varied climatic conditions and at all speeds and throttle openings; that is, no matter what the demand and its rate of fluctuation for fuel by the engine. Great difficulties arise from the different nature of the two fluids, one a mixture of permanent gases, oxygen and nitrogen, and the other a more or less volatile liquid. The mechanical characteristics of the engine (valve setting, induction pipe arrangement, etc.), the great and rapid fluctuations in demand for fuel and the variations of temperature and humidity of the atmosphere introduce further serious difficulties and it is therefore small wonder that the perfect carburation system does not exist, each design having its good features and its limitations.

Before entering on the consideration of the chemical and physical properties of the various fuels suitable for the ordinary internal combustion car or lorry engine, the mechanical process of measuring out and atomising the fuel will be dealt with, as it is in this first process that the greatest difficulties arise.

11.1   Engine suction

When an internal combustion engine is revolving, either under its own power or by the agency of the starting motor or handle, the displacement of the piston on the induction stroke represents potential ability for forming a vacuum, or depression, in the cylinder, the degree produced depending on the speed of the engine and the size of the apertures admitting air and vapour to the cylinders (these apertures being the throttle opening and any leakage openings into the induction pipe), and to some extent also on the ratio of clearance volume to swept volume.

The opening through the inlet valve is 'in series' with the above openings, but it becomes a determining factor only at high speed and full throttle openings for under average conditions the smallness of the throttle opening, in relationship to the valve opening, results in the former being, as the name implies, the chief factor in controlling the flow of gas – using that term to denote the combustible mixture of air and petrol vapour – to the cylinders.

The suction displacement of the piston in a four-stroke engine takes place only once every two revolutions, thus a cylinder of 1-litre swept volume at 2000 rev/min represents a suction capacity of 1000 litre/min. If the cylinder had no clearance volume, was at atmospheric temperature, and if there were no restriction to the flow at the throttle or the valves, 1000 litres of gas would be drawn in per minute, the pressure in the cylinder during induction being equal to that of the atmosphere. Except by supercharging (Chapter 13), no greater *quantity* of gas could be introduced into the cylinder, and provided the mixture were correct, the combustion force or mean effective pressure would have its greatest possible value. If at the same time the engine were running at its maximum permissible speed, then the power developed would be a maximum, it being assumed here that the limit of speed is determined from purely mechanical considerations.

11.2   Volumetric efficiency

In an actual engine the effect of clearance volume and the high temperature of that portion of the previous charge left in the clearance space reduce both the volume and density of the fresh charge drawn in, and the effect of restricted openings at the valve and throttle, which increases as the speed increases, reduces the pressure and therefore the density of the charge still further. The ratio of the weight of fresh charge actually drawn in, to that which would fill the swept volume at atmospheric temperature and pressure is known as the *volumetric efficiency*. Even in the best modern engines this ratio seldom exceeds about 80%, and the actual value fluctuates with the speed and throttle opening. It is also very dependent on valve timing, and it is not possible with fixed timing to maintain the highest volumetric efficiency at all speeds.

11.3   Throttling

From what has been said it will be apparent that should a reduced power be required, as for instance when after climbing a hill in top gear it is desired to maintain the same speed on a subsequent level stretch of road, it is necessary to reduce the *quantity* of the charge by restricting the throttle opening.

The smaller opening results in a greater degree of depression being produced in the cylinders and induction pipe by the movement of the pistons. The weight quantity of the charge – which determines the force of combustion – is thus decreased by the lower density resulting from the decreased *pressure* in the cylinders. Under these conditions the flow through the carburettor is reduced and there is less depression at the choke than under full throttle conditions.

The throttle may therefore be regarded as a means of preventing the full suction of the engine from acting on the carburettor when less than the maximum explosion or torque is required. This may occur at low or high speed, and therefore at low or high power.

The diagrams in Fig. 11.1 show the pressure differences arising in the induction system under different conditions of engine speed and throttle opening, but for the sake of clarity the degree of suction, vacuum or depression through the carburettor has been exaggerated in relation to the perfect vacuum or zero pressure line. The carburettor indicated is of the

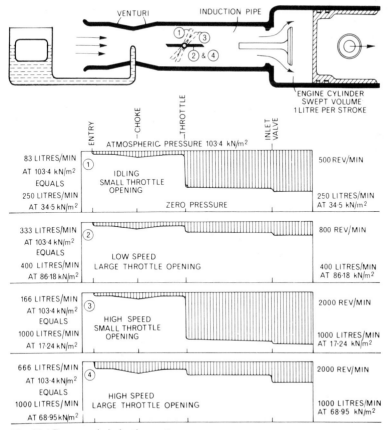

Fig. 11.1 Pressures in induction system

fixed choke type with a properly formed venturi, which results in a recovery of pressure after the relatively low value reached at the choke.

In constructing these diagrams it has been assumed that the flow is steady and that the amount of depression at any point is constant for any given values of engine speed and throttle opening. This is an ideal condition which is only approximately realised in actual practice. Clearly in a single-cylinder engine the suction impulse occupies approximately only one quarter of each cycle or 25% of the total time, thus giving rise to a pulsating flow. This is damped out to some extent by the capacity of the induction pipe and the restricted throttle opening, and in a multi-cylinder engine with four or six cylinders fed from the same carburettor an approximately uniform flow is realised through the carburettor, but these pulsations of depression still remain a source of difficulty owing to the different inertia effects arising in the two fluids. The heavy liquid petrol is far more subject to lag than the relatively light and elastic air, particularly if the passages to the jet are long and restricted. This results in the flow of petrol in relation to the air being too small at some moments and too great at others, thus causing a patchy mixture and an uneven supply of fuel to the various cylinders, or bad *distribution* as it is called.

This problem is intimately concerned with the shape and size of the induction pipe, with the valve timing and with the position of the carburettor. Its solution is largely a question of patient experiment on the part of the manufacturer, and can be touched on only briefly in a work such as this. For our purposes we will assume that for any given engine speed and throttle opening the depression and consequently the flow are steady.

Four sets of conditions are indicated in Fig. 11.1 –

(1) *Low speed, small throttle opening.* As when the engine is idling.
(2) *Low speed, large throttle opening.* As at the commencement of acceleration, or when labouring on top gear.
(3) *High speed, small throttle opening.* As when running down hill.
(4) *High speed, large throttle opening.* As when developing maximum power.

Since the air forms almost the whole of the flow (with a chemically correct mixture only about 2.2% of the volume consists of petrol vapour) we may assume without serious error that the amount of fluid passing each constriction or orifice is the same. The flow of air in litres per minute, reduced to atmospheric pressure, is indicated on the left of each diagram, the maximum piston displacement assumed at 1000 litre/min, that is a one-litre engine at 2000 rev/min. The figures are, of course, approximate only and are given for purposes of illustration. The depression diagrams illustrate the relative pressure loss throughout the induction system under the different conditions of throttle opening and speed, the depth of the shaded area representing the drop of pressure below atmospheric. The depression at the carburettor is exaggerated for the sake of clearness. In actual practice it is of the order of 1.7 to 3.5 kN/m².

It will be noticed that the depression in the cylinders and induction pipe is greatest when the throttle is nearly closed, as for idling, but at high speed down hill. The smallest possible weight of charge is required during idling and this is secured by the small volume due to the low speed, and the low density arising from the low pressure. The low pressure in turn results from the big pressure difference required to force the charge through the very small throttle opening. If the throttle is opened slightly, the flow increases and an increase of power results, appearing first as an increase in combustion torque and pressure, which will result in either an increase of speed or merely the overcoming of an increased resistance, as on a hill, or a combination of the two.

The depression at the carburettor on the other hand depends on the rate of flow only and not directly on the throttle opening, but only indirectly, because the rate of flow is itself determined by the combination of throttle opening and engine speed. The suction or depression at the jet and choke is seen to increase steadily as the flow, reduced to atmospheric conditions, increases from 83 to 666 litres/min. Thus, in Fig. 11.1, (2) and (4) show the same throttle opening, but very different depressions at the choke and jet, while in (2) and (3) the carburettor depressions do not differ, but the speeds and throttle openings do.

11.4   Factors which determine air and petrol flow

To force a given quantity of fluid per minute through an orifice of given size requires a certain difference of pressure between the two sides of the orifice.

The pressure difference which causes the flow of petrol may arise from the hydrostatic head of the liquid petrol – if the jet is below the petrol level in the float chamber – from the difference of air pressure between the float chamber and jet outlet, due to the depression at the choke, or to a combination of these two, while the flow of air through the choke is due to the excess of atmospheric pressure or supercharger pressure at the entry to the carburettor over the pressure on the engine side of the choke. In studying carburettor action it will be found helpful to realise that flow takes place as a result of excess pressure *behind* the fluid, whether the general pressure be above or below atmospheric – there is no such thing as suction in the sense of lifting or pulling a fluid, but only in the sense of reducing the pressure which opposes the flow, by the application of a vacuum pump effect, whether due to the human lungs or the piston displacement of an engine.

In order to maintain, or artificially increase, the final density of the charge in the cylinder, a supercharger may be employed to raise the pressure behind the flow in place of relying on the reduction of pressure opposing it.

No matter how the pressure difference may be caused or measured, for purposes of calculating the flow it must be expressed in terms of head of the fluid which is flowing, in order that the fundamental fluid flow formula $v = \sqrt{(2gh)}$ may be used.

This formula gives not only the velocity acquired by a body falling freely *in vacuo* under the acceleration of gravity, but also the velocity of efflux from an orifice or jet as the result of a pressure difference corresponding to a head h of the fluid which is flowing.

Any convenient units may be used (say, feet and seconds, or centimetres and seconds), provided that they are consistent throughout.

Table 4 – PRESSURE, HEAD AND VELOCITY

Pressure		Head and corresponding velocity					
		Water $D = 1000$ kg/m^3		Petrol $D = 753$ kg/m^3		Air $D = 1.298$ kg/m^3	
kN/m^2	mm(Hg)	Head m	$v = \sqrt{2gh}$ m/s	Head m	$v = \sqrt{2gh}$ m/s	Head m	$v = \sqrt{2gh}$ m
0.069	0.518	0.00070	0.368	0.00094	0.430	5.482	10.36
0.186	1.397	0.00192	0.612	0.00254	0.703	14.63	16.76
0.690	5.180	0.00704	1.171	0.00932	1.351	54.25	32.61
0.938	7.03	0.00957	1.369	0.0127	1.577	73.15	37.80
1.87	7.97	0.0192	1.934	0.0254	2.254	146.3	53.30
3.45	14.09	0.0351	2.620	0.0467	3.048	272.5	73.15
6.9	25.9	0.0703	3.715	0.0932	4.269	54.25	103.65
101.3	762	1.034	14.21	13.716	16.34	7920.0	393.0

Table 4 shows pressures and the corresponding heads and velocities for water, petrol and air, the density for air being taken as that corresponding to 101.3 kN/m^2 and 0°C. The velocities are calculated from the formula quoted above and represent the conversion, without loss, of potential energy of head or pressure into kinetic energy of velocity. Just as when a body falls through the atmosphere it meets with air resistence which prevents its velocity from attaining the full amount given by the formula, so the viscosity of liquid petrols causes their velocity of flow through carburettor jets to follow a slightly different equation from the one above, which, however, serves with reasonable accuracy for the air flow, as air approaches more closely to the ideal of a perfect fluid.

The depression in fixed choke carburettors ranges, during normal running, from approximately 100 to 500 mm of water column, corresponding to air speeds of 39.6 to 85.3 m/s. The corresponding petrol speeds are, of course, much less.

11.5 Volume flow and mass flow

The volume flow through an orifice in cubic feet per second or in cubic centimetres or millimetres per second, according to whatever units may be convenient, is obtained by multiplying the velocity by the cross-sectional area of the jet –

$$\text{Volume flow} = A \times \sqrt{(2gh)}$$

It is now the general practice to test all carburettor jets for flow, and to stamp them with the flow in millilitres – that is, cubic centimetres – per minute under a standard head of 500 mm. This flow testing is carried still further by certain firms who submit each complete carburettor to a flow test before assembly on the engine. Such tests give valuable information and ensure consistency in setting, though it is naturally impossible to reproduce exactly all the final running conditions.

In combustion calculations it is often desirable to determine the mass or weight flow per second or per minute, so that in the above formula the volume must be multiplied by the density D to give –

$$\text{Mass flow} = A \times \surd(2gh) \times D$$

Further, the head h may be expressed in terms of the effective pressure difference by the relationship –

$$h = \frac{(p_1 - p_2)}{D}$$

in which p_1 and p_2 are the absolute pressures on the two sides of the orifice and D is the density of the fluid (air or petrol), all measured in SI units.

The formula for mass flow thus becomes –

$$\text{Mass flow} = A \surd(2g) \surd(p_1 - p_2) \surd D$$
$$= \text{Constant} \times A \surd(p_1 - p_2) \surd D$$

where the constant in addition to the quantity $\surd 2g$ may be taken to include a coefficient to correct for the discrepancy between the actual flow and the 'no friction' flow. This discrepancy depends on the viscosity coefficient of the fluid and the form and proportions of the jet, the 'coefficient of discharge' being from 0.6 to 0.8 for ordinary carburettor jets.

For a given form of jet the coefficient does not vary very much with the size of the jet, nor does the density of a given petrol change appreciably with change of temperature. Changes in density of the air are, of course, important, and result in enrichment of the mixture on a warm day or at high altitudes owing to the reduced weight of air consequent on its lower density. If changes of density are disregarded, there remain two variable quantities in the above formula, namely pressure difference and orifice area, which control the rate of mass flow.

11.6   Two main classes of carburettor

Carburettors may therefore be divided broadly, though not rigidly, into two classes in one of which, the *constant choke* class, the orifice area is constant and the pressure difference or depression is varied, while in the other, the *constant vacuum* class, the area of the orifice is varied to meet the changing demand, the depression being kept constant or approximately so.

11.7   Fixed or open-choke type

Fig. 11.2 shows in simple diagrammatic form the essentials of a constant choke carburettor of the vertical type. The choke A is the air orifice and the jet B, placed at the narrow waist of the choke, forms the fixed petrol orifice. The float chamber C, of the now obsolescent bottom feed type, is shown on the left, the float acting on the needle valve D through the levers E so as to close the former when the petrol level reaches the proper height. This level is thereby maintained slightly below the level of the jet orifice. A small vent-hole is provided in the lid of the float chamber to ensure that the surface of the petrol is subject to atmospheric pressure.

It will now be realised that when the engine is running, the air and petrol orifices, namely, the choke and jet, will be subject to the same depression, or lowering of pressure below that of the atmosphere, and if the relative areas are suitably chosen, having regard to the density of the two fluids, air and petrol will flow into the choke in suitable fixed proportions.

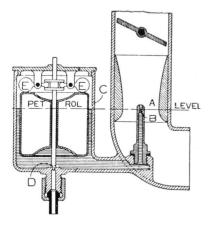

Fig. 11.2 Simple jet carburettor

The density of average petrol is about 753 kg/m³, while that of air at normal temperature and pressure is about 1.28 kg/m³. Thus the ratio of the densities of petrol to air is 587:1. The ratio by weight of air to petrol in a chemically correct combustible mixture is about 15:1. Hence, it follows that for a given suction or depression acting on both air and petrol orifices, the relative areas should be –

$$\frac{\text{Area of choke}}{\text{Area of jet}} = \frac{15}{1} \times \sqrt{\frac{587}{1}} = 363$$

$$\frac{\text{Diameter of choke}}{\text{Diameter of jet}} = \sqrt{363} = 19.$$

If air and petrol were ideally perfect fluids, and if friction, etc., could be eliminated, this simple carburettor would give a constant ratio of air and petrol liquid by weight, and would therefore fulfil the first function of a carburettor quite satisfactorily.

Unfortunately these conditions do not hold. Air is a mixture of permanent gases and, as already mentioned, approximates closely in behaviour to the perfect fluid, while the viscosity, surface tension and inertia of the liquid petrol cause its behaviour to follow a somewhat different and more complex equation than that given for perfect fluids. With steady flow, inertia effects do not arise, and the curve shown by a full line in Fig. 11.3 gives the relationship between the depression acting on the jet and the experimentally determined mass flow for a Zenith jet No. 110, the specific gravity of the petrol being 0.75 and temperature 0°C.

The depression is shown in centimetres of water column, and the corresponding scales of petrol and air column are added.

Three other parabolic or 'square root' curves have been added to represent the air flow through three alternative choke tubes suitable for the jet. Scales of air and petrol speed through choke and jet have been added, the former to be read from the uppermost air flow curve which may be taken to represent the theoretical relationship $v = \sqrt{(2gh)}$.

The petrol speed is calculated direct from the experimentally determined mass flow, and will be found to be about 65 to 70% of the speed given by the formula above. The scale for mass flow of the air is so chosen that coincidence of the air and petrol curves would represent chemically correct mixture in the ratio of 15:1. It will at once be noticed that owing to the distorted shape of the petrol curve coincidence with the parabolic curves – which may be taken to represent the air flow very closely – cannot be obtained, the best that can be done being an intersection representing correct mixture at some one value of the depression depending on the size of the choke selected. It should be realised that the same general effect would be obtained if – as would be the usual procedure – the jet were altered instead of the choke. There is an inherent tendency towards enrichment of the mixture with increase of depression, owing to the

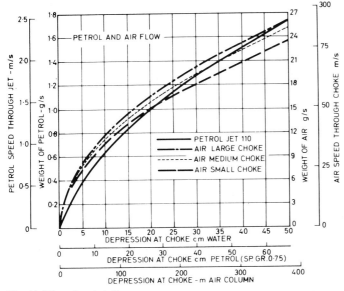

Fig. 11.3 Petrol and air flow

straightening of the petrol flow curve. With the large choke the mixture is weak throughout the whole range up to 50 cm depression, at which it becomes chemically correct. With the small choke, the chemically correct proportions are reached at a depression of 20 cm, the mixture being weak below that point and rich above it. The correct mixture may be obtained at any point desired by a suitable choice of the ratio of choke to jet, but the curves cannot be made to coincide. To obtain a constant air-fuel ratio throughout the range, whether in the correct chemical proportions or not, requires some form of compensation in order to correct the natural tendency to enrichment described above.

11.8   Compensation in fixed-choke carburettors

Compensation is the process of adjusting the mixture strength either by weakening it at large depressions or by enriching it at small, so that throughout the whole range sensibly constant proportions are maintained. Many devices have been introduced with varying degrees of success and the following list is representative –

(1) Extra air valve, hand or automatic.
(2) Hydraulic devices incorporating compensating jets.
(3) Air 'bleeder' arrangements whereby the jet is partially relieved of the choke tube depression at the upper part of the range.

The third has, in general, superseded all others, as in addition to enabling a great range of automatic correction to be realised, the air entering the bleed holes leads to a high degree of atomisation of the petrol stream and so aids distribution and vaporisation.

11.9   Extra air valve

Carburettors of the motor-cycle type are still fitted with a hand-operated extra air valve or slide which can be opened at large depressions to prevent excessive enrichment of the mixture. Here the correction or compensation is entirely experimetal, and though, if the driver is willing to take the trouble, better results can usually be obtained by this means than with any automatic device, the extra complication and manipulation involved is regarded by many as a serious objection.

11.10   Hydraulic means. The submerged jet

A very ingenious and successful method of compensation is that known as the *Baverey compound jet arrangement*, employed in the popular Zenith carburettor. The petrol supply is drawn through two orifices, ultimately mixing in the choke with the air stream which may be regarded as consisting of two parts, one fed with petrol from the main jet and the other from the compensating jet.

In Fig. 11.4, which is a purely diagrammatic illustration, A is the main jet and B the compensating jet, which is submerged, while C is the compensating jet delivery tube. It will be seen that the main jet is fed directly from the float chamber in the ordinary way, with the result that in

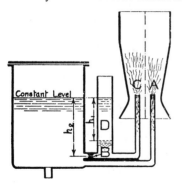

Fig. 11.4 Diagram of Zenith jets

respect of its own portion of the air stream it gives an increasingly rich mixture as the suction increases, for the reasons already explained. The compensating jet, on the other hand, discharges into a well D which is in direct communication with the atmosphere.

When the petrol in the well is level with that in the float chamber, there is no flow through the compensating jet since the surfaces of the petrol on both sides of it are level and subject to the same pressure – atmospheric. As the throttle is opened the resulting depression in the choke causes petrol to flow from the well through the delivery tube and consequently the petrol level in the well falls. The rate of flow through the compensating jet depends on its size and the difference of level h of the petrol in the well below that in the float chamber. An intermediate condition as the well empties is shown by h_1, while h_2 is the maximum head which can act on the compensating jet.

Thus when the well is emptied at quite a small depression, the compensating jet flow reaches a maximum and thereafter remains constant, no matter how great the depression at the choke may become, owing to the fact that atmospheric pressure is maintained in the well.

The further increase in the depression in the choke will, however, increase the air flow and hence it follows that the portion of mixture formed by the petrol which passes through the compensating jet will become progressively *weaker*. This balances the increase in richness of the mixture from the main jet, and the total mixture remains of appreciably constant strength provided a suitable combination of main and compensating jet sizes is chosen.

Since this Baverey method of compensation is still incorporated in Zenith carburettors, though in combination with the air-bleed principle, it will be instructive to study the flow curves in more detail by graphical plotting, particularly as other curves of fundamental importance may be readily derived therefrom.

In Fig. 11.5 are drawn mass or weight flow curves for main jets 90 and 100 and for compensating jets 110 and 135 and also the air flow curve for the large choke of Fig. 11.3.

It will be noticed that the compensating jet flow lies above that of the main jets in both cases as the head increases from zero up to 3 cm of water, that is 4 cm of petrol, which is the limiting value of h_2 in Fig. 11.4. After this point the flow remains constant. On combining the flow through the main jet 100 with compensator 110, and main jet 90 with compensator 135, it will be found that in each case the totals coincide with the air curve, indicating chemically correct mixture, at 20 cm depression. The jets were chosen to give this result, but it will be found that at other parts of the range the two combinations give different mixtures. The larger main jet with small compensator gives reasonably correct mixture throughout, though with definite slight over-compensation.

The other combination gives considerable over-compensation, which we shall see presently is a desirable result. To the left of the point of correct mixture there is considerable enrichment, while to the right is a progressive weakening, thus reversing the conditions in the simple carburettor.

In Fig. 11.6 these same curves are plotted in another way, showing quality of mixture (both as a percentage and a ratio) plotted against weight

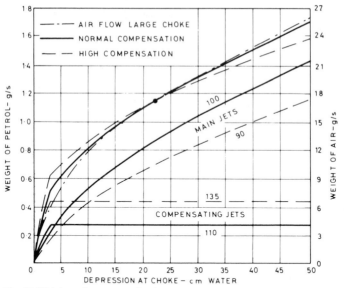

Fig. 11.5 Main and compensating jets

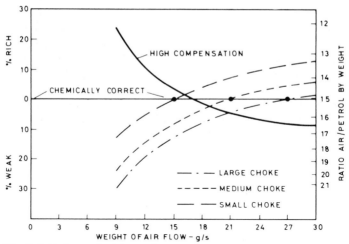

Fig. 11.6 Air flow and mixture ratio

of air flow. The three curves from Fig. 11.3 and the high compensation curve from Fig. 11.5 may thus be compared on an important and helpful basis. The reader should appreciate that these curves represent hypothetical rather than wholly experimental results, though they are based on actual behaviour.

11.11 Air bleed compensation

Before proceeding to discuss whether, by a high degree of compensation, all requirements are met, the process of compensation by air bleed devices will be described.

The earlier Solex carburettors, the main jet assembly of which is shown in Fig. 11.7, provide a simple example.

The jet orifice O is submerged, the jet tube G being inserted in a well forming part of the carrier *t* and secured by the cap A which makes metallic contact with the flange at the top of the jet tube. The petrol level is at *m n* at the neck of the choke K. Air bleeder holes are drilled at *a* and for high compensation also at higher points in the jet tube. As the jet tube becomes emptied by the suction these bleeder holes become uncovered and are then

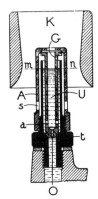

Fig. 11.7

in direct communication with the atmosphere through holes *s* drilled in the cap. The result is that the jet orifice is subject to less than the full depression in the choke, the amount of relief depending on the size of the bleeder holes in relation to the internal diameter and length of the jet tube body U.

In Figs. 11.8 to 11.11, which are diagrammatic, are shown the air bleed arrangements in the now obsolete Claudel-Hobson, and the most widely used constant-choke carburettors, namely the Solex, Stromberg and Zenith. In each case V is the choke or venturi, M the main jet and A the air metering plug for the bleed. There is also in most types of all makes an additional bleed resulting from reverse air flow through the idling jet when the well or feed passage becomes emptied. For the Solex the arrangement shown is known as *assembly 20*, and it will be noticed that the single calibrated air plug A replaces the bleed holes in the jet tube of the older type shown in Fig. 11.7.

This enables the bleed to be altered without changing the jet, and so makes tuning more flexible and definite. The downdraught form of this assembly is shown in Fig. 11.27.

It will be noticed that in the up-draught form the petrol on its way to the choke must pass through the holes in the emulsion tube, owing to the necessity for supporting this from the bottom. This makes no difference to the principle of the bleed action, for the lowest row of holes is quite sufficient to pass this petrol, as the upper holes become uncovered to pass the bleed air when the depression increases. There should be no difficulty in visualising this action if the atmospheric pressure is regarded as a positive pressure forcing air through A and petrol through M, the two fluids sharing the holes in the emulsion tube and meeting to form an emulsion in the stand pipe on the way to the choke. In the Claudel-Hobson

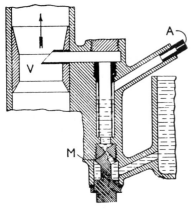

Fig. 11.8 Claudel-Hobson air bleed

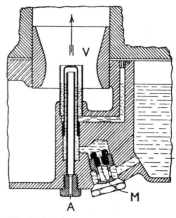

Fig. 11.9 Solex 'assembly 20'

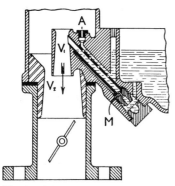

Fig. 11.10 Stromberg air bleed

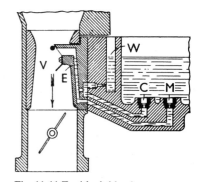

Fig. 11.11 Zenith air bleed

and Stromberg arrangements the petrol and air meet *inside* the emulsion tube, but there is no fundamental difference in the action. In each case a series of air jets penetrates the rising column of petrol producing an atomised emulsion, and by their 'atmospheric leak' effect relieve the main jet of some portion of the choke depression.

The action is progressive and the degree of compensation can be modified by changing the size of the air bleed plug.

11.12 Double diffuser

In the Stromberg down-draught arrangement illustrated, the two chokes V_1 and V_2 represent a device for intensifying the depression and therefore the air velocity at the outlet from the emulsion tube. In a smooth and gradually enlarging venturi tube, the absolute pressure at the outlet is higher than at the throat, as indicated in Fig. 11.10, so that with the outlet from V_1 placed at the throat of V_2 it is possible to obtain the highest local depression and velocity just at the point where the emulsion meets the first main air stream, which results in the formation of a rich and homogeneous mixture ready to join the final air stream through the main choke.

11.13 Zenith V-type emulsion block

In the down-draught Zenith diagram, Fig. 11.11, which represents generally the special features of the V type, C is the compensating jet, placed with the main jet in the bottom of the bowl and delivering, not as formerly directly to the well W, but to an intermediate chamber formed in the emulsion block E. The depression in this chamber will be intermediate between the atmospheric pressure in the well and the depression in the choke, depending on the size and characteristics of the communicating holes and the resistance of the main passage in the emulsion block. This principle of the intermediate chamber is discussed somewhat more generally in Section 11.19. It will thus be seen that the flow through the compensating jet is controlled partly by choke depression, and not solely by hydrostatic head as formerly.

The air bleed or leak effect is clearly also communicated to the main jet petrol, at a point intermediate between the main jet and the outlet from the emulsion block to the choke, and it becomes impossible to forecast with any certainty the flow curves for any particular jet sizes. The flow characteristics of the mixed petrol-air fluid, and the form of the passages are too complicated for any quantitative estimate to be made, and recourse must be had by designer and tuner to experiment.

As a well-known research engineer has remarked, every carburettor man has his own pet bleed holes and drillings, and development involves much drilling and plugging alternately before the desired flow characteristics are obtained.

11.14 Secondary suction effects

It is sometimes stated that the petrol flow through the jet is due to the velocity of the air past the jet. This is not fundamentally true. It is possible to interrupt the petrol flow entirely by applying the necessary degree of suction to the float chamber vent hole, though the air flow through the choke may be uninterrupted. This principle of modifying the pressure behind the petrol to reduce the net depression which causes its flow is applied in altitude controls for aircraft.

There are, however, certain secondary suction effects due to the aspect of the jet outlet or the obstruction that it causes, arising from the partial vacuum ordinarily formed on the down-stream side of such an obstruction. The chamfered emulsion outlets of the Claudel-Hobson and Zenith arrangements, and the 'distributor bar' shown in black circular section in the Zenith diagram, are examples of such obstructions. They introduce modifications to the flow which must be determined experimentally.

11.15 Mixture requirements for economy and power

The results of physical theory and research have shown that the chemically correct mixture is not the best for either economy (high thermal efficiency) or for power (high bmep and torque). For the former, weak mixtures down to 20 or more to 1 are desirable, provided that such weak mixtures can be properly distributed, ignited and burned, while for high bmep, mixtures of slightly more than 10% rich are required.

The physical and thermal properties of the products of combustion are such that high thermal efficiency is aided if, combustion being complete, there remains in the mixture a minimum of carbon dioxide and water vapour in proportion to nitrogen and residual oxygen. This enables the best use to be made of the *fuel*.

High bmep and torque, on the other hand, require that the best possible use be made of the *air* that is aspired, and this necessitates the burning of the air to produce carbon monoxide rather than carbon dioxide, though the latter is always present in considerable quantity and represents the final product of combustion of carbon. Thus incomplete combustion of the fuel, but complete combustion of the air, results in high bmep and torque, while combustion of a weak mixture leads to high thermal efficiency, except at small throttle openings, when a richer mixture is required to compensate for greater dilution by exhaust gas. To summarise, a weak mixture is required for economy, and a rich mixture for power and acceleration.

11.16   Carburettor characteristic

Fig. 11.12 is an 'ideal' carburettor characteristic suggested by D. Finlayson (see *Proc. Inst. Aut. Eng.*, Vol. XIX). The mixture becomes progressively weaker for the sake of economy up to, say, 80 or 90% of full load, at which point the throttle opening should give the maximum weight charge in the cylinder. Further movement of the throttle should enrich the mixture

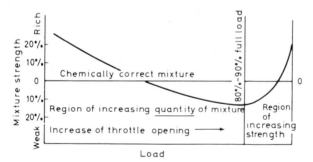

Fig. 11.12 Ideal carburettor characteristic

without decreasing its quantity in order that maximum torque shall be obtained. It is thus seen that mixture strength should depend on throttle opening no matter what the speed, depression or flow may be.

From Fig. 11.1, obviously conditions arise in which the throttle opening in (3) is such that the flow through the carburettor, and therefore the depression, is the same as that in (2) but the speeds and throttle openings are, nevertheless, widely different. The mixture required in (2) is a rich one in order that the utmost values for the mean effective pressure and engine torque may be obtained so that full throttle opening may result in rapid acceleration, while in (3) a weak mixture is desirable in order that economy at moderate loads may be realised. Condition (4) again requires a righ mixture in order that maximum power at full throttle may be attained. With the carburettor of Fig. 11.3 the same mixture would be delivered for both (2) and (3), since the flow and choke depression are the same, and there is moreover no recovery to a rich mixture at maximum delivery.

Thus a carburettor in which the mixture strength depends on the choke depression or flow only cannot meet all requirements, and the mixture ratio must be controlled by other factors. Nowadays, of course, an over-riding consideration is the need to meet the requirements of emissions regulations as discussed in Sections 11.58 to 11.65.

11.17 Mechanically-controlled power jet

Apart from the enrichment at low speeds and part throttle which is required by most engines to prevent stalling, and for which special provision is sometimes made, enrichment for maximum torque and power is required only at the larger throttle openings, and may therefore be effected by bringing into action an additional 'power jet' by the last few degrees of movement of the throttle lever.

Fig. 11.13 illustrates three arrangements for providing this enrichment mechanically. At (*a*) is shown the power enrichment valve added to the

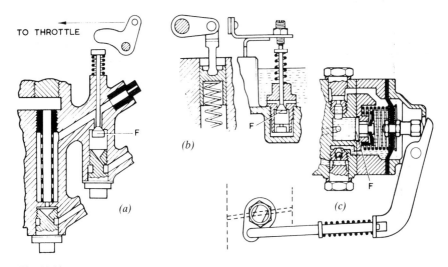

Fig. 11.13

Claudel-Hobson carburettor of Fig. 11.8, at (*b*) the scrap view is taken from Fig. 11.28 of the Zenith W type carburetter and shows a modification of the pump operating lever which was introduced, though not widely used, to open the power enrichment valve by the last few degrees of throttle movement. Fig. 11.13 (*c*) shows the mechanical arrangement used by Solex, which functions on principles similar to those of the Zenith W-type carburettors, Fig. 11.28 (*c*). In each of the views in Fig. 11.13, F is the full-throttle enrichment valve.

There is a tendency to replace these mechanical devices by those operated by manifold depression such as are described in Section 11.32 and illustrated in Fig. 11.23.

11.18   Dual characteristic

It thus becomes possible to plot on a basis of mass flow – grams per second or kilograms per minute – two characteristic curves of mixture ratio, one for full throttle opening and the other for part throttle, corresponding to, say, normal cruising speed on the level.

For each of these throttle openings a range of flow corresponding to the full range of engine speed may be plotted against the experimentally determined mixture ratio.

A generalised example of the type of characteristic to be aimed at is shown in Fig. 11.14, in which the method of plotting conforms with that used in Fig. 11.6. The part-throttle characteristic extends to the lowest value of the flow, corresponding to the lowest speed, and under these conditions a rich mixture is required to counteract the effect of dilution by exhaust gas, which may be greatly intensified by valve timing overlap.

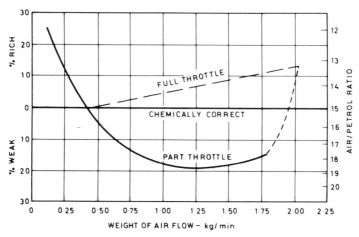

Fig. 11.14 Dual carburettor characteristic

As the flow increases with increase of speed a weak economy mixture is provided, which continues throughout the part-throttle range, until this range may be supposed to meet the full-throttle characteristic by a final opening of the throttle, indicated by the fine broken line. This curve is closely comparable with that of Fig. 11.12, and it will of course have to be further modified to meet exhaust gas emissions regulations in some countries.

11.19   Principle of the intermediate chamber

A principle which is applied in various forms in different carburettors, and particularly in idling adjustments, is the device of the intermediate chamber in which the jet or its effective outlet is placed, and through which the necessary air, or some part of it, passes on its way to the choke. In general, both the inlet and outlet of this chamber are adjustable, as for instance, by air and throttle slides in the two lever motor-cycle carburettor, or by throttle stops and air-bleed screws in idling and starting devices.

The principle is illustrated in Fig. 11.15. The absolute pressure p_2 in the intermediate chamber, on which the discharge of the jet depends, is intermediate between p_1 and p_3 depending as it does on the flow and the relative areas of inlet and outlet. At (*a*) the inlet is larger than the outlet, thus causing the depression *d* in the intermediate chamber to be less than half that in the induction pipe. At (*b*) the relative sizes of the openings are reversed and adjusted so as not to alter the rate of air flow, with the result that the depression at the jet is more than half the total depression in the induction pipe. This will clearly cause an increase in petrol flow and a

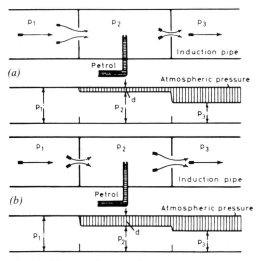

Fig. 11.15 Intermediate chamber

richer mixture. Obviously the adjustments may be made with such a degree of fineness as to produce any required change in mixture strength with constant quantity, or the quantity flowing may be altered with or without modification of the quality of the mixture.

11.20 Idling and starting devices

In the fixed choke carburettor the small flow required for idling cannot be obtained from the main choke and jet owing to the very low corresponding depression and velocities of flow.

The metering under these conditions becomes uncontrollable and atomisation is non-existent.

It is necessary, therefore, to provide idling jets and air orifices constituting in effect a small auxiliary carburettor exposed to the best depression available, which is just on the engine side of the edge of the throttle disc. The small quantity required will thus flow at high velocity, and good atomisation will result. In this connection the effect of air leaks into the induction pipe, through faulty joint gaskets or worn valve guides, should be emphasised. A small leak may represent a big proportion of the total flow under idling conditions, and will completely upset the mixture, though at large throttle openings it would be quite immaterial.

When the engine is warmed up, the idling mixture required is a normally rich one, but since the charge is of low density, it must be homogeneous in order to ensure ignition and combustion.

Such a mixture would generally be much too weak to ensure starting from cold, owing to the fact that in cold surroundings only a small proportion of the petrol vaporises. Hence arose the somewhat discredited expedients, which are now being eliminated, of using the float tickler to cause flooding and the strangler to increase the depression on the jet. These methods, at all events with the ordinary strangler, clearly gave somewhat haphazard and uncertain results.

11.21   Separate starter devices – semi-automatic

Several devices coming under this heading are in successful use. They are brought into action by the operation of a hand control, and there follows a greater or lesser degree of automatic and progressive adjustment of the mixture ratio as the engine warms up. When the engine is ready to run on the idling jet alone the starter is put out of action by release of the control.

The starter jet may be incorporated in a system which uses the ordinary idling ducts for the delivery of the petrol to the induction pipe, or it may be provided with quite independent passages which are closed by the release of the control.

The automatic and progressive weakening of the mixture which is required as the engine warms up may be controlled by depression or temperature or by air velocity, it being borne in mind that increase of depression – lowering of absolute pressure – and increase of temperature both assist evaporation, and a lower petrol:air ratio may be used.

Increased air velocity is the result of higher engine speed and greater depression, and is not strictly a third independent means of control.

11.22   Zenith starter – VE type carburettor

This semi-automatic device is illustrated in Fig. 11.16. Not now in production, it is interesting as representing the separate miniature car-burettor to supply the small quantities of rich mixture required for starting and idling. An objection to the arrangement is the difficulty of providing for 'inside air'. It consists essentially of a small fixed-choke fixed-jet carburettor proportioned to give the correct quantity of suitably rich mixture for starting, and provided with an automatic air bleed valve controlled by the depression at its own choke. This small carburettor is placed in communication with the induction pipe, on the engine side of the throttle, by the lifting of a cone valve by a cable control. Referring to the figure, C is the choke having at its neck a ring of petrol or petrol-air emulsion holes. Here the petrol metered by the jet J joins the air stream in the choke and the rich starting mixture passes through the open cone valve V to the induction pipe.

As the engine speed increases, the depression in the space S increases until it is great enough to overcome the control spring and move the air-bleed valve B off its seating. This allows air to enter through the annular area around the reduced stem of the valve. This area remains

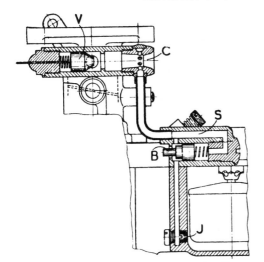

Fig. 11.16 Zenith starting device

constant as the valve opens, and adjustment is effected by changing the valve for one having a different diameter of stem as required.

Thus with increase of speed, the bleed air increases the quantity and weakens the proportions of the mixture to compensate for the improved evaporation. In this fashion a fast idling speed is maintained until warming up is complete, and there is no risk of excess petrol reaching the engine, even in the event of the control not being returned to the closed positon.

11.23   Inter-connected and automatic strangler control

The Stromberg and Zenith-Stromberg designers have adopted the principle of using the main carburettor to assist the idling devices to give the rich mixture for cold starting.

With the mechanically inter-connected strangler used on the Zenith VIG and VIM models the closing of the strangler by the dash-board control opens the throttle slightly from the idling position.

Thus a large depression is communicated to the main system on the principle of Fig. 11.15 and a rich mixture is obtained. A small automatic flap valve in the strangler provides for the admission of an increasing air flow with a sensibly constant depression in the main choke or, with further reference to Fig. 11.15, the entrance to the intermediate chamber increases with the increased demand while the main jet system is subjected to a depression p_1-p_2 the value of which depends on the area, stiffness, and deflection of the flap valve. The depression is about $3.5\,kN/m^2$, or say $35.5\,mm$ of water column.

An inter-connected automatic strangler is used also on the Zenith IV carburettor, Fig. 11.21 and Section 11.39.

11.24   Thermostatic control

Automatic control by means of exhaust manifold temperature is employed in the Solex Thermostarter. The starter unit is similar to that of the self-starter, but communication with the induction pipe is established and cut out automatically by a vacuum-operated diaphragm controlled by a thermally closed leak valve. The control box, which is mounted on the exhaust manifold, contains an adjustable bimetal strip, which on warming up closes by its flexure the leak valve referred to above, with the result that the diaphragm is then subject to a pressure difference which causes movement of the cut-out valve and puts the starter out of action.

In cases where periods of cooling are frequent, as in door-to-door delivery service, the device tends to give somewhat high consumption, and it is more suitable for applications where one or two starts per day under exceptionally cold conditions have to be accomplished.

A more comprehensive thermostatic control is that termed the 'Auto-Starter', on the Zenith CD5T and CD4T carburettors, as described in Section 11.48. Its functions are threefold: to open the throttle slightly for cranking and during the subsequent warm-up, and correspondingly to supply extra fuel during these operations and for acceleration when the engine is cold.

The additional fuel is delivered from the orifice A, Fig. 11.17, to the mixing chamber of the carburettor. Its flow rate is regulated by the tapered metering needle B, which is connected to the lever C which, in turn, is thermostatically controlled by a temperature-sensitive (bimetal) coil D.

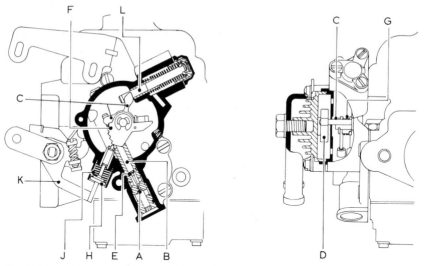

Fig. 11.17 Zenith Auto-starter

This coil is in an aluminium alloy housing, the finned outer end of which is water-jacketed. Engine coolant passing through the jacket subjects the coil to engine temperature. As this temperature increases, the coil rotates the lever C anti-clockwise, to plunge the needle deeper into the orifice and thus reduce the flow. When the engine is adequately warm, the flexible ring at E seals the orifice completely.

Adjustment of the throttle setting is effected automatically by the stepped cam F which floats on the same spindle as the lever C to which it is connected by the torsion spring G. This cam limits the motion of a sliding pin H which, in turn, serves as a stop for a lever K on the throttle spindle.

Which of the steps stops the pin H is determined by the temperature of the coil D, because the cam rotates with the lever C. Since the fast-idle pin is normally held clear of the cam by its return spring J, but is forced back onto it only when the throttle is closed, and because the connection between the cam F and the lever C is a torsion spring, the cam cannot be rotated to reset the idling speed unless the throttle is first opened to lift the lever K so that the pin can be retracted by its return spring. However, even if the vehicle is left unattended, the quantity of fuel metered through the orifice A is progressively reduced during warm-up, since the lever C is returned directly by the bimetal coil, lowering the tapered needle into the orifice.

For setting the throttle for engine cranking, a spring-actuated piston assembly L, which is retracted by induction manifold depression, rotates lever C, and therefore the cam F, clockwise. This rotation of the lever of course also withdraws the tapered needle from the orifice so that extra fuel is supplied.

Prior to starting, the throttle pedal must be depressed to release pin H from the cam F, so that the spring-actuated piston assembly L can pre-set the cam. Once the engine has started, the throttle should again be opened momentarily to release the cam so that it can be returned by the bimetal spring to a position appropriate for the prevailing temperature of the engine. In the meantime, the depression in the manifold will have retracted the piston assembly, compressing its actuation spring and leaving the end of lever C free in a lost motion slot in the end of the piston rod.

If the throttle is then opened wide, for accelerating away from rest, the pressure in the manifold rises, allowing the spring-loaded piston assembly to actuate the lever C and thus withdraw the needle from the jet orifice A. Were it not for this enrichment of the mixture, the cold engine would stall or falter.

11.25   SU automatic starting unit

As can be seen from Fig. 11.18, the ASU comprises what, at first sight, appears to be five castings on top of one another. In fact, the lower of the top two major components is a plastics moulding. The functions of these five main components, starting at the lowest, are as follows: one small casting forms the bottom cover for the lower diaphragm chamber, and clamps this diaphragm to the housing above. In this housing, but separated by a horizontal partition, are the two diaphragms, together with a return spring for the upper one, and a push rod by means of which the action of the lower diaphragm is transmitted in tandem to the upper one.

The upper diaphragm is clamped between its housing and the third casting, in which are the fuel metering needle and jet assembly and, on the right in the illustration, a spring-loaded flap valve, the function of which will be described later. This casting has also two connections: one to the induction manifold and the other for picking up extra air from over the exhaust manifold. In the plastics moulding above are carried an adjustment device at the upper end of the metering needle and jet assembly, the mixture control valve assembly with its diaphragm and, again on the

A   Bimetal assembly
B   Spring-loaded flap valve
C   Diaphragm assembly
D   Jet needle
E   Drilling
F   Jet tube
G   Jet well
H   Bimetal assembly
I   Adjustment
K   Lower diaphragm
L   Main valve
M   Vertical drilling
N   Orifice

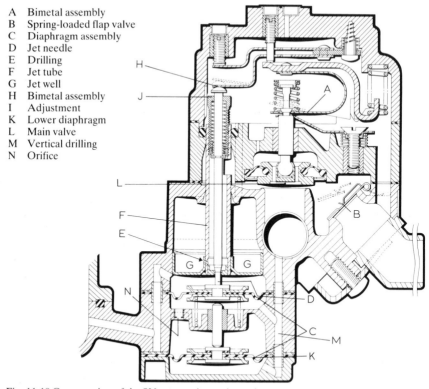

Fig. 11.18 Cross-section of the SU automatic starting unit

extreme right, the adjustment screw for this valve. Housed in the upper casting are the two bimetal strip assemblies, one for the metering needle and the other for the mixture valve.

11.26   Operation

The device draws its fuel from the float chamber of the main carburettor, on which it is mounted. When the engine is static, the level is such that, passing through the top portion of the upper diaphragm chamber, the fuel seeps past the needle jet seating, and through the drilling E into the jet well G.

Under cold starting conditions, the two bimetal assemblies are retracted upwards. This retraction frees the metering needle – on the left – so that the diaphragms below can lift it to supply extra fuel appropriately to match the manifold depression: it also lifts the main mixture valve – in the centre – so that fuel drawn up through the jet tube and out through the slot in its right-hand side can mix with the air flowing down past the mixture valve and on through the central passage into the outlet to the manifold.

During cranking of the engine, the spring-loaded flap valve B is closed for the maintenance of adequate depression in the fuel metering system. In these circumstances, a small quantity of air from the exhaust manifold, passing up the vertical passage on the extreme right in the diagram, by-passes valve B and flows over the bimetal assemblies in the upper casting. It then returns into the third casting through ports in the fourth casting to mix with fuel drawn out from the jet as it passes the mixture valve and then out through the connection to the induction manifold.

As soon as the engine fires, the increase in manifold depression opens the flap valve B and draws air in greater quantities past it to mix with the fuel and pass on to the induction manifold, as before. From this point on, regulation of the flow through the mixture valve is effected partly by manifold depression, acting on its diaphragm, and partly by the bimetal spring. For example, if the throttle is closed suddenly, so that the depression becomes high, the valve is pulled down towards its seat, reducing the extra mixture supply. The diaphragm is able to pull the valve down despite retraction of the bimental strip, by compressing the coil spring interposed between its upper end and the end of that strip.

In the circumstances just described – cold starting – the action of the metering needle controlling the extra fuel supply is as follows: while the engine is cranking, the lower diaphragm K, under the influence of both gravity and the relatively light depression, rests on the base of its chamber, while the one above it is only partially drawn down against the resistance of its return spring. This leaves the metering needle raised appropriately for supplying fuel to the jet tube. As soon as the engine fires, the sudden increase in depression draws both diaphragms down, allowing the needle to come down temporarily to the idling position. At this point, however, fuel is fed from the jet well G through the drilling E into the jet tube, above the needle jet, to provide a rich fuel supply to the manifold.

When the throttle is opened, for moving away from rest, the depression decreases and the return spring lifts the upper diaphragm, raising the metering needle. The height to which it can be lifted is limited by the end of the bimetal strip H, the position of which is determined by the temperature of the air flowing past the exhaust manifold through the by-pass duct, over the two bimetal strips and through the bleed holes in the air valve, to the induction manifold. Cap-nut J is used for adjustment of the setting of the needle, by increasing or decreasing the compression in the coil spring that is housed within it and which acts in opposition to the diaphragm return spring.

If it were not for the action of the lower diaphragm, sensitive to rate of change of depression, a sudden opening of the throttle – for acceleration – would cause a flat spot and the engine might stall. What in fact happens is as follows: when the throttle is closed, the manifold depression pulls the upper diaphragm down and, at the same time, is communicated through the bleed hole N into the chamber above the lower diaphragm; then as the pressures above and below the latter diaphragm come into balance, it sinks on to the bottom cover. As the throttle is suddenly opened, the depression collapses and both diaphragms lift together, the lower one under the influence of the retained depression above and the reduced depression below it, while the upper one is lifted by the return spring. This opens the needle valve to supply extra fuel for the acceleration and then, as the pressures above and below the lower diaphragm are equalised again by the flow through the bleed hole N, allows the needle to lower again to its equilibrium position.

As the engine progressively becomes warm, so also does the flow of air past the bimetal strips. The one above the needle lowers, to reduce the height to which it can be lifted, while that above the mixture valve also lowers but, in this instance, ultimately to close the mixture valve and thus cut off the extra fuel and air supply to the engine.

There are two screws for adjustment of the bimetal strips. One is immediately above the metering needle and its action is obvious from the diagram. The second projects through a hole in the first bimetal strip assembly, and bears on the end of an arched rocker to which the second bimetal strip, A, is riveted. This rocker, in addition to providing for adjustment, is a heat sink preventing the bimetal strip from reacting too rapidly to changes in the temperature of the air drawn in from over the exhaust manifold. When the djustment screw is turned, the rocker pivots about its lugs which seat in V-sections in the plastics moulding. The coil spring bearing down on its hooked end maintains its upper end in contact with the adjustment screw. Once these adjustments have been made in the factory, the countersunk holes containing the heads of the screws are sealed.

There is a third adjustment screw. This is in an insert in the plastics moulding beneath the hooked end of the heat sink, and it is for adjusting the height of the fast-idle device which extends the period of operation of the starter by resisting final closure of the mixture valve. The screw is of course inaccessible in service. Obviously none of these settings should be tampered with after the unit has left the factory.

By the introduction of the ASU four things have been achieved. Starting at temperatures down to $-30°C$ is virtually foolproof. Driveability of the vehicle when the engine is cold has been greatly improved. Exhaust emissions – CO and hydrocarbon under idling conditions in general, and with a cold engine in particular – are kept under much closer control. Finally, and of increasing importance now, fuel consumption in cold running conditions is reduced.

11.27   Idling systems and progression jets

A typical idling system incorporating 'progression jets' is illustrated in Fig. 11.19, which shows the arrangement used in the Zenith VE up-draught carburettor. The idling jet J draws its petrol supply by way of the emulsion block E from the main and compensating jets. This arrangement ensures that the idling jet is starved of petrol and goes out of action when the main system is in action – it does, in fact, then provide an additional air bleed to the emulsion block. On the same principle the practice of feeding the idling or auxiliary jet direct from the float chamber which was used in the early Solex carburettors has been abandoned, and the feed is now taken from the well, which becomes emptied when the main system is fully in action. In this way some tendency to excess petrol consumption is avoided.

To return to Fig. 11.19, it will be seen that the jet sprays into an intermediate chamber or duct D, into which there are three air bleeds or leaks. The outlet from this chamber is to the induction pipe above the throttle, where a high depression exists – see Fig. 11.1.

The depression in the chamber D (*d* of Fig. 11.15) is determined by induction pipe depression p_3, the size of the drilling O, and the effects of the three air leaks, which are as follows. The radial holes in the jet plug communicate with the main choke, where the pressure, with the throttle closed or only very slightly open, may be taken to be atmospheric. This fixed bleed supplies the emulsifying air.

The second bleed is provided by the adjustable air screw A, and the third by the fixed calibrated air plug P which constitutes the progression device. With the throttle closed this plug acts as a fixed air orifice supplying, with the emulsifying bleed, part of the idling air. The adjustment is thus confined to that part of the idling air entering past the screw A, and thus becomes more accurately controllable.

A further idling adjustment is provided by a slight opening of the throttle as necessary. This slightly reduces the induction pipe depression and gives a larger quantity of weaker mixture, owing to the fact that the petrol flow is reduced concurrently with the increase of air flow.

11.28 Progression or transfer action

A difficulty experienced with the fixed choke carburettor is the tendency to a flat spot on transfer from the idling system to the main system as the throttle is opened up. The opening of the throttle reduces the depression on the drilling O before sufficient depression becomes available at the main choke, but the gap is bridged by the intense local depression which then develops at the edge of the throttle disc, on the principle expressed in Bernoulli's theorem that in a fluid stream, high velocity and high kinetic energy are accompanied by low potential or pressure energy. With the throttle opened to a moderate extent as shown by the broken lines, the progression jet becomes a delivery jet for the idling system, on which depression is maintained until the main system is in action. In some instances, for example Zenith IZE, Fig. 11.32, there is more than one outlet in the progression system.

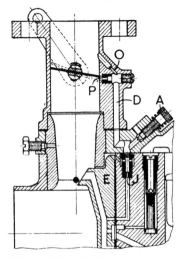

Fig. 11.19 Zenith idling system

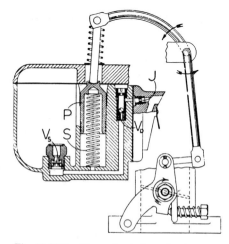

Fig. 11.20 Zenith mechanical accelerator pump

11.29   Accelerating well or pump

It has been said that the ideal carburettor should maintain correct mixture strength at all combinations of throttle opening and speed. Certain of these combinations give rise to difficulties. Thus if, after a period of low speed and light load, the throttle is suddenly opened to accelerate the engine the following conditions arise. The high depression previously existing in the induction pipe is momentarily applied to the choke, but the sudden rush of air induced is so momentary that the petrol cannot respond quickly enough owing to its own inertia. Thus the first rush of mixture is very weak. The situation is now as follows. A big throttle opening will have put the idling device out of action, while the poor vacuum producing capacity of the pistons due to the low engine speed, will be producing only a very small depression at the main jet, with the result that a very patchy and poorly atomised mixture will be produced. This will cause hesitation and misfiring.

Suppose, however, that there is a body of petrol available between the throttle and the jet, as in the well of the Zenith and in the jet tube and well of the Solex carburettors. The flow of this petrol is not controlled by the constriction of the main jet and therefore it will flow readily in response to the weak suction, temporarily enriching the mixture until the engine has gained speed. Such a 'pick-up' well is practically essential in fixed choke carburettors if satisfactory acceleration at low speeds is desired and in certain models of the majority of leading makes of carburettor this 'snap' acceleration is made still more certain by means of a positive pump which delivers a charge of petrol into the choke when the throttle is suddenly opened.

11.30   Zenith mechanically-operated pump

The pump fitted to the Zenith VIG down-draught carburettor is operated from the throttle lever by a long bell-crank lever as shown in Fig. 11.20. The pump plunger P is raised by the internal spring S and petrol flows from the bowl through the suction valves V_s. During the delivery stroke caused by rapid movement of the accelerator pedal, the petrol is forced through the double-seated ball valve and pump jet J as a fine spray into the beak of the emulsion block. The upper seat for the ball valve provides a vent to break any suction that might be communicated from the choke and so cause syphoning over. For slow movements of the accelerator, there is sufficient clearance around the pump plunger to allow the petrol to be by-passed and no delivery takes place.

Zenith use a prolonged-action mechanical pump on the Series IV carburettor, Fig. 11.21. In this instance, as the throttle is closed, the pump plunger moves upwards, drawing in fuel from the float chamber through the non-return valve in the base of its cyinder. When the throttle is opened, the piston rod A is forced down, compressing two concentric coil springs. The outer of these is the return spring, while the inner one is interposed between the piston rod – which is a sliding fit in the piston – and the piston B. It is the inner spring, therefore, that forces the piston down progressively over a period of time dependent on the rate of the spring and the size of

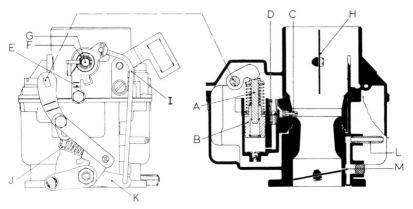

Fig. 11.21 Zenith IV carburettor, showing accelerator pump

the orifice in the pump jet C. The non-return valve D, of course, prevents reverse flow through the jet during subsequent closure of the throttle. As in the device described in the preceding paragraph, the upper vent in this non-return valve prevents syphoning of the fuel out of the pump through the jet.

The length of stroke of this pump can be changed – short for summer or long for winter operation. For this adjustment there are two holes in the end of the external lever, by means of which the pump is connected to the throttle control.

11.31   Stromberg pump: Type DBV carburettor

This pump is shown in Fig. 11.22. As the throttle is opened the pump piston rod R is pulled down and, through the compression spring S, drives downwards the pump plunger P, the pump chamber having been filled on the previous return stroke through the plate suction valve V.

The petrol is delivered through the ball valve at a rate controlled by the size of the discharge reducer D and the stiffness of the plunger spring, which by its compression will give a spread-over delivery into the choke through the spraying jet J. As in the Zenith VIG, there is a carefully controlled clearance around the piston to allow of by-passing during slow movement of the accelerator pedal.

11.32   Devices controlled by manifold depression

Variations in manifold depression may be used in various ways for the control of mixture characteristics, as also for ignition advance and retard. Fig. 11.1 shows that large throttle opening is accompanied by reduced induction pipe vacuum; that is, high absolute pressure in the inlet manifold implies a full cylinder charge, and if the fuel:air ratio is correct, high mep and power.

Thus power, economy and snap acceleration may all be controlled by sustained or sudden variations of manifold pressure.

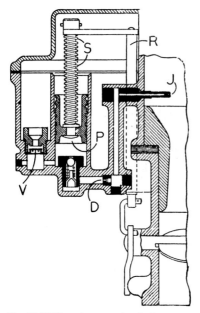

Fig. 11.22 Stromberg mechanical pump

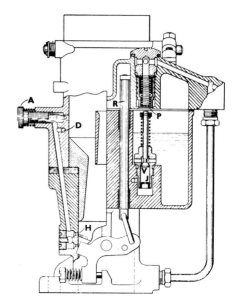

Fig. 11.23 Stromberg DBV carburettor by-pass valve and jet

In the Stromberg DBV down-draught carburettor shown in Fig. 11.23 a by-pass or power enrichment valve V is opened by the fall of the spring-loaded piston P when the depression sustaining it, and communicated by the external pipe (or in later models by internal drillings) is sufficiently reduced by opening of the throttle.

The flow is metered by the jet J.

The following additional details may be noted in Fig. 11.23: the air adjusting screw A for the idling mixture which is delivered through the discharge holes or progression jets H, and the pump operating rod R, linked to the throttle arm. D is the internal drilling through which is delivered the petrol metered by the idling jet. For diagrammatic clarity certain components are shown out of their actual position and plane in the carburettor body.

11.33 Zenith depression-actuated economiser

A common feature on Zenith carburettors is a depression-actuated economy valve. Examples are on the IZ and IV carburettors described in Sections 11.38 and 11.39 and illustrated in Figs. 11.24 and 11.25. In the IZ, the diaphragm valve closes to cut off the fuel supply to what is termed an economy jet during part throttle cruising operation, while in the IV the diaphragm opens an extra air vent to weaken the mixture under these conditions. On some of the IVEP carburettors, the IZ-type economy valve, as decribed in Section 11.38, is used; this controls the power jet in a manner similar to that of the economy jet.

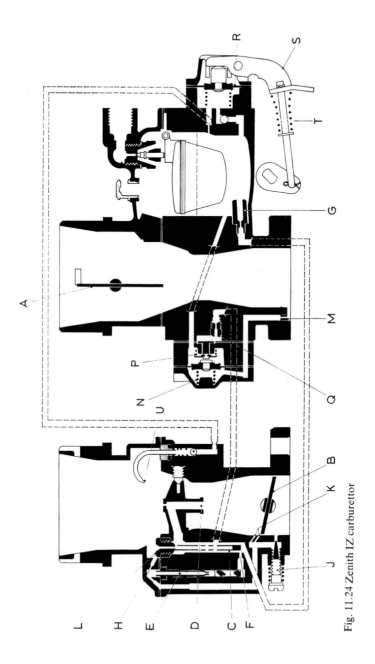

Fig. 11.24 Zenith IZ carburettor

268

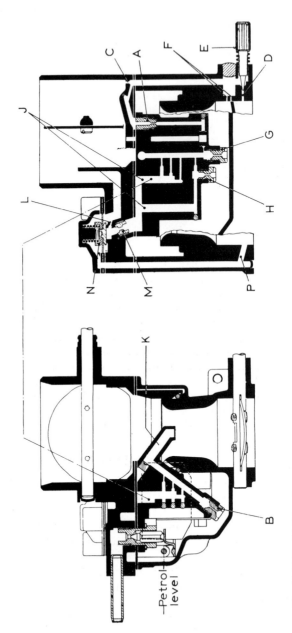

Fig. 11.25 Zenith IV carburettor

11.34 Solex vacuum-controlled accelerating pump

This membrane type of pump is fitted to certain Solex down-draught models, and is illustrated in Fig. 11.26 which is partly diagrammatic and applies to the AIP model.

P is the pump chamber supplied through a ball suction valve from the duct D which communicates directly with the float chamber.

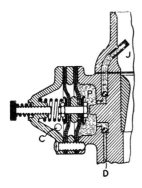

Fig. 11.26 Solex membrane type acceleration pump

The suction stroke is effected by the induction manifold vacuum on the engine side of the throttle being communicated through an internal drilling to the hole C, the membrane spring being thereby compressed. The collapse of the vacuum consequent on the opening of the throttle allows the spring to deliver the charge of petrol through the ball delivery valve and the side drilling of the jet J, which projects a fine stream into the neck of the choke. The spring may be so adjusted that the pump is filled only at suitably high values of the induction vacuum, during light running, subsequent to which rapid acceleration would be required.

Under 'all-out' high-speed conditions, the depression surrounding the jet J will become large enough to cause continuous spraying, thus providing a rich mixture at the top end of the range.

11.35 Up-draught and down-draught systems

The down-draught system has displaced almost universally both the up-draught and horizontal types of carburettor. The functional advantage claimed is that gravity assists instead of hindering the comparatively low spraying velocity of the fuel, thus aiding the atomisation and enabling a somewhat larger choke to be used with a corresponding improvement in performance.

Improved accessibility of the carburettor, with convenient accommodation for the air cleaner and silencer, is provided with the down-draught arrangement, and no difficulty is experienced with petrol supply by electric or mechanical pumps. In some installations provision is made for draining flooded petrol, which naturally falls beyond the throttle to the induction pipe, by means of an atmospheric pipe of vertical length sufficient, when filled with petrol, to overcome moderate induction pipe depression and thus allow for drainage through an upwardly-closing ball valve at the foot of the pipe. The ball valve prevents inward air leak under idling conditions.

There has been a return to the external induction manifold from the cast-in distribution systems which had become popular with the horizontal carburettor. These external manifolds incorporate hot spot contact with the exhaust manifold, and in some cases provision of thermostatic shutter control is made to regulate the local flow of the exhaust gases. Because of legislation against the discharge of hydrocarbons into the atmosphere, fuel drain pipes are of course now ruled out for road vehicles.

11.36 Solex progressive starter

The starter unit, on the left of the main view of Fig. 11.27, is operated by a manual control from the dashboard. In early models of this unit there were only two positions of this control, giving free communication of manifold depression to the starter chamber and so to the air jet Ga and to the well described in Section 11.29 through the duct D, or complete closure with the dashboard control in its off position.

No progressive action was provided in the operation of the control.

The bi-starter and the progressive bi-starter are variants of this arrangement, the former being a two-step movement with definitely-located full, intermediate and off positions. The progressive control allows for gradual change from the intermediate to the off position by regulated movement of the dashboard control.

Automatic weakening of mixture strength occurs with the exhaustion of the well.

In the intermediate position shown at Fig. 11.27 (*a*) the valve disc now presents a small dished hole Hc to the fuel duct D, and at the same time opens a second air vent Z to inside atmospheric air. The fuel and the air from this second vent share the restricted entry Hc to the starter chamber, so that a slightly larger quantity of much weaker but better emulsified mixture (for the same engine speed) enters the chamber and reaches the manifold. As the control is gradually pushed home, a progressive reduction of all the port areas takes place until they are finally closed at the completion of the fast idle warming up period, after which the action is transferred to the idle and main throttle systems.

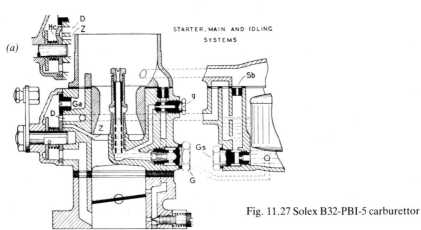

Fig. 11.27 Solex B32-PBI-5 carburettor

11.37   Zenith W type carburettors

These have basic features developed from Stromberg designs, including bottom feed to the float chamber, double venturi and air bleed emulsion tube as illustated in Fig. 11.10, mechanically-operated accelerating pump and economiser or power enrichment valve opened for full load conditions as shown in Fig. 11.28 (*c*), but closed at part throttle.

In the WIA assembly, as in the DBV type shown in Fig. 11.23, the by-pass or enrichment valve is operated by induction vacuum, but instead of a piston, a spring loaded diaphragm is used, the vacuum duct consisting of internal drillings instead of the external pipe shown in Fig. 11.23. At part throttle the induction pipe vacuum lifts the diaphragm and allows the valve to close.

For the WI type a direct mechanical control was developed, an adjustable degree of lost motion ensuring that the valve opened only in the last stages of throttle movement. This has not been widely used but is illustrated in Fig. 11.28 (*d*).

Both models include direct mechanical operation of the accelerating pump, with spring return of the piston instead of the spreadover spring delivery shown in Fig. 11.22. Seasonal adjustment of the pump stroke is provided by three alternative pin holes in the driven lever of the operating linkage. On a larger version, the 42W, an accelerating pump similar in principle to that in Fig. 11.21 is used, but with a different valve arrangement.

The strangler flap is urged by its spindle spring to the shut position but, through its lever and follower pin which bears on the starting cam, is prevented from closing until the cam is rotated by the strangler control cable to permit of the spring closure, the throttle being simultaneously cracked open for the start by the connecting rod and lost motion crank.

Fig. 11.28 shows in a diagrammatic manner how provision for these various phases is made.

A general section is shown at (*a*) through the float chamber, large and small venturis, and the main jet plug M and emulsion or main discharge tube T.

If Fig. 11.10 is compared, it will be seen that the correction or bleed holes are now placed on the under side of the inclined discharge tube T.

This view also shows the strangler flap in the fully open position, and the inside air drilling by way of which bleed air reaches the idle jet discharge by internal drillings.

Fig. 11.28 (*b*) shows the idling system, the accelerating pump inlet valve and operating crank, and the vacuum duct from the induction manifold to the chamber housing the spring loaded diaphragm which opens the economiser valve. At the bottom of the view, on the right, are the usual features of progression holes at the edge of the throttle disc, and the adjusting screw for *quantity* of idling mixture.

Fig. 11.28 (*c*) shows a full section of the diaphragm chamber and economiser valve operation, and the pump delivery valve and control jet. This view shows the inclined delivery duct by which the enrichment petrol is led to the outside of the main discharge tube, in which, after passing

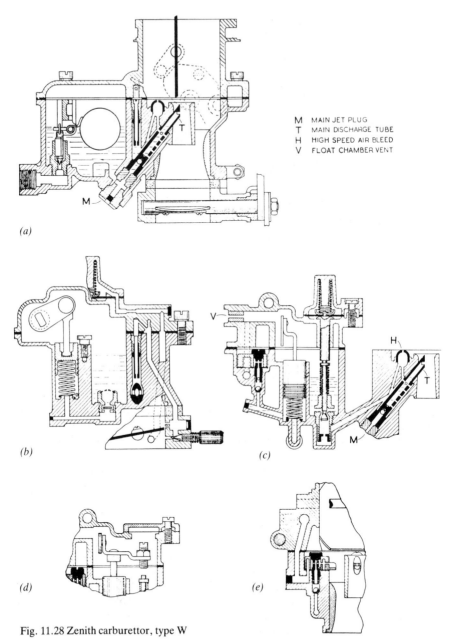

M   MAIN JET PLUG
T   MAIN DISCHARGE TUBE
H   HIGH SPEED AIR BLEED
V   FLOAT CHAMBER VENT

(a)

(b)

(c)

(d)

(e)

Fig. 11.28 Zenith carburettor, type W

through the bleed holes, it joins the main emulsion for delivery to the throat of the small venturi.

The scrap view (*e*) shows the method of delivery through the pump discharge nozzle into the main choke.

The external view of Fig. 11.29 will give some idea of the actual construction.

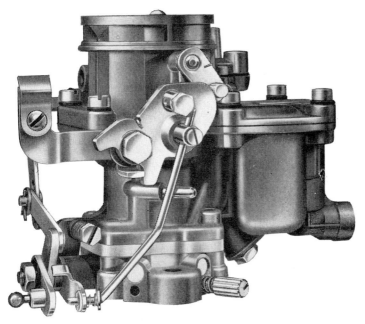

Fig. 11.29 Zenith carburettor, type W

11.38   Zenith IZ carburettors

Each carburettor in the IZ series, Fig. 11.24, has an offset manual strangler, for cold starting, a prolonged-action-type accelerator pump, a depression-actuated economy device and volume control of idle mixture. Another refinement is a filtered slow-running tube, togther with jets and passages designed to provide maximum protection against dirt or other foreign matter liable to have adverse effects on performance.

For starting from cold, operation of the choke control closes the strangler flap A. Simultaneously, a cam interconnection opens the throttle a predetermined amount to allow the manifold depression to reach the choke tube and mixing chambers for drawing off the fast idling mixture from the main well C. This mixture is discharged through the orifice D. As soon as the engine fires, the increased depression partially opens the strangler against the closing force applied to it by the torsion spring connecting it to the choke control. The degree of opening of course depends upon the throttle movement. However, the choke control must be fully released as soon as the engine temperature has risen sufficiently.

In normal idling conditions, without the strangler, the mixture is supplied by the slow running tube E, which is enclosed in a gauze filter. The fuel is drawn initially through the restriction F, from the metered side of the main jet G, and the air enters, to emulsify it, through the calibrated bleed orifice H, from the air intake. Ultimately, the emulsified mixture is drawn down a vertical channel to the idle discharge hole – into which projects the tapered end of the volume adjustment screw J. While the throttle stop screw is used to set the idling speed, the volume adjustment screw regulates the quantity of emulsified idling mixture supplied for mixing with the air passing the throttle. Smooth transfer from the idle to main circuits is obtained via the two progression holes K, which come in turn under the influence of the local venturi effect caused by the proximity of the edge of the throttle to them.

As the throttle is opened further, the increasing depression in the waist of the choke brings the main system into operation. From the main jet G, the fuel passes into the well C. Air, metered through the orifice L, passes down the central emulsion tube and, passing through radial holes in it, mixes with the fuel before it enters the main discharge orifice D in the narrowest part of the choke. As the engine speed increases, the fuel level in the main well falls, uncovering more radial holes in the emulsion tube so that an increasing quantity of air can mix with the fuel to correct the mixture strength.

A depression-actuated economy device is attached by three brass screws to one side of the float chamber. At cruising speeds, the relatively high induction manifold depression is transmitted, past a calibrated restriction M to the chamber between the diaphragm and its outer cover. This overcomes the load in the return spring N and moves the diaphragm to the left, as viewed in Fig. 11.24, allowing the chamber between the diaphragm and the main body of the device to fill with fuel, and the spring-loaded valve P to close. Since closure of this valve puts the jet Q out of action, fuel can now be drawn only from the main jet.

As the throttle is opened further, and the depression in the manifold becomes less intense, the diaphragm return-spring extends, moving the diaphragm to the right and opening the spring-loaded valve P. Fuel, metered by jet Q, then passes into the main well to enrich the mixture for increasing the power output.

For acceleration, especially from cruising speed at the weak mixture setting, a prolonged action diaphragm pump R is incorporated. This pump functions on principles similar to those described in Sections 11.29, 11.30 and 11.34. In detail, however, it differs in several respects. The prolonged action is obtained by arranging for the link with the throttle control to slide in a hole in the pump actuation lever S, and transmitting the motion through a compression spring T interposed between them. From Fig. 11.24, it can be seen that there is a small back-bleed hole interconnecting the pump delivery chamber and the float chamber. This is to prevent discharge of fuel through the pump jet U, owing to thermal expansion of the fuel if the carburettor castings become very hot – for example, if the engine is stopped immediately after a period of operation under high load.

11.39   Zenith IV carburettors

The IV series of carburettors is a development of the V type. Among the improvements is the incorporation of twin floats, set one each side of the choke and with their centroids and that of the float chamber itself as close as practicable to the jets, Fig. 11.25, so that the fuel level above the jets is virtually unaffected by changes in inclination of the vehicle, or by acceleration, braking and cornering.

All the jets, and the accelerator pump are carried in an emulsion block, which can be readily removed with a screwdriver and a 7/16″ spanner. The outlet from this emulsion block, or jet carrier, passes into a discharge nozzle, which is cast integrally with the block and which takes the mixture to the venturi. A single casting combines both the choke and float chamber integrally and, since there are neither screws nor plugs in the exterior of the float chamber, there are no potential external leakage points below the fuel level.

The principle of the accelerator pump has been described in Section 11.29. For other conditions of operation, the jets and systems that come into operation are as follows: on starting from cold, operation of the choke control pulls lever E, Fig. 11.21. This lever, through the medium of a torsion spring F, rotates the strangler spindle G and closes the strangler H. Simultaneously, the rod I, interconnecting the strangler and throttle, opens the latter to set it for fast idle. After the engine has fired and is running, the increased depression will open the strangler against the torsion applied by spring F, to prevent over-choking. As the engine warms up, the choke control must of course be released to reduce the idling speed to normal.

For idling, the mixture is supplied through the slow running jet A, Fig. 11.25. Fuel reaches it from the main jet B – that is, from the base of the emulsion block – through a calibrated restriction. After discharging from the slow-running jet, the fuel is emulsified by air bleeding from orifice C into the vertical channel which takes it down to the idle hole D, through which it is discharged downstream of the throttle.

The tapered end of the volume control screw E projects into the idle hole D. Adjustments to idling speed are made as follows: turn the throttle stop screw, J in Fig. 11.21, until the required speed is obtained – clockwise to increase, anti-clockwise to decrease. Then turn the volume control screw, E in Fig. 11.25, to obtain the fastest possible idling speed at that setting of the throttle stop. Repeat both operations as necessary. Where stringent emission controls are in force, it may be necessary for the volume control to be set – clockwise rotation weakens the mixture – by the vehicle manufacturer by reference to an exhaust gas analysis and then sealed.

As the throttle is opened, the local venturi effect between its edge and each of the progression holes F, in turn, draws additional fuel through them until the main jet system can take over. The size and positioning of these two holes is of course critical and no adjustment is allowed. Incidentally, the pipe L in Fig. 11.21 is the connection for the automatic ignition advance, and the small hole M, through which it communicates with the throttle bore, is carefully calibrated.

With further opening of the throttle, and the consequent increase in the depression in the waist of the choke tube, fuel is drawn from the outlet from the emulsion block. This fuel comes from the main jet G and compensating jet H. As the level of the fuel in the channels above these jets falls, air takes its place in the capacity wells J, above the main and compensating jets, and then bleeds through the emulsion holes into the outlet K. The rate of flow of this air is controlled by the full throttle air bleed hole L and, at times, by the larger orifice in the ventilation screw M, which depends for its extra air supply on operation of the economy diaphragm-valve N. Fuel, already emulsified by the time it leaves the outlet, is further atomised as it is swept away by the air flowing through the choke tube.

The arrangement of the economy device is as follows: it is housed in a small casting secured by three screws on top of the float chamber, adjacent to the air intake, and the diaphragm valve N is held on its seat by a spring. The chamber above the diaphragm is connected to an outlet P downstream of the throttle butterfly valve.

At part throttle, when the depression downstream of the butterfly valve is high, the diaphragm valve is lifted off its seat, allowing extra air to flow from the air intake through the ventilation screw M, to increase the emulsification of the fuel and thus to weaken the mixture, for economical cruising. When the throttle is opened further, calling for high power output, the manifold depression falls, allowing the spring to return the diaphragm valve to its seat, and the mixture is therefore enriched.

11.40   Adaptation for emission control

Zenith fixed-choke carburettors adapted for emission control carry the suffix E on their designations. These include the IZE, IVE and WIAET. The letter T, incidentally, is used to indicate that an automatic strangler is incorporated.

Among the features incorporated is a solenoid-actuated slow-running cut-off – used on some of the IVE carburettors. Because of the weak setting of the idling and slow-running mixtures on emission-controlled engines, the resultant abnormally high temperatures of combustion can cause auto-ignition when the engine is switched off. To avoid this, the slow-running supply is automatically cut off with the ignition. The device used is simply a conical-ended plunger, which is forced on to a seating by a spring. When the engine is switched on, the solenoid is energised, to lift the plunger off the seating, thus opening the slow running supply system.

On the IZE, instead of the drilled hole and dust cap on the float chamber, there is either a two-way venting system or a simpler internal vent. The simpler system is a vent channel running within the float chamber cover casting and breaking out into the upper part of the carburettor air intake. This satisfies requirements in respect of evaporative emission control and, by subjecting the float chamber to air intake pressure, obviates all possibility of enrichment of the mixture as a result of abnormally high depression over the jets due to a clogged air intake filter element.

A disadvantage, however, is that when the engine is idling, fumes from the float chamber vent can enrich the mixture and adversely affect emissions. Additionally, because of the accumulation of fumes in the air intake after a hot engine is switched off, restarting may be extremely difficult.

For these reasons, in some applications, the dual venting arrangement may be necessary. With this arrangement, the internal vent A, Fig. 11.30, is permanently open, but an external vent is brought into and out of operation by a plunger type valve actuated by the accelerating pump lever.

The valve assembly is a press fit in a boss on one side of the float chamber cover. Its plunger is spring-loaded towards its outer position, in

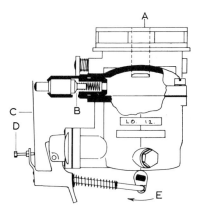

Fig. 11.30 Zenith dual venting system

which the float chamber is freely vented to atmosphere through hole B. A spring steel blade C, attached to the accelerator pump control, is used to close the valve when the throttle is opened. This leaves the float chamber under the influence of air intake depression, through the internal vent. The proximity of the steel blade to the plunger is set, using screw D, during manufacture and should not be altered subsequently.

Another device used, in one form or another, in several carburettors including the Zenith IVE, is an over-run control valve. This is necessary because, on sudden closure of the throttle, the intense depression draws into the engine all the condensed fuel clinging to the walls of the manifold. This initially enriches the mixture and, subsequently, leaves it over-weak. In each condition, the hydrocarbon emissions in the exhaust become unsatisfactory.

The over-run-control device is a spring-loaded, poppet-type, non-return valve in the throttle butterfly, as shown in Fig. 11.31. For normal operation, including tick-over, this valve is kept closed by its spring but, if the throttle is closed for deceleration and the manifold depression is therefore high enough to suck it off its seat, two things happen. First, the depression is relieved sufficiently to avoid the over-enrichment phase and, secondly, extra mixture bleeds through holes beneath the head of the poppet valve, to maintain proper combustion in the cylinders and to relieve the depression slightly.

Because the idle and light throttle opening positions are critical as regards emission control, it is sometimes desirable to have a pre-set relationship between the edge of the throttle valve and the idling progression holes and, on some carburettors required for meeting the US emissions regulations, a suction retard port for the ignition. Consequently, on some IZE carburettors, the throttle stop is adjusted during manufacture and thereafter sealed, so another method has had to be introduced for adjusting idling speed in service.

For this purpose a throttle by-pass system has been introduced. As can be seen from Fig. 11.32, a channel runs from A below the choke to an outlet B downstream from the edge of the throttle. Air flow through this channel is adjusted by means of a taper-ended screw, C, near the inlet – if turned clockwise, it reduces the idling speed, and *vice versa*. The idling mixture is controlled by the volume control screw D, in the outlet. When

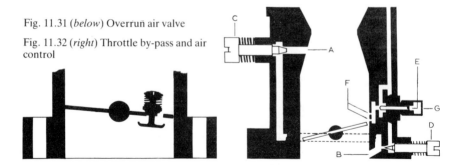

Fig. 11.31 (*below*) Overrun air valve

Fig. 11.32 (*right*) Throttle by-pass and air control

the throttle is opened, the depressions at the inlet and outlet of the by-pass channel become much the same, so it ceases to function, the progression holes taking over the function of supplying a suitable mixture.

It is of interest that the emission-controlled versions of the W type carburettors are adequate without any of the devices described in this section. Their emission control is effected by close tolerances in production, and subsequent testing.

11.41   Solex MIMAT carburettor

The MIMAT is a down-draught, twin-choke carburettor, with throttles compounded to open one after the other – the throttle in the secondary choke does not start to open until that in the primary is about two-thirds open. Both chokes of course are the same diameter. This twin-choke arrangement mitigates the disadvantages of a fixed-choke carburettor, which are a tendency towards poor atomisation at low air-speeds and strangulation at high speeds. Although careful design and setting is necessary to obtain smooth change-over from single- to twin-choke operation, the difficulties associated with the maintenance of synchronisation of two carburettors throughout the range in service are avoided.

From Fig. 11.33, the arrangement of the main jets can be seen, while the slow-running system is shown in Fig. 11.34. The method of operation of the main jets is obvious from the illustration, but one or two details need clarification.

In Fig. 11.33, the nozzles A through which the mixture is delivered to the choke are held in position by spring retaining devices, which can be seen one each side of the siamesed central portion of the choke tube. The main jets are at B, and the illustration shows only the primary choke in operation. There are two air-bleed passages to each diffuser tube assembly, which comprises a central tube drawing its air supply from C, and an outer tube the air supply to which comes from D. These air supplies pass respectively through calibrated restrictors E and F. Fuel enters the outer tube through its open lower end, into which air bleeds through radial holes to the annular space between the two tubes.

The idling and slow-running progression system is more complex, since it comprises three different circuits: two are identical, one serving the primary and the other the secondary choke tube, while the third supplies

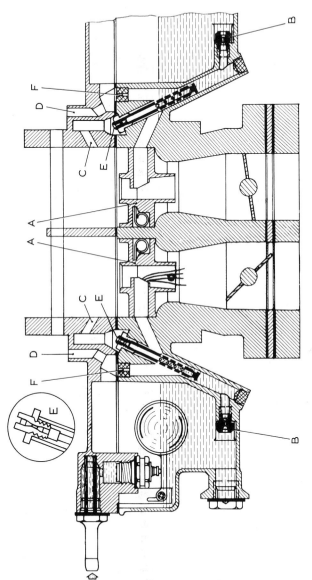

Fig. 11.33 Solex MIMAT carburettor, main jet system

280

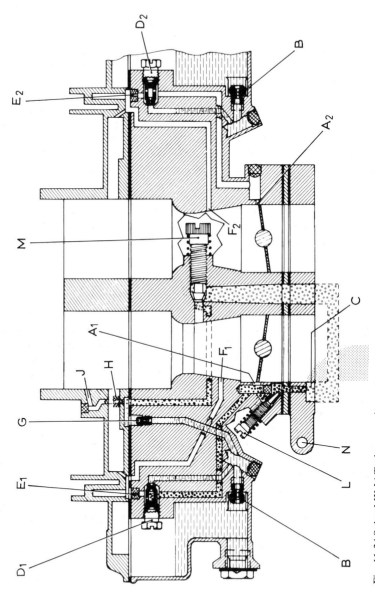

Fig. 11.34 Solex MIMAT, slow-running system

only the primary system. The first two draw their fuel from the metered supply from the main jets B, in Fig. 11.34, while the third takes it also from a jet B but only the one serving the primary choke.

In Fig. 11.34, both throttles are shown closed. Consequently, the edge of that in the secondary choke tube is downstream of the idling mixture outlet A_2, which is circular, and therefore renders the idling system for that choke inoperative. Although the outlet A_1 in the primary choke tube is a slot, for obtaining the required progression as the throttle is opened, its lower end is closed by the edge of the throttle, so this outlet too is unaffected by any local depression.

In these circumstances – hot idling – the mixture is supplied through a throttle by-pass system serving only the primary choke tube. Manifold depression is transmitted through the mixture outlet C, in the bottom flange of the carburettor, and draws fuel from two sources: one is the slow-running jet D_1, into which air is bled through orifice E_1 from the inlet F_1 below the waist of the primary choke, while the other is the jet G, into which air is bled through orifice H from both J, in the primary air intake, and K, just below the waist of the primary choke. The relative positions of all these inlets and outlets are such that, when the throttles in their chokes are open, the pressures in the mixture passages are not low enough to draw any fuel from the jets.

Jets D_1 and D_2 are not for adjustment in service, nor is screw L, which is adjusted in the factory for setting the idling air:fuel ratio. On the other hand, screw M is a volume adjuster for regulating the quantity of mixture passing, and thus the idling speed in service.

As the primary throttle is opened, the progression slot A_1 comes into operation, under the influence of the local depression, until the edge of the throttle valve swings clear of it. At about two-thirds primary throttle opening, the secondary throttle begins to move, and therefore, the progression hole A2 comes in to play, drawing fuel from jet D_2 and air from orifice E_2.

For cold starting, an automatic strangler and fast idle system, Fig. 11.35, operates. The strangler is opened by a spiral bimetal strip A and closed by a diaphragm B, actuated by manifold depression. For opening the throttle for fast idling, there is a stepped cam rotated by a second spiral bimetal strip C. The first mentioned bimetal strip is subjected to engine coolant temperature by a water jacket D, while the second is under the influence of ambient air temperature.

One end of the first bimetal strip is anchored to the water-jacket casting, while the other is connected to a lever E on a spindle F, which is linked, by another lever K and a rod, to the strangler G. The setting of the bimetal strip A is such that it tends to open the strangler above a pre-set low temperature, generally about $-20°C$.

The bimetal strip C, subject to ambient air tempeture, is anchored to the spindle D, its other end being connected to a stepped cam, which is free to rotate on that spindle except in that it tends to be rotated anti-clockwise by the bimetal strip with decreasing temperature. There are two sets of steps on the cam: one is for limiting the closure of the primary throttle by lever G, and the other for limiting the upward motion of the stop-screw H at the bottom of tie rod J.

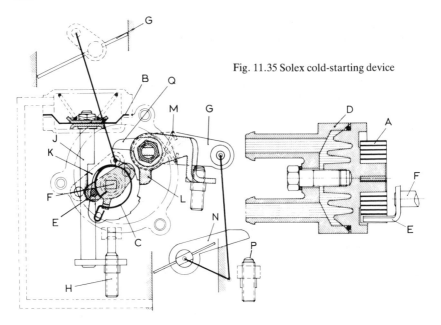

Fig. 11.35 Solex cold-starting device

The tie-rod is actuated by the diaphragm B which, prior to starting, is pulled down by its return spring. This allows lever E, a pin on which projects into the long notch in the tie-rod, to be pulled downwards by bimetal strip A. The strangler can be opened again by either manifold depression or increasing engine coolant temperature, or by over-ride devices to be described later, but its upward motion is limited by the cam, the position of which is determined by ambient air temperature acting upon bimetal strip C.

This cam also limits the closure of the primary throttle in cold conditions, by acting as a stop for lever L, which is secured to lever G by a spring M. The positions of the levers G and L, relative to each other, are adjustable by means of the screw stop on the latter, and the closure of the throttle in warm conditions is limited by stop P acting on lever N.

Before starting from cold, the driver presses the throttle pedal down once and then releases it. This allows the cam, under the influence of bimetal strip C, to take up a position appropriate to the ambient air temperature. In Fig. 11.35, the ambient temperature is assumed to be $-20°C$, so the strangler is appropriately closed by bimetal strip A.

When the engine starts, the increasing manifold depression, acting on the diaphragm, opens the strangler an amount limited by the stop at the lower end of its tie-rod, which is pulled up against the cam. Should the ambient air temperature subsequently rise, the cam will be progressively rotated clockwise by the bimetal strip C, so that the strangler can be opened further step-by-step.

As the engine coolant temperature rises, rotation of the spindle F, by the bimetal strip A, of course rotates the strangler actuating lever – until it is fully open – its end moving upwards within the notch in the diaphragm tie-rod.

If the engine is to be started from cold, but in a moderate ambient temperature, perhaps about +10°C, a larger throttle opening than that set by the position of the cam might be required. This opening is set by a peg projecting from the end of the lever K. As the strangler is closed, this peg comes into contact with the peg that connects the cam to its bimetal strip, pushing it round to set the throttle stop accordingly. When the engine starts, the first light pressure on the accelerator pedal releases the cam, which then takes up its normal position.

Should the engine fail to start, owing to an over-rich mixture, the accelerator pedal should be pushed right down. This causes the strangler to be opened by contact between projection Q, from the throttle actuation lever G, which rotates lever K against the loading applied to it by the bimetal strip A. The engine is then rotated to ventilate the cylinders, before attempting to start it again in the normal manner.

To avoid icing in cold and humid operating conditions, an engine coolant supply is taken straight through the bottom flange of the carburettor by connections to each end of the hole N in Fig. 11.34. This heats the region of the butterfly valves, the slow running outlets and the throttle by-pass circuit.

The accelerating pump, Fig. 11.36, is diaphragm-actuated by a lever, the end A of which bears on a cam B mounted on the spindle carrying the secondary throttle. It therefore operates only when the secondary throttle is in use, which helps as regards fuel economy. Spring C is provided to prolong the action of the pump.

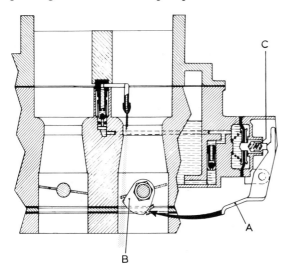

Fig. 11.36 Solex acceleration pump

Another device that operates only in the secondary choke tube is the compensating jet A, Fig. 11.37, which is controlled by a diaphragm valve subject to manifold depression. This valve is held open by a return spring but, when the manifold depression is high – light throttle operation – it is closed and sealed by an elastomeric ring on its seating face. As can be seen from the illustration, when the valve is open, the fuel flows through jet A into the diffuser well serving the secondary choke. Solex also can supply a

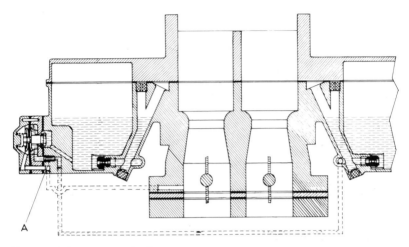

Fig. 11.37 Solex compensating jet system

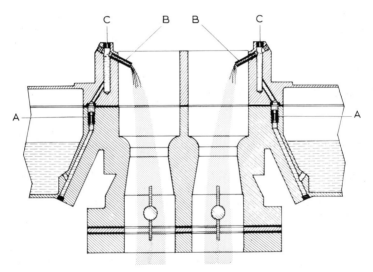

Fig. 11.38 Solex Econostat power-jet system

similar valve, but operating in the opposite sense – that is, enriching the mixture at wider throttle openings, instead of weakening it at light openings.

These diaphragm-actuated devices should not be confused with the Econostat power-jet system, Fig. 11.38. In this, the fuel, coming directly from the float chamber, is metered through jets A and discharged through nozzles B into the air intakes upstream of the chokes. By virtue of their position and the fact that fuel can be drawn off only when the depression in the air intake drops to a certain value, they cannot discharge fuel except at high speed and load. The level of depression at which these jets come into operation is determined by the size of the air bleed orifices C.

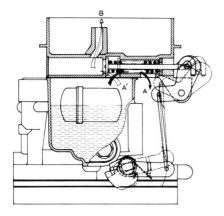

Fig. 11.39 Solex two-way vent

One more detail of interest on this carburettor is the two-way vent system for the float chamber, Fig. 11.39. Under slow-running conditions, the valve is spring-loaded on to its innermost seat so that the float chamber is vented externally at A. However, when the throttle is opened, an interconnecting linkage moves the valve to the right, as viewed in the illustration, on to its other seat. This opens the port to the internal ventilation system connected at B.

11.42 Multi-barrel carburettors

The intensive development in the USA of high-powered V-eight engines has naturally been accompanied by corresponding carburettor development by the leading corporations.   These modern instruments, which are all of the open choke type, have become somewhat complicated units, though in only one major feature do they incorporate any new combination of established principles. This is in the provision of two separately fed venturis with linked throttles which are brought into action successively to full parallel operation on maximum load.

The limitations of the simple or basic open or fixed choke class of carburettor are mentioned in Section 11.20 in connection with starting and idling devices. A small depression applied to a large orifice is unsatisfactory from the points of view both of metering and spraying or atomisation. Conditions are most unsatisfactory in the main choke in the early stages of transfer from the idling system, and progressively improve as the speed and load increase. The desire to provide full flexibility of performance, with, in some cases the highest degree of press button automaticity, has led to the extreme exploitation of the advantages of fixed orifices provided by the constant choke class of carburettor.

This has resulted in complication, but not necessarily in reduced reliability, and flexibility of performance is generally greater than is obtainable with the constant vacuum class, which has its own merits of simplicity and high full load performance.

Nomenclature is not standardised, but the terms *dual* and *duplex* are both applied to the two linked venturis mentioned above, which provide jointly the quantity and quality of mixture required through the full throttle range, while avoiding the disadvantage of excessive choke area at lower throttle openings.

What are usually referred to in Britain as the *five phases* of carburation, namely *starting, idling, part throttle, acceleration* and *power,* are usually described in American textbooks and makers' handbooks in relation to the metering and atomising jet systems, by which the required conditions are provided. The float chamber mechanism may be included as a sixth system. There is no divergence of objective in the phases or systems, merely in the degree of completeness and elaboration with which they are provided in each make and model of carburettor. Details vary but basic methods have become largely standardised.

The four-barrel instrument, used on large V-eight units, duplicates in one assembly this 'dual' or 'duplex' combination, each of the two combinations serving a selected group of four cylinders in the two banks which has been found to give the best distribution in relation to a particular firing order.

11.43   Constant-depression carburettors

In Section 11.7 an explanation was given as to why compensation devices and multi-jet systems are necessary with a carburettor having a choke of fixed diameter. With this type, the choke diameter in any case is a compromise: if it is too small, engine performance is limited by the restriction on its breathing; on the other hand, if it is too large, the accuracy of metering of the fuel and atomisation and mixing are poor at the lower end of the range.

In principle, these disadvantages can be overcome by using an automatically variable choke carburettor, such as the SU or Zenith-Stromberg units. The object is to obtain a constant air-velocity, and therefore constant depression – generally about 230 mm water head – over the jet, the size of which is varied to control the air-fuel ratio. Thus a single jet can be employed, and additional compensating devices are generally unnecessary.

Automatic variation of the size of the choke to maintain constant air velocity, is effected by having a rectangular choke, in which a piston, or diaphragm actuator, is used to raise or lower its upper portion termed the *air valve* – away from or towards – its fixed bottom portion, termed the *bridge*, in which is mounted the jet. The lowering is effected by the weight of the piston plus a very light return spring, while the raising operation is done by the depression just downstream of the choke, which is communicated to the top of the piston or diaphragm.

A pendant tapered needle fixed to the moving portion of the choke rises and falls with it and thus varies the size of the jet orifice – into which it dips – and therefore the rate of flow of fuel. The taper of the needle is not straight, but is profiled to vary the air:fuel ratio appropriately to the throttle opening – that is, for starting, idling, cruising and maximum power.

From Fig. 11.40, it can be seen that, as the throttle butterfly is opened, the manifold depression is communicated increasingly to the body of the carburettor and, through the duct V, to the chamber above the piston. The piston will rise, allowing increasing quantities of air and fuel to pass

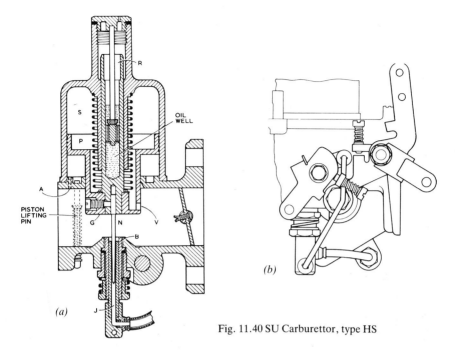

Fig. 11.40 SU Carburettor, type HS

beneath it, until the depression is just sufficient to balance the weight of the piston plus the force exerted by its low-rate return spring. Consequently, since the height of the piston is a function of the mass of air passing beneath it, the depression over the jet in the bridge is maintained constant regardless of the demand. The designer of the carburettor arranges that the value of this depression is adequate for good atomisation of the fuel, but not so great as to restrict the breathing or filling of the cylinders to an unacceptable degree.

Enrichment, to compensate for inertia of the fuel – which causes its flow to accelerate too slowly to cater for sudden throttle opening – is effected simply by damping the upward motion of the piston, so that the suction over the jet is temporarily increased until the piston finally arrives at the equilibrium height. Downward motion of the piston is virtually undamped.

Mechanically-controlled variable-choke carburettors have been produced in the past, but of course are no longer used on cars. Their controls have been either manual or interlinked with the throttle. Such controls in any case would be unsuitable for meeting modern requirements.

The advantges of an automatic variable-choke, or constant-depression, carburettor can be summarised as follows: mixture compensation is unnecessary, so only a single jet is needed. Consequently, there is no possibiity of the flat spot that could otherwise occur during change-over from one jet to another. A separate idling system may also be unnecessary, as is an accelerator pump. Optimum filling of the cylinder at the top of the speed range is obtainable without detriment to the low speed performance. Moreover, metering of the fuel can be precise throughout the whole of the range.

11.44 SU constant-depression carburettor

The SU carburettor type HS, without its extra emission control features, is illustrated in Fig. 11.40. An air valve G is integral with the piston P and securely attached to the piston rod R, which slides in the close-fitting bore of the suction chamber S. The depression just downstream of the air valve is transmitted through a pair of holes, V, to the suction chamber, above the piston. Because of the very low rate of the return spring, the load to be supported by the vacuum is practically constant, being mainly the weight of the piston. The underside of the piston is vented through hole A to the entry to the carburettor.

Also rigidly attached to the piston assembly is the tapered needle N which therefore, as the piston moves, simultaneously varies the annular orifice between itself and the jet. The jet sleeve J can be raised or lowered for over-riding the setting, for idling or starting. This is done by means of a cam and link connection to the throttle and cold start controls. Petrol is delivered through a nylon tube to the lower end of the jet sleeve, from the float chamber – which can be bolted on to either side of the carburettor body, to suit the particular installation.

In Fig. 11.40, the jet tube J is a close fit in the flanged bush B, which is a clearance fit in the bridge. On assembly in the factory, the jet tube and bush are together centred relative to the bore of the suction chamber – and thus the piston and needle assembly – and then the upper of the two nuts is tightened to lock the setting by clamping the flange of the bush securely against the shoulder beneath which it seats. The lower nut is used subsequently for mixture adjustment.

For damping the motion of the piston, a plunger is secured beneath the screw-cap on top of the suction chamber. This plunger therefore remains stationary as its cylinder, which is the oil-filled hollow rod of the air piston, moves up and down.

With the advent of emission-control regulations, additional features have had to be introduced. These, which are also incorporated in the HIF series of carburettors, are as follows: compensation for changes in viscosity of the fuel with temperature; spring-loading of the needle to one side of the jet to avoid variations in orifice coefficient, and therefore fuel flow, owing to concentricity errors; an over-run limiting valve, for maintaining proper combustion in the over-run condition; integral crankcase ventilation control; and a linear ball bearing, interposed between the stem of the piston and its housing, for minimising the sliding friction. These features are described fully in the next section.

11.45 SU carburettor type HIF

The HIF (Horizontal, Integral Float Chamber) carburettor was designed specifically to meet the requirements for exhaust emission control. At the same time, a noteworthy degree of compactness has been achieved by arranging the float and float chamber concentrically with the jet tube, as can be seen from Fig. 11.41. With this arrangement, too, the petrol level in the float chamber, immediately beneath the jet, is only minimally disturbed by changes in inclination of the vehicle, braking, acceleration and cornering. The principle of operation of this carburettor is the same as of that previously described and, in detail construction, it is much like the HS series. However, certain additional features have been incorporated.

Among these is the spring-loading of the needle against one side of the jet, so that it is positively located radially and therefore the orifice coefficient invariable – with a centrally-disposed needle, any movement off centre alters the orifice coefficient. A coil spring is used; it is axially in line with the needle and bears on a collar around its upper end. A peg, screwed radially into the piston to project beneath one side of this collar, tilts the needle by virtue of the resultant offset reaction to the spring force until it is stopped by its lower portion contacting the side of the jet orifice. The

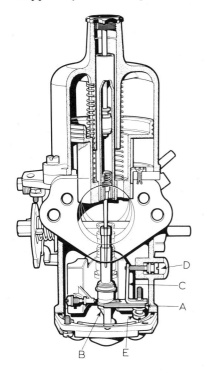

Fig. 11.41 A sectioned HIF4 carburettor

direction of bias of the needle can be either up- or down-stream. Since the flanged bush in which the upper end of the jet tube is carried does not have to be centred, it is a close fit in its hole in the bridge. The jet is pressed into the top end of an aluminium tube, the lower end of which is pressed into a plastics moulding, known as the *jet head*. Fuel enters the open lower end of this moulding and thence passes up into the jet tube.

On the throttle butterfly, there is an over-run limiting valve, which is a small spring-loaded non-return plate valve. Under over-run conditions, the intense depression in the manifold opens this valve, as described in Section 11.39 and illustrated in Fig. 11.31, so that a small quantity of air-fuel mixture can pass through to maintain regular combustion in all the cylinders – irregular combustion of course would cause the discharge of unburnt hydrocarbons into the exhaust.

For provision of a good quality mixture at small throttle openings, there is a part throttle by-pass emulsion system, taking mixture directly from the jet. At its outer end, the by-pass passage breaks out into a slot – immediately downstream of the jet – in the bridge, while its other end breaks out in line with the edge of the slightly open throttle, so that the local high velocity of flow, and therefore depression, will atomise the fuel and mix it more thoroughly than if it had been drawn through the carburettor body in the usual way.

Additional mixture for cold starting is supplied by an enrichment device, Fig. 11.42. This is a small rotary valve through which fuel is drawn from the float chamber, mixed with air from a bleed hole, and discharged through an outlet immediately downstream of the bridge. Housed in a hole in the side of the carburettor body, the device comprises a cylindrical valve body with a seal at each end and a spindle passing through it. The outer end of the spindle is threaded to receive the cam follower lever by means of which the valve is actuated.

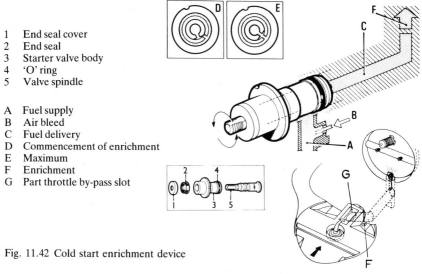

1   End seal cover
2   End seal
3   Starter valve body
4   'O' ring
5   Valve spindle

A   Fuel supply
B   Air bleed
C   Fuel delivery
D   Commencement of enrichment
E   Maximum
F   Enrichment
G   Part throttle by-pass slot

Fig. 11.42 Cold start enrichment device

Fuel is drawn by the depression over the outlet hole, up a passage in the wall of the float chamber, past a bleed hole through which air is drawn in to emulsify it. This mixture is then taken on up into an annular space between the housing and the cylindrical body, and thence in through radial holes to a counterbore in the inner end of the valve spindle and to the outlet hole behind the bridge. The flow is of course cut off when the spindle is rotated so that its radial hole no longer aligns with that in the cylindrical body. A groove is machined tangentially across the end of the hole in the spindle so that, as the spindle is rotated, the fuel flow is started and stopped progressively, as shown at D and E in Fig. 11.42.

To compensate for variation of viscosity of petrol with temperature, a bimetal strip regulates the height of the jet tube assembly relative to the needle. The arrangement can be seen from Fig. 11.41. A bimetal strip A carries at one end the jet head B. It is pivot mounted at the other, where it is riveted to a bell-crank lever C. A spring beneath it, around the screw E, pushes it so that the upper end of the bell crank moves outwards until it is stopped by the adjustment screw D. The adjustment is made on assembly – clockwise rotation of the screw D lowers the jet, and therefore enriches the mixture. When adjustment is complete, a plug is fitted over the screw head, in its countersink, to seal it.

For crankcase emission control, the constant depression chamber, between the throttle valve and air valve, is connected by a hose to the engine breather outlet. This draws crankcase fumes into the carburettor and thence, with the air-fuel mixture, to the cyinders. The fumes are replaced in the crankcase by fresh air entering through the oil filler cap breather or, on cars equipped with evaporative-loss emission control, through an absorption canister. Because the connection is made to the constant depression chamber, no valve is needed to safeguard against either excessive depression in the crankcase or interference with the slow-running mixture supply.

11.46 Zenith-Stromberg CD and CDS carburettors

The design of the Stromberg carburettors is basically similar to that of the SU types, but they differ structurally, as can be seen from Fig. 11.43. Among the major differences is the use in the Stromberg units of a diaphragm-, instead of piston-actuated, air valve. The concentric float chamber beneath the jet assembly is a feature of all the current Zenith-Stromberg designs.

On the CD carburettor, provision for cold starting is as follows: a semi-cylindrical bar seats in a groove across the bridge, to conform with its profile, as shown in Fig. 11.43. For cold starting, however, it is rotated by the choke control, to lift the air valve slightly and, at the same time, mask

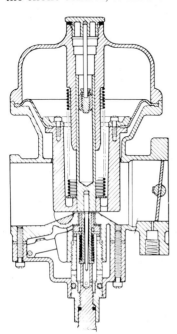

Fig. 11.43 Stromberg CD carburettor

the choke opening and thus restrict the air flow. The consequent lifting of the needle of course enriches the mixture. Simultaneously, because of interconnection with the throttle control, by means of a cam, the throttle is opened an amount determined by the setting of a fast-idle stop screw, which serves as a follower on the cam. This carburettor is now superseded by the CDS unit.

The CDS is the CD unit with, instead of the semi-circular bar just described, a rotary disc valve for supplying additional fuel for cold starting. This is described in more detail in Section 11.48.

11.47   Zenith-Stromberg CDSE emission carburettor

This is basically the CDS unit, but modified to tighten the tolerances on metering and fuel flow. Idle adjustment is effected by what is termed the idle trimmer screw, instead of by raising or lowering the jet – the latter is now fixed. The end of the idle trimmer screw is in the form of a needle-valve, which regulates the amount of air passing through a duct from the intake into the mixing chamber: this relieves the depression in the suction chamber above the air-valve control diaphragm, and thus allows the needle to fall and weaken the mixture. It has a limited range of adjustment, because it is intended only to cater for variations in the stiffness of rotation of new engines. The adjustment is made to limit the output of carbon monoxide, as indicated by an exhaust gas analyser.

There is also a temperature compensator. This is a flat bimetal thermostat spring. It senses the temperature of the body of the carburettor and regulates the axial position of a tapered needle in an orifice, through which extra air passes to the mixing chamber. The effect of this air bleed is similar to that of the idle trimmer.

To prevent an increase in the flow of unburnt hydrocarbons through the engine during deceleration, there is a throttle by-pass duct. Through this duct, a small quantity of mixture is delivered downstream of the throttle, and this ensures continued combustion in the cylinders. The air is drawn from upstream of the throttle, and fuel is added through a jet orifice in the duct. This device is brought into operation by manifold depression, acting on a small spring-loaded diaphragm and disc valve.

The jet needle is biased, by spring loading, to one side of the orifice. This and the other features of the CDSE are similar in principle to, though differing in detail from, those of the CD4 and CD5 described in Section 11.48.

11.48   Zenith-Stromberg CD4 and CD5 carburettors

These carburettors were designed specifically to meet the then current emission requirements. They are similar to the earlier CD units but differ slightly in layout, as can be seen from Fig. 11.44.

Where an Auto-Starter, described in Section 11.25, is fitted, the letter T is appended to the type designation. It is in fact fitted on the CDSET, CD4T and CD5T. Apart from this, the principal new features of the CD4 and CD5 are as follows: for starting from cold with the manual starter, the choke control actuates a lever on the side of the carburettor, which rotates a disc drilled with a series of holes of different diameters, A in the scrap view Fig. 11.44. In the fully rich position, all the holes are in communication with the starter circuit and, as the choke control is released, they are progressively blanked off.

Petrol is drawn from the float chamber, up a vertical channel adjacent to the main jet, through the disc device, and thence to the mixing chamber – between the air valve and throttle plate. In the meantime, the cam B on the starter lever, acting on the fast-idle screw C, has opened the throttle sufficiently to prevent stalling of the cold engine.

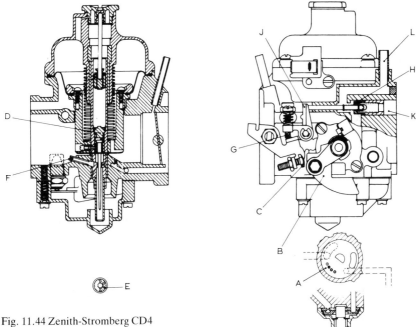

Fig. 11.44 Zenith-Stromberg CD4

Once the engine has been started and is warm, the operational principle of the carburettor is similar to that of the earlier CD series. On the CD4, however, provision is made for adjustment of the mixture strength by raising or lowering the metering needle relative to the jet orifice. This is done from above, by lowering a special tool down the damper tube, to rotate the adjustment screw D, Fig. 11.44. The method of biasing the needle to one side of the jet orifice is similar to that in the SU carburettors, except in that the needle is spring-loaded in a carrier within the piston assembly. The light bias spring is retained by the head of the needle which is tilted by either a swaged tag or a small pin. This arrangement is used also on many CDSE and CD3 carburettors, the latter being the CDSE without a temperature compensator.

A commendably simple device is used to avoid the need for a mechanical device to compensate for variations in fuel viscosity with temperature. Four emulsion holes are drilled radially in the metering orifice, as shown at E in the scrap view. They are in the semi-circular segment opposite to that in which the biased needle seats. Air is metered to them through a calibrated jet F. Without this device, enrichment due to reduction of viscosity, and other factors, with rising temperature would adversely affect the metering performance and stability of running, especially under idling conditions.

An additional feature has been introduced to improve the mixture control for idling. It is termed the *downstream discharge circuit with idle air regulator*. A small proportion of the metered fuel from the main jet is sucked by manifold depression into a calibrated hole A, Fig. 11.45, and discharged downstream from the throttle butterfly, through a port B. The position of this port is such that, once the throttle valve has been opened beyond a certain point, the system ceases to operate. Air is introduced into this system past an djustable metering screw C, so that the air:fuel ratio of the mixture can be regulated over the idling range. This screw, which is for

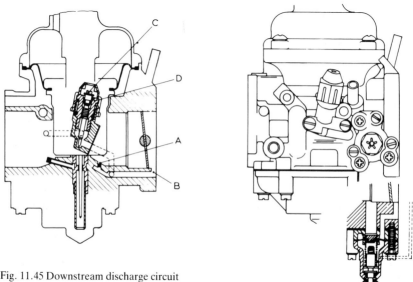

Fig. 11.45 Downstream discharge circuit

fine adjustment, is carried in a coarse adjustment screw D. The latter is set and locked in the factory, and the further fine adjustment can vary the mixture strength by no more than plus or minus half an air:fuel ratio, depending on the engine layout. Idling speed is adjusted by the throttle stop screw G in Fig. 11.44.

Float chambers are generally vented to the air cleaner. However, if the vent is taken to a point downstream of the filter element, fuel vapour can collect there when, in a recently stopped engine, heat has soaked through to the float chamber and evaporated fuel from it. This can tend to inhibit restarting the engine when hot. On the other hand, venting to the outer side of the filter element can lead to enrichment of the mixture if the element becomes clogged, since this will increase the depression over the jet.

In the CD4 and CD5, therefore, a ventilation valve H is actuated by the throttle linkage through lever J, Fig. 11.44. Under normal running conditions, the valve closes the external channel L and opens the float chamber to the internal ventilation channel K, but under idling conditions the valve moves to the right, as viewed in the illustration, to close the internal vent K and open the external one L. This system is also used on the CDSE V carburettors, the V indicating incorporation of the vent valve.

In these carburettors, the over-run valve is generally in the body casting instead of on the butterfly valve, though there are some instances of the use of a poppet valve on the butterfly. It is simply a depression-actuated non-return valve in the base of what is, in effect, a U-shape channel the upper ends of the arms of which break out, one upstream and the other downstream of the butterfly valve, into the main induction passage.

This allows enough mixture from the mixing chamber to by-pass the throttle valve and thus maintain regular combustion in all cylinders in over-run conditions.

The CD5 carburettor is a derivation of the CD4. Its principal difference is the provision made for regulating the over-run mixture strength. This is done by the introduction of an adjustment device for controlling the fuel supply to the by-pass valve intake.

11.49 Mixture ratio curves

Mixture ratio curves may be drawn for these carburettors of the same form as those in Fig. 11.14, the weight of air flow being plotted horizontally, but with no dual characteristic.

This weight of air flow may be taken as directly proportional to the lift of the cylinder, since the rectangular choke area is proportional to this lift, and is subjected to a constant depression or head.

For each position, that is for each value of the flow, there will be a definite ratio of jet area to choke area and therefore a definite mixture ratio dependent on the diameter of the needle. The anular form of the jet area, it should be noted, renders it subject to viscosity effects, and the flow is not exactly proportional to this area since it is not of geometrically constant form. Fig. 11.46 illustrates the manner in which any desired curve can be obtained by modifying the profile of the needle.

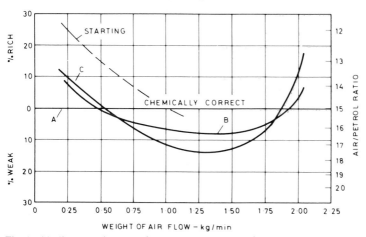

Fig. 11.46 Mixture ratio curves for constant-vacuum carburettors

At A the profile is so chosen as to make the petrol flow just proportional to the air flow and in the chemically correct ratio. If now the needle were changed for one having a slightly larger diameter than the first at all points near the middle of its length, but reduced at its two ends, curve B would be obtained, while C, giving a 12% weak mixture over the middle range and considerable enrichment at the two ends, would result from still further reduction at the ends of the needle and enlargement of its centre portion. It should be realised that, just as in the ordinary fixed choke carburettor, the mixture ratio is a function of flow only, and not of throttle opening, so that the double characteristic of Fig. 11.14 is obtainable only by use of the over-riding jet control shown in Fig. 11.40(b). In certain special models thermostatic and throttle controls are provided.

11.50   Automatic governor

The dangers of excessive speed will have been appreciated by the reader in studying the chapter on balancing, in which the nature and magnitude of the inertia forces were discussed. These dangers are intensified in vehicles with specially low emergency gear ratios, and it is possible for modern high-performance engines to suffer serious damage from over-speeding without the driver appreciating the danger, owing to the relatively low speed of the vehicle.

The provision of a mechanical centrifugal governor operating on a separate throttle has been resorted to from time to time by commercial vehicle makers, but the objections of increased cost, liability to derangement or deliberate tampering on the part of the driver, and interference with mixture distribution by the second throttle have militated against their general adoption.

A fleet operator desiring to protect from over-speeding the vehicles in his charge, which may include a variety of designs with and without governors, will naturally welcome any simple and reliable device which may be readily fitted to any engine.

Such a device should be inexpensive, so designed and installed that it cannot easily be tampered with, and it should not restrict engine performance beyond the essential function of limiting the maximum speed to a safe value. The precise performance of an accurate centrifugal governor is not required.

11.51   Velocity governor

A device successfully meeting these requirements is the *velocity* governor illustrated in Fig. 11.47. Originally associated with and developed by the Solex Company, it is now more widely available, and has been successfully adapted to certain assemblies of the Zenith carburettor.

The air velocity past a specially formed and mounted butterfly, which takes the place of the normal throttle, is used to obtain automatic closure when the piston speed reaches a desirable maximum value.

Fig. 11.47 illustrates an up-draught form of the assembly.

The butterfly is mounted on an offset spindle which is hardened and ground and furnished with a race of needle rollers to give the greatest possible freedom of movement.

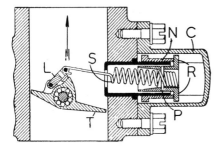

Fig. 11.47 Solex automatic governor

The spindle takes its bearing in the usual way in the throttle barrel and is rotated by the operation of the accelerator pedal. The butterfly is free to rotate relatively to the spindle in the closing direction, but is held against a limiting dog on the spindle in the other direction by the control spring.

The equilibrium position of the butterfly is thus controlled by three factors as follows –

(1) The action of the spring S always tending to open the throttle.
(2) The pressure due to the air flow always tending to close it in virtue of the greater torque in the counter-clockwise direction caused by the greater area of the tail portion T of the butterfly.
(3) The limit to the opening imposed by the accelerator pedal, movement of which against its own return spring permits the governor spring to open the throttle to the required degree. Failure of the governor spring would immediately result in the closure of the throttle by the air flow, even if the accelerator pedal remained depressed.

The mode of operation is as follows –

Suppose the operation of the accelerator pedal has permitted full opening of the throttle at a moderate engine or piston speed. The pressure on the butterfly – which is partly due to static pressure difference between the two sides of the throttle and partly due to impact pressures – will be light, and will not overcome the spring. Induction pipe depression will be small.

If the external conditions result in an increase of road speed there will be an increase of air speed, accompanied by an increase of pressure difference and closing torque on the butterfly, and the spring tension may be so adjusted as just to be overcome at the highest desired piston speed. The butterfly will then begin to close, and for the same piston speed the air speed, pressure difference and closing torque will increase sharply. If the spring force or moment did not increase correspondingly the throttle would snap shut and unstable hunting would be initiated.

For each throttle position there is, for a given piston speed, a certain pressure difference, air velocity and closing torque on the throttle (see Fig. 11.1, and Table 4 on page 242).

The stiffness of the governor spring and its effective moment may be arranged to balance this closing torque with a suitable degree of accuracy, so that the throttle will close independently of accelerator movement when the air velocity reaches the value which, for the particular throttle position concerned, corresponds to the desired limiting piston speed.

The spring may be adjusted for stiffness by cutting out a suitable number of coils by rotating the regulating sleeve R, when the diametral steel peg P, which forms the spring anchorage, will alter the number of active coils. The initial tension of the spring is adjusted by means of the tension nut N. After adjustment the locking and sealing cover C is secured.

The spring anchorage link L enables the spring leverage to be maintained practically constant, so that the moment increases with the spring force from, say 0.113 N/m with 6.35 mm of throttle opening to 0.288 Nm when the throttle is shut, the exact figures depending on requirements.

11.52   Petrol injection

Conventional carburettor and induction systems have three inherent shortcomings. First, volumetric efficiency is limited by both the need to pre-heat the mixture and the restriction of the air flow by the carburettor choke. Secondly, it is virtually impossible to distribute the mixture uniformly to all the cylinders, even with a separate carburettor for each; therefore a richer mixture than otherwise might be necessary must be supplied, to avoid the onset of detonation in the cylinders that receive the weakest mixtures. Thirdly, fuel deposition on the walls of the induction manifold in cold running conditions presents problems.

The use of petrol injection, therefore, offers the following potential advantages. Because of the absence of both the choke and pre-heating of the charge, specific fuel consumption, torque and maximum bhp are potentially higher. Improved torque is obtainable particularly by virtue of the relative ease with which the porting can be designed to take advantage of intake pulse tuning. Furthermore, with modern injection equipment, it is possible to match fuel supply more accurately to load throughout the speed range and under transient conditions, with the result that driveability of the vehicle is improved, especially during engine warm-up, and exhaust emissions are easier to control. Other advantages include freedom from icing problems, easy cold starting, fuel deposition in cold conditions can be minimal, absence of disturbances due to the effects of cornering or braking on the contents of a float chamber, and greater freedom as regards fuel formulation.

The disadvantages are high cost, complication, and the difficulty of providing adequate servicing facilities. All these, however, apply only when the comparison is made between petrol injection and the simple carburettor, and they tend to be offset when complex carburettors are required for large V engines and for exhaust emission control. Consequently, the future of petrol injection looks bright for countries that have stringent regulations regarding emissions and fuel economy. Moreover, as the quantities of injection equipment produced increase, costs will come down and it will become potentially attractive for the more expensive cars in all countries.

11.53   Injection systems

Direct injection into the cylinders has some severe disadvantages which preclude it from serious consideration. The pressures against which

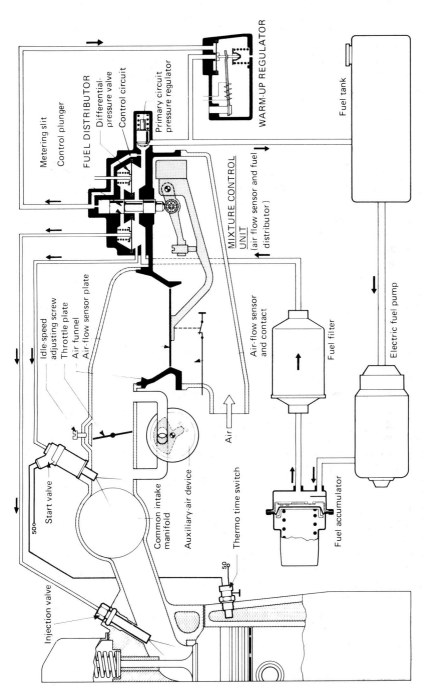

Fig. 11.48 Bosch K-Jetronic petrol-injection system

injection would have to be effected would be high and the time available for injection short. Consequently the system would have to be robust and heavy; it would have to be manufactured to extremely close tolerances; the cost would be high; and, if a plunger type pump were employed, special provision would have to be made for lubrication of the plungers – whereas diesel fuel is capable of performing this function, petrol is not. Such a system would tend to be noisy too.

With indirect injection, the injectors are generally in one of three positions. Perhaps the most favoured is in the port, immediately before the inlet valve. Here the risk of maldistribution of fuel by back-flow to one of the other cylinders is minimal, as also is that of temporary loss of mixture strength due to condensation in the port. Moreover, the relatively high temperature of the inlet valve head helps in evaporation of the fuel. The principle disadvantage of this position is the additional complexity introduced into the cylinder head to accommodate the injectors.

Next in order of popularity is a single injector, situated just downstream of the throttle valve, serving all cylinders. This has the considerable advantage of simplicity, but reintroduces the old problems of obtaining equal distribution to all cylinders, and deposition of fuel on the walls of the manifold when cold. The third possibility, screwing the injectors into the manifold branches, has few advantages and most of the disadvantages already mentioned.

Commercially, the most successful injection systems are those based on the principles pioneered by Bendix, in the USA, a development of which was described in *Automobile Engineer*, Vol. 47, No. 6, 1957. Outstanding among these are the K-Jetronic and L-Jetronic systems developed by Bosch in Germany, who have greatly refined and advanced the concept. The K-Jetronic system, Fig. 11.48, has a mechanical control unit, while the L-Jetronic scheme, Fig. 11.52, has electronic control. These systems all have the advantage, relative to diesel injection systems, that no drive from the engine is required. For the K-Jetronic system, the electric fuel pump delivers at about 4.7 bar, and this pressure is reduced to 3.3 bar as the fuel is metered into the pipes serving the injectors. In the L-Jetronic system there is only one pressure, of between 2 and 3 bar, which is set to suit the particular engine and, in operation, is varied in proportion to induction manifold pressure. A significant difference between the two systems is that, in the former, injection into the ports is continuous while, in the latter, it is intermittent – twice per injector per four-stroke cycle.

11.54   Bosch K-Jetronic system

In more detail, the operation of the K system is as follows: fuel is drawn from the tank by the electrically-driven pump and delivered into what is termed the *primary circuit*, at a pressure of 4.7 bar. It passes first into a hydraulic accumulator, the function of which is to maintain the pressure in the system for a long time after the engine has been switched off. This is to avoid vapour formation in the system while the engine is still warm, which would tend to inhibit hot starting.

From the accumulator, the fuel goes through a filter to the mixture control unit which houses, among other things, the primary circuit pressure regulator valve. Fuel in excess of requirements is dumped by this valve straight back to the tank. An extension of the primary circuit goes up to the cold start valve, which sprays extra fuel into the manifold only during cold starting. Operation of this valve is controlled electrically by a thermo-time switch screwed into the water jacket of the engine or, in an air-cooled engine, into the cylinder head. The solenoid actuating the valve is energised to open it when the engine is cold. It is closed by a return spring as the engine becomes warm enough for the sensor to signal de-energisation of the solenoid. A swirl device in the nozzle helps to atomise the fuel passing through. Should the engine fail to start within a pre-determined time, the thermo time switch – actuated by either engine heat or, in this situation, by an electrical heating element around the bimetallic strip – interrupts the circuit to the solenoid to avoid flooding the engine cylinders with petrol.

The mixture control unit is of course the key component of the system. Essentially, it comprises an air flow sensor and a fuel metering system. A disc mounted on the end of an arm extending out from a pivot in the mixture control unit is suspended by that arm in a funnel-shape air intake. If the air flow is zero, the plate falls into the narrowest section of the funnel. When the engine is started, the air pressure differential across the disc lifts it until the air flow through the annular gap between its periphery and the walls of the funnel has increased sufficiently to reduce the pressure differential to a level at which it exactly balances the force tending to pull the disc downwards. This force is independent of gravity, because the masses of the arm and plate assembly are accurately balanced about its pivot, by means of counterweights. The force tending to lower the disc is therefore solely that applied to the arm by the control plunger, the upper end of which is acted upon by fuel pressure in what is termed the *control circuit*, Fig. 11.51.

This circuit goes, through a restrictor, from the primary circuit and thence, through another restrictor, into the upper end of the cylinder in which the control plunger slides. A connection is taken from a point between these two restrictors to the warm-up regulator, which is a valve that maintains the control pressure at a constant 3.7 bar once the engine is warm. During warm-up, however, this regulator reduces the pressure to as low as 0.5 bar, so that the control plunger can rise higher and deliver extra fuel to the injectors, and thus increase the power, compensate for the loss due to condensation from the mixture on to the cold walls of the combustion chambers and induction passages.

The function of the first-mentioned restrictor, therefore, is to prevent the passage of too much fuel from the primary circuit through the control circuit and thence back to the tank by way of the warm-up regulator valve. That of the second restrictor – at the entrance to the upper end of the plunger cylinder – is to damp the motion of the plunger under conditions of pulsating air flow, for instance at low engine speeds and high load. Under such conditions, the air flow sensor disc would tend to move too far from its base position. This restrictor also damps the transient motion of the plunger during sudden acceleration when, again, the air sensor disc would tend to swing too far upwards.

A bimetallic strip controls the setting of the warm-up regulator valve, Fig. 11.49. When hot, its end lifts, allowing the return spring to close the valve to the point at which it maintains the pressure at 3.7 bar. On the other hand, when cold the bimetallic strip acts against the return spring, thus lowering the pressure in the control circuit. The unit is mounted on the engine cylinder block so that, once the engine is warm, the valve remains under the sole control of its spring. Because of the time lag between the warming of the engine to the point at which no enrichment is

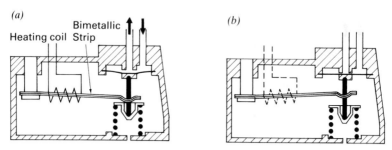

Fig. 11.49 Warm-up regulator, (a) with cold engine, (b) with warm engine

necessary and the heat soaking right through to the warm-up regulator unit, the bimetallic strip is also heated electrically by means of a coil, which is switched on automatically as soon as the engine is started, and switched off again automatically when the engine temperature is high enough to lift the end of the bimetallic strip clear of the return spring.

Compensation is needed also for power lost owing to the high viscosity of the oil when the engine is cold. This is provided by supplying extra air to the engine, bypassing the throttle valve. The auxiliary air device is a rotary plate-valve in the by-pass passage. This valve is opened by a bimetallic strip and closed by a return spring, Fig. 11.50. At normal operating temperatures it is closed. When the engine is cold, however, the end of the

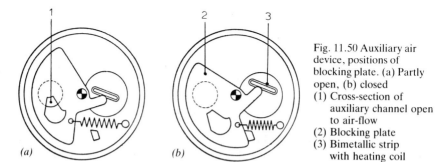

Fig. 11.50 Auxiliary air device, positions of blocking plate. (a) Partly open, (b) closed
(1) Cross-section of auxiliary channel open to air-flow
(2) Blocking plate
(3) Bimetallic strip with heating coil

bimetallic strip, bearing against a lever integral with the rotary plate valve, opens it. As in the case of the warm-up regulator, this valve unit is mounted in a position such that the bimetallic strip is subject to engine temperature, and it is also electrically-heated automatically as soon as the engine is started. When the engine is warm, and the bimetallic strip lifts clear of the end of the lever, the current to the heating coil is cut off.

11.55   The fuel distributor

When the fuel enters the mixture control unit, at the 4.7-bar pressure of the primary circuit, it passes into a series of chambers, which are each divided into an upper and lower portion by a metal diaphragm. There is one of these chambers for each cylinder of the engine. Their lower portions are all connected to an annular groove around the control plunger, so all are at the same pressure. When the plunger is lifted by the air-flow sensor lever, fuel passes from this groove radially outwards through vertical metering slits into the upper portions of the chambers and thence out through pipelines to the injectors.

The metering of the fuel to each of the injectors is accomplished by controlling the length of slit uncovered by the plunger and maintaining the pressure difference across the metering slit constant. Obviously the length of slit uncovered is dependent on the height to which the control valve is lifted which, in turn, depends upon the air flow past the sensor plate. The pressure difference is determined by the position of the diaphragms separating the top and bottom halves of the chambers relative to the ends of the discharge ports through which the fuel passes into the pipelines to the injectors, Fig. 11.51. A coil spring pushes this diaphragm downwards

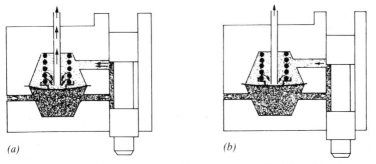

(a)   (b)

Fig. 11.51 Metering slit and diaphragm. (a) At high rate of fuel flow, (b) at low rate of fuel flow

against the opposing force exerted on its underside by the 4.7-bar pressure in the primary circuit. The compression in this spring is such that the diaphragm is maintained in equilibrium with a pressure differential of 0.1 bar between the upper and lower chambers. If the control plunger is lifted to allow more fuel to flow through the metering slit into the upper chamber, the pressure differential tends to be reduced, allowing the spring to push the diaphragm down. This uncovers the discharge port and allows fuel to flow at a greater rate through the pipeline to the injector. However, the equilibrium, at a differential pressure of 0.1 bar – 4.6 bar in the upper chamber – is still maintained since a higher pressure would open the port wider, allowing the fuel to flow through at an even higher rate, and a lower one would close it. The deflection of the diaphragm is in fact only a few hundredths of a millimetre.

From this it can be seen that the injection valve has no metering function. It is closed by a spring and opens automatically when the pressure in the delivery pipe rises above 3.3 bar. At this pressure the fuel is finely atomised as it passes through the discharge nozzle into the engine inlet valve port.

The only adjustments that can be made to this system in service are those of the engine idling speed and mixture. For adjustment of idling speed, there is a screw that restricts the flow of air through a passage that bypasses the throttle valve when it is closed. The greater the degree of restriction of course, the slower is the idling speed. To increase idling speed, therefore, the screw should be turned anti-clockwise.

The idling mixture strength is adjusted by another screw, which acts on the arm by means of which the motion of the air sensor plate is transmitted to the control plunger. Access can be gained for this adjustment, using a screwdriver, without any dismantling of the mixture control unit. As can be seen from Fig. 11.48, the idling mixture screw is on the end of a lever swinging about the same pivot as, and approximately parallel to, the arm that carries the air sensor plate. The end of the screw seats on that arm so, when it is screwed clockwise, it increases the angle subtended between the smaller lever and the arm. This raises the control plunger slightly, thus supplying more fuel to the injectors and therefore enriching the mixture.

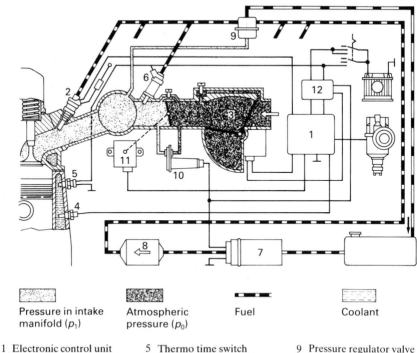

Pressure in intake manifold (p_1)	Atmospheric pressure (p_0)	Fuel	Coolant

1 Electronic control unit	5 Thermo time switch	9 Pressure regulator valve
2 Injection valve	6 Start valve	10 Auxiliary-air device
3 Air-flow sensor	7 Electric fuel pump	11 Throttle-valve switch
4 Temperature sensor	8 Fuel filter	12 Relay set

Fig. 11.52 Bosch L-Jetronic system

11.56   Bosch L-Jetronic system

In the L-Jetronic system, Fig. 11.52, the electronic control unit performs the same function as the mixture control unit of the K system. It does this, however, by controlling the duration of opening of the solenoid-actuated valves in the injectors. The advantage of electronic control is that there are fewer mechanical components liable to wear or to stick and thus to malfunction. Moreover, ultimately, more accurate control is possible because the system can be made more easily to respond to a wider range of variables than when a mechanical system is used.

Because the injectors are solenoid-actuated, Fig. 11.53, lower delivery pressures are possible than those needed to open the pressure-actuated delivery valves of the K system. Another advantage is that delivery can be

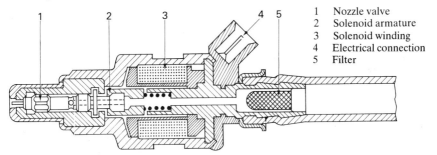

1	Nozzle valve
2	Solenoid armature
3	Solenoid winding
4	Electrical connection
5	Filter

Fig. 11.53 Cross-section of the injection valve

made through all the valves simultaneously, which means that the injection system can be simpler than if each had to be opened individually. Actually, to ensure that the distribution of fuel is uniform, to all cylinders, half the required amount of fuel is injected into each port twice, over two separate intervals, during each four-stroke cycle – that is, for each 360° rotation of the camshaft, Fig. 11.54.

The start of each injection pulse is signalled to the electronic control unit by the contacts in the ignition distributor. However, the control unit has to respond to only every second signal from the contact breaker in a four cylinder engine and every third in a six cylinder unit – since they have four and six sparks per cycle whereas only two injections are required in each case.

A load signal, which helps in determining the duration of pulse required, is obtained from an air flow sensor. This sensor differs from that of the K system in that it is, as can be seen from Fig. 11.52, a pivoted flap, spring-loaded to the closed position. The angular displacement of the flap is sensed by a potentiometer, and transmitted to the control unit. This displacement of course increases with the rate of air flow into the engine, until a balance is struck between the suction force on the flap and the restoring force of the spring.

As the illustration shows, a second flap, of the same area, is attached to the first. This second flap swings in a damping chamber, to reduce any tendency towards oscillation of the system. Additionally, because both flaps are of the same area and the suction forces on them tend to rotate the assembly in opposite directions, oscillations owing to fluctuating back

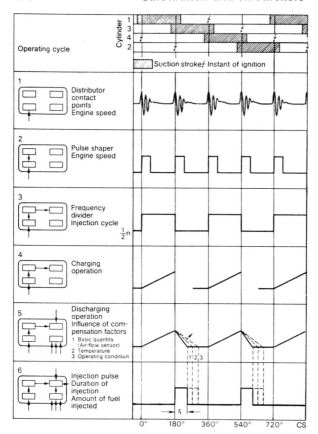

Fig. 11.54 Pulse diagram

pressure have no effect on the operation of the sensor. A non-return valve in the air flow sensor flap, Fig. 11.55, protects it against damage in the event of a serious surge of back pressure, such as might occur if the engine were to backfire.

Although the basic signal determining the duration of injection is that from the air flow sensor, it has to be modified by a number of other signals received by the electronic control. One is engine speed, which is signalled by the frequency of operation of the ignition contact breaker. A throttle valve actuated switch indicates whether enrichment is needed, for either full load or idling. As in the K system, there is a temperature sensor, but it influences the duration of injection instead of the pressure. It is necessary because the density and therefore mass of air drawn into the cylinders is greater in cold than in hot conditions. An enrichment device for acceleration is unnecessary in either system since the air flow sensor gives its signal in advance of acceleration.

A solenoid-actuated start valve comes into operation for cold starting. This is the same as in the K system, as also is the auxiliary air device for by-passing the throttle valve to compensate for the high friction losses. Here, however, there is a relay set. When the ignition is switched on, this relay set switches the battery voltage to the electric fuel pump, start valve, thermo-time switch for switching off the start valve, and auxiliary air device. When the engine starts, the power supply for the pump and auxiliary air device is maintained through a contact actuated by the air sensor. If, on the other hand, the engine fails to start, a thermo-time switch interrupts the circuit to the solenoid-actuated start valve, to avoid flooding the cylinders.

With no control-valve unit, the fuel supply is simpler than before: it passes from the pump through a filter to a pressure regulating valve and thence directly to the injector and start valve. With such a simple and direct supply a fuel accumulator is unnecessary.

As can be seen from Fig. 11.56, the fuel pressure regulator valve is of conventional design. The fuel flows radially in one side and out the other, while fuel in excess of requirements passes out through the connection at the top of the unit and thence back to the tank. With the L-Jetronic system,

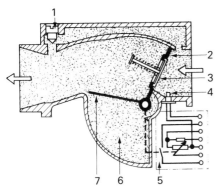

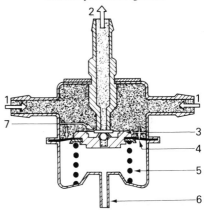

1 Fuel connection
2 Return line to fuel tank
3 Valve support
4 Diaphragm
5 Pressure spring
6 Connection to intake manifold
7 Valve

Fig. 11.56 (*below*) Cross-section of the fuel-pressure regulator

1 Mixture adjustment screw
   for the idle range
2 Air-flow sensor flap
3 Non-return valve
4 Air-temperature sensor
5 Electrical connections
6 Damping chamber
7 Compensation flap

Fig. 11.55 (*above*) Cross-section of the air-flow sensor

the fuel delivery pressure is either 2.5 or 3 bar, according to the type of engine. It is maintained at its set value by a spring-loaded diaphragm, which causes a valve to tend to seat on the port for the return line to the tank. Any increase in pressure pushes the diaphragm down and opens this port. To avoid variations in back pressure on the nozzles due to changing induction manifold pressure, a pipeline connection is taken from the manifold to the chamber below the diaphragm.

Bosch also produce a petrol injection system in which the engine load signal is obtained by sensing the depression in the inlet manifold. This is the D-Jetronic system. It will not be described here, however, since the L system is the more advanced one and therefore of greater importance. In any case, wear of the engine causes its manifold depression characteristics to change.

11.57   Further development

To meet the stringent requirements of the American and Japanese governments regarding exhaust gas emissions, Bosch has developed another sensor for use with petrol injection systems. This is the Lambda probe, which was first used by Volvo in 1976. Its name is derived from the fact that the Greek letter lambda is used in Germany and some other countries as a standard symbol for air ratio – which is the ratio of the actual quantity of air supplied to that required for complete combustion. The function of this sensor, which is screwed into the exhaust manifold, is to detect departures of the air ratio from $\lambda = 1$, by assessing the oxygen content of the exhaust gas.

From Fig. 11.57, it can be seen that the oxygen-sensitive component is a thimble shape piece of zirconium oxide, with its inner and outer surfaces coated with a thin layer of platinum in a manner such that it is permeable to gas. To protect the outer surface of the end of the thimble, which is exposed to the hot exhaust gas, a layer of porous ceramic is applied over it.

The thimble behaves like an electric cell in that, when the concentration of oxygen inside differs from that outside, an electric potential develops between the inner and outer platinum coatings. Thus, the voltage between the outer coating, which is earthed, and the inner one, from which a connection is taken, is a measure of the difference between the two oxygen

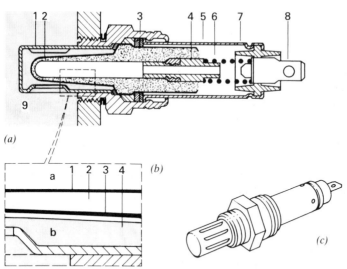

(a)	*Cross-section of the probe*	(b)	*Section from* (a)
1	Protective tube	a	Air side
2	Ceramic body	b	Exhaust gas side
3	Housing	1	Electrically-conductive layer
4	Contact bushing	2	Ceramic body
5	Protective sleeve	3	Electrically-conductive layer
6	Contact spring	4	Porous ceramic layer
7	Ventilation opening		
8	Electrical connection	(c)	*The complete unit*
9	Exhaust gas		

Fig. 11.57 The Lambda probe

concentrations. The inside of the thimble is of course open to the atmosphere.

Even when excess fuel is supplied, there is still some oxygen in the exhaust. For example, at λ = 0.95 the unburnt oxygen is between 0.2 and 0.3 per cent, by volume, of the exhaust gas. By careful development of the materials used, Bosch has been able to make a probe that is particularly sensitive to changes in oxygen content over a small range about λ = 1, Fig. 11.58. Because of this high sensitivity, the voltage changes can be used as signals and passed directly to the electronic control, so the probe becomes

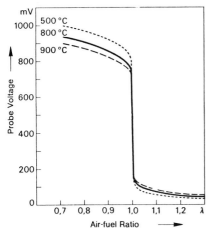

Fig. 11.58 Operating characteristic of the Lambda probe

part of a closed loop control system. This means that if the injectors are not supplying the amount of fuel required to form the correct air:fuel ratio, the sensor in the exhaust signals this back to the control unit, which instantly changes the duration of injection appropriately to correct the mixture strength. Such a device is especially valuable where catalytic systems are used to purify the exhaust gases, since these systems become overloaded and deteriorate rapidly if the air:fuel ratio is not correct.

Among improvements that have been made to the K-Jetronic systems is the development in 1977 of variable differential pressure valves, so that the distribution of fuel to the cylinders can be accurately adjusted. In 1978 an aluminium fuel-distributor was put into production, and this has fabric instead of metal diaphragms. In the same year, the surface roughness of the valve seats in the injectors was improved from 0.2 μm to about 0.1 μm, which of course is one ten-thousandth of a millimetre.

For the L-Jetronic system, an electronic cold start system delivering the extra fuel through the injectors replaces the start valve. In addition, by using integrated circuits, instead of discrete components in the control unit, the size of this assembly has been greatly reduced. A particularly interesting change, that has not reached the production stage at the the time of writing, is the use of an electrically-heated platinum wire as an airflow sensor. Since the quantity of heat removed from this wire by the airflow is a function of both density and velocity, this system senses air mass flow, so the air-fuel mixture is kept constant regardless of changes in altitude. The quantity of heat removed is indicated by the current flowing through the wire, which is a function of its temperature. Both the suspended disc and the swinging flap sensors are only half as sensitive as carburettors to changes in air density.

A digital, instead of analog, microcomputer is used for the control of this new system. This has the advantage of greater accuracy and it can be made compatible with other electronic control systems – for example for automatic transmission – which might be used in the future. Bosch are also considering the introduction of a single point injection system – injector just upstream of the throttle valve – to reduce the cost of installations for the lower priced cars.

11.58   Emission control

The smog of Los Angeles led to a spate of legislation on exhaust emissions. Pollution has been acute there because of the basin-like layout of the land, atmospheric inversion which tends to retain the polluted air in the basin, and the photo-chemical effects of exceptionally brilliant sunshine over long periods. The subsequent legislation requiring manufacturers to limit the output of certain constituents has added so much to the cost of engines throughout the world that it has been said that it would have been cheaper to have moved Los Angeles!

Among the constituents recorded as objectionable, and in some instances even poisonous, are carbon monoxide, carbon dioxide, unburnt hydrocarbons, oxides of nitrogen, lead salts, polyaromatics, soots, aldehydes, ketones and nitro-olefins. Research originally narrowed this list down to three principal undesirables: these were carbon monoxide which, because of the quantity produced, is most significant so far as Europe is concerned, unburnt hydrocarbons and oxides of nitrogen. Now, however, controversy is raging over lead salts. Although there is no widely accepted evidence that any of these substances are present in the atmosphere in quantities large enough to present health hazards, public concern has been

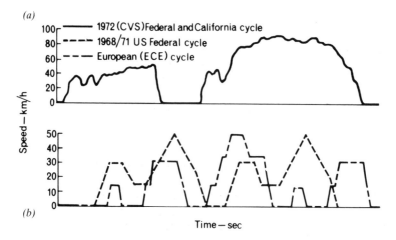

Fig. 11.59 (a) The 1972 US cycle for checking the exhaust emissions of private cars compared with (b) the 1971 US and European test cycles

aroused and legislation is being prepared, or has been enacted, in many countries.

These regulations are so complex that it is not possible to give a meaningful brief summary. Some idea of the severity of the controls can, however, be gained from the complexity of the test cycles that have to be run for the exhaust gas analyses to be made. Three of these are illustrated in Fig. 11.59. In Japan, all new models must pass two tests, one hot and the other cold, each with different limits on the individual noxious emissions. Some of the limits, according to information kindly supplied by the Society of Motor Manufacturers and Traders, are listed in Table 5, but the form of presentation here is considerably abbreviated and should be viewed as only a vague indication of the requirements.

Table 5 – A SUMMARY OF SOME OF THE PERMISSIBLE LIMITS ON EXHAUST GAS EMISSIONS, g/mile

State	*Year*	*Test*	*HC*	*CO*	*NO$_x$*
Japan	1978	hot	0.39	2.7	0.48
		cold	9.5	85.0	6.6
USA	1981		0.41	3.4	1.0
California	1983		0.41 (0.39)	7.0	0.1 (0.4)

The Californian limits differ from the US ones in that the figures in brackets are alternatives, but refer to NO$_2$ only. This is because NO is irrelevant except insofar as it may be subsequently converted in sunlight and in contact with unburnt hydrocarbons into NO$_2$, which is the only oxide of nitrogen from which the noxious peroxyacetal nitrates can be formed. The chemical changes involved are outlined in GLC Research Memorandum 485, and briefly reviewed in *Automotive Engineer*, Vol. 1, No. 7.

Test procedures are designed to represent typical journeys. The 1971 US and proposed European test cycles, together with the 1972 US cycle, are compared in Fig. 11.59. The latest cycle is of a random nature over a period of 1371 seconds and comprises 92 modes, as compared with the seven modes of the earlier US cycle. Whereas the earlier American cycle had to be repeated seven times, and the European test cycle four times, the later American one is not repeated. The 15-mode European test is intended to be more representative of driving conditions in our crowded cities, while the US test is obviously based on conditions on their highways into and out of town. They are carried out mainly with the vehicle on a chassis dynamometer, all the exhaust gases being collected in a very large plastics bag, for subsequent analysis.

It is important to distinguish between concentrations and quantities of pollutants. For example, concentrations of carbon monoxide and hydro-carbons in the exhaust gas are greatest during acceleration and idling, but the quantities produced in these conditions are small. As regards oxides of nitrogen, on a weight per mile travelled basis, these tend to occur in larger quantities during acceleration.

11.59   Carbon monoxide and hydrocarbons

Fig. 11.60 shows the effect of air:fuel ratio on the output of pollutants. From this it can be seen that, to reduce both carbon monoxide and hydrocarbon emissions, leaner mixtures must be employed. An alternative is to use either direct flame afterburners or catalytic converters in the exhaust system. Catalytic convertors, however, are relatively quickly choked by lead salts. Their protagonists, therefore, aver that cars should be run on unleaded gasoline, and it has also been suggested that the lead discharged to the atmosphere is a serious health hazard – so far not proved.

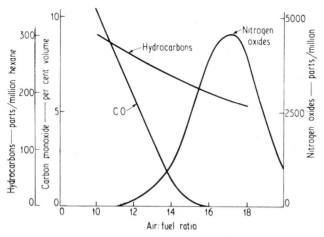

Fig. 11.60 Effect of air:fuel ratio on exhaust emissions

Unfortunately, as can be seen from the illustration, leaner mixtures, because they increase the temperature of combustion, tend to produce more oxides of nitrogen. It is thought that the critical temperature is about 1650°C.

Hydrocarbons in exhaust gases originate from the quench layer on the walls of the combustion chamber – a few hundredths of a millimetre thick, in which the flame is extinguished by cooling. Therefore the surface:volume ratio must be kept as small as possible and the design free from crevices and corners where quenching might occur. It is also necessary, however, to prevent discharge to atmosphere of hydrocarbon vapours from the fuel tank, carburettor and crankcase, even though such evaporation losses would represent only about 2 to 5% of the total pollution.

There are several ways of reducing emissions and, as regulations become progressively more stringent, it seems that a combination of several or of all of these measures will be necessary. The least expensive is modification of the carburation and ignition systems of the engine. A commonly used additional measure is the injection of air into the exhaust manifold, to oxidise the carbon monoxide and unburnt hydrocarbons. This, of course, is costly. Finally, catalytic or thermal converters can be employed. An alternative and entirely different approach might be the use of petrol injection, because of the close control that can be exercised over the fuel supply, using the lambda sensor described in Section 11.57.

11.60 Oxides of nitrogen

Nitric oxide NO and nitrogen dioxide NO_2, in the pollution context, are generally known as NO_x. They form in the engine cylinder when the combustion temperature exceeds about 1650°C. Consequently, the quantity produced per combustion stroke is a function of both temperature above that critical level and the dwell time at that temperature. For reducing the output of NO_x, therefore, the aim is primarily at reducing combustion temperature, or at least the time spent above the critical temperature. This may entail a reduction in compression ratio, modifying the exhaust valve timing to allow a small proportion of exhaust gas to remain after the exhaust valve has closed, and delaying the ignition.

11.61 Engine design for low hydrocarbon emissions

Basically, the changes needed are centred around the burning of weak mixtures, to reduce both unburnt hydrocarbons and carbon monoxide, and reducing maximum temperatures to prevent the formation of oxides of nitrogen. Combustion chambers, as mentioned earlier, may have to be rendered more compact and of a clean and simple form, free from quench areas and pockets.

A carburettor capable of metering fuel to within close tolerances is also required. It supplies a lean air:fuel mixture, which reduces the carbon monoxide too. During idling and deceleration, a calibrated flow of air and fuel is fed to the cylinders, so that irregular combustion is obviated. Changes needed in the ignition timing, however, affect the idling, increasing the speed – an embarrassment with automatic transmissions liable to creep. The exhaust gas dilution of the charge during deceleration is reduced, too, again promoting better combustion. Typical idling speeds in the USA are now 550 rev/min with automatic transmissions and 700 rev/min with manually controlled transmissions.

When the throttle is closed suddenly, the rapid increase in the depression of the manifold may draw off extra fuel, which will not burn completely and will therefore contribute considerably to the emissions. To overcome this, a gulp valve, letting extra air into the induction manifold, may be incorporated. Details of such a valve are given in Section 11.63.

Various measures are used to exercise close control over the idling mixture. One is described in connection with the Zenith CDSE carburettor. General Motors, on the other hand, have incorporated in their carburettor an air bleed screw, which is set on the production line and sealed so that it cannot be disturbed in service.

Another requirement for the slow running condition is the retarding of the ignition. This is done by fitting an extra pressure-sensitive capsule to the advance and retard mechanism. The tapping for the depression is taken from a point adjacent to the closed position of the throttle, so that the depression is effective only in this condition. This also has the effect of improving engine braking during deceleration, and there is no sacrifice of either power output or part throttle economy. General Motors, on some models, have retarded the ignition 15° by this method and, in addition, have retarded amounts varying from 5 to 15° on the centrifugal unit.

Because of the consequent lateness of burning, the heat rejection to coolant is increased, and provision has to be made to dissipate this in the cooling system. In one of the Ford systems, a thermostatic device is incorporated to advance the ignition again should the engine become overheated.

11.62   Warm-air intake systems

Apart from setting the coolant thermostat to open at higher temperatures to improve combustion in cold conditions, several manufacturers have introduced automatic control of the temperature of the air drawn into the carburettor. The General Motors system is built into a conventional air cleaner. There are two valves, operated by vacuum-actuated diaphragm mechanisms, and controlled by a thermostat. One valve lets warm and the other cold air into the intake.

The thermostat, mounted on the air cleaner, senses the temperature inside, maintaining it at 40 to 45°C. This thermostat operates another two-way valve, and this directs either induction system depression or atmospheric pressure to the actuator, according to whether cool or warm air is required. The warm air is taken from a jacket around the exhaust manifold.

Ford have developed a similar system. In this case, however, the thermostat senses under-bonnet temperature, and provision is made, by means of a vacuum-actuated over-ride, to enable maximum power output to be obtained during warm-up.

The BL Cars design is outstanding for its simplicity. It is a banjo-shaped pressed steel box assembly, the handle of which is represented by the air intake duct to the air cleaner. In both the upper and lower faces of the box is a large diameter port, and a flap valve is poised between them. This flap valve is mounted on a bimetal strip which, when hot, deflects to close one port and, when cold, to close the other. The latter port simply lets air at the ambient temperature into the intake, while the former is connected by a duct to a metal shroud over the exhaust manifold and therefore passes hot air into the intake. It follows that the temperature of the incoming mixture from both ports is regulated by its effect on the bimetal strip, which deflects the flap valve towards the hot or cold port, as necessary.

11.63   Air injection

The AC-Delco air injection system is a British version of a General Motors scheme. Its basic essential is an engine-driven air pump delivering into an air manifold, and thence through nozzles into each exhaust port. At the junction between the delivery pipe and the manifold, there is a check valve, to prevent back-flow of exhaust gas into the pump and thence to the engine compartment: this could happen in the event of failure of the pump or its drive.

A pipe is also taken back from the check valve to a gulp valve. When the throttle is closed suddenly after acceleration, this admits extra air to the induction tract to ensure that there is enough air passing into the cylinders to burn the consequent momentary surge of rich mixture and to prevent explosions in the exhaust system. The gulp valve comprises two chambers.

Of these, the bottom one is divided into two by a spring-loaded flexible diaphragm, from the centre of which a stem projects upwards to actuate a valve in the upper chamber. Air from the pump enters at the top and, when the valve is open, passes out through a port in the side, to the induction manifold (Fig. 11.61).

Manifold depression, introduced through a smaller port in the side of the housing, is introduced above the diaphragm. Therefore, a large transient increase in depression lifts the diaphragm, which subsequently returns under the influence of the spring. The duration of the lift is determined by the size of a balance orifice in the centre of the diaphragm. A period of opening of about 1 to 4 seconds is generally adopted. Slower variations in depression, which occur in normal driving, are absorbed by flow through the balance orifice.

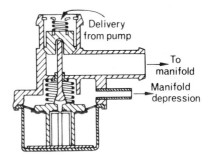

Fig. 11.61 AC-Delco gulp valve, for admitting extra air to the induction tract when the throttle is suddenly closed

In the AC-Delco system, there is also a simple spring-loaded pressure relief valve, which can be equipped with a small air silencer. This limits the pump delivery pressure and prevents excess air being injected into the exhaust ports under high speed conditions of operation.

Another system is the Lucas-Smiths Man-Air-Ox. This also comprises an air pump, gulp valve and check valve. As with the AC-Delco unit, there is an alternative to the gulp valve: a dump, or by-pass, valve can be used. This, instead of admitting a gulp of air to the induction tract, opens to atmosphere a delivery pipe from the pump. Thus, it effectively stops the supply through the nozzles, and prevents the possibility of explosions in the exhaust system. It, too, is suction controlled, but is a two-way valve. The sudden depression produced by the over-run condition lifts the valve, venting the air delivery to atmosphere, and at the same time seating the valve on the port through which the air was formerly being delivered to the manifold.

Although air injection may be used to cool the exhaust valves, the use of special steels may be necessary to offset the oxidation tendency. On the other hand, hot spots, such as ribs, may be incorporated in the exhaust manifold, to encourage after-burning.

11.64   Zenith duplex system

This system is employed in conjunction with the Zenith-Stromberg CDSE emission carburettor, Section 11.47. Basically, it is a by-pass induction tract in which is a heat exchanger, through which exhaust gas is passed, for warming the mixture and thus improving distribution to the cylinders by

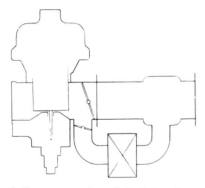

Fig. 11.62 An extra butterfly valve regulates flow through the by-pass tract of the Zenith duplex emission control system

fully evaporating all fuel droplets. As can be seen from Fig. 11.62 there are two throttle valves, one in the main tract and the other in the smaller diameter by-pass. The two are interconnected in such a way that first the valve in the by-pass opens and then, at about two-thirds of the pedal travel, the other begins to open, the full throttle condition being reached simultaneously by both.

It is easy to envisage alternative positions for the butterfly valves, and these have in fact been tried – some successfully – by Zenith. There are also variants of the system for use with multi-carburettor layouts. Although it is possible to over-ride the system, by full throttle acceleration, the time spent in this condition in normal driving apparently is not significant.

11.65   Other measures to reduce hydrocarbon emission

About 55% of the hydrocarbon pollution is in the exhaust, crankcase emissions account for a further 25% and the fuel tank and carburettor evaporation makes up the other 20%. These figures, of course, vary slightly according to the ambient temperature. In general unburnt hydrocarbons from these two sources amount to no more than about 4 to 10% of the total pollutants.

Many vehicles for sale in the USA now incorporate a trap to prevent evaporated fuel from being discharged to atmosphere. The vent pipe from the tank is taken to a canister containing a charcoal pack. When the engine is started, the canister is purged of fumes by suction through a pipe into the air intake – to this end, there is a small hole at the bottom of the canister, through which air is drawn. Filter pads prevent the entry of dirt into the charcoal and also stop charcoal granules from passing into the pipe to the engine air intake. Fuel vapour from the carburettor float chamber is passed directly into the induction system.

Crankcase fumes are drawn into the induction manifold by a closed circuit, positive ventilation system. One pipe is generally taken from the interior of the air filter to the rocker cover, and another from the crankcase to the induction manifold. Thus, air that has passed through a filter is drawn past the rocker gear into the crankcase and thence to the manifold, whence it is delivered into the cylinders, where any hydrocarbon fumes picked up from the crankcase are burnt.

There are three requirements for such a system: first, the flow must be restricted, to avoid upsetting the slow running condition; secondly, there must be some safeguard to prevent blow-back in the event of a backfire and, thirdly, the suction in the crankcase has to be limited. AC-Delco produce a valve for insertion in the suction line to meet these requirements. It comprises a spring-loaded disc-valve in a cylindrical housing. When there is no suction – engine off, or backfire condition – the valve seats on a port at one end, completely closing it. With high depression in the manifold, slow running or over-run, the valve seats on a larger diameter port at the other end, and a limited flow passes through the holes which, because they are near its periphery, are covered when it seats on the smaller diameter port. Flow through the larger port is restricted by the valve stem projecting into it. In normal driving, the valve floats in equilibrium between the two seats, and air can pass through the clearance around its periphery as well as through the holes, Fig. 11.63.

Smiths Industries, too, offer a crankcase ventilation system. It is designed to maintain an approximately constant depression in the crankcase. The through-ventilation principle is applied, but the flow passes through the diaphragm chamber of the valve assembly. The pipe from the crankcase is connected to the side of the chamber and the outlet to the manifold is taken from the base, Fig. 11.64. The top is closed by the flexible diaphragm, to the centre of which is attached the valve stem, which projects down into the valve orifice. Between the orifice and a seat on the

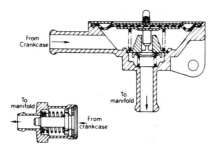

Fig. 11.63 Smiths Industries crankcase emission control valve Mk 2. The valve stem projects between guides above the valve orifice, and there is a separate non-return plate-valve beneath the orifice

Fig. 11.64 AC-Delco crankcase ventilation control valve. With zero vacuum in the manifold, the valve seats on the right-hand orifice and with maximum vacuum on the left-hand one. In normal running it floats between the two

outlet port is a plate-valve, spring loaded upwards. Suction draws the plate off the orifice and, in the slow running condition, it seats on the outlet port to limit the flow. In the event of a backfire into the manifold, the plate again seats on the orifice, thus acting as a non-return valve. In normal running, the depression pulls the diaphragm down against its return spring, the valve stem increasingly restricting the orifice, until a balance is struck between the forces applied to the diaphragm by suction and the spring.

Chapter 12

Fuel supply: air cleaning

Developments in body design, considerations of safety, and the general adoption of down-draught carburettors, involving a high position of the float chamber, rendered obsolete the simple arrangements of gravity feed from the fuel tank that were popular in early cars and many commercial vehicles.

In modern designs the rear position of the tank for private cars and the side position for commercial vehicles have become standardised, the level being at or below that of the side members of the frame. With a down-draught carburettor situated at the top of the engine, this may involve a vertical lift of 0.61 m or more in addition to the overcoming of the resistance of a considerable run of pipe from the tank to the carburettor.

Thus some means of pumping or forcing the petrol from tank to carburettor must be provided. The principle, at one time popular, of sealing the tank and maintaining in it by a hand-operated air pump sufficient pressure to force the petrol to the carburettor, has been abandoned except for certain special applications, and after a period of general adoption of the Autovac system, the modern practice of installing one or more pumps of the diaphragm type has become standardised. These pumps may be electrically or mechanically operated, both types being in wide general use. The former enables the carburettor float chamber to be filled independently of engine rotation, and since they may be fitted close to the tank and below the fuel level, the whole pipeline can be under positive pressure, thus minimising the risk of vapour lock as compared with the mechanical pump located on the side of the crankcase, where it must exert a suction lift and is exposed to higher temperatures; but these advantages are partly negatived by what is generally regarded as the superior reliability of the mechanically-operated types.

Rotary pumps of the gear or multi-plunger type which are in general use on aircraft engines are less suited to the large-scale economic manufacture necessary in automobile work.

12.1 Positive displacement pumps

The Autovac, which utilised the induction pipe depression to raise the fuel to a high-level auxiliary tank, was until the nineteen-thirties extensively used in the fuel supply of large petrol engines, but is now generally superseded by the positive displacement type of pump, for both petrol and diesel engines. Such pumps used to be of either the metallic bellows or the fabric diaphragm type, there being a tendency towards the general adoption of the latter.

The metallic bellows has proved an extremely reliable device in thermostatic applications, in which it is frequently referred to as the *sylphon* from the proprietary name used by the firm to which its commercial development is largely due, but with the rapid and continuous flexure arising in pumping applications there is some risk of failure of the metal due to fatigue, which results in the development of cracks.

Fabric diaphragms are not immune to the development of punctures, but very reliable types are now widely available by virtue of woven reinforcement, which is now used in both electrically- and mechanically-operated pumps.

12.2 SU pump

A successful pump of the electrically-operated diaphragm type which is in wide use in this country is the SU horizontal pump which has superseded the SU Petrolift. This is shown in longitudinal section in Fig. 12.1. The diaphragm D consists of a number of layers of impregnated fine gut fabric. The middle of the diaphragm is clamped to the armature A, which is centred in the stepped mouth of the magnet pot M by a ring of spherical discs or rollers, which swing with a rolling action as the armature moves to right or left. These roller discs also serve to support the free portion of the diaphragm.

The steps at the mouth of the magnet pot are so proportioned that as the lines of force passing across vary in density and direction to find the shortest path, so the component axial pull on the armature remains approximately constant throughout the travel.

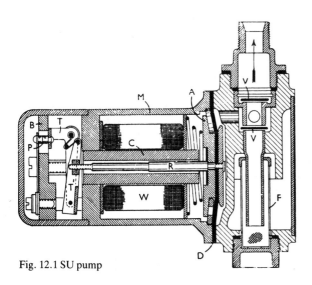

Fig. 12.1 SU pump

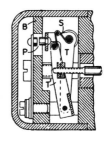

Fig. 12.2

The magnetic circuit is completed through the core C over which is threaded the winding spool W. A fibre disc is inserted in the central recess of the armature to prevent metal-to-metal contact of armature and core, which, as a result of residual magnetism, might prevent the return of the armature under the action of the delivery spring. The suction stroke occurs when the armature and diaphragm are moved to the left by the magnetic pull, and petrol then enters the pump chamber through the filter F and the lower of the two plate valves V. On the breaking of the circuit by the flick-over mechanism the diaphragm is returned by the compression spring, and petrol is delivered to the float chamber of the carburettor through the upper plate valve. Should the float chamber be so full as to close the needle valve, the diaphragm will remain at rest (with the electric circuit broken) until further delivery is required.

The float mechanism of the carburettor must be matched with the spring of the pump so that flooding cannot occur.

The stroke of the pump is about 3 mm and the maximum delivery pressure about $6.89 \, kN/m^2$. A wide margin of delivery capacity is provided.

The flick-over mechanism for the make-and-break of the current is operated by the rod R, the outer end of which is pivoted to the primary rocker T'. This controls the outer twin rocker T, which carries on a cross yoke one of the contact-breaker points P. The bottom ends of both rockers are pivoted on a pin passing through two of the legs of the plastics moulding B. The second contact point is carried on a spring blade which rests against this moulding when the contacts are open. The auxiliary diagram Fig. 12.2 should make clear how the movement of T' causes T to flick to the right and open the contacts under the action of the coil spring S mounted on a floating pin. This spring acts as a compression spring between the two rockers.

12.3   Mechanical diaphragm pump

A successful and reliable mechanical pump which is very widely used is the AC, one form of which is illustrated in Fig. 12.3. The particular model shown is adapted for high level application to a V-eight engine, where it is operated from the camshaft by a vertical push rod engaging with the inverted cup at the end of the level L_1. This lever is maintained in close contact with the push rod by the compression spring shown.

In the majority of applications the pump is mounted on the side of the crankcase at camshaft level, and the operating lever L_1 takes the form shown by the broken lines, acting as a flat cam follower. This lower position of the pump is preferable as it reduces the suction lift. In faulty installations trouble may arise through vapour lock caused by too close proximity of the petrol pipe to the hot exhaust pipe. The high temperature combined with reduced pressure due to excessive suction lift leads to vaporisation of the petrol and interference with the flow. A typical installation can be seen in Fig. 7.6.

To return to Fig. 12.3, the inner portion L_2 of the operating lever fits between the jaws of L_1 and is free to rotate on the bush B. The cross spindle R forms the pivot on which the combined lever turns. L_2 will be driven in a counter-clockwise direction by the rise of the push rod if there is contact at the heel H of L_2.

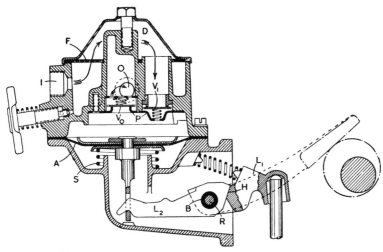

Fig. 12.3 AC fuel pump

This will draw down the diaphragm A, compressing the spring S and providing the suction stroke of the pump. Petrol enters at I and, passing to the dome D through the circular filter gauze F which surrounds the central turret, enters the pump chamber through the inlet valve V_1. This valve with the outlet valve V_0 is mounted in a brass plate P screwed to the under-side of the turret. The valves are small octagonal shaped discs of reinforced plastics, which allow for passage of the petrol while keeping the valve central. The outlet to the carburettor is indicated at O which leads to a union on the outside of the pump body.

The illustration shows the diaphragm in the lowest position. If the float chamber control of the carburettor permits delivery, the spring S will raise the diaphragm as the push rod falls. If not, the diaphragm and L_2 will remain at rest and lost motion will arise at H.

12.4   Air cleaners and silencers

When it is realised that in only one hour's normal running a 2-litre engine consumes the air content of a large room, some idea of the quantity of grit and dust that might pass through the engine can be formed.

Air cleaners may be classified as dry filters, centrifugal separators, and the washer type in which the air is actually drawn over oil-coated surfaces. An early and successful form of the dry filter type is the Vokes Protectomotor shown in Fig. 12.4. The air is cleaned by being drawn through a thickness of a special felt which, as can be seen, is supported on a star-shaped frame. In this way a very large area is obtained in a small space. A large area is required for two reasons, first to reduce the restriction to the passage of the air to the minimum, and second to make the 'life', before cleaning is necessary, as long as possible. The filter is arranged with the felt vertical, so that the air passes through it horizontally and the dust that is intercepted tends to fall off to the bottom of the device.

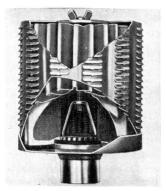

Fig. 12.4 Vokes filter

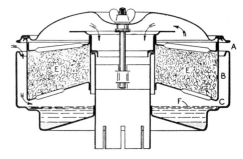

Fig. 12.5 AC oil-bath air cleaner

12.5   Oil-bath cleaner : air silencing

Fig. 12.5 illustrates a section through the AC oil-bath type cleaner. Entering at the circumferential gap A, the air passes down the annular space B to the restricted gap C at the oil level F. Impinging on the surface of the oil at high velocity after the right-angle turn, the bulk of the heavier particles are deposited at once in the oil bath and sink to the bottom as sludge. An oil mist is whipped up from the surface and entrains the finer particles which are arrested by the oil-wetted mesh of metal wool E, after which the cleaned air passes down the vertical intake to the carburettor or induction manifold of the ci engine. An outer casing can be provided to protect the unit from rain, if used in the open, and to facilitate the fitting of a single entry.

Under bad conditions of dirty and dusty atmosphere regular servicing of these cleaners is essential, by washing in paraffin or petrol and refilling with oil to the correct level, in accordance with the makers' instructions.

A variety of assemblies is available incorporating centrifugal extraction of the larger particles by means of abrupt changes in direction of the air stream by deflector vanes and catchment louvres and, in cases where the silencing function is to be combined with cleaning, units can be supplied with suitable resonance chambers and absorbent pads adapted to individual designs of power unit.

12.6   Paper-element air cleaners

The successful development of paper-element fuel and oil cleaners has been followed by an extension of the method to carburettor air intake systems.

It is now possible to provide air cleaners with the high efficiency of the oil-bath type at a lower cost and with simpler maintenance.

Delco-Remy and other makers now market paper-element cleaners having a filtering efficiency of 99.1 to 99.7% when tested in accordance with BS 1701.

The following advantages are claimed: they are lighter and more compact than most oil-bath cleaners, and do not normally require supplementary support brackets.

Resin-impregnated paper elements, which must be discarded and replaced usually at every 16 000 to 19 000 km, are easy to change and cost very little.

A large filtering surface area provides minimum air flow restriction and maximum dirt retention capacity.

The surface area of the paper element is related primarily to the air flow requirements of the engine, and may range from 2900 cm^2 for a flow of 1.699 to 2.265 m^3/min to 8700 cm^2 for a flow rating of 5.66 to 7.08 m^3/min, or about 1370 cm^2/m^3. Silencing is effected partly by tuning; that is, choice of an appropriate length of air inlet tube, Fig. 12.6.

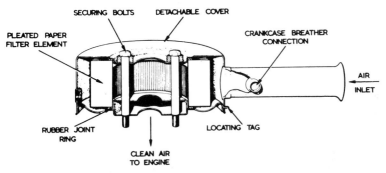

Fig. 12.6 Paper-element air cleaner

To minimise the head-room required under the bonnet, especially for engines of the V-layout with down-draught carburettors on top, filters of pancake form are now available. In other words, they are of large diameter so that, for a given filtration area, they are very shallow.

Chapter 13

Supercharging and superchargers

Increased output for a given size of engine is becoming more and more desirable in view of the trend towards weight reduction. It is also important because of the increasing emphasis on the need for providing, within the limits imposed by legal and practical restrictions on overall dimensions, the greatest possible space for pay-load.

There is more scope for supercharging in commercial vehicles than private cars, mainly because the diesel engine offers greater opportunities of gain and fewer consequential difficulties than does the petrol engine, in which the possibilities are limited by risk of detonation and all the troubles of greater waste heat disposal.

Considerably more heat can be handled in a well designed diesel engine than is represented by unblown conditions, provided sufficient air is supplied and utilised by adequate combustion arrangements.

Low speed torque may be improved and a flat torque-speed curve maintained without increased risk of bearing troubles if maximum speed is not increased. Recent years have witnessed a great increase in interest in the various systems of supercharging, and the development of new forms of supercharger.

The characteristic curves of speed, mean effective pressure, and power output shown in Fig. 4.6 illustrate the loss of power arising at high speeds from the failure to charge the cylinder completely by the agency of the atmospheric pressure alone. With aircraft engines at high altitudes this loss becomes serious, and there is full practical justification for the adoption of positive methods of forcing the charge into the cylinders in order to maintain at such altitudes the full mean effective pressure and torque obtainable at ground level. Here the extra complication and weight of the supercharging apparatus is necessary to avoid loss of performance.

In competitive track and road racing under rating rules based on cylinder swept volume, the use of specially-tuned blown engines became universal, and such engines have made a natural appeal to the private owner of a sports model, apart from organised professional and amateur racing, with its prestige value.

These engines are, however, in no sense normal production engines, being usually fitted with specially stiffened crankshafts, high compression heads and valves of special and expensive steels. They use specially blended fuels of high octane rating.

Attempts to increase the performance throughout the whole range of speed, or to increase the normal peaking speed of a standard engine by fitting a supercharger, are liable to develop serious bearing and waste-heat troubles.

Fig. 13.1 illustrates two aspects of supercharging and its effect on bmep (or torque) and power.

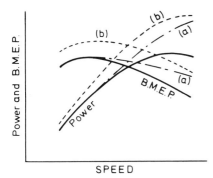

Fig. 13.1 Supercharging

The full lines represent the performance curves of an unblown engine with a somewhat steeply falling bmep characteristic. The broken lines (*a*) and (*b*) represent two different degrees of supercharge applied to the same engine.

The curves (*a*) indicate a degree of progressive supercharge barely sufficient to maintain the volumetric efficiency, bmep and torque, at their maximum value, through the speed range.

There would be no increase of maximum piston load or maximum torque, though there would be an appreciable increase in maximum road speed if an overspeed top gear ratio were provided – the engine speed range remaining the same.

Curves (*b*) show an increase of power torque throughout the whole range, due to a greater degree of supercharging. The *maximum* values of piston loads and crankshaft torque would also be increased unless modifications to compression ratio and possibly to ignition timing were made with a view to reducing peak pressures. This would have an adverse effect on specific fuel consumption, and would tend to increase waste heat troubles, but the former might be offset by fuel saving arising from the use of a smaller engine operating on a higher load factor under road conditions, and careful attention to exhaust valve design and directed cooling of local hot spots would minimise the latter risk.

13.1   Supercharging of commercial petrol engines

Spark ignition petrol engines consume virtually all the air supplied to them, and the power developed depends almost entirely on the breathing capacity of the unit. Supercharging can be applied to increase the maximum power but this tends to lead to detonation and high thermal loading, particularly on the piston, rings and exhaust valves. The tendency to detonation can be reduced by lowering the compression ratio, but this leads to a reduction in thermal efficiency over the cruising range. Increased maximum temperature of the cycle leads directly and indirectly to loss of thermal efficiency and higher fuel consumption, with increased waste heat troubles.

This aspect of supercharging is appropriate to specially tuned engines for racing purposes, where maximum performance from given cylinder dimensions is the all important objective. In commercial vehicle applications maintenance of torque at low speeds with a light engine, and utmost possible fuel economy for a given cost, weight and bulk of the power unit are the paramount considerations.

In the USA the petrol engine is in more extensive use for commercial purposes than the diesel engine, since fuel running cost is of less importance than engine first cost. Petrol engines of low cost and high power have been very extensively developed, and supercharging developments have been related to petrol engines to a greater extent than in this country, where fuel costs have encouraged the development of the more economical diesel engine.

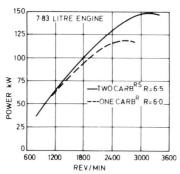

Fig. 13.2

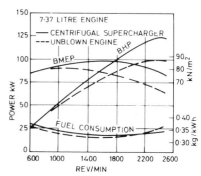

Fig. 13.3

Figs. 13.2 to 13.4 record results obtained some years ago on General Motors six-cylinder petrol coach engines. Fig. 13.2 refers to an engine of 7.83 litres and Fig. 13.3 to one of 7.37 litres. They both show improvement in performance of the same nature and similar amount to that indicated in the curves (a) of Fig. 13.1, but obtained by quite different means. The improvement in performance of the 7.83-litre engine of Fig. 13.2 is due to the substitution of two carburettors for one and increase of compression ratio from 6.0 to 6.5. The breathing characteristics of the engine and the thermal efficiency were susceptible of improvement by normal means.

The 7.37-litre engine of Fig. 13.3 was by contrast supercharged by means of a centrifugal blower, driven by belt and gearing at ten times crankshaft speed. No clutch provision was made in the blower drive, and the compression ratio was lowered slightly to avoid any alteration in the octane requirement of the fuel.

Fig. 13.4 shows the results obtained with and without supercharge on a 7.67-litre engine, the blower in this case being of the Roots type, arranged

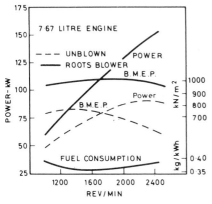

Fig. 13.4

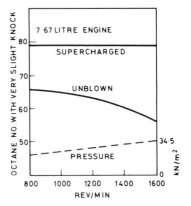

Fig. 13.5

so that its drive is engaged by a magnetic clutch only after full throttle conditions are reached.

It is recorded that the supercharged power output of the 7.67-litre engine was equal to the normal output of a larger engine of 10.1 litres capacity, with a relative petrol saving thereto of about 20% under road conditions.

No alteration of compression ratio was made in this case, but a higher octane fuel was used, and it was found that 79 octane fuel was satisfactory throughout the whole speed range with the Roots type supercharger in contrast to increasing octane requirement at lower speeds when not blown, as shown in Fig. 13.5, in which the broken line indicates the boost above normal atmospheric pressure.

The effect of supercharging on the specific fuel consumption is seen to be small in these instances.

13.2 Diesel engines

Because the mixing of fuel with air in diesel engines has to take place within a period of 35 to 40° of crank rotation, it is possible to utilise a maximum of only about 80% of the air supplied. For a given maximum power output, the cylinder dimensions are therefore larger than those of the spark ignition engine. At maximum speed and power output, the thermal loading is generally about as great as the engine can safely withstand, unless it has been specially designed for supercharged conditions. At lower speeds, however, the margin is greater, and thermal loading is not a critical factor, and full benefit may be obtained from a blower with good low-speed characteristics giving an engine torque which rises with decrease of speed and obviates the need for frequent gear changes.

This capacity to 'lug' at low speeds is one of the most valuable features of the diesel in modern applications.

The denser air of the supercharge tends to reduce the delay period, and gives better control over the rate of pressure rise. As a result, to double the normal torque calls for an increase in maximum pressure of only about 30%.

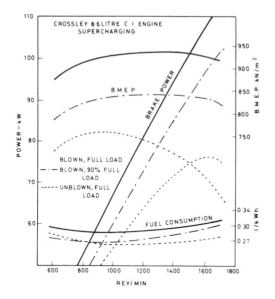

Fig. 13.6 Performance curves of supercharged Crossley ci engines

Running is smoother and quieter. A smaller engine, with higher maximum speed may be used for a given power.

Fig. 13.6 shows the performance curves obtained with Roots blowers in a series of supercharged Crossley engines supplied to the Netherlands State Railways, a full description of this important contract being given in *Automobile Engineer*, Vol. 38, No. 2.

13.3 Two-stroke engines

In two-stroke engines, excess air must be supplied for scavenging of the cylinders. There is normally a wastage through the exhaust ports of about 40% of the total air delivery. This loss is not entirely without benefit, for the additional cooling obtained reduces the thermal loading on the engine components. Because of the exhaust porting normally used in two-stroke engines, it is possible to apply a reasonable degree of supercharge only if there is back-pressure in the exhaust system.

This seems to indicate that the two-stroke engine provides a suitable field for the application of turbo-blowers. From the point of view of cylinder charge, the resistance to flow through poppet exhaust valves, where used, would have the same effect, but without the subsequent utilisation of exhaust heat obtained from a turbine. Back-pressure effects are referred to in Chapter 10.

13.4 Blower characteristics

The curves of Figs. 13.3 and 13.4 bring out clearly the comparative speed-delivery characteristics of two usual types of blower, the delivery of the centrifugal type being negligible at low speeds and giving the characteristic supercharging results indicated in the (*a*) curves of Fig. 13.1.

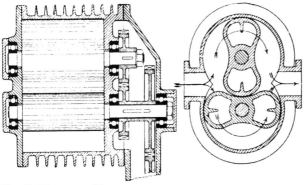

Fig. 13.7 Roots type blower

The Roots displacement type shows a positive delivery throughout the range, rising slowly with speed. The volumetric efficiency of this type increases with speed owing to the smaller proportional effect of the rotor tip clearances, but the power absorbed goes up in a greater proportion owing to the turbulence due to the right-angle turns in the flow path. The consequent warming of the charge is valuable from a carburation point of view. A blower of this type is illustrated in Fig. 13.7.

The most positive delivery at low speeds and higher pressures is given by the eccentric rotor, sliding vane type of blower, such as the Zoller, Centric and Cozette designs, but very thorough provision for lubrication is required owing to the high-speed sliding contacts, and the side loading of the blades is liable to produce distortion. This type can be made very silent.

The Centric vane type blower is of interesting construction. Fig. 13.8 shows the original construction as used for moderate powers. A central stub shaft S, on the axis of the main cylindrical casing, supports on ball bearings the balanced vane carriers C, which are interlaced in symmetrical pairs, each vane being riveted to a pair. The vanes pass through slotted trunnions of reinforced plastics in the cylindrical recesses formed at the junctions of the segmental sections of the built-up, eccentric drum D.

The drum D is rotated by the power shaft P, and carries round the vanes on their free running carriers. It will be noted that the vanes remain always radial to the outer drum, though not at a constant angular pitch. A surface seal is thus obtained at the outer edge of the vanes, as well as where they

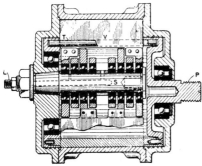

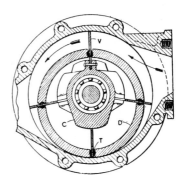

Fig. 13.8 Centric blower

pass through the revolving drum. Actual contact is avoided by providing a very slight clearance, as the vanes are accurately constrained radially by their carriers.

The construction thus provides positive and accurate driving of the vanes without high speed sliding contacts, and the internal friction is a minimum, provision for lubrication being made at L.

With units designed for higher powers and speeds it was found that there was some tendency of the stub shaft to deflect under the unidirectional forces arising from the angular acceleration and retardation of the vanes, and a new construction was developed.

In this construction, the central shaft is carried through and becomes the primary driving shaft, the drum being driven through a pinion and internally toothed ring at a speed reduction depending on the designed eccentricity. The primary drive shaft may, of course, be driven at any suitable speed through a train of gearing from the engine. The carrier bearings now undergo a relatively small oscillating movement.

Although in wide and successful use for scavenging and blowing two-stroke engines, and for supercharging of four-stroke engines to moderate pressures, the Roots blower has evinced certain limitations in efficiency and in suitability for supercharge pressure ratios higher than 1.5.

The design operates as a displacer rather than a compressor, as indeed do the other types so far mentioned, there being no general compression of the charge until the delivery port is uncovered, with the result that at high ratios, pulsations and high frequency shock waves tend to be formed, with loss of volumetric efficiency, and with high fluctuations of torque on the rotor shafts.

More recent developments are the Lysholm and Saurer types of meshing rotors which constitute true compressors. The general form of the cross-section of these is shown in Fig. 13.9, three helical lobes being used. As in the Roots type, actual contact between the meshing profiles is avoided by the mating of the precision synchronising gears at the ends of the shafts, and there is no contact with the casing, so that complete freedom from rubbing friction is obtained.

A pair of rotors of the Saurer compressor are shown in Fig. 13.10 from which it will be realised that very great problems of precision production have been overcome. Pressure ratios up to 2.0 and speeds up to 10 000 rev/min have been obtained, and at 5000 rev/min and 1.5 pressure ratio the Saurer unit has shown an adiabatic efficiency of 80% compared with 60% of a comparable Roots unit.

Performance curves of the Saurer six-cylinder diesel of bore and stroke 115 mm and 140 mm are given in Fig. 13.11 showing the naturally-aspirated and supercharged results. The blower in this case has a displacement of 2.07 litres.

13.5 Symposium of papers on supercharging

An important symposium of papers on supercharging and new forms of supercharger was presented before the Automobile Division of the Institution of Mechanical Engineers in April, 1957, by a number of acknowledged authorities.

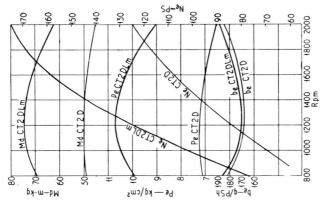

Fig. 13.11 Saurer supercharger performance curves

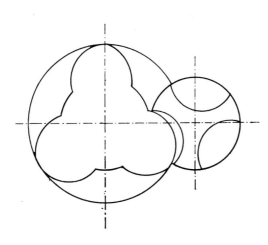

Fig. 13.10 Saurer rotors

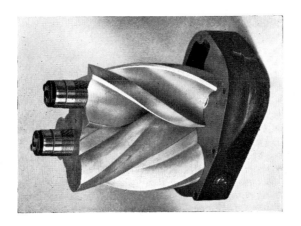

Fig. 13.9 General section of Saurer rotors

Space does not permit here of more than a very brief summary of the information given and the views expressed by the authors, and in the following discussion, published in *Proc. Aut. Div., Inst. Mech. Engineers.*

An important new form of positive displacement supercharger described and discussed was the BICERA positive compressor, designed by the British Internal Combustion Engine Research Association (now Institute). A cross-section of this supercharger is given in Fig. 13.12.

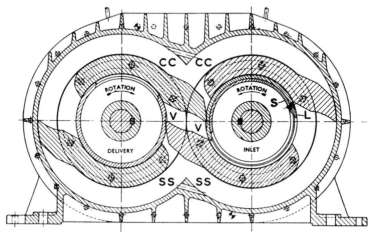

Fig. 13.12 BICERA compressor

Two interrupted drums each carry a symmetrical pair of wing-like vanes or lobes acting as pistons in the annular working spaces between their outside surface and the casing. The rotation of the drums by any suitable mechanical means is synchronised by precision spur gearing.

Intermeshing and counter movement of the vanes causes the variation of volume of the two working spaces which effects the aspiration, compression and delivery of the charge. The charge enters and leaves these working spaces by axial ducts formed by the annular spaces between the rotor bosses and shafts and the inside of two fixed sleeves fitting closely to the rotor bores.

Large ports running the full length of the rotors and extending over appropriate arcs provide communication with the working spaces. The arc of the delivery port is about 90° and of the inlet port about 170°. The latter may be varied by means of a lip L attached to an inner sleeve S which may be rotated relatively to the fixed sleeve by an external control wheel operating a toothed sector. It has been found advantageous to apply this variation of port edge to the inlet closing only.

In the position shown in Fig. 13.12 all the vane tips lie on the transverse centre line of the shafts.

It will thus be seen that the two rotating drums provide the pistons in the form of the lobes or wings and also act as the outer members of sleeve valves controlling inlet and outlet of the air. In this way rapid opening of valves of large area is provided, an essential for efficient operation of a rotary compressor, in which there is no convenient harmonic slowing of the piston movement during the opening of the valves.

There are essentially two working spaces undergoing the changes in volume which effect suction, compression and delivery.

The double annular spaces SS at the bottom of the housing form the suction volume, which is initiated as the vane tips commence to withdraw from over-lap, and reaches a steady rate of increase as the two wing tips simultaneously reach the lower point of bifurcation of the annular spaces SS, about 40° of rotation from the position shown in Fig. 13.12. This is also the point at which the previously aspired charge is split into two portions for the carry-round to the upper portion CC of the annular spaces, in which compression of the re-combined portions of the carry-round is effected, followed by delivery.

A fresh charge is aspired every half revolution, and delivery is completed one and a half revolutions later. Carry-round and direct compression of the previous charge occur simultaneously with the aspiration of the new one, and together occupy the same period of half a revolution. Delivery occupies the remaining half revolution. The cycle time of one and a half revolutions includes a dead period of about 20° between delivery and suction during which the residue of the charge occupies the constant volume clearance space VV.

The reader may care to trace the events of the cycle by means of tracings or cut-outs of the rotor sections.

The loss due to the unresisted expansion of this residual air cannot be recovered. During carry-round leakage compression takes place between the high-pressure delivery space past the rotor tips into the carry-round charge. This represents a rise of pressure at constant volume to the compression curve, and saves both volume and work at the toe of the indicator diagram. Since the rotor surfaces between the lobes have pure rolling contact, the corresponding clearances and leakages can be kept small.

13.6   Exhaust turbocharging

The development of condensing and compounded steam engines, and of low-pressure steam turbines, all represented attempts to utilise more of the energy available at the low pressure end of the expansion curve instead of discharging it to waste as previously, at pressures up to $345 \, kN/m^2$ or more according to the type of engine and conditions of working; the most heinous offender, largely in the interests of a strong chimney draught, being the ordinary steam locomotive.

A logical development of the combination of high pressure reciprocating engines with steam turbines for marine aplications is the combination of exhaust-gas turbines with reciprocating diesel engines, but unfortunately in automobile applications the power delivered from low-speed and high-speed shafts cannot readily be combined for propulsion purposes, nor applied independently as in marine propulsion.

Turbocharging, however, offers an attractive application and has been extensively used in conjunction with marine diesels, on what is generally referred to as the Buchi system. (See *Exhaust Turbo Charging of Internal Combustion Engines – Its Origin, Evolution, Present State of Development and Future Potentialities,* by A. J. Buchi, Monograph No. 1 *J. Franklin*

Inst., 1953.) The exhaust-turbo supercharger runs as a self-contained unit without any mechanical connection with the main engine, and utilises what would normally be waste heat energy, thus increasing both the power and efficiency of the power unit.

It is in this respect that the turbocharged engine shows its greatest advantages. By utilising the exhaust energy to drive the supercharger, mechanical losses associated with engine-driven blowers are greatly minimised and the performance may be from 5 to 7% better than when atmospherically charged owing to the additional work obtained from the completion of the expansion down to atmospheric pressure in an apparatus which, moreover, has a higher mechanical efficiency than that of the reciprocating engine.

Fig. 13.13 Typical turbocharger

Thanks to the pioneer work of Dr. Buchi, these benefits have long been realised in the fields of marine propulsion and stationary generating plant, where the conditions of constant speed and steady load are favourable factors in determining reliable and economical performance.

Two of the papers in the symposium dealt very fully with the problems involved in the extension of these benefits to automobile work, in which new and special problems arise.

These may be summarised briefly as due to great fluctuation of speed and load of the reciprocating engine, and the very much smaller power requirements, perhaps only one-fiftieth or less of that employed in big marine or generating installations. Moreover, the maintenance of high torque at medium and low powers, which is essential in automobile applications, is difficult of attainment with the characteristics of the rotary compressor. The high rotational inertia of these small, very high-speed units introduces difficulties during periods of rapid acceleration, when delay in response of the turbine unit will cause a temporary shortage of air delivery relative to the increased fuel delivery from the injection pump, with corresponding development of exhaust smoke.

13.7 Valve overlap and combustion conditions

To take advantage of the low-pressure periods of the exhaust pressure wave to aid scavenging it is necessary in some engines to employ valve overlap much in excess of normal amounts.

An overlap of 140° is quite common, and this results in both valves being nearly in the full open position at top dead centre.

This calls for large valve clearance slots in the piston crown, which has two disadvantages. The compression ratio is reduced, and the form of the combustion chamber may become unfavourable.

Cold starting may be adversely affected, and for this reason small high-speed engines seek a compromise between scavenge period and compression ratio.

These disadvantages do not appear to arise in all cases, for Thornycroft, who have carried out extensive development work with their 6-cylinder, 11.3-litre engine, both normally aspirated and supercharged by an Eberspacher turbocharger, state that no modification of the valve timing was called for owing to the successful matching of the turbine and engine characteristics.

The rotor is mounted on ball races and its moment of inertia has been reduced to a minimum. With these high-speed rotors (in the above case the maximum is about 35 000 rev/min) dynamic balance must be meticulously carried out to very fine limits. In more recent designs of turbocharger, plain bearings are employed because they are more suitable for high rotational speeds.

Fig. 13.13 shows a cut-away view of such a turbocharger; while Fig. 13.14, which reveals the turbine guide and rotor blading, shows how compactly the unit may be mounted and ducted; and Fig. 13.15 gives the power curves both naturally-aspirated and turbocharged. It will be noticed that there is no appreciable difference in the fuel consumption based on a one-hour rating.

Fig. 13.14 Thornycroft turbocharger

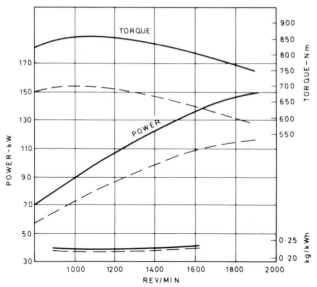

Fig. 13.15 Thornycroft turbocharged engine performance

For full information on this important development the reader should refer to *Automobile Engineer*, Vol. 47, No. 2, *How to Select and Install Turbo-superchargers*, by Hugh McInnes, HP Books, USA, and *Theory and Practice of Turbocharging*, by Bob Henderson, SpeedSport Motobooks.

Intensive development of the automobile turbo-charger is being undertaken by many firms of great repute and experience, and improvement in construction and performance should be rapid. Large scale manufacturing techniques should ensure competitive costs with other methods of improvement of engine output.

13.8   The pressure-wave supercharger

An entirely new type of supercharger has been developed by Brown Boveri, who have marketed it under the registered name Comprex. Basically, the energy in the exhaust gas is transferred directly – instead of mechanically – in the form of pressure pulses to the incoming air-fuel mixture, hence the term *pressure-wave supercharger*. With this system, maximum boost pressures of about 3 bar are said to be obtainable.

The principle is illustrated in Fig. 13.16. Energy interchange between the exhaust and induction gases occurs in a set of straight cells within the drum B. These cells, the ends of which are open, are arranged around the spindle on which the drum rotates, their longitudinal axes being parallel to it. Although the drum is rotated by a belt drive from the crankshaft, it absorbs no more than between 1 and 2% of the power output of the engine, since it does not have to compress the gas. Moreover, with such a large number of cells in operation, the compression process is virtually continuous, so synchronisation of this rotation with that of the crankshaft is unnecessary.

The sequence of operations is as follows: during each revolution of the drum, one end of each cell in turn passes the end of the exhaust passage A.

This allows exhaust gas, under the influence of the pressure in the exhaust passage, to flow along the cell, compressing the air that it already contains against its far end, which at this point in the cycle is closed. Further rotation opens the latter end and closes the former, so that the compressed air flows into the inlet port F. As the cell progresses beyond the inlet port it is again closed at that end, the other end being opened to the exhaust down-pipe through E, so the exhaust gas flows back again along the cell and out to atmosphere. This generates a suction wave in the cell so that, as its opposite end is again opened, this time to the inlet pipe D, fresh gas is drawn into the cell, so that the cycle can begin again.

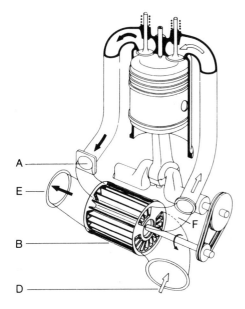

Fig. 13.16 The Comprex pressure-wave supercharger

Ferrari have been developing the system with petrol injection for application to racing cars. With carburetted engines, unless the carburettor is positioned downstream of the Comprex supercharger, the exhaust gas is brought into direct contact with the fuel-air mixture, instead of with air alone. Obviously, therefore, it is suitable principally for diesel engines.

A major advantage of the Comprex system is its virtually instantaneous response to changes in load and speed – energy from the exhaust gas is transferred at the speed of sound to the air being compressed. With the more conventional turbocharger, on the other hand, response time depends on the rate at which the rotor can be accelerated. Another advantage is that whereas, with the turbocharger, the boost at low speeds is limited because the rate of gas flow through the engine is low, the boost obtainable with the Comprex system is virtually independent of throughput of gas. Consequently, boosted power is obtainable at low speeds and, provided that the axle ratio is properly matched to this characteristic, significant fuel economy is obtainable. Finally, if the porting is timed to allow a degree of recirculation of the exhaust into the induction system, the output of oxides of nitrogen can be reduced by between 20 and 30%.

13.9   Charge cooling and two-stage supercharging

From the end of the nineteen-fifties to the close of the nineteen-seventies, turbocharging progressively gained favour, in preference to the use of mechanically-driven superchargers. This was partly because of its advantages outlined in Section 13.6, and partly owing to the emergence of materials capable of operating under severe loading at high temperatures – about 700°C – coupled with knowledge and experience gained in the design and development of very high speed machinery – about 120 000 rev/min – and especially its bearings.

Most of the mechanical problems have now been solved, though no doubt further progress will be made in respect of materials. The subsequent stage of evolution, therefore, from the beginning of the nineteen-eighties, was in the application of charge cooling.

Work done on the gas, in compressing it, raises its temperature. This has two major detrimental effects: first, it reduces the density of the charge, and therefore the weight of air that can be introduced into the cylinder; secondly, it increases the peak temperature of the gas during the subsequent combustion phase and therefore of the critical components such as exhaust valves, pistons, rings and cylinder-head gasket. Charge cooling can ameliorate both these conditions.

Cooling is effected by directing the gas compressed by the turbocharger, or for that matter by a mechanically-driven supercharger, through a heat exchanger – similar to a radiator but usually totally encased – before it is delivered to the engine cylinder. The heat transfer medium can be the water during its passage from the coolant radiator to the engine, or it can be air delivered either by a separate fan or by being diverted from the main flow of air to the radiator. Generally, water is preferred because the whole installation is then more compact.

There are two forms of charge cooling. That just described is referred to as *aftercooling*. Where two-stage supercharging or turbocharging is adopted – in effect, two superchargers or turbochargers installed in tandem to raise the boost pressure in two separate stages – the charge may be cooled after the first stage and before it is delivered to the second. This is termed *intercooling*.

Two-stage compression can be particularly advantageous with turbocharging because characteristics of the radial-flow compressors employed are such that they can be effective over only a limited range of pressure ratios, and the rates at which they deliver air increase approximately as the square of their rotational speeds. Thus, by compressing in two stages, each of which is matched so that the characteristics of the compressors are complementary, neither is called upon to operate so close to its maximum limit as to be in danger of surging, or stalling. The outcome is a wider band of speeds and loads over which the turbocharging can be effective, and therefore more advantageous engine torque characteristics. Although both intercooling and aftercooling reduce the temperature of the gas delivered to the cylinder, and therefore the final temperature in the exhaust, the principal reason for intercooling is to raise volumetric efficiency of the engine by increasing the density of the charge before it is delivered to the second stage for further compression.

Chapter 14

Fuels for automobile engines

The fuel problem may be conveniently considered under the following three heads –

(1) Commercial and political considerations of supply and cost.
(2) Power output, consumption and safety.
(3) Fuel quality, in terms of chemical and physical properties.

14.1   Commercial and political considerations

The vitally important question of engine fuels, from the point of view of national defence and supply during emergency, cannot be dealt with here, and the following summary covers, therefore, the technical aspects of commercial applications only. In these applications we are almost entirely restricted to –

(1) Fuels derived from petroleum. These are hydrocarbons principally in the liquid form, although to a limited extent and in special circumstances they may be compressed natural gases (LNG) or liquefied petroleum gases (LPG).
(2) Fuels derived from other sources. These include hydrocarbon fuels from oil shale or from coal, gaseous fuels and alcohols.

In the past, economic considerations and availability have practically confined commercial engine fuels to group (1). A limited amount of benzole is used in some countries, and alcohol fuels have been used in the past in racing engines and are still incorporated in petrols in some countries.

The use of gaseous fuels, such as producer gas and liquefied petroleum gases, in the spark-ignition engine may be mentioned in passing.

Producer gas, the chief combustibles in which are hydrogen and carbon monoxide with a large proportion of diluent nitrogen, may be made from 'capital' fuels such as anthracite and coke, or from 'income' sources represented by wood charcoal, wood shavings, seed pods and other vegetable carbonaceous matter.

During the Second World War there was a considerable development of gas generators for road vehicles on the Continent, and to some extent in

Great Britain, the solid fuel being burnt in a 'producer' fitted near the engine or, alternatively, mounted on a special trailer. The popularity of this system can, perhaps, be gauged from the rapid reversion to liquid fuel when war ended.

During the First World War some pioneer work was done in the use of coal gas carried in light rubberised fabric bags on the roof of the vehicle, the supply being obtained from the ordinary town mains at the usual pressure of a few inches of water head above atmosphere. This represented a somewhat crude improvisation with a very limited range of action, corresponding in most cases to that of less than half a gallon of petrol.

Later, town gas was experimentally compressed in special steel cylinders at about $20\,000\ kN/m^2$, by which means a range of action of 80 to 100 miles has been obtained with medium commercial vehicles.

The central compressing stations represent, however, a fixed 'anchorage' and high overhead costs, disadvantages which in times of peace prevent the system from competing successfully with the convenience and mobility of the petrol-driven vehicle, while the weight of the cylinders represents a considerable loss of net pay load.

14.2   Power output, consumption and safety

In the ordinary vehicle engine which draws in a combustible mixture there is remarkably little difference, for a given compression ratio, in the power output of a given size of cylinder as between petrol, benzole and alcohol. Ricardo has pointed out that the mixture strength or heat content per cubic unit of chemically correct combustible mixture is almost exactly the same for all the volatile hydrocarbon fuels, though the bulk and weight of fuel in which this heat is carried vary with the calorific value and density of the particular fuel under consideration. In the case of benzole the heat content per unit of weight of fuel is less, and that per unit of volume greater, than with petrol, while with alcohol both heat contents are considerably less.

Commercial paraffin or kerosene and the heavier diesel and fuel oils have heat values between petrol and benzole by weight and about the same as benzole by volume. Alcohol has the advantage of giving under comparable conditions rather better filling of the cylinder or volumetric efficiency owing to the cooling effect of its higher latent heat, that is, the heat required for vaporisation, this heat being largely picked up inside the cylinder.

Benzole and alcohol have a fairly high resistance to pinking and in this respect were formerly superior to the straight-run petrols obtained by straight distillation from crude oil. However, with the development of new refining processes, high-octane petroleum fuels have become widely available and this has been accompanied by the general adoption of high compression engines in recent years.

Thus the thermodynamic conditions for power and economy can now be met as the result of improvement in fuels and carburation.

With regard to safety, there is little to choose between the volatile fuels as marketed, owing to the necessity for including in all cases constituents which will make starting of the engine easy in cold weather. Practical immunity from fire risk can, however, be obtained by the use of heavy oils in the compression-ignition engine, in addition to the great advantages of a saving in fuel consumption of 25 to 30% which is inherent in the higher compression ratio of the diesel cycle. The relative *price* of the two classes of fuel is determined under present commercial and fiscal conditions very largely by taxation, and it must be borne in mind that the oil companies' prices for the different classes of fuel are determined by relative demand and the variation in production cost resulting from that relative demand.

The replacement for aircraft purposes of the piston engine by the gas turbine, whatever particular combination of propeller and jet may be used, has led to an increased production of specially prepared kerosene, and a reduced consumption of high-octane fuel, so better anti-knock petrols have become available for road work.

14.3   Sources and characteristics of motor fuels

Motor fuels suitable for the petrol engine are obtained from several sources, the proportion derived from each source depending on accessibility, cost, availability, and a variety of fiscal and defence problems, such as have already been suggested.

14.4   Petroleum

Almost the whole of the spirit with a world-wide distribution is of petroleum origin, and is composed of one or more of the following –

(*a*) Straight-run petrol (distilled from crude petroleum).
(*b*) Natural and 'casing-head' gasoline (very light spirits, used in blending, to produce easy starting).
(*c*) Cracked or re-formed spirits, made by thermal and catalytic treatment of certain petroleum fractions.
(*d*) Spirits made by special methods, such as polymerisation, alkylation, isomerisation and aromatisation. In all these cases various treating methods such as 'sweetening' and desulphurisation are employed to remove sulphur and to make components more stable for extended storage periods.

All petroleum products are derived from capital resources, which are being used up at a disconcerting rate.

Fortunately, prolific fields discovered in the Middle East, the North Sea, Nigeria, Alaska and Venezuela are now rapidly being exploited to supplement the long-established sources of supply from the USA.

14.5   Shale petrol

Although at present a very subsidiary fuel, petrol obtained by distillation of oil shale may assume increasing importance as the world's petroleum reserves diminish. The cost of mining, handling and processing oil shale is a formidable handicap at existing world prices of fuel.

The world possesses enormous deposits of oil shale, but these deposits are capital resources which will not last for ever, and the presence of minerals, such as uranium, in many of these shales may become an incentive towards their speedier utilisation, in view of the developments in the use of atomic energy.

Indeed, it is not impossible that the oil might become merely a by-product.

14.6 Benzole

Benzole (commercial benzene) is mainly a by-product of those industries which use large quantities of coal, such as the gas and steel industries.

It is never used alone as a motor fuel, but is normally blended with petrol at a concentration of 10 to 30%. Increasing quantities of benzene are now being manufactured from petroleum, but mainly for use as a chemical solvent or feedstock. Since for this type of use benzole commands a fairly high price, its use in motor spirit is restricted.

14.7 Alcohols

Although methanol was formerly widely used as racing fuel, where economy was not so important, the use of either methanol or ethanol as conventional motor spirit is entirely impractical. Alcohol from agricultural products such as, for example, sugar or grain, costs up to four times as much as the motor spirit it would displace, yet it has only two-thirds of the heat energy content of motor spirit.

Alcohol has, however, excellent anti-knock quality, but the cost to the consumer for octane improvement would be nearly twenty times as much as with TEL (tetra-ethyl lead). In the case of methanol, its tendency to absorb water creates problems in motor spirit distribution and storage. Water causes the alcohol to separate from the motor spirit in an alcohol-water layer.

14.8 Manufactured fuels

A miscellaneous collection of fuels is made by chemical processes; they represent a relatively small poportion of world output, but tend to increase each year. They include –

(*a*) Petrol made by hydrogenation of bituminous coal or brown coal.
(*b*) Petrol made by hydrogenation of certain types of coal tar products such as low-temperature tar and creosote.
(*c*) Petrol made from 'synthesis' gas, specially made for the purpose, such as mixtures of carbon monoxide and hydrogen.
    This includes the important Fischer-Tropsch process.
(*d*) Actual hydrocarbon compounds of 'technical' purity possessing very high octane rating such as *iso*octane, *iso*decane and triptane, made by special processes.
(*e*) Tetra-ethyl lead (TEL) and tetra-methyl lead (TML), though not strictly fuels, should be included, as they are widely used in petrols to improve anti-knock characteristics.

14.9 Chemical and physical properties

Practically all petroleum hydrocarbons found in motor fuels are members of four groups – paraffins, olefines, naphthenes (cycloparaffins) and aromatics. Crude oil does not contain olefines and these result from certain refinery processes.

Paraffins: These occur as chain structure hydrocarbons. The hydrogen and carbon atoms are related to each other by the general formula $C_{2n}H_{2n+2}$, in which n indicates the number of carbon atoms. Table 6 lists a number of paraffinic hydrocarbons and illustrates some of the characteristics of all hydrocarbons.

Hydrocarbons listed in Table 6 are called *normal hydrocarbons* when they have a straight-chain structure, as in normal octane. However, starting with butane, it is possible to have two or more distinctly different compounds, called *isomers*, with the same number of hydrogen and carbon atoms (see numbers in parentheses, Table 6). Many of these compounds

Table 6 – PARAFFINIC HYDROCARBONS AND THEIR CHARACTERISTICS

	Name of paraffin[a]	Formula	Usual form at room temperature	Approx. boiling point (°C)	Major uses
	Methane	CH_4	Gas	−161	As gas for industrial and domestic fuel; source for petroleum chemicals
	Ethane	C_2H_6	Gas	− 90	
	Propane	C_3H_8	Gas	− 42	
(2)	Butane	C_4H_{10}	Gas	− 1	In gas and motor fuels
(3)	Pentane	C_5H_{12}	Gas and liquid	36	Motor fuels
(5)	Hexane	C_6H_{14}	Liquid	69	Motor fuels[d]
(9)	Heptane	C_7H_{16}	Liquid	99	Motor fuels[d]
(18)	Octane	C_8H_{18}	Liquid	126	Motor fuels[d]
(35)	Nonane	C_9H_{20}	Liquid	150	Motor fuels[d]
(75)	Decane	$C_{10}H_{22}$	Liquid	174	Kerosene and motor fuel
	Hexadecane	$C_{16}H_{34}$	Solid	290[b]	Dissolved in heavy oils
	Pentatria-contane	$C_{35}H_{72}$	Solid	74.4[c]	Waxes

[a] Numbers in parentheses at left indicate numbers of isomers which can exist.
[b] Melting point 17.7°C.
[c] Melting point.
[d] Usually converted to other forms for motor fuel (see isomers).

have been isolated in the laboratory and, for example, one of the *iso*octanes, C_8H_{18}, is well known as a component of the reference fuel used in the octane number determination. This is a branched-chain compound. The more compact arrangement of *iso*octane, compared to that of normal octane, has a marked effect in engines. *Iso*octane is rated 100 octane number; normal octane, in contrast, is less than zero.

Petroleum companies have spent millions of pounds on research to develop processes for converting normal hydrocarbons to isomers of higher anti-knock value or to other types of hydrocarbons.

Olefines: Similar to paraffins, these compounds have two hydrogen atoms fewer and contain one chemical 'double bond' between the carbon atoms. As in the case of paraffins, isomers of olefines can exist, such as *iso*butylene. Olefines are generally much less stable than paraffins and have a greater tendency to react with oxygen, with other compounds and with each other. Apart from open-chain olefines, there are a number of ring-type olefines and diolefines.

Naphthenes (cycloparaffins): Compounds of the general formula C_nH_{2n}, C_nH_{2n-2} etc., can also occur in a ring structure such as cyclohexane.

This family of hydrocarbons is known as *cycloparaffins* and behaves quite differently from the paraffins and olefines, in both anti-knock quality and stability. Pennsylvania crude oil is very high in its percentage of paraffins whereas the asphaltic or naphthenic crude oils of the USSR, California and parts of Texas are lower in their percentage of paraffins but much higher in their percentage of naphthenic materials (cycloparaffins).

Aromatics: This term was originally applied to benzene and its derivatives because of their distinctive odour. Aromatics form part of the ring-type hydrocarbons of the general formula C_nH_{2n-6} and contain three double bonds in the ring. The basic structure of aromatics is typified by benzene itself but aromatics include many hundreds of related compounds such as toluene (methyl benzene), xylene (dimethyl benzene) and cumene (*iso*propyl benzene).

Typical physical properties of commercially-available fuels are listed in Table 7.

14.10 Pinking

Perhaps the most important property of a fuel from a performance point of view is its freedom or otherwise from liability to what is known as *pinking*, the popular term used to describe the results of an extremely rapid rate of combustion which yet falls short of the phenomenon of practically instantaneous detonation which occurs in high-explosive shells. The phenomenon is accompanied by the generation of pressure waves of very great intensity but of too short duration to be recorded by ordinary indicators. The impact of wave fronts on each other and on the walls of the combustion chamber give rise to the characteristic sound of pinking. Its occurrence results in rough running, overheating and loss of efficiency. The phenomenon *follows* ignition, and represents a very greatly accelerated rate of combustion due to compression at the flame front. The effects are sometimes confused with those of early ignition due to excessive spark advance or pre-ignition due to glowing carbon and other incandescent points in the cylinder.

This pre-ignition results in a normal process of combustion and rate of pressure rise, but occurring too early in the cycle with the result that excessive negative torque arises at the crank, with bumpy running.

The chemical and physical processes associated with pinking are still matters of controversy, but the nature of the fuel is so definitely the fundamental factor that the relative merits of fuels can be consistently indicated by an octane number, such that a fuel of high octane number will be less liable to pinking than one of low octane number, in the same engine. This does not mean, however, that a given fuel will show the same actual tendency towards, or immunity from, pinking in all engines, even of the same compression ratio. The pinking tendency is aggravated or reduced by the form of the combustion chamber and the position of the sparking plug, as well as by the compression ratio. The two former factors determine the extreme distance which the flame front has to travel and whether the last portion of the charge to be ignited – the 'end-gas' – will be in a hot or a well-cooled portion of the combustion space.

If the final stages of combustion occur on a flame front of wide area near the hot exhaust valve, and remote from the sparking plug, detonation is extremely likely to occur, while if the last part of the charge to be ignited is situated in the narrow clearance space between the piston crown and the head, it is attacked on a narrow flame front and is so adequately cooled by the high surface volume ratio that excessive rate of pressure and temperature rise is prevented. The old T-head cylinder, in which the most remote part of the charge was situated near the hot exhaust valve, was a notorious offender from the detonation point of view.

An important paper by G. D. Boerlate and Dr. W. J. van Dyck on the causes of detonation is published in Vol. XXVIII of the *Proc. Inst. Aut. Engineers*. In the paper and in the discussion as to the chemical causes of detonation, the possible influence of peroxides, formed in the early stages of combustion, as activating agents, was referred to.

14.11   Octane number

The earlier *toluene number*, introduced by Ricardo and his associates in connection with his original variable compression engine, has been superseded by the general adoption of the *octane number* as determined by the variable compression engine of the Co-operative Fuel Research (CFR) Committee using either the earlier Midgley 'bouncing pin' indication of pinking or one of the modern electronic indicators.

The anti-detonation quality of toluene is somewhat higher than that of *iso*octane, but the latter has proved more convenient and more consistent in behaviour, when mixed with normal heptane, as a standard of comparison. Normal heptane and normal octane are two members of the paraffin series that are present in ordinary petrols.

The tendency towards pinking of the paraffin series increases with the size of the molecule, octane being worse than heptane. The compound *iso*octane, which contains the same number of carbon and hydrogen atoms in the molecule as normal octane, but in a different grouping, has on the other hand high *anti*-pinking properties.

Table 7 – PARTICULARS OF TYPICAL COMMERCIAL FUELS

	Premium grade	*Regular grade*
Specific gravity at 15.6°C	0.740	0.715
Initial boiling point °C	30	30
Final boiling point °C	200	200
Aromatics (% by wt)	30	15
Tetra-ethyl lead ml/l	0.44	0.44
Research octane number (F1)	97	83

The octane number of a fuel is determined by comparison in the CFR engine of the fuel with a mixture of normal heptane and *iso*octane, the percentage of the latter in the mixture (which gives the same tendency to pink on the gradual increase of the compression ratio as does the fuel under consideration) being known as the *octane number*.

Thus, if a fuel shows the same tendency to pinking as a mixture of 15% heptane and 85% *iso*octane, its octane number is 85. With this system the octane number of heptane is 0, and of *iso*octane 100.

Two somewhat different techniques are in use, the 'research method' and the 'motor method'. The first is less severe than the motor method and, as a result, most fuels will have a higher octane number by the research method.

The research octane numbers of fuels ordinarily obtainable from road-side pumps range from about 83 for ordinary motor spirit to about 98 for highest grade spirit.

Special fuels can be produced, if circumstances justify the cost, which are much more highly resistant to pinking than *iso*octane, with octane numbers higher than 100, and suitable for use in special engines with very high compression ratios. Such fuels are widely available for aircraft use.

14.12   Fuels for high-performance engines

Development and supply of high octane fuels for the general public came practically to a standstill in Great Britain during the Second World War, owing to the demands of the fighting services, and it was not until 1953 that premium fuels became available again.

Progress in the USA was steadier because less restricted, but with the removal of military and economic barriers, the British petroleum industry has made immense strides and more than equalled progress in the USA.

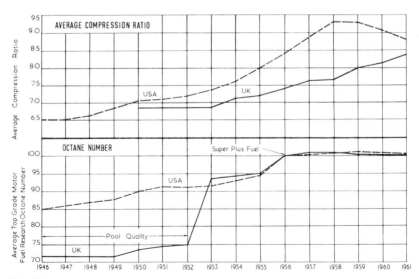

Fig. 14.1

Fig. 14.1, which is based on an authoritative article by J. G. Withers and H. J. Eatwell in *Automobile Engineer*, Vol. 46, No. 12, shows in a striking manner both the actual and relative progress of the two countries.

The upper half of Fig. 14.1 shows the progress made in average compression ratio in the first ten years after the war, and as has been mentioned elsewhere in this book, these figures have since been greatly exceeded in high-performance engines.

The lower half of Fig. 14.1 illustrates the corresponding progress in the provision of the special high octane fuels that enable these high compression ratios to be used, with the direct thermodynamic gain which results.

14.13   Other properties

Besides high resistance to pinking, there are many other properties which a good motor spirit must have. Thus its volatility, normally measured by distillation characteristics and vapour pressure, must be carefully balanced. The volatility must be high enough to ensure ready starting and rapid warm-up but is limited by the necessity to give freedom from vapour lock, carburettor percolation and carburettor icing.

In practice this means that the volatility of a petrol is adjusted to the particular climatic conditions in which it will be used, and in this country, for instance, it varies according to the season of the year.

The storage stability of a petrol is another important property. It must be refined and specially treated so that it will be capable of being stored without appreciable oxidation with the resulting formation of gum. Some typical characteristics of fuels are listed in Table 7.

14.14   Fuels for compression-ignition engines

Among fuel technologists the name 'diesel' is still in wider use than the phrase 'compression-ignition' (ci) when describing fuels, which are referred to as light, medium and heavy diesel fuels and by such industrial or trade names as Gas Oil, Solar Oil, Diesolene, Derv, etc.

For the high speed automotive diesel engine, a fully distillate fuel is required. This is a gas oil, with certain specially selected characteristics, and has a boiling range of 180 to 360°C approximately, and SG of between about 0.83 and 0.86. It should conform to the requirements for a Class A1 fuel in BS 2869:1970. The Class A2 is for high speed diesel units for applications other than automotive.

Larger stationary and marine diesels may be less fuel sensitive and can use blends of gas oil and fuel oil. These are covered by Classes B1 and B2 of BS 2869:1970, but even heavier residual fuels have been used.

14.15   Ignition quality and cetane number

The most important quality of a fuel for a high-speed ci engine is its ignition quality, or its readiness for self-ignition with the minimum desirable delay after the start of injection.

Just as *iso*octane is an effective anti-knock fuel, so a hydrocarbon of good self-ignition quality for comparative testing purposes is found in hexadecane, or cetane as it is more usually called, which has replaced cetene for this purpose. The complementary fuel of very low ignition quality with which cetane is blended is alpha-methyl-naphthalene ($C_{10}H_7CH_3$). The percentage of cetane in a reference mixture of these two compounds, which gives the same ignition characteristics as the fuel under consideration, is called the *cetane value* of that fuel. This figure ranges from 30 to 70. In general a high octane number implies a low cetane number.

14.16   Diesel index

Alternative methods, which do not require the involved procedure of an engine test, may also be used to express ignition quality, and the most common of these is known as the *diesel index*. The ignition quality of a fuel depends on the relative proportions of the different types of hydrocarbons which are present in the fuel; thus it can be measured by means of a simple laboratory test known as *aniline point*.

The aniline point is defined as the lowest temperature at which the fuel is completely miscible with an equal volume of aniline and when this has been determined, as well as the specific gravity (which is then converted to °API), the following equation is used –

$$\text{Diesel index} = \frac{GA}{100}$$

where G is API gravity
A is aniline point in °F

The diesel index will be found to give a reasonable assessment of the ignition quality of a fuel, but in value it will be numerically different from the cetane number and the exact relationship between these two methods will depend on the hydrocarbon make-up of the fuel. Because of its simplicty, the diesel index is widely used to express ignition quality; however, it cannot always be relied on to give a true estimate. Moreover, it will not be raised, as will be the cetane number, if ignition improvers are added to the fuel.

A more accurate method of assessing ignition quality is the calculated cetane index, using an empirical formula which has as its variables the mid-boiling point and the specific gravity of the fuel.

14.17   Fuel dopes

Corresponding to the anti-knock petrol dopes, there are certain ignition accelerators which may be added to diesel fuels in proportions ranging from 1 to 5%, which is higher than the corresponding percentage of ethyl fluid in petrols.

These reduce the delay period, and so tend to suppress diesel knock in the second phase of combustion, in virtue of the smaller accumulation of fuel in the combustion chamber at the commencement of burning, the rate of pressure rise being consequently reduced.

Typical substances are ethyl nitrate and amyl nitrite. The effects of such an addition on the delay period and rate of pressure rise in the second

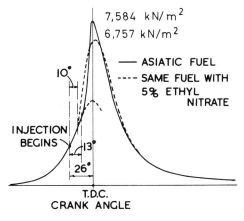

7,584 kN/m²
6,757 kN/m²

—— ASIATIC FUEL
---- SAME FUEL WITH
5% ETHYL
NITRATE

10°

INJECTION
BEGINS
13°
26°

T.D.C.
CRANK ANGLE

Fig. 14.2 Ignition accelerator

phase of combustion are shown in Fig. 14.2, which was taken from an AEC engine.

The speed in each case was 1000 rev/min and the bmep 575.7 kN/m². It will be seen that the delay period was reduced by the addition of 5% of ethyl nitrate from 13 to 10°, while the rate of pressure rise during the second phase of combustion was reduced from over 413 kN/m² per degree to less than 40. There was a corresponding reduction in maximum pressure of over 689 kN/m² with much improved running.

It must not be assumed that these results would be obtained in all circumstances. Modern high speed diesel fuels are usually of sufficiently high quality to satisfy the needs of even the most critical engine, and hence these additives do not enjoy a wide commercial use.

14.18 Diesel fuels from coal

Early pioneer work on fuels made by the distillation of coal or its by-products were disappointing, as the ignition quality of the fuels obtained was much inferior to that of the paraffin hydrocarbons, and supplies were dependent on by-products of major industries, with corresponding uncertainty as regards availability.

Considerable progress has been made in Germany and South Africa where Fischer and Tropsch as well as later workers have developed a complicated but successful process, whereby on final distillation a high-speed diesel fuel of excellent characteristics is obtained.

14.19 Gas turbine fuels

Even the most optimistic forecasts of progress in thermal efficiency of the gas turbine accept that for some years it will remain considerably below that of the piston engine and, unless cheap fuels can be successfully used, the fuel running costs will exceed those of existing prime movers. Capital and overhead operating costs then become the determining commercial consideration.

Apart from improvement due to higher turbine operating temperature as new materials for blades are developed, higher thermal efficiency involves bulky and troublesome heat interchangers.

Further, the use of low-priced liquid and pulverised solid fuel would almost certainly call for more complicated and far more bulky types of injection equipment and combustion chamber than those at present in use with aircraft plants.

For automobile work, bulk and weight are ruled out, and the automobile turbine will, for the sake of simplicity and lightness, be compelled to shoulder the handicap of high consumption of a fuel of similar nature to present diesel or light furnace oils, showing little or no price advantage apart from differential taxation.

The fuels used for aircraft jet engines are of two types –

(1) Avtur: A grade of kerosene with special characteristics.
(2) Avtag: A 'wide cut' gasoline, i.e. a fraction boiling over the gasoline and kerosene ranges. It contains no TEL.

Fuels having a high calorific value per unit volume are most desirable for automotive gas turbine use and Table 8 gives net calorific values for various fuels.

Table 8 – NET CALORIFIC VALUES FOR VARIOUS FUELS

Fuel	Specific gravity	Net calorific value kJ/kg
Premium grade petrol	0.740	4,380
Avtag	0.756	4,353
Avtur	0.790	4,331
Gas/diesel oil	0.835	4,276
Light fuel oil	0.935	4,122
Heavy fuel oil	0.970	4,078

14.20 Filtration of diesel fuel

The question of fuel cleanliness regarding compression ignition engines is quite different from that problem when dealing with petrol engines. With carburettors, jets must be kept clear and any sliding parts free from small particles of grit, sand or dirt that may get into the petrol, but this can be satisfactorily achieved by the use of very fine gauze filters. With fuel injection equipment, however, the pump elements, delivery valves, and nozzles are finished to exceptionally fine precision fits, of almost optical standards of perfection, on account of the very high pressures which have to be handled.

The working tolerances are very small (the plunger has only 1 micron – one thousandth of a millimetre – clearance in its barrel, the two being hand-lapped together). Fuel cleanliness is therefore of the utmost importance; gauze filters are quite inadequate for the purpose, and only filters specially designed for the purpose are permissible.

Even the finest of dust carried in suspension in the air is liable to cause trouble by wear and scuffing of the fine surfaces. Even with care in fuel delivery, storage and filling up, some dust enters the system through breathers and filter caps, etc., and efficient filters are the only safeguard. These must be serviced regularly according to the makers' instructions.

Chapter 15

Lubrication

The purposes of a lubricant are primarily two in number –

(1) To reduce the resistance to relative motion between two surfaces in contact under pressure.
(2) To reduce wear of the surfaces and eliminate as far as possible any danger of seizure.

The resistance to relative motion between two bodies in contact depends on a variety of factors and their various possible combinations. Three broad types of contact are recognised, but the conditions in an actual bearing rarely fall exactly into one of these divisions, being usually intermediate between two.

15.1 Dry friction

Here complete absence of lubricant is assumed. The frictional resistance is proportional to the load on the bearing and independent of the area of contact, and usually decreases somewhat with increase of speed. The coefficient of friction is high and fairly constant, and depends on the materials and fineness of finish, since there is actual contact between the surfaces. Continuous running under load would not be possible under such conditions owing to the excessive amount of heat developed.

15.2 Boundary friction

Here some lubricant is present but not sufficient to completely separate the surfaces. The coefficient of friction is reduced, but the resistance to motion is still dependent on the load and the nature of the surfaces. Oils differ considerably in their lubricating quality under these boundary conditions, the animal and vegetable oils, such as sperm, rape and castor, being somewhat superior to mineral oils in the maintenance of a film at high pressures and low speeds. They suffer, however, from the tendency to gum at high temperatures, and experience has shown that the greater freedom from carbonisation and the freer running with high-class mineral oils, particularly in combination with suitable additives, are not offset by any greater risk of failure of the film if the lubrication system is correctly designed.

It is only in recent years that physicists and chemists have made appreciable progress in understanding the phenomena of lubrication, and the boundary conditions are now known to involve far more complicated phenomena than was formerly supposed. The existence of an extremely thin adsorbed layer is now recognised, where the lubricant enters into some form of chemical or physical bond with the bearing metal of such a nature that, after being once formed, it can be removed only by mechanical polishing, by abrasive means, or, under certain conditions, by desorption.

Substances which have valuable properties under these boundary conditions are zinc oxide and colloidal graphite – that is specially purified graphite in an extremely fine state of subdivision, the suspension of which in a suitable carrier oil is maintained not only by the fineness of the subdivision but also by the application of a suitable electric charge to the particles. The exact mechanism involved in the action of these substances has been the object of painstaking research. Certain compounds involving sulphur and chlorine have also found application in this field.

15.3   Viscous friction or fluid friction

Under certain conditions of oil-bath, flooded or force-feed lubrication it is possible for the surfaces of the bearing to be completely separated by the lubricant. In these circumstances, the resistance to relative movement is a fluid one arising from the viscosity, or resistance to shearing of the oil film itself. This viscosity increases considerably with pressure, especially at very high pressures, and decreases, in some cases rapidly, with increase of temperature.

The resistance to motion is proportional to the area in contact, the speed and the viscosity coefficient and inversely proportional to the thickness of the oil film. It is far less than in the preceding cases.

It should be realised that the viscosity of the oil is itself a source of resistance, which in certain circumstances may make the total resistance with lubrication greater than without any lubrication. This may readily be tested with a valve stem and guide. If no side thrust is exerted, it will be found that the addition of lubricating oil will produce a resistance which was not previously present, the resistance arising from the process of shearing the oil film. As the clearance is increased and the viscosity of the oil reduced, the resistance to motion decreases.

This is one reason why the pistons of racing engines are made an easy fit, and the design of the slipper piston is due to the realisation by racing men of the necessity for reducing to a minimum the area of the film to be sheared between the piston and cylinder wall, the areas in contact being reduced to the least amount that will safely take the side thrust and at the same time allow for conduction of heat from the piston body to the cylinder walls. The importance of this reduction will be realised from a study of Fig. 15.1, which shows curves, due to Ricardo, of mean effective pressure required to overcome the various sources of friction in a certain engine at different speeds. It will be seen that piston friction forms about 60% of the whole.

From the foregoing it will be seen that, in order that the resistance to motion should be a minimum, the oil film should have considerable

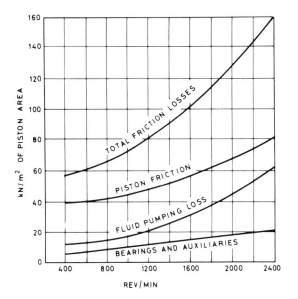

Fig. 15.1 Sources of engine friction

thickness and small extent, while the viscosity should be low. Unfortunately, these conditions are mutually incompatible, as it is impossible to confine a thin oil in such a manner as to maintain a thick film. It is necessary to use in internal combustion engines an oil of such a nature that under the high temperature of operation the viscosity will still be sufficiently high to prevent the film from being completely squeezed out and so avoid conditions approaching those of dry friction which would lead to immediate disaster.

In most engine bearings the conditions are somewhere between the boundary and flooded conditions, so that both the pressure on the bearing and the viscosity of the oil are factors in determining the resistance.

15.4 Choice of viscosity

The provision and maintenance of a suitable viscosity in the oil to meet all requirements and conditions of use is a difficult matter. To give easy starting under cold conditions, to ensure rapid and early distribution of lubricant to all working parts as the engine speeds up, and to minimise oil drag under all conditions, an oil of low viscosity is required; while to ensure the continued maintenance of a lubricating film under difficult conditions of high temperature and extreme bearing loads, and to reduce oil consumption arising from excessive pumping past the piston rings at high speed and small throttle opening, the viscosity should not fall below some suitable minimum value depending on the conditions of service.

The physical property of viscosity does not in itself imply lubricating value, and the research into extreme pressure lubrication has shown that the best local protection against the scuffing effects of excessive bearing pressures, such as arise in some forms of tooth gearing, is given by the addition of certain organic compounds of quite low viscosity, or other additives.

15.5   Change of viscosity with temperature: viscosity index

To meet the requirements of low resistance or breakaway torque at starting, combined with adequate viscosity at normal operating temperature, the oil should have a high *viscosity index*, that is, while having a suitably low viscosity when cold, it should be of such a nature that the rise of temperature as the engine reaches normal running conditions will not lower the viscosity unduly. The viscosity-temperature curve should be as flat as possible.

The index is a number based upon an empirical scale having 100 for the best Pennsylvanian blends, and 0 for certain asphaltic oils which show a very steep viscosity-temperature curve.

Modern refining methods, and particularly the new solvent extraction processes whereby the less desirable asphaltic constituents of the oil are abstracted by suitable solvents, have resulted in the marketing of oils of high viscosity index. In recent years further improvements have been effected by the use of additives.

These oils have suitably low viscosity to provide the required conditions for starting, while the viscosity is well maintained at higher temperatures.

15.6   Heat generation and wear

The work done against friction appears as heat, which will cause the temperature of the bearing to rise to a point where the loss by conduction, convection and radiation is just equal to the rate of generation. If the temperature so reached is high, the viscosity of the oil may be reduced so much that the oil film will be broken, when actual metallic contact will occur, and seizing or running of the bearing metal may take place. The great virtue of the modern system of forced lubrication, presently to be described, is its action as a cooling system to the crankshaft and big-end bearings. The excess of oil flowing over the surfaces effectively cools them and prevents undue reduction of the viscosity.

It is now generally recognised that the best combination of materials for resisting wear is one in which the materials differ widely in hardness. Mild steel on mild steel is notoriously bad, mild steel on phosphor bronze is not good, whereas case-hardened steel on phosphor bronze and mild steel on whitemetal are excellent. The accepted explanation is that the small particles of foreign matter which cause wear must so readily embed themselves in the softer of the two metals as to minimise their capacity for cutting the harder.

With metals of equal hardness the particles are not pressed into one metal sufficiently deeply to prevent their abrading the other. It has been observed that, when wear does take place in a bearing formed of two metals of different hardness, it is usually the harder metal which shows the greater amount of wear.

In any case, the more completely the oil film is maintained, the less will be the wear, though it is open to question whether a supply of oil largely in excess of what is used in maintaining this film is advantageous from the point of view of wear. Though its cooling effect is good, it is possible that a larger amount of abrasive material is thereby carried into the bearing.

15.7 Corrosive wear

Extensive researches into the phenomena of cylinder bore wear, which is notoriously greater under conditions of frequent starting under cold or partially warmed conditions, have shown that corrosion, as distinct from abrasion, plays a very large part. This corrosion is caused by the condensation on the walls of acid products of combustion at coolant temperatures below about 70°C, and hence arises the necessity for rapid warming up and free distribution of the lubricating oil. The use of lower viscosity oils and the fast idling starting devices of modern carburettors have led to considerable improvement in this direction, while the use of special alloy cylinder irons, and hardened or chromium-plated liners, has further reduced both abrasive and corrosive wear.

15.8 Systems of lubrication

Modern *full forced* systems of lubrication have developed by stages from the crude *all loss* system as represented by the early motor-cycle engine in which a pumpful of oil was delivered to the crankcase at uncertain intervals by the action of the rider, the oil being splashed around by the internal flywheels and connecting rod, and reaching the cylinder walls and various bearings in a somewhat fortuitous manner.

Unless the rider was careful and attentive, the engine suffered from alternate periods of over-oiling and starvation, occasionally with disastrous results.

In multi-cylinder engines a phase of pump circulation to distribution and dipper troughs followed, dippers on the big-end bearing caps, sometimes but not always of hollow scoop form, picking up oil from the troughs and leading it to the crankpin bearings. There was no drilling of internal oilways through the crankshaft.

Lubrication became a little more regular, and the objectional splashing of a large body of oil in the crankcase was avoided, but the direction of oil to the vital bearings was insufficiently positive and certain.

15.9 Full forced system

In the full forced system, which has now replaced the earlier systems referred to above, the oil is drawn from a sump as in the trough system, and is delivered at a pressure of from 35 to $500 \, kN/m^2$ to a system of ducts or pipes which carry it to the main crankshaft bearings and other points. After entering the main bearings a certain amount escapes along the bearings and either drains directly back to the lower half of the crankcase and so to the sump or is splashed from the crank webs to the cylinder walls, etc. The remainder of the oil delivered to the main bearings finds its way through holes drilled diagonally from the bearing journals through the crank webs to the adjacent crankpins, thus carrying a full flow of oil to the big-end bearing. Each big-end bearing is thus lubricated under pressure from an adjacent main bearing.

In the full forced system, strictly speaking, oil is led from the big-end bearings through pipes secured to the connecting rods, or through holes drilled in those rods, to the gudgeon pins, but in the majority of systems, which are called full forced, the gudgeon pins are lubricated by the oil which escapes along the big-end bearing and which is flung off by centrifugal force. Very occasionally in special cases pipes lead oil direct to the cylinder walls and pistons, but usually those parts are lubricated by the fling-off from the big ends. Other leads also go to the camshaft bearings, timing gears, etc., but again the fling-off is frequently relied upon.

Another method of camshaft lubrication, where the camshaft is in the crankcase, is to place it in an oil bath fed by a separate pipe.

Overhead camshafts are almost always lubricated by a separate pipe conveying a portion of the pump discharge to the camshaft bearings, and the camshaft itself is sometimes drilled along its axis so that oil can be led to the cam faces through suitable radial holes. In most cases oil is also led directly to the hollow valve rocker shafts and thence through holes drilled in those shafts to the rocker bearings.

Fig. 15.2 illustrates a full forced system. The gear type pump A has its suction branch protected by a gauze filter and is fitted with an integral relief valve K which returns a portion of the oil from the delivery side direct to the suction in the event of excessive pressure arising in the system when starting in cold weather with an oil of high viscosity. The pump is

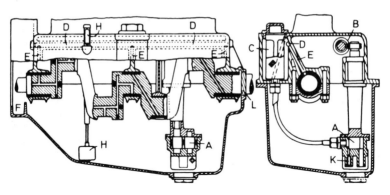

Fig. 15.2 Full forced lubrication system

driven by a vertical shaft through the skew gears B from the camshaft, and can be withdrawn as a unit after removing the sump. C is a large high pressure filter of which the gauze is readily accessible for cleaning without sacrificing the bulk of the oil, as is sometimes unavoidable in cases where a filter is provided only on the suction side. D is a gallery or delivery pipe with branches E to the three main bearings, whence it reaches the crank pins by the drilled passages shown, two alternative methods of drilling being indicated. The connection to the pressure indicator on the dashboard is usually taken from the gallery.

H is a float type level indicator with a pointer outside the top half of the crankcase (generally, a dipstick is used), while F is an oil bath for the timing gears (often fed by the overflow from a relief valve), and L a screw type oil thrower or baffle.

15.10 Wet and dry sump systems

With the forced system of lubrication either the 'wet' sump or the 'dry' sump system may be employed. The former is that already described, where there is only one pump which draws its oil from the bulk supply contained in the sump formed in the lower half of the crankcase.

The dry sump system, which is universal in aircraft engines and in other engines which frequently operate at a considerable inclination to the horizontal, employs two pumps. Very little oil is retained in the crankcase sump, from which the oil is scavenged by a pump and delivered to a main oil tank situated in any convenient position. This tank is often arranged as a cooling radiator. From the main tank oil is drawn by the second, or pressure, pump and is circulated under pressure through the piping system, to the various bearings and gears.

Occasionally two scavenge pumps are fitted, one at each end of the crankcase, each in a small sump. When a single scavenge pump is fitted, it is usually placed at the centre, in a deep sump, if the engine is likely to operate at large inclinations. The scavenge pump is of larger capacity than the pressure pump, as its work is liable to be intermittent owing to the variation of oil level in the sump and also because of aeration of the oil as it is flung off the moving parts.

15.11 Comprehensive lubrication system

A well-thought-out lubricating system which incorporates most of the features already referred to is illustrated in Fig. 15.3 in semidiagrammatic form. The provision of dipper troughs in addition to pressure oil ways and a drilled crankshaft is unusual, but the additional oil-mist formed by the pick-up of the connecting-rod peckers should materially assist the general distribution of the oil and by splashing it to the crankcase walls, ensure its better cooling.

The pump P is of unusual construction, comprising twin pumps each containing three meshing gears. The centre gears are driven by the vertical splined shaft, and the four outer gears thus all revolve in the same direction. Two suction ports are provided, one of these taking oil from the front of the sump through the pipe S_1 while the other S_2 draws its supply from the rear end. The front intake supplies oil to the suction space between the centre and offside gears of both the upper and lower pump, while the rear intake S_2 feeds the suction spaces of the centre and near side gears. The dual deliveries of the upper pump feed in parallel the gallery G_2 which supplies the troughs T. The corresponding dual deliveries from the lower and larger pump lead to the external filter F.

When the engine is level both suction ports are in action, but when considerably tilted, as in cross-country vehicle applications, either inlet may be uncovered and draw air, but under these conditions both pumps can still obtain their supply of oil from the other inlet and no interference with the flow will occur. An insert diagram of the pump is given.

The main delivery from the pump passes to the externally-mounted Autoklean filter F, whence it passes by an internal transverse pipe to the capacity chamber C, which contains a readily accessible cylindrical filter screen. From this chamber, where a steady pressure is maintained, the oil

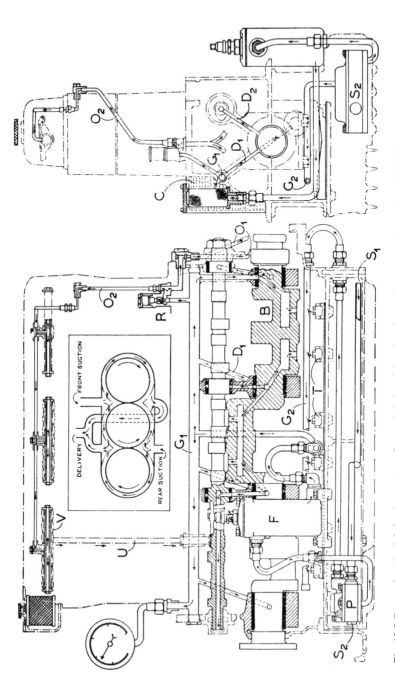

Fig. 15.3 Comprehensive lubrication system of an early industrial engine. In modern automotive engines, drilled passages have replaced most, and sometimes all, of the pipes

enters the gallery G_1, and is led by the ducts D_1 to the four main bearings, and thence by the crankshaft drillings to the six crankpins B. A further set of ducts D_2 leads to three of the camshaft bearings, while oil reaches the fourth by the centre drilling of the rear portion of the camshaft.

The pressure gauge and relief valve R are in direct communication with the main gallery G_1 and the oil which is by-passed at the relief valve is taken to the timing chain wheels, and the valve rockers V, through delivery pipes O_1 and O_2 respectively. The return oil from the valve rockers, together with the oil required for replenishment which is inserted through the filler and breather in the valve gear cover, passes to the crankcase through the tappet rod tunnels as indicated at U. The sump is protected by a flat filter screen of large area and, if required, an oil cooler may be inserted in place of the short external pipe delivering oil to the gallery G_2.

15.12 Pumps

The pumps used for oil circulation have taken a variety of forms, but that now almost universally used, on account of its simplicity and reliability, is the double gearwheel type illustrated in Fig. 15.4. It consists of two meshing gearwheels, one of which A is driven by the engine by means of the vertical shaft C which carries a skew gear meshing with another gear integral with the camshaft, while the second wheel B is driven by the first.

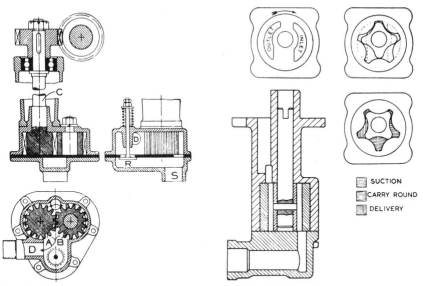

Fig. 15.4 Gear type pump   Fig. 15.5 Hobourn-Eaton pump

The two are mounted in a casing with clearances as small as possible. The casing is provided with suction and delivery ports S and D. The wheels do not mangle the oil through, as might be thought at first sight, but it is carried round the outer peripheries as indicated by the arrows, in the spaces formed by the tooth spaces and the walls of the casing. The meshing of the teeth displaces the oil from the tooth spaces and it is thus forced through the delivery port. R is a relief valve.

This type of pump cannot be regarded as a strictly positive one owing to the inevitable leakage at high pressures, but if it is used 'drowned', that is, immersed in the oil at the bottom of the sump, and if it is the proper size for its work, no trouble is likely to occur in operation. Should it be necessary for any reason to mount it in such a position that it has to lift the oil on the suction side, some arrangement should be provided for 'priming' it, that is, for filling it with oil in the event of its becoming empty through standing. In that event the pump might fail to draw the oil up, as owing to the clearances in the pump the air would escape back from the delivery side to the suction side and thus prevent the pressure on that side being reduced sufficiently to draw up the oil. The housing can act as an oil reservoir, if the inlet and outlet are at the top.

15.13   Hobourn-Eaton oil pump

This pump, shown in a simplified form in Fig. 15.5, is of the internally meshing double rotor type. Its patent specifications cover a variety of devices and arrangements aimed at automatic control of the by-passing of surplus delivery at high speeds.

The pump is intended more particularly for servo applications such as power-operated steering, where the demands may at times be only a small fraction of the available displacement volume during periods of high-speed operation of the prime-mover. It is highly desirable under these conditions that surplus delivery should be by-passed to the suction side of the pump without noise, excessive pressure or emulsification.

As a lubrication pump, units of simplified form such as that illustrated can be supplied.

From Fig. 15.5, which is partly diagrammatic, it can be seen that the driven, internal rotor has four teeth, meshing with and driving the external annular rotor, which has five tooth spaces. Displacement of oil from suction to delivery side takes place in a similar manner to that in the more usual externally meshing gear pump.

Larger pumps employ a greater number of teeth and spaces, but these always differ by one in number.

15.14   Filters

It is not possible even with the finest gauze to intercept all the minute particles of grit and abraded metal which cause wear of bearings, and it is essential to have in the oil circuit adequate filters of large total area for the interception of all dangerous abrasive material.

It is usual to provide two filters in the circuit, one, the low pressure, being placed on the suction side of the pump, and the other on the delivery side. The low-pressure filter is of comparatively coarse mesh so as to minimise the risk of strangling the suction. It takes the form, in some cases, of a large shallow cylindrical float secured by a hinged connection to the pump suction. The intake periphery is protected by a medium mesh wire gauze, and as this entry is always completely submerged below the surface of the oil but clear of the bottom, both floating matter and sediment are unlikely to be picked up.

15.15   High-pressure filter

The thorough filtering of the oil, which should ideally remove all abrasive particles large enough to span the oil films in the various bearings, is accomplished on the pressure side of the system between the pressure relief valve and the delivery galleries.

The filtration may be of the full flow or the by-pass type; in the latter, the filter is arranged as a shunt to the main flow, and passes only a portion of the total oil stream. This proportion will depend on the relative hydraulic conductivities of the two circuits through the filter to the sump and through the various bearings to the sump, just as does the amount delivered to any particular bearing depend on its conductivity relatively to its fellows. If one of a pair of adjacent big ends, for instance, fed from the same main journal, is worn or adjusted with too great clearance, it will rob its neighbour of the proper share of oil. In the event of bearing seizure, attention is not always given to the bearing which is the real source of the trouble.

It is not possible to estimate accurately the time that will elapse before every oil-borne abrasive particle will be carried to the filter, as it depends on the element of chance and the rate of introduction of new particles. It is, however, clearly related to the rate of pump circulation as compared with the total oil capacity of the system, and the relative quantities of lubricant flowing through the filter and by-passing it.

Should a large quantity of dirt be carelessly introduced to the sump during topping up, there is serious risk with the by-pass system that much of this dirt will reach the bearings before it reaches the filter.

The reason for the introduction of the by-pass system was the difficulty (experienced when the paper or fabric type of fine filter was first introduced) of providing a sufficiently large filter area to deal wth the rapid rates of circulation used in present-day lubricating systems.

This difficulty has been largely met by the use of long filter strips folded into multi-point star formations on a suitable perforated frame, or incorporating a sandwich arrangement of wire gauze and fabric. There should be no serious difficulty in designing *ab initio* for a full flow filter of adequate size to pass at moderate pressure the full delivery of the oil pump, thus eliminating the risks associated with the partial flow, by-pass system.

There may be many applications in industrial work where it is necessary to make provision for cleaning the filter without stopping the engine, but in these cases a duplicate installation with change-over cocks and suitable access doors is the correct solution.

15.16   Relief valve incorporated in filter

A fabric-type filter for use on the pressure side of the pump, incorporating good features of design, is the Vokes outward flow arrangement shown in Fig. 15.6. Both entry and exit are at the top of the container, and the relief valve which short-circuits the element is formed by a synthetic rubber ring bearing on an annular seating formed in the head casting.

The whole filter element slides on a central rod and bears on a coil spring which determines the limiting pressure difference permitted on the ele-

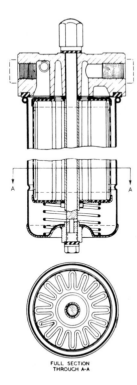

FULL SECTION
THROUGH A-A

Fig. 15.6 Vokes full-flow filter

ment, this difference being small owing to the provision of a very large filter area.

With this arrangement it will be seen that there is no risk of the accumulated silt being discharged into the delivery either by opening of the relief valve or on removal of the element for cleaning or replacement.

It is claimed that the danger of the relief valve being prevented from seating by a particle of dirt, as is possible with the metallic cone or ball valve, is eliminated by the capacity of the rubber seating to accommodate small particles without causing leakage.

15.17   Purolator Micronic filter

An interesting filtering material has been introduced in the Purolator filter to which the name Micronic has been given in reference to the physicist's unit of very small measurement, the micron. This is one thousandth of a millimetre, and the material, which is a plastics-impregnated paper, is claimed to be able to stop particles approaching this size. Even very much larger particles would be unlikely to cause damage to bearings.

Relatively high rates of oil flow are possible, and it is claimed that the extraction of additives in detergent-type oils is negligible.

The element is easily and cheaply renewed as necessary in place of cleaning.

15.19   Circulation indicators

Some indication that the lubrication system is functioning correctly is desirable, but it is to be regretted that in the majority of instances the only indicator provided is of the pressure gauge type, which is no certain guide to the oil circulation either qualitatively or quantitatively, and which may lull the driver into a false sense of security.

Any abnormal pressure, whether high or low, should be regarded as an indication that something is wrong, though changes in the viscosity of the oil due to changes in temperture produce changes of pressure.

15.20   Oil-level indicators

The oil level in the sump must be maintained between certain limits to ensure that the pump is never starved, while at the same time excess is avoided. One of the simplest devices, and one which gives reliable indications if carefully used, is the dip stick marked for high and low levels. In using this it should be removed and wiped and then reinserted to take an observation, otherwise a false reading may be obtained, owing to creep and splash of the oil.

In all cases it is desirable to check the oil level only after the engine has been running and has reached its normal temperature so that the variation in sump level due to the quantity of oil in circulation and increase in volume with rise of temperature may be allowed for.

The float type of indicator illustrated in Fig. 15.2, while giving an immediate indication, is somewhat liable to derangement from puncture of the float or bending of the rod.

Chapter 16

Engine cooling

The high working temperatures of the internal combustion engine which are the cause of its high efficiency are at the same time a source of great practical difficulty in construction and operation. No known materials are capable of enduring continuously the high temperatures to which the cylinder, piston and valves are subjected while at the same time retaining sufficient strength to withstand the high working loads.

The maximum temperature during combustion is approximately the melting point of platinum and the temperature even of the exhaust gases is above that of aluminium. It is thus essential that heat be abstracted from the parts enumerated above at a sufficient rate to prevent a dangerous temperature being reached, for, unfortunately, it is quite impossible to prevent heat entering the metal from the hot gases.

Nevertheless, it must always be borne in mind that such abstraction of heat is a direct thermodynamic loss, and if high thermal efficiency is desired the abstraction of heat should not be more than is necessary to prevent dangerous overheating and consequent distortion of the cylinder, etc. Excessive cooling will also prevent proper vaporisation of the fuel, leading to further waste and also to objectionable dilution of the crankcase oil by unvaporised fuel, which gets down past the piston. On the other hand, too high an operating temperature is bad from the point of view of the power developed, since it results in reduced volumetric efficiency on account of the excessive heating of the incoming charge with the consequent reduction of charge weight and thus of power.

In any given set of conditions there is some particular operating temperature which produces the most satisfactory results, and only experience with a particular engine will determine this temperature. If it were not for the loss of water and the interference with cooling as a result of boiling in an ordinary water-cooled system, the temperature of boiling at atmospheric pressure, namely 100°C or even higher, would not be too high a general operating temperature in the majority of engines. To prevent boiling a lower operating temperature is necessary, as local overheating must be guarded against. It is usually in the neighbourhood of 75° to 90°C unless a pressurised system is used (see Section 16.3).

To come to the actual cooling means employed, whatever these may be, the ultimate result is the dissipation of the dangerous heat to the surrounding air. Direct dissipation of heat from the cylinder barrel and head to the surrounding air, or air-cooling as it is called, is feasible with small engines and is practically universal with motor cycles. The heat is dissipated by radiation and convection from thin cooling fins cast on the cylinder head and barrel.

Natural flow air-cooling is at best very difficult to regulate, and as the size of the cylinder increases the difficulties become very serious, for the heat developed increases as the cube of the linear dimensions, while the radiating surface increases only as the square.

In multi-cylinder engines the flow of the air is controlled by suitable cowlings so as to be distributed equally to all the cylinders. However, in large engines, if air-cooling is used, it is generally in conjunction with a large fan which delivers a considerable volume of air to the cylinders, and this fan besides being bulky requires a considerable expenditure of power to drive it, so that unless other considerations enter into the question the chief gain, which is the elimination of the necessity for a radiator and water jackets to the cylinders, with the consequent saving in weight, is not always realised. Air-cooled engines have the reputation of being noisier than the water-cooled form, and very few instances of large fan-cooled engines are on the market, though in the special application of large power units to armoured fighting vehicles, important developments have recently taken place in the US Army. Extremes of climate, difficulty in replacing water lost by evaporation, and all the complications involved in frost precautions in operational theatres, added to the probable greater vulnerability of liquid cooling, are powerful inducements towards the adoption of direct air-cooling in this field.

For the normal medium and large passenger and commercial vehicle water-cooling is practically universal.

Heat is far more readily transferred from metal to water than from metal to air, while the final transfer of heat from the water to the air, in order that the water may be returned to circulate through the engine jackets, can be readily accomplished in a radiator provided with a large cooling surface in contact on one side with the hot water from the engine and exposed on the other side to a strong current of air arising from the motion of the car, aided by a fan driven from the engine.

A steady operating temperature will be reached when the difference between the temperatures of the air and radiator is sufficient, in conjunction with the area of radiating surface and air flow to dissipate heat at the same rate as it is being received from the jackets. During a long climb with a following wind equilibrium may not be reached and the water will boil.

The radiator is normally placed in front of the engine, but whatever the position may be there are two methods in general use for circulating the water through the engine jackets and radiator, namely –

(1) Thermosyphon system.
(2) Pump system.

In the former the water circulates in virtue of the pressure difference arising from the difference in density between the hot water in the jackets and the cooler water in the radiator. For success in operation the passages through the jackets and radiator should be free and the connecting pipes large, while the jackets should be placed as low as possible relatively to the radiator, in order that the 'hot leg' shall have as great a height as possible.

In operation the water level must on no account be allowed to fall below the level of the delivery pipe to the radiator top, otherwise circulation will cease.

Fig. 16.1 shows as simply as possible the essentials of the system, X X showing the critical water level.

In general the thermosyphon system requires a larger radiator and carries a greater body of water than the pump circulation system and a somewhat excessive temperature difference is necessary to produce the requisite circulation. On the other hand to some extent it automatically prevents the engine from being run too cold.

The defects mentioned have resulted in the pump circulation system becoming universal in high-powered vehicles. The pump is either a radial flow centrifugal pump, driven in the larger engines by positive gearing, and forcing the circulation from the bottom of the radiator to the bottom of the jackets, or a simpler axial flow impeller, placed usually at the outlet from the cylinder head, and driven by an all round belt drive including the dynamo. This arrangement is used with some smaller engines, and the fan is usually mounted on the impeller spindle. These impellers have less forcing power than the centrifugal type, but give appreciable assistance to the circulation.

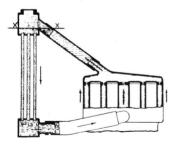
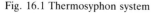
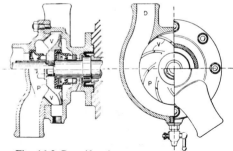

Fig. 16.1 Thermosyphon system   Fig. 16.2 Centrifugal pump

Neither type is a positive pump in the sense of being able to force a fixed rate of flow independently of the hydraulic resistance of the circuit.

Fig. 16.2 shows the construction of a centrifugal pump. It consists simply of a casing inside which an impeller P, provided with vanes V, is rotated. The water enters the casing at the centre of the impeller and, being caught up by the vanes, is whirled round. Centrifugal force causes the water to pass to the periphery of the impeller where it is thrown out into the stationary casing. The kinetic energy imparted to the water by the impeller is converted in the stationary casing into pressure or potential energy so that a pressure difference is established between the inlet and the outlet D of the pump. A seal is provided where the impeller spindle passes through the casing, in order to maintain a water-tight joint. This seal is made in modern designs by means of the face contact of a graphitic carbon ring which may revolve with the impeller or be stationary in the housing, on either the suction or pressure sides, according to convenience in design. The face contact avoids wear of the shaft, and the carbon, bearing on a suitable alloy iron, hardened steel or phosphor bronze surface, develops a hard, wear-free surface which requires no lubrication and provides an effective seal against leakage.

Alternative arrangements of the Morganite Unit Seal, supplied by the Morgan Crucible Company as a proprietary fitting, are shown on the left of the Figure. The carbon ring is bonded to a flexible rubber casing which takes the friction torque. Inside the casing is a light stainless steel spring proportioned to give appropriate pressure between the rubbing surfaces. The whole provides a readily inserted unit assembly requiring renewal only at long intervals.

Pressure relief holes may be provided through the impeller boss to prevent the delivery pressure developing undue end thrust on the back.

A pump circulation system is illustrated diagrammatically in Fig. 16.3. A is the centrifugal pump delivering to the bottom of the jackets and B shows a thermostatically controlled by-pass valve by which the radiator can be short-circuited and the water returned to the pump suction until its temperature reaches a desirable value. In the diagram the valve is in a mid position.

16.1 Temperature control

There are broadly two methods of regulation in use, the first being practically universal in automobile practice –

(1) Automatic control by means of a thermostat.
(2) Hand control by means of radiator shutters.

The thermostat consists of a concertina or bellows-like vessel of thin metal, similar to those employed in the aneroid barometer but filled with a suitable liquid. In some cases expansion is magnified by a system of levers to operate the valve. In most modern designs, the large movement necessary for the valve is obtained directly from the bellows by *evaporation* of the liquid, which should be one boiling at about 60 to 80°C. Such liquids are acetone, alcohol, etc.

The valve may control a by-pass as in Fig. 16.3, or it may simply be placed in the main circuit as depicted in Fig. 16.4, where (*a*) shows the valve as part of the engine construction and (*b*) illustrates the convenient and simple

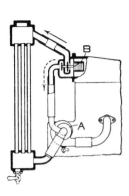

Fig. 16.3 Pump circulation

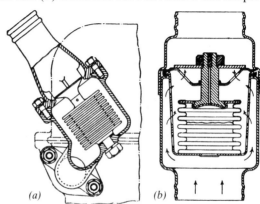

(a)   *(b)*

Fig. 16.4 Bellows type thermostat

Motorstat hose-line type, which can be readily installed in any engine in place of the hose connection to the top of the radiator.

Where the thermostatic valve closes the main circuit without a by-pass, which has been the usual practice, it must be capable of closing the circuit against the pressure developed by the centrifugal pump, but no great difficulty is experienced in meeting this condition, since the bellows can be arranged to act as a tension spring, the initial tension being regulated to give any opening temperature desired within the vapour pressure and temperature characteristics of the liquid employed.

When carefully designed and installed these devices are reliable, and their use in various forms has become general in all engine cooling systems.

16.2   Wax-element thermostats

Thermostats of the wax-element type are incorporated in most pressurised cooling systems. Western-Thomson Controls Ltd. of Reading were the first to introduce this type of unit into the UK, for the British diesel and gasoline engine manufacturers.

The waxes used are broadly in the microcrystalline group which covers the higher melting point range of paraffin waxes. In many cases the wax is mixed with a very finely divided copper to increase the thermal conductivity of the charge as a whole. This results in a more thermally sensitive element. Over the working range the wax remains in the plastic state, having a coefficient of volumetric expansion of about 0.9%/degC. A maximum lift of 9.525 mm and a thrust of no less than 15.9 kg are given by the standard automotive element.

A tapered piston rod is enclosed in a synthetic rubber boot sealed in the upper end of the capsule (a brass pressing) which contains the wax. The upper end of this rod is screwed into a central hole in a bridge carried by the main seating ring, and after adjustment for calibration, the screw is locked by solder.

As the wax expands on heating, it forces the body of the capsule downwards against the return spring carrying with it the valve which opens against the pump pressure.

To avoid the harmful effects that might arise from a stalled water pump when the valve is shut in a closed circuit, the makers recommend a by-pass system, and when this cannot be arranged without extensive modification, a suitable bleed orifice may suffice.

Failure of the wax capsule would cause the valve to remain closed, with possible disastrous consequences, but the same results would arise with a punctured or cracked bellows. The wax capsule is claimed to be less liable to failure owing to its robust construction and freedom from fatigue effects which may arise in the bellows type due to cyclical distortion.

Fig. 16.5 illustrates a wax element thermostat in one of its simpler forms. The valve, side-shutter type, is pressed on to the outside of the capsule against the swell in diameter, and seats on the main annular pressing which carries the bridge and return spring abutment. The form of the rubber boot and seal will be clear.

The authors are indebted to the makers for information, and a full decription will be found in *Automobile Engineer* for March 1962.

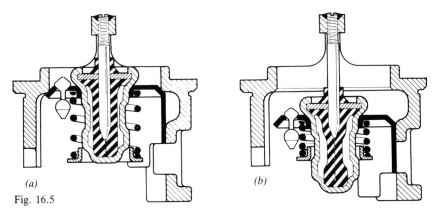

(a)

(b)

Fig. 16.5

The second means of regulation, namely by hand-operated shutters, has both the advantages and diadvantages of being under the direct control of the driver. By the use of these shutters, placed usually in front of the radiator, the air flow may be wholly or partly blanked off in order to obtain the desired working tempeature. The shutters and their controls require to be well designed and made if they are to be free from rattle. Radiator shutters controlled by a thermostat have been used.

The radiator and bonnet muff so much used in Great Britain, while useful in cold weather to prevent cooling off while the car is standing, is at best a makeshift and unsatisactory means of control.

16.3 Pressurised cooling system

Experience with evaporative cooling systems in closed water jackets of complicted form appears to have emphasised the danger of local steam pockets forming at critical positions around exhaust valve pockets and spark-plug bosses.

In such locations rapid extraction of heat from the metal is essential, but stagnant or superheated steam which is not rapidly scoured away by fresh supplies of water at boiling point is relatively a very poor agent for the purpose, and local overheating and water hammer action is very likely to take place.

A system which combines the reliability of the more familiar arrangements with some of the advantages of steam cooling is the pressurised system incorporating a light relief valve with an automatic vacuum break valve, the relief valve being spring-loaded to open at a pressure of 20.68 to 27.6 kN/m^2 above prevailing atmospheric pressure. This is illustrated in Fig. 16.6, which shows a combined pressure and vacuum relief valve.

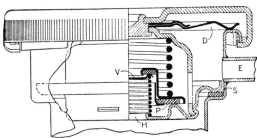

Fig. 16.6 Pressurised cooling system

The pressure inside the radiator block is communicated through the central port H to the pressure disc valve P and the vacuum valve V. These are loaded to pressures of about 24 and 6.9 kN/m² respectively. An escape pipe is provided at E. To guard against spurting on removal of the cap, the spring disc D does not leave its seating until the main body is well clear of the sealing washer S, and the pressure is reduced to that of the atmosphere.

In a closed water system of this type the pressure reached depends upon the temperature attained according to the following Table –

Temperature (°C)	94	100	107	121
Pressure (kN/m² abs.)	82.7	103.3	131	206.8

The pressure of 82.7 kN/m² corresponds to an altitude of 6000 to 7000 ft, so that boiling would occur at 94°C at this altitude in an open system, whereas in a closed system loaded to 20.68 kN/m² the temperature would be raised to the normal sea level figure before loss occurred. At sea level a margin of 6 or 7° is provided by the pressurised system. These increases may well prove sufficient to avoid the necessity of stopping to cool off in order to prevent loss of water under arduous conditions of hill climbing at high altitudes. The heat-dissipating capacity of the radiator surface would be appreciably increased by such a temperature increase.

A higher loading of the relief valve up to, say, 103.3 kN/m² would give such a gain in temperature that economy in size of radiator might be possible, though the probable necessity of strengthening the block would rule out any having in weight. With the lower figure of 20.7 to 27.7 kN/m² above atmosphere special provision for strengthening will not normally be necessary.

16.4   Twin thermostats

With diesel engines, the rate of heat flow to coolant is relatively low. Consequently, in the large engines used in heavy commercial vehicles, the water jackets of which contain a large volume of coolant, the attainment of normal working temperature after starting from cold takes a significant time and, when a correspondingly large thermostat opens, a flood of cold water may pass quickly through the jacket. For vehicles engaged on stop-start delivery, this can happen many times a day, so thermal fatigue – due to alternating stresses induced by repeated local thermal expansion and contraction – can cause cracking around hot areas such as exhaust valve seats, or fretting of joints and gaskets.

To avoid this, twin thermostats are sometimes employed, one opening at say 77°C and the other at perhaps 82°C. This not only reduces the volume of water suddenly flowing through the jackets, but also has other advantages. First, it is easier to pass a large volume of coolant through two open thermostats than through one, since the ratio of total periphery to area of the ports is larger in the former. Secondly, there is a safety factor in that a partial or even a total failure of one will not be so serious if there is a second thermostat.

16.5 Renault R4-L sealed coolant system

An interesting development of the pressurised cooling system is the sealed arrangement first adopted on the R4-L Renault front-engine vehicle.

Described as a *sealed for life* system, both temperature and pressure controls are provided. Communication with a relatively large expansion tank situated under the bonnet is opened by a thermostatic valve when the coolant reaches a temperature of 100°C. The expansion tank is provided with a pressure relief valve set to about $48.26 \, kN/m^2$.

The coolant is a 50-50 mixture of water and glycol charged and sealed permanently subject to abnormal leaks. The air capacity of the expansion tank is sufficient to prevent the pressure (at 100°C) from rising above the relief pressure, and in any case only air would be discharged.

Fig. 16.7 indicates the arrangement diagrammatically. All connections are made with rubber hose including those to the space heater for the passenger compartment.

16.6 Directed cooling

Considerable care is taken in modern designs of cylinder head to provide carefully directed jets of coolant to local hot spots such as valve seats and spark-plug bosses. This may be accomplished by means of a suitably drilled gallery pipe fed directly from the water pump, or by nozzles pressed into the head casting at each of the communicating holes between the cylinder block and head jackets. In the Vauxhall head, shown in section through the exhaust valve in Fig. 16.8, the nozzles take the form of thimbles provided with one or two ports suitably positioned in each case to direct vigorous local streams to the spots desired. A pressed locating snug ensures correct positioning in each case. The six-cylinder head has a total of ten of these jets directed in general towards the exhaust valve pockets.

16.7 Radiator construction

Copper radiators have now evolved into two types of water-tube construction, the early honeycomb or cellular construction shown in Figs.16.9 and 16.10 being obsolete. Though having certain advantages in appearance, ease of repair and smaller proportionate immobilisation by a single obstruction, the earlier types suffer from the important heat transfer defect that the ratio of metal-air to water-metal dissipating surface is practically unity instead of being many times that figure.

In modern tubular constructions, appearance and protection are provided by the ornamental grille which is now universal in passenger vehicles, and the radiator block can be designed simply as an efficient heat exchanger of the lightest possible weight.

Fig. 16.11 shows the vertical water tube type which is to be found on heavier types of commercial vehicles. The construction consists essentially of cast light alloy top and bottom tanks bolted to cast side pillars. The cooling element consists of a nest of copper tubes soldered into brass upper and lower tube plates which are bolted to the top and bottom tanks. This construction is inexpensive and makes for accessibility and ease of repair.

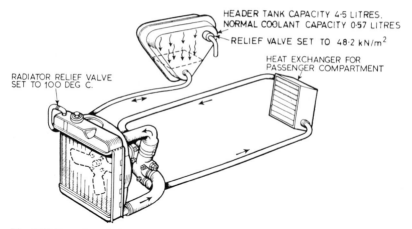

HEADER TANK CAPACITY 4·5 LITRES.
NORMAL COOLANT CAPACITY 0·57 LITRES

RELIEF VALVE SET TO 48·2 kN/m^2

HEAT EXCHANGER FOR
PASSENGER COMPARTMENT

RADIATOR RELIEF VALVE
SET TO 100 DEG C.

Fig. 16.7 Renault sealed system

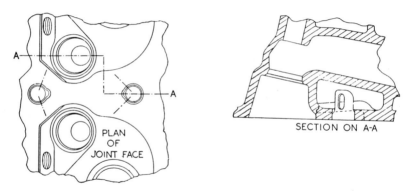

PLAN
OF
JOINT FACE

SECTION ON A-A

Fig. 16.8 Directed cooling in Vauxhall cylinder head

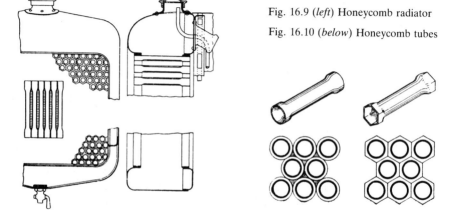

Fig. 16.9 (*left*) Honeycomb radiator

Fig. 16.10 (*below*) Honeycomb tubes

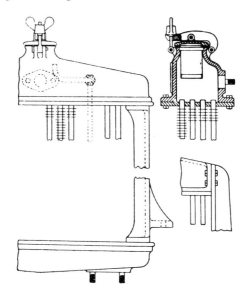

Fig. 16.11 (*right*) Radiator
construction for heavy commercial
vehicles
Fig. 16.12 (*below*) Radiator tubes
Fig. 16.13 (*below right*) Flattened
tubes, with plate gills

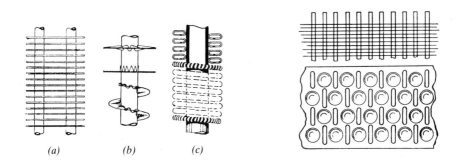

(a)   (b)   (c)

The tubes take various forms, and if of normal circular section, are usually provided with external gills to give additional surface to aid transfer of heat from metal to air. Various forms are illustrated in Fig. 16.12. At (*a*) is indicated a construction in which a nest of six or eight tubes, running from back to front of the block, is sweated into common gill plates.

Different forms of plate gill applied to individual tubes are shown at (*b*), while (*c*) shows the efficient and widely used Still tube which employs a continuous coil of copper wire wound spirally around, and sweated to, the plain tube.

Fig. 16.13 shows a popular current form of flattened tube and plate gill type, which can be assembled and sweated up to the size of block required. The flattened tubes give a more favourable ratio of transfer area to water weight than the circular tube, and they are fabricated from very thin strip metal with a folded and sweated longitudinal joint. The ratio of air surface to water surface can be varied very conveniently by the appropriate choice of the number of gill plates through which the tubes are threaded. The dimples help to ensure the desirable turbulent motion of the air.

Fig. 16.14 illustrates the extreme development of the film-tube type in which the core is built up of units formed from thin embossed copper strip of a width equal to the required thickness of block. This is normally from two to three inches thick.

The block is built by first forming air-way units of the full height of the block. This is done by folding the embossed strip round serpentine dimpled strip to provide the additional air surface, locating dimples being provided on the embossed strip to position the serpentine strip until the final soldering operation.

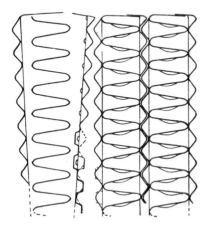
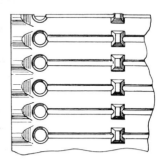

Fig. 16.14 Film tube construction
(actual size)

These air-way units are then assembled in a jig in the required number and sweated together at the corrugated edges, leaving straight vertical water-ways of a lateral width equal to the full depth of the edge corrugations. The embossing of the strip provides, in addition, strengthening flutes and spacing supports on the vertical centre line. The actual-size drawing of Fig. 16.14 should make the construction clear. The ratio of air area to water area in the example illustrated is about 5:1.

Aluminium radiators have been available for many years but have not been widely used. They are mostly of brazed construction. Because of the high temperatures involved in this method of manufacture, the aluminium becomes annealed, so relatively thick sections have to be used. With the current call for weight reduction to improve fuel consumption, either aluminium or composite radiators – such as plastics tanks with either aluminium or copper tube blocks – are likely to become increasingly attractive.

16.8   Horizontal disposition of copper tubes

The marked tendency towards wider and lower bonnet lines has encouraged designers to test the merits of the horizontally disposed radiator block. As pump or forced circulation is now practically universal, thermosyphon action has little significance, and the high and narrow constructions of block previously called for can no longer be accommodated easily. Increase of width and reduction of height of the block result in a less favourable surface/weight ratio, owing to the greater proportional weight of the top and bottom headers. The larger number of shorter tubes calls for a greater number of soldered joints and increased risk of leakage. Favourable proportions are restored by laying a 'long tube' block on its side, and if desired, introducing baffles so that inlet and outlet may be on the same side of the bonnet, the water traversing the bonnet width twice.

The increased length and smaller total cross section of the flow area naturally increase the hydraulic resistance, but by careful pump design and choice of speed, the power consumption need not be excessive. The flattened tube type of block shown in Fig. 16.13 is well suited to this horizontal lay-out.

A comprehensive series of articles on cooling system design, by S. I. G. Taylor, was published in the April, May and June 1970 issues of *Automobile Engineer*.

16.9 Fan drives

With increasing emphasis on fuel economy, the traditional pulley-driven directly-coupled pressed steel fan is tending to give way to more efficient systems. Moulded plastics – nylon or polypropylene – fans are lighter, easier to balance, look better and, above all, can be made more efficient aerodynamically. Incidental benefits are reduced noise and vibration, and less risk of serious injury if the rotating fan blades strike fingers carelessly contacting them.

Basically, there are two approaches. One, by far the simplest, is to incorporate in the hub of the fan a clutch that slips at a certain torque, thus limiting the amount of power that can be transmitted to, and therefore absorbed by, the fan. A good example is the Holset torque-limiting drive, which comprises a disc which is the driving member secured to the V-belt pulley, and a casing which is the driven member within which the disc rotates and on which is mounted the fan. The casing is finned to dissipate heat generated by slip and there is a closely controlled small clearance between it and the front and rear faces of the disc. This clearance is filled with a viscous silicone fluid, the shearing of which allows the drive to slip. Typical characteristics of such a drive are shown in Fig. 16.15.

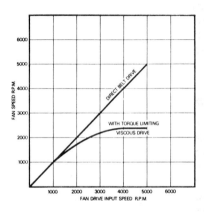
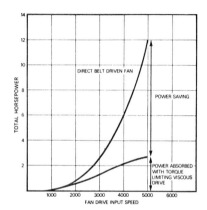

Fig. 16.15 Typical characteristics of a fan drive

The second approach is to introduce a thermostatic control either to limit the torque transmitted to the fan, or to cut it out altogether when the coolant temperature falls below a predetermined level. Again, one of the simplest is the Holset air temperature sensing fan illustrated diagrammatically in Fig. 16.16. This is similar to the drive described in the previous paragraph except in that its casing is divided by a separator plate into two chambers. Of these, the rear one houses the driven disc, while the front one is a reservoir. A scoop mounted on the separator plate continuously removes oil from the rear chamber and passes it into the reservoir. Thus, the tendency is for the viscous drive clutch chamber to be emptied so that no drive can be transmitted. However, the oil is allowed to re-enter the

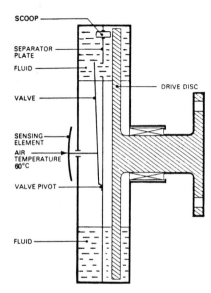

Fig. 16.16 Holset air temperature sensing fan

clutch chamber through a port nearer than the scoop to the centre of the disc, so that the fluid is therefore distributed over the disc by centrifugal force. This port is controlled by a thermostatically-actuated valve which opens when the engine coolant becomes too hot. The thermostatic control element is a bimetal plate on front of the coupling where it is exposed to the airstream issuing from the radiator.

More elaborate systems are used for some heavy commercial vehicles. These range from thermostatically-controlled hydrostatic drives to the Dynair system, which has a thermostatically-controlled air-actuated cone clutch. With most of these arrangements, the controller is a thermostatic switch, the sensor of which is in the coolant – usually in the radiator outlet. Similar controls are used also in conjunction with electric motor-driven fans – for cars as well as commercial vehicles. The advantages of this and the hydrostatic drive systems is that, because the fan is driven independently of the engine, both it and the radiator can be installed anywhere on the vehicle. Electrically-driven fans are therefore widely employed in cars having transversely-mounted engines.

Chapter 17

Potential for future development

The appliction of the gas turbine to the smaller types of road vehicle is a revolutionary and conjectural possibility, though the successful enterprise of the Rover Company in producing the first turbine-driven car attracted world-wide interest. Since these post-war developments, research and technical advance have continued, but though the great US corporations and many European firms of high standing are patenting and developing a great variety of appliances, there is no evidence yet of pending large-scale applications in the automobile field. Even under the threat of severe, restrictive anti-pollution legislation, no practical alternative to the internal combustion engine has evolved.

17.1   The gas turbine

The gas turbine, which for many years was the dream of inventors, has inspired a wealth of technical literature and experimental enterprise, but had shown very limited practical and commercial progress until the last four decades, in which we have seen the spectacular development of the turbo-jet propulsion of aircraft. This type of power unit is still considered by some as likely to become a serious competitor of the piston engine for road vehicles.

The following articles, published by the *Automobile Engineer*, should be consulted for further reference: F. R. Bell, *The Gas Turbine Car*, Vol. 43, No. 3, and *Gas Turbine Arrangements*, Vol. 43, No. 8. Additionally, a paper on the Chrysler gas turbine car was presented before the Automobile Division of the Institution of Mechanical Engineers on 13th April 1965. Readers interested in the theory of the design of gas turbines are advised to consult *Jet Propulsion Engines*, edited by O. E. Lancaster and published by the Oxford University Press, London (1959).

17.2   Two fields of successful application

The ultimate objective of automobile and power plant engineers is the replacement of the complicated, noisy, and vibration-prone reciprocating piston engine by a self-contained power unit which shall deliver energy by direct rotative motion.

The valuable features of mechanical simplicity, lightness, and ultimately cheapness, can certainly be achieved, and if fuel economy and reasonable reliability and life can be realised, the piston engine will gradually be superseded.

Unfortunately very great difficulties arise in satisfying these latter conditions, and the two fields in which successful development has taken place represent special applications in favourable circumstances.

The first of these is in the use of the turbine as an adjunct to the piston engine for supercharging purposes, on which some notes are included in Section 13.6, and the second as a means of supplying kinetic energy to the jet used for the propulsion-by-reaction of high speed aircraft.

It should be realised that jet populsion is quite unsuitable for the efficient propulsion of low speed vehicles, apart from traffic conditions.

The turbo-prop system represents an approach to the self-contained unit delivering shaft power, but in an application where economy and endurance are not factors of over-riding importance as in ordinary commercial fields. The system has a higher efficiency than the pure jet system at lower altitudes and speeds.

Fig. 17.1 represents in simple diagram form the turbo-jet and turbo-prop jet systems. The success achieved represents a remarkable advance in overcoming two of the main problems of the rotative unit, the provision of an efficient rotary compressor and the production of turbine blade materials which will give an acceptable endurance in this application.

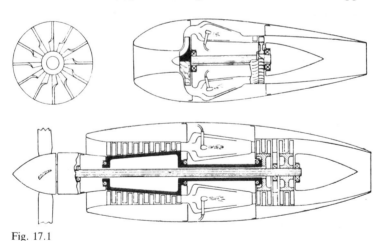

Fig. 17.1

In Fig. 17.1, a centrifugal compressor is indicated in the pure jet system, feeding multiple combustion chambers which usually fill the available annular space. An enlarged front view of the impeller is shown on the left, and indicates how the blades are curved to provide for axial entry to the eye with the minimum of shock. It should be noted that as the vanes have no curvature in diametral planes, centrifugal force has no tendency to distort their shape.

The lower diagram indicates an axial flow compressor, this type showing higher efficiency than the centrifugal type. It will be noticed that the two turbines are mechanically quite independent, but utilise the combustion gases in series. The compressors are required to supply a great excess of air over that required for complete combustion, not only to prevent excessive heating of the parts, but also to provide the necessary mass-velocity characteristics of the propulsive jet.

17.3   Essential processes in ic power units

The three essential processes in any internal combustion power unit are compression of the air charge, combustion of the fuel, and expansion of the products as completely as possible to produce mechanical work. The greater the degree of compression and expansion, and the greater the range of temperature effectively utilised, the higher will be the thermal efficiency and the lower the specific fuel consumption. These conditions apply to both piston and turbine engines.

The piston engine can accomplish the first two processes with high efficiency and reliability, but is less successful with the third owing to its unsuitability for handling the large volumes at the low pressure end of the expansion, this being incomplete unless continued in a turbine, which is admirably suited to deal with large volumes at low pressure. Hence, as explained in Chapter 13, the exhaust turbo supercharger forms a mechanically independent but not thermodynamically self-contained high-speed unit which increases the power of the main engine but does not require to be geared to the low-speed power shaft. Moreover, since the gases reach the turbine blades at a manageable temperature, no insoluble temperature-stress-time factor arises with the material of the blading.

17.4   Essential organs in turbine unit

In a self-contained turbine unit separate organs must be provided for all three processes, the compressor as well as the turbine being of the rotary form, and driven by the main or an auxiliary turbine. The combustion chamber or chambers must receive the compressed air, the liquid fuel must be injected, and the combustion be completed before the products are passed to the turbine. This combustion must be done in a light and compact arrangement, capable of withstanding the high temperature of continuous combustion over an acceptable working life.

In the present stage of the art, and with available materials, it is not possible to produce organs which in combination can approach the efficiency of the piston unit, in spite of the ability of the turbine to provide complete expansion.

The most successful rotary compressors yet built achieve at best only about 80% of the efficiency of their piston counterparts, owing to the inherent aerodynamic difficulty of controlling by high-speed rotary means the flow of light fluids. The pressure ratios that can be used are restricted both by the limitations of the compressor and also indirectly by the inability of the turbine blading and rotor to withstand for sufficiently long periods the combination of high temperature and high centrifugal stresses that are involved in the subsequent expansion process.

The net useful output of the plant is the difference between the power developed by the turbine and the power absorbed by the compressor, and it is interesting to note that the net 1489 kW of the Brown-Boveri gas turbine locomotive, corrected for losses in electric transmission, is the difference between the turbine output of about 7457 kW and the compressor consumption of nearly 5970 kW. (See *Proc. I. Mech. E.,* Vol. 141, No. 3, and *Automobile Engineer*, Vol. 32, No. 6.) It will be readily realised that a reduction of 10% in efficiency of both units would eliminate this net difference, and the early days of gas turbine development involved a succession of failures in which the output of the turbine proved insufficient to drive its own compressor. Thus fundamental aerodynamic difficulties in compressor design and material limitations in the turbine have resulted in efficiencies so low as to make the specific fuel consumption of the most successful gas turbine units greater than the average steam plant and far above the best diesel engine practice.

On the other hand, there are many actual and prospective advantages which fully justify expenditure on research and development.

In the case of jet propulsion there are certain favourable factors which are not realised in industrial applications. The low air temperature at high altitudes results in the turbine blading being exposed to less destructive temperatures than would normally arise. The time period during which the blades are so exposed is less, both on account of load factor and the limited endurance that is required or expected, fuel economy is not a first consideration, and finally in the pure jet unit the useful power output is not subject to turbine blading losses as is evident in the case of power delivery by shaft.

17.5   Gas turbines for road transport

Here the situation is much less favourable, in spite of the ultimate advantages of lightness, simplicity and compactness, absence of necessity for a cooling system and negligible oil consumption, all added to the much acclaimed advantage of direct production of rotative effort. This latter may even prove to some extent an embarrassment owing to the extremely high rotational speeds involved relatively to road wheel speeds, necessitating a large gear reducton.

17.6   Essential characteristics of turbine prime movers

When the energy of expansion of high-temperature gases is expanded in giving kinetic jet energy to the gases themselves, gas velocities of several thousand feet per second are generated, depending on the temperature range of the expansion, which in turn is limited by the maximum temperature to which the turbine blades may be continuously exposed.

The efficient extraction and utilisation of this energy involves correspondingly high speeds of movement of the parts operated upon, whether these parts are the blades of a turbine or the vehicle on which a propulsive jet reacts.

As with the Pelton water-wheel, which is the simplest form of impulse turbine, for maximum efficiency the blade speed should be about half the jet speed, and with single-stage impulse wheels peripheral blade speeds of 350 to 365 m/s are now normal practice in gas turbine work.

These speeds may be reduced by using multiple stages, and a gas turbine impulse wheel may be provided with two rows of blades with stationary deflector vanes between them. With this arrangement the gas velocity is extracted in two steps, and the peripheral blade speed may be about one-third of the initial gas velocity. Even so, since the power normally required for automobile work can be obtained from wheels of 152 to 203 mm diameter, rotational speeds of 40 000 to 50 000 rev/min will have to be provided for in design. The high rotational inertia consequent on such speeds leads to troublesome time-lag in response to throttle control.

A turbine is a high-speed, unidirectional prime mover capable of handling very large volumes of fluid flow with high mechanical efficiency – actually of the order of 85 to 90% if correctly designed – and its torque will increase with a decrease of speed for given input; but this will be accompanied by loss of efficiency, since the fixed angles of the blading are correct only for certain relative speeds of jet and blades.

17.7   Automotive power unit

For automobile work it becomes necessary to use either electric transmission, which is expensive and heavy, or a separate work turbine independent of the turbo-compressor shaft. This power turbine is geared to the road wheels, while the compressor unit can be run up to speed with the car stationary. The exhaust from the compressor turbine would thus develop a fluid drive effect on the power turbine and exert on it a starting torque. This arrangement of the power unit is shown in simple diagram form in the upper diagrams of (*a*) and (*b*) in Fig. 17.2. A single combustion chamber CC feeds the compressor turbine CT and the power turbine PT in series.

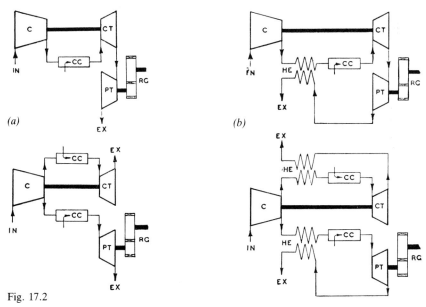

Fig. 17.2

The lower diagrams show two combustion chambers in parallel, so providing independent control for the power turbine. Diagrams (*a*) show the simplest possible layout for each system, while diagrams (*b*) indicate the use of heat exchangers HE which improve thermal efficiency by transferring some of the waste heat in the exhaust to the combustion air between the compressor and the combustion chamber. RG is the reduction gearing between the turbine and the propellor shaft, a very large ratio being required.

17.8   Fuel consumption

Low thermal efficiency remains the great stumbling-block. Unless a heat exchanger is used, the specific fuel consumption will probably be twice that of the average petrol engine and three times that of the diesel, though possibly of a cheaper fuel. While the commercial user will assess lower capital and maintenance costs as a set-off against higher fuel consumption and cost, this aspect will appeal less to the private motorist, whose accounts rarely include depreciation and interest.

It will, moreover, be many years before a low selling price can be realised, even with reduced production costs, owing to the necessarily very high cost of development work.

All things considered, the gas turbine for the private car can be regarded only as a somewhat remote prospect.

17.9   Heat exchangers

Heat exchangers are essential in large plants to reduce fuel consumption, but their bulk and weight are objections in automobile applications. Much theoretical and practical research is being devoted to improve their construction and performance, and the ultimate position of the turbine power plant in the automobile field will depend vitally on these developments.

Heat exchangers for the application under discussion may be classified into two types. Firstly, the static recuperative type, in which the heat passes by conduction from one fluid stream to the other through plate and tubular surfaces. This type is familiar in great variety of domestic and industrial applications. In relation to performance the type is bulky and heavy. Secondly, the regenerative, or change-over type, in which the two streams alternately deposit in, and extract the heat from, the refractory material, which in large industrial applications usually consists of a nest of fire bricks, through which the streams are directed in turn.

For light power applications attention is now concentrated on the development of compact revolving units, in which matrices of a suitable material in mesh form are carried in a drum revolving at 20 to 30 rev/min, the two streams passing continuously, each through an appropriate portion of the rotor profile. Each portion of the matrix picks up and deposits heat as it passes from one stream to the other. The Ford research organisation has published information in regard to a rotor construction in which a dual band of stainless steel strip is wound between a 101.6-mm diameter hub and an outer drum about 508 mm in diameter. The drive is through a small pinion engaging a toothed ring on the periphery of the drum.

(See *Engineering Details of Ford Rotary Heat Exchanger for Gas Turbine Engines*, by W. Wai Chao, Section Supervisor, Combustor and Heat Exchanger Section, Scientific Laboratory, Ford Motor Co. Abstract of a Paper presented by the Author at the 17th Annual Meeting of the American Power Conference in Chicago. *Automotive Industries*, 15th May, 1955, p. 54.)

The strips, 0.0508 mm thick, are alternately plain and corrugated, giving an extremely high surface:volume ratio, and a number of flow passages estimated at a quarter of a million. This ensures that the matrix is an extremely efficient means of transfer of heat for its bulk and weight. This is known as the *flame trap system*.

Clearly, means of pressure sealing are required where the rotor profile passes through the boundary wall separating the two streams, and formidable construction difficulties call for solution.

17.10 Turbine developments

The Rover Company achieved striking success in the 1963 and 1965 Le Mans 24 hours race with their Rover–BRM sports car, the first turbine-powered car to compete in this race.

In 1963 no regenerator was fitted, and the fuel consumption was naturally high at 2.445 km/l, but power output and mechanical reliabiity enabled the car to finish eighth at an average speed of 173 km/h.

In 1964 a heat-exchanger of the regenerator type, incorporating ceramic drums, had been developed, but time for reliability tests was limited, and it was decided not to enter for the race.

The race of 1965 saw a remarkable step in fuel economy, achieved by the use of the heat exchanger referred to above, though unfortunately it was necessary to limit performance owing to a mishap to the blading of the compressor turbine early in the race. Nonetheless the car was the leading British entrant, and was placed tenth in a field of 51 of which only 14 finished. At an average speed of 158.3 km/h the consumption was at 4.77 km/l – little more than half the 1963 figure. This was with the 2S/150R gas turbine.

An informative illustrated article will be found in *Automobile Engineer*, Vol. 55 No. 9.

The Firebird II Chassis, which has been developed by General Motors, is powered by the GT-304 Whirlfire turbine unit which incorporates a rotary regenerative type heat exchanger.

All the basic components were under test in combination, and some reliable forecast of eventual efficiencies should be possible. Improvement in aerodynamic efficiency of the compressor and turbine units will be a slower and less spectacular long-term advance, though since final power output is the net difference between positive and negative powers of the same order, relatively small improvements result in considerable gains.

Metallurgical advance and manufacturing techniques determine cost and endurance rather than thermodynamic efficiency.

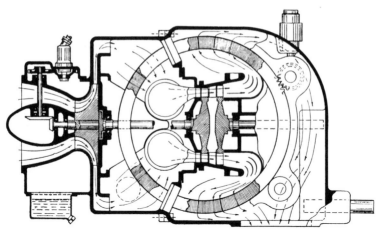

Fig. 17.3 General Motors' GT-304 Whirlfire unit

The general lay-out of the GT-304 Whirlfire unit is shown diagrammatically in Fig. 17.3. This specially-drawn schematic illustration is based on information given in one of two papers, describing the Firebird II chassis and its power unit, by four members of the research staff of General Motors and published in *J. Soc. Automotive Eng.*, Vol. 64, 1956. The present Authors are much indebted to the above Society for permission to make this brief extract.

The general lay-out consists of an accessories section incorporating a gear-driven hydraulic pump for powering the hydraulic motors which drive the rotary regenerators, fuel injection control and lubricating apparatus, and other auxiliary units.

The gasifier section comprises a single-stage centrifugal air-compressor delivering to a plenum from which the compressed and warmed air passes radially through a symmetrical pair of revolving-drum type regenerators. The heat picked up by the matrix of each regenerator as it passes through the hot exhaust stream is imparted to the air as it passes to the four symmetrically-placed 'can' type combustors. From the combustors the high-temperature gases pass through the nozzle ring mounted in a dividing bulkhead to the turbine chamber. The velocity acquired in the nozzle ring is extracted in the two separate single-stage impulse turbines in series, the power turbine discharging the hot exhaust to a deflector ring which directs the stream to pass radially outwards through the regenerators. The matrices are thereby heated and the cooled exhaust passes out at the bottom of the casing.

The driving pinions, suporting rollers and floating seals where the regenerator drums pass through the dividing bulkhead, are indicated. The construction of the seals is the subject of intensive research and development, and little information is available.

Reduction gearing is provided to the power output shaft, whence a long transmission shaft leads to the final gearing at the rear of the chassis. The normal speeds of the compressor and power turbines are 35 000 and 28 000 rev/min respectively, and the regenerators revolve at 20 to 30 rev/min.

17.11   Ford power unit

Automobile Engineer, Vol. 49, No. 8, and Vol. 59, No. 12, contain descriptions of a gas turbine power unit under development by the Ford Motor Company of America. This unit, known as the 704 Model, exemplifies successful attack on the problem of high fuel consumption by novel arrangement of the various units, giving a somewhat complicated assembly.

Two-stage compression, with intercooling, is employed, the compression ratio of each stage being 4:1. The secondary, or high-speed compressor runs at the very high speed of 91 000 rev/min as compared with 46 500 rev/min of the low speed unit. There are also two combustion chambers, the first interposed between the heat-exchanger and the high-speed inward flow radial turbine, from which the gases pass to the secondary combustion chamber where a further supply of fuel is introduced. The exhaust products

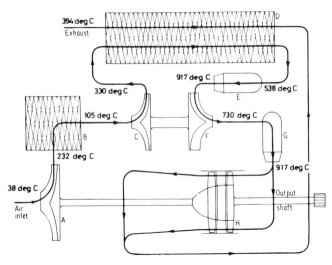

A	Low-speed compressor	E	Primary combustion chamber
B	Intercooler	F	Radial in-flow turbine
C	High-speed compressor	G	Secondary combustion chamber
D	Heat exchanger	H	Axial-flow turbine

Fig. 17.4 Ford 704 Model gas turbine power unit

then pass to the main axial turbine which drives the low speed compressor and the output shaft. The arrangement of the components is shown diagrammatically in Fig. 17.4 with approximate gas temperature at the various stages.

The weight is stated to be 294.84 kg for a power output of about 224 kW, or about one-quarter of the weight of a corresponding diesel engine. The overall dimensions are about 965.2 mm long, 736.6 mm high and 711.2 mm wide. A wide variety of fuels can be used, with a consumption of only 0.294 to 0.353 kg/kWh according to load.

17.12 Chrysler turbine car

In 1963 the Chrysler Corporation achieved limited production of a completely new turbine driven car which they then supplied to selected customers in order to obtain user experience.

The basic arrangement of the power plant follows the generally accepted system of two mechanically independent turbine wheels of the single-stage impulse type, through which the gas stream passes in series. They are axial flow wheels, the front one driving the single stage radial compressor with an extension shaft serving the auxiliaries.

Of the two, the rearmost is the power turbine. This is larger than the compressor wheel, and is provided with a novel arrangement of variable angle guide vanes which is one of the many interesting features of the power unit. The direction of the gas stream on to the turbine blading may be varied from maximum power, through economy and idling to a braking position. The operating gear is one of the hydraulic auxiliaries all fed from a single pump.

A heat-exchanger system consisting of a symmetrical pair of rotary regenerators of the multicellular type is employed. These regenerators are about 381 mm in diameter and driven by spur reduction gearing from the

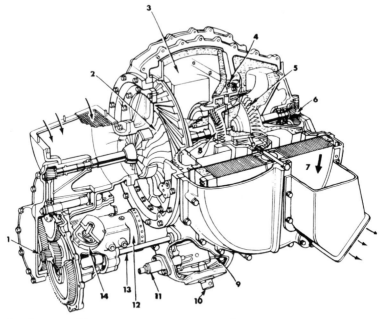

1	Accessory drive	8	Gas generator turbine
2	Compressor	9	Burner
3	R/h regenerator rotor	10	Fuel nozzle
4	Variable nozzle mechanism	11	Igniter
5	Power turbine	12	Starter-generator
6	Reduction gearing	13	Regenerator drive shaft
7	L/h regenerator rotor	14	Ignition unit

Fig. 17.5 Chrysler turbine unit

compressor shaft at 9 to 22 rev/min. Designed for axial flow, the compactly arranged and well insulated ducting leads the air-flow from the compressor volute through the front halves of the regenerator wheels, where it is pre-heated, to the single combustion chamber mounted underneath the main casing. The housing of the outer diametral seal of the left-hand regenerator may be noted in Fig. 17.5. No details of the sealing strips are available.

As it is injected the fuel burns with excess air, and the combustion products pass first, through fixed guide vanes, to the compressor turbine, and thence through the variable angle guide vanes for the second stage of expansion in the power turbine.

The hot exhaust is ducted to the rear halves of the interchangers where the wheels absorb heat and transfer it to the contrary air stream from the compressor. A pair of aluminium alloy ducts leads the exhaust to the rear of the car.

In the part-sectioned pictorial view, Fig. 17.5, is shown the general arrangement, and many of the details can be seen.

The heat exchangers and ducting are skilfully and compactly arranged, and indeed a great part of the total bulk is due to the auxiliaries and their drives, and the front air intake and cleaner.

Fig. 17.6 gives torque and power plotted against output shaft speed, and the valuable feature of high torque at low speed will be noted.

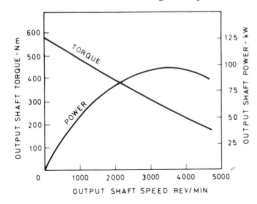

Fig. 17.6

The power turbine may be stalled to zero speed, but will continue to develop full torque, as the compressor unit will run independently.

An informative article giving particulars of transmission and automatic controls, and further structural details, will be found in *Automobile Engineer*, Vol. 53, No. 12.

17.13 Leyland gas turbine

In March 1967, the Rover team engaged in gas turbine work was regrouped to form Leyland Gas Turbines Ltd. They have developed a new, larger unit developing 260–300 kW intended for commercial vehicles. This engine is the type 2S/350/R and in design it is basically similar to the 2S/150 R, mentioned in Section 17.10. A minimum fuel consumption of 0.2373 kg/kWh at 20°C is quoted. At 26.7°C, the mass flow of air is 1.7 kg/sec.

The compressor idling speed is 19 000 rev/min, and the output speed range at full load corresponds to a power turbine speed-range of 0–32 500 rev/min. This power unit, including ducts and auxiliaries, weighs less than 454 kg.

Its radial-flow impeller is approximately 230 mm in diameter and is produced in two portions. The front part, comprising the inlet guide vanes, is a steel casting, while the remainder is an aluminium alloy forging. Both are shrunk on to the shaft, on the rear end of which is the axial flow turbine. The latter is pressed on to a spigot and its hub bolted to the shoulder on the shaft.

The compression ratio of 4 : 1 is relatively low. At the inlet to the compressor turbine, the maximum temperature of the gas is more than 1000°C. A ratio of 2 : 1 is quoted for the maximum output torque of the power turbine at stall to that in the maximum power condition.

Provision has been made for a very large exchange of heat between the gas leaving the power turbine and the air flowing from the compressor. The heat exchanger is basically similar to that of the earlier model. It comprises two 711-mm diameter ceramic discs disposed vertically, one each side of the engine, and rotated at 1/1800 of the speed of the impeller shaft, from which they are driven. This heat exchanger is of the rotary regenerator type, and the temperatures quoted are as follows: air inlet 180°C, air outlet 700°C. The pressure loss across each disc is only 2.70 kN/m². The exhaust gas is ducted to the rear half of the inner faces of the discs and the air goes through the front halves.

Each disc is driven by a pinion meshing with teeth machined on a peripheral steel ring. The pinion is driven by means of a worm and wormwheel on a transverse shaft. A full description of this turbine was published in *Automobile Engineer*, December 1968.

17.14   Gas turbine prospects

With the maximum permitted loading of vehicles likely to become something of the order of 44 tonnes, and a legal requirement of something between 8 and 10 hp/tonne under consideration, engines of about 400 hp (300 kW) will be required for commercial vehicles. For this output, the gas turbine is worthy of serious consideration and, because of its advantages already outlined, it is virtually certain to come into use for heavy commercial vehicles. Another favourable factor is the widespread development throughout the world of motorway networks on which relatively constant speeds of operation for long periods are practicable.

At present, the biggest disadvantage of the gas turbine is the bulk of its heat exchanger. It seems likely, however, that this problem will be overcome when materials better able to withstand loading at high temperatures are developed. There are great hopes for ceramic materials, which currently are being intensively developed for nozzles, blades and perhaps discs. When such materials are available, a higher degree of compression and higher temperatures at the entry to the turbine will be feasible, though the formation of No_x, polluting the exhaust, might present a problem. Later it might be possible to use multi-stage turbines to get even more work out of the expanding gas, so that a heat exchanger will be unnecessary. This will entail the use of both turbines and compressors of the axial flow type. In other words, the development of the road vehicle gas turbine engine might follow on the lines of that of the aircraft version. In fact, turbine designers have been talking of using rotors of the order of 96 mm diameter. In these circumstances, such an engine could be suitable for the private car.

A good insight into some of the problems associated with the design and development of new materials can be gained from an article on the Ricardo Keramos project, *Automotive Engineer*, Vol. 2, No. 2, April/May 1977.

17.15 Stratified-charge engines

With the rapid increase in crude oil prices over the period 1973–4, attention was drawn to the fact that oil reserves could be exhausted shortly beyond the turn of the century. Suddenly, fuel economy seemed even more important than control of exhaust emissions. In fact, the search for both economy and emission control – especially of unburnt hydrocarbons and carbon monoxide, generally abbreviated to HC and CO respectively – has resulted in intensified efforts to find ways of burning weak mixtures in spark ignition engines. After all, one of the reasons for the relatively high thermal efficiency of the diesel engine at part load is the excess of air over fuel in the charge.

At this stage, it is important to understand the implications of varying the air:fuel ratio. The air:fuel ratio required in theory for complete combustion is approximately 14:1, and this is called the *stoichiometric ratio*, or $\lambda = 1$. Spark ignition engines in general develop maximum power, however, at about 10% air deficiency, $\lambda = 0.9$, but of course the exhaust is then contaminated with HC and CO. The reasons for the higher power output are: first, a slightly higher volumetric efficiency, because of the cooling of the charge by the latent heat of vaporisation of the extra fuel; secondly, the greater amount of heat generated because of the virtual total combustion of all the oxygen in the charge and the lower peak temperatures, and therefore less dissociation – reverse chemical reactions that occur at very high temperatures.

When excess air is supplied, not only are the peak temperatures higher but also the power output is reduced too because combustion is slower. When λ rises above about 1.25, or falls below about 0.4, ignition of the charge by the spark can no longer be relied upon. The optimum ratio for producing the cleanest possible exhaust in a conventional engine is about $\lambda = 1.1$. At weaker mixtures, the higher temperatures and slower combustion – and therefore longer dwell at those high temperatures – tend to cause the production of oxides of nitrogen. With very weak mixtures, on the other hand, temperatures fall off again.

Although mixtures weaker than $\lambda = 1.25$ cannot be fired by an ignition source as small as a spark, they can be by a flame. Consequently, if an ignitable mixture can be fed directly to the sparking plug points, it will not only fire locally but also the flame will spread throughout the remainder of the charge even though it be much weaker. The weakest overall fuel ratios that have been used successfully in stratified charge engines are of the order of 64:1, but for best fuel economy and lowest possible emissions, the optimum probably lies between about 20:1 and 25:1.

This has provided the incentive for the development of stratified-charge engines. The earliest work in this field, with the aim of reducing overall fuel consumption, was in 1915 by the late Sir Harry Ricardo. Otto, however, in his Patent No. 532 covering his invention of the four-stroke cycle, proposed the admission of only air at the beginning of the induction stroke, to form a layer next to the piston, for cushioning the effect upon it of the explosion of the subsequently entering combustible mixture.

17.16 Single-chamber versions

Some of the earliest work in this field was done using carburetted mixtures. An example is that of the Société Français du Pétroles, Fig. 17.7. The aim was to feed a rich mixture, through a separate pipe, past the inlet valve and to generate a swirl in the cylinder so that, with the weak mixture entering in the normal way also through the inlet valve, a vortex comprising alternate layers of rich and weak mixtures was formed in the cylinder. Since the rich portion of the mixture was directed initially over the sparking plug points, it could be ignited and, on burning, ignite also the weak mixture.

At much the same time, the Texaco TCCS engine, Fig. 17.8, was being developed on a similar principle, but using direct injection into the cylinder to produce the layer of rich mixture swirling past the sparking plug points.

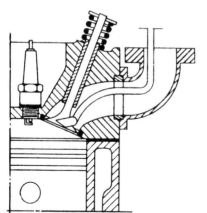

Fig. 17.7

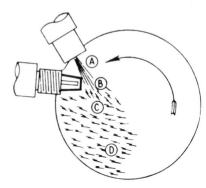

Fig. 17.8 A – atomised fuel, B – air/fuel mixture zone, C – flame front, D – products of combustion

Much later Mitsubishi actually put into production another injected version, but with a bowl-in-piston combustion chamber, Fig. 17.9. Another example of this type is the Ford Proco, Fig. 17.10. These arrangements give better control over the swirling charge, especially since turbulence can be increased by use of the squish effect between the piston crown and cylinder head.

With all these single combustion chamber engines, the principle difficulty is the control over swirl and stratification throughout the range of loads and speeds. Consequently, the Mitsubishi engine is basically an industrial power unit, for running mainly at constant speed, or over a relatively narrow speed range. A major difference between the Texaco and Mitsu-

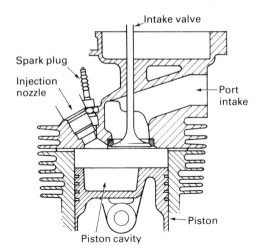

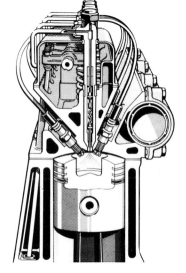

Fig. 17.9 (*left*) Mitsubishi stratified-charge industrial engine

Fig. 17.10 (*right*) Cross-section of Ford Proco engine showing bowl-in-piston combustion chamber, special injection system and dual ignition

bishi systems is that the former has early injection, while in the latter it is late. The advantage of late injection in such an engine is that control over stratification is more precise.

By early injection we mean 60° or more before TDC. Late injection is affected as the piston approaches TDC. With early injection, most of the fuel is evaporated before ignition, so combustion is similar to that in a carburetted engine. Late injection, on the other hand, entails combustion on the same principle as that in a diesel engine, though with spark ignition. That is, it occurs as the droplets evaporate. The rate of swirl is such that, when the mixture is ignited, the flame front cannot advance upstream towards the injector nozzle, which it would foul, but spreads only downstream.

The MAN FM engine, originally a diesel unit, was further developed for running as a multi-fuel engine and, later, for stratified charge. As can be seen from Fig. 17.11, fuel is injected directly towards the opposite wall of a bowl-in-piston combustion chamber. Fuel spreading in a thin film over the wall, is evaporated by the air swirling in the chamber to form the stratified charge. This charge is fed progressively to the combustion centre, which of

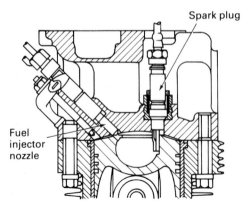

Spark plug

Fuel
injector
nozzle

Fig. 17.11 MAN FM engine as a
stratified-charge unit

course originates at the sparking plug points. These points are extended
down in a groove in the wall of the chamber, so that the spark occurs in the
layer of rich mixture. In one version of this engine, a single-electrode plug
was used, the spark jumping the gap between it and the piston itself.

17.17   Dual-chamber versions

The main sub-divisions of categories of stratified charge engines are those
with single combustion chambers, as just described, and those with dual
chambers. Both can be further divided into carburetted, and early and late
injection. The dual-chamber versions are in general similar to indirect
injection diesel engines, in that they have a small pre-chamber, generally in
the cylinder head, but of course they are spark ignited.

A dual-chamber engine supplied with carburetted mixture is the Honda
CVCC unit, Fig. 17.12, which was the first stratified-charge engine to go
into production for a car. The Porsche SKS engine, Fig. 17.13, is early
injected and the Ricardo experimental engine with a Comet MkVB Fig.

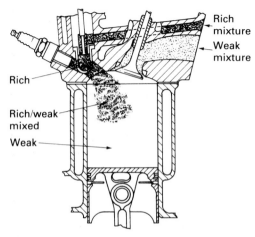

Rich
mixture

Weak
mixture

Rich

Rich/weak
mixed

Weak

Fig. 17.12 Honda CVCC engine, carburetted, at end of induction stroke

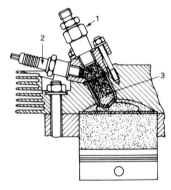

Fig. 17.13 The Porsche SKS

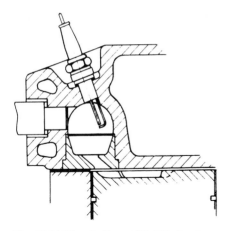

Fig. 17.14 Ricardo Comet Mk VB diesel combustion chamber adapted with special sparking plugs for stratified-charge operation

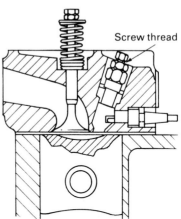

Fig. 17.15 Daimler-Benz DB-TSC engine

17.14, is late injected. A carburetted main chamber and injected pre-chamber engine, the Daimler-Benz DB-TSC, is shown in Fig. 17.15. In each of these examples, a rich mixture is supplied to the pre-chamber where it is ignited, discharging flaming gas into the main chamber to ignite the weak mixture there. Some of these engines have a third poppet valve, for scavenging the pre-chamber, while others do not.

Generally, the pre-chambers are designed for one of two totally different combustion processes. The Honda CVCC, for example, has a pre-chamber with a short but relatively large diameter throat. Consequently, when the combustion and consequent expansion of the rich mixture in the pre-chamber forces the burning gases out, the flame front spreads progressively over an ever-widening front through the weak mixture in the main chamber.

With the second system, the throat of the pre-chamber is longer and narrow, generally with sharp edges at both ends. As a result, the stream of burning gases passes through in a turbulent state and at high velocity. In these circumstances, as they pass through the throat, the rate of heat transfer – gases to metal – is so high that they are partially quenched. As they issue into the weak mixture in the main combustion chamber, the stream is torn into a cascade of tiny eddies, each of which becomes a centre of ignition of the weak mixture. This is because much of the ejected rich mixture of partially quenched gases, even though there is no longer any visible flame, is in the ionised state of the initial stages of combustion and therefore extremely unstable and highly chemically-active. The result is a rapid spread of combustion throughout the weak mixture in the main chamber.

Similar combustion phenomena appeared to have been observed in the BL Cars experimental engine, Fig. 17.16. This is a three-valve carburetted unit, the third valve being for scavenging the pre-chamber. Ciné photographs showed no visible burning in the jet until it was slowed and spread in the proximity of the opposite wall of the cylinder. In this case, however, it was subsequently discovered that, by improving the photographic technique, burning could be observed in the jet.

The effect of sparking plug position is as follows. If it is at the end of the pre-combustion chamber remote from the throat, the combustion kernel, growing from the centre of the spark, rapidly ignites the gas at that end, forcing rich unburnt gases out through the throat ahead of the burning gases. This presumably happens in the Porsche engine.

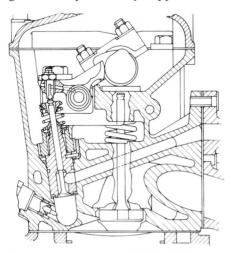 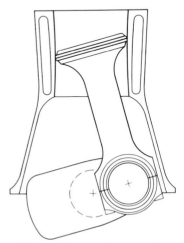

Fig. 17.16 Cross-section of BL Cars' 1.85-litre stratified-charge cylinder head

Fig. 17.17 The Saltsman rocking-piston engine

In the BL Cars engine, the plug is at an intermediate point in the pre-chamber and, moreover, directly opposite the throat. Consequently a much higher proportion of the rich mixture will be ignited before it passes into the throat, so one would expect more active ionised particles to be ejected into the main chamber.

An example of late injection into a pre-chamber, without a scavenge valve, is the Ricardo Comet system. As the piston comes up to TDC compression stroke, air from the main chamber is forced through a tangential throat to generate rapid swirl in the pre-chamber. The fuel is injected against the direction of swirl – tending to reduce its speed locally – but straight at the plug points, which extend to a position somewhere near the centre of the vortex. In this position, the linear velocity of the swirling gases is in any case relatively low, so the flame kernel is able to develop and spread throughout the pre-chamber without risk of its being quenched before it has time to do so.

That there are so many different types of stratified-charge engine is due to the fact that we are still in the early stages of the development of the principle. Ultimately, one or two forms will no doubt emerge as the most suitable, and the others will be dropped. An especially promising unit is that invented by Charles Goodacre, and developed in co-operation between him and Fiat, described in the August/September 1981 issue of *Automotive Engineer*.

An entirely different system, which might be regarded as a compromise between the single- and dual-chamber combustion chamber arrangements, but in which the emphasis is on the use of a high compression ratio, is the high-turbulence, high-compression, lean burn system adopted by Jaguar and described in Section 7.18. Ford, Porsche and Ricardo, too, have done a lot of work on such systems.

17.18 Rocking-piston engine

An ingenious Swiss engineer, W. Salzmann, of Solothurn, has focussed attention on the complexity and weight of current gudgeon-pin arrangements, the close tolerances entailed in their manufacture and the time spent in assembly. He has developed and run experimentally an engine that is conventional except in that its piston and connecting rod are rigidly connected, Fig. 17.17. If further development proves it to be satisfactory, it could have a considerable impact on engine design.

As can be seen from the illustration, the piston is almost in the form of a disc, and it reciprocates in a waisted cylinder. Production is not difficult: a rotating boring tool is used to machine the cylinder while the crankcase is mounted on a table that is rocked approppriately as the tool cuts its way down the bore. Alternatively, the tool drive-head is mounted on a crankshaft, which rotates as the machining progresses so that the plane in which the tool rotates executes the same reciprocal and rocking motion as the piston, but of course at a much slower speed.

There are many advantages. Because of the absence of a gudgeon pin and skirt, the piston is only about half the weight of its conventional counterpart. This, in turn, means that primary vibration forces are reduced by about 50%. Since the ratio of connecting-rod length to crank throw is larger, because of the absence of a gudgeon pin, the angular motion of the rod, and therefore the secondary vibration forces, are lower – about 40% of normal values. All this means that such an engine with fewer cylinders than a conventional one is without unacceptable levels of vibration.

Because gas forces act perpendicularly to a piston, their resultant in the Salzmann engine is always reacted by pure compression in the rod. This, and the reduction of lateral acceleration forces owing to the light weight of the piston, virtually eliminates piston slap. The inertia forces are at all times less than the gas forces between the rings and the bores, nor do the maximum values of each occur simultaneously – lateral components of inertia forces are zero at the ends of each stroke. Consequently, ring flutter should not occur and the rate of wear of the rings and bores should be low.

By virtue of the absence of a piston skirt, oil drag ought to be about 4% of that of a conventional piston. Therefore cold starting should be much easier so a smaller battery and starter motor would be needed. Additionally, the length of cylinder bore to be machined is only about two thirds of that conventionally required.

Many of these advantages would be of especial benefit for diesel engines for cars, and Mr. Salzmann has also designed a two-stroke version with rectangular, instead of circular pistons. With the latter, because of the rocking motion of the pistons, asymmetrical timing of the opening and closing of the inlet and exhaust ports can be arranged – for this purpose, the piston has a specially-shaped skirt, but only on each edge that covers and uncovers the ports.

With both rectangular and circular pistons, the major part of the development work will obviously have to be devoted to sealing. However, the seals are all in one plane, and both their rubbing velocities and total length in direct contact with combustion gases are considerably less than those of, for example, the Wankel engine, for which the sealing problem has been solved. Mr. Salzmann has patented a special form of seal for his engine.

This rocking piston design is an interesting concept, since it demonstrates the principle that nothing, no matter how long established, should be accepted as sacrosanct: reappraisals from time-to-time will reveal where, possibly because of changed circumstances, further advances can be made.

PART 3:

TRANSMISSION

Chapter 18

Transmission requirements

From the foregoing chapters, it can be seen that the internal combustion engine, as used in road vehicles, has the following requirements and characteristics –

(1) To start it, some form of external energy must be applied.
(2) Its maximum torque is small compared with that of a steam engine or electric traction motor of the same maximum horse power.
(3) Its maximum power is developed at a relatively high speed – ranging from about 1700 rev/min for heavy commercial vehicles to 12 000 rev/min and more in racing cars.

In consequence, it must be used in conjunction with a transmission that differs in many respects from those of either steam- or electrically-powered vehicles.

Various methods have been used for starting engines – for instance, from energy stored in a spring or flywheel, or chemical energy in a cartridge – but the general rule of course is to use a battery-electric starter. To keep the starting system as compact – and therefore as inexpensive – as possible, provision must be made for disconnecting the engine from the drive-line during the starting operation. Connecting it again to the drive-line, for propelling the vehicle, must be effected as smoothly as possible, both for the sake of passengers and to prevent damage to the vehicle mechanisms.

In passing down the drive-line, the torque of the engine is modified, stage-by-stage, until it becomes the propulsive force, or tractive effort, at the interface between the tyres and the road. If rapid acceleration is required, either when starting from rest or in any other circumstances – for overtaking, for example – that tractive effort must be increased. This is done partly by increasing the torque output of the engine but, since this alone may not be enough, the gear ratios will generally have to be changed too.

In this context, gear-changing can be likened to altering the leverage between the engine and the road-wheels, so that the relatively small torque available can be translated into a large tractive effort. A large leverage may also be required for climbing hills or traversing very soft or rough ground.

Since a large leverage implies a correspondingly reduced movement at the output end, this implies a big reduction of rotational speed between the engine and the road-wheels. Consequently, the leverage must be reduced as the speed of the vehicle increases, otherwise the engine speed would become too high and the maximum potential speed of the vehicle would be unattainable. Moreover, as explained in Chapter 4, the relationship between torque, power and the speed of rotation of the engine is such that torque falls off as speed increases. For this reason too, therefore, some simple means of varying the leverage – changing gear – is necessary.

Consider a car having road-wheels 0.66 m diameter and cruising at 60 mph. Under these conditions, the engine speed would have to be about 3500 rev/min and the road wheels would be rotating at about 800 rev/min. Consequently, the overall ratio of the gearing between the engine and the road wheels would have to be about 4.5:1. In practice, this ratio would differ to some extent, depending on the weight of the car and size of the engine. For example, until recently a car with a large engine might have an overall ratio of 3:1, a medium weight commercial vehicle 5.5:1 and a heavy truck 10:1 or even higher. Now, the demand for fuel economy is tending to encourage the use of overdrive gearboxes, and overall gear ratios as high a 6:1 could become common on, for instance, cars with five-speed gearboxes.

While the basic principles of transmission remain the same for virtually all classes of road vehicle, the actual arrangements vary – for instance, some may have four-wheel drive and others either front- or rear-wheel drive. Where, as in the majority of instances, the engine is installed at the front and the axis of its crankshaft is parallel to, or coincident with, the longitudinal axis of the vehicle, ultimately, the drive must be turned through 90° in order that it may be transmitted out to the wheels the axes of which are of course perpendicular to that longitudinal axis. Such a turn, however, is not necessary if the engine is installed transversely, though other complications, such as a need for dropping the driveline to a level below that of the crankshaft while turning it through 180°, may arise.

Another requirement for the transmission stems from the fact that, when the vehicle is cornering, the outer wheels must roll faster than the inner ones which will be traversing circles of smaller radii, yet their mean speed, and therefore both the rotational speed of the engine and the translational speed of the vehicle, may be required to remain constant.

Then again, to reduce the transmission of vibrations to the chassis frame, the engine is universally mounted on it, while the driving wheels, attached to the frame by the road springs, also have a degree of freedom of movement relative to it. Both these movements must be accommodated by the transmission.

In summary, therefore, the requirements for the transmission are as follows –

(1) To provide for disconnecting the engine from the driving wheels.
(2) When the engine is running, to enable the connection to the driving wheels to be made smoothly and without shock.
(3) To enable the leverage between the engine and driving wheels to be varied.
(4) It must reduce the drive-line speed from that of the engine to that of the driving wheels in a ratio of somewhere between about 3:1 and

10:1 or more, according to the relative size of engine and weight of vehicle.

(5) Turn the drive, if necessary, through 90° or perhaps otherwise re-align it.
(6) Enable the driving wheels to rotate at different speeds.
(7) Provide for relative movement between the engine and driving wheels.

There are several ways in which these requirements can be met, and transmissions fall into three categories –

(1) Mechanical.
(2) Hydraulic, (a) Hydrostatic,
  (b) Hydrodynamic.
(3) Electric and electromagnetic.

While the first of these is the commonest, combined mechanical and hydrodynamic transmissions are becoming increasingly popular, even on certain types of heavy commercial vehicle. Road vehicles with all-hydraulic transmissions have been built but have not gone into large-scale production. On the other hand, such transmissions are not at all uncommon in tractors for agricultural and, more especially, constructon and similar industrial equipment, such as diggers, in which transitions from idling to full load may be required to be effected suddenly and repetitively. With a hydraulic pump driving separate motors on each wheel of a pair, there is no need for a mechanical differential gear.

The same advantage can be claimed for some electric transmissions in which a generator or battery supplies power to separate wheel motors. Electric transmissions have been used in tanks and some road vehicles in the past and are still extensively employed in diesel-electric locomotives. With the current revival of interest in electric road vehicles, they are being reconsidered for wider application. Mostly, however, both hydraulic and electric transmissions have some mechanical elements in common. For instance, the hydraulic component generally simply replaces the clutch and gearbox of a mechanical transmission.

Most mechanical transmissions fall into one of the following three categories, each of which has three main elements –

(1) Clutch, gearbox and live axle.
(2) Clutch, gearbox and dead axle.
(3) Clutch, gearbox and axleless transmission.

18.1 Clutch, gearbox and live axle transmission, general arrangement

This system is shown diagrammatically in Fig. 18.1. The engine is at the front, with its crankshaft parallel to the axis of the vehicle. From the engine, the drive is transmitted through a clutch and a short shaft c to the gearbox. In cars, this short shaft is almost invariably integral with the primary gear in the gearbox but, in some commercial vehicles, it is a separate component, generally with flexible or universal joints at each end and, in some instances, with a sliding joint at one end. From the gearbox, a

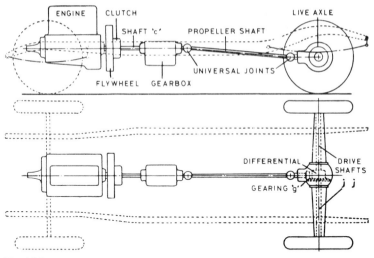

Fig. 18.1

'propeller shaft' or 'cardan shaft' – also with a sliding joint at one end and a universal joint at both ends – takes the drive to a live back axle. A live axle is one through which the drive is transmitted, while a dead axle is one that does not transmit the drive. Bevel or worm gearing g within the axle turns the drive through 90°, and *differential gears* divide it equally between the two drive shafts, or *halfshafts*, j, which take it out to the wheels.

The functions of the components are as follows. A clutch is used for disconnecting the engine from the driving wheels and it must also enable the driver to connect the engine, when it is running, without shock to the driving wheels. Since the clutch is kept in engagement by a spring-loading mechanism and is disengaged by pressure of the foot on a pedal, it cannot be disengaged except when the driver is in the vehicle. Therefore, when the driver wants to leave the vehicle with the engine running – and preferably for starting the engine, too – he has to disconnect the engine from the driving wheels by use of the gear-shift lever, which he sets in a 'neutral', or gears-disengaged, position.

The principal function of the gearbox is to enable the driver to change the leverage between the engine and driving wheels to suit the prevailing conditions – gradient, load, speed required, etc. As the propeller shaft transmits the drive on to the back axle, the universal joints at its ends allow both the engine-and-gearbox assembly and the back axle to move relative to one another, as their spring elements deflect. The sliding joint, usually integral with one of the universal joints, accommodates variations in length of the propeller shaft as its rear end rises and falls vertically with the back axle and its front end pivots about the universal joint just behind the gearbox. Gearing g, in what is called the *final drive* unit, turns the drive through 90° and reduces the speed in a ratio of about 4 : 1, since the driving wheels must rotate much more slowly than the engine. Within the final drive unit too is the differential gearing, which shares the driving torque equally between the two road-wheels while allowing them, nevertheless, to rotate simultaneously at different speeds while the vehicle is cornering.

In Fig. 18.1, the gearbox is shown as a separate unit, but two other variants of this front engine rear-wheel-drive layout are in use. One is a 'unit construction' – almost universal on cars – in which the gearbox casing is either integral with or bolted rigidly to the clutch 'bellhousing' which, in turn, is similarly secured to the engine crankcase. This has the advantages of cleanliness, lighter weight, neatness of appearance and lower manufacturing costs. Its chief disadvantage is relative inaccessibility of the clutch. In addition to accessibility of both the clutch and gearbox, the layout in Fig. 18.1 enables a shorter, and therefore lighter, final drive propeller shaft to be used, thus obviating potential problems associated with whirling and other vibrations.

The second variant entails incorporation of the gearbox into the back axle, to form what the Americans call a *transaxle* unit. For three main reasons, this arrangement is used only rarely: first, it tends to be significantly more costly than the others; secondly, it entails the use of either a dead axle or an axleless transmission as decribed in Section 8.3; thirdly, it is extremely difficult to mount a heavy transaxle in such a way as to accommodate the motions, torques, and forces of the input and output drive shafts yet to isolate it to prevent the transmission of noise and vibration to the vehicle structure.

With certain types of gearbox – notably epicyclic – the clutch action is performed within the gearbox itself, to which the drive from the engine is therefore transmitted either directly by a shaft or through a fluid coupling or torque converter. The shaft can be either separate or integral with the gearbox mechanism.

Live axles are built in several forms. That in Fig. 18.1 is called a *single-reduction axle*, because the reduction in speed between the propeller shaft and final drive is effected in one stage, in the final drive at g. In some heavy trucks, because the reduction ratio may have to be much higher, this reduction is done in two or even three stages, a *double-* or even *triple-reduction axle* being used.

18.2   Layout of rear-engine vehicles with live axles

The rear-engine and live axle arrangement has advantages for buses and coaches, primarily because it allows the floor to be set at a low level and to be flat and clear throughout virtually the whole length of the chassis. In Fig. 18.2 the engine and gearbox are built as a single unit, which is installed transversely behind the rear axle. The clutch is interposed between the engine and gearbox, while at the other end of this box is a bevel gear pair termed the *transfer drive*.

To transmit the drive to the rear axle, the driven gear of the bevel gear pair is coupled by a universal joint to a relatively short propeller shaft, which is similarly coupled at its other end to the pinion shaft of the final drive unit. Obviously, the shorter the propeller shaft, the greater is the angle through which it has to swing to accommodate the relative movements of both the engine on its mountings and the axle on its springs. Therefore, the final drive unit is incorporated at one side of the axle, instead of near its centre. The drive is turned through much less than 90° from the propeller shaft at both its final drive and transfer drive ends,

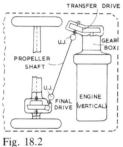

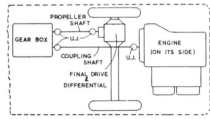

Fig. 18.2   Fig. 18.3

which simplifies the design of both pairs of gears. A difficulty with this layout is the accommodation of the long engine, gearbox and transfer drive within the overall width of the vehicle.

For this reason, several manufacturers have installed their engines longitudinally behind the rear axle. This layout has been adopted in Fig. 18.3, where the gearbox is mounted separately, in front of the axle. Because the universal joints on the coupling shaft between the engine and gearbox have to accommodate only relative movements due to deflections of the mountings and vehicle frame or structure – instead of movements of the axles – they can be of a simple type. Constant-velocity joints are needed, however, on the short propeller shaft.

In Fig. 18.4 again, separately-mounted transverse engine and gearbox units are employed, but the differential can be nearer to the centre of the axle. Disadvantages of all rear-engine installations include the lengths of the control runs from the driving position and the fact that the driver may not be able to hear the engine and judge its speed, for changing gear, especially in noisy urban traffic. The latter problem does not arise, however, if automatic transmission is used.

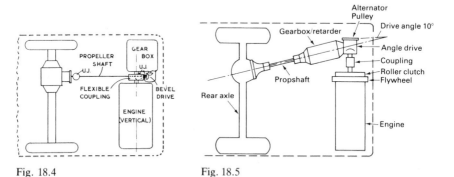

Fig. 18.4   Fig. 18.5

Transverse rear-engine installations obviously call for an angle drive, and several transmission manufacturers produce such a unit. It generally consists of a bevel gear pair in a casing that can be bolted on to the gearbox or engine and clutch or torque-converter assembly. In Fig. 18.5, a retarder – transmission brake – is incorported in the gearbox, which is bolted to the angle-drive casing. A coupling connects the angle drive shaft to the engine and clutch assembly in this MCW metrobus installation.

18.3 Dead axle and axleless transmission arrangements

An advantage of the dead-axle arrangement is a considerable reduction in unsprung weight, which improves both the ride and road holding. Incidentally, the suggestion that a rigid axle always holds its wheels perpendicular to the road is a fallacy – with many independent suspension systems, a bump under one wheel has the same effect on the angularity of both wheels as it would on only one.

Chain drive, Fig. 18.6, now rarely used, is one form of dead-axle transmission. The layouts of vehicles with chain drive are generally similar to those with transaxles, in that the gearbox and final drive unit are in one casing. So, from the engine and clutch, the drive is taken by a propeller shaft to the gearbox and ultimately, in the final drive G, is turned through 90° and divided equally between the two shafts J. At the outer ends of these shafts are the chain sprockets K, around which are the driving chains L for the chain wheels M, which are rigidly secured to the road wheels on the ends of the dead axle D.

Because there is a reduction in the speed of the road wheels owing to the different sizes of the chain sprocket and chain wheel, either a smaller reduction is needed in the final drive gear or, for example in very large tractors, an extra large overall reduction can be obtained. Relative movement between the axle and the frame, as the road springs flex, is accommodated by rotation of the loops of chains about the axes of the chain wheels and sprockets.

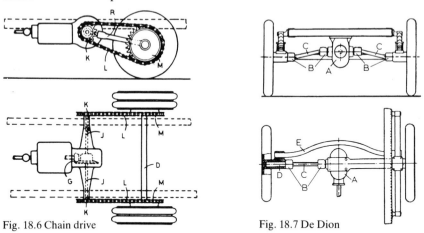

Fig. 18.6 Chain drive   Fig. 18.7 De Dion

Another, and more commonly used, dead-axle layout is based on that employed by the de Dion Company in their early cars, Fig. 18.7. It is most suitable for low cars with firm suspension, and therefore is favoured by some sports car manufacturers. This is partly because of its inherent suspension characteristics, which will be elaborated upon in Section 34.17, and partly because it is more suitable for limited quantity production than the admittedly better, independent rear suspension systems.

The transmission arrangements for the de Dion axle layout and for the axleless systems with independent suspension are similar. From the engine, clutch and gearbox, the drive is taken through a propeller shaft to a final drive unit A, which is mounted on the structure of the vehicle, instead of contained within the axle. Having been turned through 90° and divided equally between two short drive shafts C, it is then transmitted out to the wheels, which rotate on bearings carried in brackets fixed to the outer ends of the dead axle E, or to the suspension mechanism if an independent suspension system is used. Movements of the road wheels relative to the vehicle structure are accommodated by universal joints B at both ends of drive shafts C, and the corresponding variations in lengths – or telescoping – of the shafts C are obtained by making them in two parts joined by some form of splined or sliding coupling. The springs interposed between the dead axle E and the structure of the vehicle seat on the ends of the dead axle, generally on the same bracket that houses the wheel bearings. A de Dion system can also be used with a so-called *transaxle*, the only difference being the interposition of the propeller shaft between the clutch and transaxle unit instead of between the gearbox and final drive unit.

The main advantages of the de Dion layout as compared with a live axle, are that it relieves the axle of the weight of the differential and final drive unit and the wheels remain in a fixed relationship to each other – either parallel or with a slight inwards inclination towards the top, to resist rear-end drift when the vehicle is acted upon by centrifugal force on cornering. At the same time, the troubles involved in the use of chains are avoided.

One disadvantage is the shortness of the drive shafts, and consequently large angles, through which they move, which entails the use of fairly costly universal joints. Another is the fact that, when one wheel alone rises, the contact points between the two tyres and the road move sideways, which momentarily produces a slight, but marked, rear-end steering effect and therefore adversely affects stability and handling.

When there is no axle, the road wheel connections to the frame and the springing arrangements are made in the various ways described in Chapters 34 and 35. With some of these layouts, it is possible to dispense with the outer universal joints and with the sliding coupling on the shafts C.

A front engine and rear-wheel-drive layout with independent suspension is shown in Fig. 18.8. Although the engine, clutch and gearbox unit and the separate final drive unit are all carried on the frame, or basic structure, of the vehicle, universal or flexible joints are still used at the ends of the propeller shaft. This is to accommodate the slight differential movement that can occur between these two units because of deflections of both their flexible mountings and the structure of the vehicle. The forces on the mountings for the final drive unit are by far the greatest problem, owing mainly to reaction from the final drive torque. Loading associated with vibration isolation and supporting the weight of the unit under dynamic conditions is not nearly so severe and therefore calls for softer mountings.

An axleless transmission for a front-wheel-drive vehicle is shown in Fig. 18.9. This represents diagrammatically an installation in a car in which the engine is mounted longitudinally forward of the front wheels and the gearbox to the rear of them, the final drive being interposed between the two. The gearbox in this instance is of the all-indirect type, as described in Section 21.24. Consequently, its output shaft is below its input shaft, instead of the more common arrangement in which the two are in line. The pinion of the hypoid final drive unit is on the end of the gearbox output shaft and meshes with the crown wheel, which is bolted to the cage that carries the differential gears.

On each side the differential gear and crown wheel assembly is carried in bearings in the casing that houses the engine, clutch and gearbox unit. The very short shafts carrying the differential gears and projecting from this casing are coupled by universally-jointed drive shafts and sliding joints to the road wheels.

The transmission layout used in the BL *Mini* – as designed by Sir Alec Issigonis – is illustrated diagrammatically in Fig. 18.10. In both the engine and the gearbox, the axes of all the shafts are transverse relative to the longitudinal axis of the car, so spur gears transmit the drive from the driven member of the clutch, downwards to the input shaft of the gearbox.

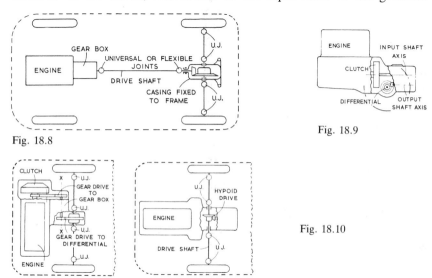

Fig. 18.8

Fig. 18.9

Fig. 18.10

Similarly, spur gears take the drive from the shaft at the output end of the gearbox to the final drive unit, which is positioned virtually on the longitudinal axis of the car. The gearbox is, in effect, in the engine sump, and the final drive unit immediately behind it but in the same casing. All three units share the same lubricant.

Both these front-wheel-drive layouts are suitable for small cars. That of the Mini is best of all though, because the whole of the space behind the final drive unit is available for unobstructed accommodation of the occupants. A disadvantage, in addition to the shortness, and therefore potentially wide angles swept by the driveshafts, is the inherently high stiffness of such a short drive line between the clutch and final drive. This may entail the incorporation of extra flexibility in the hub of the driven plate of the clutch, to obviate shock and harshness of take-up of the drive as the clutch is engaged. Another disadvantage is that the final drive torque, which is that of the engine, multiplied by the gearbox and final drive ratios, has to be reacted by the engine mountings, or special arrangements must be made to react it in some other way.

So far as effectiveness of traction is concerned, front-wheel-drive is better than rear-wheel-drive, especially on difficult terrain, including ice or snow. This is partly because the weight of the engine on the front wheels enables them to grip the surface better, which of course also applies to rear-engine rear-wheel drive vehicles. Principally, however, the advantage is gained by virtue of the fact that the tractive effort is in all circumstances delivered along the line on which the front wheels are steered. Another factor is that front driven wheels tend to climb out of holes or ruts, whereas rear driven wheels tend to thrust the front wheels deeper down and, in any case, not necessarily in the direction in which they are steered.

18.4   Four-wheel-drive transmission

A typical four-wheel-drive transmission layout is shown in Fig. 18.11. The engine, clutch and gearbox unit is conventional, but the transfer box – for transferring the drive to both the front and rear axles – is mounted behind it.

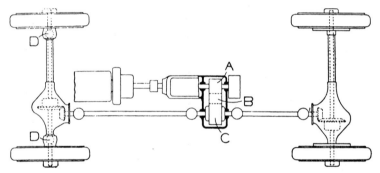

Fig. 18.11 General arrangement of four-wheel driven chassis

In this box is a pinion A, driven by a coupling from the gearbox output shaft. The pinion, through an intermediate gear B, drives a third gear C, mounted on the cage of a differential gear assembly. From the differential gears, one shaft is taken forward to the front axle and the other rearwards to the back axle. Both the axles house their own differentials and final drive gears, but that at the front carries at its outer ends the universal joints D, which are necessary to allow the front wheels to be steered.

The differential at C, in the transfer box, is necessary to distribute the drive equally between the front and rear axles and to allow for the fact that, when the vehicle is driven in a circle, the mean of the speeds of the front wheels is different from that of the rear wheels and therefore the speeds of the two propeller shafts must differ too.

Provision is usually made for locking this differential out of operation, to improve the performance and reliability of traction when the vehicle is driven on slippery ground. For vehicles intended mainly for operation on soft ground, the central differential may be omitted from the drive line, but some means of disengaging four-wheel-drive, leaving only one axle to do the driving, is generally provided for use if the vehicle is required to operate on metalled roads.

Since, as can be seen from Fig. 32.2, the steered front wheels always tend to roll further than the wheels on the fixed-geometry rear axle, because their radius of turn is always the larger, a one-way clutch, or freewheel (see Section 21.20) can be substituted for the inter-axle differential. When the driver wants four-wheel-drive, he gets out and rotates a locking device on the hub of each front wheel. As soon as he again drives his vehicle on firm ground, however, he must remember to unlock the hubs to allow the front wheels to roll freely their further distances than the rear ones. Should the rear wheels spin, on the other hand, and therefore rotate further than the front ones, the drive will automatically be transferred to the front wheels even if they are in the freewheeling mode.

In the locked condition, the overall-frictional resistance throughout the transmission is higher than in the two-wheel-drive state, and of course the transmission shafts and gearing will progressively wind up and become highly stressed so long as the wheels on the two axles are rolling different distances. On soft ground, when this wind-up becomes too high the wheels can slip and thus relieve the stresses, but this may not be possible on metalled roads, and a fractured shaft may be the result.

With independently-sprung wheels, the transmission is the same, except in that the final drive units are carried on the frame, or structure, of the vehicle. Consequently, universal joints have to be used on both ends of the drive shafts to the road wheels, as with the de Dion layout.

Four-wheel-drive offers two main advantages. First, there is the increased traction obtainable from four driven wheels, which is especially useful on soft or slippery ground. Secondly, if the front wheels drop into a ditch they tend to climb out, whereas with rear-wheel-drive they tend to be forced downwards, unless the vehicle is driven in reverse. Even in the latter event, only two-wheel-drive traction is of course available. The principal disadvantages are increased weight, bulk and cost.

Chapter 19

Clutches

Clutches are mechanisms which enable the rotary motion of one shaft to be transmitted at will to a second shaft, whose axis is coincident with that of the first. They are of two types –

(1) Positive clutches.
(2) Gradual engagement clutches.

In positive types the clutch is either 'in', so that the the two shafts are rigidly connected and must revolve at the same speed; or it is 'out', when the shafts are entirely disconnected. It is obvious, therefore, that this type of clutch is not suitable for use between the engine and gearbox. The positive clutch is used inside the gearbox, and in other places, and will be described later.

In gradual engagement clutches it is possible for one shaft to be revolving rapidly while the other is either stationary or revolving at a lower speed. As the engagement of the clutch proceeds the speeds of the two shafts gradually become the same, and when the clutch is fully engaged the shafts revolve as one. This is the type used between the engine and gearbox. In the motor car the gradual engagement clutch depends for its action upon the frictional force which acts between two bodies when they are pressed together. Such clutches are called *friction clutches*. There are, of course, hydraulic and other gradual engagement clutches employed in engineering, but since they are not used on motor cars they will not be described.

19.1 Principle of the friction clutch

Consider the two shafts A and B shown in Fig. 19.1. They are supported in bearings C and D and are free to rotate about the common axis XY. Keyed on to the ends of the shafts are circular discs E and F which face each other. Suppose the shaft A and its disc to be revolving while the shaft B and its disc are at rest, and let the two shafts be pressed together endways. Then as soon as the faces of the discs come into contact a frictional force will act between them tending to slow down the disc E and to speed up the disc F.

At first, when the force pressing the discs together is small, the frictional force may not be large enough to overcome the resistances to the motion of the shaft B, but if the force pressing the discs together is gradually increased the frictional force will increase also, until it is sufficient to overcome the resistances and cause the shaft B to move. That shaft will then gradually speed up until ultimately it will be going at the same speed as the shaft A, the clutch being then fully engaged.

Until the clutch is fully engaged the disc E is going faster than the disc F, so that slip is taking place between the faces of the discs. When the clutch is fully engaged the discs are rotating at the same speed and there is no slip between them.

This is the basic principle of all friction clutches. In motor car clutches a spring is used to press the discs together. The spring tends to keep the clutch always in engagement, and when it is desired to disengage the clutch the discs are separated by pulling one of them back against the pressure of the spring.

19.2 Torque transmitted

Suppose the spring used to press the discs together exerts a total force of P newtons, being the normal force between the discs, upon which depends the magnitude of the frictional force tending to prevent slip between them. The value of the frictional force will be $\mu \times P$ where μ is the coefficient of friction. This frictional force is the sum, or resultant, of a large number of small component frictional forces acting all over the surfaces in contact, which, in this case, it will be noticed are comparatively narrow rings near to the outsides of the discs. The resultant frictional force may be taken to act at the mean radius of the ring of contact and it will act, of course, tangentially. If the mean radius of the ring of contact is R metres, then, since the frictional force is $\mu \times P$ newton its moment about the axis of the shafts is $\mu \times P \times R$ newton metres, or Nm. This moment is the torque tending to stop the shaft A and to drive the shaft B, that is, it is the torque transmitted by the clutch.

If the ring of contact were not comparatively narrow there would be some inaccuracy in taking the resultant frictional force to act at the mean radius. By making the ring of contact very narrow, and thereby increasing its mean radius, the torque that the clutch can transmit will be increased. The ring must not be made too narrow, however, or the wear that occurs when the clutch is slipping during engagement will be excessive. While the area of the ring of contact affects directly the amount of wear that will occur, it only affects the torque that the clutch can transmit in that it affects the mean radius at which the frictional force acts.

The torque that a clutch can transmit depends therefore upon three factors: the coefficient of friction, the spring force, and the mean radius of the contact surfaces.

The coefficient of friction depends upon the materials composing the friction surfaces, and has a definite maximum value which cannot be exceeded. Constructional difficulties prevent the mean radius from being increased beyond a certain amount, and the spring force is limited to that which a driver can overcome without undue effort when provided with the maximum leverage conveniently possible. When all these three factors have been made as large as possible, a clutch of the elementary form considered would not transmit the large torques met with in large cars and lorries, and the constructional form of the clutch has to be modified so that it will transmit a greater torque. The basic principle involved remains the same, however.

The practical adaptations of this principle have resulted in three principal types of construction in motor car clutches. They are –

(1) Cone clutch.
(2) Single-plate or few-plate clutch.
(3) Multiple-plate clutch.

The cone clutch, however, is no longer used and the multiple-plate clutch is used only in certain epicyclic gearboxes but it has been thought advisable to retain descriptions of them for historical purposes and because cone clutches are used in the synchromesh mechanisms in gearboxes.

19.3 Cone clutch

In the cone clutch the contact surfaces of the members corresponding to the discs E and F are made portions of cones for a reason that will be explained later.

A typical cone clutch is shown in Fig. 19.2. The flywheel A is attached to the crankshaft by bolts passing through the web of the flywheel and a flange integral with the crankshaft. The male member is made in two parts, the cone B being bolted to the centre C by bolts D. This enables the cone to be mde of aluminium so as to secure lightness while the centre is made of steel to ensure the necessary strength. The composite male member is carried on the crankshaft spigot F, a bush E being provided. The spring G presses the male cone into the female cone of the flywheel. The spring reaction is taken through a ball thrust bearing on to the cover plate H which is bolted to the rim of the flywheel by a number of hexagon headed screws, two of which are seen in the drawing.

To disengage the clutch so that the engine no longer drives the gearbox shaft, the male cone is drawn back along the spigot F against the pressure of the spring. The faces of the cones are thereby separated and the flywheel no longer drives the male cone. If the latter comes to rest while the flywheel continues to revolve relative motion must occur either between the spring G and the male cone C or between the spring and the plug J. Actually it will occur between the last-named members because there is a ball thrust bearing between them. This bearing is essential as otherwise the friction would be considerable and it would be impossible entirely to disconnect the drive between the engine and gear box and, moreover, excessive wear would occur.

19.4 Reason for using cones

The reason for using cones for the engaging surfaces is to enable greater torques to be transmitted without having to employ extremely heavy clutch springs.

It has been seen that the frictional force between two surfaces depends upon the *normal* force between them. By using conical surfaces the normal force between them can be increased considerably without increase of spring pressure, because a wedging action is introduced. Referring to Fig. 19.3, the axial force P of the clutch spring gives rise to a normal force Q between the surfaces of the cones. This force Q is actually distributed all over the cone surfaces as a pressure. We may, however, so far as the frictional force is concerned, consider it to act at a point at the middle of the cone surface as shown. Now the only forces acting on the male cone in the axial direction are the spring force P and the axial component H of the normal force Q. This axial component must therefore be equal to the force P. The axial component H is obtained by drawing the triangle *abc*, in which *ac* represents the force Q, and *bc* the component *h*. Obviously Q is much greater than H and therefore than P.

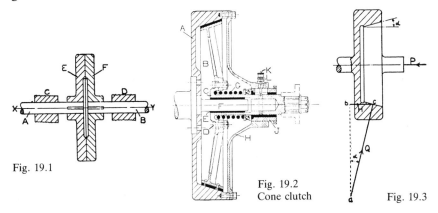

Fig. 19.1

Fig. 19.2
Cone clutch

Fig. 19.3

Usually the angle of the cone is such that H is about one-fifth of Q so that Q is about five times as large as P. The frictional force between the cones is equal to $\mu \times Q$, that is, equal to about $5 \times P \times \mu$ and the moment of the frictional force about the axis of the clutch is $5 \times P \times \mu \times R$ where R is the mean radius of the cones. If this mean radius is equal to the mean radius of the ring of contact in the elementary clutch shown in Fig. 19.1, and if the spring force and the coefficient of friction are the same in each clutch, then the cone clutch will transmit about five times the torque that is possible with the elementary clutch.

The angle of the cones cannot be made much smaller than about 20° because the male cone would tend to bind or stick in the female cone and the clutch would be difficult to disengage, and also because a small amount of wear on the cone surfaces would result in a considerable axial movement of the male cone, for which it would be difficult to allow.

19.5   Clutch linings

Cone clutches have been used in which the metal male cone engaged with the metal female cone thus giving a metal-to-metal contact. Such clutches were usually enclosed so that oil could be kept in them to lubricate the engaging surfaces. The oil, of course, reduced the coefficient of friction between the engaging surfaces, but made the engagement more progressive.

Most cone clutches ran 'dry', oil being kept away from the engaging surfaces and the male cone was covered with a friction fabric or a composition lining, so that the coefficient of friction was higher than with a metal to metal contact. The lining was secured to the male cone usually by means of copper or aluminium rivets which passed through both the lining and the rim of the cone as seen in Fig. 19.2. The rivet heads were sunk well below the surface of the lining so that they did not come into contact with the surface of the female cone.

19.6   Friction materials

There are two main types of friction lining, namely –

(1) Woven type.
(2) Moulded or composition type.

The first type is made by spinning threads from asbestos fibres, sometimes on brass wire, weaving this thread into a cloth and then impregnating it with a bonding material. This type of material can be sub-divided into two classes; (*a*) the laminated variety and (*b*) the 'solid' woven variety. The former consists of layers of cloth placed on top of each other and held together by the bonding material sometimes aided by stitching. The second variety is woven to the required thickness in one operation and the result, being an interlocked structure and not a layered one, has a much greater mechanical strength. Both types may incorporate metallic (usually brass) wire. This was originally used because it was impossible to spin asbestos fibres into a thread without using a metallic wire to provide strength but this is now possible and the wire is not always used. With the first three types of bond mentioned in Section 19.7 woven materials are usually used.

The moulded or composition type of lining is composed of asbestos fibres in their natural state mixed with a bonding material and then moulded in dies under pressure and at elevated temperatures. Metallic wires are sometimes included but only to increase the wearing qualities and to eliminate scoring of the metal faces against which the lining rubs.

19.7   Bonding materials

A very large number of different bonding matrials have been used but they can be roughly classified as follows –

(1) Asphaltic bases with additions of natural gums and oils.
(2) Vegetable gums.
(3) Rubber.
(4) Synthetic resins, (*a*) alcohol soluble.
                        (*b*) oil soluble.

The frictional properties of the materials depend chiefly on the bonding material and the above bonds have broadly the following characteristics –

(1) Coefficient of friction from 0.3 to 0.4 at any temperature up to about 250°C. The coefficient tends to rise at higher temperatures due largely to exudation of the bonding material. Higher coefficients can

be obtained by using excessive bonding material but such coefficients are not maintained after the excess of bond has been driven off by a rise of temperature. The wearing properties of materials (usually fabrics) impregnated with this bond are good, particularly when the product is die pressed.

(2) Coefficient of friction from 0.35 to 0.45 up to about 250°C. The wearing properties are rather better than type (1) but otherwise it has similar properties.

(3) The coefficient of friction can be made to have almost any value up to about 0.6 by the incorporation of filling materials and the vulcanisation of the rubber may be arranged to produce either a flexible or a rigid product. Both types tend to disintegrate under severe conditions, the flexible type being very bad in this respect. The rigid type has very destructive effect on the surfaces on which it runs. Both types are more affected by water than the other types of bond.

(4) (*a*) Coefficient of friction from 0.4 to 0.5 at any temperature up to about 230°C but at higher temperatures the coefficient falls off, *fades*, and may become as low as 0.1. This fading has been eliminated in some recent materials using this type of bond. This type of bond is not affected by lubricating oil and can withstand heavy pressures; it consequently finds a field of usefulness in epicyclic gearboxes, etc.

(4) (*b*) Coefficient of friction from 0.35 to 0.38 which is maintained at quite high temperatures. Vegetable gum and asphaltic bases are often used in conjunction with this type of bond. Both (4)(*a*) and (4)(*b*) have excellent wearing qualities.

The rubber-bonded materials are very little used.

While most asbestos friction materials will stand surface pressures up to 1380 kN/m² or more, such pressures are not often used in clutches although they may be approached in brakes. In clutches the surface pressure is usually about 100 to 200 kN/m². The fabric materials being more porous than the moulded materials will absorb oil more readily and though this makes the effect of very small quantities of oil less, the effect persists longer than with the moulded materials.

Cotton is occasionally used instead of, or mixed with, asbestos and such fabrics can be made to give high coefficients of friction, up to 0.6, but materials containing cotton cannot withstand a temperature exceeding about 150°C without being charred and ruined. They are used only for clutches. Cork is also used occasionally for clutches, almost always being arranged to run in oil. It has a coefficient of about 0.3 and surface pressures up to about 140 kN/m² may be used.

19.8 Single-plate clutch

A simple single-plate clutch is shown in Fig. 19.4, from which the principle of operation may be gathered. The flywheel is a simple disc with a thick rim having a flat face, into which are screwed six studs A. These studs carry a thick plate B, which is thus fixed to the flywheel as regards rotation; it is, however, free to slide axially along the studs. In between the plate B and the flywheel is situated the driven plate F; this is riveted to the flange of a hub G, which is connected with the clutch shaft C by splines E. When the parts are disposed as shown there is no tendency for the flywheel to turn the plate F, but if the plate B is moved along the studs so as to squeeze the plate F between itself and the flywheel the frictional forces set up between the surfaces in contact will prevent slip between them.

The necessary axial force is applied to the plate B by a number of springs which are usually arranged to surround the studs A. The latter are then provided with nuts as shown at the bottom of the figure. The face of the flywheel and the inner face of the plate B are sometimes lined with some form of friction fabric or composition, but usually the linings are riveted to the faces of the plate F. The latter arrangement has the advantage that the heat generated when the clutch is slipping during engagement is more easily dissipated, as it can be conducted directly away into the body of the flywheel and outer plate B.

In the former arrangement the heat has to pass through the linings before it can be absorbed and, as the linings are not good conductors of heat, the absorption and dissipation are not so rapid and the clutch will heat up more rapidly. On the other hand, the second arrangement increases the rotational inertia of the driven element which is undesirable; this does not outweigh the advantage obtained.

19.9   Torque transmitted

It will be observed that if slip occurs at one face of the plate F it must also do so at the other face, so that there are two frictional forces tending to prevent slip, each of which will be equal to μP where P, newtons, is the total spring force and μ the coefficient of friction. Each of the frictional forces acts at the mean radius of the ring of contact, so that if that radius is R metres the torque transmitted will be $2\mu PR$ newton metres (Nm).

To transmit the same torque as a cone clutch of equal overall diameter a single-plate clutch would generally have to be provided with a greater spring force because the wedging action of the cones is lost and also the mean radius of the ring of contact is, owing to constructional exigencies, smaller. The reduction due to these causes is offset by the fact that there are two frictional surfaces in the single-plate clutch as against the single surface in the cone type, but the net result is a reduction necessitating an increased spring pressure.

The spring pressure necessary may, however, be reduced by using more than one driven plate, as is done in the clutch shown in Fig. 19.5.

There are three driven plates which are riveted to hubs that are free to slide on the splined clutch and these are gripped between the flywheel, the pressure plate B and the intermediate plates. Thus there are six slipping surfaces and the clutch is able to transmit three times the torque that a similiar single-plate clutch having only two slipping surfaces could do. The intermediate plates are positioned on and are driven by square-headed pegs A A which engage slots formed in their peripheries. The pressure plate B is positioned and driven by three lugs C formed on the cover plate of the clutch and which engage three slots machined in the pressure plate. The force pressing all the plates together so as to transmit the drive is supplied by a single coil spring D; this bears at one end against the pressed steel cup E which seats in a hole in the cover plate, and at the other end against the housing F. Secured to the latter are three plungers G that are free to slide in holes in the cover plate and which engage the ends of the three levers H. These levers are pivoted on pins carried by small brackets J and, at their outer ends, they bear against renewable hardened pads fixed to the pressure plate. The force of the spring is thus increased by the

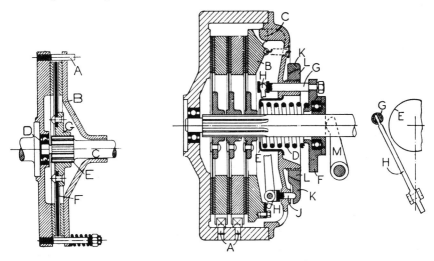

Fig. 19.4 Single-plate clutch   Fig. 19.5 Triple-plate clutch

leverage of the levers H. To ensure that all three of the levers press equally on the pressure plate the brackets J are not fixed in the cover plate but their stems are left free to slide in the holes in which they are placed and, at their outside ends, they bear against a disc K which seats on a spherical surface on the nut L. Because the disc K is free to rock in any direction on its spherical seating the forces acting on the brackets J, and hence the forces applied by the levers to the pressure plate, must be equal. The nut L, being screwed on the boss of the cover plate, enables the pressure plate to be adjusted bodily to the left to take up any wear that occurs. The clutch is disengaged by the withdraw fingers M which press against the inner member of the thrust race housed inside the member F, thereby pressing the latter to the left and relieving the pressure plate of the spring force. The pressure plate is pulled back by a number of small coil springs one of which can be seen at the top, and spring loaded levers, not shown, then separate the intermediate plates. The levers H are not arranged radially but as shown in the scrap end view where it will be seen that they pass to the side of the cup E; this enables a longer lever to be used than could otherwise be got in. In the figure the plunger G is shown out of its true position.

The use of a single spring in this manner is, however, no longer current practice.

19.10   Multi-spring single plate clutch

A typical clutch actuated by a number of coil springs on a pitch circle near its periphery is shown in Fig. 19.6. It is a Borg & Beck clutch, made by Automotive Products Ltd., and is for installation where the engine clutch and gearbox assembly form a single unit. The driven shaft, which normally is a forward extension of the gearbox primary shaft, is supported at its front end in a ball bearing in a hole in the centre of the web of the flywheel, which is spigoted and bolted on to a flange at the rear end of the crankshaft.

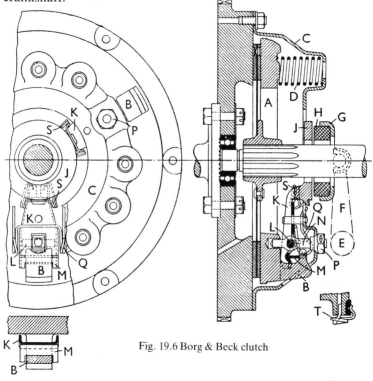

Fig. 19.6 Borg & Beck clutch

A pressed steel cover C, bolted to the rear face of the flywheel, houses the clutch mechanism. In this clutch, nine coil springs D, seating in pockets in the cover C, force the pressure plate A forwards, to clamp the driven plate between it and the rear face of the flywheel. Three lugs B extend rearwards from the periphery of the pressure plate through slots in the cover C, both to locate the pressure plate and to cause it to rotate with the rest of the assembly. The driven plate of course is splined on to the shaft.

When the clutch control pedal is depressed, to release the clutch, it rotates the spindle E, the ends of which are carried in bearings in the bell housing between the engine and gearbox. This causes a pair of fingers F, one each side of the driven shaft, to push the housing G, in which is the graphite-impregnated bearing ring H, forwards into contact with the annular plate J. The interconnection between the fingers F and the thrust bearing housing G is a pair of diametrically-opposite trunnions, which seat in slots in the ends of the fingers and are retained by the springs T, as shown in the scrap view, bottom right in Fig. 19.6. As the pedal is further depressed, plate J presses on the inner ends of the three levers K, causing them to swing about their fulcrum pins L, so that their outer ends push against the small struts M seating on lugs on the pressure plate. This pushes the pressure plate to the rear, against the influence of the nine coil springs, thus releasing the driven plate.

This arrangement of levers and struts, at first sight rather complex, is necessary for reducing to a minimum the friction in the system, which would otherwise make the clutch control action too stiff. The fulcrum pins L are carried in diametral holes in eyes in the bolts N. Nuts P on the ends of these eyebolts N seat in hemispherical depressions in the cover C, and springs Q press the ends of the levers constantly against the ends of the

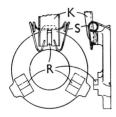

Fig. 19.7

struts M, to retain them. These struts cannot move laterally, because they are of a channel section into which the projections B register, as shown in the scrap view, bottom left in Fig. 19.6. From Fig. 19.7, it can be seen that lugs R, which project forwards from the annular plate J, in Fig. 19.6, register in slots in the ends of the levers K, where they are retained by the springs S, so these three levers constitute the sole support for the annular plate J.

When the clutch pedal is depressed, the three levers roll round their fulcrum pins, the eyebolts N of which are free to swing about the spherical seats of their retaining nuts P. At the same time, the struts M swing too, to accommodate the small radial motion that this rolling action implies. Obviously the friction in such a system is much less than if pivot pins were employed instead of the rolling contacts. As a further refinement, a bush of bearing bronze is in some instances carried in the holes into which the front ends of the eyebolts N project, to reduce to a minimum the friction between them and the pressure plate as it is pulled clear of the driven plate and flywheel.

On assembly in the factory, the nuts P are adjusted until the face of the plate J is truly perpendicular to the axis of the clutch. They are then staked over to lock the setting. If this adjustment is subsequently disturbed, new eyebolts N and nuts P must be fitted, otherwise faulty operation is virtually a certainty.

Among the various measures that in some instances have been taken by Borg & Beck to reduce friction in the clutch actuation system is the support of the eyebolts N in a three-arm spider bolted to the cover. This spider reacts the centrifugal force on the eyebolts, which would otherwise have to be reacted between their ends and the sides of the holes into which they project in the presser plate. For greater durability most vehicles now have a ball-thrust bearing instead of the carbon-impregnated ring H.

19.11　The diaphragm-spring clutch

At high rotational speeds, problems can arise with multi-spring clutches owing to the effects of centrifugal force on both the springs themselves and the levers of the release mechanism. These problems are obviated when diaphragm-type springs are used, and a number of other advantages are experienced.

Among these advantages is improved durability, which arises for three reasons. First, by virtue of the compactness of a diaphragm spring in an axial sense, a heavier pressure plate can be accommodated within the same overall length. This increases the thermal capacity of the clutch for absorbing heat generated by friction, so its working temperatures are lower. Secondly, it is easy to design a diaphragm spring so that it will maintain the optimum clamping pressure regardless of the degree of wear on the driven plate facings. Thirdly, the distribution of the clamping load over the facings is more uniform with a diaphragm spring.

Use of the diaphragm spring also reduces pedal loads. This is because of the deflection characteristics of the diaphragm as between the clutch engaged and released positions. Moreover, the total control-travel required for releasing such a spring is generally less than that for a coil spring clutch, and the friction in the moving parts increases less over the life of the clutch.

For a given size of clutch, the diaphragm-spring type has a higher torque capacity. This is partly because of the leverage obtainable due to the geometrical relationship between the diameter of the circle on which lay the ends of the fingers at the centre of the spring, Fig. 19.8(*d*), the diameter of the fulcrum ring G about which the spring pivots, and the diameter of the circle on which the spring applies its load, at J, to the presser plate. Another factor is the compactness of the diaphragm-type spring, as an energy store, and therefore the ability to provide a higher clamping load for any given size of clutch.

The inherent compactness for any given load is a major advantage of the diaphragm-spring clutch. Another is that there are fewer parts and so it is simpler in construction.

In this type of clutch, two examples of which are shown in Figs. 19.8 and 19.10, the basic form is the same as that of Fig. 19.4: the driven plate A, in Fig. 19.8(*a*), is clamped between the flywheel B and the pressure plate C, but the clamping is done by the single diaphragm spring D. This is a steel disc which, when unloaded, is of conical form as indicated in the upper half at (*b*). During assembly of the clutch on to the flywheel, the cover pressing E has to be forced axially, to close the gap *a*, during which the diaphragm is flattened, almost into a simple disc, as seen in the view (*a*). A number of slots are machined radially from the centre of the diaphragm as indicated at (*d*), thus forming the 'fingers'.

The spring is held between two circular wire rings G, which are carried on the shouldered pins F (nine in number) and which form a fulcrum for the diaphragm when the clutch is being disengaged. This is done by forcing the centre of the diaphragm to the left, so that it again becomes a cone but now with the apex, as in the lower half of (*c*). Spring clips S ensure retraction of the pressure plate when the spring pressure is thus removed.

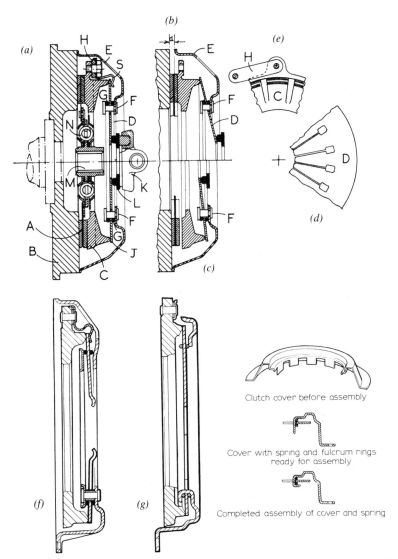

Fig. 19.8 (a) When assembled, the diaphragm spring is flattened. (b) Prior to assembly, the spring is of conical form, as in the top half here. (c) When assembled but disengaged, the apex of the spring is pushed over to the other side, as in the bottom half. (d) The spring has radially inward-pointing fingers. (e) One of the three straps linking the pressure plate to the cover. (f) Supported fulcrum ring in a Borg & Beck clutch. (g) Borg & Beck DST clutch

The method of centring and driving the pressure plate in this clutch is different from those used in the clutches described previously. Three strap links are used, one of which is seen at H in the views (*a*) and (*e*) of Fig. 19.8. These are pivoted at one end to the pressure plate and at the other to the cover pressing. The principle involved is shown in Fig. 19.9. The small axial movement for disengagement of the clutch is of course easily accommodated by the straps.

Disengagement is effected by the release bearing K which, in the illustration, is a graphite ring but which is more often a ball-thrust bearing. The graphite ring bears against the cast iron ring L, which is carried by three straps in the same manner as the presser plate, and which pushes the inner ends of the fingers of the diaphragm spring forwards to release the clutch. If a ball-thrust bearing is used, the ring L is usually replaced by the inner race of the bearing, the end face of which is appropriately rounded to form a similar section. The latter arrangement eliminates the need for both the ring L and its carrier straps, though the ball-thrust bearing is of course more costly than a graphite bearing.

In recent years, a number of improvements have been made to diaphragm-spring clutches. First, for heavy duty applications, especially for diesel engines, it has been found that the shouldered rivets F serve better if case-hardened. Secondly, these shouldered rivets were then replaced by plain rivets in hardened sleeves which served as distance pieces between the annular support plate and cover, and located the wire rings G and the diaphragm spring, Fig. 19.8(*f*). This arrangement provided continuous support around the whole periphery of the wire rings, improved the durability of the clutch and increased its efficiency, by reducing the deflections of the fulcrum rings.

Even better support for the fulcrum rings, together with economies in respect of both weight and cost, have been achieved in the Borg & Beck DST clutch. The initials 'DST' stand for *diaphragm spring and turnover*. Basically the clutch is the same as before, but the method of securing the fulcrum rings is as illustrated in Fig. 19.8(*g*). It has neither rivets nor annular support plate: instead, tags formed in the cover pressing are passed through the diaphragm spring and fulcrum rings, and then bent around them to complete the assembly. This has reduced the number of separate components by up to 19 and has saved about 0.5 kg on a typical clutch for a car, and the durability is even better than that obtainable from the best types of riveted design.

A further refinement has been a minor modification to the ends of the radial fingers of the diaphragm spring, which has had a major effect on

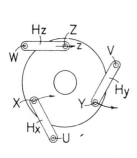

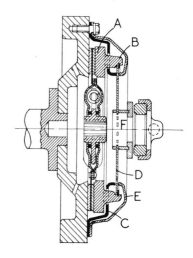

Fig. 19.9 (*above*)

Fig. 19.10 (*right*)

their durability. With the arrangement in Fig. 19.8, the radial sliding motion of the fingers over the rounded section of the ring L, or of the bearing race, together with sliding due to any slight eccentricity between the bearing and the drive shaft, causes wear of the ends of the fingers, ultimately forming a groove in each. Moreover, the eccentricity then causes chatter which is liable to loosen the rivets. To avoid these problems, the face of the ring L, or of the bearing, is now ground flat and the ends of the fingers curved, as shown in Fig 19.8(*f*). As a result of this simple modification the radial loading is greatly reduced and, because forming the curved ends of the spring fingers work-hardens them, they offer significantly higher resistance to wear.

The Laycock design of the diaphragm clutch is shown in Fig. 19.10. In this the pressure plate A is centred in relation to the flywheel, and is driven by six lugs B which fit into slots formed in the pressing C. The diaphragm spring D is carried in a recess formed inside the lugs and is kept in place by a circlip. The fulcrum for the spring is formed by the lips of the pressings C and E, which are bolted to the face of the flywheel. The diaphragm has 18 radial slots at its centre and the inner ends of the fingers thus formed engage the sleeve F which is pressed to the left by the clutch release bearing when the clutch pedal is depressed.

19.12 Pull type diaphragm-spring clutch

The rotating components of transmissions for heavy commercial vehicles are themselves heavy, and consequently synchronisation for gear shifting can take an unacceptably long time. To overcome this problem, a small brake is sometimes incorporated on the front end of the gearbox to stop free rotation of the primary shaft when the clutch is disengaged prior to selecting or changing a gear. Obviously it is advantageous if both control motions are in the same direction, so a release mechanism that is pulled instead of pushed to disengage the clutch has been introduced, Fig. 19.11. Then, the initial rearward motion of the clutch release bearing is utilised to disengage the clutch, and its further rearward motion to bring it to bear on a disc brake for stopping the rotation of the primary shaft. This enables the driver to use the brake at his discretion for the initial selection of bottom gear and for subsequent upward changes. Both single- and twin-plate versions of the pull type clutch are made, the latter being required for some tractors and for the powerful engines needed for the modern very heavy trucks.

As can be seen from the illustration, the periphery of the diaphragm spring bears on the fulcrum ring, while the diaphragm itself bears against a ring integral with the presser plate to hold the clutch in engagement. This arrangement has three advantages: first, by virtue of the proximity of the fulcrum ring to the rim of the cover of the AP clutch, it is inherently rigidly supported; secondly, less metal is required in the cover, which is therefore lighter and cheaper; thirdly, it is easier to obtain a high mechanical advantage for operation of the diaphragm spring which, for a heavy vehicle, of necessity has to be powerful. From the illustration it can be seen that, in the Fuller twin-plate clutch, the fulcrum ring is carried within the flywheel assembly.

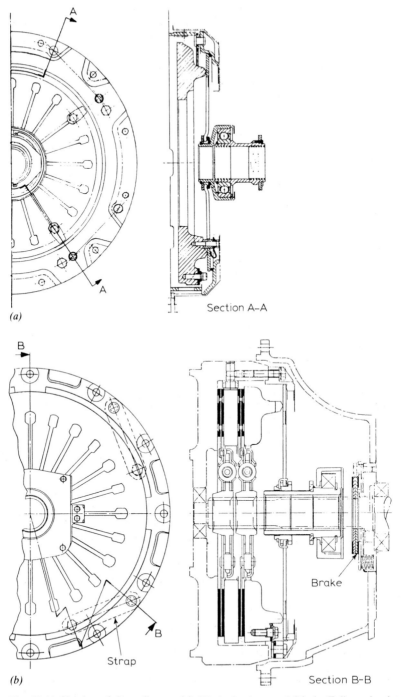

A

Section A–A

(a)

B

Strap

B

Brake

(b)

Section B-B

Fig. 19.11 Clutches of the pull type. (a) AP single-plate, and (b) the Fuller twin-plate. In (b) the details above the centre-line are of the 600 Series and those below it relate to the 900 Series

In the AP single-plate clutch, a Belleville, or disc-type, spring is interposed between the release bearing housing and the ends of the fingers of the diaphragm spring. This clamps the outer race carrier firmly enough to the fingers to prevent it from rotating but with a certain degree of resilience for accommodating the angular movement of the fingers. The rearward extension of the tubular component carrying the inner race of the bearing actuates the disc brake on the front end of the gear box.

19.13 Belleville direct-release clutch

The Borg & Beck direct-release clutch, with a Belleville spring – no fingers extending radially inwards – was first introduced for front-wheel-drive cars with transverse engines, the aim being to reduce to a minimum the space required, beyond the tail end of the crankshaft, for accommodation of the clutch. As can be seen from Fig. 19.12, the release bearing thrusts against a plate attached to the centre of the clutch cover, and both the driven and presser plates of the clutch are on the opposite side of the flywheel. The outer periphery of the Belleville spring seats in the cover, while its inner periphery pushes against a ring formed integrally on the flanged hub of the flywheel.

Movement of the clutch release bearing towards the flywheel thrusts the cover in the same direction, against the influence of the Belleville spring, and carries with it the presser plate on the remote side of the flywheel. This releases the driven plate, which was clamped between the presser plate and flywheel by the Belleville spring.

The advantages of this arrangement are its axial compactness and low rotational inertia. Its disadvantage is that the clamping and release loads are equal. This arises because of the absence of any leverage, which is obtainable only where radially inward extending fingers are incorporated as on the diaphragm type spring, so that a fulcrum can be provided.

19.14 Driven plate

With the traditional front-engine rear-wheel-drive car, the easiest way to overcome transmission noise problems at the prototype stage is, in most instances, to alter the flexibility of the propeller shaft. With front-wheel-drive cars, however, which have short, stiff drive-shafts, this option is no longer open. As a result, manufacturers have turned to adjustment of the flexibility of the driven plate of the clutch instead.

Originally, the spring centre was incorporated in driven plates solely to absorb shock-loading during engagement of the clutch. Now, however, more complex arrangements are used.

First, to ensure that the drive is taken up progressively, the centre plate, on which the friction facings are mounted, is crimped radially so that as the clamping load is applied to the facings the crimping is progressively squeezed flat. On the release of the clamping load, the plate springs back to its original radially-crimped section. This plate is also slotted so that heat generated does not cause the distortion that would be liable to occur if it were a plain flat plate – this plate of course must be thin, to keep rotational inertia to a minimum.

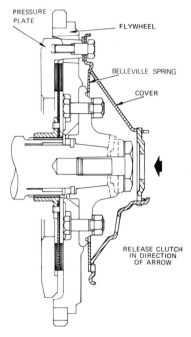

Fig. 19.12 (*left*) Direct-release clutch with
Belleville spring
Fig. 19.13 (*below*) Multi-plate clutch

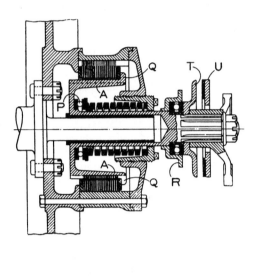

   Secondly, the plate and its hub are entirely separate components, the
drive being transmitted from one to the other through coil springs
interposed between them. These springs are carried within rectangular
holes, or slots, in the hub and plate, and arranged with their axes aligned
appropriately for transmitting the drive, as for example in Fig. 19.8. In a
simple design, all the springs – perhaps six – may be identical, but in more
sophisticated designs they are arranged in diametrically-opposite pairs,
each pair having a different rate and different end clearances in the holes
that accommodate them. The lowest rate pair have zero end clearance, and
therefore are the first to take up the loading. As this pair deflects and the
end clearances for the other pairs therefore begin to be taken up, the
second pair comes into operation, increasing the overall torsional rate,
until the third pair similarly is brought into play, still further reducing the
end clearances of any that remain, and increasing the rate, and so on. As
many as five stages have been used, though usually there are no more than
about three or four. As a further refinement, the flange around the hub is
clamped between the two slotted plates that house the springs, sometimes
with friction facings interposed between them, to provide a degree of
damping for this spring action.

19.15   Multiple-plate clutch

The multiple-plate clutch is now practically obsolete as a main clutch but is
still used in epicyclic gearboxes and one example, shown in Fig. 19.13, will
be briefly described. Bolted to the flywheel is a drum which on its inner
circumference is splined to carry a number of thin metal plates; these must
consequently revolve with the drum but are able to slide axially. Inter-

leaved with these outer plates is a number of inner plates that are splined to an inner drum A which is coupled rotationally to the gearbox shaft. This drum is supported on a spigot extension of the crankshaft, a suitable bearing bush being provided. Between the web of the inner drum and a sleeve screwed into the cover plate of the outer drum is a strong coil spring. The inner drum is thus pressed to the left and, being provided with a flange Q, it squeezes the outer and inner plates together so that friction between them transmits the driving torque from the outer drum to the inner one. The clutch is disengaged by pulling the inner drum to the right against the pressure of the spring. The fingers of the withdraw shaft bear against the flange R of the housing of the clutch withdrawal thrust race. A ball bearing P eliminates friction between the spring and the inner drum when the clutch is disengaged. The screwed cup at the right-hand end of the spring enables the spring force to be adjusted. The plates of multiple-plate clutches were at one time made alternately of steel and phosphor bronze but now are all of steel or one set may be lined with a friction material. With metal to metal contact lubrication is essential and so the clutch is made oil-tight and is partly filled with oil. The oil tends to make the plates drag when the clutch is disengaged and so a clutch stop or brake is fitted. It consists of a disc T fixed to the inner drum hub and which comes into contact with a spring loaded disc U carried by any convenient part of the gearbox casing or clutch housing; the disc U has a friction material lining.

19.16 Dry multiple-plate clutches

Multiple-plate clutches are also made to work dry, that is, without any oil. The driving plates are then lined on each side with a friction fabric. In such clutches the driving plates are sometimes carried on a number of studs screwed into the web of the flywheel in the same way as the outer plate of a single-plate clutch is sometimes carried. This construction is inconvenient when oil is used. Several small springs can be used instead of a single spring.

19.17 Clutch release gear

The disengagement of almost all clutches involves the axial movement of a shaft or sleeve that is rotating and this involves the use of a bearing that will permit the motion and transmit the force. A ball bearing is frequently used and is nowadays a dual-purpose bearing capable of supporting both axial and radial loads. In the past bearings which could support only axial loads were used, an example being shown in Fig. 19.13, and the housing R of the bearing had itself to be supported by letting it bear on the clutch shaft. Instead of a ball bearing a graphite block bearing may be used, as has been mentioned, and in this case the housing of the block can itself be supported by the fingers which transmit the axial thrust as is shown in Fig. 19.6. Referring to that Figure the shaft E has to be connected to the clutch pedal and this used to be done by means of links and rods, a method that is still sometimes used in commercial vehicles. But the drawbacks to such a linkage are that it would be difficult to arrange it in modern vehicles where the clutch and the clutch pedal are not conveniently near to each other and that, because the engine is carried on the frame or body structure on rubber mountings and the clutch pedal is mounted on a separate part of the body or frame, the relative movements that occur between these two units give rise to poor engagement of the clutch and also to rattles. Hydraulic actuation of the clutch is therefore now used. The units employed are similar to those used for brake actuation and which are described in Chapter 30. The pedal actuates a piston which forces fluid through piping into an actuating cylinder carried on the bellhousing surrounding the clutch and whose piston is connected to a lever carried by the shaft on which the withdraw fingers are fixed. Part or all of the piping can be made flexible and thus both of the difficulties associated with mechanical linkages are obviated.

19.18   Clutch brakes or stops

When a clutch is disengaged while the engine is running the inertia of the driven member will tend to keep it revolving. This inertia is proportional to the weight of the member and to the square of the 'radius of gyration' which is the equivalent radius at which the weight may be considered to act. Since this tendency to continue revolving rendered gear changing difficult, small brakes have been arranged to act on the driven member when the clutch was *fully* withdrawn. The stop member or brake was sometimes backed up by springs so that a gradually increasing pressure acted on the brake. One of the advantages of the single-plate clutch is the small weight and radius of gyration of its driven member.

19.19   Automatic clutch action

Many attempts have been made to produce motor vehicles that can be controlled by the accelerator pedal and brakes only; this can be done in several ways. A centrifugal clutch which automatically disengages itself when the speed falls below and which re-engages when the speed rises above some predetermined values may be used. Alternatively, a fluid coupling, a fluid torque converter or some special form of clutch may be employed. Examples of each of these solutions of the problem will be described in the following Sections.

19.20   Centrifugal clutches

The principle of these is shown in the simple arrangement in Fig. 19.14(*a*) where a single-plate clutch of ordinary construction has its presser plate A actuated by the 'centrifugal' forces acting on masses B formed on the ends of bell-crank levers pivoted on pins in the cover plate C. This arrangement has two principal drawbacks. Firstly, there would be some force acting on the presser plate whenever the clutch was rotating and thus the clutch would never be completely disengaged. Secondly, if the force P due to the centrifugal force CF were sufficient to engage the clutch fully at say 1000 rev/min then it would become nine times as great at 3000 rev/min and it would require nine times the force necessary with an ordinary clutch to produce disengagement at that higher speed by pulling the presser plate back in the ordinary way, and it is desirable to be able to disengage the clutch in that way.

The first drawback can be overcome by putting in springs D (shown dotted) which apply a force Q opposing the force P. The centrifugal forces will then not give rise to any pressure on the driven plate until they have increased sufficiently to overcome the force Q and until then the clutch will be completely disengaged. By choosing the magnitude of Q suitably, the commencement of the engagement can be made to occur at any desired speed. Usually in motor car clutches a speed of about 500 rev/min is chosen. The second drawback can be overcome by modifying the construction as shown at (b) where the bell-crank levers press on a floating plate E between which and the presser plate are placed springs F. These springs transmit the force P from the floating plate to the presser plate. A stop G limits the outward motion of the masses B and thus limits the amount the springs F can be compressed. The force that must be applied to the presser plate in order to pull it back so as to disengage the clutch is now limited to the difference between the force Q and the force exerted by the springs F when the masses (having come against the stops G) have compressed them

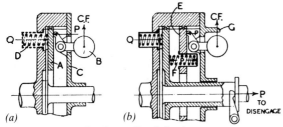

Fig. 19.14 Principle of centrifugal clutch

fully. This difference can be made to have any desired value. The pressure exerted on the driven plate will now be represented by a graph whose shape is the shaded line in Fig. 19.15. The curve OLMH whose ordinates are measured from the line OX as axis shows how the centrifugal force varies with speed. If a new axis O_1X_1 is drawn so that OO_1 equals the force Q exerted by the springs D then the graph O_1LH measured from O_1X_1 gives the pressure on the driven plate when the springs D are fitted. Finally, if the line MN is drawn so that its height above OX is equal to the force exerted by the springs F when fully compressed the graph O_1LMN will represent the pressure on the driven plate in the modified arrangement of Fig. 19.14(b). This is what is desirable for the variation of pressure with speed, that is, no pressure at speeds below about 500 rev/min, a rapid increase of pressure between 500 rev/min and about 1000 rev/min so that at the latter speed the clutch is fully engaged, and no great increase in pressure at speeds above 1000 rev/min. In Fig. 19.15, S is the force that must be used to disengage the clutch at speeds over 1000 rev/min and R the force required to enable the clutch to transmit full engine torque. If the torque developed by the engine is less than full torque (that is, if the throttle is not wide open) then a force less than R will enable that reduced torque to be transmitted and the clutch will be fully engaged at some speed less than 1000 rev/min.

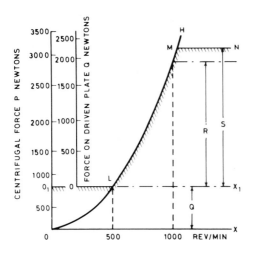

Fig. 19.15 Centrifugal clutch characteristic

19.21   Eddy current couplings

The constructional form of one of these is shown in Fig. 19.16. There are two main members, A and B, which are coupled respectively to the engine crankshaft and the input shaft of the gearbox. The member A resembles and, if required can form, the flywheel but its rim is cut away by a number of semicircular recesses as shown in the view (*a*). The metal left between the recesses forms a series of axial bars – connected together at their ends by the continuous portions of the rim. The member A thus resembles the rotor of a squirrel-cage electric motor.

The shape of the outside of the member B is shown in the view (*b*). There is an electrical winding running round the annular space C and the ends of this winding are connected to slip rings D and E on which stationary brushes bear, so that current can be passed through the winding from a battery or generator. When this is done, a magnetic field is built up whose direction will be as shown by the dotted line. The field will take this path rather than pass from the fingers F to the fingers G because the air-gap between these fingers is large compared with the gap between the members A and B and the magnetic 'resistance' or reluctance is consequently less through the latter.

If the member A now rotates relative to B, the magnetic flux will cut the bars of the member A and eddy currents will be generated in that member. There will consequently be a magnetic drag between the members which will tend to make B rotate in unison with A. Some difference of speed will, however, always exist because if there were no such difference, there would be no eddy currents and no drag.

The torque that can be transmitted from A to B depends on the difference in speed that exists between them, on the magnitude of the exciting current (up to that value which will produce saturation of the magnetic circuit) and on the size of the coupling. When transmitting the full designed torque, the difference in speed will usually be about 3% of the speed of the driving member. The variation of the percentage slip (i.e.,

100 × (speed of A − speed of B)/(speed of A)) with the torque transmitted and for two values of the magnitude of the excitation current is shown in Fig. 19.16(*c*). The take-up characteristics of this type of coupling are very similar to those of a fluid coupling (see Section 19.25). Take-up is brought about by increasing the speed of the driving member and by controlling the value of the excitation current.

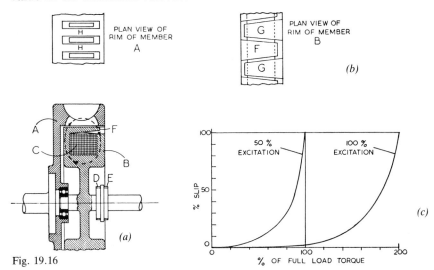

Fig. 19.16

It should be noted that the output torque from the coupling is for all practical purposes equal to the input torque so that the device is the equivalent of a clutch and not of a gearbox or torque converter. Couplings of this kind are largely used in industrial applications and have been employed in a few automobile vehicles. By fixing the member B relative to the chassis and by driving the member A off the propeller shaft, the device can be used as a brake and this has been done to some extent in heavy lorries.

19.22 The Ferlec electro-magnetic clutch

This is basically a single-plate friction clutch in which the clamping force is provided by an electro-magnet instead of by springs. Its construction is shown in Fig. 19.17, the driven plate A has a spring damper hub which is splined on the output shaft B. The latter is carried in a spigot bearing at the left and in a bearing in the gearbox at the right. The pressure plate C is bolted to an armature disc D which itself is secured to the flywheel by three tangentially disposed links K, as shown in the scrap end view. These links isolate the flywheel from the armature disc magnetically while positioning it and causing it to rotate with the flywheel. The links K also permit the small axial movement required for the engagement of the clutch. There is an air-gap of 0.45 mm between the armature and the face of the flywheel when the clutch is disengaged. When the winding F is energised the armature D with the pressure plate C is attracted to the flywheel so that the driven plate is squeezed between the pressure plate and the member G, which is rigidly bolted to the flywheel at three points, as indicated in the scrap end view at the bottom of the figure. The current for energising the winding is led in and out through brushes which bear on slip rings H and I, connected to the ends of the winding.

To provide a smooth engagement the energising current is made to build up gradually, either automatically as the dynamo speed increases or, when the battery supplies the current, by two variable resistances (one for low and one for high gears) which are decreased as the accelerator is depressed. The change from one resistance to the other is made by the

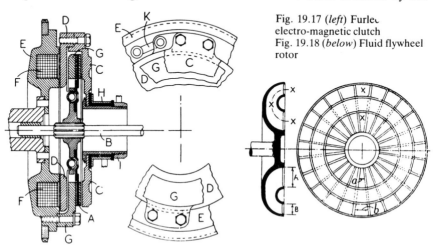

Fig. 19.17 (*left*) Furleⅽ electro-magnetic clutch
Fig. 19.18 (*below*) Fluid flywheel rotor

selecting movement of the gear lever, the striking motion of which also provides an interruption of the current to the clutch coil and gives the momentary clutch disengagement to enable a gear change to be made. A cam actuated by the accelerator pedal also opens a switch when the pedal is in the idling and starting position, thus ensuring disengagement of the clutch at starting and during idling.

19.23   Fluid flywheel

This consists of two castings (called *rotors*), almost identical in form, one of which is fixed to the crankshaft of the engine and the other to the gearbox shaft. These castings are roughly circular discs in which passages XX (Fig. 19.18) are formed. Since the areas of these passages perpendicular to their centre line (XXX in the sectional view) must be kept approximately constant and since the circumferential width of the opening a is less than that of b the radial size of the opening A is made greater than that of B. In a simplified form the passages may be represented by tubes A and B with right-angled corners as shown in Fig. 19.19.

Imagine these tubes to be full of fluid and suppose them to be rotating about the axis XX with speeds N and n. Then if the outer end of the tube A were closed by a diaphragm C the fluid would be exerting a pressure P_a on that diaphragm, and this pressure can be shown to be proportional to N^2. Similarly, if the tube B were closed by a diaphragm D the fluid would be exerting a pressure P_b on that diaphragm. Now if n is less than N the pressure P_b will be less than the pressure P_a and if the diaphragms were removed the fluid in the tube A would commence to flow in the direction of the arrow E and would force the fluid in the tube B to flow in the direction of the arrow F against its inclination to flow the other way. Thus if the speeds N and n are unequal, the fluid in the tubes will be caused to circulate round and round. If N is greater than n then the circulation will be as indicated by the arrows E and F, that is, clockwise, but if n were greater than N then the circulation would be in the opposite direction and if the speeds of the rotors were equal there would be no circulation at all. Since there will always be some resistance to the flow of the fluid the speed at which the fluid will circulate will reach a steady value which can be shown to be proportional to the difference betweeen N^2 and n^2. Of course, if the speeds of the rotors are not equal then any particular tube A will not always be opposite any particular tube B but there will always be a tube B for the fluid from any tube A to flow into although there may be a certain amount of impinging of the fluid on the walls of the tubes, that is, on the webs of metal between the passages XXX in Fig. 19.18.

Having seen that a difference in the speeds of the two rotors will cause a circulation of the fluid from one rotor to the other it can now be explained how the energy developed by the engine is transmitted to the gearbox. Consider Fig. 19.19. At K is indicated a particle of fluid which is at a distance r from the axis XX. This particle has to rotate in a circle radius r with the angular speed of the tube, that is, N. Its linear speed in the circle is thus $2\pi rN$ and its kinetic energy is

$$\tfrac{1}{2} \frac{w}{g} (2\pi r) N^2$$

where w is the weight of the particle.

Now if the fluid is circulating as described above (N being assumed greater than n) the particle K will, in a short space of time, arrive at L. It will then be rotating in a circle whose radius is R at the speed N and its kinetic energy will be

$$\tfrac{1}{2} \frac{w}{g} (2\pi RN)^2.$$

Since R is greater than r the kinetic energy of the particle when it arrives at L is greater than it was at K. The increase in the kinetic energy of the particle as it moves from K to L is derived from the energy developed by the engine, the whole of which is utilised in increasing the kinetic energy of the fluid as it flows from the centre to the outside of the tubes A.

Continuing our consideration of the particle we find that a short time after it was at L it will have arrived at M. It will then be rotating in a circle radius R as at L but now at the slower speed n. Its kinetic energy is now

$$\tfrac{1}{2} \frac{w}{g} (2\pi Rn)^2$$

and since n is less than N the kinetic energy at M is less than it was at L. Some of this difference in the kinetic energy will have been passed to the rotor B but some will have been converted into heat by impact with the webs of metal between the tubes and will for all practical purposes be lost.

Finally, a short time after the particle was at M it will have arrived at N where it will be once more rotating in a circle of radius r but now at the speed n. Its kinetic energy will be

$$\tfrac{1}{2} \, \frac{w}{g} \, (2\pi r n)^2$$

and is less than it was at M. Thus, as the particle moves from M to N it loses kinetic energy and the energy it loses is passed to the rotor B and thus to the gearbox.

19.24 Prevention of leakage

It has been tacitly assumed that the fluid cannot escape between the faces of the rotors and it might be thought that those faces would have to be in rubbing contact in order to prevent such leakage. In actual fact, however, there is a gap of about 1.5 mm between the faces and escape of the fluid is prevented by making one rotor with a cover which embraces the other rotor as will be seen in Fig. 19.20.

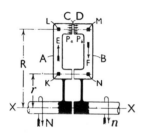

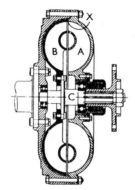

Fig. 19.19 (*above*)

Fig. 19.20 (*right*)

The relative position of the rotors has been changed in that Figure to correspond with the disposition generally adopted in fluid flywheels for motor vehicles. The rotor that is fixed to the flywheel is now the right-hand one A which is bolted to the rim of the flywheel while the left-hand rotor B is fixed to the gearbox shaft C. Fluid does escape between the faces of the rotors and fills the space between the outside of the rotors and the inside of the flywheel. Centrifugal force keeps this fluid in position and maintains a pressure at X which prevents escape of fluid from the insides of the rotors once sufficient fluid has accumulated outside to enable a state of equilibrium to be reached.

19.25 Characteristic of the fluid flywheel

The characteristic which is of chief importance is the way in which the *percentage slip* varies with the speed of rotation. The percentage slip is defined as the quantity $(N-n) \times 100/N$ and is a measure of the difference in the speed of the two rotors. If n were equal to N then the percentage slip would be zero and if n were zero then the percentage slip would be 100.

When the percentage slip is plotted against engine speed (*N*) the resulting graph is of the form shown in Fig. 19.21. At any speed less than about 600 rev/min (this speed can be made to have any desired value by suitably modifying the design) the percentage slip is 100, that is, the gearbox shaft is stationary and we have the equivalent of a completely disengaged clutch. As the engine speed increases from 600 to 1000 rev/min the percentage slip falls rapidly to about 12. This corresponds to the period of actual engagement of an ordinary clutch, the speed of the gearbox shaft being rapidly brought up to roughly the same value as the engine speed. From 1000 rev/min up to the maximum speed the percentage slip decreases comparatively slowly from 12 down to possibly as little as 2. The percentage slip at any engine speed depends, however, on the torque being transmitted, the curve above being based on the assumption that the engine exerts full torque at every speed. If the engine torque is reduced below the full torque (open throttle) value then the percentage slip will be reduced. Thus under easy running conditions when the throttle is only

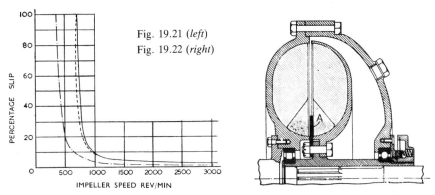

Fig. 19.21 (*left*)
Fig. 19.22 (*right*)

slightly opened the percentage slip may be less than 1%. The chain dotted curve indicates the variation of the percentage slip with the speed for such conditions, that is, level road and no head wind. Whatever the value of the percentage slip, however, it represents a direct loss of energy and thus an increase in the petrol consumption. Thus it is an abuse of the fluid flywheel to allow the engine speed to fall to the region between 1000 and 600 rev/min, full throttle, when the percentage slip becomes considerable and such use is comparable to the slipping of an ordinary clutch, which also increases the petrol consumption, the difference being that whereas an ordinary friction clutch would be damaged by prolonged slipping the fluid flywheel will not suffer any damage although it may become so hot as to burn one's hand if one touches it.

19.26 'Open circuit' fluid coupling

In an alternative design of fluid flywheel the 'torus-ring' that forms the inner wall of the passage round which the fluid circulates is omitted, as is shown in Fig.19.22. A baffle plate, as shown at A, is also sometimes fitted. The open circuit and baffle ring modify the characteristics of the coupling slightly as may be seen from the dotted curve in Fig. 19.21. The most important difference is a reduction in the drag torque when the coupling is stalled.

Figs. 19.23 and 19.24 illustrate the modern forms of seal used with fluid couplings and torque converters. The sealing surfaces are the flat faces of a steel ring C and a bronze or graphite ring D which are pressed together by a spring or springs E. The sealing faces are finished to optical limits of flatness and to ensure proper seating one ring is carried on a flexible diaphragm or bellows F. The design shown in Fig. 19.23 takes up less axial but more radial space than that of Fig. 19.24. In the latter the graphite ring D is left free to float between the metal faces on either side of it.

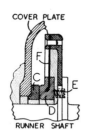

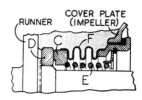

Fig. 19.23 (*left*)

Fig. 19.24 (*right*)

It can be shown quite easily that the torque exerted by the flywheel on the gearbox shaft is equal to the torque exerted by the engine on the fluid flywheel.

Thus the fluid flywheel does not give any increase of torque and is not the equivalent of a gearbox, the chief function of which is to give an increase of torque when required.

In addition to giving accelerator pedal control the fluid flywheel also reduces the shocks transmitted by the engine to the transmission and *vice versa*.

The qualities required of the fluid are high density, low viscosity, chemical stability and absence of corrosive action and the fluid that is generally used is a very thin engine oil. A thick, viscous oil would increase the percentage slip, other factors being the same, and would thus reduce the efficiency.

The only important drawback of the fluid flywheel is that even when the percentage slip is 100%, there is a drag on the gearbox shaft which renders gear changing with ordinary types of gearbox very difficult. Consequently, the fluid flywheel is generally used in combination with epicyclic gearboxes which eliminate the difficulty. In the fluid coupling made by MAAG of Zurich and used in the automatic gearbox of their design, the driven member is carried on the output shaft on a quick-pitch screw thread so that, when the speed of the driving member falls below that of the driven member, and the latter therefore tends to drive the former, the driven member is itself 'unscrewed' along the thread and moves away from the driving member. This reduces the drag in the coupling and assists in the gear changing.

When it is desired to use an ordinary type of gearbox a friction clutch is sometimes used in conjunction with a fluid flywheel. This clutch is intended to be used only for gear changing and not for taking up the drive during starting and acceleration of the car; it can therefore be made with smaller friction surface areas than a clutch that had to take up the drive but it must, of course, be capable of transmitting the full engine torque. However, if the engine is accelerated with the friction clutch disengaged and then the clutch is engaged it will have to take up the drive. To obviate this misuse of the clutch it may be interconnected with the accelerator pedal so that the latter cannot be depressed while the clutch is disengaged.

19.27 Fluid-friction clutch

The losses that occur in fluid couplings due to the continuous slip at normal running speeds are eliminated in a combination of fluid coupling and centrifugal clutch made by Self-Changing Gears Ltd. of Coventry, and called by them the *fluid-friction clutch*. Its construction is shown in Fig. 19.25. The impeller A is bolted to the flywheel and the driven member C is fixed to the output shaft D in the usual way. A spider E is also fixed to the shaft D and carries four shoes F lined with friction fabric. These shoes are pivoted on pins carried in blocks H which are free to slide radially in slots formed in the flange of the spider E. At low speeds the shoes are held out of contact with the inside of the flywheel B by a spring J, which encircles flanges formed on the shoes, but when the speed rises beyond a certain

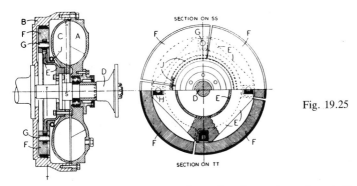

Fig. 19.25

value, the shoes move outwards under the action of centrifugal force and engage the flywheel. The slip between the latter and the driven shaft D is thereby reduced to zero. Thus the smooth take-up of the fluid coupling is retained but the continuous slip associated with it is eliminated. The shoes can be mounted on their pivots so that they either trail or lead (see Section 30.5).

19.28 Connection between the clutch and gearbox

The driven members of the clutches shown in Figs. 19.2 and 19.13 are fully supported by the spigot bearings provided within the clutch. The driven members therefore revolve about the same axis as the crankshaft, and they have to be coupled up to the gearbox shaft.

If a *rigid* coupling is used to join two shafts which have to revolve, it is essential that the axes of the shafts shall always coincide. Otherwise very heavy loads will be imposed on the bearings supporting the shafts and on the shafts themselves.

When the engine and the gearbox are independently mounted on the frame it is impossible to ensure that the axes of their shafts, which have to be coupled together, shall always coincide. Although initially the shafts may be *in alignment*, as it is termed, unavoidable flexures of the frame will upset that alignment. A rigid coupling cannot then be used; the coupling must be able to allow for the alignment. The latter may be of two kinds, an angular displacement as in Fig. 19.26, or a bodily displacement as in Fig. 19.27.

The first kind of misalignment can be allowed for by using either a flexible coupling or what is known as a *universal joint*. These will be dealt with in Chapter 24. The second kind of misalignment necessitates the use of two such joints and a short intermediate shaft as shown in Fig. 19.27. When the engine and the gearbox are separate units, therefore, the driven member of the clutch, or the clutch shaft, will be coupled to the gearbox by an intermediate shaft with a flexible or universal joint at each end.

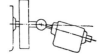
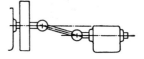

Fig. 19.26 (*left*)
Fig. 19.27 (*right*)

When the gearbox is made integral with, or is rigidly bolted to the crankcase of the engine, so as to form a single unit with the latter, it is possible to ensure the permanent coincidence of the clutch and gearbox shaft axes. Those shafts may then be coupled by a rigid coupling, but usually the clutch shaft will be one with the gearbox shaft. In that case the single clutch gearbox shaft will be supported at one end in the spigot bearing of the clutch and at the other end in the gearbox bearings. The clutches shown in Figs. 19.5, 19.8 and 19.10 are intended to be used in this manner.

Chapter 20

Object of the gearbox

In order to explain the object of the gearbox it will be necessary to consider briefly the resistances to the motion of a vehicle. When a car is moving along a road at a uniform speed there are various forces opposing its motion, and in order to keep it moving at that speed a driving force or *tractive effort* (TE) equal to the sum of all the opposing forces has to be applied to it. If the tractive effort should exceed the sum of all the resistances then the excess tractive effort will accelerate the vehicle. On the other hand if the tractive effort is less than the sum of the resistances then the excess of the resistances will decelerate the vehicle.

The forces opposing the motion can be divided into the following three groups –

(1) Air, or 'wind', resistance.
(2) Gradient resistance.
(3) Rolling resistance.

20.1   Air resistance

The air offers a resistance to the passage of bodies through it. This resistance depends on the size and shape of the body, and upon its speed through the air. Thus, the resistance to the motion of an airship that is stream-lined is very much less than it would be for a simple cylinder with flat ends. However, the effect of the shape and size of a vehicle on its air resistance need not be considered here, because for any given vehicle the shape and size are fixed quantities. The effect of speed on the air resistance must, however, be considered, and this is illustrated in Fig. 20.1, which is a graph of air resistance plotted against speed. It will be seen that when the speed is zero the resistance is zero and that as the speed increases so does the air resistance, the rise being at an increasing rate as the speed gets higher. In practice the air resistance is taken to vary as the square of the speed, so that if the speed is doubled the resistance is increased four times.

It should be clear from the graph that for slow-speed vehicles, such as farm tractors, the air resistance will be very small and may be neglected, but with high-speed vehicles it becomes important. In racing cars it is of paramount importance.

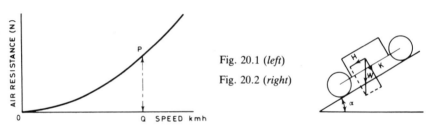

Fig. 20.1 (*left*)

Fig. 20.2 (*right*)

Since it is the speed of a vehicle through the air that determines the air resistance, the latter may be considerable even for lorries if a strong head wind prevails.

20.2   Gradient resistance

Fig. 20.2 shows a car standing on a gradient, and it will be seen that the weight of the car, which of course acts vertically downwards, can be resolved into two components H and K. The component K is perpendicular to the road surface and the component H is parallel to that surface. To prevent the car from running down the gradient a force equal and opposite to H must be applied to it, while if the car is being propelled up the hill part of the driving force goes to neutralise the force H. That force is an additional resistance to the motion of the car and may be called the *gradient resistance*. It depends simply on the steepness of the gradient and the weight of the car. It is not affected by the speed of the car up the gradient.

20.3   Rolling resistance

Under this heading are included all the remaining external resistances and also, sometimes, the internal frictional resistances of the transmission system. However, in what follows the latter is not so included and, if not neglected altogether, is dealt with by deducting it from the driving effort due to the engine.

The rolling resistance in this restricted sense is due chiefly to the deformation of road and tyre, and to the dissipation of energy through impact. It depends chiefly on the nature of the road surface, the nature of the tyres with which the vehicle is fitted and the total weight of vehicle and load. On soft, muddy and sandy roads it is greater than on hard dry macadam or wood paving; it is less with pneumatic than with solid rubber or steel tyres and it is generally taken to be directly proportional to the total weight of vehicle and load. That part of it which is due to impact undoubtedly depends also on the speed and springing of the vehicle and the remainder probably does so to a small extent. However, on roads having a hard dry surface free from large bumps and holes, the impact losses are probably only a small part of the total rolling resistance, and the effect of speed on the latter will not be great. Reliable information on this matter is lacking, however, and in what follows the rolling resistance has been assumed to be independent of the speed, but even if this assumption is not justified the value of the present chapter will be but slightly reduced.

20.4 Total resistance

The total resistance to the motion of a vehicle is the sum of the above three resistances and is thus composed of two parts that are independent of the speed of the vehicle – the rolling resistance and the gradient resistance – and of one part that is dependent on the speed – the air resistance.

A curve of total resistance against speed is therefore obtained by shifting the curve of Fig. 20.1 up vertically by the amount of the rolling and gradient resistances as is shown in Fig. 20.3.

Thus when the speed is OS km/h the total resistance SP is composed of the rolling resistance SR, the gradient resistance RQ and the air resistance QP. If either the gradient resistance or the rolling resistance increases or decreases then the curve would simply shift up or down by the amount of the increase or decrease.

Fig. 20.3 (*below*)
Fig. 20.4 (*right*)

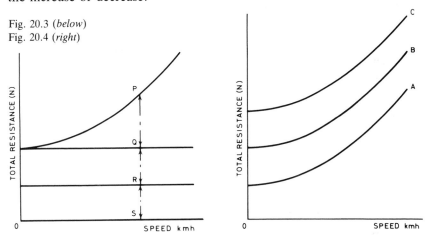

In Fig. 20.4 the curves A, B and C are the curve of Fig. 20.1 shifted up by various amounts, they therefore represent total resistance curves for a given vehicle on roads of either different surfaces or different gradients. Considering the road surface to remain unchanged then curve A might represent the total resistance on the level, curve B the total resistance on a gradient of say 1 in 30, and so on.

20.5 Tractive effort

Having dealt with the resistance to the motion of the vehicle, let us turn to the tractive effort (TE). The source of this is the engine, which turns the clutch shaft with a torque *T*. This torque is transmitted to the gearbox. Now by applying the principle of the conservation of energy as stated in Section 3.14, we shall find that if frictional losses are neglected, and if there is no storing of energy, the whole of the energy put into the gearbox at the engine end must be given out at the propeller shaft end. Since the work done in unit time is measured (when rotations are considered) by the product of the torque and the speed, it follows that the product of the engine torque and the speed of the clutch shaft must equal the product of the torque acting on the propeller shaft and the propeller shaft speed. If, therefore, the propeller shaft speed is $1/n$th the engine speed, then the torque acting on the propeller shaft must be n times the engine torque. We have then, propeller shaft torque $= n \times T$, n being the gearbox gear ratio between the speeds of the engine and the propeller shaft and T being the engine torque.

The propeller shaft drives the road wheels through the final drive where another reduction of speed occurs. If the road wheel speed is $1/n$th of the propeller shaft speed then the torque acting on the road wheel (the two wheels being considered as a single wheel) will be m times the propeller shaft torque, again neglecting frictional losses and energy storage. The torque acting on the road wheel is therefore $t = n \times m \times T$ where n is the gearbox ratio, m the final drive ratio and T the engine torque.

The way in which this torque produces a driving force to propel the car along the road is shown in Fig. 20.5. If the wheel there shown is regarded as being in equilibrium (as defined in Chapter 3, on mechanics), then the forces that act upon it must be in equilibrium and the couples also. Now at every instant the wheel can be considered as a lever (as shown by the dotted lines) fulcrumed at the point of contact of the wheel and the ground.

Under the action of the torque t the lever will tend to rotate about the point of contact with the ground and the centre of the wheel will tend to go forwards and to take the axle and the vehicle with it. At its centre therefore the wheel is pressing forwards on the axle casing with a force which we will call P_1. The reaction P_2 of this force (P_1) acts backwards on the wheel. Since the wheel is in equilibrium there must be an equal and opposite force P_3 acting on it. This is the adhesive force between the wheel and the road.

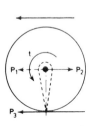

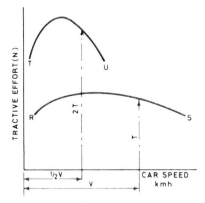

Fig. 20.5 *(above)*

Fig. 20.6 *(right)*

The forces $P_2\ P_3$ constitute a couple tending to turn the wheel in the clockwise direction and since the wheel is in equilibrium, and the couples acting on it are therefore also in equilibrium, the couple $P_2\ P_3$ must equal the couple t applied to the wheel by the driving shaft. Now the magnitude of the couple $P_2\ P_3$ is $P_3 \times R$ where R is the distance between the forces $P_2\ P_3$, in this case the radius of the wheel. Hence $t = P_3 \times R$ and since

$t = n \times m \times T$ we have $n \times m \times T = P_3 \times R$ or $P_3 = \dfrac{n \times m \times T}{R}$.

Now the values of the final drive ratio m and the wheel radius R are, for any given vehicle, constants, and for any particular gearbox gear the value of the ratio n is constant. Hence for any particular gearbox gear the value of the fraction $\dfrac{n \times m}{R}$ is a constant which may be called K.

The tractive effort is then given by the equation $P = K \times T$ where T is the engine torque and K is a constant whose value depends upon the road wheel radius, the final drive ratio and upon the gearbox gear ratio.

20.6   Variation of the tractive effort with speed

Now, since the engine is geared to the driving wheels, a particular engine speed corresponds to a particular vehicle speed, and since the tractive effort is proportional to the engine torque, the variation of the tractive effort with the variation of the vehicle speed will depend upon the variation of the engine torque with the variation of engine speed. This last relation has already been considered and a curve showing it is given in Fig. 4.7. The curve showing the relation between tractive effort and vehicle speed will be of the same shape; in fact, the same curve might be used provided that the scales were suitably altered.

A tractive-effort vehicle-speed curve for a given gearbox ratio, a given final drive ratio and a given road wheel radius is shown at RS in Fig. 20.6. If the gearbox ratio is altered we shall get another curve of tractive effort. Thus if the gearbox ratio is altered so that the total gear ratio between the engine and the back wheels is double what it originally was then the curve RS will become the curve TU, the relation between the curves being that all the horizontal distances of RS are halved and the corresponding vertical distances are doubled to give curve TU, since for a given engine speed doubling the total gear ratio will halve the vehicle speed but will double the tractive effort.

20.7   Performance curves

Having thus obtained curves showing the variation, with varying vehicle speed, of both the tractive effort and the total resistance to be overcome, let these curves be plotted to the same scales and on the same sheet of paper, as has been done in Fig. 20.7. In that figure the curves A-F are curves of total resistance for a road with a uniform surface but of varying gradient, curve A being the level and curve F the steepest gradient. Curves RS, TU and VW are curves of tractive effort for three different gear ratios, RS being, say, the top gear, TU the next lower gear, etc.

Suppose the vehicle is travelling on the level at a speed represented by OX. Then the resistance to be overcome is XY, while the tractive effort available is XZ. The tractive effort available is therefore greater than the resistance to be overcome and the excess tractive effort YZ will go to increase the speed of the vehicle. Now as the speed increases the resistance also increases but the tractive effort, it will be noticed, falls off. The excess tractive effort, given by the intercepts corresponding to YZ, which is available for acceleration, becomes smaller and smaller as the speed increases until, when the speed is OM, the tractive effort available is only just equal to the resistance to be overcome. There is therefore no excess tractive effort available for acceleration, and the speed cannot be increased further, OM represents the highest speed the vehicle can reach on the level road to which the curve A applies.

The curve RS represents the tractive effort with the engine running with the throttle wide open. If it is not desired to increase the speed beyond the value OX then the throttle would be closed until the tractive effort was equal to XY, and the speed would be maintained but not increased.

Now suppose the vehicle is travelling on the level at the maximum speed OM, and that it comes to a gradient to which the curve B applies. At the speed OM on the gradient B the resistance is MN, but the tractive effort available is only MH. Hence the excess resistance HN will slow the vehicle down and the speed will fall to the value given by the point I, at which the tractive effort is equal to the resistance to be overcome.

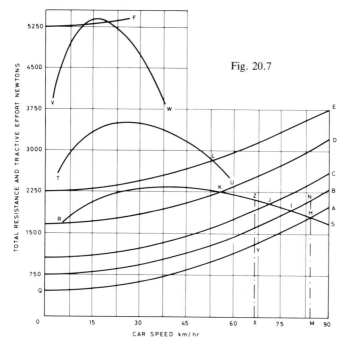

Fig. 20.7

Now suppose that the gradient becomes steeper and steeper so that we pass in succession from curve B to curve C and so on. The speed that can be maintained gets progressively lower as indicated by the points J, K, etc., and it will be seen that we cannot traverse the gradient E at any speed since the tractive effort curve lies everywhere below the resistance curve.

Now, with ordinary sized engines, if the gear ratio is such as to give a reasonable maximum speed on the level, then quite a medium gradient would bring about the conditions represented by the curve E, and the vehicle would be brought to rest. But if the gear ratio between the engine and the driving wheels can be altered we can pass from the tractive effort curve RS to the curve TU and then the gradient E can be traversed at the speed given by the point L.

Thus in order to permit a reasonably high maximum speed on the level and at the same time to be able to climb medium gradients we require to have available two different gear ratios. Similarly in order to permit reasonably high speeds up medium gradients and yet be able to climb steep gradients, we need a third gear ratio, and a fourth or fifth ratio may be desirable.

It should also be clear that at the lower speeds, when quick acceleration is especially desirable, there is a greater excess of tractive effort available on a lower gear than on a higher one.

The above is the complete explanation of the *raison d'être* of the gearbox, and it should be clear that the ideal gearbox would provide an infinite range of gear ratios so that the engine speed could be kept at or near that at which maximum power was developed, whatever the speed of the vehicle. This assumes that maximum speed is the objective. If maximum economy is desired, the engine requires to be run at the highest torque possible for a given power output. Many of the developments in transmission, such as the various hydraulic and electrical mechanisms, have as their principal object the multiplication of the number of ratios available. In general though, a compromise is adopted and three, four or more gear ratios are provided depending on the size of engine fitted and other considerations.

20.8   Clutch action

Fig. 20.7 also serves to show how the clutch enables a car to be started up from rest. When the car is at rest the resistance to be overcome before the car will move is, for the level road A, given by OQ. If the engine were in permanent connection with the driving wheels it would, of course, be at rest and the tractive effort would be zero. The clutch, however, allows the engine to be run at a speed at which a torque giving a greater tractive effort than OQ is developed and enables this torque to be transmitted to the driving wheels, though at the start the latter are at rest.

20.9   Constant power TE-speed curve

If the engine of a vehicle could be made to give its maximum power at all speeds then, since *Power = TE × Speed*, it follows that the TE will be inversely proportional to the road speed. The graph of the TE plotted against the road speed would then be like the full-line curve in Fig. 20.8.

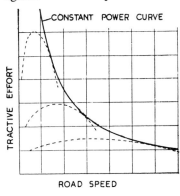

Fig. 20.8

The TE curves for an actual engine and gearbox combination will touch this constant power curve at one point (corresponding to the engine speed at which the engine gives its maximum power), but will lie everywhere else inside it, as shown by the dotted line curves. The constant power curve is the ideal form of TE curve and its shape is approached by those of a steam engine and of traction electric motors; it could be obtained with any engine if an infinitely variable gearbox of 100% efficiency were available.

20.10   Performance curves on a horsepower basis

Instead of considering the performance as a balance between the tractive effort available and the resistance to be overcome, that is, as a balance of forces, we may consider it as a balance between the rate of producing energy by the engine and the rate of using energy at the road wheels, that is, as a balance of powers. This is shown in Fig. 20.9. The curves A and E represent the horsepower required to overcome the resistances represented by the curves A and E of Fig. 20.7 at corresponding speeds, and the curves RS and TU represent the horsepower available at the road wheels on the two gears corresponding to the curves RS and TU of Fig. 20.7. The power available at any moment is, of course, equal to the power developed by the engine at that moment if frictional losses are neglected, the only effect of a change of gear ratio being to alter the road speed corresponding to a given engine speed.

The greatest speeds possible on the roads to which A and E refer are given by the intersections of the horizontal line representing the maximum horsepower of the engine and the curves A and E, and the best gear ratios for those roads will be such that at those greatest road speeds the engine speed is that at which the maximum power is developed. Any variation of gear ratio from these optimum values will result in a lowering of the maximum speed attainable. The maximum speeds possible with the gear ratios for which the curves RS and TU are drawn are given by the intersections H and L respectively.

The process of settling the gear ratios for a vehicle is ultimately an experimental one, but approximate values which will serve as a starting point may be derived as follows.

A curve corresponding to the curve A of Fig. 20.9 is drawn, and from its intersection with the line of maximum engine horsepower the greatest possible road speed found. The top gear ratio is then made such that this road speed corresponds to the engine speed at which maximum horsepower is obtained. Next the maximum gradient that is to be negotiable must be assumed and the corresponding gradient resistance found. This gives the maximum tractive effort required, and the maximum engine torque being known the gear ratio necessary to enable this tractive effort to be obtained may be determined. The top and bottom gear ratios are thus settled and the remaining ratios may be put in so that they form a geometric progression, this step being justified as follows.

The engine has a certain range of speed within which the power developed is not very much less than the maximum, and the gear ratios should be such that the engine speed can be kept within that range. Let the lower limit of the range be L rev/min and the higher limit be M rev/min.

Suppose the car to be moving in lowest gear and the engine to be speeded to the higher limit.

If the engine speed is to be kept within the specified range the gear must now be changed. Immediately after the change has been made the engine speed should be down to the lower limit L while the road speed of the car will be unaltered. If the low gear ratio is A to 1 then the road speed corresponding to an engine speed of M rev/min will be equal to $K \times M/A$, where K is a constant depending on the size of the road wheels, and if the next gear ratio is B to 1 the road speed corresponding to an engine speed of L rev/min will be equal to $K \times L/B$. But these two road speeds are the same; hence $K \times M/A = K \times L/B$ or $B = A \times L/M$, that is, $B = c \times A$ where c is a constant equal to L/M. By similar reasoning it will be found that the next gear ratio C to 1 is given by $C = c \times B = c^2 \times A$. Hence the gear ratios form a geometric progression.

Now for an engine having a sharply peaked horsepower curve c will be greater than for an engine having a flatter curve, and the number of intermediate gears required to bridge the gap between the top and bottom

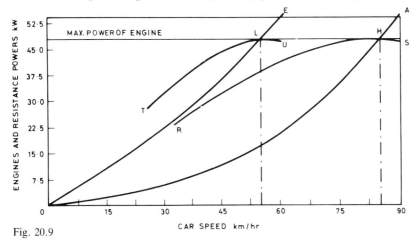

Fig. 20.9

gears will be greater. Hence a peaked horsepower curve calls for a multiplicity of gear ratios, while a flatter power curve needs but two or three. As an example, suppose the top gear is to be $4:1$ and the bottom gear $16:1$. Then if $c = 0.5$ the ratios will be $16:1$, $8:1$, $4:1$; while if $c = 0.63$ the ratios will be $16:1$, $10.1:1$, $6.35:1$, $4:1$, so that in the first case three gears are required and in the second, four.

If performance curves on a tractive-effort basis are now plotted, using the ratios found as above, the performance can be examined and modifications tried.

The number of gears required, however, depends also on the duty for which the vehicle is to be used. For example, a cross-country vehicle obviously will need higher numerical gear ratios (lower gearing) than an equivalent car used only on the road. If the cross-country vehicle is to be used also on the road, and a high top speed is required of it, five speeds will be desirable as compared with, for example, four for the comparable road-only vehicle.

In the heavy range, the requirements vary even more widely according to not only the terrain – gradients, altitudes, etc. – but also the range of loading to be expected. A lightly laden or empty vehicle, for instance, may need only four to six gears, whereas the same vehicle fully laden may need eight to twelve. To meet these requirements we have range-change and splitter gearboxes, as described in Section 21.21. Requirements depend also on the traffic which, if dense, may require that the driver of a heavy vehicle change gear frequently. He will need also more gear ratios so that he can keep with the other traffic without running his engine outside its economical speed range and thus seriously increasing his rate of fuel consumption. With very heavy vehicles – 40 tonnes and over – as many as 16 or 17 gear ratios may be necessary.

Chapter 21

Constructional arrangements of gearboxes

The gearboxes which are, or have been, used in motor vehicles may be divided into those in which the drive in every ratio is transmitted through gear teeth which mesh together, and those in which a direct drive is provided for one of the ratios while for the others the drive has to be transmitted through gear teeth. Gearboxes may also be classified in the following types –

(1) Sliding-mesh.
(2) Constant-mesh.
(3) Epicyclic.

Gearboxes which are a mixture of two of these types are not uncommon. Spur gearing is used in all three types, the differences between which lie in the manner in which the gears are brought into action.

The sliding-mesh type is the simplest and historically is the oldest; it may conveniently be dealt with first although the constant-mesh type is now the most widely used type.

21.1 Sliding-mesh gearbox

A sliding-mesh gearbox is shown in Fig. 21.1. The engine is coupled, through the clutch and clutch-shaft, to the short shaft A which is integral with the spur pinion B. The shaft A is supported in two journal ball bearings and is fixed axially in a manner that will be described later. The pinion B meshes continuously with the spur wheel D secured to the layshaft E, which is arranged parallel to the shaft A and carried at its ends in the ball bearings shown. Secured to the layshaft (which is splined throughout its length) are four other spur gears, F, G, H and J. The latter is continuously in mesh with a pinion Q which is free to revolve on a pin fixed in the casing. A third shaft (usually called the *mainshaft*) is arranged in line with the shaft A, being supported at one end in a ball bearing housed in the casing C_2 and at the other end by the spigot L which is part of the shaft K and which fits in a bushed hole in the shaft A which, incidentally, is sometimes termed the *primary*, or *first motion*, shaft.

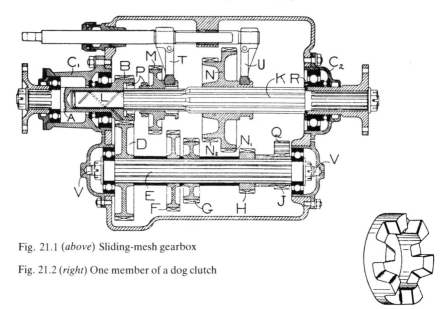

Fig. 21.1 (*above*) Sliding-mesh gearbox

Fig. 21.2 (*right*) One member of a dog clutch

The shaft K is splined for nearly its whole length and carries the independent members M and N. M is a single spur gear while N is a double gear, being in effect two gears N_1 and N_2 made in one piece. The gears M and N can be slid along the mainshaft when required by selector forks T and U respectively. These forks are secured to rods that can slide in bushed holes in the casing as shown, and their prongs fit into grooves cut in the bosses of the gears so that the latter can revolve freely, but must slide axially when the forks are moved. Teeth P, similar to spur gear teeth, are cut on the boss of the gear M and corresponding internal teeth are cut inside the constant-mesh pinion B and when the gear M is slid along its shaft to the left its teeth P fit into the spaces of the teeth P of the pinion B thus locking those members together. This arrangement is one form of positive clutch; an alternative form is composed of two members, each like that shown in Fig. 21.2. This latter form gives rise to the name *dog-tooth clutch*.

The mainshaft K is connected, through the propeller shaft, to the road wheels. The layshaft is fixed axially by thrust buttons V. The spigot L has a spiral groove cut on it to lead oil to the bearing and at its left-hand end bears, through a thrust button, against the engine shaft A. The mainshaft is thus fixed axially by the thrust button at the left and at the right by the single-thrust ball bearing in the casing C_2. The engine shaft A is fixed axially at the right by the thrust button bearing against the end of the mainshaft and at the left by the single-thrust ball bearing in the casing C_1. The proper clearance for the thrust bearings is obtained by grinding the washer R to the proper thickness. Separate ball thrust bearings are not always provided, the journal bearings being arranged to position the shafts axially.

The gearbox shown provides four forward speeds and one reverse, and the operation is as follows –

21.2 First or low gear

The gear M occupies the position shown in Fig. 21.1. The gear N is slid along the mainshaft K until it occupies the position shown in Fig. 21.3(a). It then meshes with the gear H of the layshaft. The drive comes from the engine shaft through the constant-mesh gears B and D to the layshaft, is then transmitted through that shaft to the gear H and thence through the gear N_1 to the mainshaft. The *gear ratio*, or the ratio between the speeds of the engine and mainshafts, is –

$$\frac{\text{Speed of engine shaft}}{\text{Speed of mainshaft}} = \frac{\text{No. teeth in D}}{\text{No. teeth in B}} \times \frac{\text{No. teeth in N}}{\text{No. teeth in H}} = n_1.$$

The torque driving the mainshaft is now n_1 times the torque acting on the engine shaft.

21.3 Second gear

The gear M continues to occupy the same position, but the gear N is slid over to the left as shown in Fig. 21.3(b). It then meshes with the gear G of the layshaft. The drive is from the engine shaft through the constant-mesh gears to the layshaft, through that shaft to the gear G thence to the wheel N_2 and the mainshaft. The gear ratio is –

$$\frac{\text{Speed of engine shaft}}{\text{Speed of mainshaft}} = \frac{\text{No. teeth in D}}{\text{No. teeth in B}} \times \frac{\text{No. teeth in } N_2}{\text{No. teeth in G}}$$

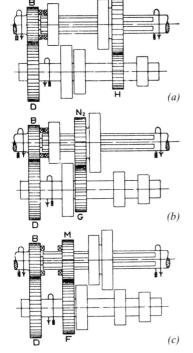

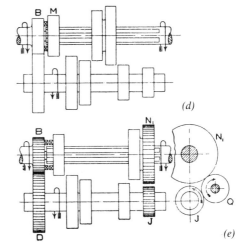

Fig. 21.3 Four-speed gear showing the various ratio combinations

21.4 Third gear

The gear N occupies the position shown in Fig. 21.1. The gear M is slid to the right into the position shown in Fig. 20.3 (c), where it meshes with the gear F of the layshaft. The drive is from the engine shaft through the constant-mesh gears to the layshaft, thence to the gear F, through that gear to the gear M and the mainshaft. The gear ratio is –

$$\frac{\text{Speed of engine shaft}}{\text{Speed of mainshaft}} = \frac{\text{No. teeth in D}}{\text{No. teeth in B}} \times \frac{\text{No. teeth in M}}{\text{No. teeth in F}}$$

21.5 Fourth or top gear

The gear N occupies the position shown in Fig. 21.1, while the gear M is slid over to the left as shown in Fig. 21.3 (d). The dog teeth on M then engage in the spaces between the dog teeth on B, thus connecting B and M and giving a direct drive between the engine and the mainshaft. The gear ratio is then 1:1. The layshaft now revolves idly.

On all the above gears the direction of rotation of the layshaft is the opposite to that of the engine shaft, while the direction of rotation of the mainshaft is opposite to that of the layshaft. The mainshaft rotates in the same direction as the engine shaft.

21.6 Reverse gear

The member M occupies the position shown in Fig. 21.1. The gear N is slid over to the right, but farther than when first gear was being obtained. It reaches the position shown in Fig. 21.3 (e), but in this position it does *not* mesh with the pinion J of the layshaft, since that pinion is made small enough to clear the gear N_1. The gear N_1 does, however, mesh with the reverse idler Q which is carried on a shaft on which it is free to revolve. The shaft is fixed in the gearbox casing and the idler Q is constantly in mesh with the pinion J of the layshaft.

The drive is from the engine shaft through the constant-mesh gears and the layshaft to the pinion J, thence to the idler Q, and thence to the wheel N_1 and the mainshaft. The direction of rotation of the idler Q is the opposite to that of the layshaft, and hence is the same as that of the engine shaft. The direction of rotation of the gear N_1 is the opposite to that of the idler Q, and hence is opposite to that of the engine shaft. The gear ratio is –

$$\frac{\text{Speed of engine shaft}}{\text{Speed of mainshaft}} = \frac{\text{No. teeth in D}}{\text{No. teeth in B}} \times \frac{\text{No. teeth in } N_1}{\text{No. teeth in J}}$$

It will be noticed that the number of teeth in the idler does not affect the gear *ratio*, but only the direction of rotation.

A different method of engaging the reverse gear is shown in Fig. 21.4, which shows a gearbox otherwise identical with that just described. The layshaft now carries only four gears, the constant-mesh gear, the third-speed gear, the second-speed gear and the first-speed pinion H. Instead of a simple reverse idler there is now a compound one Q_{1-2}, the two portions of which are of different diameters. This idler is carried on a shaft arranged parallel to the mainshaft, but besides being free to revolve on that shaft it can also be slid axially along it in order to engage the reverse gear.

In the position shown at (*a*) the idler is in the neutral position and there is no drive between the engine shaft and the mainshaft. If, however, the idler is slid to the right, to the position shown at (*b*), the part Q_2 will engage with the pinion H of the layshaft, while the part Q_1 will engage with the gear N_1 on the mainshaft. The drive will then be from the engine shaft through the constant-mesh gears and the layshaft to the pinion H, which

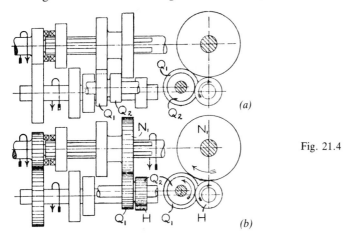

Fig. 21.4

then drives the idler Q_2; Q_1 being integral with Q_2 is also driven, and in turn drives the gear N_1 and thus the mainshaft. As before, the mainshaft goes in the opposite direction to the engine shaft, thus giving a reverse drive. The gear ratio is –

$$\frac{\text{Speed of engine shaft}}{\text{Speed of mainshaft}} =$$

$$\frac{\text{No. teeth in D}}{\text{No. teeth in B}} \times \frac{\text{No. teeth in } Q_2}{\text{No. teeth in H}} \times \frac{\text{No. teeth in } N_1}{\text{No. teeth in } Q_1}$$

The chief advantage of this method of obtaining the reverse is that the mainshaft and the layshaft can be made shorter than when the first method is used. The deflection of the shorter shafts under a given load will be less than that of the longer shafts, if the diameters are the same, and one cause of noisy operation is reduced. If the longer shafts are sufficiently stiff then the shorter shafts may be made smaller in diameter. A gearbox of the second type will generally be less bulky than a similar one of the first type. The second construction, however, involves the use of three sliding members instead of two, and makes the control mechanism slightly more complicated.

21.7 Control mechanism

The sliding of the members M, N and (when required) Q, is effected by means of selector forks, an example of which is shown in Fig. 21.7. The fork fits into a groove formed in the boss of the gear to be moved, so that although the gear is left free to revolve, it must partake of any sideways movement that is given to the fork. There will be a selector fork for each sliding member in the gearbox. The selector forks either slide on rods fixed in the gearbox casing or are fixed to rods which can slide in that casing, the rods being parallel to the shafts upon which the gears slide. The necessary sliding motions are given to the selector forks by the motion of a gear change lever actuated by the driver, but since there is only one gear change lever and there are two or three selector forks, the driver must be able to select the one belonging to the gear he desires to move. The principal forms of the mechanism that enables this to be done will now be dealt with.

21.8 Sliding type selector mechanism

This type is now hardly ever used but it has been thought advisable to retain a description of it. In the example shown in Fig. 21.5 (1) is a sectional elevation, the plane of the section being indicated by the line SS in the end view (2). The latter is a section on AB. The third view is a part plan. There are three moving members in the gearbox into which this particular mechanism is fitted so that there are three selector forks, C, D and E. The forks C and D slide on rods F and G fixed in the casing, while E is carried by a pivoted lever Q which is actuated by a member that slides on the third rod H. The forks are moved by a fore and aft rocking motion of the gear lever J which is carried by a shaft L pivoted in the casing and to the

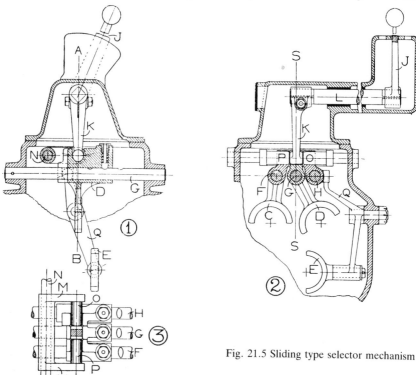

Fig. 21.5 Sliding type selector mechanism

inner end of which is secured the striking lever K. The particular fork that is to be moved is selected by a sideways sliding motion of the member JLK. To hold the forks in their various positions spring plungers, one of which is seen in (1), and which spring into grooves cut in the rods FGH, are fitted.

To prevent two forks from being moved at once a locking piece M is provided. This slides on a cross rod N fixed in the casing, and is provided with horns O and P which project into the slots in the sliding members. Between the horns O and P is situated the end of the striking lever K so that the sideways movement of the latter causes the member M to slide on its rod. The gap between the horns O and P is only slightly wider than each of the sliding members, so that the latter can be moved only one at a time.

21.9   Ball type selector mechanism

In this form of selector mechanism, shown in Fig. 21.6, the control lever is mounted on the transmission casing. Some can have this control on the steering column, as in Fig. 21.10, in which case it is connected by rods and levers to the mechanism on the box, which in principle remains unaltered. The selector forks A and B slide on rods fixed in the gearbox lid, which in this design carries the whole of the selector mechanism. The shape of the forks is shown by the perspective sketch Fig. 21.7; they are provided with slots C to receive the end D of the striking arm. The latter is the lower end

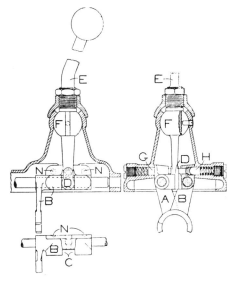

Fig. 21.6 (*left*) Ball type selector
Fig. 21.7 (*below*) A selector fork

of the gear lever E which is ball jointed in the casing at F. By rocking the lever sideways its end D may be brought into engagement with either of the selector forks, when a fore and aft rocking motion will slide that fork along its rod.

No gate is provided, but small plungers G and H prevent both forks from being moved at once. When both the forks are in the neutral position, and the slots C are opposite each other, the plungers are forced by small springs into holes in the forks, and before either fork can be moved the plunger that locks it must be pressed back into the casing. This is done by the sideways motion of the gear lever. Obviously when one plunger is pressed in to release one of the forks the other plunger is out, and is locking the other fork. These plungers also serve to lock the forks in position when the gears are properly engaged, being arranged to spring into shallow recesses NN in the forks.

Another selector mechanism, suitable for the remote control of the gearbox, is shown in Fig. 21.8. The gear lever A is carried in a ball-and-socket bearing O and its spherical lower end engages a cylindrical hole formed in an arm fixed to a shaft C that is free both to turn and to slide in bearings.

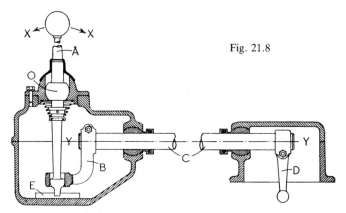

Fig. 21.8

This shaft is coupled rigidly to a shaft carried in the gearbox casing (see also Fig. 21.14). The striking arm D is fixed to the latter shaft and its lower end engages the selector forks. A sideways rocking motion of the gear lever produces a rotation of the shaft and enables the striking arm to select any desired selector rod and a fore and aft rocking motion of the gear lever then slides the shaft and thus the selector fork that has been engaged, thereby engaging the gears as required. The use of spherical bearings for the intermediate shaft accommodates any relative movement between the gearbox and the bracket that carries the gear lever, alternatively plain cylindrical bearings may be used and universal joints be provided at each end of the intermediate shaft. The lower end of the gear lever engages a grooved plate E which prevents reverse gear being engaged inadvertently. The lever must be lifted up to clear the plate E in order to engage reverse.

Gear change levers situated at the steering wheel were popular at one time but are not now used to any great extent. They are still used however in some vehicles and the principle they employ is applicable to forward control vans. A typical example is shown in Figs. 21.9 and 21.10. The gearbox concerned is a four-speed and reverse type and there are three striking forks A, B and C, of which A is for the reverse and B and C for the forward gears. The striking forks are slid along their rods by the striking lever D when the lever E is rotated about the axis OO. The appropriate fork is selected by moving the lever F, the lever G then rotates the interlocking member H about the axis XX and pivots the lever D about the pin J, thereby bringing it into engagement with the appropriate fork. The other forks are locked in the neutral position by the fingers K and L of the

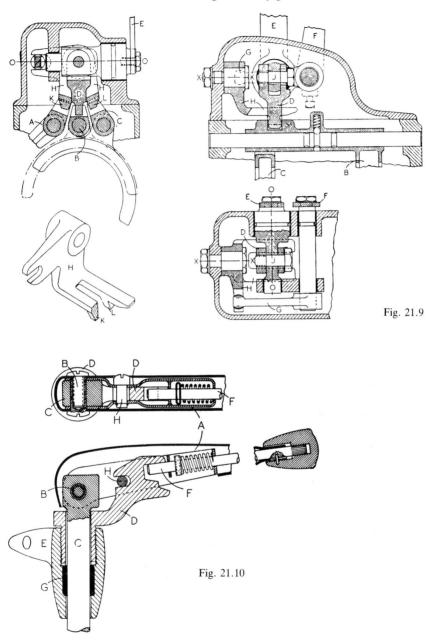

Fig. 21.9

Fig. 21.10

interlocking member which is shown separately in perspective in the lower left-hand corner of the illustration.

Fig. 21.10 shows the steering column mechanism in which the lever A is pivoted to the end of a rod C and the pin H engages a slot in the bracket D which can rotate about the axis of the rod but cannot move axially. An up-and-down motion of the end of the lever about the pin H raises or lowers the rod C; this is connected by linkage to the arm F of Fig. 21.10 and this provides the selection. Fore and aft motion of the lever rotates the rod C and an arm at the bottom end of this is coupled to the lever E of Fig. 21.9 to give the striking motion to the striking forks. The selecting motion of the gear lever is normally limited by the engagement of the rod F with a recess in the bracket D so that only forward gears can be selected. By pulling the knob out against the spring the lever can be moved down far enough to select the reverse gear striking fork.

21.10   Constant-mesh gearbox

There are many different forms of constant-mesh gearbox, in some of which the various gears slide axially along their shafts, while in others they have no axial freedom. The characteristic feature of this type of gearbox is, however, that all the pairs of wheels are always in mesh.

The principle of the commonest form of constant-mesh gearbox is shown in Fig. 21.11; the engine shaft A is integral with a pinion B, which meshes with the wheel C on the layshaft. The latter is, therefore, driven by the engine shaft. Wheels E, F and G are fixed to the layshaft just as in a sliding-mesh gear box, and the mainshaft D is also similarly arranged. The

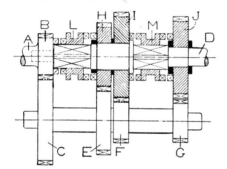

Fig. 21.11 Constant-mesh gearbox

gears E, F and G (the latter through a reverse idler) are, however, in constant mesh with the wheels H, I and J, which are perfectly free to turn on the mainshaft, bronze bushes, or ball or roller bearings, being provided between them and the shaft. The gears H, I and J, therefore, are constantly driven by the engine shaft, but at different speeds, since the wheels E, F and G are of different sizes. The wheel J, being driven through an idler, revolves, of course, in the opposite direction to the engine shaft.

If any one of the gears H, I or J is coupled up to the mainshaft then there will be a driving connection between that shaft and the engine shaft. The coupling is done by means of the dog clutch members L and M, which are carried on squared (or splined) portions of the mainshaft. They are free to slide on those squared portions, but have to revolve with the shaft. If the member M is slid to the left it will couple the wheel I to the mainshaft giving the first gear. The drive is then through the wheels B, C, F and I and the dog clutch M. The other dog clutch is meanwhile in its neutral position as shown. If, with the member M in its neutral position, the member L is slid to the right, it will couple the wheel H to the mainshaft and give second gear, the drive being through the wheels B, C, E and H and the dog clutch L. If the member L is slid to the left it will couple the mainshaft directly to the pinion B and give a direct drive, as in a sliding-mesh gearbox. The reverse gear is engaged by sliding the member M to the right when it will couple the wheel J to the mainshaft. The drive is then through the wheels B, C, G, the idler, J and the dog clutch M.

This type of gearbox has several advantages over the ordinary form of sliding-mesh box. It facilitates the use of helical or double helical gear teeth which are quieter than straight teeth; it lends itself to the incorporation of synchronising devices more readily than the sliding-mesh box; the dog clutch teeth can be made so that they are easier to engage than the teeth of gear wheels, and any damage that results from faulty manipulation occurs to the dog clutch teeth and not to the teeth of the gear wheels. Now, when once the dog clutches are engaged, there is no motion between their teeth, whereas when gear teeth are engaged the power is transmitted through the sliding action of the teeth of one wheel on those of the other. The teeth have to be suitably shaped to be able to transmit the motion properly, and if they are damaged the motion will be imperfect and noise will result. Damage is, however, less likely to occur to the teeth of the dog clutches, since all engage at once, whereas in sliding a pair of gears into mesh the engagement is between two or three teeth.

On the other hand, the wheels on the mainshaft must be free to revolve so that they must either be bushed or be carried on ball or roller bearings. If bushes are used lubrication is difficult, wear will occur and noise will arise. If ordinary ball or roller bearings are used wear is avoided but the gearbox becomes bulky and heavy.

The use of needle-roller bearings overcomes both difficulties.

21.11 A five-speed gearbox

The gearbox shown in Fig. 21.12 is an example of a mixed type of box, the first and second speeds being by sliding-mesh gears and the others by constant-mesh gears. The shaft A is coupled to the driven shaft of the clutch and has the pinion B formed integrally on it. This pinion drives the layshaft to which the gears C, D, E and F are splined. The mainshaft G is supported at the left in a roller spigot bearing housed inside the pinion B, in the centre by a ball bearing carried in an intermediate wall of the gearbox casing and at the right in a combined roller and ball bearing assembly. The ball bearing part of this assembly is used to position the mainshaft axially and to take any thrust that may come on it while the roller bearing takes the greater part of the journal loads. The double gear H is free to slide on splines on the mainshaft and gives first and second speeds when slid to right or left so as to mesh with C or D respectively. The gear J is free to rotate on a bush on the mainshaft and is kept in place by the split ring K which fits in a groove turned in the mainshaft. The split ring itself is kept in place by the overlapping portion of the washer (sectioned in full black) between it and the gear J. The latter is in permanent mesh with the gear E of the layshaft, and when coupled to the mainshaft by sliding the gear L to the right so as to engage the dog clutch teeth M, gives third speed. Fourth speed is a direct drive and is obtained by sliding L to the left so as to engage the dog clutch teeth N. Fifth speed is an overdrive, the ratio being less than unity, and is given by sliding the sleeve P (which is splined to the boss of the gear Q) to the left. The dog clutch teeth R of the sleeve P then engage the teeth S formed on the boss of the gear E and thus the gear Q is coupled to the layshaft, on which it has hitherto been free to revolve on the sleeve provided for it. The drive is then from B to F, through the teeth S and R to the gear Q, thence to the gear L and the mainshaft. Since the gear Q is larger than the gear F the mainshaft goes faster than the engine shaft A. Reverse is obtained by sliding the reverse idler UV to the left so that the teeth U engage those of the gear H and the teeth V those of the gear C.

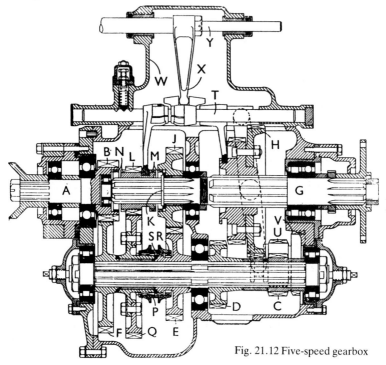

Fig. 21.12 Five-speed gearbox

The layshaft is carried in a ball bearing in the intermediate wall of the gearbox casing and in roller bearings at the ends. It is positioned axially by the screwed studs shown in the end covers.

The selector forks, by which the various members are slid in order to engage the various gears, are fixed to rods T free to slide in the cover casing W. The selector rods are positioned by spring-loaded plungers as shown. The reverse idler is operated from its selector rod through a rocking lever (shown dotted) pivoted on the wall of the casing. The striking arm X turns about the axis of the shaft Y, to which it is fixed, in order to select the appropriate selector rod and then slides axially in order to slide that rod. The connection between the shaft Y and the change gear lever will be on the lines of that shown in Fig. 21.8. Packing rings are provided in the ends of the bushes carrying the shaft Y and special sealing devices (not shown) are provided where the engine and mainshafts pass through the cover plates in order to prevent the leakage of oil.

21.12 Another example of a constant-mesh gearbox

A modern design of five-speed gearbox in which all the gears except those giving first gear are in constant mesh is shown in Fig. 21.13. The shaft A, which is coupled to the clutch shaft, is supported in two ball bearings the right-hand one of which positions the shaft axially. The pinion B is integral with the shaft A and meshes with the layshaft gear C. The layshaft consists of a splined shaft having an integral pinion E and on which are mounted the gears G, S, I, K and C. It is carried in roller bearings at the ends and a ball bearing in the middle; the left-hand roller bearing positions the shaft axially, both its races being provided with lips for that purpose. The outer

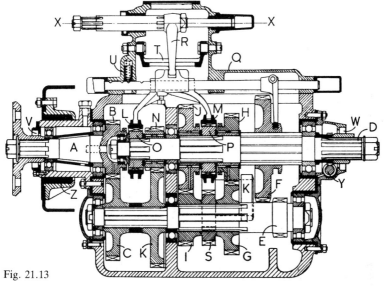

Fig. 21.13

races for the roller bearings are mounted in steel shells that are held in the cast aluminium casing of the gearbox by the studs and nuts that secure the end covers.

The gears G, I and K mesh with the gears H, J and N which are free to revolve on the mainshaft D on needle roller bearings, hardened steel sleeves being provided on the shaft for these bearings to run on. The bearings and gears are secured axially by hardened steel washers fixed on the shaft by reason of the nut at the left-hand end. The gears H, J, N and B are coupled to the mainshaft, when required, by the dog clutches L and M; these take the form of sleeves having internal teeth to fit the external teeth of the members O and P which are splined to the mainshaft. The teeth of the sleeves L and M fit the small diameter toothed portions of the gears H, J, N and B to enable the different ratios to be obtained.

Reverse gear is obtained by sliding the gear F to the left to mesh with the portion K of the compound reverse idler; the other toothed portion of this idler meshes permanently with the pinion S of the layshaft.

The gear F and the sleeves M and L are actuated by striking forks carried by rods that are free to slide in the cover casting Q and which are moved by the motion of the striking arm R along the axis XX. Selection is done by the rotation of the arm R about the axis XX and a pivoted interlocking member T, similar in principle to that shown in Fig. 21.9 and described previously, prevents two gears from being engaged at once. The selector forks are held in their various positions by the spring-loaded plungers, one of which is seen at U.

Oil seals are housed in the recesses V and W and a speedometer drive is provided at Y.

The box is supported at the front by a rubber bushing Z carried by a cross member of the frame and at the back on two lugs (not shown) which also seat on rubber pads.

21.13   BL Cars overdrive, five-ratio gearbox

With fuel economy now a prime requirement, most car manufacturers are turning to five-speed gear boxes with overdrive top gear and, usually, direct-drive fourth speed. Formerly, four-speed boxes were the general rule for all but the more expensive cars, some sports models, and medium weight commercial vehicles, the last-mentioned of course because of the wide range of their weights, from empty to fully laden. A particularly good five-speed design is that developed by British Leyland, in the first instance for Triumph and Rover cars. Fig. 21.14 is a diagrammatic illustration clearly demonstrating the basic principles, but it should not be taken as an accurate representation of that box. The main difficulty when five speeds

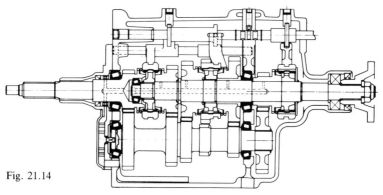

Fig. 21.14

have to be accommodated is that the shafts tend to become long. This has two main disadvantages: first, the whole structure becomes both costly and difficult to accommodate; secondly, the shafts are more liable to deflect under load and this, by throwing the gear teeth slightly out of mesh, increases the noise, vibration and rate of wear.

These problems have been overcome in this box by carrying the shafts in five taper-roller bearings, and making the overdrive gear pair overhang behind the rear pair of bearings. These two bearings are housed in an intermediate wall clamped between the rear cover and the main portion of the gearbox casing, while the two at the front ends of the main and layshafts are housed in the front wall. The fifth taper-roller bearing is in a counterbore in the primary, or first-motion, shaft and receives the spigot end of the mainshaft.

Taper-roller bearings have many advantages. One is that, because they take both axial and radial loading, no extra provisions have to be made for taking the thrust of the helical gearing. Because of the line contacts between their rolling elements and races, relatively small diameter rollers can be employed and the overall diameter is smaller than that of an equivalent ball bearing, with its point contacts. Alternatively, for a given overall diameter, a larger diameter shaft can be used

In general, for given size, taper-roller bearings have about double the life of the ball type. Another advantage of the taper-roller is that the clearances in the races can be adjusted after assembly: ideally, this clearance should be zero, since any increase tends to leave only one or two rolling elements carrying all the load, while a pre-load obviously takes up some of the capacity of the bearing for carrying the working load. Assembly of the gears into the box is easy and can be done through one end, so there is no need for side covers – the outer races are inserted into their housing and the caged rollers and gears assembled on to the shafts before they are put in the box.

Other factors ensuring adequate stiffness include the use of a live layshaft. To facilitate the machining of the gears and for ease of assembly into the box, most cars have dead layshafts, with a cluster of gears integral with a sleeve rotating on bearings around it. Live – that is, rotating – layshafts are more widely used on commercial vehicles. Their advantage is that, because no bearings are needed between them and the gears, the shafts can be both larger in diameter and integral with the gears, and therefore much stiffer. In this box, some of the mainshaft gears run directly on the steel shafts, without bearings. This has necessitated the incorporation of an oil pump, driven from the front end of the layshaft, for lubrication of these gears. Pressure lubrication, however, is in any case an advantage and has been used before on some high quality cars.

By overhanging the overdrive gear pair – which of course transmit relatively light torques – the length of shaft between bearings has been kept to only 227 mm – again helping to reduce deflections. The sort of usage pattern that can be expected is: 40% of all running done in fifth gear, 40% in direct fourth gear, 15% in third, 4% in second, and 1% in first. With a four-speed box the averages are the same for first and second, 20% for third and 75% for direct top gear.

21.14   Synchromesh devices

These are used to simplify the operation of changing gear, so that this can be done by unskilled drivers without the occurrence of clashes and consequent damage. The principle of all the devices is that the members which ultimately are to be engaged positively are first brought into frictional contact and then when the friction has equalised their speeds the positive connection is made. The devices can be applied to sliding-mesh boxes, but are almost always used with constant-mesh boxes.

The five constructional arrangements described below cover practically all the different arrangements commonly used.

In Fig. 21.15 the mechanism is shown applied to the direct drive and the next lower gear of an ordinary constant-mesh box whose general arrangement is as shown in Fig. 21.11. Thus A is the engine shaft and the integral gear B meshes with a wheel fixed to the layshaft (not shown) while the gear C is free to rotate on the mainshaft D and is permanently meshed with another wheel fixed to the layshaft. Both B and C are formed with integral dog tooth portions E and F and conical portions G and H. The member J, which is free to slide on splines on the mainshaft, has conical portions K and L to corrrespond with G and H. Thus if J is slid sideways to the left the cones K and G will come into contact and the friction between them will tend to equalise their speeds. The outside of the member J is formed with teeth which are exactly similar to the teeth E and F and the member M is free to slide on these teeth except that spring-loaded balls N engaging recesses in M tend to prevent such sliding. There are usually six of these balls. If the balls N are overcome, however, and M is slid to the left along the outside of J, the teeth on the inside of M will engage the teeth E and there will be a positive drive between A and D through the teeth E, and the members M and J. The member M is actuated by the selector fork P and thus by the gear lever. In changing gear the gear lever is brought to the neutral position in the ordinary way but is immediately pressed in the direction it has to go to engage the required gear; supposing this to be top gear the effect is to press M to the left. The spring-loaded balls N however cause J to move with M and thus the cones K and L are brought into frictional contct. When the speeds of G and J have become equal a slightly greater pressure on the gear lever overcomes the resistance of the balls N, and M slides along J so that its teeth engage the teeth E, thus establishing the positive connection. Unless the gear lever is pressed so as to force the cones G and K together there will be no synchronising action. If the member M is slid along J before synchronisation has been effected a clash will result. This may occur if the gear lever is moved too rapidly and will tend to occur if the springs beneath the balls N are too weak. Synchromesh mechanisms of this type are usually called *constant load* synchromesh units, because an applied load of constant value – the same in all circumstances – effects a gear change.

The construction shown in Fig. 21.16 is that of Fig. 21.15 turned inside out. Thus the cones K and L are formed in the ends of a sleeve M free to slide on a member J which is splined to the mainshaft. The sleeve M must, however, rotate with J because of the projecting pieces Q which engage slots cut in M. The selector fork engages the ring P which is secured to the projecting pieces Q. Spring-loaded balls N again tend to make M move with J. The action is very much as before, thus pressure on the gear lever tends to slide J to the left, say, and the balls N cause M to move with J, thus bringing the cone K into contact. The resulting friction will, given time, produce synchronisation and then an increased pressure on the gear lever will slide J along inside M and the dog teeth E and R will engage, thus establishing the positive connection.

The construction of Fig. 21.15 is rather more convenient where the wheels B and C are small.

When the member M is slowing the wheel B down (as it is in all the early stages of a change up) there will be a pressure between the sides of the projections Q and the sides S of the slots as shown in the part plan. At the moment of synchronisation the pressure will become zero and after

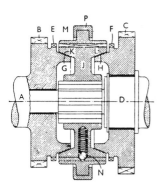

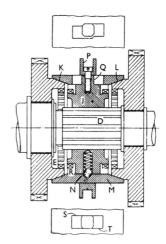

Fig. 21.15 (*above*)
Fig. 21.16 (*right*)

synchronisation (supposing the dog clutches are not engaged) the pressure would be between the other sides of the projection Q and the side T of the slot. The friction consequent on these pressures will help in preventing J from being slid along before synchronisation has occurred and this latter occurrence can be almost entirely prevented by shaping the slots as shown in the part view at the top of Fig. 21.16.

21.15 Baulk type of synchromesh

The mechanism used by Vauxhall Motors (and other General Motors concerns) works on a principle different from that used in the types described previously. It is shown as applied to the direct-drive engagement in Fig. 21.17. The cone A is loosely carried on the male cone of the gear B and has three fingers D whose ends engage the spaces between the splines of the mainshaft E but with considerable clearance as shown in the end view and plan. Thus while A has to rotate at the same speed as the shaft E it can move relatively to that shaft through a small angle. The gear B has internal dog clutch F which can engage the external teeth G on the member H, which is splined to the mainshaft and which has three slots J cut in it. These slots are just a little wider than the fingers D. Springs C are carried by the member H as shown.

The action will be described as it occurs when top gear is being engaged. Because of the small amount of friction always present between the cones in A and B there will be a drag on the former member which will keep the fingers D up against one side of the space between the splines of the shaft E, as shown in the plan and end view. This drag will be accentuated as soon as an attempt is made to move the member H along so as to engage the teeth G and F, because firstly the springs C will press against the fingers D and secondly the corners of the slots J will bear against the corners of the fingers D. Thus the cones will be pressed together and the friction between them will tend to bring about synchronism. The clutch being disengaged, synchronism will in due course come about and, if the dog clutch teeth were not then engaged, the speed of B, which has up to now been higher than that of E, would become lower. The fingers D would then be pressed against the opposite sides of the spaces between the splines of the shaft E.

Consequently at about the moment of synchronisation the fingers are about to leave one side of the spaces between the splines and pass over to the other side. The pressure on the sides of the fingers D is thus, at about the moment of synchronisation, quite small and so the force acting on the member H, in conjunction with the bevelled corners of the fingers D and slots J, can move the fingers slightly so that they come opposite the slots J.

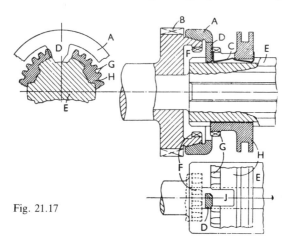

Fig. 21.17

The member H can then be slid over so as to engage the teeth G and F, the spring C being slightly depressed as this is done. Clearly until synchronisation is almost effected the greater the force that is applied to the member H the greater will be the force pressing the cones together and the greater will be the friction between them and the sooner will synchronisation be brought about. This is an advantage over the first type above, where the maximum force that can be used to press the cones together is limited by the strength of the springs pressing the retaining balls into contact with the cone members. Because the engagement of the dog clutch is baulked by the fingers D until synchronisation occurs, this synchromesh unit can be said to be of the *baulk* type.

21.16 Baulk-ring synchromesh

A further example of a synchromesh mechanism is shown in Fig.21.18. The dog clutch sleeve A is free to slide on splines on the hub B, which is fixed to the mainshaft C, and is controlled by the striking fork of the gear change mechanism. When moved to the right its internal splines *a* ultimately engage the dog teeth D to give third gear and when moved to the left they engage the dog teeth G to give fourth gear. The synchronising action is provided by the baulk rings H and J, which are coned internally to engage the cones formed on the gears E and F and which have external teeth *h* and *j* similar in form to the dog teeth D and G and are therefore the counterpart of the internal splines *a* of the sleeve A.

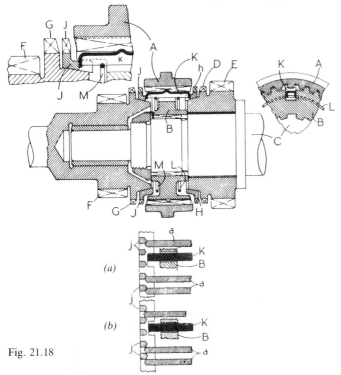

Fig. 21.18

The hub B has three grooves formed in it, as shown in the upper part of the elevation and in the scrap plan and end views, and fitting freely in these grooves are three fingers K. At their ends these fingers engage grooves in the baulk rings H and J but these grooves are wider than the fingers K so that although the baulk rings are constrained to rotate at the same speed as the hub they can rotate slightly relative to that hub. The fingers K are pressed outwards by circlip springs L and M and thus the ridge in the middle of the fingers is kept in engagement with a groove formed in the middle of the splines of the sleeve A.

Consider the action when a change from third to fourth gear is being made. At the beginning of the change the gear F will be rotating at a higher speed than the mainshaft, hub B and the baulk rings. When the gear lever is pushed so as to try to engage fourth gear it tries to press the sleeve A to the left but this merely causes the fingers K to push the baulk ring J against the cone of the gear F. Friction between the cones then tries to speed up the baulk ring and, conversely, to slow down the gear F. The baulk ring is thus forced into the position shown in the scrap plan view (*a*). In this position the teeth *j* are half opposite the splines *a* of the sleeve A. Thus even if the pressure applied to the sleeve A by the striking fork is sufficient to depress the fingers K against the force of the spring M the sleeve cannot move to the left and the pressure will merely be transferred to the baulk ring by the contact between the ends of the splines *a* and the teeth *j*. Thus the harder the gear lever is pressed the greater will be the friction, between the baulk ring and the cone of the gear F, which is tending to synchronise those members.

When synchronism is attained the frictional drag between the baulk ring and the gear F is reduced to zero and the pressure applied to the sleeve A is able, in conjunction with the inclined ends of the teeth *j* and splines *a*, to rotate the baulk ring slightly to its central position as shown in the lower plan view (*b*) and the sleeve A can then move across so that the splines engage the dog teeth G thus clutching the gear F to the hub B and mainshaft.

21.17   Smith synchromesh mechanism

Smiths Industries Ltd. synchromesh, while basically similar in principle and arrangement to the mechanism described above, differs in that it employs multiple cones and thus increases the frictional torque tending to produce synchronisation, other factors being the same. This reduces the time required to bring about synchronism and makes gear changes faster. The arrangement of the mechanism is shown in Fig. 21.19, in which the parts have been annotated with the same letters as the corresponding parts in Fig. 21.18. The important difference is that the cones J and H are now

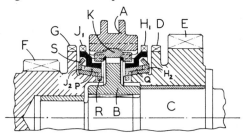

Fig. 21.19

made in two parts J_1 and J_2 and H_1 and H_2 and between these parts there are intermediate cones P and Q. The outer cone J_1 is driven by the member K as in Fig. 21.18 and the inner one by the projection S which engages a recess formed in J_1. The intermediate member P is driven by the projection R which engages a slot formed in the cone of the member F. When the shaft C is rotating relative to F there are now three slipping surfaces in the cone assembly whereas in Fig. 21.18 there is only one and hence for a given axial force on the sleeve A and with the same dimensions the synchronising torque will be approximately three times as great.

21.18   Porsche synchromesh

The principle of this will be explained with reference to Fig. 21.20 which shows a design used by Henry Meadows Ltd. of Wolverhampton, in some of their gearboxes. The gear G is on the end of the clutch shaft and drives the layshaft; H is the mainshaft of the gearbox. When changing up to the direct drive, the sleeve A, which is splined to the three-armed spider K, is moved to the left by the gear lever, and the conical inner surfaces of its splines make contact with the conical outer surface of the ring B. Friction then causes the latter to move relative to the member C so that the clearance at X is taken up and the end of the ring bears against the key E. The friction on the ring then tends to expand it and this increases the pressure between the ring and the sleeve A and makes it virtually impossible to move the latter any further to the left. When synchronism is achieved, the frictional force on the ring B is reduced to zero and it becomes easy to move the sleeve A over so that its internal splines engage the splines or teeth formed on the member D, which is itself splined to the gear G. This provides a positive drive between the gear G and the shaft H.

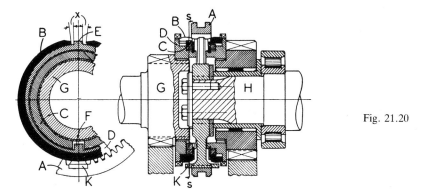

Fig. 21.20

The ring B is thicker at its centre, opposite to the key E, than at its ends though this is not very apparent from the drawing. This tapering is designed to obtain a uniform pressure between the ring B and the sleeve A, and to accommodate it, the outer surface of the ring C is made eccentric to the inner surface. The key F compels the ring C, and thus the ring B, to rotate with the gear G.

21.19   Lubrication of the gearbox

The lubrication of gearboxes, other than epicyclic types, which will be considered later, is usually effected by putting enough oil into the box to ensure that at least one gear will dip into the lubricant. When the gears are rotating the oil will be thrown about inside the box, thus lubricating the various parts.

The oil required is different from that suitable for an engine, the conditions being quite different. Temperatures are much lower and carbonisation has not to be considered. On the other hand, the pressures to which the oil films may be subjected may be much heavier than in an engine. The instructions of makers and the advice of reputable oil companies should always be followed.

It should not be thought that filling a gearbox to a higher level than that recommended will reduce the frictional losses in the box. On the contrary, the loss due to the churning of the oil will be greatly increased. However, over-filling is usually obviated by suitable placing of the filler spout.

Special oil seals of various patterns are fitted where the gearbox shafts pass through the casing and these usually give no trouble, but leakages might be caused by the expansion of the air enclosed in the box, and a vent should always be provided. Large washers are sometimes fitted on the inside of the ball bearings supporting the shafts of gearboxes to keep any particles of grit or chips from the gear teeth, from the bearings.

Some of the exterior parts of the selector and gate change mechanisms are best lubricated with a thin machine oil or with engine oil.

21.20   Freewheel devices

These are sometimes termed *one-way clutches*, since they transmit torque in one direction only and are generally used to disengage the drive automatically when torque is applied in the reverse direction. They have been placed in drive-lines, usually on the rear end of the gearbox, so that the engine could idle at a controlled speed under overrun conditions, without need for selecting neutral in the gearbox. This can be useful with two-stroke engines, which tend to fire very irregularly under overrun conditions, and it can also facilitate gear changing since it automatically de-clutches the drive when the throttle pedal is released. However, overrun braking by the engine is of course lost, which is why the device is installed so rarely. More common applications are in four-wheel drive vehicles, Section 18.4, and in automatic transmissions, as in Sections 23.1 and 23.3.

There are two main types of one-way clutch, or freewheel. Both are generally contained within the annular space between two hardened steel rings, rather like the inner and outer races of roller bearings. The inner one is keyed or otherwise fixed to the shaft and the outer one to a hub, or sleeve, from which the drive is ultimately taken.

Of the two types, one is the Borg-Warner, or sprag, type (Fig. 21.21), the essential elements of which are a series of rocking tumblers, called *sprags*, held together within a cage, also comprising two rings but with a crimped ribbon-spring in the annular space between them. All three components of the cage are pierced to accommodate the sprags.

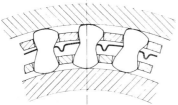

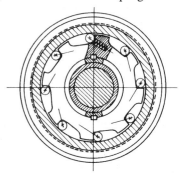

Fig. 21.21 (*above*) Borg-Warner sprag type freewheel
Fig. 21.22 (*right*) Roller type freewheel, with rollers retracted against their springs

The ribbon-spring tends to push the sprags upright, into a radial disposition between the inner and outer rings, or races. However, the radial clearance between these rings is not enough for the sprags to rock right up to their TDC positions, so they jam. Consequently, so long as the drive is in the direction tending to keep the sprags thus jammed, the torque can be transmitted from the shaft to the outer ring. If, however, the drive is reversed, the sprags tend to lay down, or trail, against the influence of the ribbon-spring, so no torque can then be transmitted.

The second type of freewheel is exemplified by the ZF unit, Fig. 21.22. This is usually called the *roller* type, because it has rollers instead of sprags. These rollers are generally housed in what resemble splines in either the inner or outer hardened steel ring. However, the base of each spline is not tangential to a circle centred on the axis of the shaft but, instead, is inclined, as viewed from the end of the assembly. Consequently, when the shaft is rotated in one direction, the rollers run up the inclines and therefore jam between the inner and outer rings. If the shaft is then rotated in the other direction, they run down the inclines again and are freed in the annular clearances between the two rings. The effects are similar to the jamming and unjamming of the sprags in the Borg-Warner unit. To obviate backlash in the system, the rollers are generally lightly spring-loaded up their short inclined tracks.

21.21   Auxiliary gearboxes and overdrives

The gear ratios adopted in all vehicles have to be a compromise since the factors concerned in their choice are conflicting. Thus for good acceleration in top gear, a ratio that is low in comparison with that which would give the best top speed on a good level road would be used. Again, for the best fuel economy higher ratios would be used than if a lively performance was the chief requirement.

The provision of a large number of ratios reduces the element of compromise and so there is a tendency to employ gearboxes giving a large number. This can be done in two ways: one is to provide the large number of ratios in a single box of more or less conventional form and the other is to use an auxiliary gearbox in tandem with a main gearbox giving only three or four ratios. The first method complicates the construction of the box and may make gear-changing a difficult operation but gearboxes giving five ratios are common in lorries and are becoming so in cars.

If an auxiliary gearbox is used, it may be an entirely separate unit but it is usually attached to the main box so as to form a single unit; it is, however, sometimes housed in the driving axle. The auxiliary box usually provides only direct drive and one reduction and this may be such that, when in use, all the overall ratios are lower than those when direct drive is used; this is the common practice with 'off-the-road' vehicles and the auxiliary box is kept in direct drive for road work and in reduction ratio for cross-country use. The auxiliary box may, however, have a reduction ratio such that when it is in use the overall ratios fall between those given when the direct drive is in use; this gives a split ratio box and all the ratios are then used in sequence. Auxiliary boxes may be simple constant-mesh types with a layshaft or may be epicyclic. The change-over is often power-operated, compressed air being generally used. Sometimes the auxiliary box takes the form of an overdrive unit, either automatically or electro-mechanically controlled, for obtaining a ratio of less than 1:1 in top gear and thus reducing engine speed during long-distance high-speed cruising, or to obtain a more suitable 3rd gear ratio for cruising in semi-urban conditions, or for overtaking at higher speeds. Where such a system is applied to all gears, it is generally termed a *range-change* box.

21.22   A Leyland ten-ratio gearbox

This provides a good example of the first of the above methods. It will be seen from Fig. 21.23 that the shaft arrangement is conventional, the mainshaft being in line with the clutch shaft and the layshaft below on a parallel axis. Two pairs of gears AB and CD provide alternative drives to the layshaft, the gears B and D being connected to it as required by muff type dog clutches. The muff E of the dog clutch for coupling the gear D has gear teeth on its exterior and provides a power take-off, the drive for which goes from A to B and thence to E which will be in its neutral position as shown. As there are two alternative drives to the layshaft the four pinions on it, which mesh directly with gears on the mainshaft, will provide eight ratios; the direct drive between the clutch shaft and the main shaft gives the ninth ratio while the tenth is an overdrive and is obtained by clutching the gear F to the layshaft. It should perhaps be pointed out that the drive from

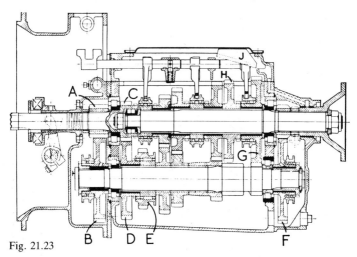

Fig. 21.23

the gear G to the mainshaft is obtained by clutching it to the gear H which is splined to the mainshaft. The reverse ratios are given by sliding a reverse idler into mesh with the gear H. The ratios are

Low 1st	9.352	1st	6.988
Low 2nd	5.764	2nd	4.308
Low 3rd	3.552	3rd	2.655
Low 4th	2.147	4th	1.605
Top	1.0	Overdrive	0.76

The gearbox is lubricated by splash provided by partly immersing the layshaft and reverse idler in oil. A trough J catches and feeds oil to the plain bearing on the outside of the hub of the output coupling.

21.23 The Fuller twin-countershaft gearbox

This provides an example of the second method of obtaining a multiplicity of ratios but also embodies a principle which enables the size of the box to be reduced. By using two layshafts (or countershafts) the tooth loads are halved and so the gears can be made only a little more than half as wide as they would have to be if only one layshaft were used. This will, however, be successful only if the torque is in fact equally divided between the two layshafts, and the way in which this is ensured is described later.

The gearbox shown in Fig. 21.24 comprises a five-speed and reverse box followed by a two-speed one, the combination thus providing ten forward and two reverse ratios. The input shaft A ends at the right in a narrow

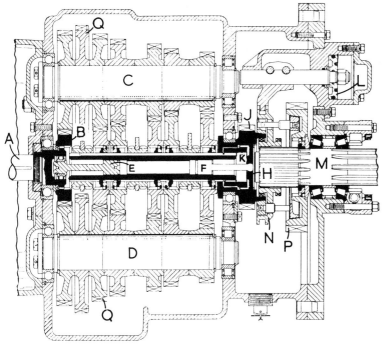

Fig. 21.24

splined portion which engages splines inside the pinion B but enough clearance is provided between the splines to allow the pinion to float radially by several thousandths of an inch. The pinion meshes with gears on the two layshafts C and D which are identical and are carried in ball and roller bearings in the casing so that they rotate about fixed axes. The gears are driven by keys which ensure that they are assembled in the correct relative positions to enable them to mesh correctly with the main shaft gears. The latter are free radially of the shaft and are positioned axially in pairs by collars, thinner ones being fixed inside the gears and the outer ones to the shaft and whose faces abut. The mainshaft is supported at each end by relatively flexible dumb-bell shaped members E and F; one end of each of these is fixed inside the mainshaft and the other ends are supported respectively in the spigot bearing inside the shaft A and in the boss H which is, in effect, part of the gear J. The latter is carried in the casing in a large ball bearing. The mainshaft gears are coupled to the shaft when required by sliding dog clutches. Because the mainshaft is free to float radially it will move slightly, if the tooth loads are unbalanced, until the upward tooth load at one side of the gear which is clutched to it is balanced by the downward tooth load at the other side. The torques transmitted by the layshafts are thus equalised. In order not to compromise the freedom of the mainshaft to move in this way it is connected to the output member J through an intermediate member K which is splined on the inside to the mainshaft and on the outside to the member J; both sets of splines are made with sufficient clearance to allow the freedom desired. The reverse ratio pinions on the layshaft (at the right) engage idlers which are carried on roller bearings and which mesh with the reverse gear on the mainshaft. The gears QQ are for a power take-off.

The auxiliary gearbox is housed in the right-hand part of the casing and a direct drive is obtained by clutching J to output shaft M by means of the dog clutch N which is operated by air pressure applied to the piston L. The low gear is obtained by engaging the dog clutch with the gear P, the drive then going from the member J through the two layshafts (not shown in the view because they do not lie in the plane of the drawing) to the gear P. The layshafts are carried in the casing on ball-and-roller bearings and rotate about fixed axes. The gear P, however, is free radially and can thus float sufficiently to enable the layshaft tooth loads to balance each other. The dog clutch N is provided with synchromesh for both its engagements.

21.24　An all-indirect gearbox

A good example of an all-indirect gearbox is illustrated in Fig. 21.25. This layout is especially suitable for rear-engine rear-wheel-drive or front-engine front-wheel-drive cars in which the engine is installed longitudinally.

Clutch shaft A is coupled to the input or driving shaft B by a splined muff C. Five pinions are either integral or fixed to the shaft B and four of these pinions mesh with gears that are carried on the driven or output shaft D on needle roller bearings N. The driven shaft is made integral with the pinion E of the hypoid final drive and is carried in the casing on taper roller bearings. The input shaft is carried at the right in a needle-roller bearing

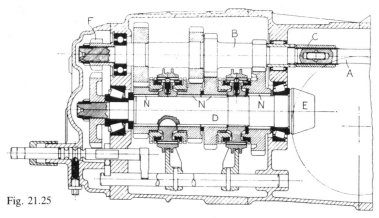

Fig. 21.25

and at the left in a ball bearing. The gears on the driven shaft are coupled to that shaft when required by dog clutches and synchromesh is provided. Reverse is obtained by sliding a reverse idler (not seen in the view) into mesh with the pinion F, which is fixed to the tail of the shaft B, and the corresponding gear fixed on the end of the driven shaft; both these gears are outside the end wall of the gearbox casing and are housed in the end cover. Now that gears can be made with sufficient accuracy to ensure reasonable silence in operation there is no real objection to the absence of a direct drive and the convenience of the all-indirect design is very great.

Chapter 22

Epicyclic and pre-selector gearboxes

Hitherto we have dealt only with what is termed *ordinary gearing*, the characteristic feature of which is that the axes of the various gears are fixed, the motions of all the gears being simply rotations about their own axes. The characteristic feature of *epicyclic gearing* is that at least one gear not only rotates about its own axis but also rotates bodily about some other axis. An example of epicyclic gearing is shown in Fig. 22.1. A spur pinion A, integral with its shaft, is free to rotate about its own axis XX, being carried in bearings in the frame E. A cranked shaft or arm C is also free to rotate about the same axis XX and carries on its crank pin a spur pinion B. The latter is free to rotate about its own axis YY but must also rotate bodily about the axis XX when the arm C is rotated in its bearings. The pinion B meshes with the pinion A and also with an internally toothed ring or annulus D which forms part of the frame E and is therefore fixed. The annulus D is, of course, circular and is concentric with the axis XX. This arrangement is an epicyclic train of gearing providing a definite and fixed speed or gear ratio, between the shaft A and the shaft of the arm C; it is *not* a gearbox.

The action of this gear train will be understood on reference to Figs. 22.2 (*a*) and (*b*), in which the effective part of the pinion B, the only part which for the moment is useful, has been blacked in. It will be seen that this

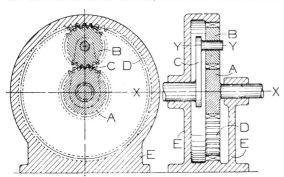

Fig. 22.1

portion constitutes a lever, the end P of which fits in a tooth space of the annulus D, the other end fitting in a tooth space of the pinion A. At its centre R the lever is pivoted on the pin of the arm C. Now suppose the pinion A to be turned through a small angle as shown at (*b*). The tooth space of A moves round to the left slightly, taking with it the end Q of the lever. Since the other end P of the lever is in a tooth space of the fixed annulus D the lever has to pivot about that point P as fulcrum. In so doing the centre R of the lever will move to the left, but since R is nearer than Q to the fulcrum P the point R will not move as far as Q. Now the lever PQ is attached at R to the arm C, hence the end of that arm moves round to the left a smaller distance than did the tooth space of A, and since the point R is farther from the axis XX than is the tooth space of A the angular movement of the arm C will be still smaller than that of the pinion A.

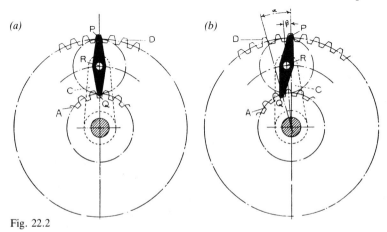

Fig. 22.2

The above action can only be supposed to take place for very small movements of the pinion A because obviously for large movements the lever PQ will go out of engagement with the pinion A and the annulus D. But we have in reality not a lever such as PQ but a complete pinion which acts as a succession of such levers so that the action is kept up, and as the pinion A is turned so the arm C is turned at a slower speed in the same direction.

22.1 Another epicyclic train of gearing

The arrangement of gears just decribed is only one of many different forms of epicyclic gearing; different, that is, in their mechanical arrangement. Fig. 22.3 shows a second arrangement.

The wheel A, integral with its shaft, is free to rotate about its axis XX in the frame E. It meshes with the teeth B_1 of a compound pinion which is free to revolve on the pin of the arm C. The latter is carried in the frame, being free to revolve about the axis XX. The portion B_2 of the pinion meshes with a wheel whose axis is XX but which, being part of the frame, is fixed. When the arm C is turned the wheel A is driven round in the same direction as the arm but at a lower speed.

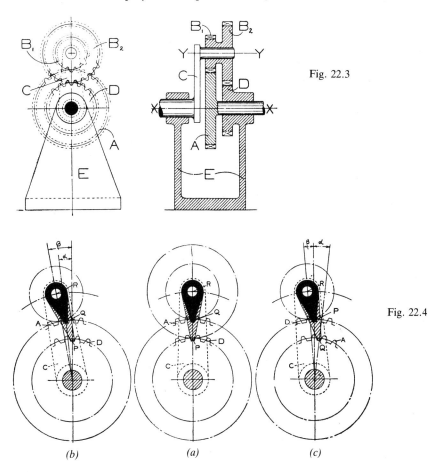

Fig. 22.3

Fig. 22.4

(b)   (a)   (c)

To illustrate the action Fig. 22.4 (*a*) and (*b*) have been drawn, in which the effective portion of the pinion is blacked and shaded and, again, it can be regarded as a lever, although the resemblance is not so easily seen as in the previous example. The end P of this lever engages a tooth space of the wheel D which is a fixture, the other end Q engages a tooth space of the wheel A, while at R the lever is pivoted to the arm C. Imagine the arm C to be turned through a small angle, as shown at (*b*). The point R of the lever is moved slightly to the left and, as the only motion possible to the lever PQ is to pivot about the point P, it turns about that point as a fulcrum. The end Q will, therefore, move in the same direction as the point R but, being nearer to the fulcrum, it will move a shorter distance. Thus the wheel A will be moved, as shown, in the same direction as the arm C, but through a smaller angle. As there is actually a complete pinion B instead of a lever PQ the action can be sustained.

It will be noticed that the fixed wheel D is smaller in diameter than the driven wheel A. When the fixed wheel is larger than the driven one the latter will be driven in the opposite direction to the arm. This is shown at (*c*). As before, when the arm C is turned through a small angle the point R of lever PQ is moved a small amount to the left, and the lever turns about the point P as fulcrum. Now the end Q of the lever is on the opposite side of the fulcrum P to the point R which moves to the left. The end Q of the lever, therefore, moves to the right taking with it the wheel A with which it engages. Thus the driven wheel A moves in the opposite direction to the arm C.

The wheels that are carried on the rotating arm in epicyclic gearing are generally called *planet wheels*, while the wheels at the centre about which the planet wheels roll are called *sun wheels*. Epicyclic gearing is sometimes referred to as *planetary gearing*.

22.2   Other forms of epicyclic gearing

There are many other forms of epicyclic gearing using both spur and bevel gears, but the two forms described are the most important as regards motor vehicles. If the working of these is thoroughly understood no difficulty should be experienced in following the working of other forms. An example of an epicyclic train using bevel gears is shown in Fig. 28.7 and the ordinary differential dealt with in Chapter 26 is nothing more than a simple epicyclic train. In the following paragraphs it is shown how the gear ratio of an epicyclic train may be worked out and the method is applicable to all the various forms of epicyclic gearing.

22.3   Gear ratio of epicyclic gearing

Consider the epicyclic train shown in Fig. 22.1. The gear ratio of the train is the ratio between the number of turns made by the arm and the (consequent) number of turns made by the sun wheel. If the arm C is turned once round (keeping the annulus D fixed) then the sun A will be turned a certain definite amount. Now, provided that in the end we arrive at the result that the annulus D has not moved and that the arm C has made one turn, the number of turns made by the sun A will be the same however we arrive at that result. This may be seen by considering as an analogy a wheel rolling on a board, as shown in Fig. 22.5. If the wheel is rolled one half turn (the board being fixed) it will move along by the amount S (half the circumference of the wheel). The result of the operation is that the wheel has turned half a turn about its axis and has moved bodily the distance S, while the board has not moved at all. Suppose now that from the original position the board and the wheel are moved solidly, both together, the distance S. The position will then be as at 2a. Now, keeping the wheel at B, let the board be moved back under the wheel to its original position (2b). The board must, therefore, be moved back the distance S under the wheel, and in so doing it will turn the wheel half a turn.

It should be clear that when the board has arrived back in its original position the result is the same as before. The board (having arrived back into its original position) has not moved. The wheel has moved bodily the distance S and has made half a turn about its axis. We have arrived at the same result in two steps instead of in a single step. By adopting a similar procedure with epicyclic gearing the motions of the various members are easily found. We arrive at the desired result in two steps instead of in one

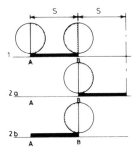

Fig. 22.5

and we so arrange the steps that in one of them we *turn every member the same amount*, and that in the other step we *keep the arm of the train fixed*, so that for that step the train works as ordinary gearing, which can easily be dealt with. An example will make the process clear, especially if the steps are recorded in tabular form.

Thus, considering the gear shown in Fig. 22.1, suppose the wheels to have the following numbers of teeth: A, 40; B, 20; D, 80. We are concerned with the motions of the various wheels and the arm and our Table will have four columns –

	Arm C	Annulus D	Sun wheel A
First step			
Second step			
Desired result	+ 1	0	?

Now when we have arrived at the desired result the arm C must have made one turn and the annulus D no turns. These figures may, therefore, be inserted as shown. Secondly, it is required that in the second step the arm of the train shall be fixed, hence we must have zero for the arm in the second step, thus –

	Arm C	Annulus D	Sun wheel A
First step			
Second step	0		
Desired result	+ 1	0	?

It follows that the motion of the arm in the first step must be + 1, and since we want all the members to have the same motion in the first step all the members must receive + 1 turn, thus –

	Arm C	Annulus D	Sun wheel A
First step	+ 1	+ 1	+ 1
Second step	0		
Desired result	+ 1	0	?

Again, it follows that the motion of the annulus D in the second step must be − 1 in order that the two steps shall add up to zero. The minus sign indicates that in this step the annulus is to be turned *backwards*. Now, considering the second step, the arm is going to be fixed and the annulus is going to be turned backwards one turn. The wheel B will then turn in the same direction as the annulus, that is, backwards, while the sun wheel A will turn in the opposite direction to B and hence in the opposite direction to the annulus. In the second step, therefore, the sun wheel moves forward so that whatever the amount of the motion the sign is +. Care must be taken to get the sign of the motion right. The amount of the motion is given by the rules of ordinary gearing as −

$$1 \times \frac{\text{No. teeth in annulus}}{\text{No. teeth in pinion B}} \times \frac{\text{No. teeth in B}}{\text{No. teeth in A}}$$

This becomes −

$$1 \times \frac{80}{20} \times \frac{20}{40} = 2.$$

Our Table now appears as under, and on adding up the motions of the sun wheel in the two steps its resultant motion is found −

	Arm C	Annulus D	Sun wheel A
First step	+ 1	+ 1	+ 1
Second step	0	− 1	+ 2
Desired result	+ 1	0	+ 3

Since the sign of the resultant motion of the sun wheel A is positive, that wheel moves in the same direction as the arm, so that the gear is a forward one. The gear ratio −

$$\frac{\text{Arm C}}{\text{Wheel A}} = \frac{1}{3}$$

so that the sun wheel A goes three times as fast as the arm. If an epicyclic train of this type is to be used in a motor car it will have to be with the engine driving the sun wheel A and with the arm C coupled to the driving wheels. As will be seen later, a train of this type is used in the Wilson epicyclic gearbox.

A pair of planet pinions meshing with each other is often used to replace a single pinion as is shown in Fig. 22.6(a). One pinion meshes with the sun and the other with the annulus. If the annulus is assumed to be the fixed member and the sun to be the driving member, the ratio of the train becomes −

$$\frac{\text{Sun}}{\text{Planet carrier}} = \frac{S - A}{S}$$

and as S must necessarily be smaller than A the ratio is negative, i.e. a reverse is obtained. One of the pair of pinions may also be made a compound pinion having two sets of teeth as in Fig. 22.6(b) where S

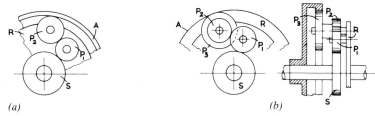

Fig. 22.6 Double planet pinions

meshes with P_1, P_1 with P_2 and P_3 which is integral with P_2 meshes with the annulus A. The ratio of this train with the annulus as the fixed member is –

$$\frac{\text{Sun}}{\text{Planet carrier}} = 1 - \frac{A - P_2}{P_3 \times S}$$

22.4 Clutch action of epicyclic gearing

In the train of gearing shown in Figs. 22.1 and 2, when the pinion A was turned the lever PQ pivoted about the point P and thus caused the arm C to turn. Now suppose that the annulus D is made a separate member from the frame E, free to revolve about the axis XX, then when the pinion A is turned, instead of the lever PQ pivoting about the point P and thus moving the arm C, the latter will remain stationary and the lever PQ will pivot about its centre R and cause the annulus D to revolve in the opposite direction to the pinion A. If now a brake is applied to the annulus D so as to slow it down and finally bring it to rest, then the arm C will be gradually speeded up and will finally rotate as it would do if D were part of the frame E. Therefore, by making what will ultimately be the fixed member of the train free, and by gradually bringing that member to rest, the driven member will gradually be speeded up and there is no longer any necessity for a separate clutch such as is required with ordinary gearboxes. The clutch action by which the engine is gradually coupled to the driving wheels is obtained in the epicyclic gearing itself. Hence cars employing epicyclic gearboxes have no clutch in the ordinary sense of the word.

22.5 Epicyclic gearboxes

So far we have dealt only with epicyclic trains giving a single ratio between two shafts. We go on to consider boxes giving a number of ratios but will point out that any single epicyclic train can be arranged to give a 1:1 ratio in addition to its epicyclic ratio by providing a clutch to lock any two of its members together. It is then necessary to leave free the member of the train that is fixed during epicyclic action and to fix it when that is required; this is generally done by means of a friction brake, though the more costly multi-plate clutch alternative is employed because it requires less attention in service.

Multi-ratio epicyclic boxes can be built up in three principal ways. In the first, the members of a single train are arranged so that each can be used either as the input, the output or the fixed member; in a simple three element train (e.g. sun, annulus and planet carrier) seven different drives are possible but the unsuitable values of some of the ratios and the complexity of the construction make the method of little practical value. In the second method, several separate trains are arranged in sequence so that each can provide its own ratios when required, i.e. a reduction or a 1:1 ratio, and by locking all the trains an overall 1:1 ratio is obtained . The number of ratios obtainable by this method theoretically increases very rapidly with the number of trains used, thus with four trains 15 ratios could be obtained but, in practice, it would be found impossible to use all of these. The trains can be all of the same type or be of different types. Fig. 22.7(*a*) shows two sun and annulus trains in tandem and (*b*) two double-sun trains so arranged. By making some of the members function as part of both trains the constructional problems are simpified but the number of ratios theoretically available is reduced. Thus in (*c*) the two sun gears of (*a*) have been joined together and the planet carrier acts for both the trains, each of which acts as a simple epicyclic train; the arrangement gives three ratios as compared with the four of (*a*). In (*d*) two double sun trains are arranged with a common planet carrier and one sun, S, and its mating pinion function for both the trains. The brake B_2 when applied gives a

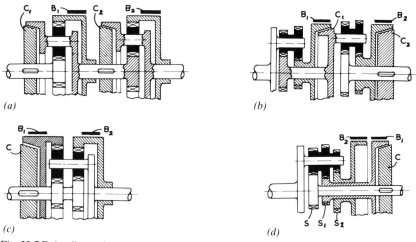

Fig. 22.7 Epicyclic gearbox arrangements

reverse gear because the sun S_2 is larger than the driven sun S whereas S_1 which gives a forward gear when the brake B_1 is applied is smaller. This ability to provide a reverse gear easily made the arrangement popular in the past but it is now little used.

The third method of getting a multi-ratio epicyclic gearbox is by compounding a number of simple epicyclic trains. The Wilson boxes, developed more than half a century ago and still widely used, employ this method and one of these will now be described.

One train of epicyclic gearing is used for all the various ratios, its sun S_1 (Fig. 22.8 (*b*)), being secured to a shaft D coupled permanently to the engine and its arm R_1 to the shaft E which is coupled permanently to the driving road wheels and the various ratios are obtained by driving the

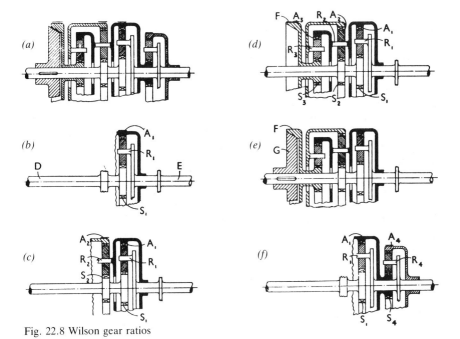

Fig. 22.8 Wilson gear ratios

annulus A_1 at different speeds in relation to the engine speed. Supposing the latter to be constant at say 1000 rev/min, then if the speed of the annulus A is zero (that is, it is held at rest), then the speed of the arm R_1 would be 1000 $S/(A + S)$, where A and S represent the number of teeth in the annulus and sun respectively. Taking a numerical example, suppose $A = 100$ and $S = 25$ then the speed of R will be 200 rev/min and the gear ratio is 1000 to 200 or 5:1. Suppose now that the annulus instead of being held at rest is driven in the same direction as the engine at, say, 100 rev/min then (the engine speed being 1000 rev/min as before), the speed of the arm R will be 280 rev/min, instead of 200 rev/min. Thus a higher gear is obtained. Similarly, if the speed of the annulus was made 200 rev/min, then the speed of the arm would be 360 rev/min. If the annulus were driven in the opposite direction to the engine then the arm would rotate slower than when the annulus was fixed. Thus, if the speed of the annulus were, say, 400 rev/min backwards then the speed of the arm (engine speed still 1000 rev/min) would be -120, that is, backwards, thus giving a reverse gear. Thus, by driving the annulus at different speeds (in relation to engine speed), the driven shaft is driven at different speeds, that is, different gear ratios are obtained.

To enable the annulus of the main train to be driven at these different speeds, auxiliary epicyclic trains are used. Thus, for second gear the train $S_2 R_2 A_2$ (Fig. 22.8 (c)) is utilised. In this train the sun S_2 is fixed to the engine shaft D, the annulus can be held at rest by a brake and the arm R_2 is coupled to the annulus A_1. If the annulus A_2 is held at rest and the engine drives the suns S_1 and S_2 then, considering train $S_2 R_2 A_2$ it should be clear that R_2 will rotate in the same direction as the engine but at a lower speed.

But R_2 is secured to A_1 and so A_1 is rotated in the same direction at the engine and R_1 will rotate at a higher speed than it did on first gear when A_1 was fixed.

To get third gear, the arm R_1 has to be made to rotate faster than on second gear and to do this the annulus A_1 and thus the arm R_2 must be made to rotate faster. To do this the annulus A_2 is now caused to rotate in the same direction as the engine. This is brought about by the train S_3 R_3 A_3, of which the sun S_3 is held at rest by the brake on its brake drum F, while the arm R_3 is coupled to the annulus A_2 and the annulus A_3 is coupled to the arm R_2. Considering the train S_3 R_3 A_3 if S_3 is fixed and A_3 is rotating in the same direction as the engine then the arm R_3 will also be rotating in the same direction as the engine. But R_3 is coupled to A_2 and so in the train S_2 R_2 A_2 both the sun S_2 and the annulus A_2 are rotating in the same direction as the engine and thus the speed of the arm R_2 must be greater than when A_2 was fixed. The speed of the annulus A_1 is thus greater than on second gear, that is, a higher gear is obtained.

The direct drive for top gear is obtained by locking S_3 to the engine shaft D by sliding the male cone G, which is splined to D, along so as to engage the female cone formed in the drum F which is fixed to S_3. This has the effect of locking the gear so that it must all revolve 'solid'.

To obtain a reverse gear the auxiliary train S_4 R_4 A_4 is brought into action. The sun S_4 of this train is secured to the annulus A_1, the arm R_4 is fixed to the driven shaft D and the annulus A_4 can be held at rest by a brake.

Considering train S_4 A_4 R_4 if A_4 is fixed and R_4 is rotating backwards then S_4 will be rotating backwards at a higher speed than the arm and thus in train S_1 R_1 A_1, although the sun S_1 is rotating forwards, the annulus A_1 is rotating backwards at such a speed that R_1 goes backwards also. This explanation can only be made convincing by working out the gear ratio as follows.

Suppose the numbers of teeth $S_1 = 25$, $A_1 = 100$, $S_4 = 40$, $A_4 = 80$. Keeping A_4 fixed, let R_4 be rotated backwards one turn, the motions of the members of train S_4 R_4 A_4 may be obtained by the method previously described and as shown in the Table Fig. 22.9. Now considering train S_1 R_1 A_1 is secured to S_1 it has received -3 turns and since R_1 and R_4 are both fixed to the driven shaft D the arm R_1 has received -1 turn the same as R_4. Hence in train S_1 R_1 A_1 the motions of R_1 and A_1 are settled and the consequent motion of S_1 may be found as shown in the Table Fig. 22.10.

Thus the engine shaft has turned $+7$ turns and the driven shaft has turned -1 turn and a reverse gear ratio of $7:1$ is obtained.

R_4	A_4	S_4
-1	-1	-1
0	$+1$	-2
-1	0	-3

Fig. 22.9 (*left*)

Fig. 22.10 (*right*)

R_1	A_1	S_1
-1	-1	-1
0	-2	$+8$
-1	-3	$+7$

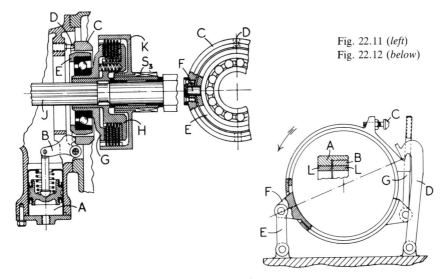

Fig. 22.11 (*left*)
Fig. 22.12 (*below*)

The clutches used to give the direct drive in modern Wilson boxes are multi-plate designs as shown in Fig. 22.11. Compressed air, or occasionally fluid pressure, is used to engage the clutch and acts in a cylinder A to rotate the lever B and thus move the lever C, which is in the form of a ring, about its fulcrum at D. The ring C is pivoted on pins F at both sides of the housing E and through the ball bearing compresses the plates of the clutch between the presser plate G and the hub H. The latter is splined on the input shaft J and carries the inner plates while the outer plates are housed in the drum K which is splined to the hub of the sun S_3.

The brakes are in two parts: an outer band A, Fig. 22.12, anchored by the hook link D and the inner band B which is anchored by the lug F that projects through a slot cut in the outer band. The two bands are thus anchored at diametrically opposite points thereby making the fairly large anchorage forces cancel each other so that no large force has to be sustained by the bearings supporting the brake drum. The outer band is pulled up at its free end by a rod G in order to apply it while the inner band is brought into action by the overlapping part of the outer band. This obviates the need for two separate actuating mechanisms. An example of the actuating mechanism is shown in Fig. 22.13. Air pressure on the piston A lifts the strut Q and rotates the lever B about its fixed axis O, the roller C then acts on the cam surface of the lever K and lifts it so as to pull up the end of the outer band. The cam surface is made so that initially the lift of the lever K for a given piston travel is large and the clearances in the brake are taken up rapidly while subsequently the lift is reduced so that maximum leverage is obtained and the large operating force is provided with the minimum effort. This action is also promoted by the approach of the point P of the lever B to a dead-centre position above the axis O and similarly by the lever K. In order to keep this mechanism in its proper operating condition as the brake linings wear an automatic adjuster is used; this is seen at the top of the pull rod and its action is illustrated in Fig. 22.14.

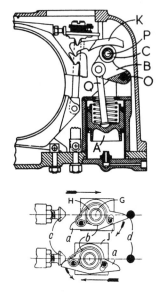

Fig. 22.13 (*left*)
Fig. 22.14 (*below left*)
Fig. 22.15 (*below*)

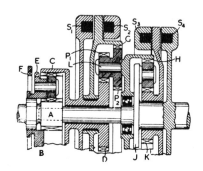

22.6   Automatic adjusters

The action of the automatic adjusters will be made clear by reference to Fig. 22.14. Surrounding the nut H on the top of the pull rod is a coil spring *b*, one end of which is secured to a pin fixed in a plate *a* which is free to turn round the nut H. The spring is coiled round the nut a few turns, is looped round the pin in the plate *a* again and finally is secured to a pin passing through a slot in the plate *a* and fixed in the knife edge plate J. When the pull rod is moved upwards by the bus-bar its upper end moves over and the plate *a* approaches the stop *c* fixed to the brake band (to the gear box casing for top gear). When the brake is in proper adjustment it comes on fully just as the plate *a* touches the stop *c*, but if wear has occurred the plate hits the stop and is rotated about the nut H in an anticlockwise direction. This rotation does not turn the nut, however, because the spring *b* uncoils and becomes free on the nut. When the pull rod is released its upper end moves back and the plate *a* hits the stop pin D, fixed in the casing. This causes the plate to rotate in a clockwise direction and this rotation *is* communicated to the nut H because for this direction of rotation the spring *b* coils up and grips the nut. The nut being turned slightly the brake is tightened up slightly. The action described occurs every time the brake is applied and released, until the nut has been tightened up so much that when the brake is fully on the plate *a* only just reaches the stop *c*; the brakes are then in proper adjustment. Thus, provided the stops *c* are positioned properly and that the automatic adjusters work regularly the brakes will be maintained always in the proper adjustment.

For public service passenger vehicles, in which Wilson boxes are widely used, it is important that the motion of the vehicle when starting and when gear changes are being effected should be smooth and the accelerations should not be unduly high. This is ensured by means of a semi-automatic operation of the gear changes.

These are initiated by the movement of a small lever by the driver but the operation of the solenoid controlled valves admitting air to the brake and clutch actuating cylinders is dependent on the prevailing conditions, in particular the road speed and the position of the accelerator pedal. The pressure of the air supply to the actuating cylinders is also modulated in accordance with the gear being engaged, a lower pressure being provided for the lower gears than for the higher ones. The pressure is also varied during the engagement of the brakes and the clutch, being increased towards the end of the engagement to ensure that this is complete.

22.7 Cotal epicyclic gear

This is shown in Fig. 22.15. The wheel A is integral with the engine shaft and meshes with pinions carried by a spider B which is free to slide along the outside of the engine shaft. When the spider B is slid to the left its teeth E mesh with teeth F of an annulus which is fixed to the gearbox casing. The pins of the spider then form fixed bearings for the pinions, and so the annulus C with which the latter mesh is driven in the opposite direction to the wheel A. This gives the reverse drives. When the spider B is slid to the right its teeth E engage the teeth of the annulus C and then the wheel A, pinions, spider B and annulus C revolve 'solid'. This gives the forward drives.

The four forward ratios are obtained by means of two epicyclic trains arranged in tandem. One consists of the sun D (fixed to the annulus C), the compound planets $P_1 P_2$ (carried on the pins L of the arm which is integral with the annulus H of the second train) and the annulus G which can be held fixed.

When this is done the annulus H is driven in the same direction as the sun D but at a lower speed. The second train consists of the annulus H, the sun K and the arm J which is fixed on the output shaft. The sun K can be held at rest so that the train gives a reduction between the annulus H and the arm J and it can also be locked to the output shaft so that the train must revolve solid. The annulus G can also be locked to the sun D so that the first train must revolve solid.

The fixing and locking of the members is done by electromagnets whose windings $S_1 S_2 S_3 S_4$ are energised as may be required. For first gear S_2 and S_3 are energised and both epicyclic trains provide a reduction since both annulus G and sun K are fixed. For second gear, S_2 and S_4 are energised and the second train revolves solid, the only reduction being in the first train. For third gear, S_1 and S_3 are energised, the first train is locked solid and the only reduction occurs in the second train. For fourth gear S_1 and S_4 are energised and both trains revolve solid so that a direct drive is obtained.

The windings S_1 and S_4 are carried by parts that sometimes rotate and so these windings are connected to slip rings on which brushes bear. The current for energising the windings is supplied by the battery or generator of the car and is between two and three ampères.

The control is extremely simple consisting merely of a switch which connects the appropriate winding to the battery. This switch is usually mounted at the centre of the steering wheel.

Chapter 23

Torque converters and automatic gearboxes

A torque converter is a device which performs a function similar to that of a gearbox, namely, to increase the torque while reducing the speed, but whereas a gearbox provides only a small number of fixed ratios the torque converter provides a continuous variation of ratio from the lowest to the highest.

Constructionally, a torque converter is somewhat similar to a fluid flywheel from which it differs in one important aspect, namely, in having *three* principal components instead of only *two*. Torque converters all consist of (*a*) the driving element (*impeller*) which is connected to the engine, (*b*) the driven element (*rotor*) which is connected to the propeller shaft, and (*c*) the fixed element (*reaction member*) which is fixed to the frame. It is the last element which makes it possible to obtain a change of torque between input and output shafts and, as has been seen, the fluid flywheel, which does not have any fixed member, cannot produce any change of torque.

A three-stage torque converter is shown in the several views of Fig. 23.1. The impeller, shown in sectional perspective at (*d*), is a conical disc provided with blades A the outer ends of which are tied together by a ring *a*. If this impeller is immersed in fluid and rotated then the fluid between the blades will be flung out more or less tangentially and a flow will be established from the centre or eye of the impeller to the periphery. The velocity of a particle of fluid on leaving the impeller is indicated by the line V_a in the view (*a*); this velocity may be resolved into a purely tangential component V_t and a purely radial component V_r.

The rotor or driven element is sectioned in black in the views (*a*), (*b*) and (*c*) and is shown in sectional perspective at (*f*). It consists of a portion similar to the impeller, comprising the disc member *b*, which carries the blades F, and the hollow annular member *g* which is carried by the blades F and which in turn carries blades B and D; these latter blades are tied together at their outer ends by rings as shown.

The fixed, or reaction, member consists of a drumlike casing *h* fitting the shaft portions of the impeller and rotor at the centre and thus enclosing

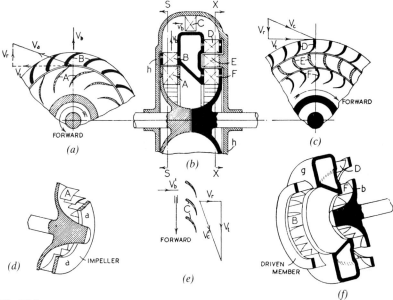

Fig. 23.1

those members. The reaction member carries blades C all round its periphery and blades E project, in a ring, from the right-hand end wall.

The action of the converter is as follows: the fluid flung out at the periphery of the impeller impinges on the blades B of the rotor and is deflected by those blades, the tangential component of the velocity of any particle, for example, V_t in view (a), being abstracted, more or less completely, so that the velocity of the particle on leaving the blades B is more or less radial as indicated by the arrow V_b. The particle being considered has therefore lost momentum in the tangential direction and this momentum has been gained by the blades B, that is, by the rotor. In being deflected backwards by the blades the fluid applies a pressure forwards on the blades. On leaving the blades B the fluid is guided round by the fixed casing and enters the blades C. In passing through these blades the velocity of the particle is changed from a more or less purely axial velocity, as V_b^1 in views (b) and (e), into a velocity having a considerable tangential component, as V_t in view (e). In deflecting the fluid in this way the blades C, and thus the fixed casing, receive a backwards thrust and unless the reaction member were fixed these thrusts would make it rotate backwards. The particle of fluid is now guided round by the fixed casing and enters the blades D of the rotor with a velocity V_c in view (c), which again has a considerable tangential component V_t and again on passing through the blades this tangential component is abstracted and the momentum associated with it is acquired by the rotor. The particle of fluid now enters the blades E which restore the tangential component of velocity once more and finally it enters blades F which finally abstract the tangential momentum, which is acquired by the rotor. The particle of fluid has now found its way back to the eye of the impeller and the cycle commences all over again.

The rotor or driven element thus receives three driving impulses, one from the blades B, one from the blades D and one from the blades F, and this converter is consequently called a *three-stage converter*.

The characteristics of a torque converter of this kind are shown by the graphs Fig. 23.2 (*a*) and (*b*).

The graphs (*a*) show the manner in which the torque-increase and efficiency vary when the rotor speed varies from zero to the maximum value (2700 rev/min), the impeller speed being constant at 3000 rev/min. When the rotor speed is zero (because the resistance opposing its motion is large enough to hold it fixed) the torque tending to rotate it will be nearly 6½ times the torque developed by the engine at its speed of 3000 rev/min.

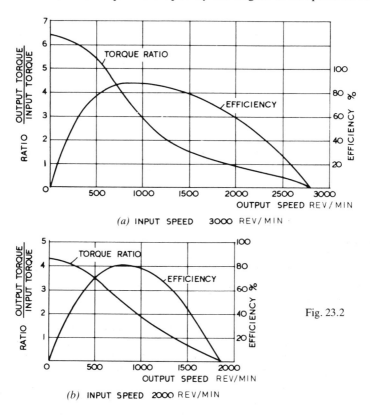

(a) INPUT SPEED   3000 REV/MIN

(b) INPUT SPEED 2000 REV/MIN

Fig. 23.2

If the resistance to the motion of the rotor now decreases so that the rotor starts to rotate, then as it gathers speed so the driving torque action on it falls off. At a rotor speed of 1000, for example, the driving torque would have fallen off to about three times engine torque, at 1900 rev/min the driving torque would be only just equal to engine torque, while at 2700 rev/min the driving torque would have fallen to zero. The efficiency on the other hand starts at zero when the rotor speed is zero, because although the driving torque acting on the rotor is then large no rotation occurs and the torque does no work; thus no work is being got out of the converter but a lot of work is being put in by the engine and so the efficiency is zero. As the rotor speed increases so does the efficiency and a peak efficiency of 86 to 90% is reached at a rotor speed of about 1000 rev/min. As the rotor speed continues to increase the efficiency falls off again and at 2700 rev/min becomes zero once more, this time because although the rotor is revolving rapidly the driving torque on it is zero and no work can be got out of it.

The graphs (*b*) show the same things but for an impeller speed of 2000 rev/min instead of 3000 rev/min. It will be seen that the driving torque acting on the rotor when it is stalled, that is, held at rest, is now only 4⅓ times engine torque and it falls off to zero at a rotor speed of 1800 rev/min. The efficiency reaches a maximum value of only about 80% instead of 85 to 90%.

It is thus seen that only over a rather narrow range of rotor speeds is the efficiency reasonably good and it must be borne in mind that if the efficiency is, say, 60%, then 40% of the power developed by the engine is wasted, being converted into heat which raises the temperature of the torque converter fluid and which has to be dissipated by some means, commonly a radiator. The fall-off of efficiency at the low speed end of the range can be tolerated because those speeds are normally used only for short periods when starting and climbing severe hills, but the fall off at high speeds cannot be tolerated and must be circumvented. There are two principal ways in which this can be done, (*a*) by substituting a direct drive for the torque converter at high speeds and (*b*) by making the torque converter function as a fluid flywheel at the higher speeds.

23.1   Torque converter with direct drive

Referring to Fig. 23.3, a double clutch, provided with two separate driven plates A and B, is situated between the engine and the torque converter (TC), only the impeller and part of the rotor of which are shown. The plate A is connected to the shaft C which is permanently coupled to the propeller shaft while the plate B is connected to the impeller of the torque converter. The rotor of the latter is connected through the free-wheel D to the shaft C and thus to the output shaft. The intermediate plate E of the clutch can be pressed either to the left or to the right. When pressed to the right it grips the plate B and thus drives the impeller of the torque converter and the drive passes through the torque converter and the free-wheel D to the output. If now the plate E is pressed to the left the plate B (and torque converter) will no longer be driven but the drive will pass direct through plate A to the shaft C and output which will override the rollers of the

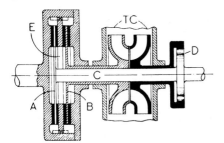

Fig. 23.3

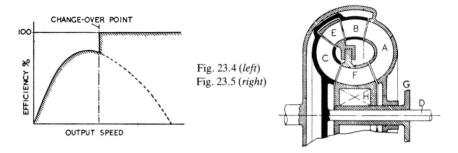

CHANGE-OVER POINT

EFFICIENCY %

OUTPUT SPEED

Fig. 23.4 (*left*)
Fig. 23.5 (*right*)

freewheel D; the rotor of the torque converter will thus come to rest. The efficiency of the direct drive is 100% and the combined efficiency curve will be as shown in Fig. 23.4. The change-over from converter to direct drive is done by the operation of a lever or pedal by the driver. Three-stage converters are no longer used in road vehicles because single-stage ones used in conjunction with gearboxes have been found adequate.

23.2   Turbo-Transmitters converter

The second method of obviating the fall-off in efficiency at the higher output speeds is used in the Turbo-Transmitters converter unit shown diagrammatically in Fig. 23.5.

The impeller is seen at A and is permanently connected to the engine crankshaft; it differs from that of the Leyland unit (Fig. 23.3) in having blades that extend over nearly half of the complete fluid circuit instead of over only about a quarter of that circuit. The impeller thus more nearly resembles the impeller of a fluid flywheel from which it differs chiefly in having blades that are curved in the end view whereas the blades of a fluid flywheel impeller are straight. The driven member, shown sectioned in solid black, has two sets of blades B and C and is fixed to the output shaft D. The reaction member also has two sets of blades E and F. The blade unit E is carried on the unit F on which it is free to rotate in the forwards direction but is prevented from rotating backwards by pawls that engage rachet teeth on F. The member F in turn is free to rotate on the fixed member G but again only in the forwards direction. Backwards rotation is prevented by a multi-plate clutch, situated at H, which engages and locks F to G whenever the member F tries to rotate backwards but which disengages when F tries to go forwards, which motion is thus allowed. This clutch is shown in Fig. 23.7. The converter is a two-stage one, two driving impulses being given to the driven member, one when the direction of the fluid is changed in the blades B and a second when the direction of the fluid is changed in the blades C. When the torque acting on the driven member BCD is greater than the engine torque applied to the driving member A, there will be a reaction torque acting on the blades E and F; this will be transmitted by the pawls and ratchet teeth from E to F and by the clutch at H to the member G. Whenever the torque acting on the blades B and C tends to fall below the torque applied to A, a forwards torque will be applied to the blades E and F; this will merely cause those blades to rotate forwards and the converter will then function as a fluid flywheel; the percentage slip will then be quite small, say about 5 or 6%, and will decrease as the speed of the driven member increases.

The characteristics of this converter will thus be somewhat as shown in Fig. 23.6, which shows torque increase and efficiency curves for an input speed of 3500 rev/min. The converter being only a two-stage one, the maximum torque is only about four times engine torque as compared with 6½ to seven in the Leyland converter, but otherwise the curves are very similar in general shape. The change-over point, at which the reaction members E and F begin to rotate forwards, and the unit commences to function as a fluid flywheel, is at 1200 rev/min, and from that speed onwards the output torque will be approximately equal to the input torque and the output speed will be only some 5 or 6% less than engine speed.

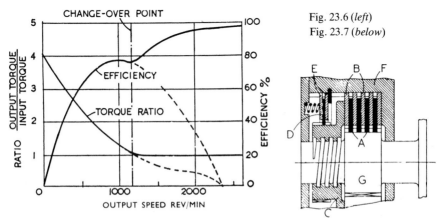

Fig. 23.6 (*left*)
Fig. 23.7 (*below*)

When the engine speed is less than the maximum 3500 rev/min assumed above, and when the throttle opening is reduced so that the engine torque is less than maximum, then the change-over speed will be lower than the 1200 rev/min corresponding to maximum engine speed and torque.

The fact that the change-over is quite automatic is important and is responsible for the good performance of this type of converter at part throttle loads and medium engine speeds.

23.3 Other arrangements of torque converters

Four arrangements of single-stage converters are shown in Figs. 23.8 to 23.11.

In Fig. 23.8 the reaction member R is permanently fixed, which makes it unsuitable for use in motor vehicles unless some form of direct drive is provided and the converter is emptied when the direct drive is engaged.

The design shown in Fig. 23.9 is widely used, being simple constructionally; the one-way clutch S is sometimes placed outside the casing by providing the reaction member with a sleeve which passes through the cover of the impeller member.

In Fig. 23.10 an auxiliary impeller I_2 is provided and is carried on a one-way clutch S_3 on the main impeller I_1; the reaction member is also divided into two portions R_1 and R_2, each of which is anchored separately

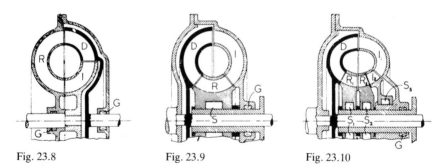

Fig. 23.8   Fig. 23.9   Fig. 23.10

by the one-way clutches S_1 and S_2. This arrangement, which was introduced on Buick cars some years ago, is claimed to increase the efficiency of
the converter and to make the change over to coupling action smoother.

In the Borgward converter shown in Fig. 23.11 the whole reaction
member RR_1 and the impeller I on which the reaction member is mounted
on ball bearings B, is moved to the left when engaging the cone clutch H
and is done by the reaction of the pressure that exists inside the coupling at
L and which acts on the exposed area of the driven member D. To obtain
direct drive, oil under pressure from the gearbox control unit is passed to
the space K and moves the reaction member and impeller to the right so as
to engage the cone clutch M. The one-way clutch S enables the output
member E to drive the impeller, and thus the engine, in the forwards
direction and so permits the engine to be used as a brake or to be started by
towing the car.

The arrangement of a two-stage converter shown in Fig. 23.12 differs
from that of Fig. 23.5 in that only a single reaction member is used and so
the second driven member D_2, which is bolted up to the member D_1,
discharges direct into the inlet of the impeller. The single plate clutch C
gives a direct drive when it is required; the method of engaging the clutch is
not shown but various means are used; a very convenient one when the
converter is associated with an automatic gearbox is to make the pressure
plate of the clutch function as a piston in a cylinder formed in the flywheel
and to engage the clutch by admitting pressure oil to this cylinder.

Fig. 23.11 (*left*)
Fig. 23.12 (*below*)

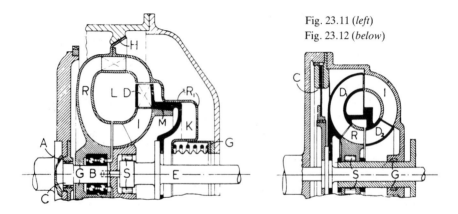

23.4   Chevrolet Turboglide transmission

This is a combination of a converter and an epicyclic gear and is shown in Fig. 23.13. The converter has five elements, the pump P, three turbine or driven elements T_1, T_2 and T_3, and a reaction member R. The latter is free to rotate in the forward direction on the freewheel F_1 and is provided with a set of blades B, whose angles are adjustable; the mechanism for making the adjustment is not indicated.

The first turbine element T_1 is coupled by the shaft D to the sun S_2 of the second epicyclic train; the second turbine T_2 is coupled through the sleeve E to the annulus A_1 of the first epicyclic train and the third turbine T_3 is coupled to the output shaft H by the sleeve G_1, the clutch C_1 (which is always engaged except when neutral and reverse are selected), the sleeve G_2 and the planet carrier R_2. The sun S_1 is normally prevented from

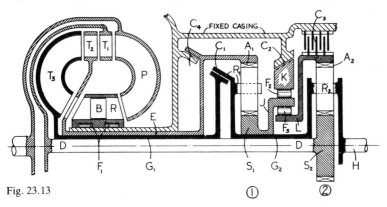

Fig. 23.13

rotating backwards by the freewheel F_2, since usually the clutch C_2 is engaged and the member K is fixed so that the sleeve J cannot rotate backwards. The annulus A_2 is also prevented from rotating backwards by the freewheel F_3 which locks it for such rotation to the sleeve J. Engagement of the clutch C_3 fixes the annulus A_2 against forwards or backwards rotation, and this is done when 'low' is selected so as to reduce the load on the freewheel F_3, when the engine is pulling hard under adverse road conditions, and to allow the engine to be used effectively as a brake on down gradients.

At low forward speeds of the output shaft H relative to the engine speed, the sun S_1 and annulus A_2 will be stationary because the torques on them will tend to make them rotate backwards and this motion is prevented by the freewheels F_2 and F_3. Both epicyclic trains then provide speed reductions and torque increases, and all three turbines will be driving.

As the output speed rises, the torque passing through the sun S_2 will fall and at some point will tend to become negative, and then the annulus A_2 will start to rotate forwards and the turbine T_1 will be effectively out of action. At a higher output shaft speed, the sun S_1 will start to rotate forwards and the turbine T_2 will go out of action. The drive will then be through T_3 direct to the output shaft, the only torque magnification then being that due to the torque converter itself. Finally, the reaction member R will start to rotate forwards and the torque converter will run as a fluid coupling. The speeds and torques at which these events occur will depend on the angle at which the blades B are set.

Reverse is obtained by engaging the clutch C_4 and disengaging C_1, C_2 and C_3. The trains 1 and 2 are then compounded and give a reverse ratio, the whole of the driving torque being transmitted by the turbine T_1 and sun S_2. Forward motion of S_2 tends to drive R_2 forwards and A_2 backwards; backward motion of A_2, however, results in backward motion of S_1 (through the freewheel F_3 and the sleeve J) and so in train 1, whose annulus is fixed, the sun tends to rotate the planet carrier R_1 backwards. The backward torque on R_1 is greater than the forward torque on R_2 (from S_2), and so R_1 and R_2 will move backwards.

23.5   Automatic transmissions in general

Transmission systems that will function purely automatically without any attention from the driver of the vehicle have been sought for many years by designers, but even to-day such systems have not been fully achieved since present-day automatic transmissions still include control levers or press buttons, which have to be operated by the driver to enable the transmission to cope with the widely varying driving conditions encountered. However, systems which require no attention under ordinary road conditions and which require only the selection of the appropriate operating range when heavy gradients or very difficult terrain are to be traversed are now in extensive use. The transmissions can be divided into those which employ mechanical gearboxes, usually epicyclic, for providing all the required variations of gear ratio, and those which use a torque converter in conjunction with a mechanical gearbox.

It is very difficult to design an automatic control system for an ordinary gearbox that will function as satisfactorily under all conditions as can a really competent driver, but present-day systems will give better results than the average driver can achieve. In general, the control must bring about changes from low to higher gears when the vehicle speed rises and from high to low gears when the vehicle speed falls. However, it is frequently possible to employ the higher gears even at low vehicle speeds, for example on level roads and with following winds, when the resistances to be overcome are low.

The control system must therefore take account of the engine load and, in general, produce changes up when the load is light and changes down when the load is heavy. There are, however, occasions, such as on descending hills, when it is desirable to employ a low gear although the load on the engine may be nil or the engine may be acting as a brake. It is under these diverse conditions that the human element has to be retained in the control.

The automatic systems now in use consequently all utilise the two factors mentioned above, namely vehicle speed and engine load, in their operation. The vehicle speed factor is dealt with by employing some form of speed-sensitive unit which is driven off the output side of the gearbox and is thus responsive to vehicle speed. These units may be mechanical, hydraulic or electrical and examples of each of these are given in the descriptions which follow. The engine load factor is introduced at present only by indirect means; it is assumed that engine load is a function of the depression of the accelerator pedal and the latter supplies the corresponding control, the actual form of which will depend on whether the system is a mechanical, an hydraulic or an electrical one.

It is essential that the vehicle speed, at which any change from a lower gear to a higher one is produced when the vehicle speed is rising and the accelerator pedal position is constant, shall be higher than the speed at which, when the speed is falling and the accelerator pedal position is unchanged, the corresponding change down will occur. If this is not so, a change up is likely to be followed immediately by a change down, and this sequence may go on indefintely. This phenomenon is known as *hunting*. It is also generally desirable that in traffic, when the accelerator pedal is released and the vehicle comes to rest, the control system shall produce all the changes down from top to botton, but shall retain the gear that is in use when the accelerator pedal is released until the vehicle speed has fallen nearly to zero, and shall then engage the low gear ready for the ensuing acceleration. It is also desirable that it shall be possible to start off in 1st or in 2nd gear according to the prevailing road conditions.

The above considerations should be borne in mind when reading the descriptions of the systems that follow since many of their apparent complications are due to the necessity to comply with the requirements outlined above.

23.6 Borg-Warner Models 35, 65 and 66 transmissions

Model 35 is shown in Figs. 23.14 and 15. It consists of a single-stage torque converter IDR coupled to a three forward and one reverse ratio epicyclic gear. The driven member D of the converter is, in effect, integral with the

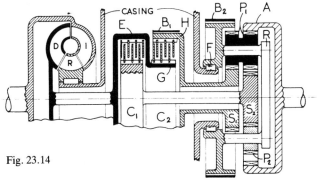

Fig. 23.14

drums E and G of the clutches C_1 and C_2. When C_1 is engaged the drive goes to the sun S_2 and if the brake B_2 is applied gives the low forward ratio while if the brake B_1 is applied instead of B_2 then the immediate ratio is obtained. The one-way sprag clutch F prevents the planet carrier R from rotating backwards but allows it to rotate forwards. By engaging both clutches C_1 and C_2 simultaneously the gear is locked solid and the direct drive is obtained. To get reverse the clutch C_2 is engaged and the brake B_2 is applied, the drive then goes from S_1 to P_1 and thence to the annulus A, the planet carrier being fixed.

The teeth seen on the outside of the annulus in Fig. 23.15 are engaged by a detent when the control lever is put into the parking position and this holds the car stationary. Two oil pumps provide the oil pressures required to engage the clutches and apply the brakes. One is housed in the left-hand end of the box and is driven off the sleeve of the impeller so that it is working whenever the engine is running while the other is seen at the right-hand side and is driven off the output shaft of the box so that it will be running when the car is in motion. The principle underlying the action of the control system is similar to that of the Hydramatic boxes which are described in Sections 23.11 and 23.12.

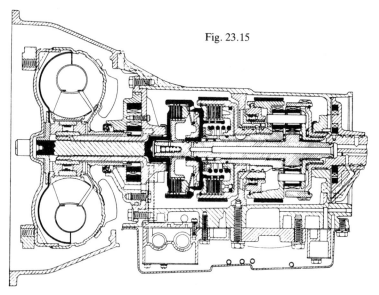

Fig. 23.15

In principle, the Model 65 is similar to the Model 35, which went out of production about 1974. Their gearsets are virtually identical, though that of the 65 is designed for heavier duty. Detail modifications have improved the quality of operation and, by lowering the brake actuation cylinders to a level below the brake bands and bringing them into the casing, the overall width of the transmission has been significantly reduced.

Further development of the Model 65 resulted in the introduction of the Model 66, which is designed for even heavier duty or for a higher level of durability in cars at the upper end of the market range. The shafting has been strengthened, and the lubrication system improved by fitting a deeper oil pan and enlarging some of the ducts. Externally, however, the dimensions remain the same.

23.7   Borg-Warner Models 45 and 55 transmissions

The demands for increasing fuel economy have tended to expand the market for cars having smaller engines. Consequently it is in this area that manufacturers of automatic transmissions must look for volume sales. This led to the introduction by Borg-Warner of a transmission specifically designed for cars in the 1- to 2-litre categories, as opposed to the 1.5- to 3-litre range associated with the Models 35, 65 and 66.

The Model 45 has four speeds and the ratio spread between top and bottom gears is thus widened without increasing the steps between ratios, so that good acceleration is obtainable with cars of modest power : weight ratios despite the use of a high final-drive ratio for good economy at cruising speeds on motorways. As in the two three-speed models previously described, a torque converter-coupling giving a conversion ratio of about 2:1 is used, but the gearset is of course different and the brakes are of the multi-disc type. Multi-disc brakes have the advantage, over the band type used previously, of not requiring any attention in service; moreover, the actuation pistons and cylinders are all coaxial with the transmission shaft, so the unit is narrower and shallower than the earlier ones. Further reductions in weight and size have been achieved by the ingenious use of steel pressings for many parts of the running gear, which has been made possible by the employment of electron beam welding for their fabrication.

The control quadrant for the gear selection, having stations marked PRND32, is similar to those of other automatic transmissions. Manual selection of either third or second gear – the last two of the stations – inhibits automatic shifting to the higher gears, P is for parking, R reverse, N neutral and D is for driving automatically.

There are three planetary trains in the gearset, giving four forward speeds and one reverse. The front train has three planet pinions and the others four. These gears are selected by means of two clutches and three brakes, all of which are applied by hydraulic pressure and released by their return springs. Additionally, there is a one-way sprag-type clutch between the ring gear of the rear train and the transmission case.

Illustrated diagrammatically in Fig. 23.16(a) is the arrangement of the gearset, clutches and brakes. When 1st gear is selected, only the rear planetary train is in operation, the other two rotating freely. The front clutch is engaged, transmitting power to the central shaft and thus the rear sun gear. Since the ring gear is prevented by the sprag clutch from rotating backwards, the planets and their carrier orbit at a speed slower than that of the sun gear – speed ratio 3:1. The planet carrier is connected directly to the output shaft.

Power flow in third speed is equally easily explained because, again, only one gear train is in operation – this time the middle one – while the others rotate freely. The front clutch is engaged and it transmits power to the ring gear of the middle train. At the same time the foremost, or 3rd gear, brake is applied, holding the sun gear and thus causing the planets to orbit at a speed ratio of 1.35:1. This planet carrier too is connected to the output shaft.

For selection of 2nd gear, both the front and middle planetary trains are brought into operation, while the rearmost ring gear rotates freely. This is done by engaging the front clutch, thus conveying power to the middle ring gear, which drives its planets and their carrier in the same direction while tending to drive the sun gear backwards, but at a rate determined by the planetary action of the front train, as follows: the planet carrier of the front train is held by the 2nd gear brake – the middle of the three. Consequently, the backwards rotation of the front sun gear – which is, in effect, integral

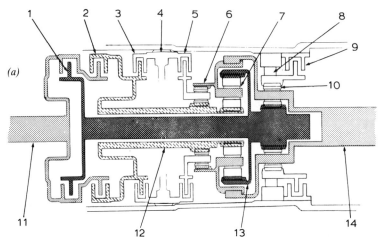

(a)

1 Forward clutch
2 Direct clutch assembly
3 3rd gear brake
4 Centre support (reaction member)
5 2nd gear brake
6 Front planetary train
7 Middle planetary train
8 Sprag clutch
9 Reverse gear brake

10 Rear planetary train
11 Input shaft and forward clutch
   cylinder assembly
12 Front and middle sun gear assembly
13 Rear sun and middle ring gear
   assembly
14 Output shaft and rear carrier
   assembly

23.16(a) Borg-Warner Model 45

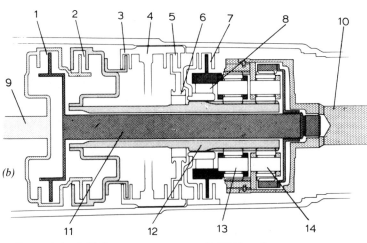

(b)

1 Forward clutch (C.1)
2 Direct clutch (C.2)
3 Brake (B.1)
4 Centre support (reaction member)
5 Brake (B.2)
6 OWC no. 1
7 Brake (B.3)

8 OWC no. 2
9 Input shaft
10 Output shaft
11 Intermediate shaft
12 Sun gear
13 Front planetary train
14 Rear planetary train

23.16(b) Borg-Warner Model 55

with the middle sun gear – drives its planets in a manner such as to cause its ring gear to rotate forwards. This ring gear is directly conected to the planet carrier of the middle train, which in turn is connected to the output shaft. The effect of coupling these two trains is a multiplication of the torque, giving a ratio of 1.94:1.

Fourth gear is a direct drive, with the two foremost clutches engaged to connect the input shaft to both the sun and ring gears of the middle planetary train simultaneously. In this condition the planet pinions are locked between the two, so the drive is transmitted through their carrier to the output shaft at a ratio of 1:1.

In common with other Borg-Warner transmissions, control over the gear changes is exercised by four basic devices. The first is the manual gearshift lever operated by the driver for selecting fully automatic drive, or limiting upward changes to either 2nd or 3rd gear, or for selecting reverse, park, or neutral. In the park position, a pawl locks the output shaft. The second control is a primary valve regulating the line pressure to the system and directing fluid at reduced pressure to the torque converter, the lubrication system and, if fitted, the oil cooler. Thirdly, there is a governor on the output shaft, which actuates a valve to regulate the pressure further in relation to vehicle speed. Finally, there is a valve actuated by the carburettor throttle. This receives fluid at line pressure and directs it, at a pressure related to throttle position, to the shift and other valves. At or beyond about seven-eighths full throttle, not only is maximum pressure attained but also ports are open for directing fluid for the 'kickdown' function, delaying upward gearshifts to obtain maximum acceleration.

The Model 55 transmission is a development of the Model 45. However, since it is intended for cars having engines ranging up to about 3 litres swept volume, it has only three forward speeds and the torque converter. As can be seen from Fig. 23.16(*b*), it has a totally different gearset, with a single long sunwheel machined on the rear end of a hollow shaft within which is the intermediate shaft. The sunwheel has two sets of four planet gears rotating around it. For the Model 55, there is an extra one-way clutch and a different brake arrangement too. The hydraulic control system also is different, and this transmission is also available with an overdrive unit mounted on its rear end.

Incidentally, a major difference between the Model 45-55 gearboxes and the 35, 65 and 66 family is the use of oil-wetted multi-plate brakes in the former to replace the brake bands in the latter. Multi-plate brakes are inherently better able to take heavy loads without showing significant signs of wear or requiring automatic adjustment devices.

23.8 The AP automatic gearbox

This is a four-speed and reverse gearbox in which bevel gears are used as ordinary gearing for some of the ratios and as epicyclic trains for the other ratios. It incorporates a single-stage torque converter whose reaction member is held by a one-way clutch up to the change-over point. The automatic changes are controlled by the speed of the vehicle through a governor driven by the output shaft of the box and by the position of the accelerator pedal. The selector lever has seven positions: reverse, neutral, 1,2,3,4 and D2, this last one giving full automaticity. The selector lever can be used to give manual control at all times, the gear selected being held until the lever position is changed. In automatic operation, kickdown changes are available.

The layout of the gearbox is shown in Fig. 23.17; there are four bevel gears S_1 S_2 S_3 S_4, the latter being always the driven gear while either S_1 or S_2 can be the input or driving gear according to whether the clutch A or the clutch B is engaged. The clutches are actually multi-plate ones and

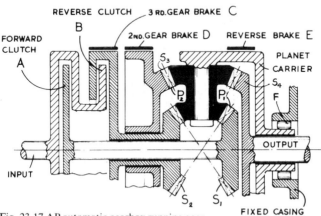

Fig. 23.17 AP automatic gearbox running gear

incorporate a piston to enable oil under pressure to engage them. The planet carrier has two compound planet pinions, only one of which is shown in the diagram. The ratios are obtained as follows –

1st	Clutch A is engaged so that S_1 becomes the driving gear, the sprag F prevents backward motion of the planet carrier which therefore remains stationary because the reaction torque that acts on it is backwards. The drive is from S_1 to P_1 and thence from P_2 to S_4, the planet pinion rotating on its fixed pin.
2nd	Clutch A remains engaged and the brake D is applied to fix the sun S_3. Rotation of the sun S_1 then causes the planet carrier to rotate forwards and so the plant P_2 drives the sun S_4 forwards.
3rd	Clutch A remains engaged but the brake C is applied to fix the sun S_2. Rotation of S_1 again causes the planet carrier to rotate forwards but gives a higher ratio because S_2 is equal in size to S_1 whereas in second gear S_3 was larger.
4th	Both clutches A and B are engaged so that the suns S_1 and S_2 are locked together and the gear has to rotate solid thus giving a 1:1 ratio.
Reverse	The clutch B is engaged and the brake E is applied to hold the planet carrier stationary. The drive is from S_2 to P_1 and thence from P_2 to S_4.

The oil pressure to apply the brakes and engage the clutches comes, when the engine is running, from a pump that is driven off the cover of the torque converter. To enable a towed start to be obtained a second pump driven off the output shaft is provided. The change-over from one pump to the other is made by the *flow-control and tow-start valve* seen at the bottom left hand corner in Fig. 23.18, where its position corresponds to that assumed when the engine is running and oil is passing from the main pump through the flow-control valve spool to the control system. In this condition the tow-start valve is held in the position shown so that the auxiliary pump can discharge freely back to the sump. When the engine is not running the flow-control valve is moved to the left by its spring and

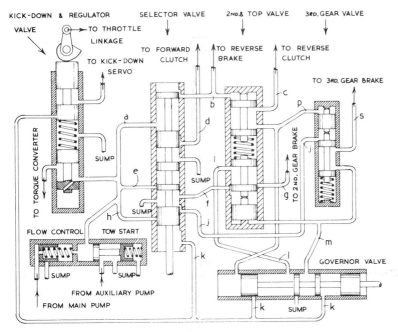

Fig. 23.18 AP automatic gearbox control system

blocks the pipe coming from the main pump, the tow-start valve spool is also moved to the left thereby closing the passage to the sump and connecting the auxiliary pump to the control system so that if the vehicle is towed the auxiliary pump can supply oil to the control system.

The pressure of the oil supply is maintained at the designed value by the regulator valve which is the lower spool in the *kickdown and regulator valve* assembly. The oil from the pump passes through the diagonal hole drilled in the spool and thus sets up a pressure that moves the spool upwards and restricts the entry of oil so that a balance of forces is reached between the upwards oil pressure and the downwards spring force.

The Control System. The box can be used either as a manually-controlled box, the gear changes being produced by moving the selector lever to the required position, or the changes, except into reverse, can be obtained automatically by putting the selector lever into the D position. Considering the manual operation Fig. 23.18 shows the selector valve in the position corresponding to N, or neutral, all the brakes being off and the clutches disengaged. If the valve is now moved upwards to Rev then oil will pass from pipe *a* to pipe *b* and so to the reverse brake; it will also pass to the top of the *2nd and top gears valve* and will move the spool downwards to open pipe *c* and so pass oil to the reverse clutch which, on engagement gives the reverse gear. When *1* is selected the valve is moved downwards and oil passes from *a* to *d* and engages the forward clutch to give 1st gear; no brake has to be applied because the planet carrier is held by the sprag. Pipe *b* is opened to the sump to release the reverse brake and the spool of the *2nd and top gears valve* moves back to its top position thus opening pipe *c* to the sump via pipe *p*. The supply to the forward clutch remains open throughout all the subsequent changes so that the forward clutch remains engaged. By moving the selector lever to *2* oil is passed from pipe *e* to *f*; it enters the *2nd and top gears valve* and raises the middle spool so that oil flows via pipe *g* to the 2nd gear brake, giving the gear. When *3* is selected the oil flows from pipe *h* to *j* and so to the *3rd gear valve* where it depresses the lower spool so that oil flows to the third gear brake via pipe *s*; at the same time the pipe *f* is opened to the sump so that the 2nd gear brake is released. When *4* is selected oil flows from pipe *h* to *k* and, if the engine speed is not low, from *k* to *p* and thence via *c* to the reverse clutch, thus locking S_1 and S_2 together and giving the 1:1 ratio.

When the selector is put in the *D* position the selector valve reaches its lowest position, pipe *a* remains connected to pipe *d* so that the forward clutch remains engaged while pipe *h* is connected to pipe *k* to give a supply of oil to the *governor valve*. As this valve moves to the left because of the increasing speed of the car it first connects *k* to *l* and thence to the 2nd gear brake via the *2nd and top gears valve* and pipe *g*, thus giving 2nd gear. Further movement causes the pipe 1 to be connected to the sump, thus releasing the 2nd gear brake and at the same time *k* is coupled to *m* and hence to the 3rd gear brake; at the same time the bottom spool in the *2nd and top gears valve* is moved upwards to give a freer flow of oil from the 2nd gear brake to the sump and take that brake off quickly. When the governor valve moves to its extreme left position the pipe *k* is connected to pipe *p* and hence to pipe *c* so that the reverse clutch is engaged as well as the forward clutch and gives the 1:1 ratio.

The kickdown changes are produced by the operation of the cam on the spool of the kickdown valve which results in oil passing from pipe *k* to *t* and so to the kickdown servo. This is a small ram which bears on an arm of the governor linkage and forces the governor valve spool to the right thereby producing the required downwards change.

23.9   AP hot-shift automatic gearbox

Conventional automatic transmissions suffer two major shortcomings. One is the inevitable energy losses in the torque converter and the other is the complexity of the epicyclic gear arrangements, including clutches and brakes, required if ratio changes are to be made without interrupting the power flow to the road wheels. Moreover, the smaller the engine the greater becomes the significance of the power lost in the torque converter relative to the total power available.

Because of the increasing prices of fuels, the trend for the future must be towards smaller engines driving lightweight cars. This stimulated Automotive Products to re-examine the prospects for developing a simpler and more efficient automatic transmission based on the traditional, highly efficient, manual gearbox. A major advantage was that both manual and automatic could, if necessary, be produced on the same production line, or at least a minimum of investment would be required in new manufacturing facilities and equipment for production of the automatic transmission.

A prime requirement was the development of a *hot-shift system* – changing gear without interrupting the power flow to the wheels. Closing the throttle and re-opening it again for each gearshift is not only a tricky operation, but also it can even be dangerous – for example, potentially initiating skids on ice – and can render emission control difficult. Consequently, a new system, based on the use of two clutches and transferring the drive from one to the other for each shift, was developed.

To understand how it has evolved, look at Fig. 23.19, ignoring the peripheral equipment, including the clutches, and concentrating attention on the mainshaft and the layshaft, top and bottom respectively. The main difference between this and the equivalent manual gearbox is that the gear pairs for 2nd and 3rd speeds have been interchanged – the order, left to right, in the conventional box would be 4, 3, 2, 1. Additionally the mainshaft has been divided, leaving 1st, 3rd and reverse gears driven conventionally through the main clutch A, on the engine flywheel, while 2nd and 4th gears are integral with a sleeve rotating freely on the mainshaft and driven through a second, smaller clutch B, mounted on the rear end of

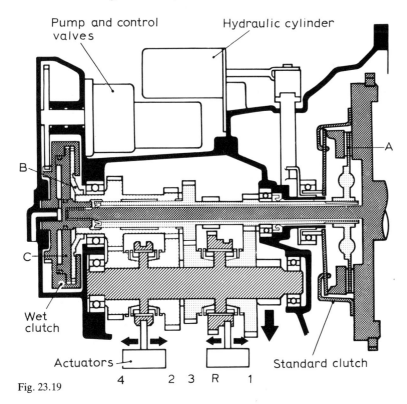

Fig. 23.19

the gearbox. This second clutch is driven by a quill shaft extending from the engine crankshaft right through the gearbox.

The main clutch is released by the hydraulic actuator, top-right in the illustration, and engaged by its diaphragm spring, in the usual way. Since the secondary clutch is not used for driving away from rest, but only for gear changing, it is not subject to much slipping and therefore can be smaller and is of the wet type. It is engaged by hydraulic pressure acting on the rear face of the pressure plate C. Hydraulic power is provided by the pump, top left, driven by the continuously rotating portion of the second clutch, and the gears are shifted by hydraulic rams, represented by the two rectangles at the bottom of the illustration.

Overall control is effected electronically by a computer, which could be designed to perform also the functions of engine control and thus optimise engine and transmission operation. So far as the transmission is concerned, the inputs to this control come from a governor, and sensors for indicating which gear is engaged, throttle-position and engine and gearbox output speeds – the throttle-position sensor of course is, in effect, a torque-demand sensor. The outputs go to control the valves for the hydraulic actuators of the clutches and gear shift rams. All gears are held in engagement by hydraulic pressure and are sprung out into neutral.

The sequence of operations is as follows: with the engine idling and gearbox in neutral, selection of drive, using the manual control, first causes disengagement of the primary clutch and then a shift into 1st gear. Depression of the accelerator initiates automatically the gradual engagement of the primary clutch, thus setting the vehicle in motion.

At an appropriate speed, the governor signals a gear change. Since the secondary clutch is already disengaged, 2nd gear can be selected by its actuator operating through its synchroniser. Then, the rear clutch engages while the front one simultaneously disengages, to perform the hot-shift. Finally, the hydraulic pressure to the 1st gear is released, so it springs out of engagement, and the primary clutch is re-engaged, to keep all parts rotating at engine speed and thus keeping the demands on the synchroniser for the next gear shift to a minimum. Subsequent gear shifts are made similarly, by transferring the drive from one clutch to the other, which is

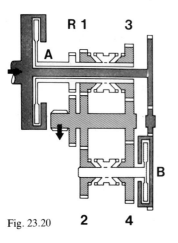

Fig. 23.20

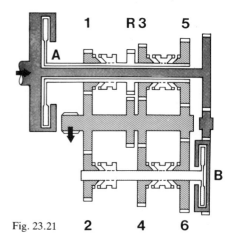

Fig. 23.21

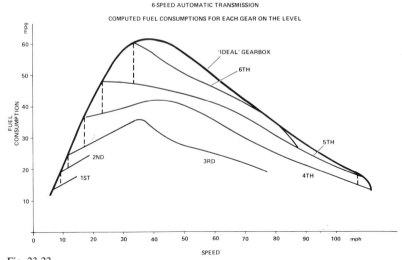

6-SPEED AUTOMATIC TRANSMISSION

COMPUTED FUEL CONSUMPTIONS FOR EACH GEAR ON THE LEVEL

Fig. 23.22

why the 2nd and 3rd gears in the box had to be interchanged for this design.

The claims made for this fully automatic transmission are as follows: its efficiency is as high as that for a manual box except in that a little power is absorbed by the hydraulic pump. Both the weight and cost are certainly no more, and are expected ultimately to be less, than for a conventional automatic box. Other advantages include ease of servicing, minimum of investment required in new tooling and the ease with which the control can be integrated with an electronic engine-management system.

For front-wheel-drive cars, a compact four-speed design is attainable, using a three-shaft layout, Fig. 23.20. Similarly, a six-speed version can be designed on a three-shaft basis, Fig. 23.21, and with so many gears it is possible to approximate fairly closely to the characteristics of an ideal continuously-variable ratio gearbox, Fig. 23.22. The outcome, AP claim, would be a potential saving of 25% in fuel consumption.

23.10 Van Doorne Variomatic and Transmatic transmissions

The twin-belt Variomatic automatic transmission developed by Van Doorne was first used in 1955 on Daf cars – more recently taken over by Volvo. By 1980, steel belt derivatives were at an advanced stage of development by Fiat, Borg-Warner and others.

The Variomatic transmission system, as originally produced, Fig. 23.23, comprises six main sub-assemblies: the propeller shaft, power divider, two belt-drive units, and two final-drive reduction gear units. Of these, the propeller shaft, with flexible couplings at each end, instead of universal joints, transmits the drive from a centrifugal clutch to the power divider, which is mounted on a sub-frame beneath the rear of the vehicle. The input shaft to the power divider has a bevel gear on its rear end, which meshes with two bevel pinions, one on each side, to turn the drive through 90°.

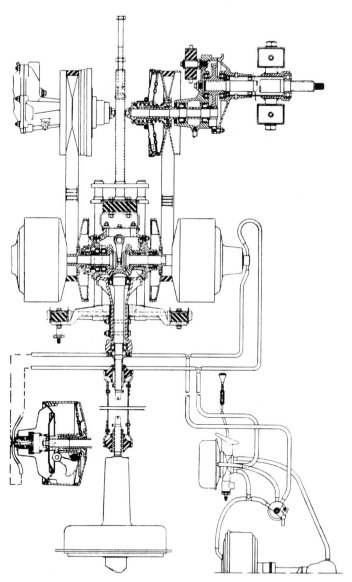

Fig. 23.23 Van Doorne Variomatic transmission

These pinions, therefore, are driven in opposite directions, but they rotate independently of their transverse shaft the outer ends of which carry the two driving, or primary, pulleys. Splined on to the centre of this shaft, and floating axially between the two pinions, is a coupling sleeve with dogs on its ends. When the coupling is in its mid-position, neither of the pinions is engaged, so the transmission is in neutral. If it is moved in one direction along the splines, its dogs engage with slots in the forward-rotating pinion and, if it is slid in the other direction, it engages the pinion rotating in the reverse sense.

One of the flanges of each driving pulley is fixed on the shaft, while the other can be moved axially on splines either to squeeze the belt outwards, if the two are closed together, or to allow it to sink deeper into the groove of the pulley, if they are moved apart. Similarly arranged flanges on the driven pulley move in the opposite sense to those on the driving pulleys, and thus vary the ratio of the drive over a range of slightly more than $4:1$. The ratio of the bevel drive in the power divider is rather less than $2:1$ and that of the final drive reduction is about $4.75:1$. In practice, the maximum overall ratio is of the order of $44:1$.

The flanges in the driving pulley are moved apart by a combination of manifold vacuum and the centrifugal force on bob-weights, and they are closed together by a diaphragm spring. This spring also transmits the torque from the shaft to the moveable pulley flange, thus obviating the need for a sliding splined joint and consequent problems due to its sticking. A control valve cuts the vacuum assistance out of operation below about quarter throttle and above about three-quarters throttle. In each case, this increases the ratio – for engine braking with the throttle closed, and for maximum acceleration with it wide open.

Unlike the driving pulleys, the driven ones are moved only by springs, but in this case a combination of a diaphragm and coil spring is used, the two together giving an almost constant closing load characteristic. Ratio adjustment is therefore controlled solely on the driving pulleys, the driven ones being automatically self-adjusting to accommodate to them.

Because of the inherent load-sensitivity of the drive, and the use of a separate pair of pulleys for each wheel, the system has a differential drive capability, which can be explained as follows: when the vehicle turns a corner, the acceleration of the outer wheel occasioned by the external forces – i.e., applied to it at its contact with the road – causes the torque transmitted by the belt to be reduced and thus lessens the tension in it. Consequently, the belt is squeezed radially outwards and the effective diameter of the driving pulley automatically increased. The converse effect of course is obtained with the deceleration of the inner wheel, which pulls the belt down deeper into its groove.

Since both the driven pulleys and the spur type final-drive reduction gears are carried by the swinging arm of the rear suspension, and the axis about which it swings intersects the neutral axis of the tension-loaded belt at the point where it leaves the driving pulley, wheel displacement neither causes misalignment of the pulleys nor varies the tension in the belts. In over-run conditions, when the opposite run of the belt is loaded in tension, the loading is so much lighter that the variations in geometry are of no consequence.

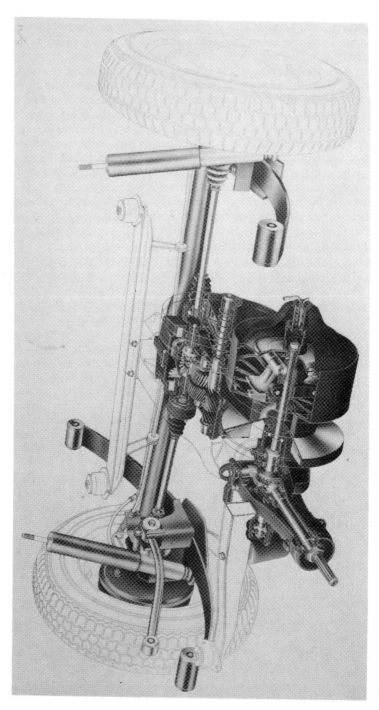

Fig. 23.24 Variomatic transmission with a single belt

A later version of the same transmission, Fig. 23.24, has a single belt, with a differential gear and final drive reduction gear together forming a transmission unit, which is carried on two transverse members secured by rubber mounting beneath the vehicle structure. A de Dion axle, with single-leaf springs is employed.

As before, the drive-line from the propeller shaft is taken to the two floating bevel gears, with a forward-or-reverse selector coupling sliding between them. Thence, however, it is taken to a single centrifugal-and-vacuum-actuated drive-pulley assembly, and through the belt to the spring-loaded driven pulley, which is splined on the end of the final drive reduction pinion spindle. The reduction gear, of the helical spur type, drives a ring gear bolted to the differential cage, the differential gears being connected by constant velocity joints to the swinging drive shafts out to the wheels.

The Van Doorne Transmatic transmission as adapted by Fiat, Fig. 23.25, is similar in principle, but much more compact and has a single segmented metal drive-belt, Fig. 23.26, hence the need for the conventional differential drive. Again the pulley ratio spread is about 4:1 but the maximum

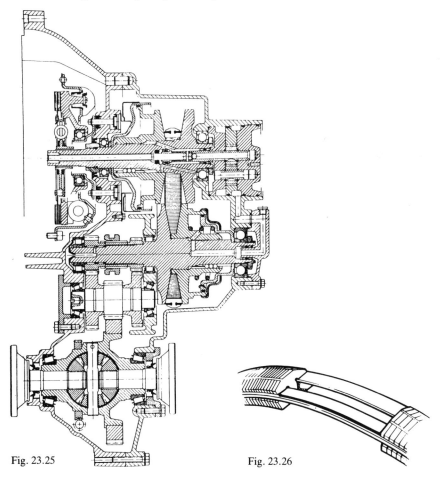

Fig. 23.25   Fig. 23.26

overall ratio is only about 25:1. This is for an experimental installation in the Fiat *Strada*.

From the illustration it can be seen that this is a transmission suitable for front-wheel-drive cars. A centrifugal clutch, top left, transmits the drive to the primary pulley and, through a quill drive, to a hydraulic pump, top right. the adjustable flanges of both the primary and secondary – driving and driven – pulleys slide axially on linear ball bearing splines, that of the primary one being controlled by hydraulic pressure in the cylinder to the left of it, while the secondary one is closed by the coil spring plus hydraulic pressure in the smaller-diameter cylinder on its right. A splined muff coupling between the two gears to the left of the secondary pulley is disengaged in its central position, engages forward drive if moved to the left, and reverse – through the medium of an idler gear – if moved to the right.

Of especial interest is the segmented steel belt. It comprises a set of plates about 2 mm thick by 25 mm wide by about 12 mm deep, with slots in each side to receive the two high-tensile steel bands which hold them together, rather like two strings in a necklace. The sides the plates slope to match the V-angle of the grooves of the pulleys in which they seat. Unlike a conventional V-belt, however, this one transmits the drive by compression, instead of tension, in the run on one side between the pulleys. The run on the other side of course is unladen and runs free. Buckling of the strand under compression is prevented by tension in the high-tensile steel bands. The principle advantage of this type of transmission is that its torque ratio is steplessly variable. Transmission efficiencies of between 90% at a 1:1 ratio and 86% at the extremes of the ratio range are claimed. The whole unit is totally enclosed in a cast housing and the belt-pulley interface is lubricated by oil passing from the primary pulley actuation cylinder through ducts into the base of the V-groove.

23.11 Hydramatic transmissions

These fully automatic transmissions were developed and are now manufactured in large numbers by General Motors and they have been made under licence by many European firms. They are essentially three- or four-speed and reverse epicyclic gearboxes having brakes and clutches operated by oil pressure and which are controlled by the joint action of a governor, whose speed is proportional to that of the car, and of a valve actuated by the accelerator pedal.

The speeds at which the changes up will occur, supposing the accelerator to be pressed hard down, are, usually, as follows: 1st to 2nd, 19–23 mph; 2nd to 3rd, 37–40 mph; 3rd to 4th, 70–74 mph. At low throttle openings these changes will occur at 7–9, 14–16 and 19–22 mph. The changes down are arranged to occur at lower speeds than the corresponding changes up in order to prevent hunting. Thus at full throttle the down change speeds are 4th to 3rd, 38–17 mph; 3rd to 2nd 13–10 mph; 2nd to 1st, 8–6 mph.

The gearbox was originally produced in 1938 and was redesigned in 1956; the constructional arrangement of the Strato-flight model is indicated in Fig. 23.27. It comprises three sun-and-annulus type epicyclic trains 1, 2 and 3, two multi-plate clutches X and Y, of which the former functions as a brake, a double-cone brake D, two fluid couplings B and C and two one-way clutches or sprags J and K. The coupling B is always filled with oil and transmits power on all the gears but the coupling C can be filled or emptied as required and is used for 2nd and 4th gears only.

The epicyclic train 3 provides the reverse gear only and will be dealt with later on; the trains 1 and 2 together provide the four forward ratios. Each of these trains can be used so as to provide either a reduction or a direct drive; thus train 1 gives a reduction of 1.55:1 when its sun S_1 is fixed and the annulus A_1, which is permanently coupled to the flywheel, drives the planet carrier R_1. The latter is integral with the driving member E of the

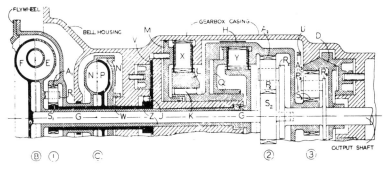

Fig. 23.27 Strato-flight gearbox

fluid coupling B and thereby drives the member F which is coupled by the shaft G to the sun S_2 of the second epicyclic train. If the annulus of the train 2 is fixed then the sun S_2 will drive the planet carrier R_2, which is the output member of the box, with a reduction of 2.55:1. The four forward gear ratios are therefore obtained as shown in Table 9.

Because some slip will occur in the coupling B the sun S_2 will be driven at a lower speed than that of the planet carrier R_1 and this slip will modify the numerical values quoted above and will make all the reductions slightly greater.

The epicyclic trains of the gearbox are essentially the same as in the models produced prior to 1956 but the methods used to control the elements of the trains in order to give either a reduction or a direct drive are different. Whereas in the earlier models the sun S_1 was fixed by the application of a band brake it is now fixed by a *sprag*, or one-way roller clutch, J which prevents the inner member of the unit, which is integral with the sun S_1, from rotating backwards. Similarly the annulus A_2 of the second train was fixed by a band brake in the earlier models and is now fixed, when necessary, by the sprag K (or the band brake H or by both together) which prevents it from rotating backwards provided the outer member L of the sprag itself is prevented from rotating by the engagement of the multi-plate neutral clutch X which locks it to the casing of the gearbox. This is done by admitting pressure oil behind the piston M. To obtain first gear the clutch X is engaged, the clutch Y is disengaged and the sun S_1 and annulus A_2 are fixed by the sprags J and K respectively. To obtain second gear the epicyclic train 1 has to be put into direct drive. In the earlier models this was done by engaging a multi-plate clutch that was

Table 9 – EPICYCLIC COMBINATIONS AND GEAR RATIOS IN HYDRAMATIC GEARBOX

Gear	Train No. 1	Coupling C	Sun S_1	Brake V	Train No. 2	Brake X	Annulus A_2	Clutch Y	Brake D	Ratio
1	In reduction Ratio 1.55:1	Empty	Fixed	On	In reduction Ratio 2.55:1	On	Fixed	Disengaged	Off	1.55×2.55 = 3.966:1
2	In direct drive Ratio 1:1	Full	Rotating	Off	In reduction Ratio 2.55:1	On	Fixed	Disengaged	Off	1×2.55 = 2.55:1
3	In reduction Ratio 1.55:1	Empty	Fixed	On	In direct drive Ratio 1:1	On	Rotating	Engaged	Off	1.55×1 = 1.55:1
4	In direct drive Ratio 1:1	Full	Rotating	Off	In direct drive Ratio 1:1	On	Rotating	Engaged	Off	1×1 = 1:1
Reverse	In reduction Ratio 1.55:1	Empty	Fixed	On	Compounded with train No. 3	Off	Rotating backwards	Disengaged	On	4.31:1

arranged between the planet carrier member R_1 and the sun S_1, and this method is used in the Dual-Range model, but in the Strato-flight model it is done by filling the coupling C, which in 1st gear was empty, so that the driving member N, which is permanently coupled to the flywheel, drives the member P which is permanently attached to the sun S_1. If no slip occurred in the coupling C then the train 1 would give a 1:1 ratio since the sun and the annulus would be running at the same speed. Because some slip must occur in the coupling C the sun S_1 will run slightly slower than the annulus A_1 and the train will give a reduction slightly greater than unity. This slip will also modify the ratios quoted above for 2nd and 4th gears. This use of a fluid coupling instead of a multi-plate clutch is to provide a much smoother take-up of the drive than was previously obtainable.

Third gear is obtained by emptying the coupling C so that train 1 goes back into reduction and by engaging the clutch Y so that train 2 goes into direct drive. This is done by admitting pressure oil behind the piston Q; this is the same as in earlier models.

To obtain reverse the clutch Y is disengaged and the coupling C is emptied while the annulus A_3 is fixed by admitting oil behind the piston D. Train 1 then provides a reduction, its sun being fixed by the sprag J, and the trains 2 and 3 function as a compound train to give a reversal of direction and a reduction in speed between the sun S_2 and the output member R_2. This action is precisely as in the reverse gear of the Wilson gearbox (see Section 22.5). During reverse the sun S_3 and hence the annulus A_2 will be rotating backwards and to permit this rotation to take place the sprag K must be made inoperative; this is done by disengaging the clutch X so that the outer member L of the sprag is free to rotate; the band brake H must also be free.

When the train 1 is being used to provide a reduction and the sun S_1 is prevented from rotating backwards by the sprag J the single-disc brake V may be employed to hold the sun against any tendency to rotate *forwards*, which tendency would arise if the car over-ran the engine: this enables the engine to be used as a brake.

The coupling C is filled by means of a large capacity vane-type pump and the emptying is done by opening a valve provided in the cover N^1 of the coupling which will permit the oil to be discharged by the action of centrifugal force. The operation of this 'dumping' valve is by means of oil pressure which is admitted to the space W and thence through passages in the cover N^1 to the valve.

When the clutch Y is engaged the engine torque is divided at train 1; part of the torque is transmitted direct from the arm R_1 through the sleeve Z and the clutch Y to the annulus A_2 while the remainder is transmitted through the coupling B and the shaft G to the sun S_2. Approximately 40% of the engine torque goes through the coupling B.

Because the coupling C runs at engine speed and has to transmit only just over one-third of engine torque it can be made smaller in size than the coupling B which has to transmit slightly over one a half times engine torque on the 1st and 2nd gears (when the clutch Y is disengaged) and which runs at a lower speed than the engine.

23.12   Hydramatic Strato-flight gearbox controls

The steering column control lever has six positions, parking (P), neutral (N), normal driving (Δ Dr), fast accelerating, driving (Dr Δ), low range (Lo) and reverse (Rev). Parking differs from neutral in that a positive lock engages the teeth U (Fig. 23.27) to lock the output shaft of the gearbox when (P) is selected.

At the rear end of the gearbox there is a governor which is driven by the output shaft and whose speed is thus proportional to the road speed of the vehicle. The governor is actually two governors in one assembly and is shown diagrammatically in Fig. 23.28. Since both governors function in the same manner only one need be described. Considering the valve B and

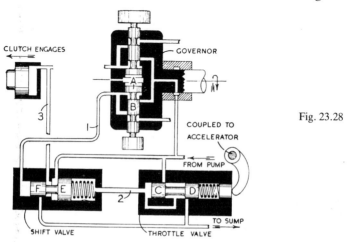

Fig. 23.28

assuming that the pump that supplies the system with pressure oil is operating, the action is as follows: The valve is shown in the equilibrium position, the upper end of the portion B is just closing the port by which pressure oil is introduced while the lower end of B seals the pipe line 1 from the exhaust port. The pressure in line 1 will be lower than the pump pressure and, as will be seen shortly, will be proportional to the rotational speed of the governor. The position is that the centrifugal force acting on the valve and tending to make it move outwards (downwards in the figure) is just balanced by the force due to the oil pressure acting on the under side of the piston A and which tends to move the valve inwards. Suppose now that the governor speed increases a little, then the centrifugal force will increase and will overcome the oil pressure so that the valve will move outwards; this will open the pressure oil inlet from the pump and the pressure in the line 1 will rise until the increased pressure acting on A is sufficient to balance the centrifugal force when the valve will move into the equilibrium position again. Thus the oil pressure in line 1 will always be proportional (up to the limit of the pump pressure) to the centrifugal force acting on the valve and thus proportional to the square of the governor speed. The reason for using two valves is that a single valve that provided sufficient pressure to control the changes at low car speed would give pressures that would be much too great at the higher speeds while if a valve suitable for the high speed changes were used it would give insufficient pressure for the low speed changes.

The governor valve B thus gives a pressure in line 1 which is dependent on the road speed of the vehicle. This pressure will be referred to as G_1 *governor pressure*, that from the other valve will be called G_2 *governor pressure*.

The throttle valve acts in a manner similar to the governor valve and is also shown in the equilibrium position, the pressure of the spring towards the left being balanced by the oil pressure in line 2 which acts on the left-hand end of the valve and tends to move it to the right. If the accelerator pedal is further depressed the balance will be upset and the valve will move to the left, the part C will then uncover the inlet port from the pump and the pressure in the space between the parts C and D will increase and this increase will be communicated by the by-pass to the left-hand end of the valve and by the pipe line 2 to the right-hand end of the shift valve. The increase of pressure will continue until the force exerted by the oil on the left hand of the throttle valve moves that valve back to the equilibrium position. The spring is now compressed a little more and the pressure in line 2 is a little higher than before. On the other hand if the accelerator pedal is released a little then the oil pressure on the left-hand end of the valve will move the valve to the right, thus uncovering the exhaust port. The pressure in the line 2 will then fall until the spring force moves the valve back to the equilibrium position again.

The throttle valve thus gives a pressure that is dependent on the throttle opening. This pressure will be referred to as *throttle-valve* (TV) *pressure*.

The shift valve shown in Fig. 23.28 is a simplified version of the actual shift valves but enables the fundamental action to be explained easily. In the position shown the governor pressure in line 1 which acts on the left-hand end F of the valve has overcome the combined force of the spring and the TV pressure acting on the right-hand end E and the valve in its extreme right-hand position in which the pipe coming from the pump is connected to line 3 which goes to an operating member of one of the epicyclic trains, say the clutch Y of Fig. 23.27. That clutch will therefore be engaged so as to give the direct drive in the train and this corresponds to the change up from 1st to 2nd or from 3rd to 4th gear.

If the speed of the car decreases or the accelerator is depressed further, then the shift valve will be moved to the left and will cut off line 3 from the pump line 1 and open it to exhaust so that the change down would occur.

The motion of the valve is made a snap motion by reason of the difference in diameter of the ends E and F and this also imparts a delay action so that the valve will not move back so as to change down again unless the car speed decreases appreciably or unless the throttle is open considerably. These actions are obtained as follows: In the position shown the forces acting on the valve to the right are due to governor pressure acting on the end F and pump pressure acting on the difference in area of E and F, whereas when the valve started to move to the right the latter pressure was absent. Hence as the part E uncovers the inlet port an additional force urges the valves to the right and makes the valve motion rapid. Again before the valve can move back to the left the force on F due to the governor pressure must fall below the force on E due to the throttle valve (or the latter must rise above the former) by an amount corresponding to pump pressure multiplied by the difference in area of E and F. The valve cannot move back, therefore, unless an appreciable fall of car speed, or an appreciable increase in throttle opening occurs and thus hunting is prevented. The snap action of the valve when moving to the left occurs because as soon as the part E covers the inlet ports and the part F uncovers the exhaust port the force due to pump pressure acting on the difference in areas of E and F disappears and the valve moves across rapidly to its extreme left position.

The complete control system is shown in Fig. 23.29, in which the manual valve is shown in the Δ Dr (drive left) position, corresponding to normal driving, and the shift and coupling valves are shown in the position corresponding to low gear; the car speed and governor pressure being assumed to be low. The main pump supplies oil to the governor which gives G_1 pressure in line 9 and thus on the left-hand end of the boost valve. The latter acts in a manner similar to the throttle valve to give a pressure in line 12 which is proportional to, but higher than, the governor G_1 pressure. This boosted governor pressure is passed via line 12 to the transition valve and then by line 13 to the left-hand end of the coupling valve. The latter, in the position shown, opens the line 15, which controls the emptying valve of the coupling C (Fig. 23.27), to exhaust so that the emptying valve is open and the coupling C is empty. The epicyclic train 1 is thus in reduction. Since pump pressure via lines 2, 6, 8 and 10 is applied to the neutral clutch (X, Fig. 23.27) the latter is engaged, thereby enabling the freewheel unit (Fig. 23.27) to anchor the annulus of the rear epicyclic which is thus also in reduction, giving 1st gear. For the moment it will be assumed that the throttle opening is kept constant and at a moderate value, then as the speed of the car rises the G_1 pressure acting on the coupling valve will rise and will eventually move the coupling valve to the right. This will cut off line 15 from exhaust and open it to line 14 so that pump pressure via line 1 will be applied to the coupling-emptying valve so as to close it. At the same time the coupling valve will open line 3 to line 16 so that pump oil will be supplied to the coupling C so as to fill it. As the coupling fills so the first epicyclic will go into direct drive, thus giving 2nd gear. Further increase in car speed and governor pressure, which acts via lines 9 and 52 on the 2–3 shift valve will cause the latter to move to the right and bring about the change up from 2nd to 3rd gear as follows. Pump pressure via line 6 from the manual valve will be passed via lines 8 and 54 to line 17, which has hitherto been opened to exhaust; thus pump pressure will be passed to the rear epicyclic clutch (Y) so as to engage it and via line 19 to the left-hand end of the transition valve. The latter will consequently move to the right, thus cutting off line 12 from line 13 and opening the latter to line 20 and thus to exhaust. The oil pressure on the left-hand end of the coupling valve will thus be released and the coupling valve will move back to the left, thereby opening lines 15 and 16 to exhaust. The coupling C will thus empty and the first epicyclic will go back into reduction. Since the rear epicyclic is now in direct drive 3rd is obtained. This action is controlled by the orifice which restricts the entry of oil into the transition valve and by the accumulator whose piston will have moved to the right before pressure can build up in the line going to the clutch Y.

519

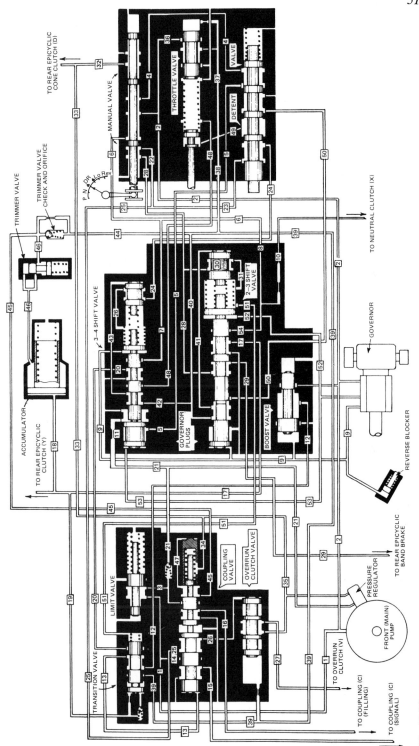

Fig. 23.29

The change up from 3rd to 4th will follow if the car speed and governor pressure continue to increase, the action being that governor (G_1 and G_2) pressures which act, via lines 9 and 53, on th 3–4 shift valve, will move that valve to the right, producing the following results. Line 20 will be cut off from exhaust and be opened via lines 7 and 6 to pump pressure from the manual valve, and this pressure will be passed via the transition valve (which is to the right) and line 13 to the coupling valve, thereby moving that valve to the right and opening lines 15 and 16 to pump pressure; the coupling C will thus be filled and the first epicyclic will go into direct drive, thus giving 4th gear. At the same time pump pressure from the manual valve via lines 4, 5 will be passed to line 21 and thus to the inner end of the pressure regulator of the pump where it will act so as to reduce the maximum pressure produced by the pump. This is desirable since it reduces the power consumption of the pump, and permissible since at all except large throttle openings, the torques in 4th gear are not heavy.

If the car speed and governor pressure fall the above changes will occur in the reverse order and the changes down will occur successively.

The effect of varying the throttle opening will now be considered. TV pressure via lines 36, 37, 38, 40, 41, 42 and 43 is applied to the right-hand ends of the 2–3 and 3–4 shift valves and via lines 44, 45 and 47 to the right-hand end of the coupling valve, and so increasing TV pressure will necessitate higher governor pressure in order that these valves may be shifted to produce the changes up and these changes will consequently occur at higher car speeds. The TV pressure also acts via line 46 on the annular area of the accumulator piston so as to tend to hold that piston down; this tends to speed up the engagement of the rear epicyclic Y on a 2–3 change as the throttle opening is increased. The TV pressure that can be applied to the accumulator is limited by the trimmer valve to 517 kN/m^2. in order that the clutch engagement shall not be made unduly harsh. It will be noticed that when the coupling and shift valves move to the right the TV pressure acting on the right-hand ends of those valves is cut off; this produces the difference in the car speeds at which the changes down will occur and also provides some of the snap action of the valves.

A part-throttle change down from 4th to 3rd can be produced, provided that the car speed is not too high, by depressing the accelerator about half-way to the bottom position. This opens line 48 to TV pressure which is thus passed via line 43 (the 3–4 shift valve being to the right) to the right-hand end of the 3–4 shift valve regulator plug which is accordingly forced to the left and thereby opens line 26 to TV pressure which is enabled to act on the large area of the shift valve and move it to the left, so producing a change down from 4th to 3rd. A forced change from 3rd to 2nd can be produced by pressing the accelerator to the floor; this moves the detent valve to the right and passes TV pressure via lines 49, 50 and 41 (the 2–3 shift valve being to the right) to the right-hand end of the 2–3 shift valve regulator plug, forcing it to the left so that TV pressure is caused to act via line 31 on the large end of the shift valve and move it to the left to produce the change down. When this occurs the coupling C has to be filled and the rear epicyclic clutch Y has to be released and it is necessary to ensure rapid movement of the transition valve to the left and of the couplings valve to the right as soon as the 2–3 shift valve moves to the left.

The transition valve is moved rapidly by passing TV pressure via the detent valve to line 50 and hence as soon as the 2–3 shift valve opens line 40, to line 39 and thus to the right-hand side of the large left-hand end of the transition valve (which is to the right), rapid movement of which is allowed by the lifting of the ball valve and by-passing of the restricting orifice. The moving of the transition valve passes governor boost pressure via lines 12 and 13 to the end of the coupling valve (which in third gear is to the left) and moves it to the right. To speed up this motion a momentary reduction of the TV pressure acting on the right-hand end of the coupling valve is produced as follows. The movement of the 2–3 shift valve to the left opens line 17 and thus lines 18 and 19 to exhaust so that the accumulator piston moves rapidly to the left (in the diagram); this produces a sudden lowering of pressure in line 46 and, because of the trimmer valve check and orifice, in line 45 also and hence via line 47 behind the right-hand end of the coupling valve. As soon as the latter moves to the right the line 45 will be closed so that although the pressure in line 45 will build up slowly through the trimmer valve orifice it will not act to move the coupling valve back to the left again.

When the manual valve is moved to the Dr Δ (drive right) position it opens line 22 to pump pressure and hence pump pressure is applied via lines 23, 24 and 26 to the right-hand end of the 3–4 shift valve; this has the effect of preventing governor pressure via lines 9 and 53 from moving the shift valve to the right except at very high car speeds so that the gearbox is virtually reduced to a three-speed box and the increased acceleration of 3rd gear is retained. Pump oil is also passed via lines 25 and 26 to the over-run clutch valve and moves that valve to the left so that line 26 is opened to line 27 and pump pressure is applied to engage the over-run clutch. The engagement of the over-run clutch is delayed until the sprag has engaged because the volume of oil trapped in the left-hand end of the over-run clutch valve has to be discharged through a restricted orifice. This enables the engine to be used as a brake in 3rd gear if required since the over-run clutch will prevent forward rotation of the sun of the front epicyclic whereas the sprag will not do so. The line 25 is cut off from line 26 whenever the coupling valve moves to the right, as it does for 2nd gear, so that the over-run clutch valve is moved back to the right-hand position and the over-run clutch is released as is necessary to enable the front epicyclic to go into direct drive.

When the manual valve is moved into the Lo position, pump pressure is passed to line 28 and thus via line 30 and 31 to the right-hand end of the 2–3 shift valve, and via line 51 to the right-hand end of the transition valve, so as to prevent that valve from moving to the right except at very high car speeds. The gearbox is thus restricted to 1st and 2nd gears. This is intended to enable very heavy going, such as in sand, to be negotiated. Since under these conditions torques will be high, oil from line 28 is passed via line 29 to the rear epicyclic band brake which thus assists the rear sprag in holding the annulus of the rear epicyclic and also holds that annulus against forward motion so that the engine can also be used as a brake in 2nd gear if required. If the car speed should increase sufficiently to enable governor pressure to move the 2–3 shift valve to the right so as to produce a change up to 3rd the shift valve will cut off line 28 from line 29 and thus release the band brake. In this position of the manual valve the line 4 is cut off from pump pressure so that pressure is not applied to the pump pressure regulator and the maximum pump pressure is not reduced.

When the manual valve is moved to the Rev position pump pressure is applied direct via line 32 to the rear epicyclic cone clutch (D) and via line 33 and 34 to the inside of the coupling valve regulator plug. The coupling valve is thus prevented from moving to the right and the front epicyclic is kept in reduction. It will be noticed that governor pressure is always to the reverse blocker so that if the forward speed of the car is higher than about 10 mph the blocker will be held out against spring pressure and will prevent the selector and manual valve from being moved to the Rev position. Line 33 is also connected via line 35 to the outer end of the pump pressure regulator so as to increase pump pressure in order to provide ample holding power to the cone clutch D. There is also a connection via line 27 to the over-run clutch so that the engine can be used as a brake in reverse.

The action of the limit valve, which has not yet been dealt with, is that it acts as an excess pressure safety valve since if the pump pressure via line 1 exceeds the maximum safe value the valve will move sufficiently far to the right to open line 1 to exhaust. The valve also acts to prevent the pressure from falling below a value of about $380 \, kN/m^2$, as it might do if a leak developed in coupling C, because at lower presures it will not move far enough to uncover line 3. Under these conditions the filling of coupling C will be done by oil from the manual valve via lines 4, 5, 11, 21 and the non-return valve into line 3.

23.13   Automatic transmissions for commercial vehicles

Automatic transmissions have been slow to gain ground in the commercial vehicle field. The principal reasons are that, because the numbers of vehicles involved are so much smaller than in the case of cars, the cost per transmission is correspondingly higher; secondly, with most such transmissions there is a fuel consumption penalty which, even though it may be only a few per cent, represents nevertheless a considerable addition to the operating costs of a vehicle travelling very large mileages at a rate of fuel consumption which, in any case, is high.

However, efficiencies have improved over the years and, with only a few very large-scale specialist manufacturers – principally Allison, Voith and ZF – producing increasing numbers of heavy-duty automatic transmissions to meet the demands from all over the world, costs per unit have been falling as the quantities sold have continuously increased. These manufacturers, while admitting that a skilful driver can get a better fuel consumption with a manual transmission than with automatic, generally assert that this is only if such a driver is positively aiming at low consumption, and that his performance will in any case fall off as the hours pass during his working day. The main argument for automatic transmission though is unrelated to fuel costs: it is that maintenance costs, including vehicle downtime, are greatly reduced since there are no clutch changes and virtually no other work to be done on the drive-line.

Types of operation for which automatic transmission may be economical are as follows –

(1) Buses – not only because of reduced drive-line maintenance but also increased passenger comfort and safety, especially for the elderly.

(2) Stop-start operation with goods vehicles – door-to-door deliveries and special-purpose vehicles such as refuse collectors.

(3) Rear-engine vehicles and vehicles that operate in conditions in which the driver may not be able to hear his engine as he changes gear – e.g., where aircraft or road works are causing high levels of extraneous noises.

(4) Where the driver has other controls to operate while operating the vehicle – e.g., road sweepers, tippers, diggers and dumpers.

(5) When dual control is required and the installation of such controls is more costly than that of automatic transmission.

(6) Where dirvers are trained and employed primarily for duties other than driving – e.g., refuse collection, telephone maintenance, etc. – or where they may successively have to take over vehicles of many different types in the course of a day's work.

(7) For emergency services such as fire appliances, ambulances and police.

(8) Operation in confined spaces close to valuable equipment, such as aircraft, that must not be damaged.

(9) For costly special-purpose vehicles where, for operational reasons, downtime for repairs to drive-lines would be expensive or unacceptable.

(10) Vehicles used among crowds of pedestrians.

The number of gear ratios required varies according to the type of operation. For instance, a light bus in a small town in a flat country such as Holland might require only a torque converter – ratio perhaps between 2.0 and 2.5:1 – and one extra forward ratio plus reverse. In general, however, a city bus might require four speeds, a coach five speeds and a long distance truck six speeds; all three types of vehicle of course would need a torque converter too, operating perhaps on only the bottom two gears.

23.14   Voith Diwamatic transmission

This is shown in Fig. 23.30 and is an example of a 'split-torque' transmission, the engine power being transmitted partly by a single-stage torque converter and partly by direct mechanical action through an epicyclic gear. A forward and reverse gearbox of conventional form is also employed. The converter is somewhat different from the usual arrangement in that the impeller I discharges directly into the fixed casing R whose passages lead the fluid into the driven member D. The division of the engine torque is done by the epicyclic train ACS in which the annulus is driven by the engine. When the vehicle is at rest and the planet carrier C is therefore stationary (assuming the dog-clutch J to be engaged with the gear E) the impeller I will be driven at a relatively high speed in the opposite sense to the rotation of the annulus A. The fluid will then develop a high torque on the driven member D and this will begin to rotate (in the same sense as the annulus) and will apply a torque to the gear E through the gears G and H,

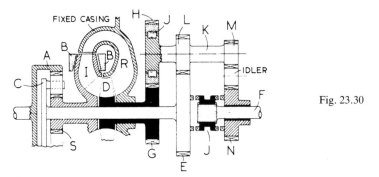

Fig. 23.30

the one way clutch J and the pinion L. A driving torque will also be applied to E direct through the planet carrier C. As the speed of the vehicle increases so the speed at which the impeller is driven will fall and the torque acting on the member D will also fall. At a speed determined by a governor driven from the output gear E the brake BB will be applied and the impeller brought to rest. The whole of the engine torque and power will then be transmitted mechanically through the planet carrier C and the dog-clutch J. The reverse drive is obtained by engaging the dog-clutch with the gear F and as this is done a cam operates a valve which empties the torque converter. The brake BB has therefore to be applied in order to obtain a drive and the application of this brake will also give the clutch action which is normally obtained from the torque converter.

23.15   ZF HP500 fully automatic transmission

As can be seen from Fig. 23.31, the ZF HP500 automatic transmission has a hydraulically-actuated lock-up clutch in front of the torque converter. Its lock-up mechanism is engaged automatically to lock the impeller and turbine wheels together, to give direct drive, at a predetermined ratio of turbine-to-engine speed. However, a kick-down switch actuated by the accelerator pedal unlocks them again to provide extra torque when called for by the driver for climbing a hill, or overtaking on one, in first or second gear. A one-way clutch in the hub of the converter prevents the stator from rotating during torque conversion, but allows it to free-wheel when the unit is operating as a fluid coupling, that is at a 1:1 ratio. A secondary oil pump, driven from the output shaft of the gearbox, can be fitted as an optional extra if a tow-starting facility is likely to be needed. In such circumstances, this pump performs the duty that is otherwise the function of the engine-driven pump.

The torque converter – maximum ratio 2.5:1 – is used only for starting from rest in 1st or 2nd gears or reverse, except under kick-down conditions, as previously decribed – hence the high overall efficiency of this transmission. Behind it is a space in which, if required, a hydraulic retarder can be installed without adding to the overall length. In Fig. 23.31, the retarder, item 4, is shown installed.

For the four-, five- and six-speed versions of this transmission, there are three planetary gear trains, but for the five- and six-speed boxes there is also an alternative internal arrangement of four gear trains and therefore a

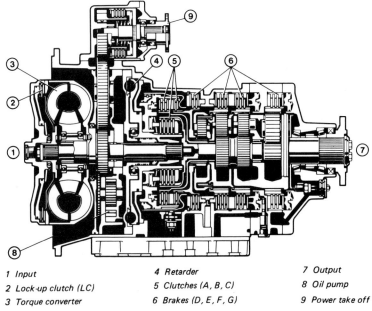

1 Input
2 Lock-up clutch (LC)
3 Torque converter

4 Retarder
5 Clutches (A, B, C)
6 Brakes (D, E, F, G)

7 Output
8 Oil pump
9 Power take off

Power-flow

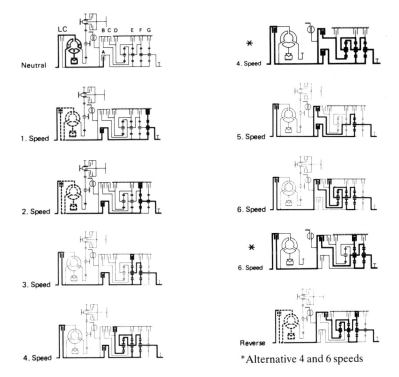

*Alternative 4 and 6 speeds

Fig. 23.31 ZF5 and 6 HP 500 automatic transmissions (version 2, with fourth gearset)

wider spread of ratios. All have a central multi-plate clutch, just forward of the group of gear sets, the other clutches and the multi-plate brakes being in an annular space between the housing and the gear sets and central clutch.

Simplest of all of course is the four-speed box, which has, in addition to the central clutch, only one annular clutch and three brakes. Then there is a five- or six-speed variant having an extra annular clutch. Finally, there is the five- and six-speed version with an extra gear train behind the others, for which there is another brake.

The fourth gear set – rearmost – is manufactured as a separate module so that it can be fitted or omitted, as required. When it is not fitted, the power flow pattern is the same, except in that 1st, 2nd, 3rd, 4th and 5th speeds are respectively as illustrated for 2nd, 3rd, 4th, 5th and 6th, and the alternative power-flow is adopted for the 6th speed. The power flow for the four-speed version is similar, i.e. 2, 3 and 4 illustrated here become 1, 2 and 3, but the alternative 4th speed power-flow is adopted.

Chapter 24

Universal joints, driving steered wheels, and alternative driving systems

A universal joint is a form of connection between two shafts, whose axes intersect, whereby the rotation of one shaft about its own axis results in the rotation of the other shaft about its axis.

The principle on which the Hooke's type of universal joint works is illustrated in Fig. 24.1. The shaft A is formed into a fork at its end and pivoted between the prongs of this fork is a cross-piece C. The cross C can therefore pivot about the axis XX relatively to the shaft A. The other shaft B is similarly forked and the other arms of the cross are pivoted between the prongs of this fork. The shaft B can therefore pivot about the axis YY relatively to the cross C and, since the latter can pivot about the axis XX relatively to the shaft A, the shaft B can assume any angular position relatively to shaft A. Or from another point of view, if the shafts A and B are supported in bearings with their axes at an angle, then when the shaft A is turned about its axis the motion is communicated to the shaft B and it turns about its axis; the arms of the cross meanwhile oscillating in the prongs of the forks.

The axes XX and YY intersect at O and are perpendicular one to the other. The axes of the arms of the cross C are also perpendicular to their respective shafts. The axes of the shafts intersect at O, which point is the 'centre' of the joint.

It does not matter how the pivoting action is obtained; all that is required is that the shaft B shall be able to pivot independently about two intersecting perpendicular axes such as XX and YY, relatively to the shaft A.

24.1 Constructional forms of universal joints

There are several types of universal joint all working on the principle outlined above, but in motor cars and lorries the joints are of two principal forms. These may be called –

(1) Cross type.
(2) Ring type.

Examples of these are shown in Figs. 24.2 and 24.3.

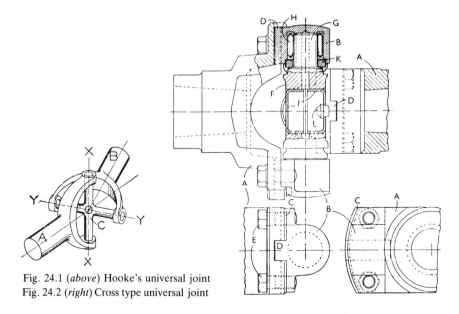

Fig. 24.1 (*above*) Hooke's universal joint
Fig. 24.2 (*right*) Cross type universal joint

A proprietary design of cross type joint is shown in Fig. 24.2. The yoke members A are secured to the shafts that are connected by the joint and carry bushes B. These are positioned by the projecting lips C of the yokes, which fit machined portions of the bushes and by the keys D integral with the bushes and which fit in keyways formed in the yokes. The keys D transmit the drive and relieve the set screws E of all shearing stresses. The two yokes are coupled by the cross member F which consists of a central ring portion and four integral pins G. The ends of the latter bear on the bottoms of the bushes B thus centring the joint. Between the pins G and the bushes B are needle bearings H. The hole in the centre of the cross member F is closed by two pressings J and forms a reservoir for lubricant which reaches the bearings through holes drilled in the pins G. The cork washers K form a seal at the inner ends of the pins and also serve to retain the needle rollers when the joint is taken apart. A single filling of oil suffices for practically the whole life of the joint. Any excessive pressure in the reservoir which might lead to oil being forced out past the seals K is prevented by the relief valve L.

Fig. 24.3 shows a ring type joint. The member A is bolted to one shaft by its flange and the fork B is secured to the other shaft by splines. The two members are coupled by the ring C. This ring is made of two steel pressings each forming half the ring and being bolted together by the nuts on the trunnion portions of the four bushes D whose shape is clearly seen in the separate plan view. The pins of the fork member B fit in two of the bushes and the ends of the pin E, which is fixed in member A, fit in the other two bushes. The space inside the ring forms a reservoir for oil which may be introduced through a nipple not shown. The joint between the two halves of the ring is ground to form an oil-tight joint and escape of oil at the points of entry of the pins is prevented by the compressed cork washers F. The shafts are centred relatively to the ring by reason of the fitting of the pins

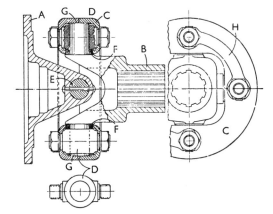

Fig. 24.3 Ring type universal joint

on faces G accurately machined inside the ring, and not by the cork washers. The nuts securing the ring are locked by a pair of tab washers H.

Another universal joint construction is shown in Fig. 24.4. It consists of a ball A having two grooves formed round it at right angles. In these grooves the forked ends of the shafts E and F fit. Obviously when the joint is put together the shaft E can slide round in its groove, thus turning about the axis XX. Similarly the shaft F can slide round in its groove, thus turning about the axis YY. This type of joint was used at one time in front wheel brake linkages. The arrangement of the shaft bearings has to be such that the shafts cannot move away from the centre of the ball, otherwise the joint would come apart. It is not suitable for use in the transmission.

24.2 Flexible-ring joints

A joint that acts by the flexure of a flexible ring is much used to connect shafts between which the angular displacement will not be very great. Such a joint is shown in Fig. 24.5. The shafts are provided with three-armed spiders, the arms of which are bolted to the opposite faces of a flexible ring, the arms of one spider being arranged mid-way between the arms of the other. The flexible ring is usually made of one or more rings of rubberised fabric made in a special way so as to provide the necessary strength. A number of thin steel discs is sometimes used instead of the

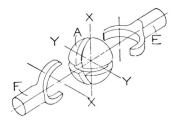

Fig. 24.4 (*above*)

Fig. 24.5 (*right*)

fabric rings. When the shafts are revolving about axes which are not coincident there is a continuous flexing of the ring. This type of joint has several advantages over the universal joints described above, the principal of which are the elimination of the need for lubrication and cheapness of manufacture. The joint cannot cope with such large angular displacements as the universal joints and when the torque to be transmitted is large it becomes very bulky.

24.3   Rubber-bushed flexible joints

Joints of this kind are now widely used and there are several forms of them, three being shown in Figs. 24.6 to 24.8. The first of these is the original Layrub; it is basically a ring type of joint. The shafts that are connected by the joint carry the two-armed spiders A and B projecting from which are bolts carrying special rubber bushes C. These bushes are housed inside the coupling ring D which is made of two exactly similar steel pressings bolted together. The rubber bushes by distorting slightly enable any misalignment of the shafts to be accommodated. Angular misalignments up to 15° can be allowed for but generally the misalignment is limited to about half that amount. The joint can also acommodate a considerable amount (up to 12.5 mm) of axial movement of the one shaft relative to the other and when two of them are used, one at each end of a propeller shaft, it is usually possible to dispense with the sliding joint that is essential when all-metal joints are used.

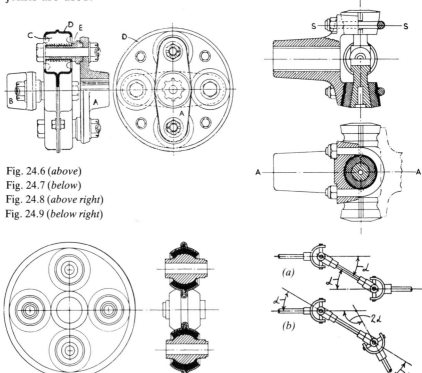

Fig. 24.6 (*above*)
Fig. 24.7 (*below*)
Fig. 24.8 (*above right*)
Fig. 24.9 (*below right*)

Since the only connection between the shafts is through the rubber bushes, the joints also assist in smoothing out vibrations; this property has been used to give a flexible clutch plate in a single-plate clutch the driven plate being connected to the clutch centre by four Layrub bushes.

The bushes are made with concave ends as shown in order to keep the internal stresses in them approximately uniform and to increase their flexibility. They are made with a metallic gauze insert on their insides and are forced on to the sleeves E which are made somewhat larger than the holes in the bushes. The outside diameters of the bushes are also greater than the diameters of the pockets in the ring D in which the bushes are housed and so when the coupling is assembled the bushes are compressed to such an extent that although when the joint flexes the distance between the sleeve E and the ring D may increase on one side the rubber remains in compression and is never in tension. The sleeves E have spigots which fit into holes in the spiders so that the bolts are not called upon to transmit the torque and are not subjected to any shearing.

Fig. 24.7 shows the very effective Metalastik unit in which the rubber bushes are bonded to the spherical pins and are compressed when the two metal pressings which form the ring of the joint are asembled together. These pressings are held together by spinning the lips of one of them over those of the other. The design in Fig. 24.8 is basically a cross type of joint and is made by the Moulton company. The rubber bushes are bonded on the inside of the tapered portions of the arms of the cross and on the outside to steel shells. The latter fit into depressions formed in the flanges of the joint and are held in place by stirrups which are bolted up to the flanges.

24.4   Constant-velocity joints

The Hooke's type of universal joint suffers from a disadvantage which is obviated in some other types of joint. It is that supposing one of the shafts connected by a Hooke's joint is revolving at an absolutely constant speed then the other shaft will not revolve at a constant speed but with a speed that is, during two parts of each revolution, slightly greater and, during the other two parts of the revolution, slightly less than the constant speed of the first shaft. The magnitude of this fluctuation in speed depends on the angle between the axes of the two shafts, being zero when that angle is zero but becoming considerable when the angle is large. This disadvantage becomes of practical importance in front wheel driven vehicles and in the drives to independently sprung wheels where the angle between the shafts may be as large as 40°. It can be obviated by using two Hooke's joints arranged as shown in Fig. 24.9 (*a*) and (*b*), the intermediate shaft being arranged so that it makes equal angles with the first and third shafts and the fork pin axes of the intermediate shaft being placed parallel to each other. The irregularity introduced by one joint is then cancelled out by the equal and opposite irregularity introduced by the second joint. Examples of front wheel drives using this arrangement are shown in Fig. 24.16 and 24.17. A slightly different arrangement using the same principle is given in Fig. 35.9.

Constant-velocity joints are joints which do not suffer from the above disadvantage but in which the speeds of the shafts connected by the joint are absolutely equal at every instant throughout each revolution. Although such joints have been known for very many years they have not been used to any extent until relatively recently.

The Tracta joint, manufactured in England by Bendix Ltd., is shown in Fig. 24.10, from which the construction will be clear. The joint is a true constant-velocity joint but the theory of it is beyond the scope of this book and those who are interested in this theory and in those of the joints

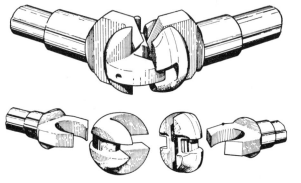

Fig. 24.10 Bendix Tracta universal joint

described below, are referred to an article by one of the authors in *Automobile Engineer*, Vol. 37, No. 1. Another true constant-velocity joint, the Weiss, which is used to a considerable extent in America, where it is manufactured by the Bendix Products Corporation, is shown in Fig. 24.11. It consists of two members each with two fingers or arms in the sides of which are formed semi-circular grooves. When the two members are assembled the fingers of the one fit in between the fingers of the other and balls are inserted in the grooves of the fingers and form the driving connection between them. The formation of the grooves is such that the balls lie always in a plane making equal angles with the axes of the shafts connected by the joint, this being a fundamental condition that must be satisfied if the drive is to be a constant velocity drive. This joint has the

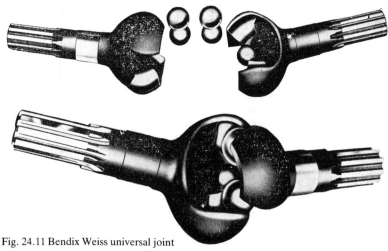

Fig. 24.11 Bendix Weiss universal joint

property that the shafts connected by it may be moved apart axially slightly without affecting the action of the joint and this axial motion is accommodated by a rolling of the balls along the grooves in the fingers of the joint members and so takes place with the minimum of friction.

A third example is shown in Fig. 24.12. It is the Rzeppa (pronounced Sheppa) and it consists of a cup member A with a number of semi-circular grooves formed inside it and a ball member B with similar grooves formed on the outside. Balls C fit half in the grooves A and half in B and provide the driving connection. For true constant-velocity operation the balls must be arranged to lie always in a plane making equal angles with the axes of rotation of the members A and B. This is ensured by the control link D and the cage E. The former has spherical ends one of which engages a recess in the end of the member B while the other is free to slide along a hole formed inside A; the link is kept in place by the spring F. The spherical enlargement G of the link engages a hole formed in the cage E which has other holes in which the balls C fit. When the shaft B swings through an angle relatively to A the link D causes the cage E and the plane XX of the balls C to swing through half that angle and thus the balls are caused to occupy the required positions for the correct functioning of the joint.

In some designs of this joint, intended for use where the angular deviation of the shafts is small, the control link D is omitted.

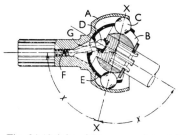

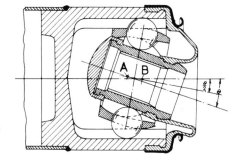

Fig. 24.12 (*above*) Rzeppa universal joint
Fig. 24.13 (*right*) Birfield
constant-velocity universal joint

A joint developed by Birfield Transmissions Ltd. which gives constant-velocity ratio transmission and allows for a plunging motion of one of the shafts relative to the other is shown in Fig. 24.13. The inner member is grooved to carry the balls that transmit the motion and its outer surface is ground to a sphere whose centre is at the point A. The balls are housed in recesses in the cage and this is ground on its inside to fit the outer surface of the inner member while its outer surface is ground to a sphere whose centre is at the point B. The outer member has a cylindrical bore with grooves formed in it to take the balls and the outer spherical surface of the cage fits the cylindrical surface of the outer member. The inner member can therefore move bodily along the bore of the outer member thus giving the plunging motion required in the drives to most independently sprung wheels and which usually has to be provided by sliding splines. The off-setting of the centres of the spherical surfaces of the cage keeps the plane of the balls at all times in the plane bisecting the angle between the shaft axes as is necessary for the maintenance of a constant-velocity ratio.

24.5   Driving and braking of steered wheels

Various methods of driving a steered wheel are shown in Fig. 24.14. In the examples (*a*) and (*b*) a rigid driven axle is assumed, but in the others independent suspensions are shown. The arrangement at (*a*) is the simplest, a single universal joint U being provided to accommodate the steering motion of the stub axle S. Unless this joint is of the constant

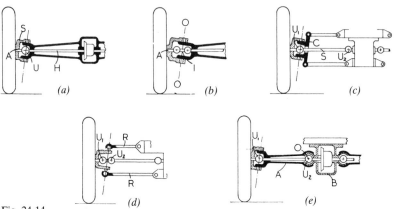

Fig. 24.14

velocity type, there will be an irregularity in the drive to the wheel whenever the sub axle is turned for steering purposes while, if the wheel is given any camber and the wheel shaft A is inclined to the half-shaft H, the irregularity will always be present. This constructional arrangement was adopted by the Four Wheel Drive Company in their lorries, which were among the earliest four-wheel-driven vehicles, and although the details of this arrangement are obsolete the general arrangement still represents current practice. An ordinary live axle is used so far as the final drive, differential and axle casing surrounding those components are concerned, but at their outer ends A, Fig. 24.15, the drive shafts are carried in bushes and are forked to form one member of a Hooke's type universal joint. The other shaft of this joint is seen at B and conveys the drive to the hub cap of the road wheel. The hub is carried on bearings on the stub-axle member, which is made in three pieces D, E and F bolted together as shown in the right-hand view. The inner spherical surfaces of the portions E and F touch the corresponding surfaces of the end of the axle casing in order to make the housing oil-tight and to exclude mud and dust, but those surfaces do not carry any loads. E and F are carried on the projecting swivel pins of the axle casing.

In the arrangement shown in Fig. 24.14 (*b*), two universal joints are used and are symmetrically disposed relative to the king-pin axis OO. When the stub axle is turned about that axis for steering purposes, the angles between the intermediate shaft I and the sheel shaft A and half-shaft H respectively will be maintained equal as in Fig. 24.9, and so a constant-velocity drive will be obtained. An example of this construction is shown in detail in Fig. 24.16. It is the design of the Kirkstall Forge Engineering Company and incorporates a second reduction gear which is housed in the

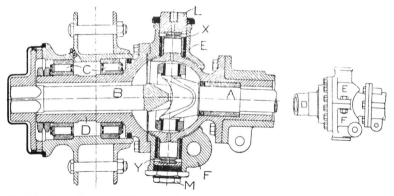

Fig. 24.15 Details of the FWD stub axle

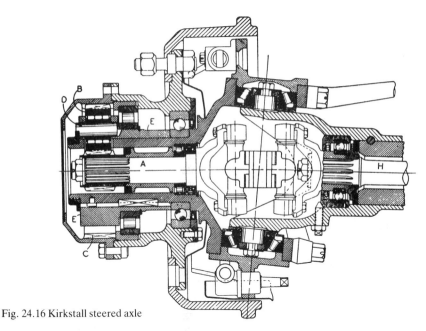

Fig. 24.16 Kirkstall steered axle

wheel hub. This second reduction is between the pinion which is splined to
the end of the shaft A and the annulus C which forms the hub cap of the
road wheel and is bolted to the hub of the latter. The intermediate pinions
B are carried on pins D, which are supported in the member E. The latter
fits the cylindrical extension of the stub axle and a key prevents rotation.
Because the intermediate member coupling the two universal joints is
rigid, and the forks of the joints are rigidly attached to the half-shaft H and
wheel shaft A respectively, one of these shafts must be left free to float
axially. This will be seen from Fig. 24.19, in which the full lines show the
position when the wheels are in the straight-ahead position, and the dotted
lines the position when the stub axle is turned for steering. It is clear that
the distance X_1Y_1 is less than the distance XY. This variation is accommodated by leaving the shaft A (Fig. 24.16) free to float. It is therefore carried

in a parallel roller bearing at the right end and is supported by the contacts with the three pinions B at the left end. The omission of a bearing at the left end ensures equal division of the driving torque between the three pinions.

The example shown in Fig. 24.14 (*c*) is a conventional double-arm type of suspension, in which a stub axle carrier C connects the two arms. The drive shaft S is provided with universal joints U_1 and U_2. The first of these accommodates the steering motion of the stub axle and, in conjunction with the second, allows for the vertical motion of the wheel assembly. Because the distance between the centres of the universal joints cannot be kept constant, the shaft S must be provided with some axial freedom. This is usually done by leaving one of the universal joint forks free to slide on the splines of its shaft. Obviously, U must be a constant-velocity joint.

In the example shown in Fig. 24.14 (*d*), the stub axle carrier is omitted and the stub axle is carried directly by the arms RR, to which it is conected by ball and socket joints which accommodate the steering motion as well as the vertical motion of the road wheel. The joint U_2 now has to be supported from the stub axle through the joint U_1, and the construction of a joint which provides this support is shown in Fig. 24.17. The joint is made by the Glaenzer Spicer Company, of Poissy, France. The forks A and B,

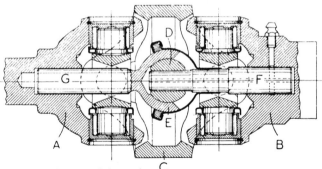

Fig. 24.17 Glaenzer Spicer axle

integral with their shafts, are coupled by four-armed spiders and an intermediate member C. The shaft B is supported relative to A by the ball and socket DE. The ball D is free to slide along the spigot shaft F, and the socket E is integral with the spigot G. The connection keeps the two universal joints and the intermediate member in the correct relationships to provide a constant-velocity drive, as described above.

Fig. 24.14 (*e*) shows a swinging-arm type of independent suspension, in which the arm A which carries the stub axle is pivoted to the final drive casing B on the axis O. Two universal joints are necessary; one (U_1) to accommodate the steering motion and the other to allow for the swinging of the arm. The arrangement does not provide a constant velocity drive unless both the joints are of the constant velocity type. The casing B is carried by the frame of the vehicle.

In the arrangement shown in Fig. 24.18 there is a gear reduction between the drive shaft and the road wheel. This makes the speed of rotation of the drive shaft higher than that of the wheel and reduces the torque the

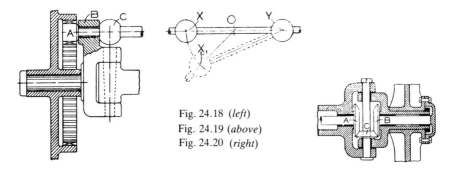

Fig. 24.18 (*left*)
Fig. 24.19 (*above*)
Fig. 24.20 (*right*)

universal joint has to transmit. The drive shafts are more exposed and difficult to protect from mud and dust but, being higher than the axle, are more out of the way of damage from the striking of obstacles. The arrangement is only very occasionally used on special types of vehicle.

The use of a universal joint can be avoided by using the arrangement shown in Fig. 24.20, where the half shaft carries a bevel gear A which drives a second bevel gear B fixed to the road wheel shaft through the intermediate wheel C. The latter is free to rotate on bearings on the swivel pin. The turning of the stub axle for steering purposes is accommodated by the rolling of the wheel B round the wheel C, and although this introduces an epicyclic action which causes an acceleration or deceleration of the road wheel this action only occurs during the time the stub axle is actually being turned. The arrangement can be made somewhat more robust than the universal joint drive, but is rather clumsy and is very little used.

24.6 Chain drive

Chain drive is beginning to be reintroduced into transmission lines, mainly as a means of dropping or raising the drive line from one level to another. This requirement is especially liable to arise between the engine crankshaft and gearbox in front-wheel-drive cars and in the transfer box for a four-wheel-drive vehicle.

The advantages include freedom of choice of centre-to-centre distance between the shafts, wider tolerance permissible than for gear drives and, because of the relative flexibility and inherent damping of a chain, it takes up the drive more smoothly than gears. It is also significantly less noisy than a gear drive, especially after wear has taken place in service. A point liable to be overlooked, too, is that simple bearings can be used for chain sprockets whereas, with helical gears, both radial and axial loads have to be reacted by the bearings. Finally, not only are sprockets easier to machine than gears, but also a chain drive is more efficient.

Obviously, the most economical arrangement is a single chain, but if the torque is too high for this to be practicable, a choice has to be made between two or three separate strands and sprockets and duplex or triplex chains. The last two mentioned are more compact but, since there is a clearance between the intermediate plates and the bearing pins, the fatigue life of the plates, and hence of the whole chain, is lower than that of a two- or three-strand drive with simple chain. Two or three strands on staggered teeth also introduce significantly less resonant vibration and noise. The employment of separate strands of chain does not necessarily entail separate chain wheels, since J. Parkinson & Son (Shipley) Ltd., a subsidiary of Renold Ltd., has developed a special technique for shaping as many as three rows of staggered teeth on a single wheel. Chain tensioners are dealt with, in connection with camshaft drives, in Chapter 6.

Another choice that has to be made is between roller and inverted tooth chain. The roller chain is lighter, less expensive and, for a given weight and life, has a higher torque transmission capacity. Maintaining the correct tension with a roller chain is easy, simply by applying a jockey sprocket or simple leaf spring, or a sprung or oil-pressure-loaded shoe to the outer face of the slack run. With an inverted tooth chain, however, these methods cannot be used because it will flex in only one direction, that is, around the sprockets.

An inverted tooth chain, on the other hand, may be the best choice for low speed, high torque applications, because the inverted tooth design has a greater number of plates per unit width, giving increased torque capacity. Moreover, for such applications, the extra weight and inertia can be tolerated. This type of chain has also been used in torque converter transmissions, where, by virtue of the absorption of fluctuations in the torque by the converter, the lower inertia and silence of roller-type chain under this type of loading may not be required. An example is the Saab range of cars. The automatic versions have an inverted tooth chain, while the manual ones are fitted with separate strands of roller chain and a hydraulic tensioner which serves also as a damper.

24.7 Belt drives

An alternative to chain drive in transmission systems is the toothed belt, pioneered by UniRoyal. Originally trapezoidal teeth were used but by the time the original patents had expired, in 1963, UniRoyal had patented a similar belt but with tooth profiles resembling those of gears. This almost doubled the transmission capacity.

The advantages of the toothed belt, as compared with the V-belt, include relatively low tension and therefore light loading on the shaft bearings, no need for adjustment of tension in service, extremely flexible, high load-carrying capacity, and zero slip.

Where silence and positive drive are important, the toothed-belt drive is the obvious choice. It is also used where relative timing – synchronisation – between driving and driven wheels is essential – a V-belt drive of course is not suitable for such applications.

Recent developments with V-belts have increased both their wear resistance and load-carrying capacity. Nevertheless, as a transmission medium, they are suitable only for auxiliary drives. Variants range from the single- to multiple-belt drives with multi-V pulleys, or the integrated banded belt which is, in effect, a number of V-belts joined at their outer edges to form a flat belt with a multi-V section driving face.

On grounds of drive efficiency, the V-belt comes off worst, its principal merits being compactness, simplicity and low cost. Even when properly adjusted its efficiency is likely to be little better than about 94%. Wear and stretch in service, allowing slip to increase, can substantially reduce this value. Largely because of the total absence of slip, the toothed belt efficiency is of the order of 98%, and this is maintained continuously. In general, toothed belt efficiency increases while that of the V-belt decreases with rising torque. The efficiencies of both types, however, decrease as the size of pulley is reduced. Speed has relatively little effect on efficiency. The efficiency of a roller chain or inverted tooth drive can be about 98% too.

Chapter 25

The differential

The differential is the device that divides the torque input from the propeller shaft equally between the two output shafts to the wheels, regardless of the fact that they may be rotating at different speeds, for instance on rounding a corner. In principle, as can be seen from Fig. 25.1, it is a set of two bevel gears with a bevel pinion between them. The bevel pinion can be likened to a balance beam pivoted at its centre, its ends registering between pairs of teeth on the differential gears.

If a force P is applied at the central pivot, in a direction tangential to the two differential gears, and if the beam either does not swing, or swings at a uniform velocity, it follows that the forces at the ends of the beam will be equal to $P/2$. Hence, equal forces are aplied at equal distances from the centres of the differential gears, and therefore the torques they transmit to the halfshafts are equal. Clearly, the force P represents the pressure between the differential pinion and its pin, while the forces $P/2$ represent the pressures between the teeth of the bevel pinion and those with which they mesh on the two differential gears.

In Fig. 25.2 is a typical differential unit in the back axle of a car. It consists of a drum-shape cage A, which is carried in ball bearings BB in the axle casing and is therefore free to rotate about the axis XX of the road wheels. Fixed to the cage A is a crown wheel C driven by the bevel pinion D. The arrangement is similar to that of Fig. 26.1, except that the crown wheel is fixed to the cage, in which the bevel gears $F_1 F_2$ and their pinions GG rotate on axes mutually at right angles. There are now two 'differential' or 'drive' shafts $E_1 E_2$, the outer ends of which are connected to the road wheels. Their inner ends pass through the bosses of the differential cage A in which they are quite free to turn. Inside the differential cage, their ends are splined into the bevel wheels $F_1 F_2$ with which the bevel pinions GG mesh. The pinions GG are free to turn on the pin H fixed in the differential cage.

It should be clear that if the differential cage is held and the wheel F_1 is turned in the forwards direction at, say 2 rev/min then the wheel F_2 will be turned backwards at 2 rev/min, since it is equal in size to F_1. Moreover, since these motions are relative to the differential cage, they will not be affected by any motion of that cage. If, therefore, the differential cage is rotating at, say, 200 rev/min in the forwards direction and the wheel F_1 is still turning at 2 rev/min forwards relatively to it, the wheel F_2 will still be turning at 2 rev/min backwards relatively to it.

The actual speed of the wheel F_1 will then be 202 rev/min, because its forward motion of 2 rev/min relatively to the differential cage is added to the forwards motion of 200 rev/min of that cage. The actual speed of the wheel F_2 will be 198 rev/min because its backwards motion of 2 rev/min relatively to the differential cage is subtracted from the forwards motion of 200 rev/min of that cage.

This is the action that occurs when a car moves in a circle: the road wheels are constrained to move at different speeds and do so by virtue of one wheel going faster than the differential cage while the other goes an equal amount slower than the differential cage. Thus the speed of the differential cage is the mean of the road wheel speeds. When the car moves in a straight line, the road wheels turn at the same speed as the differential cage, and the differential pinions do not have to turn on their pins at all.

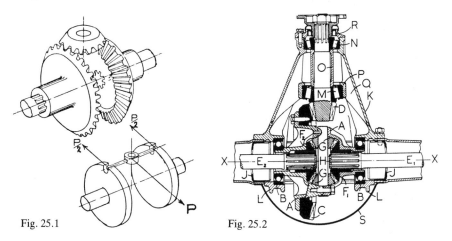

Fig. 25.1   Fig. 25.2

The above description should make it clear how the road wheels can turn at different speeds; it remains to show that when so doing they are driven with equal torques. In Fig. 25.1 the bevel wheels are shown replaced by discs having notches in their peripheries. Lying with its ends in these notches is a beam. If a force P is applied to the centre of the beam in a direction tangential to the discs as shown, then if the beam does not turn about the vertical axis, or if it turns about that axis with uniform velocity, the forces at the ends of the beam must be equal and each will be equal to $P/2$. The reactions of the forces acting on the ends of the beam act on the discs, hence equal forces are applied to the discs at equal distances from their axes, and therefore the twisting moments or torques acting on the discs are equal.

It should readily be seen that the bevel pinion acts in a manner precisely similar to the beam. Hence the torques transmitted to the drive shafts are equal and each will be equal to half the torque applied to the differential case by the final drive. In the actual differential the force P appears as a pressure between the bevel pinion and its pin while the forces $P/2$ appear as pressures between the teeth of the bevel pinion and the bevel wheels.

25.1 Spur differential

The differential described above is called a bevel differential, because it uses bevel wheels. There is another form which utilises spur wheels. Such a differential is shown in Fig. 25.3. The wheels A, B are splined to the drive shafts that drive the road wheels. Meshing with the wheel A is a spur pinion E_1, whose teeth extend nearly across the gap between the wheels A and B. The spur pinion F_1 meshes in a similar way with the wheel B, and at the centre the two pinions mesh together. The pinions are carried on pins

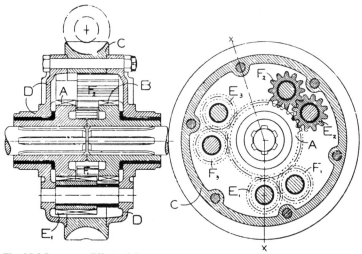

Fig. 25.3 Spur type differential

which are supported by the ends of the differential cage, which in this design is formed of the worm wheel C of the final drive and two end cover plates DD. It should be clear that if the differential cage is held fixed and the wheel A is turned in, say, the clockwise direction, then the pinion E_1 will be turned in a counter-clockwise direction, the pinion F_1 in a clockwise direction and the wheel B in the counter-clockwise direction. Hence, if one of the differential wheels goes faster than the differential cage, the other differential wheel will go an equal amount slower, just as in the bevel type.

As regards the equality of the torques, the torque on the wheel A is due to the pressure of the teeth of the pinion E_1. This pressure tends to make the pinion E_1 revolve on its pin, and this tendency is opposed by a pressure between the teeth of the two pinions at the centre. This last pressure tends to make the pinion F_1 revolve on its pin, and this tendency is opposed by the pressure between the teeth of the pinion F_1 and the wheel B. If the pinion E_1 (and therefore the pinion F_1 also) is at rest relatively to, or if it is revolving uniformly on, its pin then the two pressures acting on it must be equal. Hence, all the pressures between the teeth of the wheels A and B and the pinions E_1 and F_1 are the same, and hence the torques acting on the wheels A and B are equal. Three pairs of pinions are provided as shown.

25.2 Friction in differentials

In the consideration given to the torques transmitted to the two drive shafts it has been assumed that the various wheels and pinions can revolve without any friction on their pins, but this is neither possible nor desirable. The friction that is present may destroy the equality of the torques transmitted to the drive shafts, and the greater the friction the greater the possible inequality of the torques. Now, if one of the road wheels gets on to a patch of greasy road it may lose its grip, and any torque that is applied to it will simply cause it to spin round. Under these conditions the only torque that can be transmitted to that wheel without causing it to spin is the small torque required to overcome the friction in the wheel bearings, and the small friction between the wheel and the ground. But since the differential equalises the torques transmitted it follows that only the same small torque can be transmitted to other road wheel, and although that wheel may have a perfect grip of the road, the grip cannot be utilised. If, however, a large amount of friction is present in the differential, then a larger torque could be transmitted to the gripping wheel than to the slipping wheel, and the grip of that wheel could be utilised. With this object differentials are sometimes made intentionally with a large amount of friction.

The other method of overcoming the difficulty of a slipping wheel is the provision of a differential lock. This puts the differential out of action altogether, and then the whole torque applied to the crown wheel by the bevel pinion can be transmitted to the wheel that retains its grip of the ground. Differential locks act either by clutching one or both of the differential wheels to the differential cage by means of dog-tooth clutches, or by locking the differential pinions so that they cannot revolve on their pins. Differential locks are not used on passenger cars or light lorries, but a number of makes of heavy lorry fit them and they are generally fitted to half-track machines.

Instead of using a differential the drive shafts are occasionally driven through one-way ratchets and when the vehicle moves in a circle the outer ratchet is overriden. This arrangement avoids any trouble from a slipping wheel but does not give equality of drive between the wheels. For driving in reverse, means of putting the ratchets out of action must be provided.

25.3 Another arrangement of the bevel final drive

The bevel final drive is sometimes arranged in a different manner from that described previously, generally because some other difference in axle construction necessitates the change. The principle of this other method is shown in Fig. 25.4. The propeller shaft is coupled to the shaft A which passes right across the centre portion of the axle casing B in which it is supported. At the centre of the axle the shaft A is enlarged and formed into pins PP to carry the differential pinions CC. These mesh with the differential wheels $Q_1 Q_2$, which are integral with the bevel pinions $D_1 D_2$, of which D_1 meshes with the large bevel wheel E and D_2 with the smaller bevel wheel F. The bevel wheels E and F are supported in the axle casing and are splined on to the shafts which drive the road wheels.

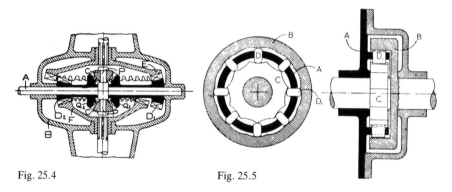

Fig. 25.4   Fig. 25.5

Of course, the gear ratio between D_1 and E is the same as the ratio between D_2 and F. The action of the differential is just the same as in the conventional axle, but the reduction of speed now occurs between the differential and the road wheels instead of between the propeller shaft and the differential cage. The differential therefore runs at a higher speed than the road wheels, enabling smaller wheels to be used in it.

It should also be clear that it is quite possible to have the axes of the shafts inclined to each other in the end view, and advantage has been taken of this feature to arch the back axle casing and to tilt the rear wheels in order to reduce the overhang on the axle and to bring the road wheels perpendicular to the curved surface of a cambered road. Arched back axles are not now used, and the form of final drive described is uncommon.

25.4 ZF differential

This device is designed to permit the half-shafts to rotate at different speeds when the adhesion of the road wheels forces them to do so but to transmit torque to one wheel only if the adhesion of the other wheel should be unduly low. Tests have shown that it is effective to some extent and it has been fairly widely used. There are two forms which are shown diagrammatically in Figs. 25.5 and 25.6. Each consists of four main elements driving member A to which is fixed the crown wheel of the final drive and which corresponds to the cage of an ordinary differential, two cam members B and C fixed respectively to the right- and left-hand half-shafts and which correspond to the differential wheels, and a set of plungers D free to slide in slots machined in the member A and which correspond to the differential pinions. Supposing the member A to be fixed and the member B to be rotated slowly clockwise then the cam surfaces of B will force the plungers D to slide to and fro in their slots but because the cam member B has a different number of cam surfaces from C the latter will be forced to revolve in the opposite direction to B. This will be seen by considering the plunger D_1, clearly clockwise rotation of B will force this plunger inwards and this will clearly force the cam C anti-clockwise. If now all three members are given an additional clockwise rotation then it will be seen that the members B and C will be rotating respectively faster and slower than the member A as in a true differential. The difference in speeds between the members B and C and the member A will not be equal in magnitude however. When the member B makes one revolution relative to A the member C will make 13/11 revolution since B has 13 lobes and C only 11. There is, however, considerable friction between the plungers D and the member A and cam surfaces so that while the device gives the difference in speed necessary for cornering it enables a torque to be transmitted to one cam member even though the resistance to the other cam member is very low.

25.5 Thornton Powr-Lok differential

This is manufactured by the Dana Corporation of Toledo, Ohio, USA, and its construction is shown in Fig. 25.7. The crown wheel of the final drive is fixed to a flange of the differential cage A, which is carried in bearings in the axle case in the usual manner. Differential wheels are splined to the ends D of the half-shafts and mesh with four differential pinions as usual. The pinions, however, are now carried on two separate cross-pins B and C, instead of on a four-armed spider, and the cross-pins are not fixed in the differential cage at their ends, but are merely located in V-shaped grooves, as shown in the view at the top of the figure. The grooves for locating the cross-pin C face the opposite way to the grooves that locate the cross-pin B.

The differential pinions are formed with cylindrical necks which bear against disc-shaped members F and H; between these and the ends of the differential cage the plates of clutches G and J are situated. The outer plates of these clutches are provided with projections, or splines, which engage with the differential cage, and the inner plates are splined to the hubs of the discs F and H, which themselves are splined to the half-shafts.

Considering the pin B, the driving forces between it and the differential cage are exerted between the faces E, and thus have components which

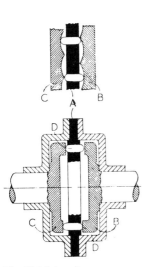

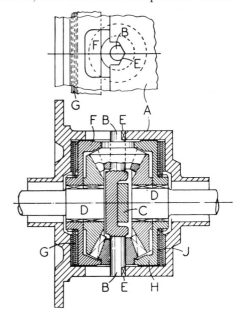

Fig. 25.6 (*above*)
Fig. 25.7 (*right*)

tend to push the pin to the left. This, in turn, causes the necks of the pinions to bear on the face of the disc F and thus to lock the clutch G. Similarly, the pin C is pushed to the right and locks the clutch J.

Thus under normal, straight-ahead driving conditions, the clutches G and J transmit a considerable part of the driving torques applied to the half-shafts, and this action also occurs even if one of the wheels slips on the ground. Thus this differential overcomes to a considerable extent the chief disadvantage of the conventional type. When rounding a corner the outer (say, left-hand) wheel tends to overrun the differential cage and this results in one of the pins (say, B) moving forwards relative to the differential cage. This reduces the forces between the faces E, and thus the clutch G is freed and the differential can function in the ordinary way.

Chapter 26

The back axle

Having dealt with the mechanical transmission system between the engine and output from the gearbox, we now turn to the three alternative final stages. As listed in Chapter 18, these are: live axles, dead axles and axleless transmissions.

26.1 Live back axles

A live axle is one that either rotates or houses shafts that rotate, while a dead axle is one that does neither, but simply carries at its ends the stub axles on which the wheels rotate. Live axles perform two functions –

(1) To act as a beam which, through the medium of the springs, carries the loads due to the weight of the carriage unit and its contents, and transmits these loads under dynamic conditions through the road wheels – rotating on its ends – to the ground. The dynamic loading is principally a result of the motions of the wheel and axle assembly over the ground and the reactions due to its mass, the flexibilities of the tyres and road springs and the mass of the carriage unit and its contents.

(2) To house and support the final drive, differential, and shafts to the road wheels, and to react the torques in both the input and output shafts.

Most live axles, therefore, are of hollow or tubular construction and usually, though not necessarily, of circular cross-section outboard of the final drive unit.

26.2 The final drive

The functions of turning the drive from the propeller shaft through 90° to distribute it to the two wheels, and of reducing the speed of rotation – thus increasing the torque – is performed by the gearing carried in the final drive unit, usually housed in the back axle. For relatively small reductions – up to about 7:1 – single-stage gearing is used; but for greater reductions, two or even three stages may be required, and the gearing for one or more of these stages may be housed in the wheel hubs. The terms *single-*, *double-* and *triple-reduction axles* are therefore used.

Generally, the first stage is either a bevel pinion and what is termed the *crown wheel*, or a worm and worm-wheel, both of which of course turn the drive through 90°. Worm drives have the advantages of silence, either a low drive-line or a high ground clearance – according to whether the worm is underslung or overslung relative to the wheel – ease of providing for a through drive to a second axle in tandem with the first, and the fact that a high single-reduction ratio can be readily provided – even as high as 15:1.

Bevel and hypoid bevel final drives are, however, far more common because they are less costly to manufacture and have a higher efficiency – the sliding action of worm teeth generates a lot of heat, especially if the gear ratio is high, and makes heavy demands on the lubricant. A hypoid bevel gear is one in which the axes of the crown wheel and the pinion are not in the same plane, and in which therefore some sliding action takes place between the meshing teeth. The one advantage is that a low propeller drive-line can be obtained, so that the floor, and therefore centre of gravity, of the vehicle can be kept down.

26.3 Single-reduction live axles

An elementary single-reduction live axle – without a differential – is illustrated diagrammatically in Fig. 26.1. It has a hollow casing A, which carries on its ends the road wheels B. The weight of the body and load is supported by the casing A through the springs which are attached to the body and to the axle in a manner which will be described later. The casing in turn is supported at its ends by the road wheels. It therefore acts as a beam and is subjected to a bending action as is shown in Fig. 26.2, where the forces *P* are the supporting forces supplied by the road wheels, and the forces *W* are the body load, applied to the casing through the springs. The casing has to be stiff enough to withstand this bending action without undue flexure.

Supported in bearings in the casing A is a short shaft D integral with which is a bevel pinion E. The shaft D is coupled by means of a universal or flexible joint, outside the casing, to the propeller shaft and hence to the mainshaft of the gearbox. Inside the casing the bevel pinion E meshes with,

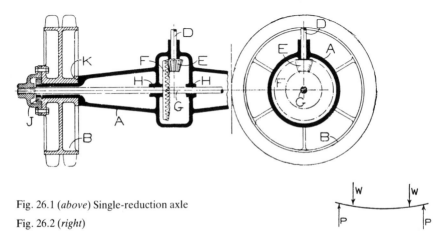

Fig. 26.1 (*above*) Single-reduction axle

Fig. 26.2 (*right*)

and drives, a bevel wheel F which is fixed to a transverse shaft G. This shaft is supported in bearings HH in the casing and is bolted to the hubs of the road wheels B at its outer ends. Obviously, when the pinion shaft D is turned by the propeller shaft the drive is transmitted through the bevel wheel to the transverse shaft G and hence to the road wheels. The road wheels are kept in place on the casing A in the end direction by nuts J and shoulders K of the casing. Although a bevel gear drive is shown, the principle would have been similar – only the gear arrangement different – had a worm drive been used.

26.4 Torque reaction

From Fig. 26.1, it can be seen that the propeller shaft aplies to the shaft D a torque which, as it is transmitted through the bevel gearing, is increased in the same ratio as the speed is reduced. This increased torque is then transmitted through the shaft G to the road wheels. From Newton's third law of motion, we know that action and reaction must be equal and opposite, so not only will this torque tend to rotate the wheel, but also the reaction from the wheel will tend to rotate the shaft G in the opposite sense. Therefore, there will be a tendency for the pinion and its shaft D to swing bodily around the crown wheel, and this tendency will be reacted by the axle casing. Some means therefore must be introduced to prevent the axle casing from rotating in the opposite direction. This may be simply the leaf springs themselves, or additional links – torque-reaction or radius rods – may be used and will be essential if coil, instead of leaf, springs are employed.

Similarly, the axle casing will tend to rotate about the axis of the bevel pinion in a direction opposite to that of rotation of the propeller shaft. However, since the torque transmitted by the propeller shaft is less than that in the drive shafts, it can in most circumstances be reacted satisfactorily simply by the suspension springs.

26.5 Driving thrust

Again, according to Newton's third law of motion, the driving thrust, or tractive effort, of the road wheels is reacted by the vehicle structure, the reaction being the inertia of the mass of the vehicle if it is accelerating, or rolling resistance of the other axle plus the wind resistance if it is not – the rolling resistance of the tyres of the driving axle involves of course purely local action and reaction. In effect, therefore, the driving axle has to push the carriage unit along, so it must be connected to the structure of the vehicle in such a way that this forward thrust can be transmitted from one to the other. This connection can be either the leaf springs or some other linkage for locating the axle relative to the carriage unit. The relevant members of this linkage are known as *thrust members*, or *radius rods*.

26.6 Torque and thrust member arrangements

In addition to the torque and thrust, sideways forces also have to be transmitted from the carriage unit to the wheels, and *vice versa*. The connections between the axle and the frame must therefore be capable of dealing with –

(1) The weight of the carriage unit.
(2) Torque reaction – from both drive-line and brakes.
(3) Driving thrust.
(4) Brake drag.
(5) Lateral forces.

Although various connection arrangements have been employed, only four are still generally accepted. These are –

(1) The springs reacting all forces.
(2) As in (1) but with separate torque reaction members.
(3) As in (1) but with torques and thrusts reacted by separate members.
(4) The springs transmitting only the weight of the carriage unit, leaving the torque, thrust and drag reactions, and lateral forces to be dealt with by separate members.

These four systems are outlined in more detail in Sections 26.7 to 26.11.

26.7   Springs serving also as torque and thrust members

This system, Fig. 26.3, known as the *Hotchkiss drive*, is the most widely used. The springs A are rigidly bolted to the axle casing B. Their front ends are pivoted in brackets on the frame or vehicle structure, and their rear ends connected to the structure by means of either swinging links, or shackles C, or simply sliding in brackets as in Figs. 33.7 and 35.18.

Obviously torque reaction causes the springs to flex, or wind up, as shown exaggeratedly in Fig. 26.4. Brake torque of course would flex them in the opposite direction. Since the front ends of the springs are anchored to the pins on the structure, they will transmit drive thrust and brake drag. The freedom of their rear ends to move fore and aft of course allows for variations in the curvature, or camber, of the spring with vertical deflection.

Wind-up of the springs under brake or drive torque causes the axle to rotate through a small angle, causing its nose either to lift, as in Fig. 26.4, or to drop. In the illustration, the spring wind-up has shifted the alignment of the final drive bevel pinion shaft from its normal attitude LO to LN, in

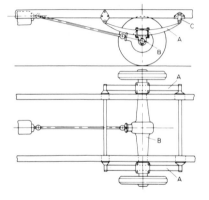

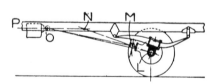

Fig. 26.3 (*left*) Hotchkiss drive

Fig. 26.4 (*below*) Spring deflection due to drive torque

which circumstances the propeller shaft would be subjected to severe bending loads were it not for the universal joints at O and M.

When the axle moves upwards relative to the carriage unit, it must move in the arc of a circle whose centre is approximately the axis of the pivot pin at the front end of the spring. The propeller shaft, on the other hand must move on the arc of a circle centred on its front universal joint. Because these two centres are not coincident, the distance between the front universal joint and the forward end of the bevel pinion shaft will vary as the propeller shaft swings up and down. This variation is accommodated by the incorporation of a sliding joint somewhere in the drive-line between the gear box output shaft and bevel pinion in the axle. Usually a sliding splined coupling is formed on a fork of one of the universal joints, but sometimes a universal joint of the pot type, as for example in Fig. 24.12, is used. The example illustrated is the Birfield Rzeppa constant-velocity joint, another would be the very neat and simple universal joint used on the inner ends of the swinging half shafts of the 1955 Fiat 600 rear-engine car. In the latter instance a rubber joint at the outboard end of each shaft accommodated the cyclic variations in velocity.

Rotation of the axle about a longitudinal axis, for example if one wheel only rises, is accommodated mainly by flexure of the springs, in a torsional sense, of rubber bushes, and by deflections of the shackles or within clearances in sliding end fittings. For cross-country vehicles, however, special forms of connection of the spring ends to the frame are sometimes used to isolate the springs from such twisting effects. Figs. 35.13 to 35.15.

26.8   Hotchkiss drive with torque reaction member

With the simple Hotchkiss-drive arrangement, making the springs stiff enough to react the torque adequately can leave them too stiff for giving a good ride. To avoid a compromise, a separate torque reaction member can be introduced, but the penalty is increased complexity. This system is now rarely used.

Ideally, since with such a system the springs do not have to react the torque, their seating pads would be free to pivot on the axle. However, to simplify construction and obviate lubrication points, rigid spring-seatings are sometimes used.

When a torque reaction member has been used, it has been mostly a triangular steel pressing, as in Fig. 26.5. Sometimes one has been employed and sometimes two. With other arrangements, a tubular torque reaction member has enclosed the propeller shaft, in some instances having its forward end carried by a ball bearing on the propeller shaft, adjacent to its front universal joint, which then has to take the vertical force necessary for reacting the torque. Whatever its form, the torque reaction member has to be secured rigidly at its rear end to the axle casing. Its front end, however, may be connected by a shackle to the frame, or structure of the vehicle. This is necessary to allow for the fore-and-aft motion of the axle resulting from the flexure of the semi-elliptic springs about their front pivots. For the avoidance of shocks, for example if the clutch is engaged too rapidly, the front end of the torque member may be sprung, as shown in Fig. 26.5.

25.9   Single combined torque-thrust reaction member, with springs taking only vertical and lateral loads

This form of construction is shown in Fig. 26.6. Bolted to the axle casing A and surrounding the propeller shaft is a tubular member B, the front end of which, C, is spherical and fits in a cup D bolted to a cross-member of the frame, or to the back of the gearbox. The springs are bolted to seats pivoted on the axle casing, and at each end are shackled to the frame. Clearly the member B will transmit the thrust from the axle to the frame and will also take the torque reaction. Since the centre line of the bevel pinion shaft will always pass through the centre of the spherical cup, if the propeller shaft E is connected to the gearbox shaft F by a universal joint situated exactly at the centre of that cup, neither an additional universal joint nor a sliding joint will be necesary, since both pinion shaft and propeller shaft will move about the same centre, namely that of the spherical cup, when the axle moves up or down. Because the axle is constrained to move about the centre of the spherical cup, the springs of course have to be shackled at each end to allow for the variation of their camber with deflection.

An alternative to the ball-and-cup construction is shown in Fig. 26.7. The tubular member B is again bolted the axle casing at its rear end, but at the front it has pivoted on it a forked member A which is pivoted on pins C carried by brackets riveted to a cross-member of the frame. By pivoting on the pins C the axle can move about the axis XX, both rear wheels moving up or down together, while by the tube B turning in the bracket A about the axis YY, one rear wheel can move up without the other. The universal joint must have its centre at O, the intersection of the axes XX, YY.

In this system the spring seats are sometimes articulated on spherical bearings on the axle casing, to relieve the springs of twisting stresses. The same advantage was sought in some early designs by attaching the spring shackles to the frame on a pivot whose axis was parallel to the centre line of the frame.

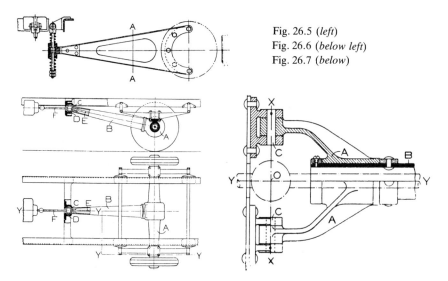

Fig. 26.5 (*left*)
Fig. 26.6 (*below left*)
Fig. 26.7 (*below*)

26.10   Transverse radius rods

Where coil, torsion bar or air springs are used, which of course cannot locate the axle, other measures have to be introduced. Two such arrangements are illustrated in Fig. 26.8 and 26.9, where transverse radius rods A, usually termed *Panhard rods*, are employed – to take the lateral loads – in conjunction with a single combined torque-thrust member B of the type illustrated in Fig. 26.6. With the arrangement of Fig. 26.8, the Panhard rod is parallel to the axle and therefore can have simple pivots at its ends. The advantage in Fig. 26.9 is that the Panhard rod is longer and therefore has less tendency to pull the axle laterally, as it moves up and down. On the other hand, its pivots must be rubber bushed, unless it can be arranged to lie parallel to the axle.

26.11   Three radius rods

The principle of a system often used is shown in Fig. 26.10. Radius rods A and B are placed parallel to the longitudinal axis of the vehicle and at the ends of the axle, while a wishbone or A-shape member C is placed at the centre. The rods A and B are provided with ball-and-socket joints at both ends, while the wishbone member if pivoted to the frame on a transverse pin joint and to the axle by a ball-and-socket joint. The wishbone member deals with all the sideways forces, while all three rods between them deal with the driving and braking thrusts and torques. The torques are transmitted to the frame by tension and compression forces in the rods. Thus the driving torque reaction (which would act in a clockwise direction as seen in the end view) produces a tension force in the member C and compressive forces in the rods A and B, while the brake torque produces a compressive force in the wishbone and tension forces in the rods A and B. An approximation to the system of Fig. 26.10 is sometimes made by replacing the triangular upper member C by two separate radius rods

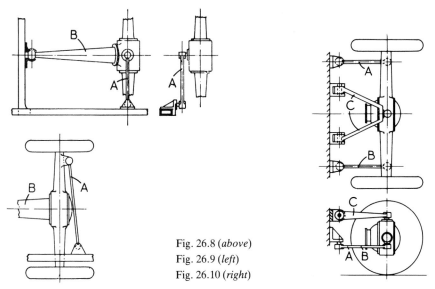

Fig. 26.8 (*above*)
Fig. 26.9 (*left*)
Fig. 26.10 (*right*)

arranged at about 45° to the axis of the vehicle and coupled at their ends by rubber-bushed joints to the frame and axle respectively.

If the upper radius rod of Fig. 26.10 is a simple link with a single pivot connection to the frame, then a transverse radius rod must be provided to position the axle sideways. These arrangements are fairly common when air or coil springs are used. Various methods of locating axles and reacting torques and thrusts are described in Chapters 33 and 34.

Chapter 27

Axle constructions

The pinion shaft of a bevel final drive and the worm shaft of a worm drive must be supported in journal bearings at two, or more, points and must be held axially. The latter can be done by using separate thrust bearings, or by means of the journal bearings.

In Fig. 25.2 is shown a differential and final drive such as might be used in a car or medium-weight lorry. The differential cage A is made in two halves which are bolted together and thus secure the pins H on which the differential pinions G are free to revolve. The tubular extensions of the differential cage carry the inner races of ball bearings B so that the cage is free to rotate about the axis XX. The outer races of the bearings B are in the differential carrier casting K, caps L being provided so that the differential cage, complete with its bearings, may be placed into position. The carrier K bolts up to the front face of the circular centre-portion of the axle casing while the rear face is closed by a pressed steel cover S. In cars this cover is frequently welded in place because the petrol tank makes it inaccessible but in lorries it is usually removable so as to give access to the final drive and differential. The centre portion of the axle casing, which is formed of steel pressings, is stiffened by pressings J and the caps L are machined so as to bear against the machined opening in the axle casing in order to give them the maximum support. The bevel pinion D is carried in two taper roller bearings M and N. The inner races are fixed to the pinion shaft by the nut at the outer end, a spacer O being provided, and the outer races are in the differential carrier casting K. The housing P for the outer race of the bearing M is supported by several webs Q that connect it to the body of the casting K. By the proper machining of the spacer O the bearings M and N are 'pre-loaded', that is, there is a load on them when the pinion is free of all load; this enables the axial deflection of the bearings due to the load applied to the pinion when driving, to be reduced in magnitude and helps in maintaining the proper contact between the teeth of the pinion and crown wheel. Similarly the bearings B are also pre-loaded. An oil seal is provided at R.

Ball journal bearings are often used for the pinion shaft instead of taper roller bearings. The outer ball bearing is then commonly used to position the pinion shaft axially, its races being fixed respectively to the shaft and the carrier casting. The bearings are frequently pre-loaded. Taper-roller bearings are frequently used instead of ball bearings to support the differential cage.

A hypoid gear final drive assembly is shown in Fig. 27.1. The pinion A, integral with its shaft, is now supported in two large ball bearings at its outer end and in a parallel roller bearing at its inner end. The ball bearings take the axial loads and position the shaft axially, a selected washer B being used between the flange of the sleeve carrying the bearings and the neck of the casting C in order to give the correct adjustment. The roller bearing is carried in the web C_2 of the casting C and this web also houses two angular contact bearings which support one side of the differential cage, the other side being supported by a parallel roller bearing housed in

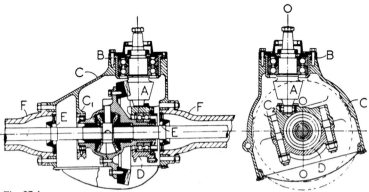

Fig. 27.1

the web C_1. Both webs are provided with caps. The axial position of the differential cage and crown wheel is determined by a selected washer interposed between the bearings and a flange of the web C_2 and cap D. Tubular arms F are bolted up to the central portion C of the axle to complete the axle structure and oil seals are provided at E.

An underhung worm-drive axle is shown in Fig. 27.2. The worm A, which is integral with its shaft, is supported by parallel roller bearings B and positioned axially by the dual purpose bearing C. As the latter is being used as a thrust bearing its outer race is an easy fit in the bore in which it is housed but is held securely against axial movement. This type of bearing is now regarded as superior to an ordinary thrust bearing of the type shown in Fig. 2.8. The bearings of the worm are carried in the cover plate casting D which bolts up to the underside of the axle casing K. In an overhead worm drive the cover plate would be bolted to the top of the axle casing. An oil seal is provided at J. The differential cage is formed of the worm wheel itself and of two end plates that are bolted up to it at each side. Ball bearings which fit on the bosses of the end plates and are carried in the cover plate casting D serve to support the differential cage. Bearing caps E enable the diferential assembly to be placed in position and these caps are arranged to bear against machined faces G on the axle casing so as to get the maximum lateral support. Washers F, which are selected of suitable thicknesses during assembly, enable the lateral position of the worm wheel in relation to the worm to be adjusted. A bevel type differential is used, four pinions being provided and carried on the arms of a cross-shaped

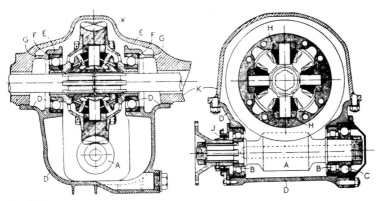

Fig. 27.2

spider; these arms fit into four rectangular blocks H that in turn fit into slots formed in the bore of the worm wheel, thus enabling the spider and pinions to be assembled, and driven by the worm wheel. The blocks H are held sideways by the end plates of the differential cage. The axle casing is a forging and is like an inverted pot at the centre; it has tubular arms which carry the spring seats and wheel bearings.

27.1 Effects of wheel bearing layout on axle loading

Some comments on wheel bearing details are given in Section 32.11. The actual layout has a significant influence on axle loading. For instance, in both the elementary axle of Fig. 26.1, where the road wheels run on plain bearings, and the more advanced design of Fig. 27.5, in which the wheel is fully supported on two bearings on the axle casing, the half-shafts carry no loads other than the driving torque. This is termed a *fully-floating* axle layout.

To reduce the cost, complexity, weight and bulk of the hub, however, other arrangements are often used, especially for the lighter cars and other small vehicles. Again, the basic principles can be demonstrated by the use of a simple diagram, Fig. 27.3, where the road wheel is mounted on the end of the half-shaft which, in turn, is carried in plain bearings in the axle casing. The vertical load applied through the spring to the axle is W, and the equal and opposite reaction is also W and is at the point of contact between the wheel and the ground.

Because of the offset between this point of contact and the outer bearing carrying the half-shaft, a bending load is applied to that shaft, Fig. 27.4 (*a*), the couple being reacted by equal and opposite loads P on the inner and outer bearings. There is also a shear load on the half-shaft, which could cause a failure of the type illustrated in Fig. 27.4 (*b*). While the shear stress is constant between the wheel and the outer edge of the bearing, the bending moment increases linearly up to this section and so the maximum combined stress will occur here.

If for any reason a side-load S is acting on the wheel, this too will apply a bending load, but in the opposite sense, to the half-shaft, Fig. 27.4 (*c*). In this instance it will remain constant up to the outer edge of the outer bearing, and will be reacted by equal and opposite loads at the two bearings. These loads, $-Q$ in Fig. 27.3, are of course opposite in sense to the loads P.

For the maintenance of a state of equilibrium of forces, if a side load S is applied at the wheel, there must be an equal and opposite reaction S. Since the half-shaft is placed in compression there must be a thrust bearing in the region of the centre of the axle, to provide this reaction.

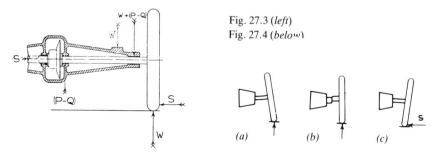

Fig. 27.3 (*left*)
Fig. 27.4 (*below*)

(a)　　　(b)　　　(c)

Thus the shaft is subjected to five different loads, and the maximum combined stresses arising from them will occur in a plane adjacent to the outer edge of the outermost bearing. The loads are –

(1) Bending under the vertical load at the wheel.
(2) Shearing due to the vertical load at the wheel.
(3) Bending arising from the couple due to the side load on the wheel.
(4) Axial loading – compression or tension – due to this side loading.
(5) Drive torque.

Between the extremes of totally supported and fully-floating axle, there are several intermediate, or *semi-floating*, arrangements in common use. In most, the centre of the single bearing used is either in or as close as possible to the plane in which the vertical load is applied to the wheel. This reduces to a minimum the bending load on the half-shaft and avoids the use of two bearings. The half-shaft, however, still has to share with the bearing the side loading and its couple.

27.2　Some actual bearing arrangements

Some typical road wheel bearings are shown in Figs. 27.5 to 27.8. The first of these is a full-floating bearing for a lorry; the hub A of the road wheel is carried on two taper roller bearings B whose inner races fit on the end of the axle casing C. One of these bearings will take any end thrust to the right while the other will take any thrust to the left. The inner races are pulled up against the spacer F by the nut D which is screwed to the end of the axle casing and locked by a bolt whose head enters a hole in the casing. The spacer E prevents excessive loads being applied to the bearing by tightening the nut too much and also enables the left-hand race to be firmly held. The spacer F is bolted up to the flange G, the backplate H of the brake assembly being placed between these two members. The flange G is welded to the axle casing. The casting K which is bolted up to the hub A and which houses the oil seal L serves to keep oil or grease from getting

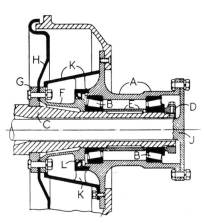

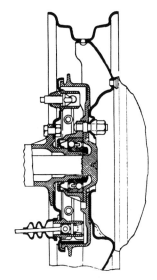

Fig. 27.5 (*above*)
Fig. 27.6 (*right*)

through on to the brake shoes or mud from getting into the wheel bearings. The wheel hub is driven by the half-shaft J whose end is formed into a flange that is bolted to the hub. The brake drum is bolted to the outer side of the flange of the hub and so can be removed without disturbing the bearings.

In the bearing assembly shown in Fig. 27.6 a double row ball bearing is used, its inner race being held on to the outer end of the axle casing by a nut and its outer race being held between the flange of the half-shaft and a member which is bolted to the flange. The pressed steel wheel centre and the brake drum are also bolted to this flange. The bearing thus takes end thrust in both directions while the half-shaft takes only the driving torque although it also assists the bearing in taking the tilting actions due to end loads acting on the wheel. The back plate of the brake assembly is bolted up to a flange that is integral with the end of the axle casing.

In the assembly shown in Fig. 27.7 the half-shaft A is formed with a flange at its end to which is bolted the brake drum E and also the road wheel (not shown). The half-shaft is supported by a single row ball bearing B whose outer race is housed in the cup C which is bolted up to the flanged end of the axle casing D. The back plate F of the brake assembly is also bolted to a flange of the member C. The outer race of the bearing B is thus held so that it can take end thrusts in both directions while the inner race abuts up against the shoulder of the half-shaft on the right-hand side and is held by the collar G, which is a force fit on the shaft, at the left. The bearing thus takes all the end thrusts but the half-shaft is subject to shearing force and bending moments. An oil seal, indicated at G, prevents the egress of oil from the axle casing.

In Fig. 27.8 the end of the half-shaft A is tapered and the brake drum E is bolted to it, a key serving to transmit the drive. A single taper roller bearing B supports the half-shaft, its inner race fitting the taper on that shaft while its outer race fits in the end of the axle casing and is held in by the plate C which, together with the oil seal housing G and the brake back

Fig. 27.7 (*below*)
Fig. 27.8 (*right*)

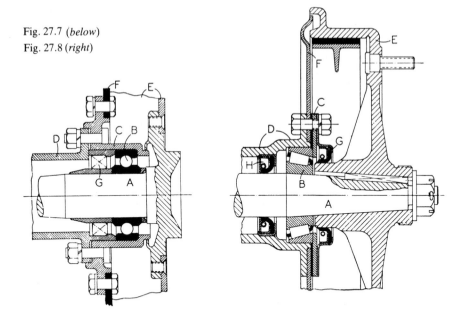

plate F is bolted up to the flange of the axle casing. The bearing B can thus take end loads acting to the right but loads to the left have to be carried through the half-shaft to the bearing at the other side of the axle. The half-shafts therefore abut at the centre of the axle. An oil seal H serves to prevent oil from escaping from the axle.

27.3 Axle casing constructions

Space is not available to allow all the axle constructions that are used to be described; only the most important types can be dealt with.

A common type when a worm final drive is used as shown in Fig. 27.9. The central portion A is a hollow iron or steel casting open at the top and having tapering extensions at each side. Bolted to the top of this member is a cover plate B in which are arranged the bearings for the worm and for the differential cage. The latter is carried in ball or roller bearings housed in the cups CC, the upper halves of which are integral with the cover plate, the lower halves being separate caps in order that the differential cage may be got into position. The caps are secured by the nuts and bolts shown, but studs screwed into the cover plate are sometimes used instead of bolts.

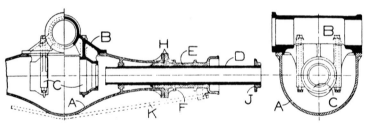

Fig. 27.9 Worm-drive axle casing

By supporting the differential cage in this way the worm and worm wheel can be adjusted to the correct relationship on the bench, and then the whole assembly can be bolted to the axle casing A. The gearing can also be easily withdrawn for inspection.

Pressed into the extensions of the central casting are two steel tubes D, which at their outer ends carry the bearings for the road wheels, ball or roller bearings being arranged between them and the inside of the wheel hubs. The springs are bolted to spring seats pivotally mounted on the cylindrical portions of the extension castings E, the latter being bolted by flanges H to the central casting. The wheels are kept on by nuts J screwed to the ends of the tubes D, while side thrusts towards the centre of the axle are taken on the ends of the members E.

This construction provides a strong and rigid axle.

Most axles have a built-up construction, the axle beam that carries the bending stresses being formed of a central member to which tubular side members are welded or bolted on as in Fig. 27.1. On the ends of the tubular sections castings are fixed, or pieces welded, to form the spring seatings and radius rod attachment point and the brake backplate. The central member may be a casting or may consist of a number of pressings welded together; it usually has an approximately circular face at the front and may also have one at the rear.

A casting that houses the final drive and differential assembly is bolted to the front circular face and a cover plate to the back one but this may be permanently closed by a cover that is welded on. This construction is shown in Fig. 25.2.

In Fig. 27.2 the axle is a single forging consisting of a cylindrical annular central portion with tubular extensions but as this is expensive to produce it is not often employed.

Chapter 28

The double-reduction axle

In this type of axle the permanent reduction of speed between the engine and road wheels is obtained in two separate steps. Double-reduction axles are used chiefly on heavy lorries, buses, etc., for the following reasons: such vehicles run at low speeds in comparison with passenger cars; thus, while cars run at speeds up to 100 mph, lorries do not exceed between 50 and 80 mph; they also have larger diameter wheels. Thus, although lorry engines run at much slower speeds than car engines, the reduction of speed between the engine and the road wheels is a good deal larger, being from 5:1 up to 10:1, as against 3.5:1 up to 6:1.

If these large reductions were obtained in a single step, using, say, bevel gearing, then either the bevel pinion would have to be made very small with few teeth, when it would be both weak and inefficient, or the crown wheel would have to be made very large, which would result in a heavy and expensive axle, and would reduce the clearance between the axle and the ground too much. Similar conditions are found, to a lesser degree, with worm final drives, and so the double reduction axle is adopted when the final drive ratio has to be large. On some vehicles they are used to enable a very low body position to be obtained.

28.1 Both steps at the centre of the axle

This type of double-reduction final drive is shown in Figs. 28.1 to 28.5. Referring to Fig. 28.1, the bevel pinion A is driven by the propeller shaft and gears with a small crown wheel B. The latter is fixed to a layshaft C, to which is also fixed a spur pinion D. The layshaft is carried in ball or roller bearings at its ends in the axle casing, suitable thrust bearings being provided to take the thrust of the bevel gears. The spur pinion D meshes with a large spur wheel E which is bolted to the differential cage F just as the crown wheel of a single reduction axle is bolted. The differential cage is carried in ball or roller bearings in the axle casing in the usual way.

The arrangement of the gearing in Fig. 28.2 is slightly different from the above. The differential is here situated between the two halves of the layshaft instead of between the two drive shafts. The propeller shaft drives the bevel pinion A, meshing with the small crown wheel B that is bolted to the differential cage. The latter is supported by the shaft C which is carried

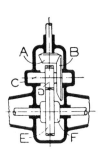

Fig. 28.1 (*above*)

Fig. 28.2 (*right*)

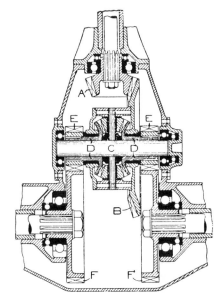

in ball bearings in the axle casing. The differential wheels DD are now integral with short sleeves free to rotate on the shaft C, and which carry spur pinions EE at their outer ends, outside the differential cage. The pinions EE mesh with spur wheels FF fixed to the drive shafts. Thus the differential action is obtained between the pinions EE instead of between the drive shafts themselves. The chief advantage of this arrangement is that the differential now revolves at a higher speed than the road wheels, and so, for a given torque on the latter, the forces on the differential wheel teeth are smaller, enabling smaller wheels to be used. To set against this advantage, two spur pinions and wheels are required for the second reduction, thus increasing the cost.

A third arrangement is shown in Fig. 28.3. The spur pinion A driven by the propeller shaft, drives a wheel B fixed to the layshaft C, to which is also fixed the bevel pinion of the bevel drive. The arrangement of the latter is normal. It will be observed that the axis of the propeller shaft is higher than it would be with a single reduction bevel gear axle, and can thus be brought more nearly into line with the mainshaft of the gearbox, so that the work put upon the universal joints is reduced. This advantage is also obtained with the other types of double-reduction axle and with the overhead worm-driven axle.

With single-reduction bevel axles and with underhung worm drives the engine and gearbox are sometimes inclined in the frame in order to obtain this advantage.

An arrangement in which the second reduction is by an epicyclic gear is used by Scammel on some of their lorries and is shown diagrammatically in Fig. 28.4. A bevel first reduction and a normal bevel-type differential are used, the differential cage being carried in bearings in the end plates A which are bolted up to flanges on the central drum-shape portion of the axle casing. The differential shafts carry pinions B which form the sun wheels of epicyclic gears of the sun and annulus type. The annuli C are

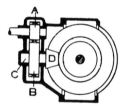

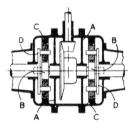

Fig. 28.3 (*left*)
Fig. 28.4 (*right*)

fixed, being formed integral with the end covers which are bolted up to the central casing on the same flanges as the plates A. The arms D which carry the planet pinions are made integral with the drive shafts and are supported in bearings in the end covers C. The tubular end portions of the axle casing are bolted up to the end covers C on flanges as shown.

28.2　Kirkstall double-reduction axle

An interesting and original design by the Kirkstall Forge Engineering Company of Leeds, who manufacture axles for all kinds of vehicles, is shown in Fig. 28.5.

The first reduction occurs between the worm and worm-wheel, the latter being fixed to the annulus member A which is carried in bearings C and D in the axle casing; the second reduction is obtained from the epicyclic action of the train consisting of the annulus A and sun S, in conjunction with the concentric spur train (not epicyclic) consisting of the pinion H and the annulus J. The annulus A meshes with three planet pinions which are carried by the member E and the latter is splined to the left-hand half-shaft F. The pinions mesh at the centre with the sun S, which is integral with the pinion H. The latter drives the annulus J through three pinions K, which are carried on pins L supported by the member M which is fixed to the axle casing. The annulus J is splined to the right-hand half-shaft. The left-hand half-shaft is thus driven in the forward direction by forward motion of the

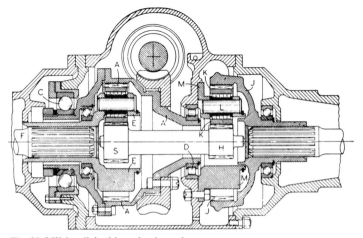

Fig. 28.5 Kirkstall double-reduction axle

annulus A, as it would be if the sun were fixed; but the sun, being free, will be driven in the backward direction so that the speed of the planet carrier E and its half-shaft will be lower than if the sun S were fixed. The backward motion of the sun S and pinion H is converted to forward motion of the right-hand half-shaft by the pinions K, and some reduction of speed occurs in this train.

In order that equal torques shall be exerted on the two half-shafts, the gear train H, K, J must have a particular ratio in relation to that of the epicyclic train A, S. This particular ratio is found as follows. Let the torque imparted to the annulus A by the worm and wheel be T, and let the number of teeth in the annulus and sun be denoted respectively by s and a.

Then the torques applied to the member E will be $\dfrac{T \times (a + s)}{a}$ and the torque acting on the sun S will be $T \times \dfrac{s}{a}$ (backwards). The torque applied to the annulus J is therefore $T \times \dfrac{s}{a} \times \dfrac{j}{h}$ where j and h are the numbers of teeth in J and H respectively. Hence if the torques applied to the two half-shafts are to be equal, we must have

$$T \times \frac{a + s}{a} = T \times \frac{s}{a} \times \frac{j}{h}$$

that is, $\dfrac{a + s}{s}$ must equal $\dfrac{j}{h}$.

The value of the second reduction produced by the trains A, S and H, J may now be found by using the tabular method described in Chapter 22. Let N_A, N_F and N_S be respectively the speeds of the annulus A, the left-hand half-shaft F and the sun S. Then we have the results shown in Table 10,

Table 10

Planet carrier E or left-hand half-shaft F	Annulus A	Sun S
N_F	N_F	N_F
O	$N_A - N_F$	$(N_F - N_A)\,a/s$
N_F	N_A	$N_S = N_F(1 + a/s) - N_A.a/s$

and the speed of the right-hand half-shaft will be $-N_S \times \dfrac{h}{j}$ or

$$N_R = \left[N_A \frac{a}{s} - N_F \left(1 + \frac{a}{s} \right) \right] \times \frac{h}{j}$$

the minus sign occurs because the annulus J goes in the opposite direction to the pinion H.

Since j/h is made equal to $(a + s)/s$, as stated above, we get

$$N_R = N_A \times \frac{a}{s} \times \frac{h}{j} - N_F$$

But in straight-ahead running $N_R = N_F$, hence

$$2\,N_R = N_A \times \frac{a}{s} \times \frac{h}{j}$$

The second reduction is therefore

$$\frac{N_A}{N_R} = 2 \times \frac{s \times j}{a \times h}$$

It will be noticed that the shaft SH is supported solely by the contacts between the teeth of the gears S and H and the planets and pinions K. This ensures equal division of the torques acting on the pinions S and H between the three pairs of teeth of each pinion which transmit the torques.

28.3   One step at centre of axle, the other at road wheels

Double-reduction axles of this type may be divided into two classes, those in which the second reduction is provided by a simple spur pinion and wheel, and those in which it is given by an epicyclic train. An example of the second type is given in Section 28.2, while an axle of the first type, to a design by Mercedes-Benz, is shown in Fig. 28.6. It will be seen that the parts required to fulfil the two functions of a live axle are to a great extent independent members. A forging A, to the ends of which are bolted the

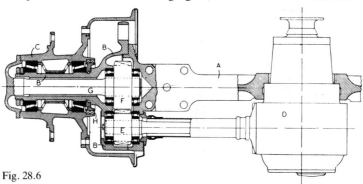

Fig. 28.6

members B, forms the axle beam and the road wheels, the hubs of which are seen at C, revolve on taper roller bearings on the ends of the members B. The springs are bolted to seats formed on the forging and the covers B. A separate casing D houses the first reduction and differential, and light tubular covers protect the half-shafts. At their outer ends the latter are splined to pinions E, which are carried in roller bearings and which mesh with the gears F. The latter are also carried in roller bearings and are splined to the shafts G, which are integral with the hub-caps and by which the wheel hubs C are driven. Seals H serve to keep lubricant in and mud out.

This arrangement has the advantage that the half-shafts revolve at higher speeds than the road wheels so that the torques they have to transmit are correspondingly smaller than if they drove the road wheels direct. The system gives a very rigid construction, and by arranging the half-shafts below the axle beam, a very low body position can be obtained. Alternatively, by placing the half-shafts above the axle beam, a very high ground clearance could be achieved, but this would introduce certain difficulties and has not become widely used. In the axle shown the half-shafts are situated behind the axle beam and the only gain in road clearance is that, because of the second reduction, the crown wheel of the first reduction, and hence the casing, D, can be smaller than otherwise.

In some early axles of this type the gear F was replaced by an internally toothed ring with which the pinion E meshed. The drawback to this arrangement was the great difficulty in providing satisfactory seals.

28.4   A bevel-gear hub reduction

A design by Foden Ltd. that uses a bevel epicyclic train as the second step of a double-reduction axle, is shown in Fig. 28.7. Splined on the end of the half-shaft there is a bevel gear A and a similar gear B is splined to the end of the axle casing C. Between these two gears is a two-armed spider on

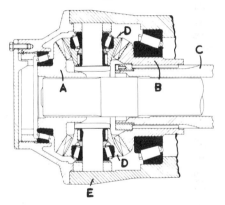

Fig. 28.7 Foden bevel-gear hub reduction

whose pins the planet pinions DD are carried on taper roller and needle roller bearings. The spider is fixed inside the wheel hub E. The bevel gear B is thus the fixed member of the epicyclic train, the gear A is the driving member and the planet carrier and wheel are thus driven at half the speed of the half-shaft.

PART 4 :

THE CARRIAGE UNIT

Chapter 29

The basic structure

So far, we have dealt with the propulsion sub-systems of road vehicles – engines, transmissions, axles and wheels. Now we come to the main assembly on which the engine and transmission are mounted, and the interconnections between it and the axle-and-wheel sub-assemblies. This of course is the carriage unit, which also includes the body for carrying the occupants in comfort and safety or, in the case of trucks, the payload safely and without damage.

29.1 The frame

Until the end of the Second World War, the overwhelming majority of cars had separate frames similar to, though of course much smaller than, those now associated with most modern commercial vehicles. The function of the frame is to carry all the major components or sub-assemblies making up the complete vehicle – engine, transmission, suspension, body, etc. In Fig. 29.1, a fairly early ladder-type frame is illustrated, but it has been drawn with dissimilar side members, to show two different types of layout. These side, or main longitudinal, members normally would be virtually identical, though opposite handed. In this illustration, that at A is straight, and therefore easy to manufacture, and it is inclined inwards towards the front; that at B, on the other hand, is cranked inwards. In the first instance the taper, as viewed in plan, and in the second, the cranked formation of the side member, are for clearing the front wheels when steered on full lock but are also convenient for taking the engine mountings. As viewed in side elevation, these members in both instances are cranked upwards near the rear to clear the back axle.

Transverse members C (often confusingly called cross members – nothing to do with cruciform members) separate the side members, contribute to the overall reaction to torsional loading, and help to support components mounted above or slung underneath – the gearbox or a transaxle for instance. Ideally, if the suspension spring or linkage is laterally offset relative to the frame side members, one transverse member is fitted between each of the mounting points, D and E, to translate the torsional loading applied to each side member – by the offset – into a bending load in the transverse member. Additional transverse members may be required to carry the body or other major units such as the engine or final drive unit – if the latter is not in the axle – and for locally supporting the side members where they are cranked inwards towards the front. The last-mentioned supports are needed because of the tendency of the side members to flex where they are kinked. Such flexure would occur owing to severe local deflections due to the tensile and compressive loads induced in their flanges – by bending in the vertical plane – and would rapidly cause fatigue failures.

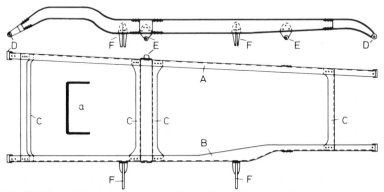

Fig. 29.1 Inset (*a*) is the cross-section of both the longitudinal and transverse members

Where the centres of the suspension spring attachment points are directly beneath the effective flexural axes of the side members, transverse support is required to take only the side loading at the spring eyes and, in these circumstances, the lateral bending may not be large. It may therefore be taken by extra-stiff front and rear extensions of the side members, at D. These extensions are called *dumb irons*.

In general, the usual reason for the omission of transverse members where one might have thought them to be essential is the need to allow clearance for the propeller shaft, as it moves up and down with the suspension, or the presence of some obstruction such as the engine sump, clutch or gearbox. In some instances, the propeller shaft passes through a vertically elongated hole in the centre of a transverse member.

Where the cranked portion towards the front of a frame is unsupported by a transverse member, substantial gusseting or some other form or reinforcement is necessary. In other instances, for example at the rear spring attachments, the frame side members may be locally reinforced to transfer the loads from the spring support brackets to the nearest transverse member.

On the lowest of the side members shown in Fig. 29.1, two brackets F extend laterally outwards. These are for carrying the running boards fitted to most pre-Second World War cars. Similar, but generally much shorter, brackets carry the body sides and other components such as engine, gearbox, and fuel tank mountings.

Early cars and most modern commercial vehicles traditionally have had channel section frame members, *a* in Fig. 29.1 – either steel pressings or fabricated from steel plate or strip. Where practicable, brackets are attached by bolting, riveting or welding them to the webs of the sections.

This avoids introducing stress raisers in the flanges, which are the most heavily stressed parts when the whole sections are subject to bending loads. For heavy commercial vehicles, bolts are frequently used in frame construction, including for the attachment of the transverse member, because such frames are usually fairly accessible and maintenance is therefore easier than on car frames. Rivets must be very skilfully fitted, preferably cold, otherwise they are liable to loosen. Welds tend to suffer fatigue failure under the severe racking loads experienced with commercial vehicles. Because of this loading and the need to avoid local high stresses due to sudden changes in overall stiffness along the length of the frame – for example between a cab and the body – torsionally rigid frames of box section are widely regarded as unsuitable for heavy commercial vehicles. Mild steel – easily pressed and welded – used to be the invariable choice for all frames, but modern heavy commercial and even some light vehicles frequently have frames of carbon manganese steel with a yield stress of about $3620 \, kg/cm^2$.

With the introduction of independent front suspension, chassis frames were called upon to take much higher torsional loading. This was because, whereas the centres of semi-elliptic leaf springs on a beam axle have to be well inboard of the front wheels to leave a clearance for steering them, the effective spring base – distance between spring centres – with independent front suspension is approximately equal to the track. In these circumstances, when a wheel on one side only rises over a bump, the upward thrust it exerts on the frame has a much greater leverage about the longitudinal axis of the car.

The outcome is that means have to be sought for increasing the torsional stiffness of the frame. Provided that their ends are closed – by, for instance, welding to them a flat or flanged plate – or are otherwise strongly reinforced so that they cannot lozenge or in any other way distort, tubular sections of any shape – round, oval, triangular, square, rectangular, etc. – are inherently very rigid torsionally. Such sections therefore began to be used for both longitudinal and transverse members on car frames. A selection of sections that have been used is illustrated in Fig. 29.2.

The transverse members most heavily loaded in torsion are of course those that support the independent front suspension. This is partly because of brake-torsion reaction which is applied by the rearward thrust of the road on the tyre contact patch and transmitted through the brake disc or

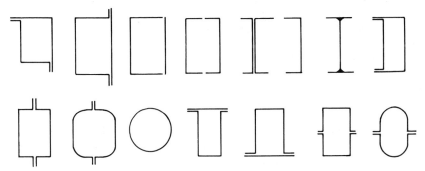

Fig. 29.2 Some chassis-frame sections

the drum brake back-plate to the stub axle, and thence through the suspension links to the frame. Additionally, an entirely different torsional loading arises in his transverse member as a result of single-wheel bumps – when the wheel on only one side rises. Such a bump, lifting one side of the front end of the frame, leaves the far side and the rear end down in their original positions, thus causing the side members to tend to twist the front transverse member and, incidentally, all the others. Hence, heavy gusseting is needed between the transverse and side members. Sudden local changes in stiffness at or near the junctions between the transverse and side members have to be avoided, otherwise trouble due to fatigue failures will be experienced.

Among the last separate frames to be designed for large cars produced in reasonable quantities in the UK was that of the Humber *Super Snipe*, Fig. 29.3. This has box section members of various cross-sections selected for the ease with which they can be accommodated beneath the floor and secured to each other. The front cross member is a top-hat section of very

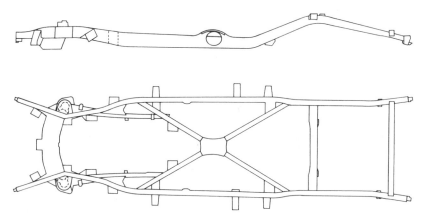

Fig. 29.3 Humber *Super Snipe*. All the main members of the frame are of 12 swg steel sheet

large proportions, with a closing plate welded to its bottom flanges. Such a section is fairly convenient for the attachment of the gussets and brackets, top and bottom, that carry the suspension link pivots, springs and shock absorber mountings. The frame has also a cruciform bracing member, made from channel sections welded back-to-back. At the centre, the top flanges of the cruciform member arch over the clearance hole in the web, through which the propeller shaft passes.

There is also extensive gusseting between the ends of the cruciform and the cranked portions of the side members. The torsional stiffening effects of a cruciform bracing member on a frame can be accounted for in either of two ways. First, together with the adjacent side and transverse members of the frame, it forms in effect, a single huge tubular member of flat rectangular section, the outer boundaries of which are, on each side, the webs of the side members at each side and, top and bottom, the flanges of the side members, transverse members and cruciform brace. From the structural viewpoint this is similar in effect to extending all the flanges to form a continuous web closing the top and bottom of the frame, to form the huge flat rectangular section. Indeed, total enclosure was in fact done successfully to solve a torsional vibration problem that was causing dash shake in the development stage of the Austin A90 *Atlantic*, and was patented in about 1949 by the author. The stiffness of any closed tube of given wall thickness, incidentally, is directly proportional to the cross-sectional area it encloses.

The alternative explanation, which applies particularly to an earlier form of cruciform bracing, is that the cruciform is in effect four tetrahedrons, Fig. 29.4 – a tetrahedron is the simplest basic geometric structure that has torsional stiffness. In most road vehicles, the front and rear tetrahedrons of

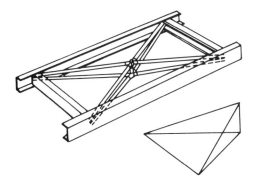

Fig. 29.4 Cruciform bracing and tetrahedron

the cruciform bracing have acute angles and those on each side have obtuse angles at their apices. There can of course be a hole through the central vertical post, to clear the propeller shaft, provided that post is suitably reinforced around the hole.

Backbone-type frames have also been used. The tubular type, Fig. 29.5, has been adopted principally for some Czechoslovakian, German and Austrian designed vehicles – Tatra, Daimler-Benz and Steyr Puch. In some instances the ends of the tubular backbone are bolted directly, at the front, to the gearbox and, at the rear, to the final drive casing, while in others, they have forked extensions, between the arms of which these components are accommodated. An example of a backbone-type frame, but made by in effect bringing the two box section side members together, side-by-side in the centre, is illustrated in Fig. 29.6. It is that of the 1960 Triumph *Herald*, probably the last quantity-produced small car to be designed in the UK with a separate frame.

The advantages of the backbone frame include high torsional stiffness at low cost, and light weight. A disadvantage is the length of the outrigger arms needed to carry the body sides. These arms tend to introduce torsional vibration problems because of their bending flexibility.

Separate frames, in general, have the merit of being capable of accepting a wide variety of different bodies – hence their attraction even for light commercial vehicles. The principal disadvantage is that, because such as a frame has to be accommodated under the floor of the vehicle, its depth is of necessity restricted and therefore its bending stiffness – proportional to the cube of its depth – and its torsional stiffness are limited. This can be overcome by the use of a space frame, of which there are plenty of examples in racing cars, but these are of complex construction and therefore costly. They are suitable where exceptionally light and simple bodywork, for instance of reinforced plastics, is to be fitted; but, where the body in any case has to be a fairly substantial structure, considerable weight saving and economy can be effected by designing the body so that it can perform the functions of the frame.

Fig. 29.5 On the Steyr Puch Haflinger chassis (a), the floor frame of the body is mounted on top of the springs, to which some of the vertical and torsional loading is directly applied through the body platform, as can be seen at (b)

Fig. 29.6

29.2 Sub-frames

Sub-frames are employed for one or more of three basic reasons. The first is to isolate the high frequency vibrations of, for example, an engine or a suspension assembly, from the remainder of the structure. In this case, rubber or other resilient mountings are interposed between the sub-frame and main structure.

Secondly, a sub-frame can isolate an inherently stiff sub-assembly such as the engine or gearbox from the effects of the flexing of the chassis frame. This is done generally by interposing a three-point mounting system between the sub-frame and main frame, one of the mountings being on the longitudinal axis about which the main frame twists, and the others one on each side.

Thirdly, a sub-frame may be used to carry, for instance, the front and rear suspension sub-assemblies, where to utilise the front and rear ends of the body structure for this purpose would increase unacceptably its complexity or cost, or introduce difficulties in either manufacture or servicing, or both. A good example of such sub-frame usage is the BL

Mini, the front and rear sub-frame assemblies of which have been used by some kit car manufactures because of the ease with which the engine and front suspension, on its sub-frame, can be bolted to the front, and the rear suspension, similarly on its sub-frame, bolted to the back of a different body designed to receive them.

29.3 Integral and chassisless construction

The terms *integral* and *chassisless* construction are often confused, but the difference is simple. Integral construction is that in which a chassis frame is welded to, or integrated with, the body. It was the first stage in the evolution of the chassisless form of construction, in which no chassis frame can be discerned. The first quantity produced vehicle in the latter category was almost certainly the Austin A30, the design of which was very fully described in *Automobile Engineer*, October and December 1952, and March and April 1954. The first two of these four references describe the vehicle itself, while the second pair elaborate on methods, developed by the author, for use in its structural design.

The details of chassisless construction are much too numerous, varied and complex to be described here. In principle, however, its advantages stem from the facts that beams formed by the body panels may be something like 50 cm deep, whereas a chassis frame for a car is only about 8 to 13 cm deep, and the area enclosed by a complete body is similarly vastly bigger than that enclosed by the cross-section of a frame side or transverse member. Since the strength and stiffness of a beam are proportional respectively to the square and cube of its depth, while both the torsional stress and stiffness of a box section are proportional to the area enclosed by it, it follows that the strength and stiffness of a body shell are potentially much greater than of a chassis frame.

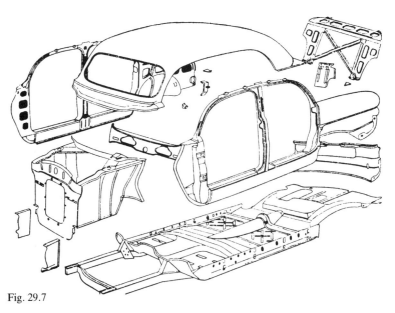

Fig. 29.7

One of the main facts to be borne in mind when designing sheet metal structures is that even a simple flange will carry satisfactorily a surprisingly large load provided that it is stabilised – supported against buckling or other forms of distortion. A useful rule of thumb is that a flange will carry a stress up to the yield strength of the material provided that its width is no more than 16 times its thickness. This is approximately valid provided that the deflection of the beam as a whole is negligible. If not, as would be the case if, for example, an inverted top-hat section beam freely supported at its ends and point-loaded by a weight on top of its centre, the component would fail prematurely.

In such a beam, the loading would induce a compressive stress in the top layers and a tensile stress in the bottom layers, that is the flanges, of the section. As the yield stress was approached, the beam as a whole would bow downwards, and the tensile loading in the flanges would cause their outer edges to tend to stretch straight – in other words chordwise – instead of following the bowed form of the remainder of the beam. This, in turn, would reduce the effective second moment of area – moment of inertia – of the section, so the stress in the stiffer portions of the flanges – adjacent to the vertical walls of the section – would be higher than the calculated values, the metal would yield and the section buckle and collapse prematurely.

A typical chassisless body structure is illustrated in Fig. 29.7. Spot-welding is used extensively in its construction, though some unstressed panels may be bolted on, for ease of replacement in the event of damage.

Chapter 30

Brakes

The operation performed in braking is the reverse of that carried out in accelerating. In the latter the heat energy of the fuel is converted into the kinetic energy of the car, whereas in the former the kinetic energy of the car is converted into heat. Again, just as when driving the car the torque of the engine produces a tractive effort at the peripheries of the driving wheels, so, when the brakes are applied the braking torque introduced at the brake drums produces a negative tractive effort or retarding effort at the peripheries of the braking wheels. As the acceleration possible is limited by the adhesion available between the driving wheels and the ground, so the deceleration possible is also limited.

When a brake is applied to a wheel or a car, a force is immediately introduced between the wheel and the road, tending to make the wheel keep on turning. In Fig. 30.1 this is indicated as the force F; this is the force which opposes the motion of the car and thereby slows it down. The deceleration is proportional to the force F, the limiting value of which depends on the normal force between the wheel and the road, and on the coefficient of friction, or of adhesion, as it is called. Since the force F does not act along a line of action passing through the centre of gravity of the car, there is a tendency for the car to turn so that its back wheels rise into the air. The inertia of the car introduces an internal force F_1 acting at the centre of gravity in the opposite direction to the force F. The magnitude of the inertia force F_1 is equal to that of the force F. The two forces F and F_1 constitute a couple tending to make the back wheels rise as stated. Since actually the back wheels remain on the ground, an equal and opposite couple must act on the car somewhere so as to balance the overturning couple FF_1.

This righting couple is automatically introduced by the perpendicular force W_1 between the front wheels and the ground increasing by a small amount Q while the force W_2 between the back wheels and the ground decreases by an equal amount Q. The forces $+Q$ and $-Q$ constitute a couple which balances the overturning couple FF_1. The magnitude of the latter is $F \times OG$, so that other things being equal the smaller the height OG the less the overturning couple. The magnitude of the righting couple QQ is $Q \times SS$, so that the greater the wheelbase SS the less the force Q, that is, the less the alteration in the perpendicular forces between the wheels and the ground.

When going down a hill the conditions are changed. From Fig. 30.2 it will be seen that the vertical force W, the weight of the car, can be resolved into two components H_1 and K. The component K is the only part of the weight of the car that produces any perpendicular force between the wheels and the ground, and is, therefore, the only part of the weight giving any adhesion. Thus, on a hill, the adhesion available is necessarily less than on the level. The component H_1, however, tends to make the car run down the hill, and if the car is merely to be kept stationary, a force H equal and opposite to H_1 must be introduced by applying the brakes. The forces H and H_1 constitute an overturning couple, which is balanced by an increase L in the perpendicular force between the front wheels and the ground, and an equal decrease in the rear.

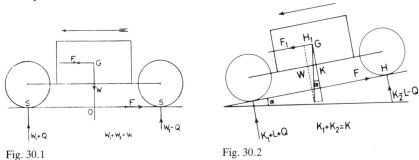

Fig. 30.1   Fig. 30.2

If, instead of being merely held stationary, the car has to be slowed down, then an additional force F must be introduced between the wheels and the ground by applying the brakes harder. An equal inertia force F_1 is then introduced by the deceleration of the car. This inertia force acts at the centre of gravity of the car, and together with the force F constitutes an additional overturning couple, which is balanced between the wheels and the ground. The perpendicular force between the front wheels and the ground is thus increased by an amount $L + Q$, and that between the rear wheels and the ground is decreased by the same amount. Thus, on a hill, the deceleration possible is less than on the level for two reasons. First, the maximum perpendicular force between the wheels and the road is reduced from W to K, and secondly, part of the adhesion is neutralised by the component H_1 and is not available for deceleration.

If the rear wheels only are braked, the conditions are still worse, because the force producing adhesion is still further reduced by the amount $L + Q$.

A little consideration will show that the opposite action occurs when the car is being driven forward. The perpendicular force between the front wheels and the ground is then decreased, and that between the rear wheels and the ground is increased, so that from the point of view of adhesion the rear wheels are a better driving point than the front wheels. This is particularly so when accelerating up a hill.

The extent of this alteration in the weight distribution depends directly upon the magnitude of the deceleration, which, in turn, assuming the brakes are applied until the wheels are about to skid, depends upon the coefficient of adhesion between the wheels and the road. When that coefficient is low the maximum deceleration is low also, and the weight distribution is altered only slightly. Under these conditions the relative effectiveness of the front and rear wheels is in the ratio (approximately) of the weights carried by these wheels, and if the weight carried by the front wheels is only a small part of the total weight little will be gained by braking them.

The decelerations possible with modern braking systems are, however, high enough to make the braking of all the road wheels desirable and this is a legal requirement in most countries.

30.1   Two functions of brakes

Two distinct demands are made upon the brakes of motor vehicles. First, in emergencies they must bring the vehicle to rest in the shortest possible distance, and secondly, they must enable control of the vehicle to be retained when descending long hills. The first demand calls for brakes which can apply large braking torques to the brake drums, while the second calls for brakes that can dissipate large quantities of heat without large temperature rises. It may be pointed out that the same amount of energy has to be dissipated as heat when a car descends only 400 yds of a 1:30 incline, as when the same car is brought to rest from a speed of 35 mph. Thus heat dissipation hardly enters into the braking question when emergency stops are considered, but when descending long hills the problem is almost entirely one of heat dissipation.

30.2   Braking systems

A driving wheel can be braked in two ways: directly, by means of brakes acting on a drum attached to it; or indirectly, through the transmission by a brake acting on a drum on the mainshaft of the gearbox, or on the bevel pinion, or worm, shaft of the final drive. A brake in either of the latter positions, being geared down to the road wheels, can exert a larger braking torque on them than if it acted directly on them. If the final drive ratio is 4:1, then the braking torque exerted on each road wheel is twice the braking torque exerted on the brake drum by the brake, that is, the total braking torque is four times the torque on the brake drum. Thus, brakes acting on the engine side of the final drive are much more powerful than those acting on the wheels directly. A transmission brake, however, gives only a single drum to dissipate the heat generated, whereas when acting directly on the road wheels there are two or more drums. Also in many vehicles a transmission brake would be badly placed as regards heat dissipation, but in commercial vehicles it can sometimes be better in this respect than wheel brakes since the latter are generally situated inside the wheels and away from any flow of air. The transmission brake has the advantage that the braking is divided equally between the road wheels by the differential but the torques have to be transmitted through the universal joints and teeth of the final drive and these parts may have to be increased in size if they are not to be overloaded. The transmission brake at the back of the gearbox is fixed relatively to the frame so that its actuation is not affected by movements of the axle due to uneven road surfaces or to changes in the load carried by the vehicle. In vehicles using the de Dion drive or an equivalent, the brakes are sometimes placed at the inner ends of the drive shafts and here again the torques have to be transmitted through universal joints and also through sliding splines which may cause trouble.

In present-day vehicles the wheel brakes are usually operated by a foot pedal and are the ones used on most occasions; they are sometimes referred to as the *service brakes*. The brakes on the rear wheels can generally be operated also by a hand lever and are used chiefly for holding the vehicle when it is parked and are consequently called *parking brakes* but as they can, of course, be used in emergencies they are sometimes called *emergency brakes*.

30.3   Methods of actuating the brakes

Considering manually-operated brakes, the brake pedal or lever may be connected to the actual brake either mechanically, by means of rods or wires, or hydraulically, by means of a fluid in a pipe. Before considering these connections, however, we must deal with the brakes themselves.

30.4   Types of brake

Brakes may be classified into three groups as follows –

- (1) Friction brakes.
- (2) Fluid brakes.
- (3) Electric brakes.

The last two types are, in practice, confined to heavy vehicles and are not used in cars. The principle of the fluid brake is that a chamber has an impeller inside it that is rotated by the motion of the road wheels so that if the chamber is filled with fluid, usually water, a churning action occurs and kinetic energy is converted into heat thereby providing a braking effort. To dissipate the heat the water may be circulated through a radiator.

The construction is somewhat similar to that of a fluid flywheel and the unit is generally placed between the gearbox and the front end of the propeller shaft but it can be incorporated with the gearbox. The chief drawbacks of this type of brake are that it is difficult to control the braking effort precisely and that while it can provide large braking efforts at high vehicle speeds it can supply very little at low speeds and none at all when the road wheels are not rotating. Thus it can be used only to supplement a friction brake and so such devices are often called *retarders* rather than brakes.

The electric brake is, in effect, an electric generator which, being driven by the road wheels, converts kinetic energy into an electric current and thence, by passing the current through a resistance, into heat.

The 'eddy current' brake employs the same principle as the eddy current clutch described in Section 19.21. The rotor is coupled to the road wheels, being often mounted on a shaft that is interposed between the gearbox and the propeller shaft, and the stator is mounted on the frame of the vehicle. The heat generated is dissipated chiefly by convection but this may be augmented by some kind of fan which may be incorporated into the rotor.

This type of brake suffers from the same drawback as the first type of fluid brake, namely, that it cannot provide any effort at zero speed and can be used only to supplement a friction brake. A fairly large number of such brakes are in use at the present time, as retarders, and have been quite successful.

The vast majority of brakes are friction brakes and these may be sub-divided into: (1) drum brakes and (2) disc brakes, according to whether the braked member is a drum or a disc. Drum brakes are still widely used and are invariably expanding brakes in which the brake shoes are brought into contact with the inside of the brake drum by means of an expanding mechanism. External contracting brakes are now used only in epicyclic gearboxes.

The principle of the internal expanding rigid-shoe brake is shown in Fig. 30.3. The brake drum A is fixed to the hub of the road wheel (shown in chain dotted lines) by bolts which pass through its flange. The inner side of

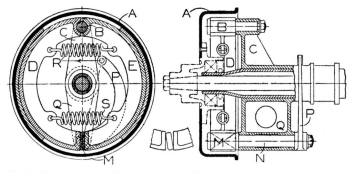

Fig. 30.3 Internal expanding rigid-shoe brake

the drum is open, and a pin B projects into it. This pin is carried in an arm C which is either integral with, or secured to, the axle casing, a rear wheel brake being shown. The brake shoes D and E are free to pivot on the pin B. They are roughly semicircular, and in between their lower ends is a cam M. The latter is integral with, or is fixed to, a spindle N free to turn in the arm Q of the axle casing. A lever P is fixed to the end of the cam spindle, and when this lever is pulled upon by a rod which is coupled to its end, the cam spindle and cam are turned round slightly, thus moving the ends of the brake shoes apart. The shoes are thus pressed against the inside of the brake drum, and frictional forces act between them, tending to prevent any relative motion. The frictional force thus tends to slow down the drum, but it also tends to make the shoes revolve with the drum. The latter action is prevented by the pin B and the cam M. The pin B is therefore called the *anchorage pin*. The magnitude of the frictional force, multiplied by the radius of the drum, gives the torque tending to stop the drum, that is, the braking torque.

The reaction of this braking torque is the tendency for the shoes to rotate with the drum, so that this reaction is taken by the pin B and cam M, and ultimately by the axle casing and the members which prevent the axle casing from revolving, that is, the torque-reaction system. Most modern car brakes do not have actual pins for the shoe anchorages but, instead, have simple abutments against which the rounded ends of the webs of the shoes bear and are kept in contact by springs, but in lorries a separate anchorage pin is often provided for each shoe, as indicated in Fig. 30.4 which shows a design of the Kirkstall Forge Engineering Company. The anchorage pins are seen at A and B and are carried in the projecting arm C of the brake anchorage bracket. The latter is a force fit on the end G of the

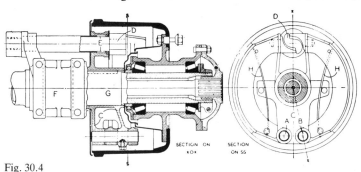

Fig. 30.4

axle case, and a key is provided to prevent any rotation. The actuating cam D is now of S-shape, which provides a greater amount of expansion of the shoes and a more constant leverage than is provided by the simple cam shown in Fig. 30.3. The cam D is integral with its shaft and is supported in needle roller bearings, one of which is seen at E. The pull-off springs H are now single-leaf springs, which are easier to remove and replace than coil springs. The seats F, to which the road springs are bolted, are formed integral with the brackets C.

The cam expanding mechanism described above is simple in construction and fairly satisfactory in action but there are others and two are shown in Figs. 30.5 and 30.6. The first, Fig. 30.5, is used in heavy lorries and is a variation of the S-cam described above, it is actually a double crank and connecting rod mechanism, it provides a greater movement with less friction than the ordinary cam; when the S-cam is used friction is often reduced by employing rollers at the shoe ends against which the cam surfaces bear. In the second example, Fig. 30.6, a wedge T is used and is pulled inwards towards the centre of the vehicle by the rod R in order to apply the brake. The wedge operates through rollers that reduce friction and forces the plungers or tappets U and V apart. The body W that houses the tappets may be fixed to the backplate of the brake assembly in which case the forces applied by the wedge to the shoes may be unequal or it may

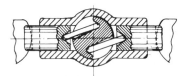

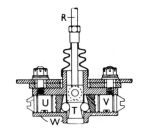

Fig. 30.5 (*above*) Brake shoe expanding mechanism

Fig. 30.6 (*right*) Wedge type actuator

be free to slide and then forces will be equalised. Equalisation of the shoe forces can be obtained although the housing is fixed by leaving the wedge free to rock or slide sideways and an example of the latter is shown in Fig. 30.31.

30.5   Elementary theory of the shoe brake

Consider the simple shoe shown in Fig. 30.7. An actuating force W will give rise to a normal force P between the shoe and the drum (this force is shown as it acts on the shoe) and this normal force will produce a frictional force μP if the drum is rotating as shown. Now the shoe is in equilibrium under the action of the forces shown, together with the forces acting at the pivot, but the latter have no moment about the pivot and consequently the clockwise moments due to the forces P and μP must be balanced by the anti-clockwise moment due to W. Hence we get the relation –

$$W \times L = P \times M + \mu P \times R$$

and hence that –
$$P = \frac{WL}{M + \mu R}.$$

Now the braking torque acting on the drum is due entirely to the frictional force μP and is equal to $\mu P \times R$, or, substituting the expression obtained above for P, we get –

$$\text{Brake torque } T_t = \frac{\mu WLR}{M + \mu R}.$$

Considering the shoe shown in Fig. 30.8, the balance of moments about the pivot gives –

$$WL + \mu QR = QM$$

and hence –
$$Q = \frac{WL}{M - \mu R}$$

so that the expression for the braking torque is –

$$T_1 = \frac{\mu WLR}{M - \mu R}.$$

It is now easily seen that T_1 is greater than T_t, the other factors being equal. Let $\mu = 0.4$, $L = 0.15\,\text{m}$, $M = 0.075\,\text{m}$, $R = 0.1\,\text{m}$ and $W = 500\,\text{N}$. Then –

$$T_1 = \frac{0.4 \times 500 \times 0.15 \times 0.1}{0.075 - 0.04} = \frac{3}{0.035} = 86 \text{ Nm}$$

while –

$$T_t = \frac{3}{0.075 + 0.04} = 26 \text{ Nm.}$$

Thus T_1 is 3.3 times T_t.

The shoe shown in Fig. 30.7 is called a *trailing shoe* while that shown in Fig. 30.8 is called a *leading shoe*. It should be clear, however, that in a conventional brake the leading shoe will become the trailing one if the direction of rotation of the brake drum is reversed, and *vice versa*.

An actual brake shoe acts in a similar manner to the simple one considered above, the only difference being that the frictional force μP will act at a larger radius than the radius of the brake drum and this will accentuate the difference between the torques developed by the shoes.

In a brake of the type shown in Fig. 30.3, however, the expanding cam will not apply *equal* forces to the shoes but will apply a greater force to the trailing shoe. Taking the data assumed above and supposing that a total actuating force of 1000N is available then the cam would apply a force of 767N to the trailing shoe and only 233N to the leading shoe. The total

Fig. 30.7 (*left*)

Fig. 30.8 (*right*)

braking torque would then be 8000Nm. If, however, the whole 1000N available for actuation had been applied to the leading shoe alone then the brake torque would have been 17 144Nm, that is, more than twice as great and this result can be obtained by making both shoes leading shoes and applying 500N to each.

If the actuating mechanism were of the type that applies equal forces to the shoes then each actuating force would be 500N and the total brake torque developed by the shoes would be 8571 + 2608 = 11 179Nm. Thus a floating or equalising actuating mechanism gives an increase in brake torque for a given actuating force but it has the disadvantage that the wear of the leading shoe (assuming the shoes to have linings of the same material) would be 3.29 times that of the trailing shoe. The brake with two leading shoes would not suffer from this drawback and, has been seen, gives an even greater brake torque. Such brakes are, therefore, widely used, particularly for front wheels. When hydraulic actuation is used it is a simple matter to make both shoes leading ones for the forward direction of rotation; the brake is arranged as shown in Fig. 30.9, two actuating cylinders, connected by a pipe, being used instead of one cylinder. For the reverse direction of rotation both shoes would be trailing shoes and the brake would be rather weak. For this reason it is usual to employ the two-leading shoe brake in the front wheels only, the rear brakes being the conventional leading and trailing shoe type.

When the brake actuation is mechanical it is not so simple to make both shoes leading ones but a relatively simple mechanism has been developed by Girling and the principle of this is shown in Fig. 30.10. The expanding mechanism does not act directly on the shoe but on one arm of a bell-crank which is freely pivoted on a pin carried by the shoe. The other arm of this bell-crank bears against a fixed anchorage (shown cross-hatched) and the shoe itself can bear on this anchorage and on another one at the top, as shown. It should be clear that, supposing the arms of the bell-cranks to be all equal in length, the force in the strut will be equal to the actuating force W and this force will act on the bell-cranks as shown; also that the bell-crank at the bottom will press on the anchorage with a force W and the

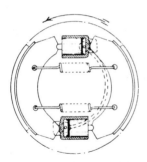

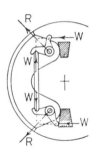

Fig. 30.9 (*left*)
Fig. 30.10 (*right*)

anchorage will press back equally on the bell-crank as shown. The resultant force on each bell-crank will thus be a force *R* as shown and these forces will press the shoe into contact with the drum. If the drum is turning clockwise the shoe will now move round clockwise very slightly until it bears on the anchorage at the top and is thus a leading shoe while if the drum is turning anti-clockwise the shoe will turn anti-clockwise and will bear on the anchorage at the bottom, being once again a leading shoe. Thus, by employing two shoes, each with the bell-crank and strut mechanism, a brake which is a two-leading shoe brake for either direction of rotation and which requires only one actuating mechanism is obtained.

30.6   Brake shoe adjustments

In order to take up the wear of the brake linings and to enable the clearance between the shoes and the drum to be adjusted the anchorages on which the shoes pivot are frequently made adjustable so that the shoes can be moved outwards. In the example shown in Fig. 30.11, the brake shoes bear on the ends of tappets carried in a housing that is fixed to the backplate of the brake assembly. These tappets can be forced outwards by screwing in the adjusting wedge, thereby reducing the clearance between the brake shoes and drum. The adjusting wedge is roughly conical but the cone is actually a series of flats; this enables the pull-off springs to lock the adjustment positively.

A design by Lockheed suitable for heavy duty brakes is shown in Fig. 30.12. The housing G is bolted to the backplate H and the tappets A and B have screwed inner members D and E that are prevented from rotating by their engagement with the ends F of the brake shoe webs. The outer members of the tappets have teeth K formed on them so that they can be

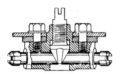

Fig. 30.11 (*above*) Wedge shape adjustment device

Fig. 30.12 (*right*) Lockheed heavy-duty brake adjusting mechanism

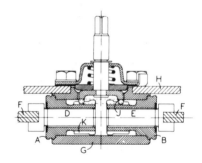

rotated from the outside by means of a simple crown wheel J and thus move the inner portions of the tappets outwards. Other designs of adjusting mechanisms can be seen in Figs. 30.14 and 30.15.

An alternative point at which an adjustment can be made is between the actuating mechanism and the ends of the brake shoes.

30.7   A modern rear-wheel brake

The brake shown in Fig. 30.13 is suitable for the rear wheels of a car because it incorporates an hand-brake actuation. It is a Girling design. The shoes bear against the flat faces of an abutment carried by the back-plate at the bottom and against the ends of the plungers of the hydraulic actuation cylinder at the top. They are held in place by two springs, only the bottom one being shown. Flat strip springs S at the middle of the shoes bear against the webs and hold the shoes against projections (two for each shoe) formed on the back plate.

The hand-brake actuation is by means of a bell-crank lever B and a connecting link or strut, made in two parts E and F. The bell-crank lever is pivoted on the upper end of a pillar C and when its long arm is pulled inwards as indicated by the arrow the short arm D applies a force to the right hand shoe and the reaction of this force moves the upper end of the pillar C to the left, this motion being possible because the pillar is carried at its lower end on a flexible rubber moulding. The motion of the pillar is transferred through the strut EF to the left-hand shoe and so the shoes are applied with equal forces.

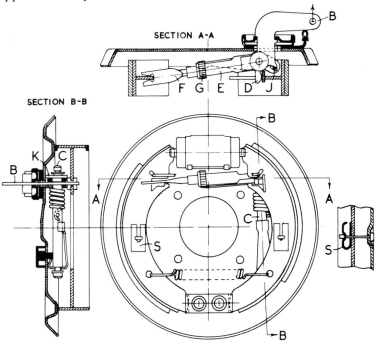

Fig. 30.13 Girling drum brake with auto adjuster

The ends of both the parts E and F of the connecting link are flat but the middle parts are cylindrical, E being hollow and F having a screw thread formed on it on which there is a nut G, rotation of which will alter the effective length of the strut. The flat end of the member E pivots on the pillar C and a ratchet lever (shown in dotted line in the upper view and seen below the strut in the main view) is also pivoted there. A slot in a short arm of the ratchet lever is engaged by the end J of the spring that surrounds the pillar so that the spring tends to rotate the ratchet lever in an anti-clockwise direction, this motion is limited by a small shoulder formed on the bell-crank. The long arm of the ratchet lever can engage teeth formed on the outside of the nut G. When the bell-crank is rotated to apply the brake the spring causes the ratchet lever to follow up the motion and if, due to wear of the linings, this is greater than normal the lever will rotate the nut G and take up the wear. When the brake is released, the shoulder on the bell-crank will move the ratchet lever back to its original position. The actuating force applied to the lever B and the force in the strut both tend to pull the pillar up against the back plate and so a roller K is provided to reduce friction when the pillar moves during the brake actuation.

An automatic adjusting mechanism made by the Lockheed company is shown in Fig. 30.14. The actuating cylinder is single-acting, i.e. it is closed at one end and its piston has an arm A secured to it. This arm carries a pin B that engages a bell-crank lever C which is free to turn on a fixed pin D.

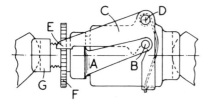

Fig. 30.14 Lockheed auto adjuster

The end E of the bell-crank forms a pawl that engages the teeth F of an adjuster sleeve that is free to turn inside the piston but must move axially with it. The tappet G is screwed into the adjuster sleeve but is prevented from rotating by the brake shoe that it engages. When the piston is moved outwards (to the left in the diagram) the pin B rotates the bell-crank and if the movement is greater than normal the pawl E will ride over one or more teeth of the adjuster sleeve F so that when the brake is released and the piston moves back the pin B will rotate the bell-crank and turn the adjuster sleeve so as to take up the wear.

Some designers prefer to use adjusting mechanisms that operate only when the brake is applied and the car is moving backwards and an example of this is shown in Fig. 30.15. The brake is a duo-servo type in which one shoe is used to apply the other through the adjusting turnbuckle whether the brake drum is rotating clockwise or anti-clockwise. The shoes are prevented from rotating very far by a fixed abutment C, against which one of the shoes will abut when the brake is applied. An expanding mechanism operated by the hand-brake linkage may also be incorporated between the upper ends of the shoes. For forward motion of the drum, which is assumed to be anti-clockwise, the shoe A is the servo shoe and it will be brought into action by the left hand piston of the actuating cylinder. The

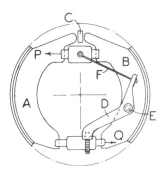

Fig. 30.15 Girling duo-servo
brake with auto adjuster

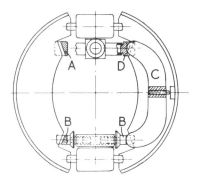

Fig. 30.16 Girling
two-leading-shoe brake

frictional force on the shoe will cause it to rotate slightly with the drum and
so acting through the adjusting turnbuckle it will apply the shoe B, causing
it to bear against the abutment C at the top. The force Q applied to this
shoe will be considerably greater than the force P applied by the piston to
the upper end of the servo shoe. For backwards motion the shoes will
change their functions and the shoe B wil become the servo shoe. The
slight rotation that it then gets will cause the lever D to rotate about its
pivot E on the shoe because the upper end of the lever is constrained by the
wire D which is anchored at its top end. If undue wear has occurred the
rotation of the lever D will be sufficient to cause the pawl at its end to
rotate the nut of the turnbuckle and so take up the wear.

Another example of a duo-servo brake is shown in Fig. 30.16 (which
illustrates the principle) and in Fig. 30.17 which shows the complete brake
and all its components. The brake is a Girling design and suitable for heavy
lorries. In the diagram, the left-hand side shows the service actuation and
the right-hand side the parking actuation but the brake is actually
symmetrical. Double-acting hydraulic cylinders at top and bottom provide
the service actuation and bring the shoes into contact with the drum when,
assuming clockwise rotation, the left-hand shoe will move round until it
comes up against the abutment at A, and the right-hand shoe will come up
against the adjuster at B. Both are fixed points, A being part of the back
plate while the body of the adjuster which carries the tappets B is fixed to
the backplate. For anti-clockwise rotation the abutments A and B will be
interchanged. The servo action is thus effective for both directions of
rotation.

The parking brake actuation is provided by a wedge type expander
which moves the tappets D outwards and through levers C applies forces to
the centre of the shoes. The lever C fulcrums on a flat formed on the tappet
B and lies in a plane that is slightly offset from the central plane of the
shoes. It will be seen from Fig. 30.17 that the wedge of the expander is free
to slide in a slot formed in the plunger of the drawlink and so the forces
that are applied to the levers C will be equalised. The adjusting mechanism
for the tappets B is duplicated and operated by small bevel gears on the
same principle as that shown in Fig. 30.12.

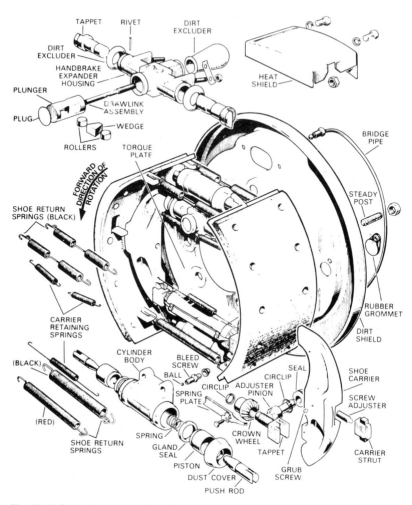

Fig. 30.17 Girling heavy-duty drum brake

30.8 Disc brakes

Brakes using flat discs as the friction surfaces have been used in the past but until the last three decades have not been so successful. They are now almost the commonest type for the front wheels of cars and are often used for the rear wheels and on some light vans. The earliest disc brakes were made on the same lines as a multiple-plate clutch but most present day designs use a single disc and almost always have sector shaped friction pads of relatively small area. The great advantages are, first, that despite the small area of the pads compared with the area of lining of a drum brake occupying approximately the same amount of space the rises of temperature are smaller and consequently the linings are less subject to fade and their life is comparable with that of drum brakes. Secondly, the action of the disc brake is unaffected by the occurrence of wear or by expansion due to rises of temperature, both of which are sources of trouble in drum brakes.

Perhaps the simplest construction is the fixed calliper double piston type shown in the diagram Fig. 30.18. The disc A is secured to the wheel hub which rotates on bearings on the axle casing or stub axle depending on whether a rear or a front brake is concerned. A calliper member C is bolted to the member B, which will be referred to as the mounting, and two pistons D and E are carried in cylinders formed in the calliper. These bear on pads consisting of a metal plate to which friction material facings are bonded. The metal backplates fit in recesses in the calliper so that they are

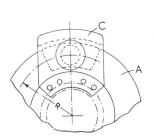 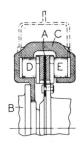

Fig. 30.18

prevented from rotating with the disc. The callipers of such brakes usually have to be made in two parts to enable the cylinders to be machined and also must have openings through which the friction pads can be removed for replacement. Their actual form is therefore more complex than as shown in the diagram.

The brake torque provided by a disc brake of this type is given by $T = 2\mu paR$ where μ is the coefficient of friction, p is the fluid pressure, a is the area of one cylinder and R is the distance from the point at which the frictional force acts to the wheel axis, this may be taken to be distance from the wheel axis to the centre of area of the pad. Calculation will show that to obtain the same torque as from a drum brake occupying the same volume the forces applied to the pads of the disc brake must be much higher than those applied to the shoes of the drum brake. This is for two reasons, firstly the radius R is necessarily less than the radius of an equivalent drum brake and secondly there is no servo action in the disc brake because the frictional forces do not help in the application of the brakes as they can do in drum brakes. It is consequently imperative that the axial forces on the disc shall be balanced and this is clearly so in the arrangement shown; it can however be obtained in other ways and these are considered later.

Although the axial forces are balanced there is an unbalanced tangential frictional force on the disc and this will have to be supported by the wheel bearings. By using two callipers placed diametrically opposite each other the brake torque can be doubled and the tangential forces be balanced although, of course, the volume of fluid that has been displaced to apply the brakes will be doubled. This arrangement is seldom used. It is also imperative to provide automatic adjustment for wear in disc brakes and this is usually done very simply. A rubber ring placed near the pad end of the actuating cylinder is carried so that when the piston moves outwards the ring distorts enough to allow the normal clearance to be taken up without any slip occurring between the ring and the piston but if the movement is more than this, slip occurs and when the fluid pressure is released the piston retracts only by the amount of the distortion and thus the normal clearance is restored.

Some methods of balancing the axial forces without using two cylinders are shown in Fig. 30.19. In (*a*) the calliper is carried on two links G pivoted at one end to the calliper and at the other end to the mounting B; it can therefore float sideways so as to equalise the axial forces. The design shown in (*b*) uses a single pivot but has the disadvantage that if the friction facings are initially of uniform thickness they will wear to a wedge shape and there will be a waste of friction material but this can be avoided by making the facings wedge-shaped initially. In (*c*), the calliper is allowed to slide along pins fixed in the mounting and in (*d*) the calliper is again carried on a single pivot but this is now placed approximately tangential to the periphery of the disc and in its central plane. If the axis of the pivot is offset from the central plane, then the tangential forces on the pads will have a moment about the axis and the balance of the axial forces will be upset but the magnitude of the effect is not likely to be great. The pads will also wear

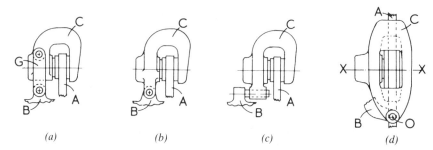

Fig. 30.19 Floating calliper disc brake arrangements

to a wedge shape when the pivot is offset but again this can be allowed for by making them wedge-shaped initially. In all these examples only one actuating cylinder is required and this is one of their chief advantages as it avoids having to put one cylinder inside the road wheel where it cannot always be adequately cooled.

The disc itself can be a simple flat one but this can sometimes lead to trouble because of the stresses that can be set up due to temperature rises; this can be mitigated by using a top-hat shape for the disc – a shape which may sometimes be forced on the designer to enable him to get the working surface into a suitable position. The cooling of the disc can be improved by venting it with radial passages so that a flow of air can be established through it. This is not much done in Europe but is fairly common in America.

A more detailed drawing of a brake in which the calliper is pivoted as in Fig. 30.19 (*b*) is given in Fig. 30.20. This is a Girling design which has an unusual indirect method of actuation. The calliper body is in one piece to which one pad is fixed directly, the other pad is carried on the cylindrical outer member assembly E, which slides in a bore in the calliper. It is moved by the piston A acting through the connecting piece D, the lever B and the inner part of the assembly E which is in two parts screwed together. By holding one part and turning the other the effective length of the unit is increased and the wear is taken up. This is done by means of ratchet teeth F and a stirrup-shaped member G; when, due to wear the lever B moves farther than usual the stirrup comes up against an abutment H and is caused to rotate about an axis at O, a projecting finger of the stirrup then engages the ratchet teeth and rotates the inner screwed portion of the assembly E. Provision is made for mechanical actuation of the brake

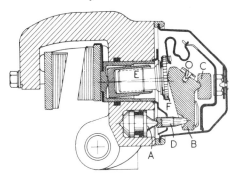

Fig. 30.20 Girling indirect floating calliper disc brake

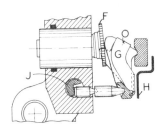

so that it can be used as a parking brake; this is shown in the scrap view where J is a rod having a lever at its outer end and shaped at its inner end so that it can also actuate the lever B. This scrap view is a section by a plane parallel to that of the main view but displaced perpendicularly to the paper slightly, the plane of the piston A in the main view is displaced slightly the other way in relation to the assembly E.

Another design by Girling that may be regarded as a sliding calliper type is shown in Fig. 30.21. The cylinder A is open at both ends and is fixed to the mounting K, it is provided with two pistons B and C, the latter bearing directly on the pad D while the former acts on the pad F through the plate E to which the pad is secured. The plate E, which is in effect the calliper, is supported in slots H formed in the cylinder and in a nylon insert J inside the piston B. Springs, not shown, take up any clearance and prevent rattle. The plate E is curved as shown in the end view to enable it to clear the disc while contacting the pad F and the piston B at their centres. The chief advantage of the plate over the conventional calliper is that as it is a steel pressing instead of a casting, it can withstand the stresses set up by the forces acting on the pads better and is appreciably lighter.

An American design of a sliding calliper brake, the Delco-Moraine, is shown in Fig. 30.22. The calliper body A is free to slide on chromium-plated bushes B that are fixed to the mounting D by the bolts C. The pad E is fixed to the calliper and the other, F, is supported by, but free to slide on, the bolts C.

A Lockheed single-cylinder disc brake is shown, somewhat simplified, in Fig. 30.23. It is a pivoted calliper type in which the calliper is again a steel plate pressing. It is supported on an angle bracket B that is bolted to the mounting and is pivoted at O on a pin that can be adjusted to a small extent in a direction perpendicular to the disc; this enables initial adjustments to be made during assembly of the vehicle. The actuating cylinder D has slots

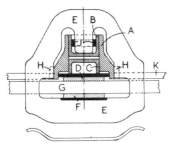

Fig. 30.21 Girling sliding calliper disc brake

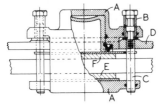

Fig. 30.22 Delco-Moraine sliding calliper disc brake

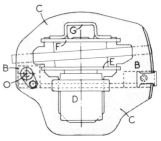

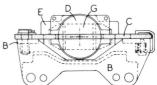

Fig. 30.23 Lockheed pivoted calliper brake

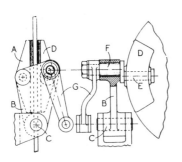

Fig. 30.24 (*left*)
Fig. 30.25 (*right*)

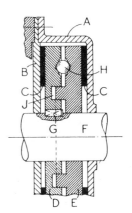

formed in a flange at its open end and can be slid into an opening formed in the calliper. The cylinder also has small slots at its corners which position its closed end by engaging the calliper plate. A spring clip, not shown, holds the cylinder in place. The pads are moulded on to back plates E and F and these fit into recesses formed in the calliper so as to transmit the tangential forces. A plate spring and split pins hold the pads in place radially. The pad F is supported by a steel pressing G which has a slot cut in its U-shaped centre part to fit the calliper plate. A spring at the pivot O and a spring-loaded clip at the other end prevent shake or rattle.

In the Tru-Stop brake, shown in Fig. 30.24, equality between the forces acting between the friction linings and the disc is obtained by leaving the link B, which carries the two shoes, free to pivot on the fixed pin C which is carried by a part of the gearbox casing. The shoe A is pivoted on a pin which is fixed in the link B while the shoe D is pivoted on the pin E of a crank or eccentric F, which is carried in bearings in the link B and to which the actuating lever G is fixed. When a pull is applied to the lever G the shoes are drawn together and grip the disc.

30.9 Self-energising disc brakes

The principle of a brake using complete annular discs for the friction elements instead of small pads and which was used on some military vehicles many years ago is shown in Fig. 30.25.

The rotating part is the drum which is made in two parts A and B and the non-rotating part is the inner member F on which the discs D and E are carried. The disc D is prevented from rotating by a key but the other one, E, rotates slightly. Both discs carry friction linings CC. On the inner faces of the discs there are several conical recesses in which steel balls H are placed. The brake is applied by moving the discs apart and in the diagram this is, for simplicity, done by admitting fluid to the annular cylinder J. The frictional force applied to the disc E as soon as it makes contact with the drum rotates it slightly and causes the balls H to force the discs apart and thus adds to the actuating force. The magnitude of the servo or self-actuating action depends on the included angle of the ball recesses.

The brake torque is given by –

$$T = \frac{2\mu p a R R_b}{R_b - \mu R \tan\alpha}$$

where μ is the coefficient of friction, p the actuating pressure, a the area of the actuating cylinder, R the mean radius of the friction lining, R_b the radius to the centre of the balls and 2α is the included angle of the ball recesses. If the angle α is made larger the denominator of the above expression will become smaller and the torque T larger; there is a limiting value for the angle α which makes the denominator zero and the torque theoretically infinite, i.e. the brake locks itself as soon as the discs make contact. This limiting value of α must not be approached too closely because it is dependent on the value of μ and this may vary.

Brakes acting on this principle are used to a considerable extent on agricultural tractors and contractors' vehicles. They may be either 'dry' or 'wet' according as to whether oil is kept away from the friction surfaces or

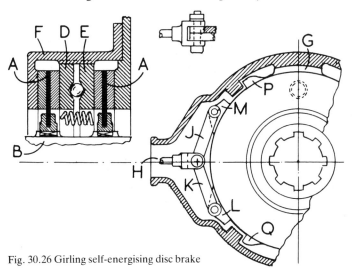

Fig. 30.26 Girling self-energising disc brake

whether they are housed inside a gearbox or axle casing and are exposed to oil. The constructional arrangement of these brakes differs from that described above and is shown in Fig. 30.26.

The rotating members are now the discs A,A which are splined to the shaft B to which the brake torque is to be applied and they are pressed outwards against the fixed casing F to apply the brake. This is done by pulling on the rod H thereby causing the links J and K to pull on the lugs L and M and cause the discs to rotate slightly in opposite directions and bring into action the self-energising forces. Depending therefore on the direction of rotation of the shaft B one or other of the discs will become anchored by its lug P or Q coming up against a stop on the casing. The discs are centred by means of projections G which are in contact with machined surfaces inside the casing. The construction of the wet form of this clutch is similar but the friction linings are of course of different material and, because of the lower coefficient of friction obtainable, the single discs of the dry form are replaced by packs of several plates as in a multiple-plate clutch.

30.10   Brake linkages

Hydraulic actuation is now almost universal for the service brakes of vehicles but linkages consisting of levers, rods and wires are often required for the operation of the parking brakes and these may conveniently be considered first. A simple linkage for applying the two rear brakes of a vehicle is shown in Fig. 30.27; it is called an *uncompensated linkage* because there is nothing to ensure that equal forces will be applied to the two brakes. This should be evident if the effect of lengthening one of the rods H or K is considered. In the linkage partly shown in Fig. 30.28, however, the beam C (which is pulled on at its centre by the hand lever)

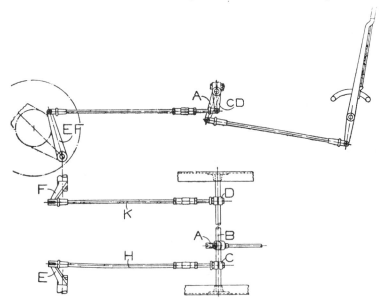

Fig. 30.27 Uncompensated brake linkage

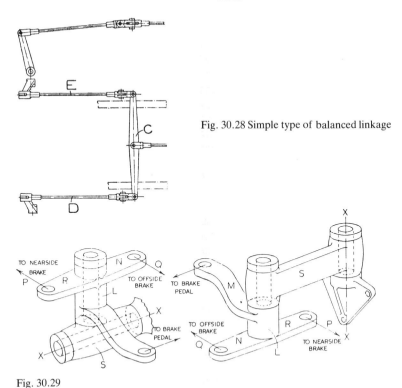

Fig. 30.28 Simple type of balanced linkage

Fig. 30.29

ensures the equality of the forces transmitted by the rods D and E to the brakes and the linkage is consequently called a *balanced* or *compensated* linkage. When a balance beam is employed however it it usually made quite short and may sometimes be arranged to lie in a vertical plane, the rod from one going direct to one brake while the other end is coupled by a cross-shaft, with levers at both ends, to the other brake.

When the application of the brakes is effected by rods that pull inwards towards the centre of the vehicle the compensation between the two sides is most easily effected by one of the arrangements shown in Fig. 30.29. The principle of both of these is that the levers L are free to move sideways and thus enable the forces P and Q to balance each other. The freedom is obtained by pivoting the levers on members S that can rotate about the axes XX. In cars, the compensation is sometimes obtained by using a flexible wire that passes round a pulley and has its ends connected to the brake actuating levers. The pulley is itself pulled on at its centre by a rod coupled to the hand lever.

30.11 Leverage and adjustment of the brake linkage

The forces that have to be applied to the brake shoes in order to produce the maximum deceleration of the vehicle in an emergency stop are very large, approximating to the weight of the vehicle, and to enable the driver to produce these forces with an effort which cannot exceed about 700 N and which is normally kept down to about one-third of that amount, the brake linkage has to provide a considerable leverage. The leverage that can be provided, however is strictly limited by several factors. First, a definite clearance has usually to be maintained between the brake shoes and drum; supposing this to be only 0.25 mm then, with a leverage between the shoes and brake pedal of 100 to 1, 25 mm of pedal travel would be required merely to take up the clearance. Secondly, the brake linkage cannot be made rigid and so when the brake pedal force is applied the parts of the linkage stretch and give slightly and to take up this stretch may use up another 25 mm of pedal travel.

Now the total travel that can be conveniently accommodated is limited to about 100 mm and so only 50 mm is available to take up the wear of the linings and this corresponds, with the leverage assumed above, to only 0.05 mm. Thus it is important to keep the leverage provided down to the lowest value consistent with reasonable pedal pressures and to keep the stretch of the brake linkage (including deformation of the brake drums themselves) as low as possible. But even when this has been done the brakes will still have to be adjusted at intervals. The best place for this adjustment is as close to the brake shoes as possible and in cars nowadays the adjustment is always either at the anchorage or between the actuating mechanism and the shoes.

30.12   Hydraulic systems

The general arrangement of an hydraulic system is as follows.

The foot pedal actuates the piston in a master cylinder and forces fluid along a piping system to operating cylinders situated in the wheel brakes. The pistons of the operating cylinders are forced out and thus operate the brake shoes. Since all the operating cylinders are connected to the one master cylinder, it follows that the pressure in all the cylinders is the same, and hence compensation is automatically obtained. It is important that all air should be eliminated from the piping system and cylinders, because if air is present then, when the piston of the master cylinder is depressed, instead of fluid being forced along the pipes into the operating cylinders the air in the piping will be compressed, and since air is readily compressible the pressure in the system may not rise sufficiently to actuate the brakes. Of course, if enough travel could be given to the master piston the presence of air would not matter, because the air could be compressed sufficiently to raise the pressure until the brakes were operated; it is not possible to do this, however. Arrangements are therefore made to keep air out of the system.

A Lockheed master cylinder is shown in Fig. 30.30. It has an integral sheet metal reservoir that should always contain a reserve of fluid in order to keep the cylinder replenished and thus prevent air from getting into the system. The piston is sealed by a cup A and a thin, slightly corrugated washer is interposed between the cup and the piston. In the 'off' position the hole B is uncovered and so fluid can flow from the reservoir to make good any losses that may have occurred. A second hole keeps the annular space C full of fluid and helps in keeping air out of the system. The valve assembly D is held against the end of the cylinder by the spring and it

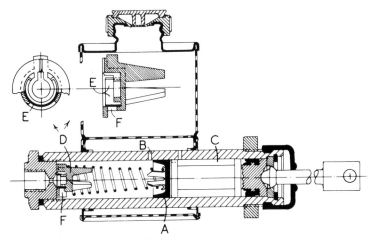

Fig. 30.30 Lockheed master cylinder

incorporates a second valve consisting of a flexible arcual strip E of copper alloy that will lift inwards when a pressure is set up in the cylinder.

When the brakes are applied, therefore, the fluid flows through the opening F into the piping system but, in order to return when the brakes are released, the whole valve D has to be lifted. This requires a difference in pressure across the valve to overcome the force of the spring and so, when the valve closes, a low pressure remains in the piping system. Such an arrangement is called a *trap valve* and it helps to prevent a sudden reduction of the pressure in the piping system if the brake pedal returns at a faster rate than the brake actuating pistons in the brakes.

30.13 Operating cylinders

Various types of operating cylinder are used according to circumstances; one type is open at both ends and is fitted with two pistons which bear, either directly or through simple struts, on the brake shoes which are operated when fluid is forced in between the pistons. This type must clearly be situated inside the brake drum and this is sometimes a drawback since the space available is very limited and also the temperature may rise considerably and thus lead to vaporisation of the brake fluid.

A second type of operating cylinder is closed at one end and has a single piston; this type may be placed either inside or outside the brake drum and may be used to operate a single brake shoe or a pair of shoes. For the latter purpose the operating cylinder is sometimes pivoted to one of the shoes and has its piston pivoted to the other shoe and is connected to the piping system by a flexible pipe. Alternatively the cylinder may be carried by the back plate of the brake but be free to slide, parallel to the cylinder axis, on that back plate; the piston then bears on one brake shoe and the cylinder on the other shoe. When only one shoe has to be operated the cylinder will be fixed to the backplate and the piston will bear on the shoe. A 'bleeder' screw is usually incorporated in the operating cylinders so that the piping system may be bled until it is free of air. The system is bled as follows.

A piece of rubber pipe is connected to the nipple of the bleeder screw and its end is kept submerged below the level of some brake fluid contained in a glass jar. The reservoir of the master cylinder is filled with fluid and is kept full during the bleeding operation. The bleeder screw is then loosed a turn or two and the brake pedal is pushed down and allowed to come *right* up several times so that fluid is pumped through the piping system and out through the bleeder screw into the glass jar and pumping is continued until the fluid coming out is seen to be free of air. The bleeder screw is then tightened. Each bleeder screw throughout the system is treated in this way.

A single-acting Lockheed operating cylinder that incorporates provision for the mechanical operation of the brake shoes is shown in Fig. 30.31. The body A is carried by the back plate B but is free to slide parallel to the cylinder axis. The piston is made in two parts C and D and bears, through a Micram adjuster, on the leading shoe of the brake. The cylinder body bears on the trailing shoe at E. When fluid enters the cylinder a force is exerted on the piston and thus on the leading shoe; the reaction of this force acts on the cylinder body and is transmitted to the trailing shoe, because, as mentioned above, the body is free to slide on the back plate. Mechanical operation is through the lever F which is pivoted on the pin G carried by the cylinder body. When the lever is pulled inwards (towards the centre of the car or upwards in the figure) it applies a force to the piston member D and thus to the leading shoe. The reaction of this force acts on the pin G and is transmitted by the cylinder body to the trailing shoe. A rubber filling piece is provided in the cylinder in order to reduce the volume of fluid enclosed inside the brake drum where it is subject to any temperature rise that may occur.

Operating cylinders that are situated outside the brake drums are less likely to be affected by temperature rises and so are used to a considerable extent on commercial vehicles. A Lockheed design is shown in Fig. 30.32.

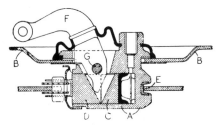

Fig. 30.31 Lockheed single-acting operating cylinder

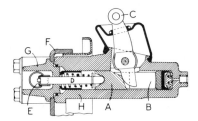

Fig. 30.32 Lockheed external actuating cylinder

The piston is in two parts A and B, the former only being moved when the actuation is mechanical while, when the actuation is hydraulic, the actuating lever itself is not moved. The brake shoes are expanded by the wedge-shaped end of the strut D acting on the plungers or tappets E. These are carried in the housing G and bear on the brake shoes. Rollers are interposed between the wedge and the plungers and these are kept in place by a cage carried on the end of the wedge. The whole assembly is clamped to the back plate F of the brake between the body H and the housing G.

30.14 Divided and dual brake systems

In most countries it is now obligatory to design the brake system in a manner such that a failure in any part of it cannot cause total loss of braking – usually any two of the four wheel brakes must remain fully effective. Duplication of the complete system would be both costly and unnecessary, so vehicle manufacturers generally install a double master cylinder, as in Fig. 30.33, which has two pistons, each serving a different part of the brake system. The system itself, therefore, is also divided into two independent sections.

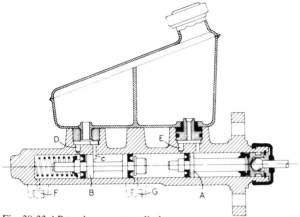

Fig. 30.33 AP tandem master cylinder

The simplest way to make such a division is to take the output from one part of the master cylinder to the front wheels and the other to the rear ones. However, for cars, even ignoring the effects of weight transfer, if the front-rear axle load ratio is 70:30 and the coefficient of friction between road and tyres is 0.8, the maximum efficiency of the rear wheel brakes acting alone cannot be more than about 25% and therefore is inadequate for emergency braking, which is when most sudden failures occur. Should it be the rear circuit that has failed, the residual braking at the front would give about 55% efficiency – the total, front + rear, is of course, corresponding to the coefficient of friction of 0.8. Such a system may, however, be used on heavy commercial vehicles which, if unladen, still have sufficient power in the front brakes to stop satisfactorily and, if laden, have a suitable front-rear load distribution for either the front or rear brakes to be effective.

A further disadvantage of such a system on cars is the possibility of loss of control as a result of locking of the two wheels being braked. Locked front wheels result in the vehicle continuing in a straight line, even if the steering wheel is turned. The even more dangerous two-rear-wheels-locked condition renders the vehicle unstable, almost invariably causing it to spin. This latter phenomenon occurs because of the difference between the static coefficient of friction between, at the front, the rolling wheels and the ground and, at the rear, the significantly lower coefficient of sliding friction between the locked wheels and the ground, which means that unless the vehicle is braked extremely accurately in a straight line and the road is level and not cambered, the lateral component of the forces on the vehicle will meet with much less resistance at the rear wheels than at the front ones, so the rear end will swing round.

Connection of one part of the master cylinder output to the two wheels on the left and the other to those on the right would be dangerous because of severe pulling of the vehicle to one side in the event of a failure. On the other hand a diagonal split – each half serving a front wheel on one side and a rear wheel on the other – is frequently used. However, this gives only 40% braking efficiency and, moreover, is unsuitable for vehicles having a significant offset between the centre of the front wheel contact with the ground and the kingpin axis projected to the ground. This is because the couple due to this offset when only one front brake is in operation will not be reacted by an equal and opposite couple on the other wheel so, again, the steering could pull suddenly and unexpectedly to one side on application of the brakes. Such a system has two advantages though: premature wheel locking is ruled out because the normal criteria for front-rear wheel braking ratios still apply; and, secondly, there will always be one freely rolling wheel on each side for steering with and for reacting any tendency for the rear end to swing.

The so-called L-split, in which each part of the divided circuit serves the two front and a different rear brake, has certain limitations. Application of extra pressure to make up for the loss of braking on one rear wheel is impracticable because it would cause locking of that rear wheel and therefore further loss of efficiency. Consequently, the maximum obtainable braking efficiency of one circuit is still only about 40%.

By far the best system would appear to be what is termed the *HI split* – one circuit serving all four wheels and therefore, if viewed in plan, can be likened to the letter H, while the other serves the front brakes only, and therefore can be likened to the letter I. With such an arrangement the circuit serving only the front wheels may be connected to large-diameter cylinders in the disc brake calliper, while that serving both front and rear brakes is connected to smaller diameter cylinders. The outcome is that, by increasing the pedal pressure, a braking efficiency of about 55% can be obtained with the I circuit alone, while that with the H circuit alone a good braking performance – about 45% – is still obtainable even though greatly increased pressure may not be practicable for fear of locking the rear wheels.

In all the systems two master cylinders are required and these are sometimes physically separate, their pistons being actuated by the brake pedal through a balance beam that equalises the forces applied to them. The motion of the balance beam is limited and so if one system fails the other can be applied although the pedal travel has to be increased to do this. The use of tandem cylinders became the most widely used arrangement however and a typical example made by Automotive Products Ltd. is illustrated in Fig. 30.33. The two pistons A and B work in a single bore in the body casting, the front one A being operated directly by the brake pedal push rod while the rear one B floats between the front one and the end of the cylinder.

In the 'off' position shown, the space between the two pistons and that between the rear piston and the end of the cylinder are open to the two parts of the reservoir via the holes D and E and this keeps these spaces and the piping systems connected to them full at all times. In normal action the brake pedal moves the front piston and as pressure is built up in front of it, so the rear piston is moved along and thus equal pressures are built up in both systems. If the rear piping system should fail, the rear piston would move along without generating any pressure but as soon as it came into contact with the end of the cylinder pressure would start to build up between the pistons and the other system would function normally except that the pedal travel would have to be greater. If the piping system connected to the space between the pistons should fail, then the front would move along until it contacted the rear one and the rear system would then function normally. In systems of this kind (including those employing separate master cylinders and balance beams) attention must be paid to the adjustment of the brakes themselves in order to ensure that the available stroke of either piston is not used up before the brakes it operates are applied.

Chapter 31

Servo- and power-operated brake systems

As vehicle weight increases then the force that must be exerted on the pedal of a simple brake system to produce the maximum deceleration permitted by the road conditions also goes up, and when the weight exceeds two to three tons the force required may become greater than a man can exert. The driver must then be given some assistance in applying the brakes. This can be done in two ways, (a) by using a servo mechanism which adds to the driver's effort although that effort remains a considerable part of the total effort applied to the brakes, or (b) by using power operation in which case the effort of the driver is a controlling effort only and is not transmitted to the brakes at all.

Servo systems are usually lower in cost than power-operated systems and can frequently be fitted as an addition to a vehicle having an ordinary brake system. They are widely used on vehicles coming within the medium weight range, say, two to six tons, whereas power operation is used for heavy vehicles where the weight exceeds six tons or so and for vehicles used with trailers.

There are two essential features of both servo and power brake systems: (1) the time-lag of the system, that is the time interval between the moment when the brake pedal is depressed and the moment when the brakes come on, must be very small and (2) the system must be such that the driver can judge the intensity of application of the brakes fairly accurately. The second feature usually requires that the force applying the brakes shall be closely proportional to the force exerted by the driver on the brake pedal.

The source of the additional effort supplied by a servo system may be (a) the momentum of the vehicle itself, (b) vacuum in a reservoir, obtained by connecting the reservoir through a non-return valve either to the induction manifold of the engine or to a separately driven exhauster, (c) oil under pressure supplied by a pump driven by the engine or some part of the transmission system, (d) air under pressure supplied by an air compressor driven by the engine.

The first servos to be introduced were purely mechanical in action but had to be very carefully designed and made in order that they should function properly, and this made them costly to manufacture. They became obsolete when cheaper vacuum-operated mechanisms were introduced.

31.1   Vacuum brake operation

Vacuum may be used in two ways in the application of brakes. In each method a cylinder fitted with a piston, or diaphragm, is used and the piston is coupled to the mechanical brake linkage.

In one method the cylinder is permanently open to the atmosphere at one end and the other end also when brakes are off. The brakes are applied by exhausting the latter end of the cylinder to the desired degree thus setting up a force on the piston equal to the pressure difference on its two sides multiplied by its area. In the other system the cylinder is closed at both ends and when the brakes are off the same degree of vacuum exists in both ends. To apply the brakes one end is open to the atmosphere so that the pressure in that end rises and gives a force on the piston which applies the brakes.

The second system is commonly referred to as a *suspended vacuum system*. Its chief advantages over the first system are that it is slightly more rapid in action and that there is a smaller amount of air that has to be exhausted either by the engine through the induction manifold, or by the exhauster, if a separate one is used. Both of these advantages arise from the fact that under the second system vacuum has to be destroyed in a volume equal to the piston area multiplied merely by the piston travel necessary to apply the brakes; whereas in the first system the volume that has to be filled, and subsequently exhausted, is equal to the piston area multiplied by the maximum piston travel possible, plus any clearance which may then remain between the piston and the end of the cylinder. By increasing this clearance volume in a suspended vacuum system, the servo cylinder can be made to function as a vacuum tank and a separate tank can therefore be dispensed with. This is done in many light commercial vehicles.

31.2   Clayton Dewandre master servo unit

The first successful vacuum-operated servo was made by the Clayton Dewandre Company of Lincoln, and as it embodied the basic principle of present-day designs and because large numbers of them are in present-day use it has been thought desirable to retain a description of one. This is shown in Figs. 31.1 and 31.2. It consists of a drawn-steel cylinder A fitted with a piston B sealed by a cup-leather C. The piston is connected by a link E to the lower end R of a balance lever F, the upper end of which bears against the valve G. In the position shown, the right-hand end of this valve is clear of the face of the valve J so that the port H through the centre of the valve G opens the passage K and the cylinder A to the atmosphere. The balance lever F is pivoted on the pin O, which is carried by the support levers MM. The latter are pivoted on the fixed pin N. The brake pedal is coupled by the rod D to the balance lever at the point Q, but the connecting pivot pin S is hollow and there is ample clearance between it

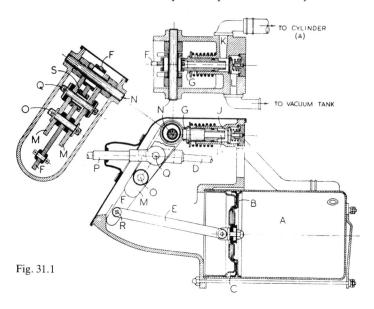

Fig. 31.1

and the pin Q. The latter serves to couple the support levers MM to the brake linkage through the rod P. The arrangement is shown in perspective in Fig. 31.2.

When the brake pedal is depressed the balance lever is rotated clockwise about the pivot pin O, and its upper end pushes the valve G to the right. This seats on the valve J and thus closes the vent H to the atmosphere. It then pushes the valve J off its seat, so that the vacuum tank is put into communication with the cylinder C via the passages L and K. The pressure in the cylinder A starts to fall so that a force, X, is exerted, which tends to pull the lower end of the balance lever to the right. When this force reaches a value sufficient to balance the force applied by the rod D, the balance lever will be rotated slightly anti-clockwise, and this will bring the valve G to the 'lap' or 'brake applied' position, the valve J being seated but the vent H being still closed. In this position the cylinder A is isolated. The force X is now balancing the force Y applied by the brake pedal, and the relation of these forces is determined by the ratio of the lever arms of the balance lever. Thus –

$$X = RO = Y = QO \quad \text{so that} \quad X = Y = \frac{QO}{RO}.$$

The resultant of the forces X and Y applied to the balance lever $\left[\text{equal approximately to } Y \left(1 + \frac{QO}{RO}\right)\right]$ is applied to the pin O and through the support levers and the rod P to the brake linkage. As the brakes come on, the support levers may rotate slightly, but this will not upset the balance of forces since in the lap position the upper end of the balance lever is concentric with the pivot N, about which the movement will be occurring.

The force transmitted to the brake linkage is thus seen to be proportional to the force applied by the driver to the brake pedal, and the degree to which the latter will be augmented by the servo is determined by the ratio of the lever arms of the balance lever.

If for any reason the vacuum formed in the cylinder A is insufficient, the brakes may be applied purely by the force Y, the action being as follows. The depression of the brake lever rotates the balance lever clockwise about the pin O until the clearance between the eye of the balance lever and the pin N is taken up. The pin N then becomes a fulcrum for the balance lever and the force Y can be transmitted through the pin O and the levers MM to the rod P. Since the rods D and P are approximately in line, the force in the rod P will then be equal to the force in the rod D.

When hydraulic actuation of the vehicle brakes is adopted, the master cylinder of the system is bolted up to the vacuum servo unit, but the latter is rearranged slightly. The rod D is now coupled to the support levers and operates the piston of the master cylinder, while the rod P is pivoted to the balance lever and connected to the brake pedal. The forces in the rods D and P will now be compressive forces instead of tension forces.

31.3 Reservoirs

The reservoirs used with vacuum brake systems are usually simple cylindrical (sometimes spherical) vessels fitted with a non-return valve in the pipes connecting them with the induction manifold or the exhauster, as the case may be. A drain plug or cock is usually fitted at the lowest point. To give a sufficient reserve to enable several brake applications to be made even though the engine has stopped requires a large reservoir; but a large reservoir takes a long time to evacuate and this is a drawback. To overcome this difficulty dual reservoirs are sometimes used. These comprise a small tank which can be quickly evacuated and a large one which provides a suitable reserve but which does not begin to be evacuated until the smaller one has been completely evacuated. The diverter valve which governs this action is shown in Fig. 31.3. Until the small or primary tank is exhausted the spring A keeps the valve B on its seat and the large or secondary tank is blanked off. As the small tank is evacuated and the

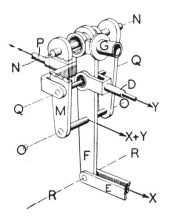

Fig. 31.2 (*left*)

Fig. 31.3 (*below*)

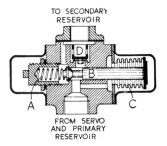

pressure in it falls a force acting to the left will be set up on the bellows C, which is subject to atmospheric pressure externally and to the pressure in the small tank internally. When the pressure in the small tank is reduced to the designed value the valve B will be unseated and the large tank will begin to be evacuated. The large tank supplements the small one when necessary because if the pressure in the small tank rises above that in the large tank the valve D will open and put the two tanks into communication.

31.4   Bendix Hydrovac

The Bendix Hydrovac was one of the earliest suspended vacuum systems and is still in extensive use, it combines a vacuum servo with the master cylinder of an hydraulic brake system. In Fig. 31.4, the size of the valve gear has been exaggerated in order to make the details clear. When the brake pedal is in the off position the valve A will be off its seat and so both sides of the piston B will be subject to vacuum and there will be no force acting on the piston. The plunger C, which is integral with the piston rod, will be off its seating in the piston H so that the hydraulic piping system leading to the brakes will be open to the master cylinder D and thus to the brake fluid reservoir. When the brake pedal is depressed a pressure will be set up in the master cylinder and this pressure will act on the plunger E of the vacuum valve. The diaphragm F will be pushed up until it seats on the valve A and then the valve G will be pushed off its seat. The left-hand end of the vacuum cylinder will thus be opened to atmosphere and the pressure in it will rise so that a force will act on the piston B to push it to the right. The movement of the piston B will first seat the plunger C on to the piston H and then will force the latter into its cylinder so as to apply the brakes. The force due to the oil pressure acting on the left-hand side of the piston H will be added to the force due to the piston B so that the system is a servo system. The pressure in the left-hand end of the vacuum cylinder also acts on the top of the diaphragm F and when the pressure reaches a value sufficient to balance the hydraulic force applied to the plunger E the diaphragm will be depressed slightly and the valve G will be seated again. The left-hand end of the vacuum cylinder will then be isolated and the pressure in it will be proportional to the hydraulic pressure acting on the plunger E, that is, proportional to the brake pedal force. If for any reason no vacuum is available then the pressure set up in the master cylinder D will be transmitted direct to the brake cylinders because the plunger C will remain off its seat.

31.5   Direct-acting vacuum servos

In many cars it is convenient to operate the master cylinder piston directly from the brake pedal but the use of servo assistance is required; for such conditions *direct-acting servos* are used.

The design by Automotive Products shown in Fig. 31.5 consists of a pressed steel body or vacuum chamber to the front of which the master cylinder is bolted and which is closed at the rear by a pressed steel cover between which and the chamber a rubber diaphragm is secured. At its centre the diaphragm is sealed to the stem of a piston E that houses the

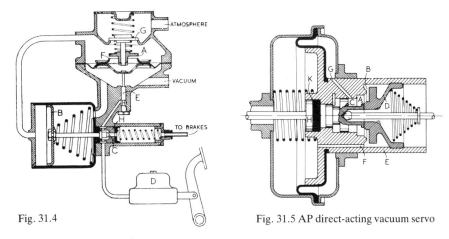

Fig. 31.4   Fig. 31.5 AP direct-acting vacuum servo

control valve. There is a sliding seal between the cover and the stem of the piston which is bored out to take a small piston H that is in effect integral with the push rod of the master cylinder and behind this piston is a rubber reaction disc K. A spring holds the servo piston in the 'off' position. The left-hand side of the vacuum chamber is connected to the induction manifold of the engine by a pipe containing a non-return valve so that a vacuum always exists in that side and in the 'off' position the same vacuum will also exist in the right-hand side because the two sides are connected via the passage F, the gap B and the passage G.

When the brake pedal is depressed the valve C is moved to the left and this permits the valve D, which is a reinforced rubber moulding, to close the gap B, thereby closing the connection between the two sides of the vacuum chamber. Further motion of the valve C then opens a gap at A and puts the right-hand end of the chamber into communication with the atmosphere so that the pressure rises and sets up a force to move the servo piston to the left. This force causes the rubber reaction disc K to be compressed and the rubber to deform until it fills up the space on its right and makes contact with the left-hand end of the valve C. The pressure set up in the rubber and therefore the forces acting on the valve C and the piston H will increase until the valve is pushed to the right to the equilibrium position where the gaps at A and B are both closed. In this condition the force acting on the piston H and thus on the master cylinder piston will be nearly proportional to the force applied to the valve C by the brake pedal.

When the brake is released the valve B is pushed off its seat by the valve C and the force exerted by the rubber K and the system returns to the 'off' position. The relative sizes of the parts in the figure have been modified in order to make the construction clear.

31.6   Power-operated brakes

These may employ either oil or air as the working medium and in what follows the term *fluid* may often be used since it covers both media and the systems using them have much in common.

A fluid system that has been widely used is the Lockheed design shown in Fig. 31.6. The pump supplies fluid to the cut-out valve and in normal operation when the pump is running and the accumulators are charged up this fluid flows from A to B and thence from C to D through the driver's foot valve and so back to the supply tank. The pressure in the pipe line BC is then only a little above atmospheric and so the pump is running light. When the foot valve is depressed the flow from C to D is restricted and a pressure builds up in the pipe line BC and as this is connected to the actuating cylinders of the front brakes these are applied. The pressure that is set up will be proportional to the force applied by the driver to the brake pedal. If the pump is not running then the front brakes will be operated by the accumulator F which is coupled by the pipe GH to the foot valve and the flow will then be from H to C. The rear brakes are normally operated direct from the accumulator R via the pipe JK and so through the foot valve to L. Again, the pressure set up in the brake-actuating cylinders will be proportional to the force applied by the driver.

The cut-out valve regulates the pressure in the accumulators by inter-rupting the supply when the upper limit is reached and restoring it when the lower limit is reached. In Fig. 31.7 the valve is shown in the position it occupies when the accumulator pressure is above the lower limit and is able to keep the sliding seat P seated on the end Q of the valve QS. The pump is assumed to be running and it will keep the valve S off its seat in the casing and will also press back the sliding member T so that fluid can flow from A to B. As the pressure in the accumulator falls so the valve QS and the sliding seat P (still in contact) will move to the left and when the lower limit for the accumulator pressure is reached the valve S will seat on the casing. The pressure in the space V will then force the sliding seat P away from the valve Q and fluid will flow into the accumulator. The pressure in the pipe line connecting the pump and the space V also acts on the non-return valve of the accumulator F (Fig. 31.6) and so if the accumulator pressure is low it also will be charged up.

The construction of the driver's foot valve is shown in Fig. 31.8. Its operation is as follows: in the position shown there is a passage from C to D and the fluid from the pump via the cut-out valve will flow without any great pressure drop. But when the brake pedal is depressed the valve spool X will be depressed through the inner spring and this will reduce the area for the flow of fluid from C to D and so the pressure in the space C and the reduced part of the valve X will rise and, as explained above, the increased pressure will apply the front brakes. The pressure in the space C is transmitted through the holes (shown dotted) in the lower end of the valve X and will act in the space between X and Y. This pressure will tend to push the valve X upwards and that valve will consequently reach an equilibrium position in which the fluid pressure acting on its bottom end balances the force exerted on its upper end by the inner spring and thus by the brake pedal. Thus the pressure in the brake-actuating cylinders is made proportional to the force applied to the brake pedal. Returning now to the lower spool Y, this has been pushed down a little by the valve X but not enough to open the passage from K to L. However, as the pressure in the space between X and Y increases the valve Y will be pushed further down and the passage from K to L will be opened. Fluid will then flow from the

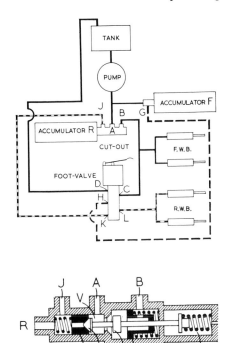

Fig. 31.6 (*left*)

Fig. 31.7 (*below left*)

Fig. 31.8 (*below*)

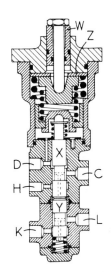

accumulator R (Fig. 31.6) to K and L and thus to the rear-brake-actuating cylinders. The pressure set up in the latter will be transmitted through the holes drilled in the lower part of the valve Y and will act in the space at the bottom of that valve. The valve will thus reach an equilibrium position in which the fluid pressure on the bottom end balances that on the top end and as the latter is proportional to the pedal force so the pressure in the rear brake actuating cylinders is also kept proportional to the pedal force. Clearly, the front brakes are independent of the rear ones and vice versa.

The purpose of the outer spring at the top of the assembly is to limit the normal vehicle deceleration to a value which will not be objectionable to passengers while still permitting greater decelerations in emergencies. The compression of the inner spring is normally limited by the plunger W coming into contact with the plate Z which is held up by the pre-compressed outer spring. But extra force applied by the driver in an emergency will compress the outer spring further and thus increase the force applied to the valve spool X and thus will increase the brake-actuating pressures.

31.7   A dual power brake system

The Clayton Dewandre system shown in Fig. 31.9 represents a modern design in which great importance is attached to the elimination of total failure of the system and all the components are duplicated so that one set is available even if the other fails.

A dual pump B driven from the engine has its two cylinders fed from the separate compartments of the reservoir A and delivers fluid through separate pipe lines to two accumulators CC and thence to a dual foot-operated valve F that is described later on. Low-pressure warning light switches D and filters are included in the pipe lines. A branch pipe line that contains a non-return valve E brings fluid to the hand-brake control valve G which is used to operate the spring-brake unit H; this also is described later on.

The dual foot valve is shown in the diagram Fig. 31.10, only one valve being shown the other being identical. The two valve plungers are depressed by the foot pedal equally between the two plungers. As only a very small motion of the plungers is needed it is possible to actuate one plunger even if there is no pressure acting in the other valve, the tilting of the beam being sufficient for this.

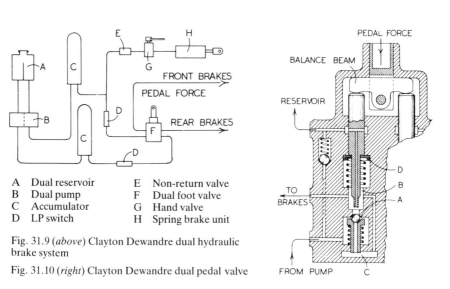

A   Dual reservoir   E   Non-return valve
B   Dual pump   F   Dual foot valve
C   Accumulator   G   Hand valve
D   LP switch   H   Spring brake unit

Fig. 31.9 (*above*) Clayton Dewandre dual hydraulic brake system

Fig. 31.10 (*right*) Clayton Dewandre dual pedal valve

When the brakes are applied the plungers move downwards and their lower ends contact the balls A thus sealing off the brake pipe from the reservoir, the balls are then pushed off their lower seats so that fluid can pass through the pump or accumulator to the brake pipes. The pressure in the pipe lines also acts in the spaces B and upwards on the reaction discs D and so tends to push the plungers upwards. The pressure will increase until the plungers do move upwards to an equilibrium position when the balls A re-seat themselves but still remain in contact with the ends of the plungers and seal off the passage to the reservoir. The plungers are then in equilibrium under the action of the downwards force applied by the brake pedal and the upward force due to the fluid pressure acting on the reaction discs D. The fluid pressure is thus made proportional to the pedal force. When the pedal is released the valve plungers move upwards and open the spaces B and the pipe lines to the reservoir through the holes in the plungers.

31.8 Compressed air systems

Most of the compressed air brake systems in use are power systems although there is no reason why compressed air should not be used in servo systems, in fact most of the units described above for vacuum could be modified so as to work equally well with compressed air.

A complete system suitable for a vehicle having a trailer is shown in Fig. 31.11. The compressor A may be driven off the engine or, in elecrically-propelled vehicles, by a separate electric motor. The compressor charges a reservoir B to a pressure which is regulated by the governor valve G. When this pressure is reached, the unloading valve U lifts the inlet valves of the compressor so that the latter runs 'light'. The air supply to the brake cylinders DD of the tractor vehicle is supplied direct from the reservoir through the brake valve C, which controls the pressure in the brake cylinders to a value proportional to the force exerted on the brake pedal. The brake cylinders D_1D_1 may be supplied in the same way if the dotted pipe line replaces the units R and K.

When the brake cylinders are at some distance from the brake valve, however, they may be operated indirectly from an auxiliary reservoir K situated close to them. In this case, the air from the brake pedal valve operates a relay valve R which passes air from the reservoir K to the brake cylinders D_1D_1 and regulates the pressure to the same value as determined by the brake valve. The reservoir K is charged from the main reservoir when the brake valve is in the 'off' position.

The trailer brakes are operated by air from the trailer reservoir S by means of an emergency relay valve X. The reservoir S is charged direct from the main reservoir on the tractor, through the emergency pipe line Y, and the brake operation is controlled by the air supply coming from the brake pedal valve via the pipe line H through the medium of the valve X.

A filter F is usually fitted, and sometimes an anti-freeze device as well. The latter feeds small amounts of methanol (methyl alcohol) into the air drawn into the compressor and this lowers the freezing point of any moisture that is in the air and prevents the system from frosting up.

Dual reservoirs are used as in vacuum systems, the smaller reservoir being charged up to full pressure very rapidly and before the larger one. The actuating cylinders employed are similar to those used with vacuum brakes but are smaller in size because of the higher pressures that can be used. Pressures of the order of 550–700 kN/m^2 are usual.

Some of the components used with compressed air systems are shown in Figs. 31.12 to 31.14. The reservoir valve that controls the pressure in the reservoir is shown in the first of these. The port A is connected to the reservoir whose pressure thus always acts on the lower side of the diaphragm B. This pressure is also transmitted to the driver's pressure gauge by a pipe connected to the port E. The valve is shown in the position corresponding to the lower limit of the air pressure. The spring has overcome the air pressure acting on the lower side of the diaphragm and has pushed the valve D off its seat, thereby opening the port F to the atmosphere through the dust protecting valve G. The port F is connected to the unloading mechanism of the compressor and with only atmospheric pressure applied to it the compressor will be functioning and passing air to the reservoir so that the pressure in the latter will rise. It will be noted that the hole down the centre of the valve C is closed by the contact with the valve D. The diaphragm is in equilibrium under the action of the spring force downwards and the air pressure upwards. The pressure acts on the area of the diaphragm minus the area of the valve C but plus the area of the hole of the latter. As the reservoir pressure increases the diaphragm will gradually move upwards until when the upper pressure limit is reached the valve D will seat on the casing and contact between it and the end of the valve C will be broken. Immediately this occurs the force tending to push the diaphragm upwards will increase by the amount due to the air pressure acting on the annular area of the valve C and so the diaphragm and valve will move up with a snap action. Air from the reservoir can now pass through the valve C and the port F to the unloading gear and unload the compressor by holding its inlet valve up. As the reservoir pressure

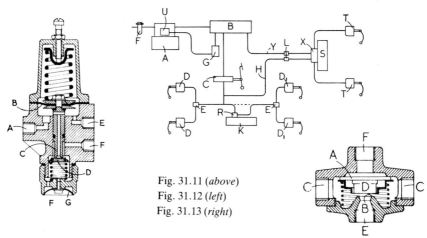

Fig. 31.11 (*above*)
Fig. 31.12 (*left*)
Fig. 31.13 (*right*)

gradually falls the valve C will move downwards until it contacts the valve D, thereby shutting off the air passage from the reservoir to the port F and pushing the valve D off its seat. This opens the port F to atmosphere so that the unloading mechanism will bring the compressor into action again. This action will also be a snap action because when the valve D is pushed off its seat the air pressure will no longer act on the annular area of the valve C and so the upward force on the diaphragm will be suddenly decreased.

A quick-release valve is shown in Fig. 31.13. The port F is connected to the brake pedal valve, the port E to atmosphere, and the ports CC to the brake cylinders. In the 'off' position shown, the brake cylinders are open to the atmosphere through the port E. When pressure air enters the port F, the diaphragm A will be moved downwards and its stem D will meet the seat B and seal off the exhaust port E. Pressure air will pass round the periphery of the diaphragm to the ports CC and the brake cylinders. When the pressure in the latter equals than in the port F, the diaphragm will reseat on the upper seating, but the stem D will remain seated on the seat B. This is the 'brake holding' position of the unit. As soon as the pressure in the port F falls below that in the ports CC, the stem D will lift off the seat

B and the air in the brake cylinders will escape to the atmosphere without having to pass along the pipe from F to the brake pedal valve.

The Bendix emergency relay valve is shown in Fig. 31.14. When the trailer reservoir pressure is low, air will pass from the tractor reservoir along the emergency pipe line (Y of Fig. 31.11) and through the non-return valve C and the space B to the trailer reservoir. The emergency line pressure is also exerted on the top of the diaphragm E and the latter will be depressed and the valve G will open, as shown. Air to the trailer reservoir can thus pass also via the space A and the valve G. If, however, the pressure in the emergency pipe line should fall below that in the trailer reservoir, the valves C and G will close and the trailer reservoir pressure will be maintained. The pressure below the diaphragm D will keep the valve N off its seat and the diaphragm itself in contact with the face X so

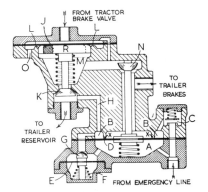

Fig. 31.14 (*left*)
Fig. 31.15 (*below*)

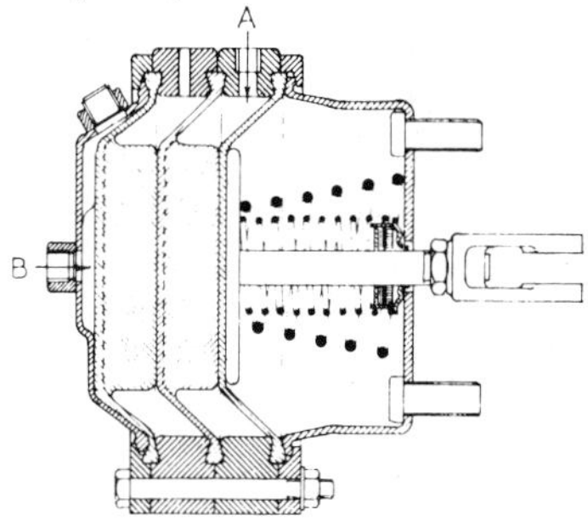

that air from the trailer reservoir can reach the trailer brake cylinders only via the valve K.

In the ordinary way the brakes will be applied by the admission of pressure air from the brake pedal valve to the upper side of the diaphragm J. This will seat the diaphragm on to the seating L and will seal off the brake cylinders and the space M from the exhaust port O. The piston R will also be depressed, and the valve K will be unseated so that air from the trailer reservoir can pass to the trailer brake cylinders. The pressure set up in the latter will be such that the force exerted on the underside of the diaphragm J just balances the force applied to the top side, and so the trailer brake pressure will be equal to the pressure set up in the service pipe by the brake pedal valve, and will be proportional to the force exerted on the brake pedal.

If the trailer is disconnected or breaks away from the tractor, the pressure in the emergency pipe line will fall to atmospheric and the trailer reservoir pressure in the space B will depress the diaphragm D and seat the valve N. Air will then pass from the trailer reservoir via the space B and round the stem of the valve N to the trailer brake cylinders, and the pressure set up in these will be approximately equal to the trailer reservoir pressure, so that a full application of the trailer brakes will result.

Power operation is especially suitable when a large number of brakes have to be operated, as, for example, on eight-wheeled vehicles and when trailers are used, because although the driver's valve proportions the intensity of the braking to the force exerted by the driver, this latter force does not increase with an increase in the number of brakes operated as it would do in a mechanically-operated system. The connection between a tractor and trailer is simpler with air operation, relative movement between the two being allowed for by the use of a flexible hose connection and having no effect on the brake operation, a condition that is not easily obtained with mechanical linkages. The trailer brakes can also be arranged to come on automatically should the trailer break away from the tractor.

31.9   Actuating cylinders for air brakes

Air pressure brakes are usually actuated by diaphragm cylinders in which the diaphragm acts as a piston but has the advantage that no sliding air-tight joints are necessary. To enable a single cylinder to be used for both foot-pedal and hand-lever operation Clayton Dewandre introduced the triple-diaphragm cylinder shown in Fig. 31.15. When the brake pedal is depressed air is admitted to the space A while operation of the hand-brake admits air to the space B. The space between A and B is open to atmosphere. For both forms of braking the force applied to the brakes will be regulated by a brake valve so that it is proportional to the force exerted by the driver. Although air pressure is used for the application of the hand brake the brake will be held on by the usual ratchet even if the air pressure should fall after the brakes have been applied.

31.10   Spring brake units and locks

In road vehicles the foot brakes are used chiefly for stopping the vehicle and for controlling its speed on gradients and the hand brake is used almost solely for parking purposes or in conditions where the driver does not have a foot free to operate the foot brake, for example when starting on a gradient.

The two systems are made independent to a considerable extent in order to meet legal requirements and no great difficulty arises in designing satisfactory systems except in very heavy vehicles and in tractor-trailer combinations. The requirements of the foot brake can be met even in heavy vehicles by using servo assistance or power operation but these do not suffice for parking brakes that must often be left on for long periods. To meet these demands springs have been used to apply the brakes and power to release them and this is done in a *spring brake unit*, which may be placed at the driver's end of an ordinary mechanical linkage as in the system shown in Fig. 31.9, or one may be used at each brake.

The system comprises a spring that is sufficiently powerful to apply the brakes fully but which is normally held so as to be inoperative by means of a piston in a cylinder to which air or fluid under pressure is admitted. The construction is shown in Fig. 31.16. Fluid from the hand-brake control valve is passed to the port F so as to hold the piston in the position shown, the spring E being then inoperative. To apply the hand brake, the control valve is moved so as to release the pressure in the cylinder and the spring then applies the brakes. As the fluid pressure can be regulated by the control valve the brake can be applied by the spring for normal applications if required. However, a separate diaphragm cylinder C is incorpo-

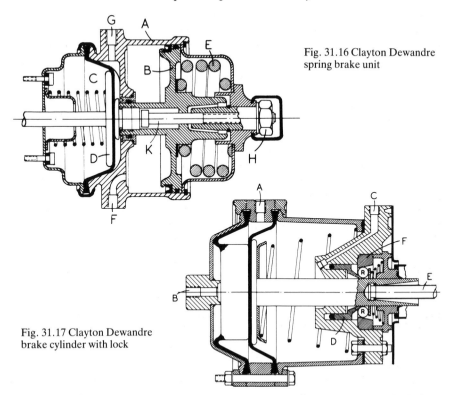

Fig. 31.16 Clayton Dewandre spring brake unit

Fig. 31.17 Clayton Dewandre brake cylinder with lock

rated and this provides for the service applications, fluid or air being admitted through the port G by the pedal valve so as to operate the piston D. To enable the unit to be dismantled when required a draw bolt K and nut H are provided to hold the spring in compression.

An alternative to the use of a spring unit is to employ a mechanical lock to hold the brakes on after they have been applied by air pressure. This is generally used when direct-acting diaphragm chambers are situated close to, or actually mounted on the back plates of, the brakes. An example is shown in Fig. 31.17.

The service brake application is obtained by admitting air to the port A from the pedal valve and the parking application by admitting air through the port B and this can, if required, be used to supplement the foot brake. To hold the parking brake on, even when the air pressure is released, locking rollers R are provided; these are normally held so as to be inoperative by the piston D to which air is admitted through the port C but to lock the brakes this pressure is released and then the spring pressing on the rollers will force them into the tapered bore of the collar F and they will jam so as to prevent the piston from moving back. To release the brake, air must first be admitted to the port B so as to relieve the pressure on the locking rollers and then these can be moved to the free position by admitting air to port C; this sequence may be provided automatically by the control valve and it prevents the brakes from being released inadvertently because after the lock has been released the parking brake has to be released in the normal way.

31.11   Brake-limiting device and anti-slide systems

When a wheel is running freely and is neither driving nor braking the vehicle, there will be almost no circumferential slip between its tyre and the road. However, if a brake is applied with a gradually increasing intensity, the slip will increase gradually at first but much more rapidly as the braking force between the wheel and the road approaches the value at which the wheel will lock and slide along the road surface instead of rolling. During the last phase of this action the angular deceleration of the wheel will be considerably greater than that which would correspond to the linear deceleration of the vehicle with no wheel slip occurring.

Now, it is a well-established fact that a sliding tyre exerts appreciably smaller braking forces than one that rolls, even if the slip is quite large. Thus, to obtain the shortest stopping distance, it is best to avoid sliding the wheels. However, even very skilled drivers cannot manipulate the brakes so as to obtain the best results at all times and particularly in emergencies. Designers have therefore been trying for a long time to devise schemes to enable optimum results to be obtained even by unskilled drivers. The difficulties were increased when the general design of cars resulted in more than 50% of the static weight being carried on the front wheels and when improved brakes enabled greater decelerations to be obtained thereby causing even more of the load to be transferred to the front wheels and increasing the likelihood that the rear wheels would slide. Hence, the earliest devices were designed to limit the application force applied to the rear-wheel brakes while allowing unrestricted forces on the front ones.

A device of this kind, designed by Lockheed (Automotive Products), is shown in Fig. 31.18. It consists of a body A that is bored to take the smaller end of a plunger B whose larger end is provided with a cup seal C and which is normally held in the position shown by the spring D. The body is closed by a screwed plug into which the pipe from the master cylinder fits, while two side bores take the pipes to the rear brake operating cylinders. The left-hand face of the plunger has radial grooves formed in it and so there is a passage for free flow of fluid from the master cylinder to the brake cylinders. But when the fluid pressure rises to the designed value, depending on the areas of the ends of the plungers and the strength of the spring, the force on the plunger will move it to the right and cause the seal C to seat on the face E and close the passage to the rear brake cylinders. The usefulness of such devices, however, is lessened when the load carried by the rear wheels is liable to vary considerably as it can do, particularly in commercial vehicles, because if the setting is right for light loads it will be unduly restrictive for heavy loads.

To overcome this difficulty, devices sensitive to the load carried by the axle whose brakes are concerned were developed. They can be used with either hydraulic or air operation and consist essentially of a pressure regulating device that is interposed in the pipe line to the brakes and whose setting is varied by a mechanical linkage that couples it to the axle, the valve being of course carried on the frame. Such a device, made by Clayton Dewandre, is shown in Fig. 31.19. It regulates the pressure set up in the brake pipe B in relation to the pressure at the inlet A and in accordance with the position of the roller D which is controlled by the distance

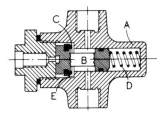

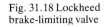

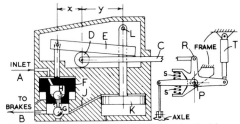

Fig. 31.18 Lockheed brake-limiting valve

Fig. 31.19 Clayton Dewandre Mk I brake-limiting system

between the axle of the vehicle and the frame. The pressure of the air at the inlet is itself regulated by the brake pedal valve so as to be proportional to the force exerted by the driver. In action, the air entering at A depresses the piston F so that the end E of the dumbell GH contacts its seating and closes the exhaust port and the end H is moved off its seating so that air can pass to the brakes. The pressure that builds up in the brake pipe also acts via the passage J on the piston K and (through the pin L which is now in contact with the beam E because of the downward movement of the piston F) applies a force to the beam and pulls the piston F upwards. An equilibrium position is reached when the valve H contacts its seating but the valve G still remains in contact. The forces at the ends of the beam are then in the ratio of the lever arms x,y and the pressures at the ports A and B are then in a ratio that is determined by the ratio $x:y$ modified by the relation between the areas of the two pistons. The ratio between the inlet pressure and the brake pressure can thus be modified by moving the roller D and this is done by any sustained motion of the axle relative to the frame by means of a linkage whose principle is shown by the diagram to the right. Rapid movements of the axle such as are due to road irregularities are accommodated by the springs S and the bell-crank member R is held virtually stationary by the damper T, but any sustained movement of the axle will move the bell-crank and thus alter the position of the roller D.

In the system described above, the magnitude of the forces acting on the roller fulcrum prevents any alteration of the pressure ratio setting during the actual brake actuation. This drawback is obviated in another Clayton Dewandre system shown in Fig. 31.20. In addition to the form shown, the device is made in two simplified forms but all three regulate the ratio between the pressure applied to the brake actuating cylinders and the pressure of the air coming from the brake pedal valve.

In the simplest form, known as the *direct type*, all the components above the line ZZ are omitted and replaced by a simple cover and the double piston T_1T_2 is replaced by a simple one-piece piston. The port A is connected to the brake pedal valve and, via the passage P and the dotted opening shown, air reaches the top of the piston T. The force thereby applied to that piston forces it down against the springs thereby closing the gap C, through which the brake actuating cylinders have been open to the atmosphere and then opening the valve D so that air from the port A can pass to the brakes. The pressure that builds up in the port B also acts on the piston F via the passage E. The forces acting on the pistons T and F are made to balance each other by means of the struts S and G which are pivoted together, a ball bearing H being mounted on the pivot pin. This ball bearing is in contact with a ramp R which is pivoted in the casing on an axis that coincides approximately with the axis of the ball bearing. The inclination of the ramp is controlled by the 'height' of the suspension through a linkage similar in principle to the one described earlier. When the pressure on the piston F reaches an appropriate value the ball bearing H moves slghtly up the ramp and the strut moves up to allow the valve D to seat so that the air from the brake valve is cut off and the system reaches an equilibrium position. The ratio between the pressures at A and B then depends on the areas of the pistons T and F and the angle at which the ramp is placed by the axle. When the brake pedal is released, the force on the piston T falls to zero and the springs open the gap at C, thus releasing the air pressure from the brake cylinders.

In the second form, known as the *relay type*, the port A is connected to a reservoir and the brake pedal to a port in the cover above the piston T. When the brake pedal is depressed air passes to the top of the piston T and the action proceeds as before except that the air to the brake cylinders comes from the reservoir via the port A instead of through the brake pedal valve.

In the third form, the *relay-emergency type*, shown in Fig. 31.20, the brake pedal valve is coupled to the port J and an emergency pipe line to the port K. Pressure is normally maintained in the emergency pipe line and this holds the valve L to the right, allowing the valve M to seat on the shoulder of the body member and leaving a gap between that valve and the end of the valve L. Thus, when the brake pedal valve is depressed, air passes via port J through the hole in the valve L and through the passage N_2 to the top of the piston assembly T_1 T_2 and the action proceeds as in the second type, the air passing from the reservoir conected to port A to the brakes via port B. The reservoir can be charged via the emergency pipe line air which can

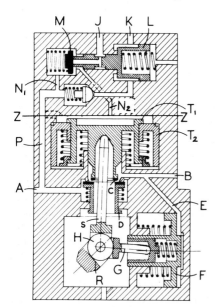

Fig. 31.20 Clayton Dewandre Mk II brake-limiting system

overcome the non-return valve so that air passes to the reservoir via the passage P. Both the relay and the relay-emergency types have double piston assemblies $T_1 T_2$ as shown and the outer piston moves down to pre-load the inner one; this provides a smoother action when the brakes are applied.

If, for any reason, the pressure in the emergency pipe line falls to a low value the valve L will be moved to the left and air from the reservoir will pass via the passage P, N_1 and N_2 to the top of the pistons to give a full application of the brakes.

But even these devices cannot take into account the changes in road conditions that occur due to icy or greasy surfaces and they can be set only for average conditions; the difficulties can, however, be almost completely overcome in the anti-lock or anti-wheel-slide systems now coming into use. The first of such systems was the Dunlop-Maxaret (Section 31.13) but present-day systems all employ the same basic principle and this will now be considered.

31.12 Basic principle of anti-lock systems

For the sake of simplicity a single wheel will be assumed in the following description.

A means of measuring the rotational deceleration of the wheel is provided and this deceleration is used to control the brake actuation. As explained above, when the wheel is slipping only to a small extent, the deceleration will be low in comparison with the value appertaining to the approach of sliding and so, when the deceleration exceeds a certain value, the control releases the brake, the deceleration of which will then fall to a low value and so the brakes will be re-applied. This release and re-application of the brakes must take place in an extremely short time if the system is to work satisfactorily and, in practice, the cycle will occur up to as high as 15 times per second.

In the early systems the wheel deceleration was measured by purely mechanical means but in present-day systems electronic circuits are used because they give much quicker responses and can be controlled more easily. These circuits are beyond the scope of this book and only an outline of their action can be attempted.

The deceleration sensor usually consists of a toothed disc attached to the hub of the wheel, and a pick-up placed near to the periphery of the disc. The pick-up is essentially a horseshoe magnet with a winding, and the projections of the disc act as a succession of keepers which bridge the poles of the magnet thus momentarily causing an increase in the magnetic flux through the winding and setting up a current in it. The frequency of this current will depend on the speed of the disc and the rate at which that frequency changes will be proportional to the deceleration of the disc. This rate can be measured relatively simply electronically and can then be used to supply a signal for the control of the brakes. The remainder of the system therefore consists of valves actuated by the signal and which control the actuation of the brakes.

A sensor may be provided for each wheel to be controlled but sometimes it is practicable to control the wheels in groups. A common system is to have a sensor for each of the front wheels and a single sensor with its disc on the propeller shaft for the two rear wheels together. It will be appreciated that the incorporation of these anti-lock systems is facilitated by the use of power operated brakes, also that they are somewhat expensive and are used therefore only on the more expensive cars and on certain classes of commercial vehicle.

31.13   Dunlop-Maxaret system

The Dunlop-Maxaret system was developed for application to the driving wheels of the tractor unit of articulated vehicles in order to prevent the vehicles from jack-knifing. The system has been most successful in doing this.

The general lay-out of the system is shown in Fig. 31.21 and details of the valves appear in Fig. 31.22. When there is no incipient wheel slide there will be no signal current from the electronic module to the control valve and so the port A (Fig. 31.22 (a)) will be open to atmosphere through the gap at C and there will be atmospheric pressure on the right-hand sides of the brake actuator diaphragms. Hence, when the brake pedal is depressed,

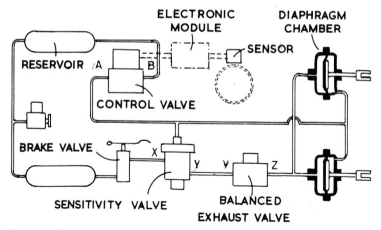

Fig. 31.21 Dunlop-Maxaret anti-slide system

air will pass freely from the service (lower) reservoir to the port Y of the balanced exhaust valve, Fig. 31.22 (b). This pressure will deflect the outer portion of the lower diaphragm against the force of the spring so that air will pass to the port Z and thence to the left-hand sides of the brake actuator diaphragms, thereby applying the brakes. Under poor road conditions depression of the brake pedal will again pass air to the brake actuators to apply the brakes but if wheel slide becomes imminent the electric modules will pass current to the solenoid of the control valve, the gap C will be closed and air will pass from the anti-skid (upper) reservoir to the right-hand side of the brake actuator diaphragms and release the brakes.

The pressure air from the control valve will also depress the piston assembly of the sensitivity valve, Fig. 31.22 (c), and this will restrict the

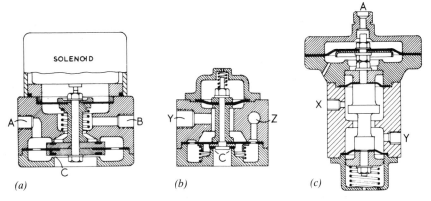

Fig. 31.22 Dunlop-Maxaret anti-slide system valves

passage of air from the brake pedal valve to the brakes. The pressure that acts on the left-hand side of the brake actuator diaphragms also acts on the underside of the balanced exhaust valve and if it exceeds the pressure acting on the upperside from the port Y the central portion of the diaphragm will be lifted so as to open the port Z to the atmosphere via the gap opened at C. Thus the valve equalises the pressures at Y and Z and the brake actuating pressure will at all times be equal to the pressure determined by the brake pedal valve.

As soon as the anti-skid pressure on the right-hand side of the brake actuators is released by the cessation of the signal from the electronic module the brakes will be re-applied. This action will be repeated with a frequency of several cycles per second as long as the wheel-slide condition continues.

31.14 Lucas-Girling WSP system

The general lay-out of the Lucas-Girling system, as applied (for the sake of simplicity) to a single wheel is shown in Fig. 31.23. It is designed for use with brakes employing fluid application. Under normal conditions the brake is applied by the master cylinder in the usual way because the valve A of the actuator unit of the system is open as shown.

The valve is held open by its spring and by fluid pressure on the left-hand side of its piston, this pressure being maintained at a constant value by a pump that is driven by the engine of the vehicle. When a signal is passed by the electronic module to the solenoid of the control valve, oil from the pump will pass to the right-hand side of the actuator piston and as the effective area of this side is greater than that of the left-hand side the piston will move to the left to close the valve. Because of the decrease in the volume of the stem of the valve that projects into the chamber B, the pressure in the brake cylinder will drop and the brake will be released. When the signal to the control valve ceases the right-hand side of the actuator piston will again be opened to the atmosphere in the reservoir and the valve will open. The action will be repeated with a frequency up to some 15 Hz, this frequency being modified to some extent by auxiliary

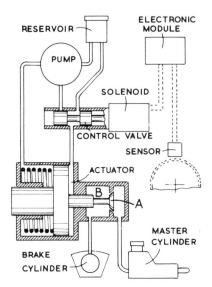

Fig. 31.23 Lucas-Girling WSP system

circuits in the electronic module. When several wheels are to be controlled each must have its sensor, electronic module circuit, control valve and actuator but the pump will be common to all.

31.15 Lucas-Girling Skidchek GX

Following some years' experience with their original Skidchek system for heavy commercial vehicles, Lucas-Girling introduced the GX version. This was virtually a redesign based on an analysis in detail of the performance of the original system in service. The fundamental considerations, they found, were as follows.

To minimise the delay between the driver's observing a need to brake and the actual application, a rapid rise in air pressure is essential. It is this that is liable to cause a skid, because of the tendency for the pressure to overshoot the target pressure level and apply the brakes too hard. Unfortunately, however, it is not practicable to reduce the rate of pressure rise for the initial application without unacceptably increasing the stopping distance, as measured from the instant the driver depresses the foot valve.

The only possibility for reduction of this tendency to overshoot, therefore, is early detection of wheel-lock. One requirement is to have a sensor on each wheel and to trigger the air pressure release sequence following detection of incipient wheel-lock on the slowest wheel of the pair on an axle, or of two pairs on a bogie. Lucas-Girling considered that to economise by using only one sensor and placing it on the propeller shaft could increase the reaction time. This is because vibrations in the drive-line can generate spurious signals and the electronic detection system then has to wait a few milliseconds to establish whether these signals are real before it can initiate an anti-lock sequence. Obviously, earlier detection of incipient wheel-lock might also be made by designing the electronic control system to respond to factors other than just wheel acceleration – for instance, to rate of change of acceleration, possibly in relation to wheel and vehicle speeds.

Once the initial brake application has been completed and the anti-lock cycles begin, however, it is possible to modify the rate of pressure build-up for each successive re-application. This is done in the GX system by the use of a modified relay valve, which memorises the pressure at which the wheels previously locked. The new valve, called the *memory-controlled relay* (MCR) valve, is illustrated in Fig. 31.24. It is similar to a conventional relay valve except that a solenoid, a latch valve and the memory chamber have been added.

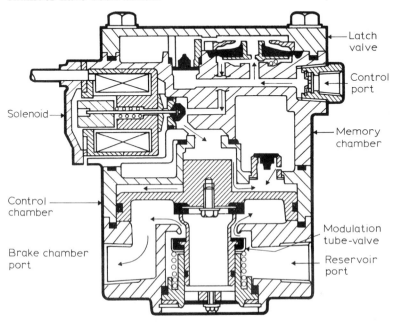

Fig. 31.24 MCR valve operation for rapid re-application of brakes

When the driver depresses the brake pedal, air from the foot valve enters at the control port. The solenoid is not energised, so this air lifts the latch valve and flows rapidly down, past the solenoid valve – seated on its exhaust port – into the control chamber, pushing the control piston down. This causes the piston to seat on the end of the tube below, which is the exhaust port for the brake application system, and to push this tube downwards against its return spring. The latter action opens the modulation tube-valve, by lowering it from its seating, thus allowing air to flow rapidly from the reservoir port, past this valve to the brakes.

When the electronic control unit detects a wheel lock, it energises the solenoid, lifting the solenoid valve off its exhaust seat and closing it on to the control pressure supply port. This allows the pressure in the control chamber to exhaust past the solenoid to atmosphere, so the control piston rises again, closing the modulation tube-valve and allowing the pressure in the brake line to exhaust rapidly to atmosphere through that tube-valve.

In the meantime, while the brakes were on, two things have happened: first, air from the control port has leaked through the restricted orifice in the centre of the latch valve and equalised the pressure above and below it;

secondly, the non-return valve in the base of the memory chamber has lifted, so the pressure in that chamber is that of the control system, as dictated by the force applied by the driver to his pedal.

Then, when the solenoid was energised and the pressure below the solenoid valve dropped to atmospheric, the valve in the base of the memory chamber dropped on to its seat, so the pressure in that chamber could fall only at the slow rate dictated by the size of the orifice on the right, just below that seat. Consequently, when – in response to a signal from the sensor indicating that the road wheel has regained its appropriate operating speed – the electronic control de-energises the solenoid, the pressure remaining in the memory chamber is dependent on both the original pressure that initiated the wheel lock and the time that the wheel has taken to recover to its normal speed. the latter time of course is a function of the grip – or lack of it – of the wheel on the road surface.

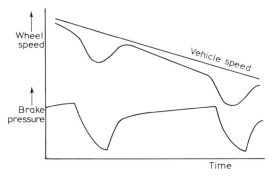

Fig. 31.25 GX anti-lock cycles

This de-energisation of the solenoid – closing its exhaust valve and opening the control valve supply port – releases the control pressure into the control chamber. The resultant drop in control pressure pulls the latch valve down on to its seat, leaving only a small passage open past the seat to the control chamber. Despite the small size of this passage, however, the flow is still enough to move the control piston rapidly downwards, so that the rate of application of the brakes is still high. This rapid action is attributable to the fact that the volume of the control chamber is very small when the piston is in its uppermost position.

However, as the control pressure rises above the residual pressure in the memory chamber, the valve in the base of this chamber opens, suddenly adding its volume to that of the control chamber, with the result that the rate of pressure rise equally suddenly falls, remaining low for the remainder of the brake re-application cycle. This reduces the tendency for the brake re-application pressure to overshoot its target value. At the same time, the point at which the fall in rate of pressure rise starts – dependent on the residual pressure in the memory chamber – is such that the target pressure for brake re-application is related to the maximum pressure in the preceding cycle and, after the initial cycle, quickly adjusts to a value appropriate to the coefficient of friction in the tyre/road contact patch. Because of the reduced rate of rise to the target pressure and the absence of overshoot, the braking force remains longer at the optimum level, as indicated in Fig. 31.25, the stopping distance is reduced, and the whole sequence of operations is much smoother, thus avoiding the excitation of vibrations of either the cab or the whole vehicle.

In Fig. 31.26, the lower sine curve represents a typical characteristic of a simple commercial vehicle anti-lock system, for comparison with that of Skidchek GX, as depicted in Fig. 31.25. The upper sine curve in Fig. 31.26 is an indication of what can be achieved with an anti-skid system for a car. The difference between the two is attributable to the faster reaction time of a small hydraulic brake control system of the car, as compared with that of a much larger pneumatic system, and the relatively small rotational inertia of car wheels. A heavy commercial vehicle wheel takes a much longer time to spin up to normal speed after it has locked, especially on a very slippery surface. Obviously, under maximum braking conditions, a small degree of wheel-slip is inevitable, the optimum being the range between the two dotted lines in Fig. 31.26.

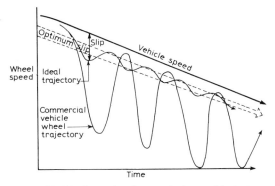

Fig. 31.26 Wheel-speed trajectory during anti-lock stop

A continuously-operating electronic monitoring unit, working in conjunction with the electronic control, causes the system to revert to normal braking, without anti-lock, and a warning lamp to be illuminated, in the following circumstances –

(1) Energisation of the solenoid for longer than 3 sec.
(2) Solenoid open circuit.
(3) Inadequate output from the sensor.
(4) Regularly missing sensor pulses – due, perhaps, to damage to the sensor ring.
(5) Low supply voltage.

Should the fault clear during the journey, anti-lock is reinstated and the warning lamp extinguished. Similarly, a spurious wheel-lock signal caused by one wheel ceasing to spin following the application of excessive drive torque is cancelled as soon as rotation of both wheels is synchronised.

Chapter 32

Front axle and steering mechanism

Generally, the function of the steering system is thought of simply as that of providing a means whereby the driver can place his vehicle as accurately as practicable where he wants it to be on the road, for selection of the course he wants to steer round corners, and so that he can avoid other road users and obstructions. It must also, however, keep the vehicle stably on course regardless of irregularities in the surface over which the vehicle is travelling.

For the achievement of these basic aims, the first requirement is that, when the vehicle is travelling very slowly, all the wheels shall roll truly, that is, without any lateral slip. In Fig. 32.1, motion of the wheel along YY is pure rolling, along XX it is wholly slip. Motion along any other axis, ZZ for example, will have both rolling and slip components.

Since for all the wheels on a vehicle to roll truly they must all move in the same direction perpendicular to their axes XX, these axes must all intersect at a common point. If the vehicle is on a straight course, this point will be at infinity, in other words the axes will be parallel. On the other hand, if the vehicle is turning a corner, this point will always be the centre about which the vehicle as a whole is turning, and the tighter the turn the closer it will be to the vehicle.

Unless both the front and rear wheels are to be steered – impracticable on grounds of complexity, except in special circumstances, such as on vehicles having more than eight wheels, in which it may be virtually inescapable – the common centre must lie somewhere along the lines of the axis produced of the fixed rear axle. As can be seen from Fig. 32.2, this means that, when the front wheels are steered, their axes must be turned through different angles so that the point O of their intersection is always on that axis produced. With a beam axle this can be done by pivoting the whole axle assembly about a vertical axis midway between its ends. However, such an arrangement is impracticable for any but very slow vehicles.

Generally, the wheels are carried on stub axles, A and B in Fig. 32.2. Except with independent suspension, these stub axles are pivoted on the

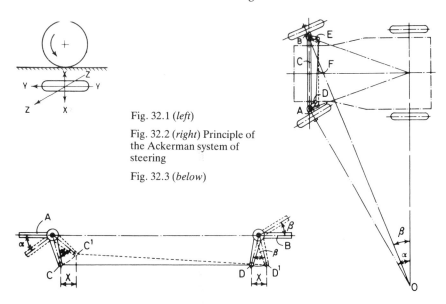

Fig. 32.1 (*left*)

Fig. 32.2 (*right*) Principle of
the Ackerman system of
steering

Fig. 32.3 (*below*)

ends of the axle beam C which, since it is connected by the road springs to
the chassis frame, remains in effect parallel to the rear axle, as viewed in
plan. With independent suspension, the principle remains the same, even
though the mechanism is different in detail. The arms D and E together
with their associated stub axles form what amounts to bell crank levers
pivoted on the kingpins and are used for coupling the two wheels so that
they move together when they are steered. These arms are termed the
track arms and are interconnected by the *track rod*. The actual steering is
usually effected by a connecting link, called a *drag link*, between the
steering gear and either what is termed the *steering arm* on the adjacent
stub axle assembly or, in some instances, part of the track rod system.

32.1 Ackerman linkage

From the illustration it can be seen that there is a difference between the
angles α and β through which the wheels on the inside and outside
respectively of the curve have to be turned. In practice, this difference is
obtained by setting the arms D and E at angles such that, in the straight
ahead position, shown dotted, lines drawn through the centres of the two
pivots on each intersect near the centre of the rear axle. The exact position
of this intersection point depends on the relationship between the wheelbase and track, and other factors.

From Fig. 32.3 can be seen how the stub axles are steered differentially
by this linkage, the full lines depicting the straight ahead and the dotted
lines a steered condition. In the latter, the stub axle B has turned through
an angle β and the end D of its track arm has moved to D′, a distance *x*
parallel to the axle beam. Neglecting the slight angle of inclination of the
track rod, it follows that the end C of the other track arm must move the
same distance *x* parallel to the axle beam. This, however, entails movement of the arm C through a greater angle than D, because the latter is

swinging across bottom dead centre, as viewed in plan, while the former is moving further from its corresponding lowest point. Although, for practical reasons, these arms may have to be curved, perhaps to clear some other part of the wheel or brake assembly, the effective arm remains that of a straight line joining the centres of the kingpin and the pivot at the opposite end.

The illustrations show the track rod behind the axle, but sometimes it is in front, again with suitably inclined arms. An advantage of placing it to the rear is the protection afforded to it by the axle beam, but it is then loaded in compression and therefore must be of stiffer construction. On the other hand, when it is in front, difficulty is generally experienced in providing clearance between its ball joints and the wheels.

With Ackerman steering, the wheels roll truly in only three positions – straight ahead, or when turned through a specifically chosen angle to the right and left. Even in the last two positions, true rolling occurs only at low speeds. At all other angles, the axes of the front wheels do not intersect on that of the rear wheels, while at the higher speeds the slip angles of the front and rear tyres usually differ and certainly those of the tyres on the outside will always differ from those on the inside of the curve. In all instances, the slip angle on both the front and rear wheels has the effect of turning their effective axes forwards.

Linkages giving virtually perfect static steering geometry on all locks have been devised, they they have been complex and in practice have not proved satisfactory because they cannot take into account the variations in slip angle. The Ackerman principle, based on the best practicable compromise – usually slip angles are assumed to be equal on all four wheels – is satisfactory in practice, probably because flexing of the tyres accommodates the errors.

32.2   Multi-wheel vehicles

With six-wheel vehicles, perfect steering geometry is unobtainable because the two rear axles always remain parallel. An assumption is made, therefore, that the vehicle turns about a centre on an axis midway between and parallel to those of the two rear axles, and the steering linkage for the front axle is laid out on this basis. There will of course be some tyre scrub on both rear axles, but this is accommodated by the lateral flexibility of these tyres. Even so, the two back axles are always placed as close together as practicable within the limitations imposed by legal requirements and the size of tyres needed to support the rear end of the vehicle in the fully laden condition.

On eight-wheel vehicles, all four front wheels must be steered. A similar requirement arises on certain special-purpose six-wheel vehicles having a preponderance of weight at the front, and which therefore may have only a single axle at the rear. Both cases are represented in Fig. 32.4. On the six-wheel vehicle, each front axle has an Ackerman linkage, that for the leading axle designed for wheelbase W_2, and that for the second axle for wheelbase W_1. For the eight-wheel vehicle, the two wheelbases would be extended to midway between the two rear axles. All four front wheels have to be steered through different angles α, β, γ and δ. These differences are

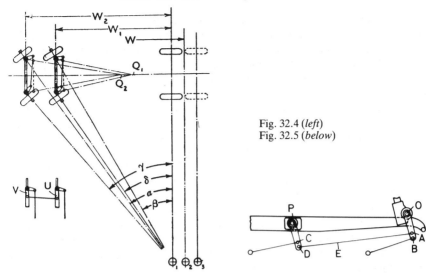

Fig. 32.4 (*left*)
Fig. 32.5 (*below*)

taken care of partly by the Ackerman linkage, there being several ways of catering also for those between the first and second axles. One is illustrated in the scrap view, in Fig. 32.4. Here, the two steering arms, V and U, on the foremost and second axles respectively are interconnected by a link. The arm U on the first is slightly longer than that at V, on the second axle, as measured between the axes of their kingpins and the pins connecting them to the link, so the leading axle is steered through the greater angle. One of these two arms is actuated in the usual way by a drag link from the drop arm on the steering box. Comments on the layout of the drag link are given in Section 33.12.

A more common method of interlinking two steered axles is illustrated in Fig. 32.5. Two drop arms OB and PD are used, one for each axle, the former being splined on to the spindle of the steering box and the latter pivoted on a bracket on the chassis frame. The arm PD is actuated by a link E connecting its end D to A on OB. Links are taken from B and C to the steering arms on the first and second axles respectively. Since PC is shorter than OB and, furthermore, OA is shorter than PD, the second axle is always moved through a smaller angle than the leading one.

32.3 Steering linkages for independent suspension

The Ackerman linkage already described is occasionally used with independent suspension, especially the sliding, or pillar, type. A system suitable for the single or double leading or trailing link type suspension is illustrated in Fig. 32.6. Its Ackerman linkage comprises two bell cranks AX and BY interconnected by the track rod C and pivoted on brackets on the vehicle structure. Two drag links G and H connect the ends of the bell cranks to the steering arms E and F, on the stub axles.

Ball joints must be used at E, F, X and Y. When the wheels are steered straight ahead, the centres X and Y must lie on the axes about which the stub axle assemblies oscillate as the suspension deflects. Then the suspension motion will not have any steering effect.

With single or double transverse link suspension systems, a divided track rod is necessary, the inner end of each part of which lies on the axis about which the adjacent stub axle assembly oscillates as the suspension rises and falls. Such a system is illustrated in Fig. 32.7, where A and B are the stub axle assemblies and OEG is a triangular link, or an acute angle bell-crank lever, pivoted at O on the vehicle structure, or frame. Links EF and GH are the two parts of the divided track rod.

Fig. 32.6 (*left*)
Fig. 32.7 (*below*)

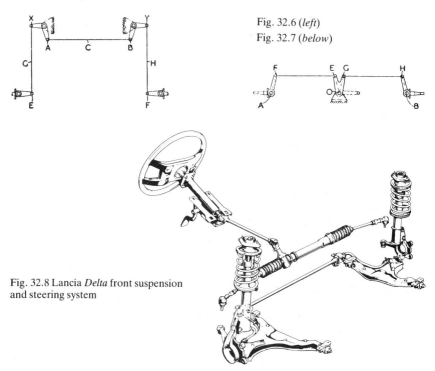

Fig. 32.8 Lancia *Delta* front suspension and steering system

Clearly the links OE, EF, FA constitute an Ackerman system for the offside wheel, and OG, GH, HB form a similar system for the nearside wheel. The arm shown dotted on the triangular link is connected by a rod to the steering gear drop arm, which is arranged so that it oscillates in a horizontal plane. Obviously, if the triangular lever cannot be accommodated as illustrated, its pivot O can be moved to the other side of the track rod, and the two pieces of the track rod do not necessarily have to be in line. Where a rack-and-pinion steering gear is used, the triangular link can be omitted and the joints E and G are either on the ends of the rack, as in Fig. 32.8, or linked separately to only one end of it.

32.4   Centre-point steering

In Fig. 32.9 it will be noticed that the axis about which the stub axle (with its road wheel) turns when steering is effected intersects the ground at the point O, while the road wheel makes contact with the ground at the point P. Now, when a car is travelling along a road there is a force acting between the front wheels and the road in a direction opposite to that of the motion. On a good road this force may be small, but on a bad road, and when the front wheels are braked hard, it may be considerable. This force acts perpendicular to the line OP (in plan) and hence has a moment, about the axis XX, which tends to turn the stub axle about its pivot pin. This tendency has, of course, to be resisted. Now, the stub axle on the other side tends to turn in the opposite direction, and since the two stub axles are connected together by the track rod the two tendencies towards rotation will, if they are equal, neutralise each other, and the only result wil be a stress in the track arms and the track rod. If, however, the two tendencies are not equal, the difference between them has to be resisted by the friction in the steering mechanism or by the driver.

In order to reduce to the minimum the moment of the force tending to turn the stub axles the point P is brought as close to the point O as is conveniently possible, and very often the points are made to coincide. When such coincidence is obtained the construction is said to give centre-point steering, and it can be obtained or approximated to in three ways –

(1) Keeping the swivel pin axes vertical the wheels can be inclined so as to bring the point P nearer to the point O.
(2) Both the wheels and the swivel pins can be inclined.
(3) A construction can be adopted that enables the swivel pin to be situated in the plane of the wheel.

Method (3) is adopted by a few makers and method (2) by a much larger number, but method (1) is now used only very rarely. Centre-point steering is, however, only approximated to and not actually obtained on most cars. It should be mentioned that designers are by no means in agreement as to whether true centre-point steering is desirable, although a fairly close approximation to it is admitted to be desirable when the front wheels are braked.

Inclination of the wheels is generally referred to as *camber* and the angle between the plane of the wheel and the vertical is called the *camber angle*.

There are one or two points which should perhaps be mentioned in connection with the use of inclined swivel pins. Firstly, the connections between the track arms and the track rod can no longer be simple pivots, but must be ball and socket joints because, as will be seen from Fig. 32.9, when the stub axles are turned the end of one track arm moves up and the

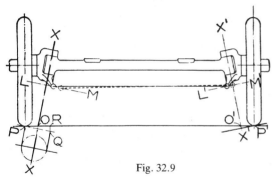

Fig. 32.9

end of the other one down, so that the track rod assumes an angular position in a vertical plane as well as in the horizontal plane. Secondly, unless true centre-point steering is obtained the front of the vehicle will have to be lifted slightly when steering is effected. This can be seen from the same figure. The point of contact of the wheel with the ground moves in a circle whose plane is perpendicular to the swivel pin axis. This plane is seen in the figure as the line PQ. If the stub axle were turned through half a turn (which, of course, is not actually possible) then the point of contact of wheel and ground would move from P to Q, and if the vehicle did not lift slightly the wheel would have to penetrate the ground to the depth QR. Actually, of course, the vehicle would be lifted the amount QR, and a similar action occurs when the stub axle is turned through smaller angles. This action tends to make the steering self-righting, so that after a turn the car automatically comes back to a straight path. This is due to the weight of the car, which tends to turn the wheels until they are in the position where the centre of gravity of the car is lowest, and this position is with the wheels set parallel.

32.5 Castoring or trailing action

The swivel axis about which the wheel is turned for steering purposes is generally inclined in a fore-and-aft direction by a few degrees so that its intersection with the ground (B in Fig. 32.10) lies slightly in front of the point of contact A of the tyre with the ground or rather, since this contact is over a small area, in front of the centre of this contact patch. The distance, x, between the two points is called the *trail*.

The object sought is to stabilise the wheel under running conditions so that the wheel tends to remain with its plane parallel to the direction of motion. Figure 32.10 shows the wheel at a slight angle to the direction of motion and the force R, acting at the road surface, which will be parallel to the direction of motion, is seen to have a moment about the point B (that is about the swivel axis) that tends to bring the wheel back into the plane of motion just as the castor wheel on a chair leg does; hence the term *castor action*. If however the force acted in the opposite direction, the trail would be disadvantageous since it would tend to make the wheel turn through 180°.

Since in front-wheel-driven cars the driving force is in the forwards direction it would seem that in such cars the trail provided should be negative and this is sometimes the case. However a compromise has to be made in any case between the requirements during driving and braking conditions.

In practice the steering of a wheeled vehicle is not quite such a simple matter as these considerations would imply, because it has been found by experiment that a wheel which is rolling along a road cannot sustain any side force unless it is held so that its plane makes an angle with the direction of motion. Thus in Fig. 32.11 if the wheel is required to travel in the direction XX while a side force P is applied to it the wheel must be held so that its plane makes an angle A (called the *slip angle*) with XX, as shown. It has been found that the side force that can be sustained is proportional to the magnitude of the slip angle for values of the latter up to

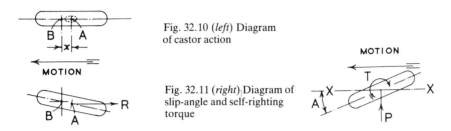

Fig. 32.10 (*left*) Diagram of castor action

Fig. 32.11 (*right*) Diagram of slip-angle and self-righting torque

about 6°. The ratio *side force sustained/slip angle* has been taken as a measure of the cornering ability of a tyre and has been called the *cornering power*.

32.6   Cornering power

The cornering power of tyres has been found to depend on many factors such as the construction of the tyre itself, the value of the vertical force between the tyre and the road (referred to in what follows as the load on the tyre), the inflation pressure, the size of the tyre and the extent of any tilting of the wheel. Thus the cornering power of a tyre falls off as the load on the tyre departs from the normal load for the tyre, but the extent of this falling off is small provided the variation in the load does not exceed plus or minus about 50% of the normal load. The cornering power increases as the inflation pressure is increased, but is smaller for large tyres than for small ones of the same type of construction. As regards camber the cornering power falls off as the top of the wheel in Fig. 32.11 is moved in the direction of the force *P* (this being called *positive camber*) and increases with the amount of negative camber. The cornering power has been found to be independent of the speed.

32.7   Self-righting torque

When a wheel is travelling along the line XX as in Fig. 32.11 there will be a torque *T* acting between it and the road which will tend to turn the wheel so that its plane becomes parallel to the direction of motion, and in order to keep the wheel travelling as shown an equal and opposite torque must be applied to the axle carrying the wheel. The torque *T* may be called the *self-righting torque* and it has been found to increase in direct proportion to the load on the wheel and to be greater for wheels with positive camber than for vertical wheels.

32.8   Steering characteristics – oversteer and understeer

The result of the above actions is that when a vehicle moves in a circular path the centre of that path does not coincide with the point of intersection of the wheel axes. This is indicated in Fig. 32.12, where O is the intersection of the wheel axes and O_1 is the actual centre of rotation. The slip angles for the wheels (A_1, A_2, A_3 and A_4) will in general all have different magnitudes.

If a side force P acts on a car that is travelling in a straight line XX (Fig. 32.13), that force must be balanced by side forces acting between the road and the wheels and the wheels must be set at the appropriate slip angles to the direction of motion. If the slip angles for all the wheels were equal then the car would continue to move in a straight line but inclined at that slip angle to the original path, but if the slip angles of the wheels are not equal then the car will generally move in some curve. If, for example, the slip angles of the back wheels are a little greater than those for the front wheels, the car will begin to move about some centre O as shown. This

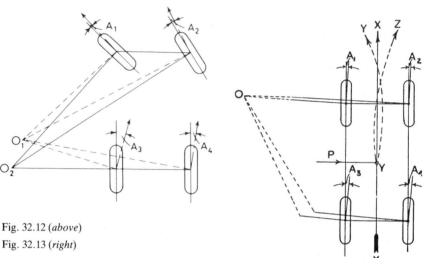

Fig. 32.12 (*above*)

Fig. 32.13 (*right*)

would introduce a centrifugal force which in effect would increase the magnitude of the side force P and would thus accentuate the action. The car will tend to move in a curve such as YY, veering towards the side force P. This action has been called *oversteer* and tends to increase with any increase in the speed, because the centrifugal force increases as the square of the speed, while the side forces between the wheels and the road do not increase with the speed but only as a result of an increase in the slip angles. A car with this steering characteristic when going round a corner may require the steering wheel to be turned back towards the straight ahead position in order to keep it from turning too sharply and is generally less stable and more difficult to handle than a car with an *understeer* characteristic. The latter would be obtained if the slip angles of the front wheels were greater than those of the back wheels, for then the centre of rotation would lie on the opposite side of the line XX and the car would tend to move in a curve such as YZ. The centrifugal force due to this motion opposes the side force P and the action will tend to decrease with any increase in the speed. A car with an understeer characteristic when turning a corner will tend to straighten out and the steering wheel will generally have to be turned a little more to counteract this tendency. Such a car is more stable and easier to handle. An oversteer characteristic can sometimes be corrected by decreasing the slip angles of the rear tyres and increasing those of the front tyres by increasing the inflation pressure of the rear tyres and decreasing that of the front tyres or by altering the weight distribution so that a smaller proportion of both the load and the side force comes on to the rear wheels.

Since both the slip angle and the self-righting torque are affected by alteration of camber the steering characteristic can be controlled to some extent by controlling the change of camber of the wheels due to a tilt of the body of the car relative to the ground. This can be done with independent suspensions of the double-arm type (see Section 34.3).

32.9 Axle beam

When the front wheels are not braked the axle beam is usually a simple forging of I section with suitable seats for the attachment of the springs and with the ends suitably shaped to carry the stub axles. The I section is adopted because it is the best adapted to withstand the bending action to which the beam is subjected. This action arises, as in the back axle, because the axle beam is supported at its ends, while the loads are transmitted to it at the spring seats which are situated nearer to its centre. The action tends to bend the beam in a vertical plane. Simple rectangular and tubular sections are also sometimes used.

The axle beam is also subjected to a bending action in the horizontal plane, but usually this action is small compared with that in the vertical plane. But when the front wheels are braked the horizontal bending action becomes considerable. In this case a rectangular or a circular section may be more suitable than an I section. Again, when the front wheels are braked the portions of the axle beam between the stub axles and the spring seats (and possibly the rest of the axle also) are subjected to a twisting action, the torque reaction of the braking torque applied to the brake drums. A circular section is best adapted to withstand this twisting action. Hence, when front wheel brakes are fitted, circular sections may be used.

32.10 Stub-axle construction

The principal methods of pivoting the stub axles on the ends of the axle beam are shown in Fig. 32.14. The first goes by the name of the *Elliot stub axle*, the second is called the *reversed Elliot*, the third is sometimes called the *Lemoine*. The third and fourth methods are sometimes used upside down, that is, with the wheel axis below the axle beam instead of above it.

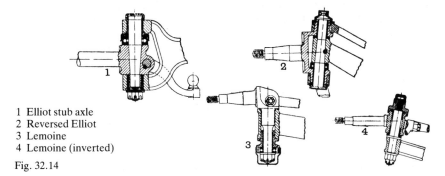

1 Elliot stub axle
2 Reversed Elliot
3 Lemoine
4 Lemoine (inverted)

Fig. 32.14

In the Elliot construction the swivel pin is usuallly fixed in the stub-axle forging and its ends therefore turn in the forked end of the axle beam. In the reversed Elliot construction the swivel pin is usually fixed in the axle beam, so that in each construction the bearing surfaces are situated as far apart as possible and when wear occurs on those surfaces the resulting angular shake or play is as small as possible.

Although the use of a front axle is still the commonest construction for commercial vehicles, they are rarely now used in cars. The above discussion of the principles involved is, however, relevant to the independent suspensions used in cars, but a description of these suspensions is deferred to Chapter 34.

32.11 Wheel bearings

On cars, wheel bearings are not severely loaded. The static load is generally in the range 250 to 400 kg and maximum speeds are of the order of 700 rev/min. In addition to the dynamic loading accompanying suspension deflections, the following loads also have to be reacted: brake drag, traction in the case of driving wheels, and centrifugal forces due to cornering. Obviously the cornering force, applied at the rolling radius of the tyre, produces a couple about a wheel centre, which has to be reacted by the two bearings and therefore adds to the vertical load – including any extra due to weight transfer – on one and subtracts from that on the other. However, on average, a car spends only about 5% of its running time cornering, divided equally between left- and right-hand turns.

Ball or roller bearings are generally used, and the impact loading on them is not normally high. After all, there are few other applications in which such bearings are cushioned on both sides – in the case under discussion, by the tyre on one hand and suspension spring on the other. The choice between ball and roller bearings is based on two main factors: first, whether radial or axial compactness is required and, secondly, the life specified.

Where the roller-type exclusively are used, taper-roller bearings are virtually essential for taking the combined axial and radial loading. Because they make line contact with their races, they tend to have long lives. They certainly are more compact radially and, for any given design loading and outside diameter, can accommodate a shaft of larger diameter than a ball bearing. Assembly is easy because a ring of caged rollers on an inner race can be placed in position on the axle independently of the outer race in the hub. Adjustment of bearing clearance, using shims between the inner races, is also easy. The principles are outlined in an article in *Automotive Engineer*, December 1979.

A typical taper roller bearing assembly for a driven wheel is illustrated in Fig. 32.15, which is that of the Ford *Fiesta*, while for a wheel that is not driven, Fig. 32.16 illustrates a good design, also Ford *Fiesta*, and Fig. 32.17 an even more compact layout. All have Timken bearings and are greased and sealed for life. Interesting features in two of these designs include the abutment of the inner races so that only the shoulder separating the two outer bearings has to be machined to close tolerances – all the other tight tolerances are in the bearings themselves which, in any case, are precision components.

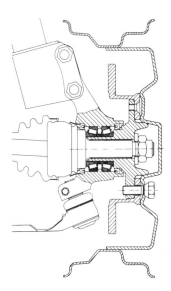

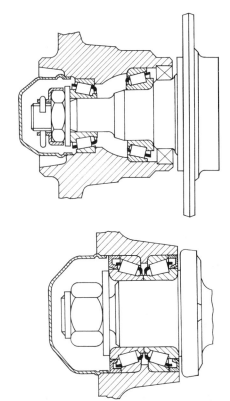

Fig. 32.15 (*above*) The Ford *Fiesta* front drive wheel bearing arrangement using set-right adjusted bearings

Fig. 32.16 (*above right*)

Fig. 32.17 (*right*)

In Fig. 32.17, a major factor in keeping the axial length of the assembly to a minimum is the housing of the seals so that they bear on the inner races. With this design, the stub axle is so short that it is loaded more in shear than in bending, which makes it inherently more resistant to failure. In the design in Fig. 32.16, on the other hand, advantage has been taken of the bending moment diagram characteristic of a cantilever to reduce the diameter of the hub and bearing at the outer end. In Fig. 32.15, full benefit has been derived from the capability of taper roller bearings to accept the large diameter shaft needed for transmitting the drive as well as serving as a stub axle.

The most widely used ball bearing arrangement is that illustrated in Fig. 32.18, because it is the most economical of all, but double-row angular contact ball bearings, as in Figs. 32.19 and 20 are being looked on with increasing favour. These are all RHP bearings and are of the angular-contact type designed to take both axial and radial loading. The illustrations are from an article on hub design published in *Automotive Engineer*, April/May 1980.

Although each ball has, in theory, only point contacts with the races, this has two advantages: first, it keeps friction to a minimum; secondly, because of the relative ease with which this tiny area of contact can be increased elastically under load without excessive generation of heat, such a bearing is more tolerant of pre-loads than are taper rollers. On the other

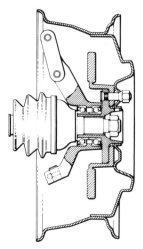
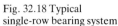
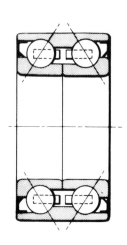
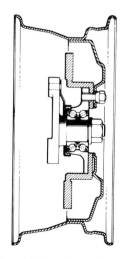

Fig. 32.18 Typical
single-row bearing system

Fig. 32.19 Double-row
ball bearing, 1st generation

Fig. 32.20 Double-row ball
bearing, 2nd generation

hand, shock loading or severe overloading can quickly cause fatigue failure.

Owing to the absence of play in pre-loaded bearings, precise control is obtainable over both steering and the concentricity of brakes, so they are favoured for racing and sports cars. Another advantage of ball bearings is that, if they fail, the symptoms are simply excessive noise, whereas a taper-roller bearing is liable to seize and therefore might be dangerous.

In all types, a most important requirement is good sealing, to keep lubricant in and dirt and water out. With a double row angular contact bearing, generally a double-lip type seal at each end bears on the inner race and is a tight interference fit in the outer race, the complete assembly being pre-greased and sealed for life. Lip type seals with garter springs are usually fitted externally with single row bearings. Shrouds, thrower rings and baffles are widely used, in conjunction with the seals at the inner ends of road wheel hubs, as in Fig. 32.15, to keep water out. The outer ends are generally well protected by hub caps and nave plates. These last mentioned terms, incidentally, are often confused: a hub cap is a small cup-shape screwed on or snapped over or into the end of the hub to retain the grease and keep the bearings clean; a nave plate is a large diameter circular disc, usually chromium-plated, snapped on or sprung into the outer face of the wheel to hide its retaining nuts and improve its tidiness and general appearance.

32.12 Steering column

Rigid steering columns are now ruled out by legal requirements in most countries, because of the risk of their penetrating or otherwise severely damaging the chests of drivers in the event of collisions. Either the steering shaft is in three parts set at angles relative to each other and connected by universal joints, as in Fig. 32.8, so that an impact will cause them to fold, or a sliding coupling is interposed in the column, or one that is made of a convoluted section that will concertina if an axial load is applied.

At some point between the wheel at the top and the connection at the bottom to the steering arm on the stub axle – usually at the bottom of the column – a system of levers or gearing is incorporated to reduce the effort that has to be applied to the wheel at the top to steer the vehicle. It follows that the steering wheel has to be turned through a larger angle than the stub axle assemblies. The actual ratio may range up to well over 25:1, according to the weight of the vehicle, size and type of tyre and other factors such as whether ladies are likely to drive, and the top speed. For cars, the average ratio ranges from about 15 to 22:1, giving between three and 4½ turns from lock-to-lock. Where power assistance is provided, the ratios are smaller. A disadvantage of a high ratio is that it may make it difficult for the driver to actuate the steering rapidly enough to correct a skid or, on heavy commercial vehicles, even to get round a sharp corner.

32.13 Reversible and irreversible steering

With most steering gears, if the road wheels are gripped, they can be swung about their kingpins, causing the steering wheel inside the car to rotate. If, however, the friction forces within the steering gear are high enough to prevent this, the gear is said to be irreversible. In general, the higher the steering ratio, the greater is the tendency to irreversibility, since a high ratio helps the driver to overcome the frictional resistance when he uses the steering wheel but multiplies that resistance if he applies his effort at the road wheels.

Early steering gears were of the screw-and-nut type. These were succeeded by the worm-and-sector, which was followed by the cam-, or screw-and-lever with first a fixed stud, or cam follower, and later a bearing-mounted stud or follower. A still later development was the recirculating-ball type, in which a train of balls was interposed between the threads of a screw and nut, with a return channel for recirculating them. Now, however, the most popular type, at least for cars, is the rack-and-pinion.

There have been many variants of these steering gears. Examples of two of the cam-and-lever type are illustrated in Figs. 32.24 and 32.25. A third is the Ross cam-and-twin lever type which is similar to that in Fig. 32.24, but the lever is forked to carry two studs, one registering at each end of the cam, or screw. Its advantages are a halving of the wear in the straight ahead position and an increasing mechanical advantage towards the extremes of wheel movement, because the relevant lever is then nearest to its top dead centre position. The worm-and-sector type is simply a variant of the worm-and-worm-wheel alternative, but only a sector of the worm-wheel is used in it. Various other forms of gearing have been employed, including straight and helical spur gear pairs and epicyclic trains.

32.14 Rack-and-pinion steering mechanism

This is especially suitable for cars with double transverse wishbone or MacPherson strut type suspension. Its principal advantages, in addition to accommodating relatively easily with the suspension geometry, are the positive feel of such a system, high efficiency, simplicity, the relative ease with which it can be rigidly mounted on the vehicle structure and the consequent precision of the system. Moreover, by increasing the spiral angle of the teeth, a high ratio is obtainable with a pinion that is small yet has teeth of adequate section for taking the loads to which they are subjected.

In Fig. 32.21, the rack is housed in a tubular casing, which has rubber bushes around its ends by means of which it is secured to the structure of the vehicle. These bushes help to absorb high-frequency vibrations and reduce the severity of shocks transmitted back to the steering wheel.

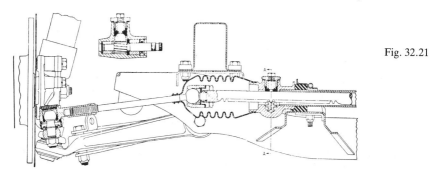

Fig. 32.21

A spring-loaded pad presses the rack into contact with the pinion, which is integral with a short spindle splined to the steering wheel shaft. This spindle is carried by plain bearings in the cast housing on one end of the tubular housing for the rack. Ball joints connect the ends of the rack to the track rods. The centres of these ball joints are approximately in line with the axes about which the stub axle assemblies oscillate, so suspension deflection does not have any significant steering effect.

32.15   Screw-and-nut mechanism

An example of this type of steering gear is shown in Fig. 32.22. A multiple-threaded screw B is free to rotate in bearings in a cast-iron casing C. Axial motion is prevented by thrust bearings DD and the screw is connected by the shaft A to the steering wheel. A nut H fits on the screw and is prevented from rotating. Hence, if the screw is turned the nut must move axially up or down the screw. This motion is caused to rotate the drop arm through the medium of a two-armed spindle L, which is carried in ball bearings in the casing and which carries the drop arm at its outer end. The two arms KK of the spindle L straddle the nut, to which they are connected by the bronze pads MM. These pads are free to turn in cylindrical recesses formed in the sides of the nut, and they are provided with parallel grooves to receive the arms of the spindle L. The pads are necessary because the nut moves in a straight line while the arms of the spindle L move in circular paths.

In this design the nut is prevented from rotating by the arms K of the spindle L. In some designs this is done by guiding the nut in guides in the

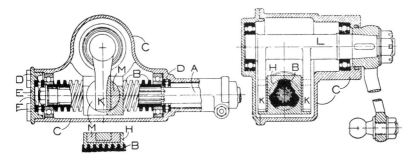

Fig. 32.22 Screw-and-nut steering mechanism

casing. In some designs also short connecting rods are used, instead of the pads, to connect the nut with the arms of the spindle L.

Backlash in the above mechanism can arise from end play of the screw and from wear of the threads of the screw and nut, etc. End play of the screw is eliminated in assembly by means of the selected washer F. Wear of the threads cannot usually be remedied except by replacement, but in view of the large area of contact between the nut and the screw the wear should be small provided that lubrication is attended to.

This type of mechanism has the advantage that the leverage provided increases as the steering approaches full lock.

A slightly different form of screw-and-nut mechanism is shown in Fig. 32.23. The screw is formed on the end of the shaft A to which the steering wheel is fixed. The nut is formed with integral trunnions BB which pivot in holes in the ends of arms CC of the fork member, which is splined to the drop arm shaft D. At its upper end the shaft A is supported in the steering column in a ball and socket joint E which secures it against axial motion but allows it to turn about its axis and also to swing slightly about an axis perpendicular to the axis the shaft itself. This last freedom is required because the trunnions BB must move in the arc XX as the nut moves to and fro along the screw, and so the lower end of the shaft A is moved slightly in the direction YY. Actually, instead of a plain ball-and-socket joint at E, a self-aligning ball bearing is used. Alternatively an ordinary journal bearing supported in a rubber bush may be used, the rubber bush accommodating the rocking of the shaft A. This arrangement eliminates the pads M of the mechanism of Fig. 32.22, reduces the number of bearings required and so cheapens the construction. The fixing of the nut against rotation is also more easily done by the arms CC than by the arms KK of Fig. 32.22.

32.16   Cam steering mechanisms

Many cam steering mechanisms have been invented but few have been commercially successful. One example which is used by many makers is shown in Fig. 32.24. It is the Marles steering gear. Carried by the drop arm spindle A on the ball bearings shown is a V-shaped roller B which engages a groove cut in the member C. The latter is keyed to the steering wheel shaft but is fixed axially. When the steering wheel is turned the spiral groove in the member C constrains the roller B to move to the right or left

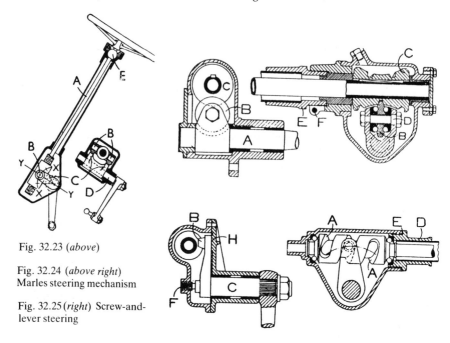

Fig. 32.23 (*above*)

Fig. 32.24 (*above right*)
Marles steering mechanism

Fig. 32.25 (*right*) Screw-and-
lever steering

from the position shown, thus turning the drop arm. End play of the member C can be eliminated by screwing the casing E farther into the steering box, a clamping screw F being provided for locking purposes. Proper meshing of the roller with the groove in the member C may be obtained by turning the pin D. The centre portion of this pin, which carries the races that support the roller, is eccentric to the end portions, hence when the pin is turned the roller is moved into closer mesh with the member C.

32.17 Screw-and-lever mechanism

This steering unit is a form of cam mechanism and an example is shown in Fig. 32.25. At the bottom end of the steering wheel shaft a helical groove A is formed, and this engages the projection B of the drop arm spindle lever. When the steering wheel shaft is turned the drop arm is rocked to and fro. End play of the steering wheel shaft is eliminated by putting in a suitable washer at E. The drop arm spindle lever is supported by bearing on the cover plate at H, and a screw F prevents it from meshing too deeply with the groove A. The pin B is sometimes made in the form of a roller, being carried in bearings in the drop arm spindle lever. A recent modification is to provide the lever with two pins which, in the central position of the gear, engage the screw near its ends. This enables increased leverage to be obtained when the steering is locked hard over.

In the Marles Weller steering gear, whose general arrangement is similar to that of Fig. 32.25, the pin B is formed with two hemispherical recesses one on each side and half-balls fit in these recesses. The approximately flat faces of the half-balls engage the sides of the screw thread.

32.18 Steering connections

The drop arm, or rack, of the steering mechanism is connected to the steering arm of the stub axle and the connections must be such as will allow of angular motion in two planes. Ball-and-socket joints are now used almost always but at one time universal joints were used. An example of modern ball-and-socket joint construction appears in Fig. 32.26, and this is a design by Automotive Products. The bush A is split on a vertical diameter and can thus be made to contact the ball member both above and below the central horizontal plane and so this bush carries all the actual steering loads, the lower member B being spring loaded to eliminate backlash and rattle. The bushes are moulded in a composition which

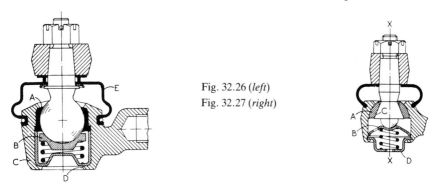

Fig. 32.26 (*left*)
Fig. 32.27 (*right*)

contains a lubricant and the joint requires no other lubrication throughout its life. The ball and bush assembly is retained in the solid eye of the link C by rolling the lip of the eye over, as seen at D. Dust and water are excluded by the rubber boot E. The surface of the ball is plated to give protection against corrosion and to provide a fine surface finish. Joints of this kind can provide considerable angular freedom in all directions.

In the joint of Fig. 32.27 the upper, load bearing, surface is formed on a bush A which is free to rotate on the conical end of the pin C. This enables a large spherical surface to be provided while at the same time reducing the relative motion between that surface and the eye of the rod. This is because motions about the axis XX will occur at the surface C. A spring-loaded cup B holds the parts in contact and limits any separation to the amount of the clearance between the bottom of the cup and the cap D. When the angular motions about XX are not large the member A is usually made integral with the pin.

32.19 Alignment of the front wheels

When a vehicle is moving in a staight line all its wheels should be parallel to the direction of motion. Unless the back axle has been badly damaged the back wheels will be so, but proper adjustment is necessary if the front wheels are to be so. In order that the front wheels shall be parallel when the vehicle is moving they must usually be set slightly out of parallel when the vehicle is stationary, the distance between the wheels in the plan view being made slightly less at the front than at the back. Then, when the vehicle is moving along the road the forces acting on the wheels will cause small deflections in the steering connections, which will bring the wheels into parallelism. This setting of the wheels is known as *toe-in* and the difference between the 'track' of the wheel rims at the front and back varies with different makers from almost nothing up to as much as 6 mm. Modern practice is to keep it as small as possible.

In independent suspensions of certain types the rear wheels are sometimes given a small amount of toe-in when the vehicle is standing with its normal load. The suspension will generally cause the alignment to change a little as the wheels move relative to the frame as it will also do in independent front suspensions.

32.20   Power steering

It has been seen that when the size and weight of a vehicle become large it may be necessary to have servo-assisted or power-operated brakes and, for the same reasons, it may also become necessary to employ power steering. Several systems have been developed by various makers and three will be described. They are all similar in principle and are all operated by oil under pressure. This oil is suppled by a pump driven off the engine, or sometimes off the rear end of the gearbox. An accumulator or reservoir is usually provided. The pressures used are fairly high, reaching 7000 kN/m^2. Systems using compressed air have also been developed but the principle of operation is the same as that of the systems about to be described. This is that the first slight movement of the steering wheel operates a valve so as to open up a passage for pressure oil from the pump and accumulator to the appropriate end of a *slave cylinder* whose piston is connected to the steering linkage. A pressure difference is thus built up across the sides of the piston which therefore moves and actuates the steering. The movement of the piston is arranged to 're-set' the valve, that is, to bring it back to the equilibrium position and so the movement of the piston and steering linkage is made proportional to the movement of the steering wheel. The systems are always arranged so that the steering linkage can be actuated direct by the steering wheel if the oil pressure should not be available. They are also sometimes arranged so that some appreciable effort must be applied to the steering wheel before the valve of the system is operated; this effort is transmitted direct to the steering linkage and, if the forces and moments opposing motions of the road wheels are small, this direct effort may be sufficient to overcome them and the steering is then done direct without any power assistance. This is claimed to give a good 'feel' to the steering. When the resistances are larger then the valve is moved and the power effort is added to the direct manual effort.

32.21   Vickers system

The principal features of the system developed by Vickers Incorporated of Detroit are shown in Figs. 32.28 and 32.29. The slave cylinder A (Fig. 32.28) takes the place of the drag link of the steering linkage being connected by a ball-and-socket joint B to the steering arm of the stub axle while the piston rod is coupled by the ball and socket joint C to the frame.

The drop arm D of the steering box is arranged to actuate the valve of the system, as will be seen from Fig. 32.29. Supposing the steering wheel to be turned so that the drop arm turns clockwise then the valve E will be moved to the left, thus opening the port x to the pressure supply and the port y to the exhaust. The pressure in the end F of the slave cylinder will therefore rise while that in the end G will fall. The cylinder will therefore move bodily to the left, thus actuating the steering. The movement of the cylinder brings the valve E back to the equilibrium position and the desired movement of the steering will have been effected, chiefly by the oil pressure but partly by the direct pressure of the drop arm on the left-hand spring of the valve. The movement of the valve is limited to a very small

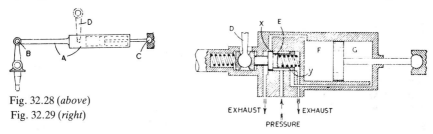

Fig. 32.28 (*above*)
Fig. 32.29 (*right*)

amount either way and if the oil pressure should not be available then the drop arm can actuate the steering direct as soon as the valve comes up against its stop. There is therefore some backlash, the amount depending on the free movement allowed to the valve, when the steering is being operated manually. In order that the slave cylinder shall not exert any drag on the system when it is being operated manually a valve is provided which opens a direct passage between the ends of the cylinder if the oil pressure fails and the movement of the control valve exceeds the normal amount.

32.22 Ross system

This is shown in Figs. 32.30 to 32.32. The steering wheel is fixed to the shaft A which at its lower end is provided with a screw or cam B, the groove of which is engaged by the pin C. The latter is carried in taper roller bearings in an arm secured to the drop arm shaft D, the drop arm E is also fixed to this shaft and is actuated by the piston of the slave cylinder through a yoke member that engages a sliding block carried on the pin G of the arm F. The latter arm is also fixed to the drop arm shaft. The shaft A and cam B are, in effect, integral with the valve of the system which is situated at H and is shown in more detail in Figs. 32.31 and 32.32. Supposing the steering wheel to be turned clockwise then for the first slight movement the pin C will remain fixed and the cam B, shaft A and valve will move to the left. The detailed action of the valve will be described later but when it moves to the left the pressure in the pipe j will rise and that in k will fall and so the piston of the slave cylinder will be urged to the left thereby rotating the drop arm anti-clockwise and actuating the steering. The anti-clockwise movement of the lever and pin C will move the valve back to its equilibrium position. The action of the valve is as follows. Referring to Fig. 32.31, the valve position, when the system is in equilibrium, will be such

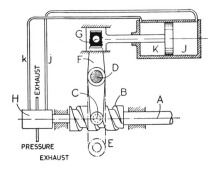

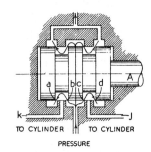

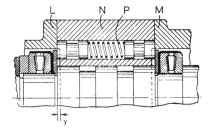

Fig. 32.30 (*above*)

Fig. 32.31 (*above right*)

Fig. 32.32 (*right*)

that the areas of the passages *a*, *b*, *c* and *d* will be equal (neglecting for the moment the effect of the piston rod of the slave cylinder), the pressure drops across the passages *b* and *c* will be equal and the pressure drops across the passages *a* and *d* will also be equal. The pressures in the recesses of the valve will therefore also be equal and these pressures are transmitted by the pipes *j* and *k* to the ends of the slave cylinder. If now the valve is moved to the left the passages *b* and *d* will be reduced in size while the passages *a* and *c* will be increased. The pressure drop across *b* will increase while that across *c* will decrease, the pressure drop across *a* will decrease while that across *d* will increase. Hence the pressure in the left-hand recess and pipe *k* will fall and the pressure in the right-hand recess and pipe *j* will rise as described above. The effect of the piston rod of the slave cylinder is to reduce the effective area of the end K of the cylinder and as the forces acting on the piston must be balanced in the equilibrium position the pressure in the end K must be a little higher than in the end J. This is obtained automatically, the valve setting itself so that the area *c* is slightly larger than *b* and the area *d* slightly smaller than *a*. The valve is provided with a number of centring springs P (Fig. 32.32), in the equilibrium position these springs exert no force on the valve because the plungers against which the springs act abut against the end covers L and M. Before the valve can move from the equilibrium position a torque must be exerted on the steering wheel which is sufficient to produce a force equal to the spring force. The reaction of this force acts on the pin C (Fig. 32.30) and is transmitted to the steering linkage. If the forces opposing the motion of the road wheels are small steering may be effected without any movement of the valve and purely by the manual effort of the driver. Under these conditions there will be no backlash in the steering. If the forces opposing the motion of the road wheels are large then the valve will be moved and the steering will be done mainly by the slave cylinder. If no oil pressure is available the motion of the valve is limited to the amount *y* (shown exaggerated in Fig. 32.32), the depth of the recess in the end of the body N of the valve housing, and the backlash is limited accordingly. The space between the plungers acted on by the centring springs is connected to the pressure side of the system and consequently when oil pressure is available the force of the centring springs is supplemented by the force exerted on the plungers by the oil.

32.23 Marles-Bendix Varamatic system

This is shown in Figs. 32.33 and 32.34. The mechanical part of the system is based on the Marles mechanism which is described in Section 32.16 while the servo part is basically the same as that of the Ross system described in Section 32.22. There are, however, some important differences. The cam A (Fig. 32.33) now has a variable pitch so that when the roller follower B is in the central position shown the ratio *angular motion of cam/angular motion of drop arm (C)*, for a very small motion, is about 21:1 but when the drop arm and follower have moved about 12° away from the central position that ratio has fallen to 13:1 and thereafter it remains constant at that value. The valve which controls the servo action now operates by the

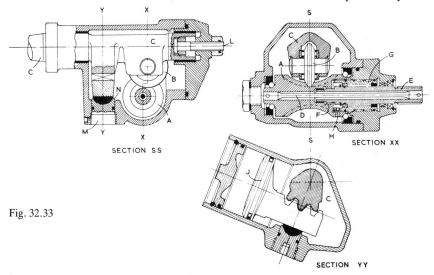

Fig. 32.33

rotational displacement of its two main components instead by their axial displacements as in the Ross system.

The cam is carried in the casing on two angular contact ball bearings and is coupled at the left-hand side to the torsion bar D by a cross-pin. At the right-hand end the torsion bar is coupled, also by a cross-pin, to the sleeve E which is splined to the steering-wheel shaft and which forms the inner member of the valve. The left-hand end of the sleeve E is formed with splines F which engage splines formed in the right-hand end of the cam A but these splines are machined so as to allow 7° of freedom of rotation and are only to provide a safeguard against over-stressing of the torsion bar when the steering is operated without servo assistance. Pipes connect the pump, which is driven by the engine, to the valve and the latter to the outer end of the servo cylinder; the inner end of the servo cylinder forms the casing which houses the cam A and follower assembly and the valve is directly connected to that space. The outer member G of the valve is coupled by the ball-ended pin H to the right-hand end of the cam A. The servo piston J is integral with a stem on which rack teeth are formed and these teeth engage teeth machined on the end of the drop arm forging C.

The principle of operation of the valve is shown by the diagrams Fig. 32.34 (*a*) and (*b*). It is really three valves in parallel, parts relative to which are denoted by suffixes 1, 2 and 3 – following the letters P and S in the diagram – but the action will be described in relation to one of them. The ports P are connected to the delivery of the pump and when the valve sleeve E is centrally placed, as shown at (*a*), fluid flows equally to each of the pockets S_1 and S_2 which are connected at their ends to the return pipe to the pump. The pressure-drops across the apertures *b* and *a* are equal to those across the apertures *c* and *d* and so there is no pressure difference between the spaces C_L and C_R which are connected to the ends of the servo cylinder. Hence there is no net hydraulic force acting on the servo piston.

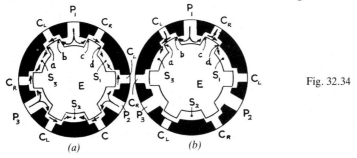

(*a*)   (*b*)   Fig. 32.34

But when a torque is applied to the steering wheel to overcome a resistance to a steering motion of the road wheels the torsion bar is twisted and relative motion occurs between the inner valve sleeve E and the outer one G, as is shown at (*b*). The passage *c* is thereby increased while the passage *d* is decreased and so the pressure in the space C_R is raised. Conversely, the passage *b* is decreased and *a* is increased so that the pressure in the space C_L is lowered. A pressure difference is thus established across the servo piston and the drop arm is rotated. As this occurs the cam and outer sleeve of the valve rotate so as to follow up the inner valve sleeve and bring the valve to a central position. The drop arm having thus been rotated the required amount the servo action ceases and the system remains in equilibrium. The use of three sets of ports provides a valve in which the radial hydraulic pressures are balanced and the required port areas are obtained with a valve only one-third the length that would be needed if only one set was provided.

Provision is made for adjusting the mesh of the roller B with the cam A; this is done by means of the screw L which, when turned, will move the drop arm shaft C in or out and thus bring the roller into closer or looser mesh. Similarly, the mesh of the rack teeth on the servo piston stem can be adjusted by means of the screwed plug M which bears on the underside of the stem through the spherically seated pad N.

Chapter 33

Suspension principles

Obviously, if the loads applied to the rolling wheels of a vehicle were transmitted directly to the chassis, not only would its occupants suffer severely but also its structure would be subjected to an excessive degree of fatigue loading. The primary function of the suspension system, therefore, is to isolate the structure, so far as is practicable, from shock loading and vibration due to irregularities of the road surface. Secondly, it must do this without impairing the stability, steering or general handling qualities of the vehicle. The primary requirement is met by the use of flexible elements and dampers, while the second is achieved by controlling, by the use of mechanical linkages, the relative motions between the unsprung masses – wheel-and-axle assemblies – and the sprung mass. These linkages may be either as simple as a semi-elliptic spring and shackle or as complex as a double tranverse link and anti-roll bar or some other such combination of mechanisms.

33.1 Road irregularities and human susceptibility

Some indication of the magnitudes of the disturbances caused by road irregularities can be gained from *Surface Irregularity of Roads*, DSIR Road Research Board Report, 1936–7. From this report it appears that surface undulations on medium-quality roads have amplitudes in general of 0.013 m or less, while amplitudes of 0.005 m are characteristic of very good roads. The average pitch of these undulations is under 4 m while most road vehicle wheels roll forwards at about 2 m/rev. In addition to the conventional tarmac roads, there are pavé and washboard surfaces, the latter occurring largely on unsurfaced roads and tracks. Representative replicas of these two types of surface are described in *The MIRA Proving Ground*, by A. Fogg, *Proc. A.D. Inst. Mech. Engrs.* 1955–56.

Obviously the diameter of the tyre, size of contact patch between tyre and road, the rate of the tyre acting as a spring, and weight of wheel and axle assembly affect the magnitude of the shock transmitted to the axle, while the amplitude of wheel motion is influenced by all these factors plus the rate of the suspension springs, damping effect of the shock absorbers, and the weights of the unsprung and sprung masses. The unsprung mass can be loosely defined as that between the road and the main suspension springs, while the sprung mass is that supported on these suspension springs, though both may also include the weights of parts of the springs and linkages.

Two entirely different types of shock are applied to the wheel: that due to the wheel's striking a bump, and that caused by the wheel's falling into a pot-hole. The former will be influenced to a major extent by the geometry of the bump and the speed of the vehicle, while the major influence on the latter, apart from the geometry of the hole, is the unsprung masses and spring rates, speed being an incidental influencing factor.

Human sensitivity to these disturbances is very complex, and a more detailed discussion can be found in *Car Suspension and Handling* by Donald Bastow, Pentech Press, London, 1980. It is widely held that vertical frequencies associated with walking speeds between 2.5 and 4 mph – that is, 1.5 to 2.3 Hz – are comfortable, and that fore-and-aft or lateral frequencies of the head should be less than 1.5 Hz. Dizziness and sickness is liable to be experienced if the inner ear is subjected to frequencies between 0.5 and about 0.75 Hz. Serious discomfort may be felt in other important organs at frequencies between 5 and 7 Hz.

33.2 Suspension system

A suspension system can be represented, in simplified form, as illustrated in Fig. 33.1. The natural frequency of the sprung mass – that at which it

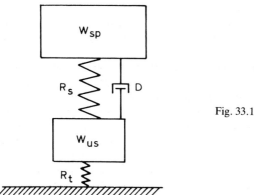

Fig. 33.1

would bounce up and down if momentarily disturbed and then left to bounce freely on its springs – is determined by the combined rate of the tyres and the suspension springs in series, which is –

$$\frac{1}{R} = \frac{1}{R_s} + \frac{1}{R_t}$$

where R is the overall suspension rate
R_s is the suspension spring rate
R_t is the tyre rate

In Fig. 33.1, the shock absorber is the hydraulic damper at D. Any friction in the suspension system will be additional to the hydraulic damping. However, whereas the hydraulic damping force of the shock absorber can be taken as proportional to the square of the vertical velocity of the sprung mass relative to that of the unsprung mass, the dynamic friction damping force is, in effect, constant regardless of velocity. It follows that while small amplitude, small velocity movements of the suspension are virtually unaffected by the hydraulic damping, the force applied by the friction damping is the same for these small movements as it is for large ones.

With, for example, a new multi-leaf semi-elliptic spring, there is only a small difference between the static and dynamic interleaf friction forces – sometimes differentiated by calling them respectively *stiction* and *friction*. When, however, the same spring becomes rusty and dirty, this difference can become considerable, with the result that mean value of the work done by the friction damping during high frequency, small amplitude motions becomes excessive. Indeed, in extreme cases, the spring may become so stiff that, for small amplitude disturbances, it in effect does not deflect at all. This can of course lead to a harsh uncomfortable ride. It must be borne in mind, too, that even the hydraulic forces are in any case transmitted directly – that is, uncushioned by the suspension springs – to the sprung mass.

Dampers have a twofold function. First, they are for reducing the tendency for the carriage unit to continue to bounce up and down on its springs after the disturbance that caused the initial motion has ceased. Secondly, they prevent excessive build-up of amplitude of bounce as a result of periodic excitation at a frequency identical to the natural frequency of vibration of the spring-mass system. This natural frequency is a function of the weight of the sprung mass and the spring rate, and in fact can be shown to be directly proportional to $1/\sqrt{\delta}$, where δ is the static deflection of the spring.

Each of two forms of disturbances can cause either of two entirely different resonances. One such form is the passage of the wheel over a series of equidistant bumps at a speed such that the frequency of the disturbance that they generate coincides with the natural frequency of the suspension system. The second is imbalance of the wheel, the out-of-balance force of which will increase as the square of the speed of rotation.

Of the two different frequencies: one is that of the sprung mass on the suspension spring system, and the second is that of the unsprung mass – the wheel and axle assembly – on the tyre. Obviously the latter is affected by the suspension spring rate, but only marginally. The former will be experienced as a relatively low frequency – perhaps about 1 to 1.5 Hz – bouncing of the carriage unit, while the latter is that of wheel hop, at a higher frequency – generally 10 to 15 Hz – and is generated almost totally independently of the motions of the carriage unit. For minimising the amplitudes of wheel hop – not only resonant but also isolated hops – the unsprung weight must be kept as small as possible. Resonances of either the sprung or unsprung masses can affect adversely, and indeed to a dangerous extent, the handling characteristics of the vehicle. Obviously, therefore, it is important to maintain the dampers, or shock absorbers, in good working condition.

These same disturbances can also cause pitching or rolling vibrations of the vehicle. In these instances, the natural frequencies are functions of the spring rates in the rolling and pitching modes and the moment of inertia of the sprung masses about the lateral and longitudinal axes respectively. Rolling oscillations of an axle alone, that is about an axis parallel to the longitudinal axis of the vehicle, are generally termed *tramp* because the effect is something like the tramping motion of a man – advancing one step at a time.

Supplementary roll stiffness can be obtained, without affecting two-wheel bounce stiffness – resistance to vertical motion of complete axle or, with independent suspension, of both wheels simultaneously – by the use of a torsion-bar spring. This spring is generally called an *anti-roll bar*, and it is mounted transversely beneath the vehicle in two bearings – usually rubber bushes – its ends being connected by levers and, sometimes, shackles to the axles. If simple pivots, instead of shackles, are used to connect the levers to the axles, these levers can be utilised as radius rods, for guidance of the axles as they move up and down, as in the MacPherson suspension illustrated in Fig. 34.10. Since the use of an anti-roll bar inevitably implies the imposition of extra vertical loading on the tyres during roll, it has an effect on steering and handling. This is because the extra vertical deflection of the tyre of the outer wheel, in the region of its contact with the ground, renders it more susceptible to lateral deflection – increases the slip angle – when the vehicle is cornering. This effect has to be considered by the designer when he decides whether to instal an anti-roll bar at the front or rear, or both.

Clearly there must be an interaction – a vibration coupling effect – between the motions of the front and rear suspensions, and this must affect the tendency to pitch. The magnitude of the interaction will depend on the frequency of the disturbances, or bumps over which the car rolls, and the natural frequencies of the front and rear suspensions. Obviously, the forcing frequencies depend on the spacing of the bumps, the speed of the vehicle, and its mass moment of inertia about the axis of pitch, while the magnitude of the response in pitching of the vehicle will depend not only on these two factors but also on its wheelbase.

It can be shown, if the rear suspension has a lower natural frequency than the front, the pitching motion tends to persist longer than if the front has the lower frequency. Moreover, if the rear suspension has the higher natural frequency, the initial pitching motion is less severe. Consequently, the natural frequency of the rear suspension is normally made higher than that of the front. The higher the speed of the vehicle, the less severe is the initial pitching motion. This effect arises because, as the speed increases, the time between the front and rear wheels striking the bump becomes a smaller proportion of the periodic time of the pitching motion of the vehicle at its natural frequency, and in theory could ultimately become zero. The principle is analogous to that of vibration isolation – for instance of an engine vibrating freely at a relatively high frequency on a rubber mounting system having a low natural frequency.

33.3 Damping

As mentioned previously, the dampers, or shock absorbers as they are sometimes called, are required to cause a rapid die-away of any vibrations forced either randomly or periodically at the natural frequency of the suspension system and thus introducing a state of resonance. To do this, they apply a force in a direction opposite to that of the instantaneous motion of the suspension. Early cars had friction dampers, which were generally packs of friction material interleaved between blades, or arms, which were attached alternately to the sprung and unsprung masses. Semi-rotary vane type hydraulic dampers have also been used. However, these were abandoned because the ratio of sealing length around their vanes to volume displaced was so high that these units were rapidly adversely affected by wear.

Modern dampers are almost invariably either telescopic hydraulic struts interposed between the sprung and unsprung masses – carriage unit and axle – or, less frequently, of the lever type, which also are hydraulic units. The body, incorporating the hydraulic cylinder, of the lever type damper is usually mounted on the carriage unit, with its actuating lever connected to the axle. If the body were mounted on the axle, the high-frequency, high-velocity motions to which it would be subjected might cause aeration of the hydraulic fluid and hence adversely affect the damping capacity of the unit. The maximum vertical accelerations of an axle under dynamic conditions can be of the order of 20 to 30 g.

Damping is effected by the damper piston, or pistons, forcing the hydraulic fluid at high velocities through small holes. Thus energy is absorbed by the fluid, converted into heat, and then dissipated partly by conduction into the surrounding structure of the vehicle, but ultimately all passing into the air stream flowing past these components. The amount of energy thus absorbed and dissipated, for any given rate of energy input, is a function of the volume and viscosity of the fluid and the numbers, sizes and geometry of the holes through which it is forced. A major advantage of hydraulic damping is that, as previously mentioned, the resistance to deflection of the damper is a function of the square of its velocity. Therefore, slow movements of the wheels can occur with relative freedom, but the resistance increases rapidly with the velocity of motion.

Ideally, the aim in damper design is to obtain maximum possible potential for energy absorption for any given size, and this would imply equal damping on the bump and rebound strokes. However, since the bump stroke is often a violently forced motion, and it is undesirable to transmit such forces directly through the damper to the sprung mass, the damping on the bump stroke is often arranged to be less than that on the rebound stroke, which of course is a gentler motion effected by the weight of the axle and the force exerted by the suspension spring. To relieve the bump stroke of all damping, and thus the carriage unit of all directly transmitted shocks, is impracticable for two reasons: first, it would halve the energy-absorption capability of the damping system; secondly, damping only on the rebound would tend to jack the carriage unit down to a mean level below that of its static deflection on the springs. The transmission of high frequency, small amplitude vibrations through the dampers directly to the carriage unit is avoided by the interposition of rubber bushes or blocks between their end-fittings and their anchorages on the axle and carriage unit – that is, on the sprung and unsprung masses.

33.4 Dampers in practice

A characteristic common to all telescopic dampers is that, as the piston moves into the cylinder, its whole area is effective in transmitting the load, and thus pressurising, the fluid but, as it moves outwards, the effective area of the piston is reduced to that of the annulus between its periphery and that of the piston rod. If equal damping is required in both directions, therefore, some compensation is obtained by adjusting, to a different value for each direction of flow, the pressures at which the valves open the small holes in the piston, through which the fluid is forced to provide the damping. Also, the total cross-sectional areas of the holes for the flows in the two directions must differ too. The latter effect can of course be obtained by use of a simple plate valve to close some of the holes during motion in one direction only.

Another effect of the intrusion of the piston rod into the cylinder is that the volumes available for accommodation of the fluid on the two sides of the piston differ. Compensation for this can be provided by the incorporation of a flexible element in the cylinder, so that the total volume within it can adjust automatically, as required. This flexible element can be an elastic sphere containing an inert gas, or a free piston with an inert gas between it and the closed end of the cylinder. An alternative is the use of the double-tube design.

33.5 Double-tube damper

A double-tube design is illustrated in Fig. 33.2. It consists of a cylinder A, to which is welded a head B. The latter is screwed into the outer tube C to which is welded a pressed steel cap and eye D by means of which the cylinder A is secured to the axle or wheel assembly. A piston E, in the cylinder A, is secured to the piston rod F which at its upper end has an eye welded to it by which it is attached to the frame of the vehicle. The part of the piston rod that emerges from the cylinder is protected by a cover welded to the fixing eye. A gland G prevents leakage where the piston road passes through the head B; any fluid scraped off by the gland packing passes down a drain hole to the reservoir space between the cylinder A and the outer tube C. At the bottom of the cylinder A is a *foot-valve* assembly L.

Piston E has two concentric rings of holes drilled through it: the outer ring is covered by a disc valve H held down by a star-shape disc spring I, while the inner ring is covered by the disc valve J held up by the coil spring K. The valve assembly in the foot is similar to that in the piston except that the lower disc valve, covering the inner rings of the holes is held up by a disc spring instead of a coil spring. This is to reduce the dead length of the shock absorber – that is, the length not available for the working stroke.

Both ends of cylinder A are completely filled with fluid, but the space between A and C is only partly filled. If the eye D is moved upwards, fluid must be displaced from beneath to above the piston E. This fluid will pass through the outer ring of holes, by lifting the valve H against the spring I. But since the increase in the volume of the upper end of the cylinder is less – by the volume of the portion of piston rod that enters the cylinder – than the decrease in volume of the lower end, fluid will also be displaced through the inner ring of holes in the foot-valve and the level of the fluid in the reservoir space will rise.

The pressure set up will depend on the sizes of the passage opened by the valves in the piston and foot-valve, and, of course, on the square of the speed at which the cylinder is moved upwards. For downward motion of the cylinder the valve J will be forced off its seating, and fluid will be displaced from the upper end of the cylinder, through the inner ring of holes in the piston, to the lower end, but the removal of the volume of the piston rod from the cylinder will cause fluid to be drawn also from the reservoir space, through the outer ring of holes in the foot-valve into the lower end of the cylinder.

An advantage of the double-tube damper is that the oil displaced from the main tube into the outer one carries heat with it, which is then readily conducted away. This tends to keep all the fluid at a moderate temperature. Obviously, the higher the level of fluid in the outer tube the greater is the heat transfer effect. Another advantage is that damage – a dent for example – in the outer tube will not interfere with the working of the piston.

33.6   Single-tube damper

A single-tube damper is shown in Fig. 33.3. The spaces immediately above and below the piston are filled with oil, and the damping action arises from the viscous losses that occur in the orifices, as in the double-tube type. However the effect of the volume of the piston rod is allowed for by the use of a volume of gas under compression at the bottom of the tube, where it is separated from the oil by a floating piston. When the tube of the damper moves upwards, the gas will be further compressed and the floating piston will be moved downwards relative to it by the amount required to accommodate the changes in the volume of the two oil spaces. This compression of the gas results in a progressive change in the characteristic of the damping, such that the force required to move the damper tube upward at a constant speed will rise at an increasing rate. In contrast, in the double-tube type, the rate of increase is constant.

In a single-tube damper, the pressure of the gas – usually nitrogen – must be higher than the maximum operating pressure in the fluid below the main piston, and may be of the order of $2.5\,MN/m^2$. This of course adds to the total spring-rate of the suspension by an amount equal to the gas pressure multiplied by the effective cross-sectional area of the piston rod.

The Woodhead Manufacturing Company. has produced a single-tube damper without a floating piston. In it the inert gas is free in the cylinder and therefore tends to emulsify the fluid. Although the gas and oil separate while the vehicle is stationary, re-emulsification occurs rapidly owing to the large flow rates inherent in the design, the performance of the unit therefore becomes normal equally rapidly. An advantage of this type of damper is the impossibility of jacking up and subsequent bending of the piston rod, in the event of leakage of fluid past a free piston. Also, again because of the absence of the free piston, the dead length of the damper is small. Moreover, the performance of these emulsion-type dampers is

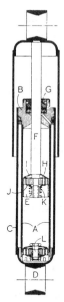

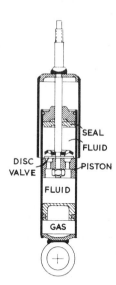

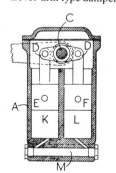

Fig. 33.2 (*far left*)
Double-tube telescopic
damper

Fig. 33.3 (*left*) Girling
single-tube telescopic
damper

Fig. 33.4 (*below*)
Lever-arm type damper

affected less than that of the fluid type by variations in working tempera-ture. Single-tube dampers in general have the advantage that, for a given overall diameter, the piston area is greater, but they have the disadvantage of a higher built-in pressure.

Telescopic dampers are also used in the MacPherson, or strut-type, suspension, Fig. 34.10. Here, a major problem arises because of the imposition of side loads at the top of the strut, and therefore bending moments on the piston rod. Because such a piston rod, taking these loads and performing guidance function, has to be of large diameter, the problems arising owing to its intrusion into the damper are aggravated.

33.7   Lever-arm type damper

In Fig. 33.4, two pistons E and F are actuated by the ends of a double lever DD carried on a shaft C, which is coupled externally to the axle. The bores K and L are interconnected by the passage M, which houses some form of orifice assembly. Damping again arises from the viscous losses that occur in the orifices. The lever arm of such a damper can be made to serve as one of the links of an independent suspension system.

33.8   Springs

The function of the suspension spring can be understood from the following. When the wheel hits a bump, it rises extremely rapidly, so if a spring were not interposed between it and the carriage unit, the shock transmitted would be considerable. With the traditional suspension sys-tem, the only force transmitted to the carriage unit is that required to compress the spring far enough for the wheel to ride over the bump. This force causes the body to accelerate upwards, but at a much smaller rate than would otherwise be experienced.

When the wheel falls into a depression, the force in the spring, acting on the relatively light unsprung mass – wheel and axle – forces it down at a rapid rate so that it generally reaches the base of the depression almost before the relatively much larger mass of the carriage unit has, owing to its inertia, had time to begin to descend. Since the variations in the spring force over such deflections are relatively small, the downward acceleration of the carriage unit supported by the spring is correspondingly moderate as compared with that which, under the influence of gravity, it would be if there were no spring.

When the disturbance has passed, whether it is a bump or a depression, the subsequent motion of the carriage unit is its free vibration on the springs, the acceleration being small. This vibration is rapidly reduced to zero by the dampers.

The following types of spring are currently in use for the suspension of cars and commercial vehicles: laminated, or leaf; taper-leaf; coil; torsion bar; rubber; air; and gas. The principal characteristics governing the choice of type of spring are: overall cost of the installation, relative capacity for storing energy, total weight of suspension system, fatigue life, and location or guidance linkages required.

Leaf springs in general have approximately only a quarter of the energy-storage capacity, for a given stress level, of either coil or torsion-bar springs. Calculated on the basis of weight for a given energy storage capacity, the ratio is about 3.9:1 in favour of coil or torsion-bar springs. For rubber springs this ratio varies according to the form such springs take, but it would probably be of the order of between 7.4 and 15:1. If the stress in a leaf spring has to be limited to $700 \, MN/m^2$, its energy storage capacity is about 50.4 Nm/kg. By using the ratios just quoted, it is easy to calculate the approximate specific energy storage capacities of the other springs.

Gas springs of course inherently have an extremely high energy storage capacity per kg, but this is considerably reduced if the weight of the ancillary equipment required is taken into consideration. This equipment may include a compressor, reservoir, gas drier, de-icer, pipework, valves, dampers and filters. On commercial vehicles, however some or all of these components may be carried in any case for the air brake system.

33.9   Types of leaf spring

In its most commonly used form on road vehicles, the leaf spring is a beam simply supported at each end, with a point load at the centre. Consequently, its bending moment diagram is a triangle, with its apex above the centre and its base a straight line extending between its end supports. If the spring were of lozenge shape, therefore, as in the top diagram in Fig. 33.5, and appropriately proportioned, the bending stresses would be uniform along its length. It follows that if we were then to cut it into strips, as indicated by the dotted lines in the diagram, and assemble them together in pairs of equal length, as in the plan and elevation below the top diagram, we should have a laminated, or leaf, spring of compact form in which optimum use was made of the material because the stresses would be fairly well distributed throughout the volume of the material.

In other words, if a leaf spring is deflected until the stresses in the outer layers of all the leaves rise to the elastic limit, the energy stored greatly exceeds that which could be stored in, for example, a solid steel spring of the same shape, as viewed in plan and elevation, similarly stressed to its elastic limit. The leaf spring is of course much more flexible because the stiffness of a beam is proportional to the cube of its depth multiplied by its width. In the case of the leaf spring illustrated, the depth is in effect that of only one leaf, though the width is the mean of that of the original lozenge shape.

Obviously, as such a laminated spring deflects, there is relative sliding between the surfaces of the leaves, and friction between them tends to oppose the motion. In an effort to reduce and control this friction, the

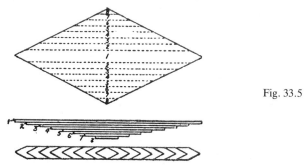

Fig. 33.5

spring leaves are often either interleaved with plastics materials having a low coefficient, or pads or buttons of similar materials are interposed between the ends of their adjacent leaves. Also, the springs themselves are wrapped and sealed to prevent the entry of dirt and water. Even so, to obviate this problem altogether, coil springs or torsion bars have now been widely substituted for leaf springs in cars. Another disadvantage of the leaf spring is that it is heavier than the coil or torsion-bar spring. Moreover, whereas two-thirds of the weight of a semi-elliptic leaf spring is carried by the axle – that is, has to be considered as unsprung weight – only half of that of a coil spring and virtually none of that of a torsion bar is unsprung weight.

33.10   Laminated spring details

On road vehicles, semi-elliptic springs are usually slung beneath the axles, but on cross-country vehicles, to give more ground clearance beneath the body and chassis, they may seat on top of them. In either case, the spring seating pad is generally either welded to the axle tube or is integral with it, and the spring is clamped between it and a saddle plate by either four bolts, or by two U-bolts either embracing grooves around the saddle or seating in separate stirrup pieces around the tube. The bolts used are generally of special steel and should not be replaced by any other type. They have been known to stretch, leaving the spring loose, so exceptionally heavy shock loading can shift the axle back along the springs. These are points that should be looked for in service.

The ends of the longest, or master, leaf of a laminated spring are usually coiled to form the eyes for receiving the pivot or shackle pins. Sometimes, however, these eyes are forged on the ends or other special arrangements made. Rubber bushes are widely used in the eyes of springs for light vehicles, but metal bearing-bushes, with provision for lubrication, are necessary for very heavily loaded springs. Sometimes bushes of threaded form are used in conjunction with similarly threaded pins, to increase their effective bearing areas and better to retain the lubricant. Although rubber bushes need no lubrication and help to prevent the transmission of high-frequency, low-amplitude vibrations to the carriage unit, if they work loose they can squeak and deteriorate rapidly. Nylon or other plastics and composite self-lubricating bearings have been used to obviate both the squeaking and the need for lubrication.

Generally, the ends of the second leaf are extended in order partly to embrace the eyes, for safety in the event of breakage of the master leaf. A single bolt, usually in a vertical hole through the centre of the spring, holds all the leaves together. The head of this bolt is generally accommodated in a hole in the spring seating pad.

Various methods have been used to locate the outer ends of the leaves laterally within the pack. For example pips, or projections, on their upper surfaces can register in corresponding recesses in the underside of the leaves above, as shown in Fig. 33.6. Alternatively, the upper and lower surfaces respectively can have ribs and grooves rolled along their whole lengths. Sometimes the clips alone, also illustrated in Fig. 33.6, are used. Their main function, however, is to distribute the load over the whole length of the spring in the rebound condition, when without the clips, the ends would drop away from the leaves above them. This separation of the leaves, due to the reversal of the load on the spring, would throw all the rebound load on to the master leaf and possibly cause it to break. Sometimes short *rebound leaves* are fitted on top of the master leaf to help to take this reverse loading.

In a patented form of spring, the leaves are symmetrically arranged above and below the master leaf. With clips, such a spring is equally effective in both directions, but such characteristics are rarely required.

The function of the shackle is of course to accommodate the variations in length of the spring, as it deflects upwards through the straight condition to an inverted semi-elliptic shape. Because of this change of length, the rate of the spring changes, being lowest in the straight condition and increasing as its effective length decreases during deflection in either direction from that condition.

Alternatives to the swinging link type of shackle include the slider-block, and rubber types, illustrated in Figs. 33.7 and 8. In the former, the ends of the two top leaves project into a slot in the cylindrical member A, in which they are free to slide. The cylindrical member is free to rotate in its housing B, which is secured to the chassis frame. A disadvantage of this scheme is that it requires lubrication, but modern commercial vehicles generally have the simpler arrangement that can be seen in Fig. 35.18, where the spring ends seat on a curved pad in a tunnel-shape member bolted to the chassis frame. There is plenty of vertical clearance between the spring and the tunnel, but the lateral clearance is restricted to an amount needed to allow a limited degree of articulation as the spring is twisted by one end of the axle rising to ride over a single-wheel bump.

With the Metalastik rubber shackle, Fig. 33.8, lateral location of the end of the spring is afforded by the wedge-shape base of the mounting, leaving it free to deflect the rubber in shear for fore-and-aft movements – with any shackle of course, fore-and-aft location of the spring as a whole is effected by the eye at its other end. Advantages of the rubber shackle include the absence of any maintenance requirement, silence of operation, and absorption of high frequency vertical vibrations, which are taken in

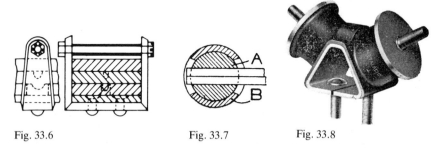

Fig. 33.6   Fig. 33.7   Fig. 33.8

compression in the rubber. Tension in the rebound condition is avoided by a rebound stop, usually a strap fitted loosely between the axle and frame. An example of the use of this system is the 1980 *Ailsa* Mk. III double-deck bus chassis.

A semi-elliptic spring arrangement is illustrated at (*a*) in Fig. 33.9. Since the axle is secured by U-bolts beneath the centre of this spring, the shorter leaves are the lower ones. In suspension arrangements such as some of those illustrated in Chapter 35, where the sprung mass, instead of the unsprung mass, is secured to the centre of the spring and the axles to its outer ends, the shorter leaves are uppermost.

Another form of semi-elliptic spring layout is termed the *full-cantilever spring* – rarely used today except possibly on special mechanisms for construction equipment. This type of spring is pivoted at its centre and at one end, these pivots being on the frame; its other end is then either pivoted or shackled to the axle, according to whether the spring is to take thrust loads and guide the axle or whether other links are to be used to perform these functions.

The quarter-elliptic spring is illustrated at (*b*) in Fig. 33.9. This is a cantilever multi-leaf spring the thick end of which is bolted rigidly to the frame, or sprung mass, and the other end is pivoted or shackled to the axle. It has the advantage of extreme simplicity; for example, its thick end can be clamped in the end of a chassis frame, which therefore can be much shorter than if a semi-elliptic spring were used.

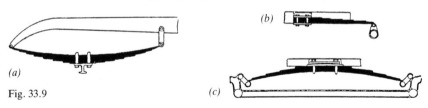

(*a*)

(*b*)

(*c*)

Fig. 33.9

Semi-elliptic springs have also been installed with their axes arranged transversely, Figs. 34.6 and 34.7, one of the last examples in a quantity-produced car being for the independent front suspension of the Fiat 600, introduced in 1955. An earlier example, used on a beam axle, is illustrated at (*c*) in Fig. 33.9. This arrangement has the advantage of economy – one spring and fixings instead of two – but the disadvantage of small vertical deflections unless thin leaves are used or high stresses tolerated, or both. Moreover, such springs can be unstable if called upon to react brake torque and drag simultaneously. With the Fiat 600 and some other independent front-suspension systems, the ends of the transverse leaf spring form the lower links of a double transverse link suspension.

33.11   Taper-leaf springs

Despite the measures taken to improve the stress distribution throughout the depth of a semi-elliptic spring, by dividing it into a multiplicity of separate leaves, the maximum stresses in each leaf still occur only adjacent to where it is supported between the adjacent leaf or leaves and its seating pad on the axle, Fig. 33.10(*a*). Therefore, because so much of the material remains relatively lightly stressed, such a spring is heavier than it otherwise might be.

In recent years, therefore, the taper-leaf spring, sometimes known as the *parabolic-leaf* or *minimum-leaf spring*, has become increasingly popular. It was pioneered in the early nineteen-sixties by the Rockwell Corporation in the USA and, later, by what used to be Rockwell's part-owned company in the UK, Bramber Engineering Ltd.

For any given maximum permissible stress level and width, the stiffness of a semi-elliptic spring is proportional to nt^3, where n is the number of leaves and t is the thickness of each. Consequently if n is halved, to maintain the same stiffness it is necessary to increase t by a factor of only $\sqrt[3]{2}$, which is about 1.26. If, for example, a spring has six leaves, each 0.5 cm thick, its overall thickness is 3 cm, so its stiffness is a constant $K \times 6 \times 0.5^3 = K \times 0.75$. So, if we halve n, t must be increased to $0.5 \times 1.26 = 0.63$ so that the stiffness again becomes $K \times 3 \times 0.63^3 = 0.75$. This reduction in the number of leaves and overall thickness, together with the fact that the

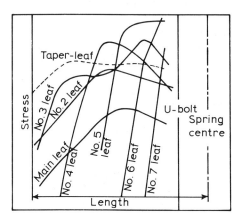

Fig. 33.10(a) Stresses in a single taper-leaf spring compared with those in a plain multi-leaf spring

leaves can be tapered from the centre to each end fairly accurately for efficient material utilisation, means that such a spring can be about 30% lighter than its conventional multi-leaf spring equivalent.

For cars, a single leaf is in many instances adequate but, for heavy commercial vehicles, two or three leaves are common, often used in conjunction with a helper spring. The upper main, or master, leaf has eyes or slider pads at its ends, as in a conventional multi-leaf spring, while the second and third leaves are shaped so that they bear on each other, or on the main leaf, only at their ends, as in Fig. 33.12, and of course they may have spacers between them at the centre. Consequently, inter-leaf friction is extremely small and remains, for all practicable purposes, constant throughout the life of the spring. The Bedford two-leaf front suspension is illustrated in Fig. 33.10(*b*). This is of interest too because the lower end of the damper is spring-mounted.

Fig. 33.10(b) The Bedford BL truck has two taper leaves in each front spring. One end of the lower leaf is wrapped around the eye at the front end of the master leaf and the other end is simply dipped beneath the rear one. Of special interest is the resilient mounting of the lower end of the telescopic damper for cushioning exceptionally severe shocks

As always, the cross-sectional area of the outer ends of the master leaf, and therefore its depth, must be adequate to take the shear plus any torsional loading that might be applied when the vehicle rolls or one wheel only deflects. Inwards from this point, while the bending load increases linearly towards the spring seating in the centre, the stress is a function of the square of the thickness of the leaf. Consequently, the taper is profiled according to an inverse square law – hence the use of the term *parabolic leaf spring*. Sometimes, such a spring is also tapered as viewed in plan, to obtain more clearance between its ends and the tyre. In this case, a straight taper is of course employed, but the ends must be wide enough to avoid instability, or twisting under combined vertical and lateral or torsional loading.

For multi-leaf springs a silico-manganese steel – 0.53 to 0.62% carbon, 1.70 to 2.10 silicon and 0.70 to 1.00 manganese – is adequate because the leaves are so thin that there is no difficulty in obtaining the necessary 80% martensitic structure at the centre of the section. Where the leaves may be up to 28.5 mm thick, however, a carbon 0.60 to 0.90% chromium steel is needed, while for even thicker sections a chromium-molybdenum steel is required. Since, owing to their through-hardening properties, the high-quality steels are employed of necessity for taper-leaf springs, and their yield points are of the order of 620N/mm^2, as compared with 448N/mm^2 for a silico-manganese steel, even further weight reduction is obtained. Moreover with these better steels, reduction in strength at the surface as a result of decarburisation is not a problem. Finally, with taper-leaf springs, no allowance has to be made for loss of fatigue strength owing to interleaf fretting and corrosion in service.

In practice, fatigue strength is further increased by 'scragging' – loading beyond the yield point, as a manufacturing operation – to leave residual compressive stresses in the surfaces that are in tension during deflection. Strain-peening – shot-peening while the spring is under load – is also used for this purpose and to round off the edges of any scratch marks left in the surface by the manufacturing operations, again improving fatigue resistance.

Despite the inherently light weight of the taper-leaf spring, the multi-leaf type can still be the better choice in certain circumstances. First, the tooling costs for the manufacture of taper-leaf springs are high, so such springs can be too costly for small quantity production. Secondly, because of the thickness of leaf, the taper-leaf spring must be longer than the equivalent multi-leaf type – stiffness is proportional to t^3 – and the chassis layout may be such as to limit the length of spring that can be accommodated. Thirdly, in some applications, the hysteresis of a multi-leaf spring may be an advantage. In some cases, the attraction of the multi-leaf spring is that it can be relatively easily made up from any number of leaves of virtually any thickness, or of various thicknesses, to meet a given design requirement.

33.12 Steering effects of leaf springs

Although leaf springs have the advantage of performing the two functions of springing and axle guidance, they have steering effects on their axles. These effects arise from two sources: the first is simply by the motion they induce in the axle, and the second is attributable to the effect of this motion on the steering linkage. The motion of the axle, if it is not regulated by any other linkage, is controlled by the motion of the spring acting as if it were a solid link pivoting about the end secured by its eye directly to the sprung mass – the other end is of course so connected by a shackle. The effective length of this link, however, is modified by the initial straightening and subsequent inversion of the curved shape, or camber, of the spring as it moves from the rebound to the full bump condition. This tends to pull the axle towards the eye as the spring deflects either up or down from the straight condition, and thus reduces the effective radius about which the axle swings. On the other hand, the effect of the shackle in tending to keep the centre of the spring horizontal, is to increase that effective radius.

A rule of thumb for calculating the effective radius of the spring acting as an axle guidance link, is as follows: assume the spring to be horizontal and deflected to zero camber. If the centre of the eye is then a height *h* above the centre of the master leaf, which is the leaf on the end of which the eye is formed, the other end of the effective link will be ½*h* below the centre of the master leaf and on a vertical line three-quarters the effective half-length of the spring from the eye, Fig. 33.11 (*a*). If the axle is clamped rigidly to the spring, the effective half-length is the distance between the centre of the eye and the point at which the spring protrudes from the clamp. Sometimes, however, a resilient pad is interposed betwen the spring and its seating, for absorption of high frequency, small amplitude vibrations; in this case the half-length will be a short distance inside the clamp and is most easily determined experimentally.

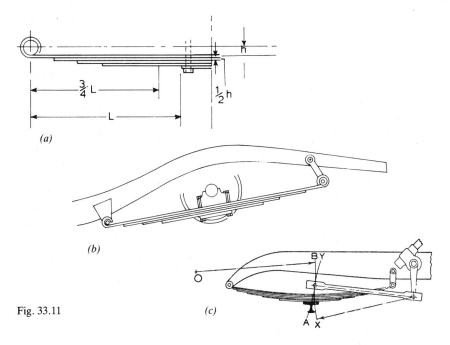

(*a*)

(*b*)

Fig. 33.11   (*c*)

The effect of the spring, acting as a radius rod about its eye, is therefore to pull the axle forward as it moves towards the full bump and rebound positions – or rearwards if the shackle is at the front end and the eye at the rear end of the spring. Consequently, when only one wheel rises over a bump, there is a steering effect on the axle, one end only being pulled forward. This phenomenon can be employed to provide what is termed *rear-end roll-steer*, and is sometimes utilised by designers to compensate for excessive oversteer or understeer arising from other factors such as unequal front-rear weight distribution or the extra deflection of the tyres on one axle owing to the effect of an anti-roll bar on that axle. A steering effect is also, and more usually, obtained by inclining the spring, front to rear as in Fig. 33.11 (*b*), so that it pulls the axle further forward when deflecting in one direction than in the other. It can be modified further by setting the axle off-centre along the length of the spring, taking advantage of the effect of the swinging of the shackle.

Nowadays only commercial vehicles have semi-elliptic springs at the front. Here, the axle-guidance effect of the spring can interact with the action of the steering rod, as shown in Fig. 33.11 (*c*), unless the centre of the eye at the lower end of the steering drop arm is in line with the axis about which the front eye of the spring pivots. Similar principles apply to the positioning of steering-rod joints with independent front suspension, but these will be dealt with later.

33.13   Coil and torsion springs

Both these types of spring were originally used mainly with independent suspension systems, details of which are given in the next Chapter. Now, however, coil springs are widely employed with both live and dead axles. Various linkage systems, as described in the latter part of Chapter 26, are used to control the motions of these axles and to react tractive and brake torques.

Coil springs have the advantage of fitting into a compact space, though the accommodation of a torsion bar parallel to the longitudinal axis of the vehicle is not necessarily difficult. Both of course are stressed in torsion, though there is some bending in a coil spring, and their lives are increased by shot-peening their surfaces to induce compressive stresses in them, and to reduce the effects of scratches in initiating fatigue cracks. Immediately after shot-peening, such springs may be given an anti-corrosion treatment, again to increase fatigue life.

Torsion bars are *scragged* – that is, overloaded in torsion during manufacture – to stretch their outer layers beyond the elastic limit. Because this leaves a residual stress in the outer layers, the maximum stress under service loading occurs beneath the surface, where it is less likely to initiate cracks. This again helps to increase fatigue life. The main reason why torsion bars are not as popular as coil springs is that their end fixings are more costly and provision has to be made for adjustment of the ride height on the vehicle assembly line.

33.14   Variable-rate springs

The rate of a spring is the increment of static load it will carry per unit of deflection – that is, in kg/cm – and with nearly all simple spring arrangements it is constant throughout the normal range of deflection. A rising rate, therefore, is one that increases, instead of remaining constant, as the spring progressively deflects. It has two advantages. First, when the vehicle is only lightly laden – either statically or dynamically – a high degree of isolation of the carriage unit from loading due to small amplitude deflections of the wheels is obtained, without the penalty of excessive deflections under heavy loading. Secondly, since the natural frequency of a mass suspended on a spring is a function of its rate, resonance will not – which it otherwise would – cause a dramatic increase in amplitude of vibration of that mass since such an increase would imply a change in natural frequency, taking the system off resonance.

A rising rate is often obtained by installing what is termed a *helper spring*, which comes into operation only towards the end of the upward deflection of the main spring. With coil-spring suspension, such a helper may take the form of either a rubber spring, or a second coil spring shorter than the main spring, which is mounted beneath the chassis frame so that the axle comes up against it only in the latter stages of its upward deflection. Alternatively, with leaf-spring suspension, a second semi-elliptic spring, having a smaller radius of curvature than the main one, can be centrally clamped on top of the latter in a manner such that its ends come up against stops on the chassis frame only on the latter stages of the upward deflection of the main spring, as in Fig. 33.12. With such an

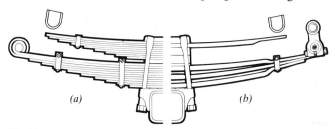

Fig. 33.12 Alternative multi-leaf (a) and taper-leaf (b) spring assemblies with helper springs designed for mounting on common fixings on a Scania range of chassis

arrangement, the rate of the helper spring increases with deflection too since, as it flattens, the slender sections of its ends progressively slide outside the span between its two stops, or supports. A progressive rate is even more easily obtained with rubber springs, as described in the next section, and it is an inherent characteristic of a gas spring compressed adiabatically, as described in Section 33.16.

33.15 Rubber springs

Various forms of rubber springs are used, mainly for commercial vehicles. They have been employed in passenger-carrying vehicles too, but the precise control of ride essential for comfort is difficult to achieve with such springs. A reasonably successful system was that used on the first *Minis* introduced by BMC. This had rubber springs similar to those in the Hydrolastic system described in Section 33.20, but each actuated directly by a rod attached to its centre, and of course without the hydraulic actuation, damping and interconnection system. Separate conventional telescopic hydraulic dampers were used.

An advantage of rubber springs is that, by designing their fixing brackets for loading them initially in shear and then progressively changing to compression they can easily be given a rising rate – because rubber is much stiffer in compression than in shear. The arrangements for the progressive change from shear to compression loading can be seen from Fig. 33.13, where a wedge-shape seating is employed.

Another advantage of this sort of arrangement is that the fatigue strength of rubber is best in compression. It is worst in tension because of the tendency for cracks to be opened out into which impurities are drawn and trapped. Consequently, some form of check-strap or tie is generally used to prevent tension loads from being applied to the rubber, in rebound conditions (see Figs. 33.15 and 16). From the operator's viewpoint, the main advantage of rubber springs is a complete absence of any maintenance requirement. Leaf springs are especially liable to break in rough conditions such as are encountered in quarrying or construction sites. The damping, due to hysteresis of the rubber, is much more predictable than interleaf friction and helps to improve the ride in the unladen condition. Furthermore with an inherently high roll centre, the roll stiffness of a rubber suspension system is good.

The suspension in Fig. 33.13 is for a Norde trailer bogie, made by North Derbyshire Engineering Co. Ltd. On each side of the bogie are longitudinal beams A pivoted, on rubber bushes B at their centres, on the ends of a transverse beam. These longitudinal beams are rubber-bushed at their

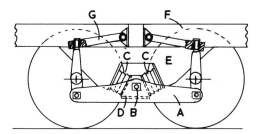

Fig. 33.13

ends too, where they are pinned to the lower ends of vertical brackets on dead axles. The upper ends of these brackets are connected to rubber-bushed radius rods G, pivoted in front of and behind the transverse member of the chassis frame. Under each end of this transverse member are two inverted V-shape brackets, D and E, one beneath the frame side member and the other mounted on the end of the transverse beam. The rubber springs C are interposed, chevron fashion, between these inverted V-shape brackets, so that they are loaded partly in shear and partly in compression.

Radius rods G are usually A-shape links as viewed in plan, to locate the axles laterally. This can be seen in Fig. 33.14, in which the outer ends – apices – of these A-shape links are attached to the tops of the differential housings of the axles, thus obviating the need for brackets. Fig. 33.14 illustrates dual-drive live axle bogie, which is fitted to a Dodge GR1600, 16-tonne tipper chassis.

Another live axle arrangement, the Norde 20-tonne bogie, is shown in Fig. 33.15, and a Foden 40-tonne arrangement in Fig. 33.16. In the latter, two pairs of rubber springs are used, to take the heavier load, and the rebound stop is a cable, instead of the twin vertical tie-rods of Fig. 33.15, which are perhaps noisier. A further difference is the use in the Foden version of metal bump stops and, in the Norde bogie, rubber ones – the latter in effect, are helper springs acting solely in compression. In each case, these stops are in the apex of the inverted V-bracket. A Norde single-axle system, with rubber-bushed trailing links and a Panhard rod for axle location, is shown in Fig. 33.17, again with a rubber bump stop.

Fig. 33.14 Norde Mk II suspension for Dodge GR1600 tipper (16 tonnes gvw)

Fig. 33.15 Norde 20-tonne bogie

In each instance, the rubber springs are interleaved with bonded-in steel plates. The primary function of these plates is to stabilise the rubbers, preventing them from bowing and ultimately being squeezed out bodily from between their abutments. They also help to conduct heat, generated by hysteresis, out from the centre of the rubber blocks.

Two other forms of rubber spring have been used to a limited extent, mainly on trailers and for special-purpose vehicles. The first is simply a steel tube within which is carried coaxially a spindle, either solid or hollow, both components being bonded to a sleeve of rubber in the annulus

Fig. 33.16 Foden 20-tonne suspension

Fig. 33.17 Single-axle 10-tonne suspension with rubber spring, rubber bumpstop, and trailing link location for axle

between them. The tube is usually secured, with its axis horizontal, to the frame. Then the spindle is connected by means of an arm to the axle, thus loading the rubber sleeve in torsion.

The second type of springing is the Neidhart system. This is similar to the first, except that both the tube and spindle are of square section, the sides of the squares of one being set 45° to those of the other, and rubber rollers are interposed between the two, as shown at A in Fig. 33.18. A variant is shown at B, and there are others, for example with hexagonal section spindles and tubes. Significant features of all these arrangements are that,

TYPE A

TYPE B

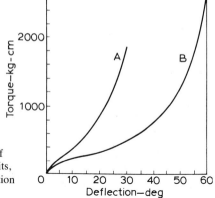

Fig. 33.18 Cross-sections of the type A and B spring units, and a typical torque-deflection curve for each

because the rubber elements roll as well as being compressed, the deflection for any given value of torque is large and, by virtue of the shapes of the members between which the rubber rollers are contained, a rising rate is obtained.

33.16 Air springs

A volume of air, enclosed either in a cylinder fitted with a piston or in a flexible bellows, can be used as a spring, as in Fig. 33.19. Under the static load, the air is compressed to a predetermined pressure, and subsequent motion of the piston either increases or decreases the pressure and consequently increases or decreases the force acting on the piston. If this force is plotted against the piston travel, a curve similar to the compression curve of an engine indicator card will be obtained, so obviously the rate at which the force varies with the piston travel becomes greater as the air pressure increases. It follows that, whereas with a metal spring, equal increments of force result in equal increments of deflection, the rate of an air spring is not constant. This varying rate is an advantage in that a low rate can be obtained for small deflections from the mean riding position while keeping the total rise and fall of the axles within reasonable limits.

Air springs are fairly widely employed on vehicles whose laden and unladen weights differ greatly. This includes principally tractors for semi-trailers, the semi-trailers themselves, and large drawbar trailers. They are also used to some extent on coaches, more especially in Continental Europe and the USA, because of the very high quality ride obtainable with them, particularly if used with independent suspension. The disadvantages are high cost, complexity of compressed air ancillary system, and therefore risk of breakdown, more maintenance than other types of springing, and freezing of moisture in the air in cold weather, which can cause malfunction of valves. Air suspension systems of this sort are, in general, too bulky and too complex for cars, though Citroën cars for instance have their hydro-pneumatic system, Fig. 33.22.

In double-wishbone type suspensions a rubber bellows, circular in section and having two convolutions, is generally used and simply replaces the coiled spring of the conventional design. Rubber bellows type springs

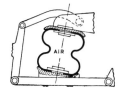

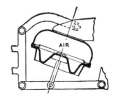

AXIS OF WHEEL ARM

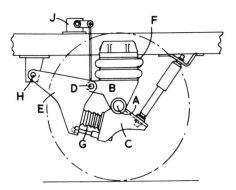

Fig. 33.19 (*above*)

Fig. 33.20 (*left*) Dunlop Stabilair suspension

Fig. 33.21 (*below*)

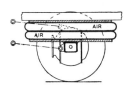

are used also in the Dunlop Stabilair suspension, Fig. 33.20. Alternatively, a metal air-container in the form of an inverted drum is fixed to the frame and a piston, or plunger, is attached to the lower wishbone. Since the piston is considerably smaller than the drum, sealing is effected by a flexible diaphragm secured to its periphery and the lip of the drum. This construction enables the load-deflection characteristic of an air spring to be varied considerably by using profiled guides, such as E and F in Fig. 33.29, to control the form assumed by the diaphragm, and thus its effective area, as the inner member moves relative to the outer one.

Elongated convoluted bellows such as are indicated in Fig. 33.21 have been used in trucks and coaches, with radius rods to deal with the driving and braking torques and thrusts, and a Panhard rod for lateral location.

33.17 Adjustable and self-adjusting suspensions

When steel torsion-bar springs are used, some method of adjusting the standing height of the suspension is needed. This is because, owing to the multiplying effect of the lever arm connected to the active end of the torsion bar, even a small tolerance on the angular relationship between the fittings at its ends can make a significant difference to the attitude of the vehicle. Moreover, it is generally difficult to maintain tight tolerances on the angular relationship between the ends, especially when the bar has been overstressed, or scragged, to increase its fatigue resistance. The adjustment device is generally a screw stop against which a short lever on the static end of the bar bears.

There are also variants of this principle, in which a worm-and-wheel drive is used, the wheel being on the static end of the torsion bar and the worm on a spindle that can be rotated by the driver whilst seated in the vehicle. Whereas the screw type adjustment is for the initial setting on the production line and only rarely used when the vehicle is being serviced, the

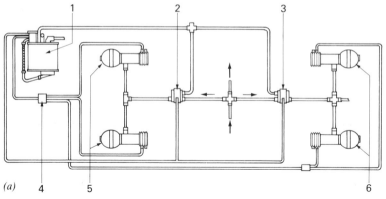

(a)

1 Reservoir
2 Front height corrector
3 Rear height corrector

4 Return reservoir
5 Front suspension cylinders
6 Rear suspension cylinders

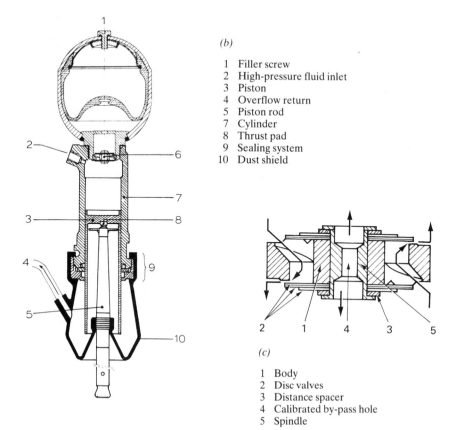

(b)

1 Filler screw
2 High-pressure fluid inlet
3 Piston
4 Overflow return
5 Piston rod
7 Cylinder
8 Thrust pad
9 Sealing system
10 Dust shield

(c)

1 Body
2 Disc valves
3 Distance spacer
4 Calibrated by-pass hole
5 Spindle

Fig. 33.22 (a) Citroën GS suspension system, (b) a spring unit, (c) damper valve

worm-and-wheel or other mechanism – sometimes actuated by a small electric motor – is employed also for adjusting the fore-and-aft trim of the vehicle to cater for variations in the load distribution – for example, when heavy luggage is carried in the boot. While provision for such manual adjustment systems is uncommon, automatic adjustment is the norm for air suspension.

There are two distinctly different types of automatic adjustment system for air suspension. One is the Citroën arrangement, Fig. 33.22, in which an engine-driven hydraulic pump supplies fluid under pressure to an accumulator and thence through levelling valves to combined air spring and strut-damper units. This is the *constant mass* system, in which the mass of the air, or an inert gas, enclosed in the spring is constant. The principle is illustrated diagrammatically, but greatly simplified, in Fig. 33.23 where the hydraulic accumulator is omitted and a floating piston P is depicted instead of the flexible diaphragm of the Citroën system, and the hydraulic damping system is omitted from the chamber O. The constant mass of gas A is compressed above the floating piston.

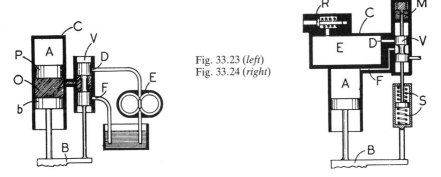

Fig. 33.23 (*left*)
Fig. 33.24 (*right*)

Space O, between the floating piston P and the piston *b* attached to the axle, is filled with oil O, which moves up and down with the pistons *b* and P, the air being correspondingly compressed or expanded. If the load is increased so that the assembly C, which is fixed to the body B, moves downwards, the valve V opens port D, so oil from the pump E passes into the space O. The piston P and assembly C, together with the body, therefore move upwards, and this continues until the port D closes again. Similarly, if the load decreases, the port F is opened and oil escapes from the space O until the port F closes again. Thus the basic ride height of the suspension can be kept constant. This self-adjusting action is damped so that the motions between the body and the axle due to irregularities of the road do not influence the basic setting of the ride height.

The second type of automatic adjustment system is the *constant volume* one, Fig. 33.24. In this, for ride height adjustment, the volume of space A must be kept constant, so air has to be pumped into and released from that space, thus varying the mass of air in it.

If the load carried by the vehicle is increased, valve spool V opens port D, so that air can pass from reservoir E through passage F into space A, until the appropriate ride height is regained. The reservoir is kept charged with air, from a compressor, through non-return valve R. If the load carried is reduced, the valve spool V drops, until passage F is connected through the waisted portion of the spool to the outlet to atmosphere. Since such systems call for a compressor, they are used almost exclusively on commercial vehicles with air suspension – for these vehicles, a compressor is needed in any case for their brake systems.

To avoid excessive air consumption, a dashpot is introduced at M to prevent rapid movement of the spool V by suspension deflections as the wheels roll over the road, but allowing the longer term adjustments in ride height to be made to cater for changes in load. The introduction of this dashpot of course necessitates the interposition of a spring connection of some kind – such as that at S or, perhaps, resembling a hairpin spring – so that, if the axle lifts or falls rapidly, the spring deflects leaving the spool valve to move only at the speed it is allowed to by the dashpot.

33.18   Interconnected suspension systems

In a four-wheeled vehicle the suspensions of the front and back axles or wheels are usually quite independent of each other, but sometimes they are connected together and then the suspension system is said to be *interconnected*, *compensated* or *equalised*. The basic principle involved is shown in Fig. 33.25, where a lever C connects the front and back springs. If the body D is assumed to move up and down so that it remains parallel to the ground, the lever has no effect, and the natural frequency of a vibration of this nature (which is commonly referred to as *bounce*) would be the same as if no lever were used and would depend chiefly on the stiffness of the springs A. But if the body is assumed to vibrate about the axis O, the frequency of this type of vibration (known as *pitch*) will depend chiefly on the stiffness of the springs B and, by making these relatively soft in comparison with the springs A, the natural frequency in pitch can be made very low while keeping the natural frequency in bounce reasonably high. This is the chief claim made for interconnected suspensions.

An equivalent arrangement which is more easily carried out in practice and which is used by Citroën in some of their vehicles is shown in Fig. 33.26.

An alternative arrangement is shown in Fig. 33.27, where the springs B are placed between the body and the axles, and only the springs A are

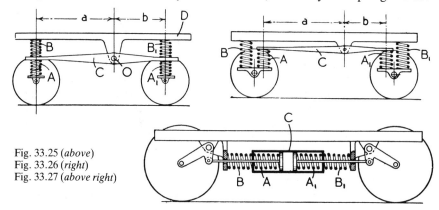

Fig. 33.25 (*above*)
Fig. 33.26 (*right*)
Fig. 33.27 (*above right*)

coupled by the lever C. This produces the same kind of effect as the previous arrangement, but the bounce frequency now depends chiefly on the stiffness of the springs B, and the pitch frequency on that of the springs A. A suspension system using this principle has been used, with torsion bar springs, by the Packard company.

An article on the theory of interconnected suspension systems will be found in the *Automobile Engineer*, Vol. 47, No. 1.

33.19   Interconnected air and liquid suspensions

The interconnection of air springs is a simple matter provided that the actual spring units are of a suitable type. It is essential that they should give an increase in spring force with upward motion of the road wheel even though the air pressure in the unit remains constant. This will be seen from the diagrams in Fig. 33.28 (*a*) and (*b*). In the first the air spring units are shown as simple cylinders such that the effective area of the piston or diaphragm on which the pressure acts remains constant as the wheel rises or falls relative to the body of the vehicle. Thus, assuming that both air

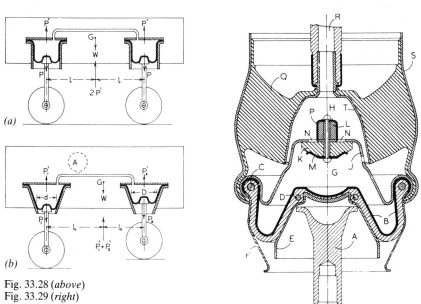

Fig. 33.28 (*above*)
Fig. 33.29 (*right*)

spring units are of the same size, it follows that the pressures in them when they are interconnected will be equal as also will be the forces P exerted by them. The resultant vertical load will thus be $2P = W$ acting at the mid-point between the wheels. The centre of gravity (CG) of the body must therefore always lie at that mid-point in order to obtain equilibrium and this is obviously impossible. Any slight shift of the CG would result in one air unit moving up to its extreme upward position and the other to its lowest.

In diagram (*b*), however, the air units are shown such that the effective area of the diaphragms increases as the road wheels move upward. Thus the effective area of the left-hand unit in the position shown is approximately $\pi d^2/4$ and that of the right-hand unit is $\pi D^2/4$ and so since the air pressure in the units is the same the force P_2 will be greater than P_1. The system will now be stable since any shift of the CG will cause one air unit to move up, thus increasing the force it exerts, while the other unit will move down, thus reducing its force, and equilibrium will be reached when the resultant of these unequal forces acts along the same line as the weight of the body.

The argument is equally valid if the areas of the units are unequal, the CG being no longer at the mid-point.

A system as shown at (*b*) would be effective if it were filled with liquid instead of air but would give a very stiff, or hard, suspension because liquids are only slightly compressible. The effective stiffness of the system can, however, be adjusted to a suitable value by making some part of the system elastic. This is indicated in the diagram where A represents a flexible container or reservoir whose volume can change considerably with changes of internal pressure. Alternatively, the reservoir can be rigid but fitted with a spring-loaded piston or diaphragm or could contain compressible material.

By putting suitable valves in the piping connecting the units of an interconnected fluid system sufficient damping can be obtained to eliminate the necessity for separate dampers.

33.20   BL Hydrolastic suspension systems

In these the elastic element is rubber acting in compression and shear and the interconnection is by fluid, with which the systems are filled. The general form of the construction is shown in Fig. 33.29, which shows a front-wheel unit for one of the BL *Mini* vehicles. It is used in an approximately vertical position but in the BL 1800 a similar unit is used in a horizontal position with its axis transverse to the centre line of the vehicle and for the rear-wheel units the position is again approximately horizontal but parallel to the centre line. The stem A is attached to a rod which bears at its lower end on the upper link of a double wishbone suspension at a point fairly close to the pivot of the wishbone so that the stem motion is only about one-fifth of the wheel movement. The wheel load is supported by the pressure acting on the upper surface of the diaphragm B. This is made of two rubber materials, one providing the required strength and the other the necessary seal for the liquid; it is reinforced by steel beads C and D. A piston member E in conjunction with a skirt F provides support for the diaphragm and helps to give the required spring characteristic. The fluid in the chamber G can at all times pass into the chamber H through a bleed hole provided in the member J which separates the chambers. A damper valve assembly K, L also provides additional passages. Thus the rubber flap valve K which is loaded by the spring M will open downwards when the pressure in H rises sufficiently above that in G, thus allowing fluid to pass through the holes N. The similar valve L, which is at right angles to K, will let fluid pass from G to H. These valves are kept from rotating out of position by fingers integral with the springs M and P which are bent down (as is seen in the case of P) so as to engage the holes N. The fluid in the chamber H acts on the underside of the rubber element Q and through the hose R is transmitted to the other wheel unit on the same side of the car. The rubber Q is bonded on the outside to the canister S which is fixed to the body structure and at its inside to the pot member T. The skirt F, diaphragm B, member J and the canister S are all secured by rolling over the edges of the metal components as shown.

33.21   Moulton Hydragas suspension

The Moulton Hydragas suspension, Fig. 33.30, superseded the Hydrolastic system on the BL car models. Moreover, since September 1977, its use has not been restricted, as it was by the original agreement, solely to this vehicle manufacturer. Now, a constant volume of nitrogen gas has replaced the rubber springs of the Hydrolastic system.

The spring unit, Fig. 33.31, is manufactured for Moulton Developments Ltd. by Dunlop. It comprises a fabricated pressed-steel container, divided into three chambers, one above the other. The uppermost chamber, beneath the domed top of the unit, contains the nitrogen gas and is

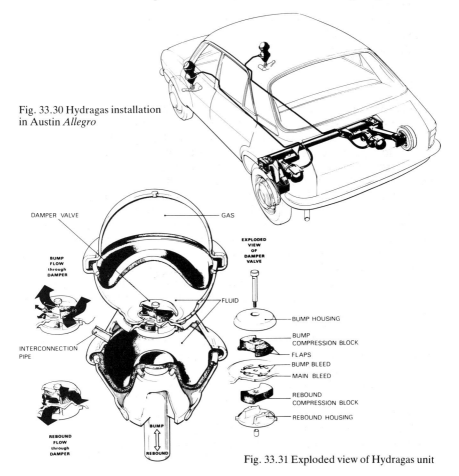

Fig. 33.30 Hydragas installation in Austin *Allegro*

Fig. 33.31 Exploded view of Hydragas unit

separated by a rubber diaphragm from the intermediate chamber below it, which is full of hydraulic fluid – water with anti-freeze agents and a corrosion inhibitor. Below this is the third chamber, again full of hydraulic fluid, and its lower end is also closed by a diaphragm. Beneath this diaphragm bears the tapered piston that is moved up and down by the suspension. The interconnection passage between the two lowest chambers contains the damper valve.

From the illustration it can be seen that, as the piston rises, it forces fluid from the lower chamber, past the elastic rebound valve block which remains seated on the valve plate, through the holes each side of it in that plate, thus lifting the elastic upper, or bump, valve block and flowing into the central chamber where, acting on the upper flexible diaphragm, it compresses the gas in the top chamber. On the rebound stroke, the flow reverses, allowing the upper damper valve block to close and forcing the lower one to open. The shapes and sizes of these two valve blocks determine which holes they cover and uncover, the arrangement being such as to give more damping on the rebound than the bump stroke. Such a spring unit in the *Allegro* rear suspension is illustrated in Fig. 33.32.

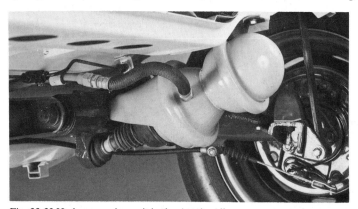

Fig. 33.32 Hydragas spring unit in the Austin *Allegro* rear suspension

With both Hydrolastic and Hydragas suspension, the spring rate increases with deflection. This rising rate is obtained in several ways: the first, in the Hydragas system only, by a progressive increase in the area of the piston contacting the diaphragm; secondly, in the Hydrolastic system only, by the progressive transition from shear to compression loading in the rubber spring; thirdly, by the geometry of the lever system – that is, the suspension – actuating the piston; and finally, the torsional characteristics of the rubber bushes in the pivots of that system. With Hydragas, the front-rear interconnection is made between the lower chambers of each unit.

33.22   Austin *Mini Metro* Suspension

The *Metro* suspension, Fig. 33.33, is a modified Hydragas system. All four wheels have gas springs but, because of the short wheelbase and potentially large variations in front-rear weight distribution, the front and rear springs are not interconnected. This avoids both a high frequency of pitching when lightly laden and a tail-down attitude with a heavy load of luggage at the back. As in the *Mini*, a twin unequal-length tranverse link system is used at the front, and a trailing link actuates each rear gas spring through a push rod, the leverage ratio being 5:1.

With only the driver in the car, a high proportion of the total load is that of the engine and suspension assembly on the front sub-frame. To provide adequate damping control, therefore, between the structure of the vehicle and both the front suspension and the engine, telescopic hydraulic dampers are installed, and there are no damping valves in the front Hydragas units.

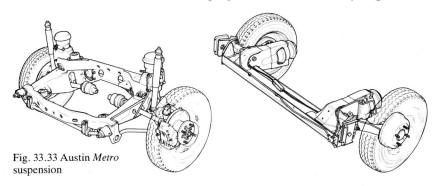

Fig. 33.33 Austin *Metro* suspension

The rear Hydragas springs, on the other hand, are internally damped, as described in Section 33.21. This avoids the need for separate shock absorbers and consequent vertical intrusion into the load space above. The spring units are installed horizontally within the confines of a U-shape sub-frame. To reduce the suspension deflection from the unladen to fully laden condition, the gas springs at the rear are pre-loaded by coil springs co-axial with the push-rods. This restricts the range of operation of the gas spring to the top part of its load-deflection curve, where the slope of that curve steepens. The front-rear attitude of the vehicle is set by charging the rear springs appropriately with fluid. These springs are interconnected laterally so a single charging connection is provided. On the other hand, since there is no front-rear interconnection, the front springs have to be charged individually – they are not laterally interconnected.

Because the front springs act independently and an anti-roll bar is installed there too, all tendency to roll is reacted at the front, while the rear end, on its interconnected rear suspension, is allowed to float freely so far as roll is concerned. This arrangement is analogous to that of a three-legged stool, which has the advantage that all the legs are at all times firmly planted on the ground regardless of whether it is horizontal, flat, or uneven. Consequently, the adhesion between all four wheels is contantly in balance and therefore road-holding is good.

33.23 Chassis lubrication

Most of the more heavily-loaded pivots and control joints in cars either have greased and sealed-for-life bearings or rubber or other types of bushes that do not need lubrication. There may still be, however, one or two points where periodic lubrication is needed, either under pressure through nipples or from an oil can through holes provided for this purpose. On commercial vehicles, where the loading is much heavier, more gun lubrication points may be provided. Oil is preferred to grease on the grounds that it will flow more readily to all parts of the bearing. To reduce the labour involved, nipples are in some instances grouped, with short pipes connecting them to the points to be lubricated.

Alternatively all the points may be fed from a centrally placed reservoir provided with a simple plunger pump which forces oil through a piping system to the lubricating points. The plunger may be spring operated so that after being depressed it gradually rises and forces the oil through the pipes, or it may be operated by the vibration of a spring-suspended mass or by the variation in the pressure in the induction manifold. The chief differences between the systems lie in the arrangements determining the oil flow to each point. One method employs restricted orifices formed sometimes by a loose-fitting screwed plug through the clearances of which the oil has to flow or by a pin fitting fairly tightly in a hole, the oil having to flow between the pin and the walls of the hole.

Another type of central lubrication system uses a pump which is driven at a very low speed from some member of the transmission or engine and which feeds oil continuously through a piping system to the various bearings, regulation of the flow being by restricted orifices.

As an example of a modern central lubrication system the Clayton Dewandre Milomatic will be described. It is shown in Fig. 33.34 and consists essentially of three units: the distributor valve, the intensifier and the delivery valve block. The distributor valve, seen in the lower view, comprises a gearbox giving a reduction of 955:1 between the input shaft A (which is driven off any convenient part of the transmission, the speedometer drive being frequently used) and the gear wheel B which carries the eccentric C. The latter is thus caused to make one revolution per vehicle mile and it operates the valve plunger F through the bell crank D and spring E. As the plunger is pushed to the left it first makes contact with the disc valve G and thus cuts off the passage from the pipe J to atmosphere which has hitherto been open through the hole in the plunger. The disc valve is then pushed off its seat so that air under pressure can pass from the inlet H, which is connected through a pressure regulating valve to the reservoir of the brake system, to the outlet J which is connected to the inlet J in the upper view. This view shows the intensifer; in the position shown the space N is open, through the valve M, to the oil tank and so is full of oil. When the distributor valve passes air to the inlet J the piston K is forced to the right and immediately releases the valve M which then seals off the inlet from the oil tank. The movement of the piston then raises the pressure in the space N and consequently in the spaces P of the delivery valve block which is shown on the right. This consists of a housing Q which is shown bolted up to the face of the intensifier unit but can be mounted as a separate unit and connected to the intensifer by a pipe. In the housing Q injector units S are mounted radially and each one is coupled by a pipe to a chassis point requiring to be lubricated. The spaces T of the delivery valve block are connected to the oil tank via the passage X or by a separate pipe if the valve block is a separate unit. When the pressure in the spaces P is

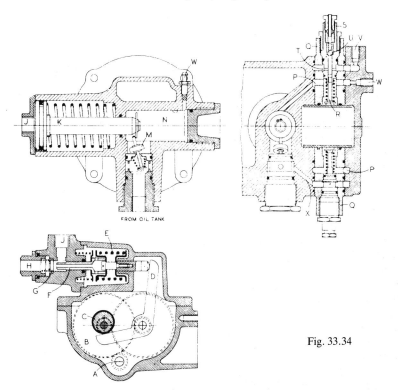

FROM OIL TANK

Fig. 33.34

raised by the action of the intensifier it acts on the area of the plungers R and forces the plungers outward. As soon as the plungers seal off the inlet ports T oil will be forced out through the non-return valves U to the lubrication point. By varying the position of the inlet port the amount of oil delivered per cycle can be varied and three standard positions are available corresponding to deliveries of 0.025, 0.05 and 0.075 cc per cycle. Initially, the system must be filled with oil and so bleeding points are provided as shown at W. Any excess oil can return to the oil tank through the pipe conected to the outlet V. Each valve unit contains 12 injector units and up to six valve units can be operated by one injector unit. The system will continue to operate satisfactorily for all the other lubrication points if one point should become blocked or if the pipe to it should be fractured.

Chapter 34

Suspension systems

Independent suspension is the term used to describe any arrangement by which the wheels are connected to the carriage unit in a manner such that the rise and fall of one wheel has no direct effect on the others. Although widely used only since the Second World War, its first employment was at least as early as 1878. Some of the reasons for the majority of manufacturers abandoning – progressively for about a decade from 1935 – the beam axle and semi-elliptic spring front suspension on cars are given at the end of Section 33.9. The benefits derived from the adoption of independent front suspension are as follows –

(1) Because of the close approximation to vertical travel of the wheels, gyroscopic kicks in the steering system are obviated – with a beam axle, these reactions, which tend to initiate wheel shimmy, are inevitable if only one wheel rises over a bump.

(2) Steering effects due to lateral movements of the tyre/road contact patch, as the wheel rises and falls, are obviated.

(3) Axle tramp, and particularly that associated with alternating wind-up and release of leaf springs subjected to brake torque, is obviated.

(4) Variations in castor angle – defined in Section 32.5 – due to this wind-up are obviated.

(5) A coil spring can be more easily accommodated close to a wheel that has to be steered than can be a semi-elliptic spring.

(6) The roll centre can be lower and the spring base wider, so the roll resistance is higher. A secondary effect of the inherently high roll resistance is that softer springing can be used which, as explained in Section 33.2, reduces the tendency to pitch.

(7) The engine can be positioned further forward, since it does not have to clear a beam axle – this leaves more space for the occupants of the car.

(8) Unsprung mass is lighter, and therefore the ride quality improved.

There are many independent suspension layouts, and they can be classified as in Table 11.

Most of these can be adapted for use with any of several different types of spring. It would be impossible in the space available to describe all the systems, but the most important types are dealt with approximately in order of merit in this Chapter.

Table 11 – INDEPENDENT SUSPENSION LAYOUTS

Types	*Examples*
Single transverse link (Sec. 34.5)	A Mercedes-Benz 300d swing axle (rear)
Double transverse link (Sec. 34.3)	Majority of modern front suspensions
Single leading or trailing link (Sec. 34.6)	Citroën 2 CV front and rear, *Mini* and Renault *Frégate* rear
Double leading or trailing link (Sec. 34.7)	VW *Beetle*, rear
Broulhiet (Sec. 34.8)	Broulhiet
Girling (Sec. 34.9)	Daimler *Regency*, 1951
Single link with pivot axis not parallel to either longitudinal or transverse axes of car (Sec. 34.19)	Triumph 2000 (1963) and Fiat 600 (1965) rear suspension
Double link with pivot axis not parallel to either longitudinal or transverse axes of car (Sec. 34.19)	Humber *Super Snipe* (1952)
MacPherson strut type (Sec. 34.4)	Many modern cars, including Ford range
Dubonnet (Sec. 34.10)	Vauxhall ranges, just prior to and after the Second World War
Slider, or pillar, type (Sec. 34.11)	Morgan

34.1 Camber angle

The overwhelming majority of cars now have a double transverse-link front suspension, though the MacPherson strut-and-link type, to be described in Section 34.4, is gaining ground. In both instances the aim is at a vertical motion of the wheel approximating to what it would be if it were mounted on an arm whose pivot was a point of infinity on the opposite side of the vehicle. This implies no changes in camber angle, which is the angle of the plane of the wheel relative to the vertical.

Camber angle is positive when the lower edge of the wheel and tyre is tucked under the vehicle, and negative when the upper part slopes in towards the centre of the vehicle – easy to remember by association of negative with knock-kneed. Negative camber, by setting the wheel at a favourable inclination for reacting the centrifugal force on the vehicle, increases its cornering ability. Positive camber, on the other hand, is sometimes adopted to help in obtaining centre point steering, as described in Section 32.4.

34.2 Roll centre

When a force acts on a car from the side, making the body tilt or roll, the motion will be about some line lying in the vertical plane containing the longitudinal axis of the car. This line is called the *roll axis*. Its position

depends on the type of suspensions at the front and rear. In Fig. 34.1 is a
front view of a car having an axle and laminated springs – the latter are
indicated simply by zigzag lines. When no side force acts, these springs will
be equally compressed and each will exert a force P equal to half the weight
carried by the axle. The vertical forces between each wheel and the ground
will also be equal to P plus half the weight of the axle and wheels. When a
side force F acts on the body it sets up forces f_1 and f_2 at the points of
connection of the body and springs. The relative magnitudes of these
forces and the exact positions at which they act will always be somewhat
uncertain. However, assuming them to be equal and to act as shown, their
resultant is a force F' equal and opposite to F. These two forces F and F'
thus constitute a couple of magnitude Fh, h being the perpendicular
distance between them which, unless the tilt is vary large, may be assumed
to be equal to OG. For equilibrium, there must be an equal and opposite
couple to balance the couple Fh. This balancing couple is supplied by an

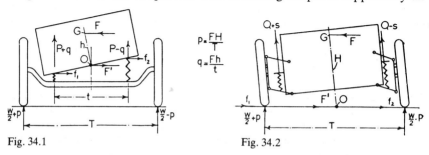

Fig. 34.1   Fig. 34.2

increase q in the left-hand vertical reaction and a decrease of the same
magnitude in the right-hand one. Consequently, the left-hand spring will
be compressed a little more than before while the right-hand one will
extend by the same amount. The body will thus tilt about the point O, on
the roll axis. Similarly there will be a corresponding centre O' at the rear,
so the line OO' is the roll axis. The change q in the spring forces on each
side will be equal to Fh/t, t being the spring base.

The forces between the wheels and the ground will change by amounts p,
where $p = $ FH/T, T being the wheel track and H the height of the line of
action of the force F above the ground. If, under the action of the side
forces f_1 and f_2 or, more accurately, under the reactions to those forces, the
springs deflect slightly sideways, the point O would move sideways and
therefore the centre of tilt would actually be slightly lower.

Considering now the car with independent suspension as shown in Fig.
34.2, the side force F again sets up a tilting couple and this has to be
balanced by an increase p in the force exerted by the left-hand spring and
an equal decrease in that exerted by the right-hand spring. If the tilt is not
excessive, these changes in spring force will be equal, one increasing from
Q to Q + s and the other decreasing to Q − s. The compression of the
left-hand spring will be increased by some amount and that of the
right-hand spring will be decreased by the same amount. Therefore the
suspension will assume the position shown and the body will have tilted
about the point O. Thus O is now a point on the roll axis and the line
joining it to the similar centre of tilt O' at the rear will be the roll axis.

For a car having rigid axles at front and back, the roll axis will be some distance above ground level while for a car having independent suspension at front and back, the roll axis will be at or near ground level. The roll axis of a car having independent suspension at the front and a rigid axle at the rear will be inclined, from approximately ground level at the front rising to about axle level at the rear.

If the roll axis lies at ground level, the overturning couple FH will be greater than Fh obtaining when the roll axis is above ground level. Although this will tend to make the tilt of the car with independent suspension greater than that of the car with rigid axles front and rear, this tendency is offset because the effective spring base of the independent suspension is the wheel track T, which is considerably wider than the spring base t. It can be shown that, for a vehicle with rigid axles, the angle of tilt is approximately proportional to $2q/t^2 = 2Fh/t^2$ while, for a car with independent suspension, it is proportional to $2p/T^2 = 2FH/T^2$. In most cases, the latter will be the smaller because of the greater effective spring base, which will outweigh the effect of the increase in the arm H of the overturning couple.

The greater the roll stiffness – resistance to roll – at one end of the car, the larger will be the proportion of the tilting couple that will be reacted at that end. Indeed, if the roll stiffness were infinite at the front, the whole of the tilting couple would be reacted there, unless the vehicle were flexible enough to deflect torsionally and thus throw some of the load on to the rear suspension. Cars are very rigid torsionally relative to the loads they carry. This is because the whole body can be regarded as a torque tube. Heavy commercial vehicles, however, because of the great weights that they must carry – relative to which their chassis frames are shallow – are flexible torsionally, which is one reason why independent suspension is not normally used on them.

In practice, however, 'roll centre' is not such a simple concept as it might at first appear. Although it is generally assumed that the vehicle rolls about an axis represented by a line passing through the roll centres of the front and rear suspension, this could be true only if the wheel and tyre assemblies were rigid and did not move sideways on the road. The roll centre, as determined from the kinematics of the suspension links, moves as the suspension deflects and does so increasingly towards the extremes of this deflection. Obviously the actual motions of the carriage unit, taking into account not only the movements of the roll centre due to variations of the suspension geometry with wheel deflection but also both vertical and lateral deflections of the tyre calls for the use of a computer. Even so, a first approximation accurate enough for practical purposes can be obtained from consideration of the suspension link geometry.

The method of finding the roll centre is illustrated in Fig. 34.3. It involves extending the axes of the suspension links until they meet at O, and then joining O and the centre of contact T between the tyre and the road. Point O is then the instantaneous centre about which rotate all parts of the suspension and its pivots on the carriage unit on that side of the vehicle. If we then do the same for the suspension on the other side, we find that the two lines OT intersect at C, which is the instantaneous centre about which the two points T rotate and is therefore the roll centre of the vehicle as a whole. By re-drawing this diagram with one suspension deflected up and the other down – the situation when the body rolls – it can be shown that the points O move down and up respectively on the two sides which of course moves the roll centre C not only up or down, according to the geometry, but also laterally, off the vertical centre-line of the vehicle. Some typical linkage systems and their roll centres, with the suspension in its static position, are shown in Fig. 34.4.

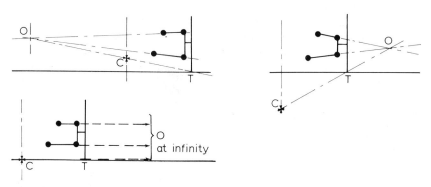

Fig. 34.3 Note: If the suspension on the other side of the vehicle were drawn, the diagram for obtaining the instantaneous centre would be a mirror image of that shown here, which is why C is always on the vertical centreline of the vehicle, except when the wheels on each side deflect in opposite directions

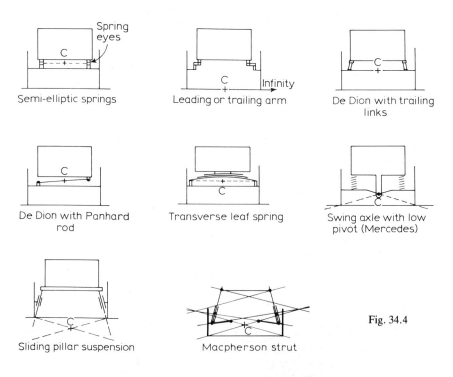

Fig. 34.4

34.3 Double transverse-link suspension

A double transverse link suspension, with a torsion-bar spring, is illustrated diagrammatically in Fig. 34.5. To eliminate wheel tilt with deflection, that is change in the camber angle ϕ, the two arms would have to be of equal lengths, which would place the roll centre at ground level. This, however, would have the effect of varying the track with roll, having undesirable steering effects and could also adversely affect tyre wear. By shortening the upper link it is possible to keep the track almost constant without introducing too much variation in camber angle. Moreover, the slight change in the camber angle is negative on the outer wheel when the vehicle is turning, which increases the cornering power. In the early independent suspension systems, these links were generally both parallel to the ground. After the Second World War, however, the practice of inclining them, to move the roll centre, became widespread. Exactly what these effects are can be seen easily by drawing sketches on the lines indicated in Fig. 34.3, but with the arms at various angles. It will be seen that sloping the upper link down towards the wheel raises the roll centre, and *vice versa*.

Where a coil spring is to be used, instead of a torsion bar, it is usually installed co-axially with the telescopic damper S in Fig. 34.5. Incidentally, it is more common for the upper ends of the spring and shock absorber to be on the vehicle structure instead of on the upper transverse arm. On some vehicles, the springs and dampers have been mounted separately, so that access could be gained more easily for servicing the shock absorber. An alternative is to arrange for removal of the shock absorber through a hole in the spring seating pan. With front-wheel-drive cars, the coil spring and shock absorber are in most instances interposed between the upper transverse link and the vehicle structure, to leave space for the drive shaft to the wheel.

With unequal-length wishbones, the end B of the steering arm, Fig. 34.5, moves in a curve that is not an arc of a circle, so vertical deflection of the suspension inevitably has some steering effect if the centre of the other end – that of the joint at its connection to the remainder of the steering linkage – is in line with the axis $X_1 X_1$ of the pivot for the lower transverse link. This problem is generally overcome in one of two ways: either a position for the centre of the connection to the remainder of the steering linkage can be chosen so that it coincides with the centre of an arc approximating to the curve through which B moves, in which case the undesirable steering effect may become negligible; or the centre of B is placed in line with the axis x_1 of the lower arm A_1, in which case, with the other connection in line with the axis X_1, the motion would be truly circular and there would be no steering effect. Similarly, the two ends could be in line with the axes X_2 and x_2 of the upper arm A_2, though this is more difficult to arrange.

Two variants of this type of suspension linkage are shown in Figs. 34.6 and 34.7. In the first, a laminated spring serves as the upper arm, while in the second, two pairs of laminated springs, one at the top and the other at the bottom, replace both transverse arms. The first can of course be inverted, as in the case of the Fiat 600, which had a wishbone-type upper link and no drag link. When the lever arm type shock absorber was widely

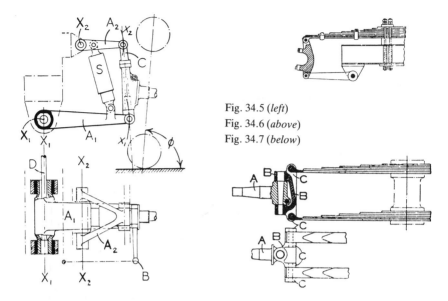

Fig. 34.5 (*left*)
Fig. 34.6 (*above*)
Fig. 34.7 (*below*)

used, its arm was sometimes made to serve as the upper transverse link, a notable example having been the Morris *Minor*.

Another variant is one in which the lower arm is replaced by the drive-shaft. One example is the Triumph *Herald*, in which the upper transverse link is formed by the ends of a transverse leaf-spring, and the lower by what is sometimes termed a *swinging half-shaft*. This shaft swings up and down about a universal joint at its inner end, where it is connected to the final drive differential gear. Provision for the necessary articulation at its outer end is made in an unusual manner. The wheel is keyed directly on to the tapered outer end of the half-shaft, and the wheel bearings are immediately inboard of it. These bearings, with the outer end of the half-shaft rotating in them, are carried in a housing that is pivot-mounted on the lower end of the vertical link to the upper end of which the eye of the transverse leaf-spring is connected. The axes of these two pivot connections are of course parallel, so that the two links can articulate together, carrying the vertical link and thus the wheel assembly up and down with them. To provide fore-and-aft location, a drag link, pivoted at both ends, serves as a radius rod between the wheel bearing housing and a transverse member further forward on the chassis frame.

A similar independent rear-suspension layout, but with coil springs, Fig. 34.8, is used on several Jaguar cars. Here the swinging half-shaft forms the upper transverse link, but it has at its outer end a universal joint instead of the pivoted bearing housing arrangement of the Triumph *Herald*, to give it the required freedom to articulate. The lower link comprises a single transverse arm and a drag link. The disc brakes are mounted inboard, on the final-drive assembly, thus considerably reducing the unsprung weight and relieving the suspension linkage of the brake torque except in so far as it is transmitted back through the swinging half-shaft to the brakes. Since the stub axle carrier pivots about the outer end of the lower link, the vertical loads applied at the wheel put the half-shaft in compression while,

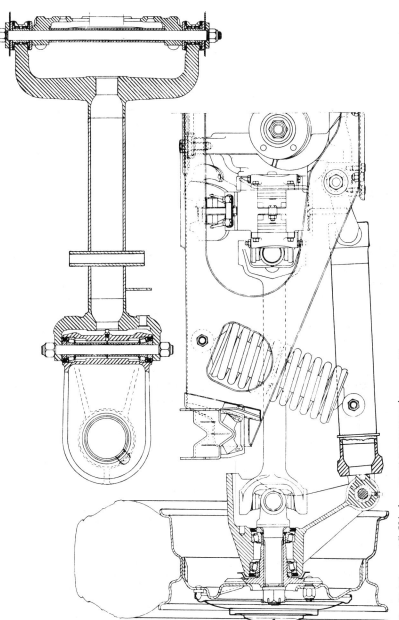

693

Fig. 34.8 Jaguar Mk X independent rear suspension assembly

during cornering, the side load on the outer wheel places it in tension, the two tending to cancel each other out. On the inner wheel, although the two loads are additive, they are in any case lighter and, during extreme cornering, fall to zero.

There are some of the variants of the double transverse link system, in which each of the two links can be a single arm used in conjunction with a drag link, as in the Jaguar system, or it may be triangulated to form what is termed a *wishbone link*. In the latter, the apex of the link is adjacent to the stub-axle carrier, and the base is secured by a pivot bearing at each corner to the vehicle structure. The more widely spaced are these bearings, the lighter becomes their loading due to brake drag and torque. There are examples in which the axis of the pivot bearings are not parallel to the longitudinal axis of the vehicle. This arrangement is usually adopted, as in the Humber *Super Snipe* chassis, simply to enable the front transverse member of the chassis frame to clear the engine sump or, in other words, to enable the engine to be installed as far forward as possible. The frame of this vehicle is illustrated in Fig. 29.3, and the wishbone links (not shown) trail at the same angle as the outer ends of the front transverse member.

34.4 MacPherson strut type

The principle of the strut type suspension is illustrated in Fig. 34.9 and details in Figs. 34.10 and 32.8. This type is common because, with its widely-spaced attachments to the carriage unit, it fits in well with the basic concepts of chassisless construction. Moreover, with transverse engines there may be no room for upper transverse links and, even if there is, the strut type leaves more space around the engine, so access for maintenance is easier. The only significant disadvantage is the radial loading on the piston, due to lateral forces during cornering and to brake torque.

Two links, one taking the lateral and the other the drag loading, and one nearly vertical telescopic strut, make up the complete mechanism (Fig. 34.9). A single transverse arm is pivoted on the structure at B and connected by a ball-and-socket joint D to the base of the strut C. Sliding in C is the member E, the upper end of which is secured to the body by the equivalent of a ball-and-socket joint – in practice, since the articulation at F is small, a rubber joint is generally used. The spring is compressed between two flanges, one on the member C and the other on E. This telescopic strut also serves as the hydraulic damper. For steering, member C rotates about the axis DF.

The fore-and-aft forces acting on the road wheel are taken by a tie or drag link, the rear end of which is pivoted near the outer end of the link A; at its other end, this drag link is pivoted to the body structure. Both pivots are usually rubber bushes. In plan view, it is usually set approximately 45° relative to the longitudinal axis of the car and, since it is in front of the link A, it is in tension. In many instances, it is formed simply by bending the ends of a transversely-installed anti-roll bar, so that they will perform the dual functions of drag links and lever arms for actuation of the anti-roll bar, which is usually carried in rubber bushes adjacent to its cranked ends.

In Fig. 34.10, the strut and stub-axle forging are made as separate components, for ease of replacement of a damper. The top end of the piston rod E is free to rotate in a bush in the centre of a large rubber mounting by means of which the unit is secured to the body. This bush serves as a swivel bearing for the steering, while the rubber mounting insulates the body from noise, vibration and strains due to deflection of the suspension unit. The lower transverse link A is connected by a rubber bush H to the drag link, which has another rubber bush for its connection to the vehicle structure.

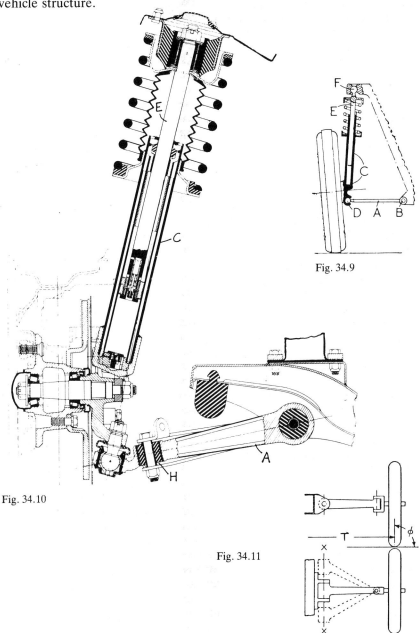

Fig. 34.9

Fig. 34.10

Fig. 34.11

34.5 Single transverse link

What might be described as a single transverse-link system was used for the front suspension of the Allard vehicles in the nineteen-fifties. In effect, the front axle beam was divided in the centre, where each half was pivoted to the chassis frame. Coil springs were interposed between the outer ends of these half-axles and the frame. Drag loads were taken by two radius rods, both pivoted beneath the centre of the front transverse member of the frame and extending rearwards and outwards to a point beneath the spring seats, where they were rigidly attached to the axle. The axis of the pivots of the radius rods were in line with those of the divided axle. Thus, each half-axle and drag rod together formed a single transverse link. This type of system has been more commonly used in rear suspensions, as the swing axle arrangement described in Section 34.18, and it suffers the same disadvantages.

Fig. 34.11 illustrates diagrammatically a front axle arrangement, the dotted line showing how a wishbone type link can be used, instead of a drag link, to react brake drag. Both the track T and the camber angle Ø change with suspension deflection. The steering rods have to pivot on ball joints the centres of which are in line with the axes X, so that the rods rise and fall parallel with the transverse link.

34.6 Single leading or trailing link

This type, shown diagrammatically, in Fig. 34.12, is the simplest but has several disadvantages, which include variations in angle of inclination θ of the kingpin axis, the difficulty of obtaining adequate stiffness to resist satisfactorily the couple due to lateral loading at ground level during cornering, and the fact that the wheels tilt to the same angle as the sprung mass when the vehicle rolls. Such a system has been used also with torsion-bar springing, including with laminated torsion bars. Normally the two torsion bars, one for the left-hand and the other for the right-hand arms, are attached one at each of the pivots X of the arms A, and their other ends are anchored to the frame or vehicle structure, usually on the side remote from the pivots, so that they overlap instead of being co-axial, and therefore can be longer.

When the wheel is steered straight ahead, the joint B on the end of the steering arm moves through arc x_1 while the stub-axle moves through arc x as the suspension deflects. Therefore, if unwanted steering effects are to be avoided, the other end of the steering rod should pivot somewhere along axis XX, which can be difficult with torsion-bar springing. Because of this and the variation of castor angle, or angle of trail, this type of suspension has been used more for rear than for front suspension systems.

34.7 Double leading or trailing link

With two parallel links, A_1 and A_2, of equal lengths and pivoting about axes X_1 and X_2, Fig. 34.13, the vertical member C, which carries the stub-axle and kingpin, maintains the angle θ constant. The end B of the steering arm moves through arc y, the radius of which is equal to that of

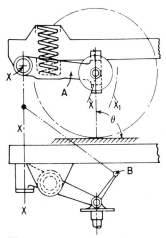

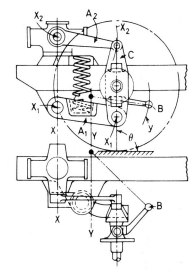

Fig. 34.12 (*above*)
Fig. 34.13 (*right*)

arcs x_1 and x_2. Therefore, if the steering rod end is pivoted anywhere on the axis YY, vertical deflection of the suspension will not have any steering effect. If torsion-bar springing is used, one bar can be connected to the upper link on one side and the other bar to the lower link on the other side.

34.8   Broulhiet suspension

The Broulhiet arrangement, Fig. 34.14, is a variant of the double transverse-link system. A single link is used at the top and a wishbone- or V-shape arm at the bottom. The bottom link is made in two parts, B and C, pinned together. This joint is not, however, a working joint so B and C could be made integral. The axes XX of all the pivots are parallel to each other but inclined – converging towards the front – relative to the longitudinal axis of the car. This arrangement places the arm C in a good position for taking the fore-and-aft forces; it is also longer than in the more conventional double transverse arm type, and therefore can more easily react brake torque. Since the pivots E and F are a considerable distance apart, it is difficult to keep their axes coincident. To allow for any slight misalignment, one or both of the pivots can be rubber bushed. Except for misalignment errors, the movements of the linkage do not involve any but ordinary pivot action at any of the joints.

34.9   Girling suspension

This is a variant of the Broulhiet system, and is illustrated diagrammatically in Fig. 34.15. The stub-axle and swivel-pin assembly is in effect carried by the arm C, and if the length of that arm is appropriately chosen, the brake torque can apply at its pivot an upward force appropriate for counteracting the nose-down effect due to weight transfer from rear to front axle. Because of the conflicting motions of the links, rubber bushes have to be used at all the pivot points, so this type of suspension is not favoured for modern cars where precise steering is required.

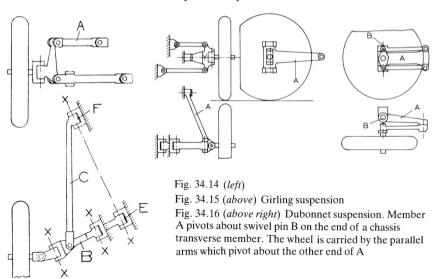

Fig. 34.14 (*left*)
Fig. 34.15 (*above*) Girling suspension
Fig. 34.16 (*above right*) Dubonnet suspension. Member
A pivots about swivel pin B on the end of a chassis
transverse member. The wheel is carried by the parallel
arms which pivot about the other end of A

34.10　Dubonnet suspension

With the Dubonnet system, Fig. 34.16, the kingpins are mounted on the
ends of a transverse beam rigidly secured to the vehicle structure, and each
stub-axle is on the end of either a leading- or a trailing-arm assembly
deflecting vertically about the end of a torsion-bar spring and, for steering
the vehicle, swivelling about the kingpin. In other words, the kingpin
bearings and steering arm are on the sprung mass, and the mechanism
allowing vertical deflection of the suspension is interposed between the
kingpin and wheel. Several American cars had such a system in the
nineteen-thirties but the most recent example was that used on Vauxhall
cars in the late nineteen-forties. Fig. 34.16 is a diagrammatic representation of the 1936 Vauxhall DX Light Six, which had a torque-reaction rod
parallel to the leading arm.

The Vauxhall system, Fig. 34.17, the 1949 *Velox* and *Wyvern* L-type,
was in fact a modified Dubonnet arrangement, in which a coil spring
supplemented the torsion-bar spring. A rigid hollow trailing arm extended
rearwards from the kingpin bearing. It contained the coil spring and
damper and carried at its rear end both the outer end of the transverse
torsion-bar spring and, just outboard of it, the bearings for the forward
extending arm carrying the stub-axle. Because of the restricted space for
the torsion-bar spring, owing to the proximity of the engine, it comprised
two co-axial halves – a hollow and a solid bar. The outer end of the solid
bar was secured to the pivot end of the suspension arm and the inner end
splined into the inner end of the hollow torsion bar, the outer end of which
was flanged and bolted to the rear end of the rigid arm housing the coil
spring and damper.

The functioning of the forward extending arm and torsion-bar spring is
simple, so no explanation is necessary. Rather more complicated, however, is the action of the powerful supplementary spring and the simul-
taneous operation of the damper. The latter is a twin side-by-side cylinder

type, hydraulic damping unit actuated by a pair of arms diametrically opposed on the pivot pin extension of the torsion bar, and therefore rocking with it as it oscillates in each direction. In principle, it is similar to the lever-type damper illustrated in Fig. 33.4.

The damper is housed behind, and the coil spring in front of the torsion bar, both of course being in the rigid hollow arm. A toggle arm extends forwards from the pivot pin extension of the torsion bar, and the coil spring is compressed between its end and the swivel-pin bearing housing assembly. When the suspension arm is in its normal static position, the axes of

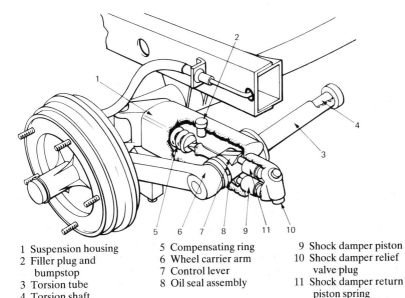

1 Suspension housing	5 Compensating ring	9 Shock damper piston
2 Filler plug and bumpstop	6 Wheel carrier arm	10 Shock damper relief valve plug
3 Torsion tube	7 Control lever	11 Shock damper return piston spring
4 Torsion shaft	8 Oil seal assembly	

Fig. 34.17 Vauxhall front suspension, sectioned view

the spring and the toggle arm are in line, so the spring has no effect on the overall spring rate. As the toggle rotates further, allowing the coil spring to extend, and thus unloading it, the overall rate increases again, ultimately approaching, at both extremes of deflection, that of the fairly short, and therefore stiff, torsion bar. The advantages of this system are light unsprung mass, variable-rate suspension, accurate steering geometry, and an anti-dive effect because the arm carrying the stub-axle tends to lift the front of the car when brake torque is applied. Its disadvantages, however, are its complexity, and shortness of the torsion-bar spring.

34.11   Slider, or pillar, type

Lancia were probably the first to introduce this type of suspension, which has been used for many years too on Morgan cars. The principle is illustrated in Fig. 34.18, in which, for steering, the stub axle A, on pillar B, swivels in plain bearings in the housing C for the coil spring D. Broulhiet produced a similar suspension but with the lower end of the pillar carried in bearings, for accommodating steering motions, in the end of a rigid transverse member secured to the frame. The slider portion of the Broulhiet pillar had splines and linear ball bearings to reduce the friction in the system. This arrangement also had the advantage of placing the steering linkage on the sprung mass.

In general, the disadvantages of the pillar type of suspension, other than the Broulhiet arrangement, include a steering effect owing to the vertical motion of the wheel in relation to the arc through which the steering rod must move. With all types, there is difficulty in accommodating a pillar and coil spring of adequate length without seriously reducing the ground clearance beneath them. Moreover, the resultant need to limit the vertical deflection can cause severe understeer when, under extreme conditions during cornering, the roll has taken up all the suspension movement and roll reaction is consequently taken mainly through the front wheels. The principal advantage is the absence of variations in camber and castor angles or track, with vertical deflection of the suspension.

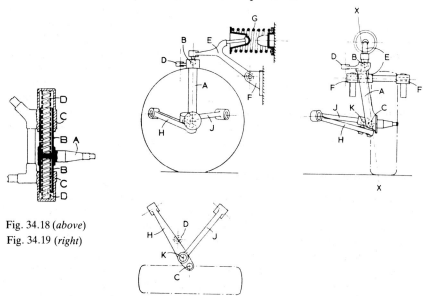

Fig. 34.18 (*above*)
Fig. 34.19 (*right*)

34.12   Rover 2000 front suspension

This type of suspension, Fig. 34.19, does not fall neatly into any of the 11 categories listed at the beginning of this Chapter. The road wheel is carried on a stub axle which is integral with the tubular member A. This member is held top and bottom by ball-and-socket joints B and C and so can turn about the axis XX for steering – the steering arm is at D. The ball of the joint B is part of a lever E, which is pivoted in rubber bushes, on the axis FF, and carried by brackets fixed to the body structure. The lever E is also used to transfer the vertical load of the wheel to the spring G and thus to the body. At the lower end of the member A, the ball of the joint is fixed in the composite wishbone member H and J, whose two parts are pivoted in rubber bushes on the vehicle structure at their inner ends and are pivoted to each other at their outer ends, at K, by a ball-and-socket joint at an angle to each other. A telescopic damper (not shown) is coupled at its upper end to the lever E and at its lower end to the body structure.

The advantages include a reduction in weight of the vehicle, because the main load-bearing structure extending foward from the dash is limited to that needed to carry the engine mountings and lower link only of the suspension. Additionally, camber and castor angles and track vary very little with vertical deflection. A major disadvantage is that, because the suspension loads are taken mainly directly by the dash, it is difficult to keep the noise out of the passenger compartment.

34.13   Driven-wheel suspension

Many of the systems previously described have been adapted for driven wheels in both front- and rear-wheel-drive cars, and others will be described in the Sections on rear suspension that follow. Some early examples had transverse leaf-springs serving also as either one or both of the transverse links on each side, as in Figs. 34.6 and 34.7. The telescopic dampers then had to be offset to the front or rear of the driveshafts.

Some of the Renault models have a coil spring and double transverse-wishbone system, but the coil spring and damper are placed above the upper link, thus leaving the space between the links clear for the driveshaft. In the Ford *Fiesta*, the MacPherson strut type suspension is adapted simply by cranking the bottom transverse link, as viewed in plan, so that the pivot at its inboard end is positioned far enough forward to clear the driveshaft as the suspension drops to the rebound position.

34.14   Rear suspension – live axle

Some comments on control systems for live axles have already been given in Chapter 26. With such a rear axle, the unsprung weight comprises that of the axle assembly – differential, its casing, the half-shafts and their tubular housings, the hub and wheel assemblies, about two-thirds of the weight of the springs, if semi-elliptic, plus that of the propeller shaft. If coil springs are employed, only half their weight is unsprung, and in any case, they are much lighter than leaf springs. On the other hand, some additional links must then be provided to control the motion of the axle and, generally, half the weight of these is unsprung. The greater the unsprung mass the larger will be the amplitudes of the hop and tramp motions of the axle and the more difficult it becomes to obtain good ride, roadholding and stability.

Another disadvantage of the live rear axle is the tendency for the propeller shaft torque to press the wheel on one side down and to lift that on the other side. In the early days, engines were designed to be started with a cranked handle, using the right hand, so they traditionally rotate clockwise as viewed from the front. When they are running, their torque, from the viewpoint of a man in the driving seat, tends to press the left-hand rear wheel down and to lift the right-hand wheel. Consequently during acceleration in low gear from a standing start – when the torque can be very high – the right-hand wheel may spin and traction be lost. Additionally, excessive roll may occur if the car is turning to the right under these conditions.

34.15 Torque reaction and axle guidance

Methods that have been used to obviate torque-reaction effects and for axle guidance include the provision of a torque-reaction tube coaxial with the propeller shaft and attached at its front end to the vehicle structure or the gearbox casing and at its rear end to the nose of the differential gear carrier. Alternatively, if a torque-reaction rod as described in Section 26.8 is used, the reaction point, at its forward end, can be offset to the right of the vehicle so that the lift due to the reaction to the torque in the half-shafts counteracts the downward pressure due to the reaction to the torque in the propeller shaft. Otherwise, the only remedy apart from the use of complex torque-reaction rods, is a de Dion or independent suspension system – in other words, either a dead axle or an axleless suspension.

To obviate the problems of interleaf friction, the unsprung weight of semi-elliptic springs, and the imprecision of motion of axles when guided only by such springs, coil springs and axle guidance and torque-reaction links are now fairly widely used at the rear. An example is the Vauxhall *Viva*, Fig. 34.20, where each extremity of the live back axle is pivoted on the trailing end of an arm, the forward end of which pivots beneath the vehicle structure. A coil spring is interposed between the rear end of the

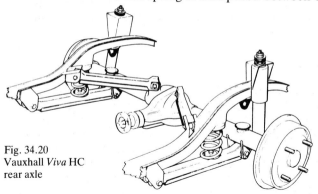

Fig. 34.20
Vauxhall *Viva* HC
rear axle

arm and the structure, or sprung mass. Lateral location is effected by two semi-trailing links, arranged V-fashion with their rear ends pivoted on top of the differential casing and their front ends in brackets outboard, again on the vehicle structure. All the pivot points are rubber-bushed, to introduce some compliance, to prevent the transmission of some of the vibration from the road to the vehicle, and to accommodate the motions due to single-wheel deflections and the skewing of the axes of the upper links relative to those of the lower ones. Brake torque reaction on the links tends to pull the rear end down, thus at least partially counteracting the front end dive effect, while drive torque tends to offset the tendency to rear end squat.

Several manufacturers use twin parallel trailing links on each side, for axle location and to react brake torque, in which case a Panhard rod is required for lateral location. To reduce lateral movement of the axle to a minimum, the Panhard rod is generally made as long as possible by attaching it to the vehicle structure on one side and, to the axle, as far away as practicable on the other side.

In some instances, the rear end of the lower trailing link on each side is pivoted to a bracket below the outer end of the axle, while a single central upper rod, triangulated in the form of an A-link or wishbone link, is pivoted at its apex to the top of the differential casing and at its base to a transverse member on the vehicle structure. Such a system, shown diagrammatically in Fig. 26.10, and used by Renault for example, has the advantage that the single triangulated link replaces not only the two upper ones, but also the Panhard rod, since it can locate the axle laterally. This practice is fairly common on heavy commercial trailer axles used with air or rubber springs, Fig. 33.14.

The single trailing link system has been used with live axles, but only rarely. A good example is the London Transport *Routemaster* bus, on which the single trailing links, one each side, project behind the axle to carry at their ends a transverse beam that extends outwards behind the rear wheels. Coil springs seat on the ends of this beam, so the spring base is as wide as possible. Air springs have also been used with this layout.

An essential with the single trailing-link arrangement is a flexible connection between the links on each side and the axle, to relieve the latter of the severe torsional loading that would otherwise be applied to it during single wheel deflection. On the *Routemaster*, this flexibility is provided by interposing on each side two Metalastik rubber sandwich type mountings, chevron fashion, between the axle and the trailing link.

34.16   Watt's linkage

Watt's linkages have been employed for both lateral and fore-and-aft location of axles, so that they will rise and fall in a straight line. However, since such an arrangement is both costly and difficult to accommodate, it tends to be used mainly on sports and racing cars, where extreme precision is important. Typically, the Watt's linkage comprises a leading and trailing link, the adjacent ends of which are inter-connected by a vertical link, as in Fig. 34.21, or for the lateral location of a de Dion axle, Fig. 34.28. To the centre of the vertical link is rigidly attached the axle. There are pivot joints at the ends of all the links so, as the axle rises and falls, it does so in a straight line. If the two horizontal links are of equal length, the axle has to be attached to the centre of the vertical one; if not, it has to be set off-centre, towards the end of the longer horizontal link by an amount such that the distance between these two centres is $LA/(A+B)$, where L is the overall centre-to-centre length of the vertical link, and A and B are respectively the centre-to-centre lengths of the longer and shorter horizontal links. The centre-to-centre distance from the axle and the attachment of the vertical link to the shorter horizontal link, therefore is $LB/(A+B)$.

34.17   Rear suspension – dead axles

The considerations applying to a dead axle at the front also apply at the rear, but without the complication inherent in the need to steer the wheels. However, except on some commercial front-wheel-drive special-purpose vehicles, and of course trailers, dead rear axles are rarely used. For cars, on the other hand, a particular form – the de Dion axle – is not uncommon.

The de Dion axle (see Section 18.3) is most suitable for cars with a low centre of gravity, hard suspension and a long wheelbase. This is because the axle location links are usually approximately at the height of the wheel centres, which makes it impossible for the roll centre to be near the ground, and therefore extra roll stiffness is desirable. Moreover, with a high roll centre, the contact point between both wheels and the ground moves sideways as one wheel is deflected upwards, and this has a steering effect. With independent suspension, even though there may be a similar degree of sideways movement on the rising wheel, it is resisted by the other wheel. A long wheelbase makes up for the absence of any anti-dive effect during braking and anti-squat effect during acceleration. Lateral location of a de Dion axle is generally effected by a Panhard rod, but a Watt's linkage is used in some instances, as in Fig. 34.28.

An especially interesting, but complex, de Dion system – that which was used on the Rover 2000 – is illustrated diagrammatically in Fig. 34.21. The stub axles of the wheels are carried in bearings B in the ends of the two parts A_1 and A_2 of the dead axle. These two parts of the dead axle are free both to slide and rotate relative to each other on the axis XX. The outer ends of the drive shafts G_1 and G_2 are coupled by universal joints to the short flanged shafts I in the wheel hubs, while their inner ends are similarly connected to the differential gear F. There are no variations in track, since their swinging motions are accommodated by the sliding joint on XX in the dead axle – the freedom of rotation in this joint allows for the differential rise and fall of the wheels on each side.

Lateral location of the wheels is effected by the shafts G_1 and G_2, and lateral location of the differential and final drive unit F by the radius rod K. This radius rod is needed because the final drive unit F is flexibly mounted to prevent the transmission of noise and vibration to the vehicle structure.

The links C and D, together with the vertical bracket carrying the bearings B, form a Watt's linkage to guide the axle vertically in a straight line and to locate it fore-and-aft. These links also react both drive and brake thrusts and torques. Disc brakes are installed inboard on the differential gear casing, the discs being mounted on the drive shafts, so the brake and drive torques are both ultimately reacted through the final drive mountings. To reduce to a minimum their vertical loading due to these torque reactions, the mountings are spaced very widely – on the ends of a transverse yoke at the rear, and under an exceptionally long extension of the nose of the final drive casing at the front.

34.18   Rear suspension – independent

At one time, the most common form of independent rear suspension was the swing axle, in which the axle tube and drive-shaft on each side formed a single transverse link, in some instances with a radius rod extending forwards to take the reaction to brake and tractive thrust. This arrangement was used for many years by Porsche, VW and Daimler-Benz. In principle, it differed from the Rover system just described in that there was a universal joint only at the inner end of the half-shaft, as shown diagrammatically in Fig. 34.22, so the camber angle changed as the wheel rose and fell.

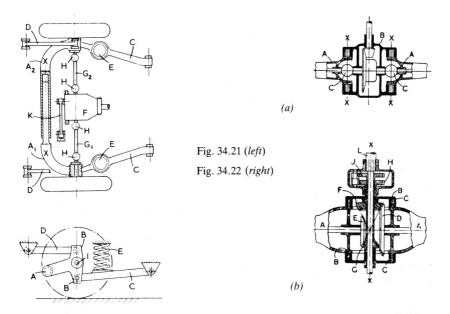

Fig. 34.21 (*left*)

Fig. 34.22 (*right*)

In Fig. 34.22, the wheel hubs are carried on the outer ends – not shown – of the axle tubes A and the half-shafts rotate in bearings in their inner ends. At (a) the axle tubes swing about trunnions, while at (b) they have semi-cylindrical flanges B on which they pivot in semi-cylindrical housings in the final drive casing C. The axes XX of the trunnions at (a) are in line with the centres O of the universal joints. At (b), rotation of the centres of the semi-cylindrical flanges is accommodated by rolling of the bevel gears D and E about the pinions F and G. These pinions are mounted on sleeves driven by the wheels H and J of a spur-type differential.

There have been many variants of the swing-axle layout, but most commonly a fabricated link was substituted for the axle tube. As with an axle tube, however, the wheel hub was attached to its outer end. The inner end was usually forked to carry the two bearings about which it swung, and the pivots for these bearings were generally in the differential casing, though in some instances the whole final drive unit was integral with the inner end of one link and the other link swung about a pivot pin common to both and mounted on the chassis frame.

On the Mercedes-Benz 220, this pin was below the final drive unit, which gave a roll centre fairly close to the ground. The object was, by making the shafts as long as possible, to reduce not only the wheel camber variations but also, by lowering the roll centre, what are termed the *tuck-under* and *jacking-up* effects. Tuck-under occurs if either the whole rear end, or one side only, is lifted so that the wheels, or wheel, drop to the rebound position. When the car falls again, the forces on the wheels are such that it will roll along for a certain distance with the wheels tucked under before they roll out to their normal positions again. Jacking-up occurs when the couple due to the lateral loading as a result of the centrifugal force on the vehicle times the height of the roll centre above the ground is greater than the righting douple due to the weight of the vehicle acting vertically downwards multiplied by the horizontal distance from the centre of the outer wheel contact patch on the ground to the projected centre of gravity of the vehicle. The latter effect leads to instability because, as the jacking-up progresses, the roll centre moves upwards, progressively increasing the overturning couple. Both effects tend ultimately to cause rear-end breakaway during cornering, which is why this system is rarely used nowadays.

34.19   Single link with angled pivot axis

Of the types of suspension listed at the beginning of this Chapter, only two remain to be discussed. These are single and double link with pivot axes not parallel to either the longitudinal or the transverse axes of a car. The single-arm systems of this type are commonly used in rear suspensions. Brief mention of a double-arm system is made at the end of Section 34.3. Its characteristics are a combination of those of the other twin-link systems – with longitudinal or with transverse pivot axes – and the principles of the single arm apply so far as roll axis etc. are concerned. Consequently, there is no need to go into it in any more detail.

The single-arm system is attractive as a rear suspension principally because of the simplicity of a single link and the relative ease with which it can be accommodated. It would be difficult to fit into the front end because the engine would be in the way.

The basis of the evolution of this system has been as follows. Swing axle systems suffer the disadvantages outlined at the end of Section 34.18, and the single trailing arm has the disadvantages set out at the beginning of Section 34.6. These include too much camber angle change with the former and too little with the latter, so a combination of the two could be just right. Again, the swing-axle system lacks fore-and-aft rigidity unless a drag link is added and the trailing arm system lacks lateral rigidity, so again a combination of both could give adequate rigidity in all directions.

We can reject the swing-axle system totally on grounds of instability when cornering, but the trailing-arm system is worthy of more serious consideration and, indeed, is used on a number of modern cars. How, then, can we improve it and combine with it some of the desirable features of the swing-axle system? The answer is to stiffen the arm by triangulating it and to set its pivot axis somewhere between the lateral and longitudinal orientations.

Consider first a simple conventional trailing arm. An obvious step is to add to it an extra bracing member pivoted inboard, on an axis in line with that of the main bearing. The whole link will then be in the form of a right-angle triangle with the wheel hub at its apex. This places the right angle at the outboard end of its base, where the pivot bearing for the trailing arm is situated; and the brace forms the hypotenuse and, where it joins the base, carries a second pivot bearing. Both bearings are carried in brackets on a transverse member of the vehicle structure. A disadvantage of this system is that either the hypotenuse becomes too long, since it is both loaded in compression and subject to fairly severe vertical inertia loading (see Section 33.3) or the two bearings are not spaced apart widely enough.

A wide bearing-spacing is important for reducing to a minimum the loading imposed on them by the couple applied by centrifugal force in a lateral direction when the vehicle is cornering. Rubber bushes are usually used for the pivot bearings and, if they are heavily loaded, they have to be made too stiff. This is an especial disadvantage when modern radial-ply tyres are used, since these are much less resilient, so far as absorption of fore-and-aft shock loading is concerned, than cross-ply tyres. With radial ply tyres, therefore, fore-and-aft resilience has to be provided by using a soft rubber in these bushes, otherwise unpleasant vibrations are felt by the occupants of the car.

A good example of a semi-trailing link rear suspension can be seen in Fig. 34.23, which illustrates that of the Triumph 2000. A similar system is used on the BMW 1500. In the Triumph suspension, the trailing arm is swept from inboard of the wheel to outboard towards its pivot. This is to widen the spread between the pivot and the bearing for the bracing arm that forms the hypotenuse of the triangulation system. That this lengthens

Fig. 34.23

the trailing arm does not matter, since it is subjected only to tensile loads when the vehicle is moving forwards. Moreover, the fact that the curvature thus introduced reduces the rigidity of the arm – since it will cause it to be subjected to bending loads – does not matter either, because some flexibility has to be introduced in any case if radial ply tyres are to be fitted.

By setting the axis of the two pivot bearings at an angle intermediate between those required for a true trailing link and a swing axle, the bracing arm, or hypotenuse of the triangle, is shortened so that it can better take the compresssion loads which, because of weight transfer during cornering, are heavier than any tension loads to which it might be subjected. The drive shafts have universal joints at both ends and sliding joints at their inner ends to cater for the variations in their lengths as the suspension arms rise and fall.

An additional advantage of this angular setting of the pivot bearings is that the transverse member on which they are pivoted, being of necessity of V-shape, can be used to carry the nose of the final drive unit. The rear end of this unit is carried by another transverse member, or yoke. Both these transverse members have circular rubber sandwich mountings at their ends, by means of which they are secured to the structure of the vehicle. On the BMW, conical mountings, which offer greater resistance to horizontal than to vertical loading, are used and, while there are two for its V-shape front member, there is only one for supporting the rear of the final drive unit. The absence of the rear transverse member and of one mounting no doubt compensates, at least partly, for the employment of the more costly conical type mountings.

On both vehicles, the innermost of the two pivot bearings on each side is lower than the outer one. The effect of this is to lower the roll centre, which reduces the variation in track as the wheels rise and fall. With a trailing link suspension, the roll centre is initially at ground level (Fig. 34.4) and, with a swing axle it is either above and half way between the two pivots or, if there is only one pivot, the roll centre will coincide with its axis.

The method of finding the roll centre with a semi-trailing link is shown in Fig. 34.24. Here it can be seen that increasing the degree of trail of the suspension arm moves the point O outboard of the wheel on the opposite side and, in effect, increases the length of the imaginary swing axle and therefore reduces the variation in camber as the wheel rises and falls. The point O in Fig. 34.24 can be arrived at by drawing in the axes of the pivots on the other side, but this is not really necessary because it can be deduced from the symmetry of the overall system.

An example of an early suspension of this type, with a transverse leaf spring and a swing axle is shown in Fig. 34.25, and similar arrangements have been used, with coil springs seating on the outer ends of the swing axles A, or on the ends of the drag links D. In the illustration, the final drive unit is carried on a sub-frame C, and a spherical bearing is employed at E. With these arrangements, the axis about which the suspension arms swing is set at an angle approximating too closely to that of a swing axle system, so the roll axis is too high and the jacking-up and tuck-under effects too pronounced.

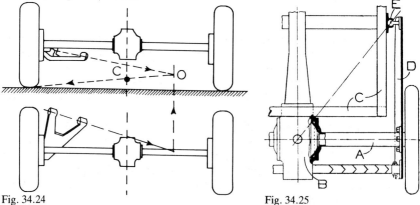

Fig. 34.24   Fig. 34.25

34.20 MacPherson strut rear suspension

A particularly good example of a MacPherson strut type rear suspension is that of the Lancia *Delta*, Fig. 34.26. With this arrangement, the springs occupy space above the wheels, which in any case is normally wasted so far as capacity for luggage in the boot is concerned. An alternative arrangement is that of the Ford *Escort*, Fig. 34.27.

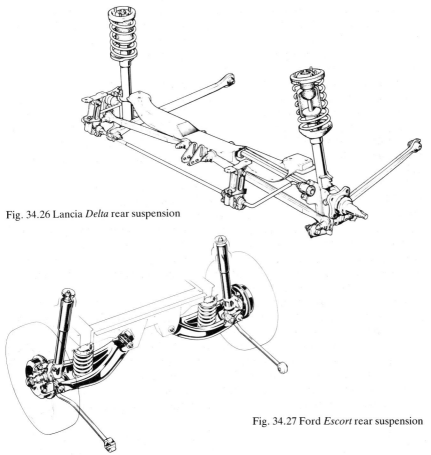

Fig. 34.26 Lancia *Delta* rear suspension

Fig. 34.27 Ford *Escort* rear suspension

Among the interesting features of the Lancia system are the use of twin transverse links pivoted close to the longitudinal axis of the car, one in front of and the other behind a substantial transverse member of the structure. A single trailing link on each side reacts the brake drag, while the torque is taken equally between this link and the top end attachment of the strut.

The axis of the spring is offset slightly relative to that of the strut, to apply a couple tending to counteract that due to the offset of the roadwheel on the strut. This relieves the piston and rod assembly of some side-load and therefore the friction between it and its cylinder. The piston rods are Teflon coated to reduce the sliding friction between them and the glands at the top ends of the cylinders.

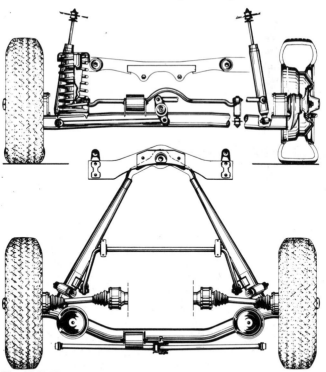

Fig. 34.28 The Alfa 6 rear suspension in elevation (top) and plan (bottom)

As can be seen from the illustration, the ends of the anti-roll bar pivot in rubber bushes on the stub-axle carrier assemblies. The straight central portion of the anti-roll bar is carried in two rubber mountings, one at each end. These mountings are on the lower ends of pendant links, the upper ends of which are pivoted on the vehicle structure. This uncommon arrangement has been adopted so that the roll bar cannot exert any constraint on the movement of the suspension strut and linkage.

In the front suspension of this vehicle, Fig. 32.8, the method of avoiding such constraint has been simply to place the rubber mountings in line with the axes of the pivots of the wishbone links. Yet another method – the use of shackles on the ends of the anti-roll bar has been adopted by Alfa Romeo for the rear suspension of the *Alfa 6*, Fig. 34.28. The *Alfa 6* rear suspension layout is virtually identical to those of the *Alfetta* and *Giulietta* models. Its drive shafts have plunge-type constant-velocity joints, as described at the end of Chapter 24, to accommodate variations in their lengths as they swing up and down. Mounted on the de Dion axle, adjacent to the centrally-pivoted arm of the Watt's linkage, is a tuned vibration damper to counteract axle hop. Fore-and-aft location of the axle is effected by a trailing V-shape link the apex of which is pivoted on a ball-joint beneath a transverse member. The ends of the anti-roll bar are connected by shackles to the arms of the V, so that they can articulate freely. Another feature of note is the installation of a combined bump stop and hollow rubber spring coaxially inside each coil spring, to give a progressively rising rate.

Chapter 35

Six-wheel vehicles

In most countries a limit is set by law to the weight that may be carried on any one axle of a road vehicle; this limit is regulated, presumably, according to the capacity of the roads upon which the vehicles will operate, but factors other than the road also set a limit, for example, the tyres. With unshod steel wheels that were used on traction engines the permissible load could be increased readily by increasing the width of the wheel, but with rubber-tyred wheels this is not so practicable. The use of twin pneumatic tyres enables the load to be approximately doubled, but this solution of the problem has many drawbacks. The great width of the wheels necessitates the use of a comparatively narrow frame and somewhat hampers the coach builder; stones get wedged between the tyres and cause damage; it is difficult to change the inner tyre and the load is not always equally distributed between the tyres. These drawbacks to the twin-tyred wheel have led to the adoption of the alternative method of carrying heavier loads, which is by using more than two axles.

Since the use of three or more axles is primarily to enable heavier loads to be carried, while keeping the load per axle within definite limits, the arrangement used ought to be such that the load carried will be properly distributed between the axles, however uneven the road may be. This requirement should, strictly, rule out the adding of axles having independent springing since, if one of these axles stood on a hump, it would obviously carry more than its proper proportion of the total load. However, this compromise is sometimes adopted and when the road surfaces are good it may be satisfactory.

There are two quite different solutions of the problem, and six-wheelers can be divided into two classes accordingly –

(1) 'Flexible' or 'articulated' vehicles.
(2) 'Rigid' vehicles.

Vehicles of the first class consist of a two- or three-axle tractor unit with, mostly, a short wheelbase, and a one- or two-axle trailer, which may be permanently or detachably connected to it. The connection between the two units to provide for road inequalities must consist of a ball and socket joint or its equivalent. The trailer wheels are almost always merely weight carriers and not driving wheels, owing to the difficulty of arranging a satisfactory drive to them. They are usually carried on a simple axle, no provision being made for steering them. The trailer then 'cuts-in' when the vehicle is cornering, and manoeuvring in reverse requires some skill. Sometimes, however, the trailer wheels are carried by an axle fixed to a turntable and arranged to steer so that the trailer wheels follow in the tracks of the tractor wheels, thus overcoming the cutting-in difficulty, which, however, is not a serious disadvantage so that steering trailers are not much used.

This type of six-wheeler cannot operate on very uneven ground, firstly, because it is not practicable to provide for sufficient relative movement between the two units to ensure constant weight distribution; secondly, because such vehicles are somewhat unstable when turning on sloping ground and thirdly, because of insufficient adhesion between the ground and the driving wheels, which can be especially serious owing to the drag of the trailer wheels.

35.1   The rigid six-wheeler

This type of vehicle has been intensively developed during the last 20 years and many different arrangements have been evolved both as regards their suspension and transmission systems. The earliest vehicles consisted essentially of a four-wheeled lorry with the addition of a third axle placed behind and as close as possible to the existing rear axle. The third axle was sometimes merely a weight-carrying dead axle and sometimes a live driving axle. This type of vehicle is still widely used, but other types have been developed.

35.2   Suspensions for rigid six-wheelers

Considering first the suspension systems, Fig. 35.1 shows four simple arrangements. In (*a*) the loads carried by the axles are equalised by connecting the adjacent ends of the springs to a balance beam A pivoted at its centre to the frame. As shown, the springs are pivoted at their other ends to the frame and are used to take the torque reactions and driving thrust, but when torque-thrust members are provided for the axles then shackles would be fitted. The balance beam cannot be made very long without making the distance between the axle centres rather large, which is undesirable because of steering considerations, and this results in either

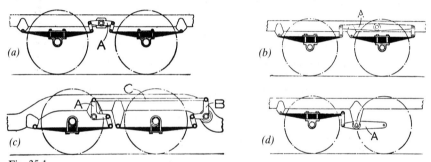

Fig. 35.1

excessive angular movement of the lever or undue limitation of axle movement. The difficulty is avoided in (*b*) where the lever is connected to the rear ends of the springs, and the arrangement at (*c*) overcomes the difficulty as regards the centre distance of the axles. In this latter arrangement the springs are connected by bell-crank levers A and B and the rod C. A variation of (*b*) is to connect the lever A to the outer ends of the springs and a variation of (*c*) is to connect the adjacent ends of the springs to the bell-cranks. The centre distance between the axle can be reduced by using the arrangement (*a*), but with the rear spring connected to the front end of the lever and the front spring connected to the rear of the lever; as the ends of the springs then overlap one has to be placed above the other, and one is usually placed on the top of the axle casing, the other being underslung. In (*d*) a single spring is used and the rear wheels are carried on the ends of levers A, no rear axle being used. The rear wheels are then not driven but are merely weight carriers. For equality of loading the lever arms must be unequal. In Fig. 35.2 (*a*) a single spring is again used and rigid lever A is pivoted to that spring at its centre and to the axles at its ends. The single spring has now to carry the total weight supported by the two axles. The same principle is used in the Scammell design described later. At (*b*) is shown a commonly used arrangement, a single laminated spring being pivoted at its centre to a bracket fixed to the frame and at its ends to the axles. When the spring is required to take the

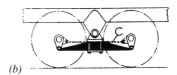

Fig. 35.2

(*a*)

(*b*)

driving and braking torque reactions it becomes somewhat difficult to obtain a satisfactory connection between the spring and the axle casings. This is achieved in one design by providing the spring with an extra leaf (as shown dotted), which is separately pivoted to the axle casings. This difficulty is avoided in the arrangement shown in Fig. 35.3 by using two springs secured rigidly to a trunnion block A at their centres and pivoted to the axle casings at their ends. The trunnion block is free to pivot on the end of a cross member of the frame. Fig. 35.4 illustrates a design used by Thornycroft, in which, again, two springs were used, but where each was separately pivoted at its centre on a pin carried by a bracket fixed to the frame.

All the above arrangements will equalise the loads carried by the middle and rear wheels when the vehicle to which they are fitted is motionless, but this equality may be destroyed as soon as the wheels are driven or braked, and a driving or braking torque reaction is set up. To maintain equality during driving or braking the system adopted for dealing with the torque reactions must satisfy certain conditions which will be considered later. However, the resulting inequality when it does occur is seldom of any great importance in vehicles operating on good or moderately good roads, but in vehicles operating on bad ground any serious inequality of loading may render the vehicle useless, and for such vehicles special attention must be

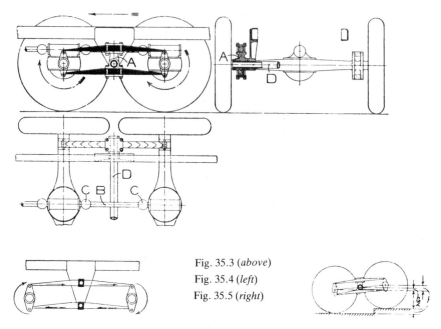

Fig. 35.3 (*above*)

Fig. 35.4 (*left*)

Fig. 35.5 (*right*)

given to the arrangements for dealing with the driving and braking torque reactions.

With any of the above systems the rise of the frame when one axle goes over a bump is only half the height of that bump, as shown in Fig. 35.5. The shocks transmitted to the frame and to the road are consequently less than in a four-wheeled vehicle, but two shocks are experienced for each bump instead of only one.

35.3   Transmissions of six-wheelers

The most important of these are shown in Fig. 35.6. That at (*a*) is probably the simplest and most widely used, the employment of worm-driven axles enabling the worm shaft of the middle axle to be extended through the back of the axle casing and coupled by an intermediate shaft to the rear axle. The intermediate shaft must be provided with two universal joints (indicated by circles) and a sliding joint S as shown. An overhead worm gives large road clearances and is used for cross-country vehicles, whereas an underhung worm gives a low body position and is used for buses and coaches. The use of bevel-driven axles is not so simple, as the diagrams (*b*) and (*c*) will show. In (*b*) a second pinion is mounted at the back of the middle axle in order to drive the intermediate shaft, and it will be seen that the crown wheel of the rear axle has to be mounted on the offside of the pinion in order to make the wheels of the two axles rotate in the same directions. The driving torque for both middle and rear axles is transmitted through the pinion and crown wheel of the middle axle, and the design of those gears is made more difficult. For a given distance between the axles this drive results in the shortest distance between the centres of the universal joints on the intermediate shaft, and thus for a given relative movement of the axles in the greatest angularity of those joints. In (*c*) the drive shaft is mounted above the axles, the drive being carried down to the bevel pinion shafts by chains or gears. By using similar axles turned back-to-back as shown, the length of the intermediate shaft is increased and the angularity of the universal joints is decreased. This arrangement was evolved and is used by the FWD Company. At (*d*) is shown an American design. The casing A is fixed to the frame and the drive is taken through a train of gears to the bottom shaft, the ends of which are coupled by universal joints to the bevel pinion shafts of the axles. The latter are provided with torque thrust tubes which are anchored to the casing A by ball and socket connections surrounding the universal joints; sliding joints are consequently unnecessary. The length of the torque thrust tubes cannot be made very great without making the centre distance between the axles large, and consequently the angles at which the universal joints may have to work may be rather large. Constant-velocity type joints are used but

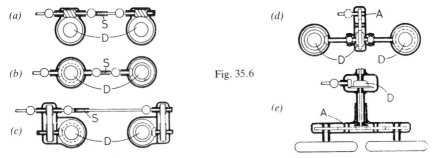

Fig. 35.6

even so it is questionable whether this transmission could be used successfully on a cross-country vehicle. For vehicles operating on good roads it should be very satisfactory, and for such vehicles the use of a third differential to divide the torque equally between the two axles is desirable and is very easily provided for as shown. A third differential can be arranged if required when transmission (*a*) is used and an example, the design of the Associated Equipment Company (AEC), is shown in Fig. 35.7. The shaft A is coupled by a universal joint to the propeller shaft coming from the gearbox and carries the four-armed spider B on splines at its right-hand end. On the arms of this spider the differential pinions C are free to turn and are kept in place by the ring D, the inside of which is made spherical to fit the spherical ends of the pinions. The ring D is itself kept in place by the overlapping portions of the teeth of the differential wheel E.

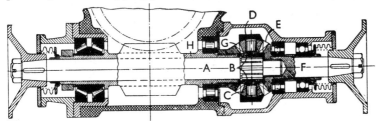

Fig. 35.7 AEC third differential

The latter is made integral with its shaft F, which is coupled by a universal joint to the intermediate shaft going to the third axle. The other differential wheel G is splined to the hollow worm shaft H. A transmission for an early Scammell six-wheeler is shown in Fig. 35.6 (*e*), a single reduction bevel driven axle being shown, but the double reduction axle shown in Fig. 28.4 can be used equally well. The drive to the road wheels is through a train of gears housed in the lever casing A. It is very difficult to arrange a third differential to divide the drive equally in this transmission, but since it is intended for cross-country work this is not of importance. A suspension

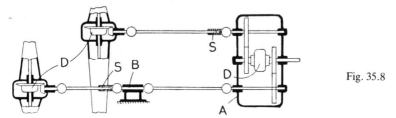

Fig. 35.8

similar to the Scammell has been used by the Saurer company, who used a shaft drive in place of the train of gears used in the Scammell, thus a bevel pinion was mounted on the end of the axle shaft and meshed with two bevel wheels mounted on longitudinal shafts housed in the lever casing; at their outer ends these shafts carried other bevel wheels that meshed with bevel wheels fixed to the road wheel shafts. Fig. 35.8 shows a transmission that has been used in America and on the Continent. Two separate propeller shafts are used, one driving the middle axle and the other the rear axle. The drive coming from the gearbox is divided between the two propeller shafts in a 'transfer' case A fixed to the frame and a third differential (the principle of whose construction is similar to that of the AEC design shown in Fig. 35.7) is sometimes provided. To enable the rear axle propeller shaft to clear the middle axle casing it is provided with an intermediate bearing B fixed to the frame. An alternative to this is to carry this intermediate bearing on the casing of the middle axle. Offset final drive axles must be used and it is difficult to provide for any great relative movement of the axles. The system is consequently used only for vehicles operating on roads. The use of worm-driven axles facilitates the design somewhat. A German Büssing chassis which used this transmission employed torque thrust tubes to take the driving and braking reactions.

35.4   A Scammell design

The general arrangement of the rear bogie transmission system of the Scammell *Constructor* chassis, which is designed for off-the-road use, is shown in Fig. 35.9. The axles A and B are each provided with a torque-thrust member, C and D respectively. These members are connected by ball joints to cross members of the frame and transmit the driving and braking efforts and torque reactions. The drive to the axle A is through a conventional propeller shaft with universal joints, H and J, at the ends. The shaft is provided with axial sliding freedom. The centre E, about which the axle pivots, is placed relatively to the joints H and J, so that the

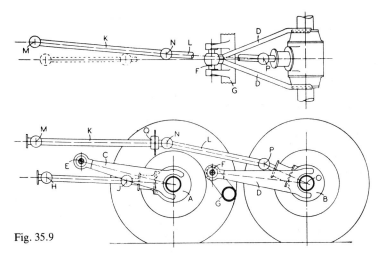

Fig. 35.9

angles between the propeller shaft and the transfer gearbox shaft and between the propeller shaft and the bevel pinion shaft of the axle are always maintained approximately equal in magnitude so that a constant velocity drive is obtained on the lines of those used in front-wheel drives and described in Section 24.4. The axle B is driven by a propeller shaft L through an intermediate propeller shaft K, which is coupled to a shaft of the transfer gearbox and which is supported in a flexibly mounted bearing Q at its right-hand end. The centre F is again placed in relation to the joints N and P so that a constant-velocity drive is obtained.

The axles are positioned sideways by Panhard rods. Flat leaf springs are employed, and these are pivoted to the frame at their centres. As the springs play no part in the positioning of the axles, the connections between them and the axles are designed to avoid any constraint of the axles and any undue distortion of the springs. They are shown in Fig. 35.10. The master leaf of the spring has a cup member B bolted to its end,

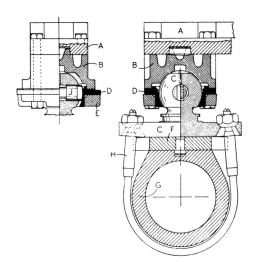

Fig. 35.10

and the spherical part of a pedestal member C fits into this cup, being retained by a collar D, made in two parts, and a cover E. The member C is free to slide on a hardened steel plate F, which is mounted on the axle casing G. The member C is prevented from rotating about a vertical axis by a pin J, whose ends engage slots formed in the collar D. A flexible wire stirrup H prevents separation of the assembly during rebounds of the axle.

35.5   Torque reaction in rigid six-wheelers

Referring to Fig. 35.3, when torque reactions are exerted on the axle casings as indicated by the arrows they will tend to turn the whole unit consisting of the two axles, the springs and the trunnion blocks about the transverse member on which these blocks are free to pivot; this tendency has to be balanced by an increase of load between the rear wheels and the ground and an equal decrease of load between the middle wheels and the ground. Calling the torque reactions t_1 and t_2 and denoting the distance between the axles by l then the magnitude of this alteration in load is given by –

$$Q = \frac{t_1 + t_2}{l}$$

In cross-country vehicles fitted with auxiliary gearboxes giving very low ratios for emergency purposes, it is possible for this alteration Q to become equal to the normal load carried by each axle so that the middle axle would be carrying zero load and would be about to lift off the ground, while the rear axle would be carrying twice the normal load. Under these conditions the rear wheels will probably sink into the ground if the latter is at all soft or sandy and the vehicle will be stalled. The same result will occur with any suspension that deals with the torque reactions in the manner indicated. During braking the reverse of the above action will occur, the middle axle load increasing and the rear axle load decreasing. The arrangement shown in Fig. 35.4 avoids the trouble, the torque reactions being transferred to the frame of the vehicle by means of horizontal forces acting in the springs as shown and which have no effect on the balance of the vertical forces, that is, the loads, acting at the axles. When this arrangement, which was evolved by Thornycroft, is used, the total torque reaction $t_1 + t_2$ is balanced by a decrease q in the load carried by the front axle and an equal increase in the load transmitted through the spring trunnions at the rear. This latter increase however will be shared equally by the middle and rear axles, whose loads will remain equal. The alteration q is given by –

$$q = \frac{t_1 + t_2}{L}$$

where L is the mean wheelbase of the whole vehicle (that is, the distance between the spring trunnions and the front axle), and since L is much greater than l the alteration q will be much smaller than Q. The same result is achieved in the War Department (WD) design shown in Fig. 35.11. The springs are bolted rigidly to the trunnion blocks D, which are pivoted on the ends of the frame cross member E, but at their outer ends the springs are pivoted to boxes A which are mounted on spherical members C which are free to slide outwards along the axle tubes for a reason that will appear later. Torque rods B, connected at one end to the axle casings and at the other end to the frame, are now used to transmit the torque and brake reactions to the frame. Comparing this arrangement with the Thornycroft it will be seen that the torque rods B are acting as the upper spring in Fig. 35.4, and the two springs in Fig. 35.11 are acting as the lower spring in Fig. 35.4. As the torque reactions are transferred to the frame by horizontal forces, the equilibrium of the vertical forces is unaltered, and this design gives the same results as the Thornycroft. Torque rods, arranged as in the WD suspension, are used by some makers in conjunction with the single spring suspension shown in Fig. 35.2(*b*).

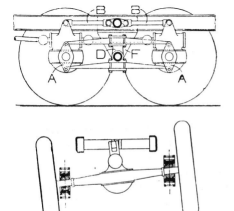

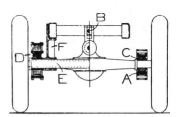

Fig. 35.11 WD type suspension

When the suspensions of Fig 35.1 are used with the springs secured rigidly to the axle casing at the centre and pivoted to the frame at one end so that they take both the torque reactions and thrusts, it can easily be shown that the equality of wheel loading is upset by the torque reactions and also by the couple due to the driving thrust being exerted at axle level and resisted at the level of the spring eyes, the alteration being however that the load on the middle axle increases and that on the rear axle decreases when the vehicle is driven forwards, the opposite action occurring during braking. When each axle is provided with a torque thrust tube then the equality of loading will depend on whether the torque reactions of the two axles are equal or unequal. In the Scammell design, Fig. 35.6 (*e*), equality of loading can only be obtained if the gear ratio between the drive shafts and the road wheels is unity and if those members revolve in the same direction. Actually the gear ratio is a little greater than 2 : 1, so that torque reaction does produce some alteration in wheel loading. Brake torques will also produce an alteration which may be much greater than that due to the driving torque. Experience has shown, however, that these alterations do not affect the performance of the Scammell design, which is outstanding among cross-country vehicles.

35.6 Spring stresses in rigid six-wheelers

The suspension systems of six-wheelers must be considered from another
point of view than that of weight distribution, namely, the effect of axle or
wheel movements on the springs themselves. When the springs are rigidly
bolted or are pivoted by pins to the axle and are connected to the frame by
pin joints, then clearly when the axles assume angular positions relatively
to the frame, as indicated in Fig. 35.12, the springs will be twisted. While
this twisting is unimportant in vehicles operating on roads where the axle
movements will be comparatively small, it is very serious in cross-country
vehicles, and if permitted would lead to fracture of the springs. It is
avoided in the WD design by the use of the ball members C (Fig. 35.11),
which allow the axles to tilt without producing any corresponding tilt of the
boxes A. Twisting of the springs is avoided in the suspension shown in Fig.
35.2 (*b*) by using the connection shown in Fig. 35.13, which is self-
explanatory. A design, used by the Kirkstall Forge company, which
relieves the springs of longitudinal twisting and of side forces is shown in
Fig. 35.14. It comprises a ball-and-socket joint, the ball of which is capable
of sliding along the pin on which it is mounted. Hardened steel pads
prevent damage to the joint when unduly large movements occur.

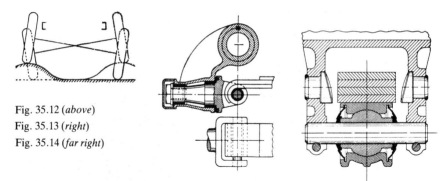

Fig. 35.12 (*above*)
Fig. 35.13 (*right*)
Fig. 35.14 (*far right*)

In the Thornycroft design the same result is achieved by using gimbals A
(Fig. 35.15), pivoted to the axle casings on trunnions whose axes are
fore-and-aft. The spring ends are pin-jointed to the gimbals. This gives the
same freedom as in the WD design while permitting the torque reactions to
be transmitted through the springs to the frame. There is another action
which must be avoided however. When the axle tilts, the horizontal
distance between the points of connection of the springs becomes smaller,
while the horizontal distance between the points of connection of the
springs and frame remains unaltered. There is consequently a side bending
action which in cross-country vehicles would be serious. It is avoided in the
WD design by leaving the balls C free to slide outwards along the axle
tubes and in the Thornycroft design by leaving the springs free to slide
inwards along their central pivots and outwards along the pins connecting
them to the gimbals. To avoid bending and twisting of the torque rods
themselves they are sometimes connected to the axle and frame by
ball-and-socket joints, but sometimes universal joints are used. In the
latter case the rods must be made in two portions free to turn relatively

about their longitudinal axis, the joint being made capable of transmitting tension or compression. Some freedom from twisting of the springs is obtained by using swivelling boxes between the spring eyes and the frame brackets or shackles, but while these are satisfactory for vehicles operating on roads it is doubtful whether they can cope with the large movements experienced in cross-country work.

35.7 Scammell articulated trailer

It has been seen that in the Scammell *Constructor* chassis the springs have been relieved of all stresses, except those due to the weight of the body. In the four-wheeled trailer portion of one of their articulated vehicles, Scammell have used the springs to take the braking forces and, in conjunction with torque rods, the brake torque reactions, but the springs are relieved of the sideways forces by transverse radius rods. Undesirable stresses are minimised by employing the connections shown in Fig. 35.16 between the axles and the springs. The end of the spring is provided with a ball A fitting in a socket B which is made in two parts for assembly and which is free to slide sideways, that is parallel to the axle, in the housing C.

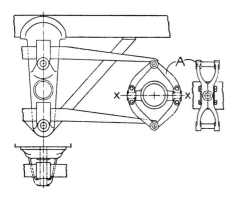

Fig. 35.15 (*left*)

Fig. 35.16 (*below*)

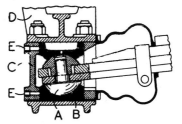

The latter is bolted to the bracket D of the axle. Lubricating nipples are provided at E. This arrangement enables the springs to take longitudinal and vertical forces, but relieves them of other actions.

The general arrangement of the suspension is shown in Fig. 35.17. The springs B are bolted to seats, which are pivoted on pins C carried by brackets. These brackets are secured to the frame members of the trailer and are braced by the cross member D. The braking forces and torque reactions are transferred to the frame by longitudinal forces in the springs B and torque rods E, and side forces are taken by the transverse radius rods F, which are pivoted at one end to the axles and at the other end to the spring-pivot brackets. Both the rods E and F are provided with rubber bushes at the pivots, and these accommodate the very small difference in the motion of the axle due to the flexing of the springs and that due to the constraint of the radius rod; they also relieve the rods E of undesirable bending stresses.

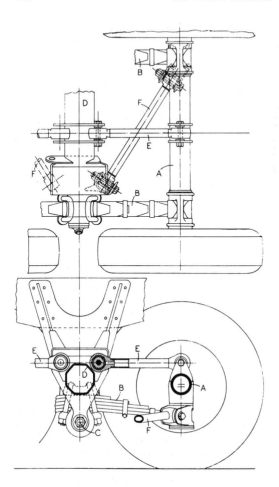

Fig. 35.17

35.8   Scammell *Routeman*

Many of the principles described in this book are exemplified in the Scammell *Routeman* and *Constructor 8* tandem drive bogie, Fig. 35.18. The drive is taken by the propeller shaft to a four-pinion, lockable, inter-axle differential unit in the top of the final-drive casing of the front axle, and then split two ways: one is through a pair of spur gears down to the final drive pinion of the front axle, and the other straight through to the rear, through a short propeller shaft, to the trailing axle. Thus, the drive is normally shared – by the inter-axle differential – between the two axles. However, to stop the wheels on one axle from spinning, in icy conditions or on soft ground, the inter-axle differential can be locked by means of an air actuated dog clutch on the leading axle. This clutch of course must be disengaged as soon as the vehicle regains hard ground, to avoid transmission wind-up in the short propeller shaft interconnecting the two axles.

These axles are of the double-reduction type. The first reduction is effected by the crown-wheel-and-pinion and the second by a planetary gear-set at the outer end of each half-shaft. Fore-and-aft location of each axle is effected by two radius rods at the bottom and one at the top. Those on top are pivoted at one end on top of each final-drive casing and their other ends are pivoted on a transvere member of the frame, above the pivot mountings for the two road springs. Each of the four lower rods, beneath the springs, is pivoted at one end under the axle tube and at the other on the bracket that carries the pivot mounting for the spring above it. Thus all the connections to the frame are grouped compactly around the transverse member forming the main support for the bogie. These rods of course also react drive and brake torques.

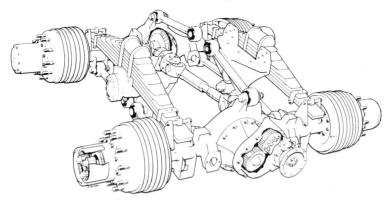

Fig. 35.18 Scammell *Routeman 3* tandem-drive bogie

Lateral location is effected by the road springs. The slipper ends of these springs seat between lugs on top of the axle tubes, and their centres of course are clamped by large U-bolts to the seating pads on top of their pivot, or trunnion, bearings. Relatively narrow pads bear on the tops of the ends of the springs, to hold them down on their seats between the lugs on the axle tubes under rebound conditions. These look like rollers but, in fact, are not free to roll. Because they are narrow, they allow the springs freedom to articulate sufficiently to accommodate vertical motions of the wheels on one side relative to those on the other.

Index